SECRETS OF JOURNALISM IN RUSSIA: MASS MEDIA UNDER GORBACHEV AND YELTSIN

SECRETS OF JOURNALISM IN RUSSIA: MASS MEDIA UNDER GORBACHEV AND YELTSIN

By G.N. Vachnadze

Nova Science Publishers

Nova Science Publishers, Inc.
6080 Jericho Turnpike, Suite 207
Commack, New York 11725

Electronic Book Production Manager:
                                      Denise Engelhardt
Cover Design: Michael A. Masotti

Library of Congress Cataloging-in-Publication Data
available upon request

ISBN 1-56072-081-6

© 1992 Nova Science Publishers, Inc.

All rights reserved. No part of this book may be reproduced, stored in a retrieval system or transmitted in any form or by any means: electronic, electrostatic, magnetic, tape, mechanical, photocopying, recording or otherwise without permission from the publishers.

Printed in the United States of America

SECRETS OF JOURNALISM IN RUSSIA

TABLE OF CONTENTS

INTRODUCTION xii

PART I

CHAPTER I   MUZZLED FOURTH POWER

How we were forced to subscribe to the party press   3
On Aug. 1, 1990 censorship in the USSR collapsed   8
The Communist Party monopoly of dispensing paper   18
Why do journalists tell lies   30

CHAPTER II   TASS, IAN, "INTERFAX", ETC.

Ministry of Information under the guise of TASS   39
Under the cover of APNL   49
The unsinkable   55
Honest journalism takes a stout heart   60

CHAPTER III   VETERAN POLITICAL PUBLICATIONS

What was interesting in Pravda   67
From Alexei Adzhubei to Igor Golembiovsky   82
Collusion on silence   88
Memoires of Komsomol   91

CHAPTER IV   THE NEW INDEPENDENTS

The court jesters in the epoch of perestroika   102
The time of "heavyweight" literary is over   114
How Literaturnaya Gazeta passed away   131

CHAPTER V	**THE PRESS THAT EARLIER WAS NOT**	
	Vitaliy Tretyakov, a friend of M.S. Gorbachev	139
	The power of the democrats has newspapers of their own	148
	In the spirit of Sergei Grigoryants' "Glasnost"	160
	The massacre of Vilinius finished off the idea of the Soviet Union	173
CHAPTER VI	**THE PRESS FOR BUSINESS PEOPLE**	
	Tough guys from "Kommersant	183
	USSR Prime Minister used to be a journalist too...	190
	"Moscow Magazine" and "Burda"	192
	Publishers in the spheres of culture and charity	199
CHAPTER VII	**BOOK PUBLISHING**	
	"Don't burn Gorbachev!"	209
	The General needs not just a few dozen books, but thousands	217
	Under Suslov censors wouldn't take bribes	226
	The last keep of GULAG in the USSR Writers' Union	239

PART II

CHAPTER VIII	**RADIO**	
	Radio Russia vs. the Politbureau of the CPSU Central Committee	253
	"Echo of Moscow" saved the honor of the nation	257
	Foreign radio stations broadcast in Russian	262
	President Yeltsin's decrees on opening bureaus of Radio Liberty in Russia	275
CHAPTER IX	**TV STARS**	
	Eduard Sagalayev, Tatiana Mitkova, Yuri Rostov vs, President of the USSR	285
	First interview with Academician A. Sakharov	297
	Information war on the air ended Aug. 21, 1991	315

CHAPTER X	TELEVISION FOR THE PRESIDENT	
	Earthquake in Georgia as the 14th TV news item from Moscow	325
	Symbiosis of the Central TV of the KGB	329
CHAPTER XI	TELEVISION TECHNOLOGY	
	The Kremlin threatens to shoot down Russia's first communications satellite	345
	Georgy Kuznetstov: Yes, we do need 20 channels	359
	In this country you can't just fo to a store and buy a TV set	371
	Cable TV	376
	Videomafia in the USSR	381
CHAPTER XII	COMMUNICATIONS NETWORKS	
	Telephone from "the big brother"	393
	Bugged by Kryuchkov	398
	COCOM refuses to sell us fiber-optic equipment	404
	Checking all the mail	410
CHAPTER XIII	WHAT LIES IN STORE	
	Some forecasts	415

Name and Subject Index 431

FOREWORD

Glasnost was the main achievement of perestroika. Yeltsin's August 22, 1991 decree promised to turn glasnost into freedom of the press.

Fundamental human-rights laws on religious organizations, political parties, the mass media and immigration and emigration procedures were adopted in 1985-91. We received democratic freedoms of which only three years earlier we could not have even dreamed. But we still had a long way to go to democracy as understood in the West. We were still overcoming the legacy of our totalitarian past and at the same time committing new and tragic mistakes, which resulted in the August 1991 attempted coup.

During the six years of perestroika, Soviet authorities and their press conducted shameful cover-ups and disseminated much pure disinformation. Glasnost is one thing, but for our media a yawning gulf lies between it and full freedom of information. The reputation of Soviet journalists was stained by preliminary censorship and Party control—witness the untruths about the bloody events in Baku and Tashkent, in Tbilisi and Nagorny Karabakh, as well as the distorted coverage of the liberation movements in the Baltic and Transcaucasian republics and cities of Ukraine and Russia.

The five-year silence over the true scale of the Chernobyl catastrophe has drastically shortened the lives of millions of Byelorussians, Ukrainians and Russians who to this day live in radioactive zones. In 1991 it was officially accepted that more than 200,000 children in the Chernobyl area are doomed to premature deaths unless they can receive bone marrow transplants—which in Russia is simply impossible due to the absence of the necessary medical equipment. All hopes rest on international aid, which so far we have been less than active in seeking.

For decades up to 1991, the role of the opposition press in the USSR was played by the foreign mass media. Yet the paradox is that it is precisely the Soviet press that is leading the processes of perestroika, the reforms begun from above by Mikhail Gorbachev with the active support and genuine enthusiasm of numerous journalists working in the official central press. Today we know that the magazine *Ogonyok*, the journal *Novy Mir* (New World), the weeklies *Moskovskiye Novosti* (Moscow News) and *Argumenty i Fakty* (Arguments and Facts) and the daily paper *Izvestia* are promoting perestroika with all their strength—and for their pains have become the principal targets of attacks from conservative forces within the country.

The information revolution in the USSR was launched by artists Galich, Vysotsky and Okudzhava. In the 1960s and the 1970s, Soviet records with their songs were not issued, but their voices reproduced by samizdat tape-recording equipment sounded throughout our evening-parties held during these times. The official authorities imprisoned people for samizdat and tamizdat publications, for video-tapes and Xerox copies and banned duplicators at home, with the exception of antediluvian typewriters. Western companies looked the other way at the fortunes being made by new generations of Soviet businessmen engaged in the piracy of copying Western books, concerts, motion pictures and computer programs. Practically everyone consumed unofficial creative productions and prohibited information. Only now is this practice gradually shifting to a legal basis. The black information economy seems doomed.

The lifting of preliminary censorship on August 1, 1990 has changed the face of our press and television. In the absence of independent court procedures that uphold citizens' interests and not the interests of the political system, the press has played and continues to play the role of a bureau of complaints. Moreover, the attitude of our supreme federal authorities to the press remained appropriate.

Dozens of new periodicals, TV and radio programs—*Nezavisimaya Gazeta* (The Independent Gazette) and the *Stolitsa* (Capital) magazine, the TV program *Vesti* (News), the illustrated monthly *Moscow Magazine*, the weekly *Kommersant*, the magazine *Nashe Naslediye* (Our Heritage), *Radio of Russia* and the radio program *Echo of Moscow*—all have become our achievements in the sphere of free journalism.

The material in this book was selected according to three broad topics: 1) a narration about those who in the 1990s have sought to dismantle the Stalinist system in the press and book publishing, in radio and television; 2) an analysis of the development of audio-and video-technology, satellite and cable television, communications and computerization; 3) the interrelationship of the problems of a free press and human rights in Russia.

PART I. JOURNALISTS SERVING PERESTROIKA

CHAPTER I

THE MUZZLED FOURTH ESTATE

How we were forced to subscribe to the party press

The communist dictatorship established itself in Russia as a result of the First World War, and as a consequence of the long cult of such ideas as Russian populism, anarchism, terrorism, socialism and the community system of the Russian raznochintsy (people of various origins who no longer belonged to a traditional group of the population). The outward attraction of socialist ideas and the skillful manipulation of them through mass media enabled Lenin and Stalin, Hitler and Mussolini to seize political power. The difference between them consists, perhaps, in the fact that the first pair managed to do away with their compatriots on a much larger scale than the second pair. Without Stalin's long economic and political backing, there could be no Hitler. The latter unleashed the Second World War, which then widened the sphere of communist expansion.

In 1990 the Rubicon was crossed. The countries of Eastern Europe acquired their freedom, and liberalization begin to gradually take hold in the Soviet Union. The West instituted a type of new "Marshall Plan" for Eastern Europe, but it will be difficult to restore what has been ruined by decades of communist rule. Not only the economy and environment bear the scars but also the people. The slave mentality prevents us from being people bear the scars. The slave mentality prevents Russians from being free persons. The Poles, on the other hand, never stopped fighting for their freedom, be it from Russians, Germans or Communists. They never gave up their resistance. They have won their freedom, at last. We shall have to fight for ours yet.

In terms of copies of newspapers per 1,000 people, the Soviet Union, with 405, was one of the world leaders, (UNESCO 1984 figures). Ahead of us were only Japan (575 newspaper), West Germany (408), East Germany (530), and Britain (421). This becomes a dubious honor if we detach ourselves from the statistics and look at the root of the problem. The majority of our newspapers consist of four sheets of ordinary or condensed print. Previously, one page was always devoted to reprints of identical TASS reports and commentaries (which were mandatory for the entire central, republican, regional, city and district press).

Up to 90 percent of newspaper printruns in the Soviet Union is distributed on a subscription basis, i.e., the annual fee is paid in advance to the publishers. Thus, with the cash safely gathered in, the state postal service feels no urgency and newspapers often reach distant rural areas not daily but in bulk weekly consignments. Part of the already paid-for print run doesn't appear at all, usually under the pretext of insufficient paper. In 1989, the USSR for the first time introduced free, i.e. unlimited, subscriptions to most periodical publications. At the same time the Party's habit of forcing members to subscribe to *Pravda* and the journals *Kommunist, Agitator* and *Politicheskoye Samoobrazovaniye* (Political Self-Education) was relaxed. The result was not long in coming—in 1990 the above-named publications lost up to 40 percent of their readership. The circulation of the Party press would have nose dived completely were it not for two circumstances: retention of the previous subscription levels by establishments at state expense, and also the emptiness of kiosks, which sell out their daily ration of fresh copies within an hour or so. *Pravda* was always the last one to go, although it should be admitted that more copies of it entered retail sale than of all the other newspapers combined.

There was, of course, a desperate shortage of paper in the country. There was enough of it only for the Communist Party and the cooperative businesses. The former flattered itself and turned out unlimited quantities of stuff fit for the shredder, while the latter pay, and as much as is necessary. Subscribers are also being forced to fork out more every year for their favorite reading, and are voting with the ruble.

The circulation of Soviet central newspapers for 1990 looked like this: *Argumenty i Fakty* 31.5 mln, *Komsomolskaya Pravda* 20.3 mln, *Trud* (Labor) 20 mln, *Izvestia* 9.4 mln, *Pravda* 6.4 mln, *Selskaya Zhizn* (Village Life) 5.7 mln, *Semya* (Family) 4.6 mln, *Literaturnaya Gazeta* 4.2 mln, *Sovetskaya Rossia* 3 mln, *Uchitelskaya Gazeta* (Teachers' Gazette) 1.2 mln, *Krasnaya Zvezda* (Red Star) 1 mln, *Rabochaya Tribuna* (Workers' Tribune) 800,000, *Ekonomika i Zhizn* (Economics and Life) 600,000, and *Sovetskaya Kultura* (Soviet Culture) 500,000. The magazines: *Ogonyok* (Spark) 4 mln, *Novy Mir* 2.7 mln, *Znamya* (Banner) 900,000, *Molodaya Gvardiya* (Young Guard) 600,000, *Izvestia TsK KPSS* (CPSU Central Committee News) 600,000, *Kommunist* 500,000, *Nash Sovremennik* (Our Contemporary) 400,000, and *Zvezda* (Star) 300,000.

Availability of certain publications has always been limited—the *Angliya* (England) and *Amerika* (America) magazines, and the weekly *Nedelya* (Week)—and there were no subscriptions to the Russian edition of *Moscow News* prior to 1990.

On August 1, 1990 the Law on the Press came into effect, abolishing preliminary censorship as well as the Party and state monopoly on publishing.

Soviet journalist no longer trembled before Party panjandrums of various ranks. The practice of compulsory official answers to criticism in the press has also ceased. Investigative reporters are no longer sacked. As rewards for stories in defense of "unjustly insulted individual workers", free flats, hospital beds and college courses are no longer handed out. Only yesterday, journalists were in the employ of an amazing public body that combined the functions of prosecutor and judge, provider of social security, and church. The most populous office of any Soviet daily was (and is) the letters department. Until recently, mail would arrive by the sackful every day—complaints and tear-jerking appeals, anonymous denunciations and simply responses to past articles. The old axiom known to every newspaper in every civilized country is only now beginning to establish itself in Russia: the journalist's weapon is the ability to influence the opinion of the public, not of an individual bureaucrat. In a law-based state, the offended takes the offender to court, instead of writing to a newspaper or Party committee for redress.

For the press to carry out its new functions and wield its new power, it requires both political and economic independence. Freedom never comes cheap, and is not something on which costs should be cut. This, evidently, was the opinion of Mikhail Poltoranin, head of the recently-established Ministry for the Press and Information of the Russian Federation. On September 9 1990 *Moscow News* interviewed him, under the headline "The Fourth Estate in Russia":

> Minister Mikhail Poltoranin gets told off by his wife. And this purely personal feature of his life has a direct bearing on his work in the ministry. Judge for yourselves: after a month and a half he still has not received any salary, and he works from 8 in the morning until it is pitch dark outside the windows of his office in a well-appointed town house. Add his staff of three, multiply by the crisis in production of and prices for paper, and do not forget the Law on the Press and the wave of new and old publishers that has swamped Kachalov street, then recall in whose pockets are most of the country's printing companies—and you will understand why the new Russian minister has anything but an easy job. The ministry appeared de jure on September 1, and within a month and a half has de facto achieved the equivalent of what it would have taken its predecessor—the Russian Federation Committee for Publishing and Printing (Goskompechat RSFSR)—an entire year.
>
> Poltoranin is preparing to issue a 90-volume edition of the works of Leo Tolstoy, complete and unabridged (two volumes more than the last such collection). And he especially wants it to be released by the Posrednik publishing house in Tula province, which was founded by Tolstoy himself and is currently in dire straits. Poltoranin has suggested to the Russian government a state monopoly on the commercial issue in Russia of copyright-expired literature. If the go-ahead is given, the Party will have to relinquish its highly-profitable printing of Pushkin, Balzac, Gogol, Conan Doyle, Jules Verne, Azimov and others. The benefit is obvious: it will become possible, without placing the price at more than 5 or 6 rubles per copy (since paper costs have risen) to offset the problem of money-losing school

textbooks, children's literature, and small-circulation and unprofitable publications in the republics.

Question: So where are you going to publish classical, adventure and other literature for which you don't have to pay the authors?

Answer: In our own printing houses, which are standing idle because they're out of paper...

From literary prose our conversation moved to more mundane questions.

Question: Everyone knows that there's a paper shortage in the country...

Answer: For example, in the USA per capita of population consumption of paper is about 300 kg annually, in little Finland about 250, and here—37! We need to raise this to at least 150. The Russian government has discussed the problem of building this stricken industry. After all, the Russian Federation produces 85% of all the country's paper. A commission has been set up, which will elaborate a government program to boost paper production. We don't need gigantic businesses. We'll be building medium-sized operations, forming joint ventures and delivering equipment to existing plants.

Question: This will probably take 10 years. Yet new publications are multiplying like rabbits, new political parties are appearing, and they're all saying: gimme! gimme!

Answer: Last year the country manufactured 6.3 million tons of paper, not including for packaging. And despite our poverty we still managed somehow to export 335,000 tons, the CPSU Central Committee took 280,000 for books and journals, and over 250,000 for newspapers. All the publishing houses of Russia subordinated to our ministry received a grand total of 165,000 tons! We put forward a draft resolution to the Russian Federation Supreme Soviet: all the paper produced in Russia (last year it came to 5.4 million tons) should be distributed by Russia. We should be in charge of our own paper and parcel it out fairly and openly—with participation of public, cultural and arts societies, and taking into account various parties' needs.

Question: So the Russian monopoly would give Russia paper, and the state monopoly on copyright-expired books will give it money. What will it be spent on?

Answer: I've already mentioned school textbooks and children's literature. But there are plenty of other problems. We subsidize 115 unprofitable provincial newspapers. We're going to continue doing so, but on one condition: they should be published by local Soviets. We're about to make suggestions on this to the government.

Question: But the ruling party has enough resources to flood the market with its own press...

Answer:	We've proposed that in Russia no Party, should possess more than 30% of the mass media.
Question:	**What levers do you have?**
Answer:	Paper and the Russian Bank. If the 30% quota is exceeded, the bank freezes the account.
Question:	**But will this not lead to the well-known principle of confiscate and distribute—albeit in a fairer form than previously?**
Answer:	No, it won't. The ministry is setting up its own commercial banks, which will provide loans to independent Soviet publishers. This is the only way to defend cultural and moral values in Russia.
Question:	**But money has to be earned.**
Answer:	The other day the Russian finance ministry registered the "Rossiiskii Dom" (Russian House) joint-stock company. Among the founders is our ministry. We're going to earn that money.
Question:	**Okay then, things are becoming clear as regards books and newspapers. But what about the other mass media? This is also one of your ministry's concerns. Will there, for example, be a Russian wire agency?**
Answer:	We've dropped this idea. Why duplicate the huge TASS outfit? There are numerous independent news agencies in Russia, whose reports, incidentally, are carried by *Moscow News* among others. We plan to create a center based on them in Moscow. By agreement with these agencies we're going to collate all their information and distribute it.
Question:	**What about Russia's own press?**
Answer:	We plan to issue two dailies and two weeklies, and 8 magazines, one of which will be called *Rossia*.
Question:	**Will we be able to watch a Russian TV service?**
Answer:	Yes, an All-Russian state TV and radio company is going to be established as part of our ministry. Part of its assets will come from central TV, but we've also signed a letter of intent with some foreign firms—we want to set up commercial television, build our own TV studios...

Mikhail Poltoranin, Russian Minister for the Press and Information, went on about the history of the Soviet press and history in general, although he worked in the new capacity for barely two months. He did not betray the hopes of those who welcomed the Law on the Press. Quite a few good laws were approved under perestroika, but nearly all of them remained on paper. The implementation of democratic laws was hindered by the apparatus, which was loath to give up even the smallest of its privileges.

It is nice that in late 1990, the sixth year of perestroika, a republican Minister of the Press proved stronger than the State Committee for the Press of the USSR and all ideological departments of the Moscow City Party Committee, Polozkov's Russian Communist Party, the USSR Communist Party

Central Committee and related organizations, such as the KGB, the Union of Writers and the Central Committee of the Komsomol.

Consequently all the above party structures, as well as our military leaders, hated Poltoranin and pinched and kicked him in their press and on the Vremya news program as much as they kicked Yeltsin.

Poltoranin was a top-class professional journalist. He worked for *Pravda* and the Novosti Press Agency, was editor-in-chief of the newspaper *Moskovskaya Pravda* and board chairman of the Moscow branch of the USSR Union of Journalists. The latter nominated him as People's Deputy of the USSR. After that Poltoranin worked on the Law on the Press as a deputy for a year. When he was appointed minister, he started implementing it. He is facing a challenging task of laying the foundation for the Fourth Estate, the power of public opinion as expressed in independent mass media.

On August 1, 1990 Censorship in the USSR Collapsed...

Today it is important not to forget that the very limited freedom of the press we have acquired was not given to us as a present. This freedom was won through the selfless efforts of people who deserve a good word about themselves.

How this happened is the subject of an article in the first issue of *Demokraticheskaya Rossia*. On August 1 1990 the Law on the Press and other Mass Media came into force. So did the country acquire a free press? Both yes and no is the opinion of Mikhail Fedotov, doctor of law and a former member of a committee working group at the USSR Supreme Soviet:

> Freedom of the press cannot be legislated into life. It is merely a branch on the tree of democracy. Until the tree itself grows, such freedom will remain, on the 'drawing board'. Attaching it to the trunk of social totalitarianism is futile and immoral. Futile because the freedom to express opinions logically runs counter to a monopoly of the economy, politics and ideology. Immoral because ritualistically proclaimed it becomes a convenient screen for brainwashing under the pretext of 'moulding of a new Man'.
>
> For seven decades our society lived under "freedom of the press" declared by Soviet constitutions to be 'in the interests of the people and for the purposes of strengthening and developing the socialist system'. Thousands of national, republican and local Pravdas restlessly drummed into our heads truths dreamed up at Staraya Square. All other thoughts were undeserving of the freedom to be expressed since, in the opinions of the custodians of the truth, they contradicted the legislatively-established, 'interests and purposes', and consequently should be punishable as 'deliberate falsehoods slandering the Soviet state and social order'.
>
> When it was obvious that only a dead-end was ahead, it turned out that the people were quite capable of defining their own interests, choosing between those striving to 'strengthen and develop', and those proposing other options. Naturally, the glasnost that was proclaimed to let off steam amounted to merely an ersatz freedom

of speech and the press. The powers-that-be simply relaxed their grip on the reins, they did not let them go. They intended to renew their grip with the help of the Law on the Press and on a fully respectable legal basis.

The fact that they never even dreamed of guaranteeing real freedom of the press is obvious from the official draft submitted to the deputies. Drawn up at Staraya Square to the standards of the press legislation in the days of Antonin Novotny and Nicolae Ceaucescu, it proposed to legalize censorship, destroy samizdat and condemn the press to the eternal role of 'the Party's powerful and trusty weapon'.

As we know, the deputies preferred an alternative draft, elaborated by Drs of Law Yu. Baturin, V. Entin and myself and printed—after an uphill fight lasting several months—in the form of a pamphlet at our own expense to be given away to deputies attending the 1st Congress. In this unofficial way it got into parliament.

But what seemed to us, the authors and deputies who were members of Nikolai Fyodorov's working group as benefits were described by our opponents as 'throwbacks to democracy' and 'a morass of bourgeois freedoms'. They did everything they could to castrate the draft, make their own changes and remove anything not to their liking. At meetings of the working group representatives of 'interested departments' attacked virtually every article, trying to plant time bombs that would later blow up the entire draft. Not only that, but strange metamorphoses constantly took place within the text: after retyping at printshops, new phrases would unfailingly appear, and on one occasion an entire article—on limitations to freedom of speech in the mass media.

Despite all this we managed to prepare an entirely respectable document for the first reading. Having enjoyed little success during the committee stage, our opponents resorted to other means. The working group decided to publish the draft for discussion by the journalistic community. At Staraya Square they forbade us to do so. We printed it as an official document of our session for distribution to deputies—Staraya Square confiscated the print run. During the first reading a scandal broke out. On the eve of the readings the deputies were handed a 'final version' of the draft that was as different from ours, as endorsed by the committee, as day is from night. On the surface it appeared the same, but the essence had been removed.

This 'finalized' draft was thrown out as an illegal lobbyist's trick and ours was passed, with a resolution that it be published for nationwide discussion and then amended. But behind the scenes the resolution was reworded: first amend and then publish. Also, in the draft there appeared 'alternative wordings proposed by a group of People's Deputies', concerning just two questions: the right to found a publication, and the independence of the editorial staff. In the first instance the right of individual citizens to found a paper was withheld, in the second, founders and publishers were allowed to dictate their will to journalists. These alternatives reversed the whole sense of the draft and instead of freedom of the press, proposed the opposite.

Incidentally, losses were sustained on the way to the second reading. Since the battle was on all fronts, something had to be sacrificed. The grounds on which a refutation could be refused for publication disappeared, as did those on which a journalist could be denied information. The representatives of 'interested departments' strenuously claimed that journalists should have the same right to information as everyone else. But the ordinary citizen has virtually no right to information! Our attempt to equate a reporter to a surgeon, who unlike others is allowed to cut a man with a scalpel to save his life, was unsuccessful.

'Politically-literate typists' also made their contribution. The members of the working group failed to notice in time that the right to close down a media outlet had been given to the authority that registered it. Imagine a registry office that itself decides to wind up a marriage!

Unfortunately, we were late in spotting this particular pearl. There were others as well. For example, from one article that established the grounds on which a media outlet could be closed down the word 'only' disappeared. The revised wording of the article was such that this absence led to the possibility of closing down a paper for any reason. Thank God we realized this meddling in time.

And what did the typist say? 'I'm also responsible for this draft law', she once replied to my rebuke. 'If you raise a fuss, we'll have you thrown off the working group'.

It took three days to get the draft passed. This was a drama with three acts.

On the first day, the deputies managed to pass just one article. But it was a good one! 'Censorship of the media shall be prohibited'. I think that the great Pushkin would have rejoiced to see that on the anniversary of his birth such a dream came true—the abolition of the censor.

On the second day the provision guaranteeing an individual the right to set up his own media outlet survived, despite a massed onslaught. I don't know what convinced the deputies more: selected quotes by Lenin, references to Herzen's, Pushkin's and Delvig's beginnings in publishing, the USSR's international obligations... The proposal to exclude individuals gathered only 84 votes. During the break we embraced and congratulated each other.

But ahead there lay defeat. Four times members of the working group and like-minded deputies attempted to remove the clause which would allow registering authorities the right to close down a media outlet. We explained thoroughly that this was an obvious mistake. Yet the typing pool's amendment became law, although at times we were just 20 votes short of victory.

The third act of this prolonged drama was packed with surprises. Firstly the splendid writer Sergei Zalygin took the microphone to call upon us to ... reject the law, because although it protected journalists it did not, in his opinion, protect *Novy Mir*.

After him a deputy from Moldavia demanded legal action against all astrologists, people with ESP and in general everyone who disseminates 'information not corresponding to reality'. To back up his proposal he referred to the panic that had taken place after the radio station Mayak had broadcast some astrologist who predicted an earthquake soon in Moldavia. He evidently didn't realize that he was inflicting a fatal wound to pluralism of opinion and freedom of speech. The solicitous 'typists' were at the ready with a polished wording for this amendment. They understood everything.

Fortunately, the Moldavian deputy's amendment failed, as, incidentally, did the majority of others. To cut a long story short, during the second reading they could not make it worse. But neither could we make it better.

Is the new law bad? No, most likely good. Worth a B plus. Or perhaps a B minus. The main thing is that more minuses weren't added on by the federal government and state committees for publishing and broadcasting. We have to be on our guard and fight for those rights given us by the Law on the Press, using all the rules set out in this and other laws. We have to fight in the parliaments, local Soviets, courts, editorial offices ... everywhere.

Nezavisimaya Gazeta (The Independent Gazette) reported on February 2, 1991 that "scholars of the USSR Interior Ministry are editing the Law on the Press, at the request of and expense of the USSR Committee for Printing, rather than at the demand of the President". The Interior Ministry's research institute has already forwarded its proposed amendments to the USSR Supreme Soviet where, according to the newspaper, they were favorably received.

This lawlessness shows both the one-sided bias of Central TV to reflect the viewpoint of the CPSU politburo, and the not insignificant detail that the Union Law on the Press was not supplied with the mechanisms to enable it to come into force. For example, the legislators drafted the RSFSR Law For example, the legislators have drafted the RSFSR Law on introducing amendments and additions to the Criminal Code of the Russian Federation. If the Russian parliament accepts this draft, censorship will become a criminal offense. The Russian Ministry for the press and Information succeeded in obtaining an explanation from the RSFSR Supreme Court that the sale of newspapers in any place does not entail a contravention of the law. Consequently an editorial office may hire schoolchildren to sell its newspaper for fair financial remuneration. For a small circulation publication on bad terms with the SOYUZPECHAT (Press Distribution Agency), this path can be quite effective.

Glasnost has always been restricted in our country. Attempts were made to muffle it to a sufficient extent for the powers that be. Although the times have changed, the censorship system which had recently been fine tuned has made it possible to conceal from our society any information disagreeable to the old ideologists.

As the newspaper *Izvestia* reported on March 25, 1991, the repeal of censorship has not caused a change in society's conceptions of the mass media, varying from "what is useful and what is not useful" to an open call voiced in the Supreme Soviet of the USSR that the operation of the Law on the Press be suspended.

> Today we must speak both about the press and glasnost, and the citizens' right to all information. And this must be regulated by appropriate normative standards. The press should be governed by democratic principles. These constitute, above all, independence from the founder, freedom of choice of the editor-in-chief and the journalists' right to express their own opinion. However, these principles have to be mastered by us. Hence this call has been raised by different groups: the press must be controlled, as it has failed to remember whom it should serve.
>
> By the way, we can cite many more theoretical arguments on the role of the press in a democratic state, but the possibilities afforded by the Law passed in June

last year are of greater interest. In the opinion of Kh. Sheinin, deputy chief of one department in the Supreme Court of the USSR, however, the USSR Law on the Press is not used today to its full extent. Above all, this concerns the statutory right of citizens to receive information, that of the mass media to supply it and of officials to provide information. He noted that he cannot understand why journalists who are denied information, do not apply to law-enforcement bodies to protect their rights. Since the appearance of the Law on the Press there has been no such case in judicial practice, although today there are requisite possibilities to initiate legal proceedings against officials who prevent the receipt of information or merely distort it.

In March 1991, *Moscow Magazine* carried an article entitled "*How much, Comrade Bureaucrat?*" Its author, American journalist Karen Dukes, remarked that during the glasnost era Soviet officials began to demand large sums of money in hard currency from foreign correspondents for any interesting information. You can no longer rely on a bottle of vodka or a blank videocassette. Vladimir Martynov, chief of the press service of the Moscow militia, said that the maximum sum collected from foreign TV reporters for one day's filming of Moscow militiamen at work amounts to 1,000 dollars. The magazine quoted the words of Yasen Zasursky, Department of Moscow University Faculty of Journalism, who asserted that officials who demand payment for information remind him of taxi drivers who extort one or two hundred rubles for a journey from Sheremetyevo Airport to the center of Moscow. According to the Law on the Press, officials are obliged to grant journalists interviews free of charge.

Undoubtedly, normal practice lagged behind the operative Law on the Press. In the opinion of V. Foteyev, former Chairman of the USSR Supreme Soviet Committee on Glasnost, much has to be achieved in the future (*Izvestia*, March 25, 1991).

But it is quite evident that the practice of replacing a law by a former purely administrative form of management of the mass media must come to an end. As a matter of fact, the Glasnost Committee has been transformed into a place where its members consider complaints demanding that press freedom be stifled. It is, however, obvious that a law our society must be guided by should exist in actual fact. The demands voiced in the Supreme Soviet to examine the particulars of articles published in the press, which are not to the liking of its deputies, must not be forgotten. Otherwise this may well backfire and provoke lawlessness and become a regular bridle on glasnost. In the opinion of V. Foteyev, the mass media today are in fact confronted by a qualitatively new task: they must shape public opinion on the basis of objective information.

The Committee sees its priority task to be the realization of the Law on the Press. It intends to draft a program which will secure glasnost: the creation of typography facilities, of the bodies for personnel training, as well as the protection of journalists and their publications. Today journalists have to work under severe pressure from publishers and founders. Here one should mention the newspaper *Nash*

Golos (Our Voice), the organ of the People's Deputies of the Krasnoyarsk Territory. The Krasnoyarsk Worker Publishers, in exchange for an agreement to print the paper, demanded that the editorial office give the publishing house a receipt, to the effect that "the paper undertakes not to subject CPSU committees to indiscriminate criticism". This symptomatic case vividly characterized the monopolism evidenced on the publishing market. Local publications are not the only ones to face such ultimatums. When some central publications expressed a desire to become the founders of *Pravda*, its publishing house refused to sign a letter of agreement.

What do people in the West think about all this? The newspaper *Novoye Russkoye Slovo*, issued by Russian emigres in the United States of America, displayed its interest in the changes in the USSR and printed the article of our former compatriot Mark Popovsky under the title "*The Word and the Axe*". This title refers to the tragic circumstances of the murder of Alexander Men', a well-known priest and writer, by an unknown assassin. Popovsky wrote in the paper, issued on December 14, 1990:

> Glasnost is already three years old. The West regards it as Gorbachev's main, indisputable achievement. In the Soviet Union the attitude to glasnost is somewhat more cautious. This attitude is shared even by those who support the President and Party General Secretary. We believe that the Law on the Press, which entered into force on August 1, 1990 has not saved the Soviet press from fear and falsehood. In any case the leadership of the weekly *Moscow News* stated on November 18, 1990: "The people must know the whole truth about the real state of affairs in the country. Semi-truth and undisguised lies uttered by statesmen must be punished". This opinion is shared by many writers and editors. They want to have the publicity framework extended. At the same time an opposite point of view is expressed, for example, by readers of the paper *Izvestia*. "The freedom and independence of press organs are needed for one purpose only–to discredit the Communist Party and help radicals seize state power", writes a Lvov resident. "If I were in charge, I would enforce a strict control of the media. If you are not controlled, you will make a real mess of things", writes a Muscovite. Readers from the town of Vsevolzhsk insist that "our society should be protected against information violence and consequently moral censorship should be introduced to serve this purpose". Residents from the city of Gorky pronounced their own final verdict: "An unsupervised press in a civilized society is inadmissible and pernicious".
>
> What does glasnost in the press, which is tolerated by Soviet authorities, look like today?
>
> It has granted our society a certain degree of freedom. Papers, journals and magazines feature articles and notes by scholars, priests, officers and rank-and-file citizens, who mentioned in their letters to the editorial board the burden they bear in everyday life.
>
> But after easing the pressure on the press, the authorities did not forget their own interests. Government propaganda has not fallen silent, but instead has merely quietened down. They keep saying to the people that the former institutions of oppression have been completely destroyed and no longer create any threat to

individual citizens. These assertions were found in numerous statements by the staff workers of the State Security Committee and the Chief Administration for the Protection of State Secrets in the Press, who were responsible for the censorship of newspapers and magazines in the country. The censors now act as friendly advisers and consultants to prevent information leaks. As the state shift to profit-and-loss management principles, the censors of the Chief Administration for the Protection of State Secrets in the Press suggested that editorial offices and publishing houses should conclude agreements and pay them for their cares. This is called means self-financing.

In connection with such changes, the headquarters of state censorship (I remember its huge building in Moscow's Kitaisky Proyezd, not far from the former CPSU Central Committee) was renamed the Central Administration for the Protection of State Secrets in the Press and Other Mass Media. In their interviews, the censors of the new Administration admit apologetically that perhaps 20 to 30 books imported from the West are detained by customs houses, since they reflect 'the spirit of the cold war' and try to undermine the Soviet system and the country's unity.

Is this a list of banned books? No, it is not. This list has not been compiled yet. The question on whether such books should be admitted or not remains to be settled... But the libraries enjoy full freedom today: only 500 books are still banned. All the rest may be read. But while the censors kept giving 'laid-back' interviews and people's deputies spent almost three years drafting and adopting the Law on the Press, the government authorities did not cease the censorship policy. During this period attempts were made to sack four editors of papers and magazines, which supplied the readers with a large volume of so called 'undesirable information'. The wrath of government bodies swooped down on the editors of the paper *Argumenty i Fakty*, the city paper of the town of Noginsk and the magazines *Oktyabr* and *Knizhnoye Obozreniye* (Book Review). The then masters of the country managed to dismiss only one rebel, but they had other powerful means of pressuring the press.

On the 22nd day of the entry into force of the Law on the Press, which announced the total abolition of censorship, a new secret 'List of information materials prohibited for publication' was issued and circulated among the officials 'who are responsible for the dissemination of information'. This list was printed together with a number of copies amounting to 20,000, sufficient for distribution among all the supervisors of the press. It was reported exclusively for their notice: journalists have no right to write about the foot-and-mouth disease infecting the livestock and are forbidden to cite figures, describing its losses; they cannot refer to the inferior condition of military discipline among the personnel of the USSR Armed Forces, inform the people about crimes and suicides in the army and about the wear and tear of railway cars and engines. The list of secret data was endorsed by the Council of Ministers on the basis of reports sent in by ministries. The principle is very simple: ministerial officials make secret all information, which describes their bad work performance and failures, the lack of talent and incompetence of their leadership. The people must not be aware that million heads of cattle die, that railway cars and engines are totally worn-out and that consequently there are railway crashes 'according to a plan', that the Soviet army is disintegrating and that its equipment and materiel are being stolen. No sooner had the Law on the Press come into being than the apparatchiks detonated the principal thesis about the abolition of censorship. At the same time another paragraph of the same Law arises: all breakers of state secrets may be sentenced by a court of law to 5 to 8 years imprisonment. The most zealous seekers, guardians and disseminators of public truth may fall into this trap.

Incidentally attempts are already being made to catch journalists who 'divulge secrets'. After *Moscow News* published in the summer of 1991 the statement made by the former KGB general Oleg Kalugin, one of the editors was 'asked' to visit the Chief Military Procurator's Office. The interrogation lasted four hours. Then an investigator from the Procurator's Office came to the editorial office and demanded a verbatim report of Kalugin's speech on whose basis the paper had prepared the article. Naturally, all this was done in order to preserve state secrets, which Kalugin and *Moscow News* had allegedly leaked.

In remote Siberia, the authorities made short work of disobedient journalists in a far simpler manner. When the independent Siberian Information Agency issued an information bulletin which upset the local regional CPSU committee the latter ordered that the entire print run be confiscated in the city airport. The publishers were accused of 'engaging in a prohibited trade' under the appropriate article of the USSR Criminal Code. In Leningrad the paper *Smena* conjectured that the KGB had prepared the crash of the plane which Boris Yeltsin flew to Spain in, and this was followed by sanctions threatening the editor with a court trial. In the Urals the persecutors of the free press keep using their own methods-- they employ the post service to remove undesirable editions. From time to time the total print run of this or that magazine suddenly disappears and consequently did not reach subscribers. This often happened to issues of the 'freedom-fighter' magazine *Dvadtsaty Vek i Mir* (The 20th Century and the World).

It was, however, far more convenient for the centralized state to suppress any objectionable papers by using centralized methods. Shortly prior to the 1991 subscription campaign it was announced that the price for newspapers and magazines would be raised sharply, perhaps by 3 to 4 times. This was allegedly necessitated by the increased cost of the printing and postal services. This was an excellent move. It was clear that *Pravda*, *Izvestia* and *Kommunist* and other "high-ranking" editions would survive such a trial, as the losses would be covered by the Party and state budgets. The young newspapers and magazines, however, which were becoming independent as well as a few of the older papers, which had broken away from the CPSU Central Committee's surveillance could go bankrupt, since the public would not be able to subscribe to very expensive publications. Vitaly Korotich, the Editor-in-Chief of the magazine *Ogonyok*, had the following comment to make about the ruling clique's decision: "Our economists calculated that if prices were to double, the subscription would also be cut in half". Pavel Gusev, Editor-in-Chief of *Moskovsky Komsomolets*, took a deeper look at the situation or perhaps ventured a greater degree of frankness: "The rise in prices is a camouflaged action, aimed at striking at the freedom of expression. Consequently those who really need information, will be deprived of it". The Editor-in-Chief of *Sovetskaya Kultura* adhered to the same opinion: "The apparatus, which wanted to suppress glasnost a long time ago has found now a new pretext--the transition to a market economy in order to curb public interest in newspapers via an increase in their cost".

This is true. Especially if we consider the fact that the circulation of many Party newspapers and magazines had dwindled five times or more during the perestroika years. In 1991 the demand for Party newspapers fell even further. Consequently mass propaganda possibilities also diminished, despite the fact that Party bosses prized the concept of brainwashing the people. But we shall not bother ourselves with the fate of the Party apparatus, as all the levers of state administration were still in the hands of its functionaries. They fully controlled public property as well. The monopoly of glasnost has been repealed, but the monopoly of printing paper has still been retained. Over half the country's supply of newsprint was provided at extremely low prices to the Party system, ministries and other government departments. Every year the Managing Department of the CPSU Central Committee devoured 500,000 tons out of the 1,800,000 tons of newsprint produced in the country. Moreover, the military consumed 150,000 tons a year. There were many other 'high-ranking' consumers, and consequently every year the remaining newspapers in Russia received only 60,000 tons of newsprint. Next year we do not expect any fundamental change in the distribution of newsprint. Book-and magazine-printing paper is distributed in the same manner. In 1990 Pravda Publishers issued 350 million copies of its low-standard Party propaganda literature, while the rest of the book trade in Russia amounts to 140 million copies. So there was no need to send special squads and KGB troops to quell the press. According to the Party apparatus' calculations, numerous democratic publications would be stifled by the rise in prices or by the shortage of newsprint. Is this Gorbachev's leadership strategy in the era of glasnost?

How is the present situation in the press assessed by professional journalists? Will the Law on the Press transform a dimly lit glasnost into full freedom of speech? Here are some of the most striking pronouncements on this score by the editors of diverse publications.

Alexander Levikov (*Literaturnaya Gazeta*):
"Glasnost and the freedom of the press are two different things. Glasnost means everything permitted by the powers that be. Generally speaking, I can't name a single printed paper or magazine as part of the free press. There is no freedom of the press in our country for it has not emerged so far during the years of perestroika?".

Alexei Pankin (*Mezhdunarodnaya Zhizn*):
"Journalists, public figures and even statesmen have strained their voices during the perestroika years and now everyone is sick of them because of their howls: 'Give trustworthy statistics to us! Reveal the share of military production in the national income!' At best the results are ambivalent and at worst they are closer to zero".

Mikhail Fedotov (a lawyer and public figure):
"Censorship means reins. Today these reins have been slackened a little bit. We are shaking our heads now. But at any minute these reins may be restored. At first we shall bristle under them, but we shall subsequently get used to be trampled under".

Anatoly Ivanov (*Molodaya Gvardiya*):

"The Law on the Press is imperfect in many respects... Our press has hardly any independence, it is still dependent on somebody!"

Vitaly Korotich (*Ogonyok*):
"Generally speaking, it is much easier to pass a law than implement it".
"As we see it, neither journalists on the 'left' or the 'right' are disposed to regarding the future of their profession in an optimistic light. The steel axe of state censorship still hangs over the free press of Russia."

The Russian legislators chose another road by submitting in May 1991, for nationwide discussion their own, republican draft of the Law on the Press. Its authors comprised those specialists who had drafted and upheld the Union Law on the Press adopted by the USSR parliament--Mikhail Fedotov, Yury Baturin and Vladimir Entin.

The authors added that the draft does not contradict the Union Law; moreover, it develops and supplements the latter. For example, if the Law had only one phrase about censorship in Article 1, the draft included a special article entitled "The Inadmissibility of Censorship".

The article says that no allowance should be made for the censorship of mass communication, which means that the officials of government bodies, organizations and non-governmental associations shall not demand that a mass media editorial office should agree in advance upon its reports and other materials (except when someone in the office is the author of an article or an interview) and no ban shall be imposed on the dissemination of reports and other materials or the parts thereof. Allowance shall not be made for the creation and financing of bodies, organizations or institutions or for the appointment of officials with the task of exercising any censorship of the mass media.

An interesting formulation was made in the Chapter "Organization of the Activity of the Mass Media": the editorial office is exempted from paying a share of its profits to the budget within two years of the first publication by the mass media.

New sections on the electronic mass media have appeared. Provision has been made for the creation and functioning of a Federal Commission of Mass Communications. In particular, it will elaborate state policy in the domain of radio and television licenses (Art. 30). Here is another provision of Article 31 License for Broadcasting: "License applications made directly or through subsidiary organizations by political parties, trade unions, religious bodies or other non-governmental associations shall not be accepted for consideration." It is clear that only professionals should deal with TV and radio broadcasting and grant equal opportunities to everybody.

The chapter "Interrelations between the Mass Media and Individual Citizens and Organizations" had a larger section on the right to receive information. It is supposed to include in this section articles concerning the request for information, any refusal and delay in granting information, confidential information. Incidentally, during the discussion of the Union Law, these articles had disappeared from the text.

Professor Ya.N. Zasursky, Dean of the Moscow University Faculty of Journalism, called the draft RSFSR Law a serious contribution to the development of legal thought about the mass media. For the first time in the Soviet state, a draft of a law pursued the underlying principle of a law-based state: "Everything not prohibited by law is allowed" (Instead of the traditional principle: "Everything that is allowed is...allowed")...

The draft RSFSR Law on the Mass Media was dedicated to the memory of the People's Deputy of the USSR Lyudmila Batynskaya, a journalist from Krasnoyarsk, who upheld in the Union parliament the right of the press to be the fourth power in the state and not "mere dust on boots". The text of the draft was published in a special issue of the newspaper *Rossia* and in a special booklet.

The Communist Party Monopoly of Dispensing Paper

What was to happen to the property previously held by the CPSU? It controlled the main typographic capacities for the issue of all periodicals. On March 16, 1991 the Moscow newspaper *Kuranty* (Chimes) noted that the RSFSR Ministry for the Press and Information had at its disposal only four per cent of the newspaper printing houses available in the Russian Federation. This is what the Minister Mikhail Poltoranin said on this score (see *Argumenty i Fakty*, July 28, 1990):

> When I familiarized myself with the state of affairs in this sector I got a shock. Nearly 60% of all paper factories have been in operation since the turn of the century. Also, 65% of all equipment is completely worn out. Over the past 20 years, growth rates in timber processing have fallen five times over. We sell raw timber abroad for peanuts. Russia has the world's largest forestry reserves—73,000 million cubic meters, yet we turn out six times less paper pulp than the USA, eight times less paper, 15 times less writing-and printing-quality paper, and 50 times less paper for hygiene purposes.
>
> The same applies to printing works. The Party's taken the best for itself, and left the rest to the state.
>
> In 1975 the best printing works were transferred to the Party's balance sheet. The Party expropriated businesses built with the working people's money, and now claims that its possessions are sacred and inviolable.
>
> Loss-making concerns were left to get by on state subsidies. The state committee for printing and publishing finances 2,115 small-circulation newspapers, 80% of which run at a loss. Sixty million rubles a year are pumped out of republican budgets to keep them going. And these publications are managed by Party committees at various levels.

The Muzzled Fourth Estate

There is virtually no machine-building sector for the printing business in the USSR. It turns out 182 types of equipment out of the 362 types that are essential—and these are 50 years out of date. During the years of perestroika, production even of these has decreased by 42%. On the one hand, they talk about glasnost, on the other—they undermine it.

So we're not starting from zero, but from minus.

Question: The ministry is assuming a wide range of tasks. Do you not fear that with time it will grow to become a monster and that fighting monopolies, it will itself become one?

Answer: No. The ministry doesn't intend to dictate its will to publishers and publications. We're going to try to pool the efforts of all organizations engaged in publishing activities and the mass media, so that they switch to a self-regulating basis and begin to more effectively serve the cause of reviving morality in Russia. We're setting up a coordinating committee, whose members will be newspaper and magazine editors and publishing house managers. Together we'll be drawing up proposals for submission to the Russian Federation Supreme Soviet and government. We see our main task in ensuring a legal framework for glasnost.

Our priority tasks? We need to set up a distribution commission, made up of People's Deputies, lawyers and economists. Let them sit down and work out what exactly belongs to the Party. Where has it come from? How? Why do Party functionaries who have led the country to the edge of the precipice receive pensions from the state and not from the Party? And how much public money have they squandered? How much money has the Party taken from the state to fit out its printing works, its clinics and treatment centers for its privileged class, its country homes with furniture, and so on? And draw up a bill. It'll then transpire not only that the Party has nothing, but actually owes the people billions. The Supreme Soviet can pass a law nationalizing the Party's assets and forcing it to repay its debts to the people.

Question: This is all in the future. What can be done now?

Answer: We need to strengthen our starting position. We're currently conducting negotiations in the USA to acquire university printing facilities for ethnic minorities in the Far North.

We know full well that we can't solve all our problems by ourselves. We'll be attracting foreign investment to develop the paper and printing industries, and to set up production facilities for video technology. Businessmen are coming to our aid, they want to get a slice of our market. Neither should we refuse charity.

Question: Is this not selling off Russia, as the hardliners like to say?

Answer: For 70 years they pumped out our resources and kept quiet about it. They sold raw materials to prop up the world system of socialism, to prop up the hierarchy—the Party, KGB, state and army mandarins. In other words, to support totalitarianism. Now things are changing in Russia—no longer are they going to swallow up foreign money. Now it will be directed towards benefitting the people. There will be tough criticism, of course. It's already started—more hints, more vagueness, less truth and less common sense. These tricks worked in the past, but now they have the opposite effect.

Answer: Mr. Poltoranin, a specific question. On August 1 the Law on the Press comes into effect. Let's suppose that I wish to start up my own newspaper. What do I do?

Answer: The Russian government has decided that Russian publications will be registered by my ministry, and those set up in autonomous republics, regions and districts—by the local state authorities.

You'll receive a license, and be able to publish your newspaper. The rest is up to you—how to get hold of paper, where to print, etc. The idea is that we'll help with this, but not now, only when we're stronger and better able to. The bank will give you a loan—go find a printer, and good luck.

Question: **More people write in this country than in any other—instructions, memoranda, regulations, explanations, and so on. And they all get published. Does the ministry have any plans to put the printing industry in order and seriously set about sharing paper?**

Answer: We need to move fast, and distribution of paper resources is an urgent issue. How come *Novy Mir* and other popular publications can't get hold of any, while the CPSU Central Committee is starting up new newspapers and magazines?

Why do the Party publishing outfits have no worries, while children's publishers have nothing to print on?

The ministry is going to make some proposals regarding distribution of paper to the government. And when we've set up a basis for glasnost, when joint ventures start operating at full steam, when the market comes into effect, the ministry's functions will become narrower...

Question: ... and you'll be out of a job.

Answer: Which will mean that the ministry's done what it was supposed to do.

Let us sum up what the minister said. It turned out fairly easy to cancel censorship and permit free and unlimited subscriptions to any publication, even to *Amerika* or *Moscow News*. For 73 years there was preliminary censorship and compulsory subscription to all the Communist Party's products, but no longer. Logically, demand in the market for all this extremely unpopular output (turgid, full of disinformation, false communist "achievements", cold-war style vilification of the capitalists and other bourgeois exploiters) should have evaporated instantly. If only this were so. As the overall production of newsprint and magazine paper fell sharply in the USSR in 1990, the government did all it could to ensure that Party publications continued to receive all their deliveries. A significant quantity of paper found its way onto the market, where it goes for colossal prices. The previous duties of the Glavlit censor or the "executive staff member" of the Party Central Committee ideology department were now carried out, and no less successfully, by bureaucrats in the federal agency that distributes newsprint on the basis of ideological reliability—the unruly are last in line and have to pay much more. There are other, and simpler, ways of pulling the carpet from under glasnost. Just a year ago, who could have imagined that printing in the Soviet Union would grind to a halt due to ... a shortage of color inks. This essential ingredient had to be acquired abroad. And the bureaucrats did not acquire it, choosing rather to save money. Production of school textbooks, children's books, passports and money has stopped. And someone in our planning and supply organizations once again lined his pockets with a fat sum by selling the precious remainder of this ink on the black market at huge profit. West German and Swiss suppliers came to our aid and dispatched urgent consignments of the required pigments and color ingredients to two Soviet factories. And in response we failed to pay the bill. Our Western suppliers indignantly halted all further deliveries. All that was needed to acquire these goods was 4 million dollars a year.

It transpired in mid-January 1991 that the country's sole supplier of high-quality zinc for printing purposes had ceased producing it. This new shortage first and foremost affected the central newspapers, which are printed not only in Moscow but throughout the country; copies of pages are transmitted by photo-telegraph to local printworks and then made into zinc plates, from which the actual printing takes place. The reason is that as of the beginning of 1991 the State Planning Committee excluded printing zinc from the state order system, i.e., allowed free-market cosmic prices for it. Incidentally, the USSR has the world's largest discovered reserves of zinc.

On January 4 *Izvestia* published a round-up of reports from its own correspondents in various parts of the country, with a large editorial on how the USSR Communications Ministry is virtually everywhere using various pretexts to sabotage the paper's delivery and distribution. A most curious thing was happening: although postal delivery charges had been upped several times over, enthusiasm for delivering *Izvestia* decreased several times. But for some strange reason the effective blockade is selective. There are no problems with *Pravda*, for example, but *Izvestia* and *Komsomolskaya Pravda* are delivered only erratically by the postal workers.

The young Russian press was having it much more difficult than veteran newspapers. How this had come about is described by *Argumenty i Fakty* (No. 46 1990) in a story called *"Russia Is Acquiring a Voice"* by the deputy Russian Federation minister for the press and information, People's Deputy of the USSR V. Logunov:

> We are voiceless in the era of glasnost ['glasnost', meaning 'openness', is derived from the word 'golos', or 'voice' 'openness', is derived from the word 'golos', or 'voice'—trans]. The Law on the Press has opened the floodgates. As of November 1

about 300 various publications coming out within the republic had been registered at our ministry.

The new newspapers have numerous difficulties. They don't have enough staff. Printing facilities are few and far between. In this respect we're about 50 years behind other countries. Our equipment is antediluvian, and we have little of it.

Russia has never had its own television or radio or publications, apart from the reasonably well-known *Sovetskaya Rossia* which, despite officially being aligned with the Russian Federation Supreme Soviet didn't belong to it. And what about dual-subordination territorial, regional, city and district newspapers? These joint publications were always ordered around by the Party committees.

Therefore the ministry, established at the end of September, began its work by setting up an independent Russian press.

What's been done? The parliament's *Rossiiskaya Gazeta* has started coming out. The pilot issue was released on November 3, and issue No. 1 on November 11. A government weekly will appear before the end of the year. A weekly is also planned, to deal with topics such as sovereignty and our federation, plus a current affairs magazine and other publications.

Principles or compromise? How did we manage to get Russian newspapers published? Well, we agreed with the CPSU Central Committee that we could use the *Moskovskaya Pravda* publishing house. In addition, we'll be jointly completing the construction of a second printworks for it (with an area of 32,000 square meters) and equipping it, after which we'll receive 40% of its capacity and the same percentage of all profits. By the end of 1991 we should have no problems putting out our own publications.

We're now being accused of "reneging on our principles" by agreeing with the CPSU Central Committee... But let's look the truth in the face: what would we have achieved by taking away *Sovetskaya Rossia*? In reality only an allocation of paper plus the name (which isn't very popular with most readers anyway). And where would we have found printers? In Tula? Geneva? Add to this the fact that the newspaper of communists in Russia has its own history and readership... and the new Russia should receive a new newspaper.

In August we circulated a letter throughout the country stating that from now on local, city and district papers with dual subordination would no longer receive subsidies from the Russian budget (which this year amounted to 70 million rubles, and next year, due to the increased price of paper, printing and distribution, would have exceeded 300 million), but also that they could expect to continue receiving 50% of the required quantity of paper (the rest would have to come from the Party's business department). In response, these papers have started breaking away—from the mastheads the traditional "publication of the area, city or district Party committee) logos have been removed (although these committees intend to continue running them, as before).

Nobody's being forced to unite or split up or whatever—this should be a purely spontaneous process. The question of subsidies will be decided by the Russian Supreme Soviet when it endorses the republican budget; that of the viability of publications will be decided by local Soviets and not the Party committees. We intend to stick to our guns. The fate of local publications means also the livelihood of 30,000 journalists...

The situation with paper is serious, and it is this that worries us most of all. There is a desperate shortage of it in the republic. On occasion we hear the traditional cry (as if by chance!) of "it's the cooperatives' fault—they buy up all the paper". But in fact they take (at 30 times the going rate) just a drop in the ocean in comparison with what various sensitive defense-sector organizations and the CPSU Central Committee business department receive. The planners have always waited for instructions from the latter as to how much paper to give to whom.

Has the situation changed today? On the surface, yes. Yet in essence the old principle of allocating paper remains as it was. For example, last year 1,800,000 tons of newsprint (a rough figure) was produced. Of this, 600,000 went to the union republics. About 250,000 tons went to other socialist countries. Of the remainder, more than 500,000 tons (over a half!) went to the CPSU Central Committee, 150,000 was taken by various government departments (the defense ministry, KGB, interior ministry, Komsomol, etc.). Russia was allocated 60,000 tons, ie., less than 4% of the total amount of paper produced within the republic! The only answer is to change the distribution system, to the detriment of those consumers who have large resources at their disposal.

Journalists have written hundreds of articles about the material basis in the USSR for glasnost. Each news shortage has its own objective reasons, the main one of which is a fight for survival of the command system. The Party apparat and ministries know full well that their dictatorship can only govern in conditions of total shortage, of poverty and denial of rights. "You'll be deprived of your food! And of everything else as well!", the communist apparatchiks screamed (to themselves, not out loud), and eagerly threw up the economic barricades to kill a good idea.

On the night of January 1–2, 1991 a USSR Interior Forces unit seized the Riga Printing House. The new USSR Minister for the Interior, Boris Pugo, denied that he had ordered the "black berets" into action, announced that he would not intervene, and advocated that a compromise be found. With whom? The Latvian communist party, which had decided to "recover CPSU property" in this way.

Izvestia (January 9 1991) quoted Kazimir Dundurs, the Printing House's director: "In 1957 ownership of the Latvian newspaper and magazine publishing house was transferred, free of charge, to the communist party. Every year from 1.5 to 2 million rubles in profit went to the party's funds. In 1972 construction of a new printworks costing 25 million rubles was started. But the work that we've done here has produced several times that sum. From 1976 to 1990, over 90 million rubles has been handed over to the CPSU. Only a year ago we turned the Printing House into a joint-stock company, our workforce gave its unanimous approval, and hundreds of our employees have already bought shares. Moreover, at the constituent assembly the shares were distributed thus: 51 percent to the printers and editorial staff members, 26 percent to the Latvian republic, and 23 percent to the CPSU. Neither courts of law nor the State Arbitration have recognized either side's claims to the Printing House".

And then suddenly in went the "black berets", on behalf of the CPSU. The workforce of Latvia's largest publishing house (1,300 people, of whom 750 are printers) flatly refused to work at gunpoint. The central (Moscow) newspapers have stopped coming out in Latvia, the republic's government newspaper, *Diena*, has moved to another printworks in Riga. The Interior Forces' actions were strongly supported by the CPSU Central Committee, central television and *Pravda*, who did their level best to inflame the situation in Riga still further.

By the beginning of 1991, Georgia, Armenia, the Baltic republics and a number of regions of Moldavia and the Ukraine had virtually no publications left. The local papers had removed the "Workers of the World, Unite!" slogan and at the same time escaped from Party stewardship and become independent. That is, their own workforces became their new founders.

But privatization, even in 1992, has yet to affect the paper industry and printing works. Paper-pulp factories in the country still work under GULAG conditions, since to this day virtually everything they earn is taken away by higher authorities. They are almost completely deprived of any degree of commercial freedom on the domestic or foreign markets, or even at their own works. Reference here to the GULAG is by no means an exaggeration. As before, it is current or former convicts that cut down the trees for pulp factories, where the workforces are blighted by bad food supplies and illness. There can be no healthy human beings in such places, since the surrounding air, land and water is poisoned by pollution. (According to official Soviet statistics, 80% of *all* children finishing school are unhealthy. The health of the remaining 20% is in doubt. The principal reason for this is the poor diet—an excess of flour-based products, sugar and animal fats, vegetables poisoned with nitrates, the absence of fruit—and the disastrous state of the environment).

Today Moscow cannot (or does not want to, as some say) correct the miserable condition of the forestry and paper complex of Russia. A good 80% of paper-pulp factories are kitted out with imported equipment, and their entire output is for export, for hard currency. A revival of these so badly neglected businesses is possible—but the death throes of the fossilized central monopolies were a hindrance. This is a pessimistic view. There is good news as well. The Stalinist command economy, it transpires, is capable of certain achievements. Thus, the clapped-out and obsolete equipment at Soviet paper factories can be put to more effective use with the help of the latest Western automated control systems. The American firm ABB USSR Business Development Inc. in August 1990 offered a credit of 22.5 million dollars, to be paid back over three years. According to the program, endorsed by the USSR forestry ministry and Council of Ministers, the joint venture IRIS (whose investors are ABB and the Soviet Neftekhimavtomatika R & D institute) will fit out 10 factories as early as

1990-1991 with equipment that will allow productivity to be increased by 5-20% and ensure international standards.

Yet we still do not have a market; the monopolist diktat remains in place. Let us imagine that we want to install new spark plugs (read: management) on all our old jalopies (read: paper factories)—and we will, we'll force ourselves to do it. And then we shall sit back and let them all go to ruin. Meanwhile, how many times will ministerial and government bureaucrats have gone on official trips to the United States? Lots. And they will have been so well received there that they will undoubtedly dream up some other huge project that is equally profitable ... for the American taxpayer.

The paradox is also that Western firms, if they get guarantees from their governments and sometimes even if they do not, are willing to invest their cash in the Soviet Union, for projects that, commercially speaking, are absolutely hopeless. Common sense might state that Westerners should help the nascent Soviet free press in exactly the same way that they did the Polish press in the 1970s and 80s, when everything conceivable was done to provide paper, money, printing technology and other essential equipment. The policy regarding the USSR is different, the direct opposite. This is how it was described by People's Deputy Galina Starovoitova in an interview with the Moscow correspondent (Yuri Mityunov) of Radio Liberty, which broadcasts in Russian and other languages spoken in the Soviet Union. The following extract has been taken from the June 8 1990 issue of the emigre paper *Russkaya Mysl* (Russian Thought):

> It seems to me that the West is preoccupied with stopping the USSR from becoming a collapsing empire, a kind of, so to speak, Zimbabwe with nuclear weapons. True, some of our journalists were in Zimbabwe recently, and they say that if we work hard for 30 years we'll live as well as the Zimbabweans do. This is not a very accurate analogy, but it's often applied in the West. And so, the West is ready to make various concessions, including granting credits; the Germans have already started doing this, to ensure that the economic crisis looming over us is averted. And it is genuinely in the West's interests to do so, because a disintegrating empire presents a danger to the entire globe. The West is interested in prolonging our stagnation, and is willing to provide loans right up to the beginning of economic reforms in our country. But are we interested in prolonging this stagnation and receiving loans or charitable gifts from the developed countries without starting reforms? I think that they will be squandered in exactly the same way as the huge international aid to Armenia following the earthquake, which went God only knows where. Our current system is incapable of putting foreign aid to effective use. I think that the West would be doing the right thing if it had any interest in how this money is used. It would be even better if we were to be given help simply in the form of technology, management techniques, specialists, and especially in setting up a framework for an independent press, which would blow away all the old cliches existing in the greater part of Soviet public opinion and holding back the

development of normal business activity. Otherwise, the crisis will only be prolonged, it will not be averted.

After 70 years of propaganda lies, it is important to revive in the Soviet Union an influential, professional and free press. So far, it is merely crawling in its nappies.

And here is another trap dug for the independent press. Not only have paper prices been sharply increased (the official state-set rates have doubled or even quadrupled, while on the free market they are sometimes 10 times higher), and printing costs made more expensive, but the USSR Ministry of Communications has increased its rates for the distribution and sale of periodical publications. Using its factual monopoly on distribution via the Soyuzpechat kiosks and postal system, it requested (i.e., demanded) from central publications (ie., national newspapers and magazines published in Moscow) one half of their cover prices as of summer 1990. From republican and all other publications seeking to extend their circulation as far as possible it decided to opt for "contractual rates", i.e., whatever it could get.

According to *Izvestia* (January 26 1991), the record price rises for newspaper delivery by post and by hand were achieved in Kazakhstan (up 16 and 26 times respectively). Local publications now have to hand over 60 percent of their revenues to the ministry, and many are in danger of closing down.

To avoid financial ruin, all Soviet periodicals were forced to raise their cover prices several times over, and some limited their number of subscribers. In 1990 one issue of a central daily newspaper cost not more than 5-20 kopecks. "Unofficial" independent publications, which are not usually independent publications, which are not usually accepted for distribution or subscription via Soyuzpechat, were usually on offer for 1 or 2 rubles, from street vendors (take into account also that they are few in number and dreadfully printed).

By artificially inflating prices the central agencies, taking advantage of their factual monopoly over the production and distribution of paper, ownership of printing works and publishers' premises and control of the press distribution network, seem to have got things their own way. The Communist Party continues to do all it can to circulate *Pravda*, *Sovetskaya Rossia* and the like either through compulsion as in the old days, at reduced rates or even for free. And what was the editorial board of *Novy Mir* to do? In 1990 only half of the year's issues left the presses.

Of course, paper factories and the postal and distribution service need a complete overhaul, and new printing capacities have to be constructed. But where are the guarantees that the difference between the old and new prices for paper, distribution and printing will go to modernizing machinery, increased wages and improved living and working conditions for timber, printing and postal workers? As usually happens in this country, all the profits, or nearly all of them, disappear into the state's bottomless pocket.

That which was achieved in the past by restricting subscriptions (you're welcome to have *Pravda* for a year, Communist Party members were coerced into taking another couple of its publications, and just one subscription voucher for *Novy Mir* would be raffled among the entire 1,000-strong workforce of an institute or other establishment) is now achieved by upping the price. Yet the apparatchiks have forgotten one thing: whatever happens now, it is the subscriber that makes the final choice. And instead of 3 or 4 papers he will now fork out only for one or two, which he really wants to read. So we'll count the chickens when they've hatched...

We still have an information famine. The poverty of our press amazes even in comparison with 1913, before the Revolution. In 1988, 1,578 journals and magazines on various themes and for various purposes were published in the USSR. Pre-revolutionary Russia had over 8,000. According to *Ogonyok* (May 19, 1990), we cannot even begin to compete with the industrialized West. In the Federal Republic of Germany, with a population one-fifth of that of the Soviet Union, there are 1,268 *research* journals alone, and in the USA 18,500! The Americans have 290 sociological journals; we have 2. A grand total of 59,609 magazines and journals come out in the USA.

But then exactly one half of all paper in the former USSR went for "socio-political" and socio-economic publications. There were pathetically few truly scientific ones among them. Soyuzpechat kiosks and library shelves from Moscow to Vladivostok overflowed with propaganda and the products of various government departments and ministries. This dead weight, which nobody read, was regularly written off to help fulfil the state waste-paper quota. It all begs the question: who in his right mind would buy with his own money or even read for free and voluntarily in a library such journals as *Problems of Peace and Socialism* (an international communist publication that comes out in Prague), or *Bloknot Agitatora* (The Agitator's Notebook, a Communist Party publication in 76 regional versions and in many of the languages spoken in the USSR), or *Sotsialisticheskoye Sorevnovaniye* (Socialist Emulation), *Slovo Lektora* (The Word from the Lectern), *Sotsialistichesky Trud* (Socialist Labor), *Raboche-krestyansky korrespondent* (The Worker and Peasant Correspondent), *Ekonomika Sovetskoy Ukrainy* (The Economy of the Soviet Ukraine), *Kommunist Gruzii* (Communist of Georgia), and many hundreds of others such?

Left without the cover of compulsory subscription, most of these "socio-political" titles have simply closed down. According to *Izvestia* (November 24, 1990), the overall picture is as follows:

> Circulation by subscription of central newspapers as of January 1, 1991 compared to January 1, 1990 stands at 64.9%, of central journals and magazines—45.4%.

Leading the newspapers, as in last year, is *Argumenty i Fakty*, with 22.7 million subscribers. Its current readership is 33.2 million. *Trud*'s subscription in November 1990 was 21.4 million; next year it will have 17 million. Next comes *Komsomolskaya Pravda*. In 1990 it came top among the dailies and claimed a place in the Guinness Book of Records with a print run of 22 million copies. It will now have 16.3 million readers.

Izvestia, with its new annual rate of 22 rubles 56 kopecks, has lost some of its subscribers, as we expected. But with 3.6 million it is still in the top 5 nationwide. In fifth place is *Selskaya Zhizn*, with 3.5 million.

Of the national papers, the greatest losses have been sustained by *Literaturnaya Gazeta* (as of January 1, 1990 4.5 million, now down to 1 million) and *Pravda* (6.8 million compared to 2 million now). The major losers among the magazines are *Dialog* (with 343,000, which is 19.6% of last year's figure) and *Izvestia TsK KPSS* (152,900, or 22.8%). The print run of *Chelovek i Zakon* (Man and the Law) has been cut by three quarters. And *Ogonyok*, which has more than doubled its cover price, has been deserted by about one third of its readers. In 1990 its print run was 4.6 million, and in 1991, 1.5 million.

By the autumn of 1991 Soviets of different levels had registered 20,000 periodicals, of which 400 had been founded by private persons. The 1992 all-Union catalogue of subscription editions includes over two thousand titles, of which nearly 300 titles are entirely new ones, while the 1991 catalogue included less than a thousand newspapers and magazines.

In 1992, the regular annual subscription to many newspapers, not to speak about scientific journals, became a luxury. The Press Distribution Agency, the Ministry of Communication and the Cabinet of Ministers took all possible measures to twist the publishers' arms and to retrieve their losses at the expense of the subscribers. Soon low-paid persons began to buy newspapers like cakes for a holiday.

Things stood differently with local newspapers in which a great part of Soviet journalists were employed. Until recently the largest and most profitable district newspapers were financed from the CPSU budget, while the smaller and unprofitable newspapers—from the local state budget. Suffice it to take any district newspaper in order to understand that the present and impending economic crisis threatens with a fatal outcome such press. It's a pity that the local journalists will have to issue their newspapers without photographs but with a blind and battered print. Two or three years back all Soviet printing houses received at least some equipment from the printing and publishing industry of the German Democratic Republic or Czechoslovakia. From 1990 this machinery may be bought only for foreign currency. But our printing houses have no hard currency of their own and lack their own typographic equipment. Newsprint is still available, but it has long since become the object of a political game on the part of the powers that be.

We must take into account the following facts: first, the pulp and paper combines systematically do not fulfil their plans and, generally speaking, reduce the total output of newsprint; second, they know very well that one ton of their newsprint even of a low quality may be sold for 470 dollars in China, India or Taiwan; third, several regions of the Russian Federation decided to limit the export of timber beyond their territory; fourth, 95 per cent of newsprint in the USSR is produced by three pulp and paper combines in Kondopoga, Solikamsk and Balakhna by 22 paper-making machines, of which 8 machines have been in operation for more than 50 years, 12 machines were commissioned 20 or 30 years ago, and the newest 2 machines have served for eight years. All these machines were manufactured abroad and the equipment and spare parts to them were imported from other countries as well. Today hard currency is in short supply in this country.

From year to year the government bought Finnish newsprint for printing a sizable part of the circulation of the newspapers *Pravda* and *Izvestia*. Every year up to 1991 the Soviet Union bought 400,000 tons of paper of all grades to a total sum of 250 million dollars. Of some interest in this respect are the following data on the production of newsprint in the leading Western countries: 9,673,000 tons in Canada, 5,300,000 tons in the USA, 2,588,000 tons in Japan, 1,975,000 tons in Sweden, and 1,874,000 tons in the USSR. The annual consumption of newsprint per head of population is as follows: 6.3 kg in the USSR, 43 kg in Switzerland, 44.5 in Sweden, and 51.6 kg in the USA.

By the amount of produced paper Japan holds second place in the world, yielding to the USA. In 1987, she produced 22.5 million tons of paper, which is almost twice of the output in the Soviet Union.

The wide and multi-purpose application of paper in the printing and publishing industry and in other spheres of production and everyday life is combined with the exclusively rational and thrifty attitude to the use of waste. According to the Japanese statistics, in Britain the old paper recycling in 1987 was 29.5 per cent of the total national paper output and in the Soviet Union the respective figure was only 19.1 per cent and in Japan 49.1 per cent.

In 1987, Japan produced 81.5 per cent of all printing paper out of the recycled scrap-paper.

In return, we can supply all the museums of the world with the specimens of obsolete polygraphic equipment. The entire world, Africa included, have long ago devolved on electronics, while even our central press is still set with linotypes.

This situation was to be corrected by Mikhail Nenashev, who headed in July 1991 the USSR Ministry of Information and the Press. As compared with his colleagues in the mass media he showed himself to good advantage. His later resignation and replacement by Kravchenko has put him in the ranks of such highly respected figures, as Bakatin, Shevardnadze, Petrakov, Yakovlev and Shatalin, who lost their government posts towards the end of 1990 in consequence of a right course in state policy.

In 1991, the mass media leadership was joined by Eduard Sagalayev, who has a good name and holds dear his reputation of a decent and serious man. He does not use words lightly. For this reason he was elected Chairman of the Board of the Confederated Union of Journalists of the USSR. But what is the Union of Journalists of the USSR? Is it a trade union? The whole point, unfortunately, is that it is not. But Sagalayev promises to set up such a trade union in time.

Why Do Journalists Tell Lies?

For decades bondage was an orderly multistage structure for Soviet journalists. A journalist, especially a little-known one, could spend months or even years to take up a job in a mass media but was dismissed 24 hours before a notice without invoking a court of law. The Soviet press was an object of extremely effective, strict total control at all levels of the hierarchy. Any district newspaper with a printing of several thousand copies was constantly controlled by all higher CPSU committees up to the CPSU Central Committee, whose respective department discharged the functions of the USSR Ministry of Information and the Press. Every issue of a small district paper was investigated through a microscope by censors and KGB officials, Party, financial and planning bodies' functionaries. A knitted-goods factory could for years send to the market up to 90 per cent of its output not registered by any government body and produced from the actually stolen raw materials, but the mass media could not put out its ideological products without the strict supervision of government and Party censors, who did not take bribes.

And what if any journalist dared to try to express to his bosses, or even worse publish, anything "scandalous" (ie., not to the liking of those above) on even the most insignificant and even non-political subject? He would immediately be out of a job, and the ranks of the unemployed on the street would be swelled by one more member. Our journalists have never enjoyed any *factual* protection in the form of a trade union, nor from the "creative" USSR Journalists' Union, nor even from the courts. The disgraced hack would be thrown out and be deprived of even the minimal level of social welfare and defense available to every rank-and-file worker whatever his trade, be he a ploughman or a teacher. Ideologically, the Soviet journalist is like a mine-detector—he can only make one mistake. And we have already mentioned that this set-up remained virtually untouched right up to the end of 1990.

The Journalists' Union Board expanded its staff over the decades, becoming a rest home for the rejects and deadbeats of the Party Central Committee and KGB. At the apparat and political police one had to show at least some kind of results—and service in the sumptuous suites of this Union was always a well-paid sinecure.

Its staff, out in the localities was made up in the main of Party functionaries. Its executive secretaries were always the leaders of Party publications, topping the press hierarchy in Moscow or provincial centers. The chairman's seat on the board was always reserved for the editor-in-chief of *Pravda*, with his deputies being the heads of TASS, *Izvestia*, the state TV and radio, APN, and so on. As one general director would depart—that of TASS, let us say—so the new one would take over his place round the table.

On February 5, 1991 the 7th Congress of the USSR Journalists' Union opened in Moscow. The majority of delegates were over 50. They leapt to the defense of Leonid Kravchenko when a long debate began as to whether he should be recalled from his duties as a USSR People's Deputy elected by the Union as a public organization. Chairman of the presidium and acting chairman of the Union Ivan Zubkov tried to remove the item from the agenda, but delegates insisted that Kravchenko report on the recent events at Gosteleradio, where a powerful assault on glasnost coincided with his arrival.

Some time later Leonid Kravchenko was expelled from the USSR Journalists' Union by the Presidium of the Moscow Journalists' Union. The USSR JU was, however, disbanded at its 7th Congress. The latter proclaimed the formation of a new Journalists' Union, this time on a confederative basis. In this way it underscored the equality and sovereignty of all organizations, which had united via mutual agreement. The new Union is a self-governing, non-governmental and politically independent organization. It must uphold the authority and rights of mass media workers, as well as the right of the viewer and reader to proper, balanced information.

As soon as the Congress of Journalists was over, the press published the Decree of the President of the USSR on the Priority Measures for the Socio-Economic Protection of Writers and Artists During the Transition to Market Relations. The new organ of the USSR Journalists' Union *Golos* (Voice) immediately responded to the important event ("publications of the JU shall be exempt from taxes") and carried in its February 1991 issue No. 8 an interview given by Deputy Minister for the Press of Russia M. Fedotov under the title "*Can the Press Be the Fourth Estate When It Belongs to Somebody Else?*"

Fedotov: After reading this Decree, I thought that we had quite recently, during the work of the 7th Congress of Journalists of the USSR, appealed to the President of the USSR, and proposed that "the editorial offices and journalist unions should be exempt of the tax and that the mass media should be provided with the requisite means to survive in the new economic conditions". Do you remember this?

Corr.: Of course. We published this appeal to the President in the seventh issue of *Golos*. But what is the purpose of this preface?

Fedotov: I consider it a swift answer to the problem we have raised.

Corr.: **Mikhail Alexandrovich, surely you believe that the President needed our appeal to promulgate the said Decree?**

Fedotov: It's difficult to say what finally led to the adoption of the given decision. But it may have been perhaps it was the Congress appeal. It is true that the question was posed in a broader manner that the tax levied on all mass media be repealed. For when prices for paper, polygraphic and communication services rise, newspapers and magazines, which in the past made huge profits (where they were invested is a different matter), now begin to incur tremendous losses. The decision by the President is a very important measure. Otherwise we would have found ourselves within six month in a society bereft of a mass media. Only purely pornographic and commercial editions supported by advertisement would be able to survive.

Corr.: **Does it mean that these two engines alone will stimulate the publication of the papers and magazines?**

Fedotov: Yes.

Corr.: **Is it true that like any other enterprise, newspaper and magazine editorial offices pay a 45 per cent tax?**

Fedotov: This is the case under Union law, but in Russia the tax amounts to 38 per cent. In addition, 50.6 per cent of income is collected by communications workers. Add to this the cost of newsprint. We know very well that the workers in the pulp and paper industry take no notice of the state price of 880 rubles per ton of newsprint. They sell it for 1,200 or 1,500 rubles and even more... Can a newspaper survive given this robbery?

The Presidential Decree creates a new situation for the mass media by exempting the JU and its enterprises, associations and organizations of the tax. From now on the editorial offices of the papers and magazines placed under the aegis of the JU will be exempted from the tax.

Corr.: **Does this mean that the papers which remain the organs of CPSU committees or Soviets will, as before, pay 45 or 38 percent tax?**

Fedotov: Quite correct. But if a paper changes its founder or becomes the press organ of a regional, city or district branch of the JU, it will be exempted from the tax?

I think that this has a definite political meaning. For in no other country of the world (I am referring to genuinely democratic countries) do you find papers acting as the tools of the state authorities—here there are so many party papers. Everywhere the press is the true fourth estate. And this fourth estate cannot and must not be the organ of the first, second and third powers. Otherwise, what kind of fourth estate is it, if it is the press organ of somebody else!

I see in this Decree the following new unexpected effect: all the mass media will start to come under the tutelage of the JU. The more so, the

	JU, as its 7th Congress stated, must be an exclusively professional and creative organization and not a commercial one.
Corr.:	**This means that *Golos* will be one of the first papers to be exempted from the tax and that the USSR JU will be our co-founder. Another question arises: how does one change from one founder to another? Should we carry the consent of the JU or should we have our paper registered as a new edition?**
Fedotov:	The second measure will be enough. The paper may adopt a new name or leave the old one, but it should of necessity stop functioning and have it registered as a new edition.
Corr.:	**Mikhail Alexandrovich, you say that only the Presidential Decree exempts the editions of the JU from the tax. But as far as I know, in the past many editions had been exempted from the tax.**
Fedotov:	That's right. There were several such editions and their names were withdrawn in favor of the JU. But how did this come about? The JU demanded: either you transfer all your income or the state will take it from you in the form of a tax. In any case the editorial offices were stripped of everything. But as of now they will be exempted from the tax on legal grounds.
Corr.:	**They may also improve their financial standing through advertising. After all, the foreign press receives its main income from advertisements and not from the sale of its issues.**
Fedotov:	Unfortunately, our papers cannot survive on advertisements. To make advertisements a stable part, we need a stable demand. But demand only appears when there is an abundance of consumer goods. Consequently our newspaper advertisements are made up of self-advertising campaigns by the managers of enterprises with extra money and nothing else to do. Consequently it cannot become a stable source of income.
Corr.:	**The Decree says that the newly-founded enterprises of creative unions may be exempted from the tax by the Ministry of Finance, in agreement with the USSR Ministry of Culture. Mikhail Alexandrovich, what, in your opinion, is the attitude of the Ministry of Culture towards the newly-founded papers?**
Fedotov:	I believe that a definite mechanism may be set up here and that the Ministry of Culture will be able to use it as a stick to whip up the creative unions.
Corr.:	**Does this mean that the Ministry of Culture will make demands on the new editions of the JU?**
Fedotov:	Why not? The Ministry of Culture may state that it exempts one paper from the tax and not another. In this case an additional dangerous mechanism of ideological control may appear.
Corr.:	**But in addition to ideological control a situation favorable for bribery may arise.**

Fedotov: That is not excluded. But the Decree says that the newly-founded enterprises and organizations are exempted from the tax by the Ministry of Finance. Consequently we shall interpret this provision in the said spirit: the Ministry of Finance is obliged to exempt them from the tax. Although it is hard to explain all this, I am inclined to think, that by introducing this norm, the drafters of the Decree have implied that if creative unions begin to set up enterprises, which have no bearing on their specialization (for example, motor car assembly or radio engineering), an end will be put to this illegal undertaking.

Corr.: **However, as well as papers and magazines, pulp and paper production may become the objects of their specialization.**

Fedotov: I think that this is quite right. In the first place the Union must now concern itself with the creation of a logistical support system for the freedom of speech. For if it does not receive the requisite material resources, the freedom of the press will amount to nothing. If there is no paper, printing or publishing industry, there can be no free press or free speech.

I believe that this Decree marks the first step by the President on the path to realizing the socio-economic problems discussed at the 7th Congress of the Journalists's Union and dealt with in the Congress appeal to the President of the USSR.

In May 1991, the JU set up a Committee to Protect the Freedom of Speech and the Rights of Journalists. It was chaired by another unemployed journalist—Pavel Gutiontov who was forced to leave *Izvestia* where he was regarded as a leading and most popular commentator, due to internal political problems. Gutiontov was now faced with an extremely difficult dilemma: whom was he to protect or defend?

Those who in the past hurled abuse at the foreign bourgeoisie, received punctually their royalties and went on business trips abroad did not believe in the things they had written. Today these persons openly employ imperial scorn and classify as "nationalists", "fascists", etc. the leading figures in Lithuania; despite the fact that they have no idea about what is going on in that republic. In Uzbekistan the USSR Ministry of the Interior imprisoned the republican leaders, who were not popular in Moscow. In Baku, local obstinate leaders were shot down by airborne troops or replaced by docile people on the instructions of the envoys of the Kremlin. A war and economic blockade were declared on the whole Armenian nation. Moreover, the Turks of Meskhetia, Ossetians and Abkhazians were played off against independent Georgia. All these disgraceful things have been perpetrated by the Center with active journalistic support. Professional liars are still to be found in abundance in our country.

Can we speak now about the respect such small people have for journalists and their profession? They can only be dreaded as much as anybody fears a meeting with an investigator, militiaman or KGB official. Mikhail Poltoranin hit the nail on the head in the international newspaper *Russky Kuryer* (Russian Courier, No. 16, June 1991):

> We are now in a different world setting than in 1958 and 1959, when we would be cursed from all rostrums. Our society does not like journalists, because it is sick. Normal journalism is revealing society's shortcomings, diseases as well as its seedy side, in short, everything which was in the past concealed. Our immature, non-democratic society shuddered, because it transpired that people had been poorly educated, lived in poverty and were badly dressed... But instead of trying to cure themselves, people began merely laid their own faults at other peoples' doors and even tried to smash them in.
>
> The second wave of public disapproval of journalism occurred, when the partocracy managed to seize control of nearly all the mass media once again. A small number of publications, which actively fought against the background of this 'well-being', were subjected to ostracism. Since August 1990, however, when independent newspapers began to emerge, in accordance with the Law on the Press, and inform the public of the things which other papers kept silent, special instructions followed: 'Don't you dare! Leave them alone!'
>
> On the other hand, the journalists have, in many ways, only themselves to blame for the public's disrespect. We were the first to adhere to market conditions. It has now been confirmed that many journalists, accustomed to live under somebody else's roof and execute somebody else's instructions, are unable to deal with the conditions which independent democratic journalism lives in. The more so, the CPSU committees have changed their tactics. Whereas in the past, in meetings with journalists, the partocrats would throw selected morsels from the lordly table, they now began to feed the journalists, who continue cooperating with the Party press: with *Pravda, Sovetskaya Rossia, Selskaya Zhizn, Rabochaya Tribuna, Moskovskaya Pravda* and central TV. They began creating for their journalists conditions, which were far better than the ones endured by those in the independent press, whom they call 'scribblers'. The journalists accorded special privileges by their chiefs were ready to execute any orders.
>
> Let us take, for example, Igor Fesunenko, who conducted the broadcasts with Russian Presidential candidates. He specially selected TV spectators' questions posed to Bakatin and Ryzhkov. He was so nice when reading the questions. But when he talked to Gorbachev, he demonstrated his full servility and obedience. He arched his back into a question-mark.
>
> The same Fesunenko sprawled in an arm-chair in an arrogant manner before Boris Yeltsin and asked questions in a boorish manner. When Yeltsin removed his jacket (it was very hot in the studio owing to the lights), he said: "I hope you will confine yourself to this". I think that in any decent society such a journalist would not be allowed to appear again on TV. When people look at such journalists, naturally enough they have no respect for them. They consequently react negatively to other representatives of our profession.
>
> I am uneasy about the split in journalist ranks. Some veer to the right, others to the left. A journalist, however, has no right to serve one particular group of people, as it is his duty to represent the fourth estate, the power of public opinion. The latter always has a tendency to be objective and avoid confrontation. It always favors

common accord and civilian peace. In no circumstances should the journalist forget this, or else he will commit something like perjury. I believe that journalists, including students of journalism, must take an oath akin that of Hippocrates. It should be based on objectivity and adherence to universal human values, Christian ideals, compassion for man and service to man, all those things referred to as civic duty. We must gradually transform our principles of partisanship in journalism to journalism in support of civil society.

The authoritarian bureaucratic system does not forgive such statements. For example, the weekly newspaper *Glasnost* (of September 20, 1990), founded by the CPSU Central Committee, accused Poltoranin of "hurling abuse at thousands of Soviet journalists" in one of his appearances on central TV. It reverted to this theme in eight successive issues and repeatedly raised the issue of Poltoranin's aptitude for the posts of Minister and People's Deputy before the then Chairman of the RSFSR Supreme Soviet Boris Yeltsin, the then USSR Procurator-General Alexander Sukharev and the then Chairman of the USSR Supreme Soviet Anatoly Lukyanov. But what did Poltoranin actually say on October 16, 1990 in his talk on central TV? Let us quote the extract from the phonogram cited by the newspaper *Sovetskaya Rossia* on July 7, 1991:

> Every person who serves the CPSU apparatus, inevitably serves the partocracy, bows down before it and should realize that, as the Russian saying goes, there will be no virtuous men or guilty parties. Consequently all those who today serve the CPSU, especially Party journalists who have made their choice, and not only journalists in general, must be aware of the fact that they are playing with fire. They are not thinking about the future of their families and generations to come.

For six months Poltoranin tolerated the personal attacks of *Glasnost*, *Pravda* and of V. Petrunya, TASS observer, but finally initiated court proceedings against these papers.

In May 1991, the USSR JU made a public statement supporting Lithuanian journalists, whereby it voiced its official protest against the military's presence in the republican TV center and the Vilnius Press House. What purpose did this action play? To be effective, the Union needs to transformed into a trade union, which protects the interests of its members before the employer. Eduard Sagalayev advocates this position. But this process may well take a very long time.

At the beginning of May 1991, the Congress of Journalists of the USSR discussed and adopted a Journalistic Code of Professional Ethics, drafted by Mikhail Fedotov, D.Sc. (Law), who is already familiar to us. He had written the code (recognized as one of the best in Europe) with Dmitry Avraamov, and ensured that it was published three years back in the magazine *Zhurnalist* (Journalist) and then translated into several languages.

June 1991 witnessed the official registration of the Fund to Protect Glasnost, launched by the Union of Cinematographers of the USSR. One hundred thousand rubles were deposited in the Fund's current account with the Commercial Bank of Oil and Gas Piping Construction. The Fund was to provide financial and legal aid to journalists and television workers under pressure, assist the families of workers, who have been dismissed or killed, support independent editions and new TV stations. It was set up on the basis of the joint efforts of the staff of the following mass media: *Moscow News, Argumenty i Fakty ' Ogonyok, Moskovsky Komsomolets* and *Megapolis-Express*. The RSFSR Minister for the Press, Mikhail Poltoranin, who took the floor at the founding meeting of the new-born Fund, warned them that the relatively propitious period for the democratic press was coming to a close.

> Now that the mass media had started to gnaw away at the roots of the regime, the latter was preparing to take offensive action. He added: "We may be called free, independent and democratic, but we continue to be printed on the CPSU-owned polygraphic facilities. Both newsprint and the printing industry are still owned by the state. It will be very simple for the latter to cut off the supply of oxygen supply of democratic editions by introducing a new type of censorship-economic pressure. Moreover, the state controls the Press Distribution Agency. We are now witnessing the way in which this Agency refuses to distribute many newspapers in various cities, alleging that the new editions are not popular." The creation of an independent economic base for newspapers and magazines now in opposition is the principal task of the Fund today. The freedom today. The freedom of speech and freedom of information must be protected. Under the flag of sovereignty many Republics shut the doors to information, as exemplified by the coverage of developments in Nagorny Karabakh. The military stationed in Karabakh are forced to resort to violence. The reports on desertion and hunger strikes are concealed.

We can note an unexpected and significant coincidence: the presentation of the Fund was held on exactly the same day as in 1922, when the Government adopted a decree on the official establishment of a Chief Administration for the Protection of State Secrets in the Press (Glavlit). The birthday of Soviet censorship thus becomes the birthday of the movement which is combatting it, for freedom of speech

It was aptly said in *Ivestia* (June 10, 1991), the times of romanticism for glasnost are over.

> The time has come to look for a way to protect glasnost. The methods to be used in this struggle are already being worked out to the last detail. In Russia, the work collectives and the RSFSR Ministry for the Press and Information founded 35 regional newspapers, independent of Party bodies and local Soviets, enjoying a circulation of some three million copies. Leningrad has set in motion a new system of press distribution, as an alternative to the Press Distribution Agency.

On August 19, 1991, during the first hours of the coup Eduard Sagalayev supported the statement by the Soviet Journalists' Union leadership in his interview to a Japanese TV company, with tanks in the streets as a background. Subsequently, he spent three days among the defenders of the White House, i.e. Russian Parliament. A similar stance was taken by the Moscow Journalists' Union headed by Pavel Gusev, *Moskovsky Komsomolets* editor-in-chief.

On August 22, the Moscow Union established special awards for the Moscow journalists who lived up to their professional duty in the days of the state coup. The Union's Secretariat presented diplomas and 1,000-ruble bonuses to the editorial boards of: *Argumenty i Fakty, Vechernaya Moskva, Komsomolskaya Pravda, Kommersant, Kuranty, Megapolis-Express, Moskovsky Komsomolets, Moscow News, Nezavisimaya Gazeta* and *Sobesednik* newspapers; as well as *Iskusstvo Kino* and *Stolitsa* magazines; to the Russian Information Agency, and Echo of Moscow and Russian Radio stations.

The Secretariat also ruled that: "Proceeding from the Moscow Journalists' Union Rules, leaders of Communist newspapers besmirched by their participation in political actions and criminal collaboration with the coup organizers, namely: G. Seleznev, *Pravda* first deputy editor-in-chief, editors-in-chief V. Chikin (*Sovetskaya Rossia*), A. Yurkov (*Rabochaya Tribuna*), A. Kharlamov (*Selskaya Zhizn*) and V. Lysenko (*Moskovskaya Pravda*), as well as G. Shishkin, TASS Deputy Director-General, shall be expelled from the Journalists' Union. To note, L. Kravchenko, Chairman of the State Radio and Television Company of the USSR, has already been expelled from the Journalists' Union."

CHAPTER II

TASS, NOVOSTI, INTERFAX, SibIA AND OTHERS

Ministry of Information Under the Guise of TASS

The Soviet authorities have always maintained a tight grip on journalists and stringently controlled the production and dissemination of political information and news, be it in the form of a wall newspaper or the announcement of an official audience in the Kremlin.

What is a wall newspaper? A few articles written by hand or typed, glued onto some thick paper with a couple of drawings or photographs added, and displayed in the corridors of all Soviet establishments, factories and schools; wherever there was a Party committee, there would be a wall newspaper as well. The removal of censorship and relaxation of the Party control throughout the country changed by 1990, the technology of these "datsybao", and now there is the opportunity, at least in theory, to print whatever you like, run off plenty of copies and hand them out to anyone who wants one.

Only for very large workforces of several thousand have there been what are called large-circulation newspapers: two or four tabloid pages, printed and available in several hundred copies. These were the only publications not obliged to reprint official reports by TASS, the Telegraph Agency of the Soviet Union, which for decades used to perform the role of a ministry of information. Or rather the mouthpiece of the Party's propaganda department. District, regional, republican and central newspapers would every day receive by teletype the texts of official announcements with detailed instructions on where and when to publish them. No independent comment or room for manoeuvre. The end result was that opening any daily paper—*Pravda*, *Izvestia* or the Georgian republican *Zarya Vostoka* (Dawn of the East)—you would very frequently find one or two identical pages, with the same announcements from the Kremlin.

In 1990 TASS continued to hand out its instructions, only now the editorial reaction was somewhat different. Those who only recently tugged their forelocks and did all they were told by Moscow now summoned up their courage. Not only did they ignore orders from above; some actually took photocopies of the teletypes and published them for the benefit of all, as did *Zarya Vostoka* on the eve of the November public holidays (issue dated November 6 1990), which have fortunately been cancelled in Georgia anyway:

ATTENTION EDITORIAL STAFFS

THE FOLLOWING PROCEDURE IS RECOMMENDED FOR THE PUBLICATION OF REPUBLICAN, TERRITORIAL AND REGIONAL PARTY NEWSPAPERS BEFORE AND DURING THE PUBLIC HOLIDAYS:

NOVEMBER 6—ALL NEWSPAPERS COME OUT AS SCHEDULED.

NOVEMBER 7—PUBLICATION OF THE WELCOMING SPEECH BY M S GORBACHEV, SPEECHES BY PARTICIPANTS IN THE CEREMONIAL GATHERING TO MARK THE 73rd ANNIVERSARY OF THE GREAT OCTOBER SOCIALIST REVOLUTION.

NOVEMBER 8—PUBLICATION OF THE REPORT ON THE PARADE AND MILITARY DEMONSTRATION ON RED SQUARE OF NOVEMBER 7. DESIRABILITY OF PUBLICATION ON NOVEMBER 9 SHALL BE AT THE DISCRETION OF EDITORIAL STAFFS AND LOCAL AUTHORITIES

-TASS-

Explanatory note. TASS has promulgated an instruction. Such instructions we have been receiving for years before every holiday or anniversary. Who issues them, why they are transmitted in TASS's name and without their authors' signatures, and what penalties will be incurred following failure to obey—we do not know. The only thing we do know is that they are supposedly mandatory.

The Law on the Press has been enacted. As yet we have no republican legislation on this subject, and thus we turned to the republican legislation on this subject, and thus we turned to the federal law. No matter how hard we looked, we could find no mention of the managing and controlling role of TASS, of its right to recommend to or impose any instructions upon newspapers, nor anything remotely resembling it.

To tell the truth, it is not of course journalists that take it upon themselves to circulate such orders to the towns and villages, but those who, ensconced in their Moscow offices, are accustomed to ruling the hearts and minds of one-sixth of the planet. Perhaps the habit of meekly complying with anonymous edicts would be less powerful were it not for the mention of the need to cover the military parade in Moscow. Do our readers really pine for panoramas of columns of tanks?

Many of the TASS branches in the republics have changed their names and political orientation. But the TASS headquarters in Moscow did not change the spirit and words of its reports. The phrase that crowned the most weighty statements of the Kremlin "TASS is authorized to state..." remained one of the official symbols of Soviet power.

TASS reports (which by no means consisted of official protocols only) were often accompanied by the note "for compulsory publication", with the required page and even newspaper stipulated. Newsmen still recall that any discrepancies with TASS's views were unfailingly intercepted.

One more curious thing: once sent out by TASS, information, so to speak, obtained a quality-control stamp. Rumors, guesses and pure invention that get onto the wire are instantly legalized and can be quoted without a twinge of conscience as proven fact (not for nothing did newspapers' verification departments never bother to check TASS despatches).

On March 7, 1991 *Moskovsky Komsomolets* carried the following article under the optimistic title "*Everything Is All Right with TASS Prestige*":

> On January 16, 1991 the newspaper *Moskovsky Komsomolets* published the statement by the Presidium of the Moscow Journalists' Union about the developments in Lithuania and assessed the TASS coverage of the conflict. The TASS leaders were outraged by the statement and gave the following answer:
> "In its statement about the events in Lithuania the Presidium of the Moscow JU has assessed the TASS activity, accusing the Agency of 'outspokenly biased information' about the developments in Lithuania, and has come the conclusion that information transmitted by its correspondents 'does not contribute to the settlement of the conflict and, moreover, deepens it by fanning up ethnic strife'.
> TASS cannot agree with this assessment of its activity, since it spread versatile information about the events taking place in Lithuania from 12 to 15, 1991. This information presented the events in their dynamic, reflected the opinions of eyewitnesses, and showed different approaches to the estimation of what was going on.
> One may easily satisfy himself, if he makes unbiased analysis of the entire flow of information on the Union and foreign TASS tapes, and also the materials of the pictorial review of the TASS and the magazine *Ekho Planety* (Echo of the Planet).
> It is not the fault of TASS that certain mass media select out of the total amount of its information only that part that corresponds to their vision of events and political views.
> The statement of the Presidium of the Moscow JU undermines the prestige of TASS as one of the world information agencies and infringes upon its rights and lawful interests.
> On the instruction of the TASS Collegium Deputy
> Director-General of TASS V.G. Talanov."
> *From the editorial board.*
> Of course, 'it is not the fault of TASS that certain mass media select out of the total amount of its information only that part that corresponds to their vision of events and political views'. It is a pity that *Pravda*, *Sovetskaya Rossia* and *Glasnost* have materials from which they may select items, while our newspaper, *Moscow News* or *Nezavisimaya Gazeta* do not have such a possibility. Although we,

honestly, every day, as you advise, analyze the flow of information coming to us from your Agency...

But, dear colleagues, is it worth taking offence? For it is your destiny to be The Telegraph Agency of the Soviet Union and not a small private firm. This means that your predestination is to do everything in the name and for the benefit of our great power. It is obvious, however, who knows better what is to be done for its benefit.

And because you bear your cross, holding your head high, you are valued and given all the conditions for productive work. That is why the personnel raised and steeled in your Agency is why the personnel raised and steeled in your Agency become the most popular people in the country. The Government, having assessed them by their merits, sends TASS leaders to pull out from the abyss the most important sectors of the information industry. And look how in the numbered days the Central TV has transformed itself!

As for the statement of the Presidium of the Moscow JU that undermines the prestige of TASS, you, dear colleagues, do not trouble: it will be at the same level as always.

It is not worth surprising that *Moskovsky Komsomolets* made an attack on TASS, for it was not accidental that the chief editorial office of Union information was headed by V. Petrunya, a talented journalist but tightly oriented on the political views of the papers like *Glasnost*, issued by the CPSU Central Committee, *Sovetskaya Rossia, Pravda, Krasnaya Zvezda*, and also of the TV news program Vremya. Actions against V. Petrunya were brought by People's Deputies of the USSR Galina Starovoitova (she won her case in a Moscow district court in February, 1991) and by Mikhail Poltoranin for his impudent public statements (he also won the case).

But what a court of law should be invoked by the Czechs who managed to hear by radio that the TASS had distorted the facts of the liberation of Prague in May 1945. On February 12, 1991 the American newspaper *Novoye Russkoye Slovo* detailed the substance of the matter in the following words:

Speaking today at the briefing, Vitaly Churkin, the Chief of the Information Department of the USSR Ministry of Foreign Affairs, fulminated against Czechoslovakia for the impending dismantling of the monument in honor of the Red Army—the T-34 tank standing on the obelisk—in the Prague district of Smihov.

Churkin said: "Following ups and downs or giving way to petty political passions, it is possible to rewrite history, but it is impossible to remodel it. We are convinced that the May days of 1945 will remain a striking page in the history of relations between the friendly peoples of the Soviet Union and Czechoslovakia, and nobody will be able to exterminate them from the memory of the rising generations."

Churkin did not wish, certainly, to remember that for the citizens of Czechoslovakia the Soviet tank is associated not only with the year of 1945, but also with the more fresh events of 1968, when the Soviet troops and the units of the Warsaw Treaty occupied the country and put an end to democratic reforms.

In connection with Churkin's statement, TASS correspondents A. Kanishchev, I. Peskov and L. Timofeyev write: "At the closing stage of the Second World War

Soviet tankmen, responding to the appeals of insurgent Prague, made an unparalleled thrust through mountains and saved the city from inevitable demolition. One of the first tanks that had broken through the enemy lines and reached the capital was placed on the pedestal."

Once more TASS tries to rewrite history. Prague was liberated not by Soviet tankmen. It was set free from Nazis by the division under the command of Colonel Bunyachenko that was a part of the army led by General Vlasov. When "the valiant Soviet tankmen' burst into Prague, the capital of Czechoslovakia no longer needed their assistance.

And Yeltsin's second decree, on the elimination of party cells in state establishments and organizations of Russia, issued in July 1991? It produced a no smaller effect than Yeltsin's announcement on his withdrawal from the party. It took the TASS leadership several hours to secure the approval for the publication of the decree, while the Vremya news program did not mention the hottest news of the day at all.

TASS is an enormous information network with hundreds of bureaux in the Soviet Union and abroad. In Georgia, for example, there used to be several hundred people working for it but they, like their colleagues in the Baltic republics, announced themselves independent of the agency, broke away, shared out the assets and switched to equal rights and contractual agreements. The head of TASS has always been the Number 2 in the journalistic hierarchy (after *Pravda*). Leonid Zamyatin, after many years in charge, left for a job in the Party Central Committee's apparat and for a good ten years of the "stagnation period" as chief of the international information department orchestrated the chorus of praise in the West for Brezhnev's policies. Then he became ambassador to London, where he remained till August 1991. Zamyatin's deputy at the Central Committee was Vitaly Ignatenko, who later for one year became the main man in the President's press liaison team and then for a few months—head of TASS. This is what happens—the best people of the "era of stagnation" smoothly enter the leading echelons of perestroika.

Zamyatin does not give interviews, and Ignatenko as a secondary figure is of no interest. Nonetheless, it is worthwhile reading between the lines of an interview with the former director of TASS, Leonid Kravchenko. This interview appeared in *Moskovskaya Pravda* on May 5, 1990 and despite the stilted language of Party cliches one could glimpse a certain degree of regret (so slight as to be almost imperceptible) regarding the state of affairs in the Communist Party:

> Question: Mr. Kravchenko, it turns out that today the mass media - the principal discussion forum of perestroika- have themselves become the object of a tough and uncompromising debate. The range of opinions is vast: from claims that the press is nothing other than the

driving force of the reforms, to accusations that our colleagues are to blame for all the failures and delays. But what never ceases to amaze me is that there are so many different views regarding the avalanche of information that has descended upon readers and listeners.

Answer: I would've been amazed if everyone was delighted about it. Our society has been half-starved for information for too long to be able to handle this new abundance without indigestion. I also think that we journalists were not fully ready for such rapid lifting of all the restrictions. In any event, what I can say is that we have nothing like a full understanding of our readership. We're only learning to foresee its reactions. We'll leave to one side the hardliners, in whose throats the truth always sticks, and turn to the vast majority of people for whom we work—who are honest and sincere. Not all of them are delighted that in order to get the news they no longer have to tune in to foreign radio stations at night. All they have to do is open a newspaper....

Question: ... from which you can almost see the smoke rising.

Answer: That's right, from news that is not always pleasant. This is something that we have to get used to. People, and especially the older generation, have become accustomed to something else. The advocates of state-sponsored optimism inadvertently taught them to read between the lines and assume that there is more to a story than what is written. For example, if some isolated shortcomings are described, it means that everything's gone awry. And now it's set out in black and white: crisis. Incidentally, the bitter lesson of Chernobyl is also that the coverage of this tragedy hopefully was one of the last lapses into the old half-truths, which were little better than straight lies.

Question: But if the essence of our profession was merely to register facts, then I don't think that the question of the media's influence on public opinion would arise...

Answer: Of course. It's not enough to simply record events dispassionately, because this can play a destructive role. Suppose you constantly remind a person of his physical handicap. You would also be telling the truth, but it would not make him any happier. It would be quite a different matter to tell him how someone with similar problems has found a role in life. Truth is the instrument of our profession, the main tool of our trade. It should be used in a constructive and not in a destructive manner.

Question: *Moskovskaya Pravda* decided to interview you not only because you are in charge of the largest information agency in the world. While working at *Stroitelnaya Gazeta* (Construction Gazette) you rose from ordinary reporter to editor-in-chief. During the first half of the 1980s you were editor of *Trud* and then deputy chairman of the State Committee for Radio and Television, and I'm sure that your tenure in these posts was not entirely unconnected with noticeable concessions made at that time to readers, viewers and listeners. We won't dwell on your time at TV and radio, although it coincided with the appearance of several programs without which today's viewing would be unrecognizable, and was a period of reform of which generations of journalists had dreamt. So, your time at *Trud*, 1980-85. A somewhat dry central trade-union newspaper suddenly became highly readable. Its circulation jumped from 9 to 19 million. And what about TASS?

Answer: TASS is a source of official material...

Question: ... which all papers from central to local level are obliged to carry.

Answer: But it's an anachronism to reduce TASS's functions to the simple circulation of government announcements. If this were the case, the agency would hardly enjoy such a reputation abroad. Our material goes out in 8 languages via 100 other agencies and is constantly received in 130 countries. The sum total of our daily output is equal to 750 newspaper pages. Not even the government of such an enormous country as ours, in which so much happens, could produce so much news all by itself! This information production line works in two directions—from the USSR abroad and vice versa.

Question: From what you've been saying it's clear that behind all this lies a colossal amount of work carried out by an army of reporters. Nonetheless when official material with the TASS logo appears in a paper, the reader regards it as the official opinion of the authorities.

Answer: Unfortunately, this applies also to reports that by virtue of their contents can't possibly be official. And when the oft-used formula "TASS is authorized to state" crops up, the author of the article quite often isn't the government at all. Or even TASS itself. Our agency is merely a go-between. In my opinion, it's absurd when one of our correspondents with a report on, say, the cultural scene, speaks on behalf of the entire agency. Incidentally, this is often the fault of newspapers, who leave the TASS logo but for some reason cross out the author's name. I'm categorically against such depersonalization, and see no reason to conceal which agency or authority is conveying the information. TASS is indeed not infrequently authorized to make this or that announcement, so why not publicize who exactly is authorizing us?

Question: Let's get back to the official announcements. Thanks to them even today our newspapers often look identical.

Answer: Let me say immediately that I'm a convinced opponent of all forms of coercion regarding newspapers. But for the sake of justice I must add that the nature of other material that goes out via our channels is such that no self-respecting publication, in my opinion, could refuse to take it. However, I repeat, I am for the removal in full of all compulsion in this matter. The editorial board should always have the final word. And as a regular reader of *Moskovskaya Pravda* I welcome its decision not to accept official reports that arrive so late that they threaten the printing deadline. Our duty is not only to release information promptly but also to do all we can to make it required reading as it is, without any TASS signatures on it.

Question: Today is Journalists' Day in the USSR. What comments, what desires, would you like to express in connection with this?

Answer: What else can I wish for on our professional day other than the good health of our cause? TASS has recently been undergoing a re-equipment program, which is continuing. This does not mean simply "patching up the holes" or even just modernization. Our service is now attaining an entirely new technical level. I won't bore your readers with a list of our acquisitions, and just say what the overall aim is. We want to set up a TASS electronic data bank, an unrivalled and unprecedented archive with a rich variety of information within virtually all fields of knowledge.

Question: But "bank" is a commercial term...

Answer: Of course it is. In these self-financing times we ought to stop being so coy about this word. The contents of the bank will not of course only be at the disposal of TASS. It will be provided to all who want it, on commercial terms.

Question: I can foresee a criticism of this: "the government's agency is becoming an information monopoly—within a multi-party system".

Answer: We don't intend to make any restrictions as to our potential clients, be they businesses, organizations or political parties. In the final analysis accurate information and truth are never to be feared if you are truly convinced of the rightness of your cause.

In December 1990 Lev Spiridonov became the new general director of TASS. He is 59, and a Candidate of Philosophy. He previously worked in the Komsomol (Young Communist League), then in the USSR foreign ministry; former editor of *Moskovskaya Pravda*, departmental chief at the CPSU Central Committee, and recently first deputy editor-in-chief of *Pravda*. As a journalist, practically unknown to the Soviet public. One of the President's new proteges (like Pugo, Gromov, Kravchenko, etc).

The activities of the largest Soviet official bodies, be they military, industrial or ideological, were always concealed from the public, or from the Soviet public at least. We were always the last ones to find anything out about ourselves.

It stands to reason that specialists knew with what business the TASS international service was occupied and expected with impatience radical changes in it. Small wonder that the weekly *Argumenty i Fakty* (No. 16, April 1991) carried a small article, entitled "*At Long Last!*" and written by deputy editor-in-chief of the TASS International Service V. Golovin under the title *"TASS Reports Are Still Secret For You"*:

> Is there an information market in our country? I bear in mind not the presence of the most independent newspapers but the quick possibility to learn about, say, the attitude of the Singapore authorities to joint ventures or to receive regular information about Poland, with which your district executive committee might set up business contracts. Alas, there is no such market in this country and information is largely distributed along the old limited channels intended for the Soviet nomenklatura.
>
> However, at the end of last year, TASS, or to be more exact, its Chief Editorial Office of Foreign Information made a step towards the formation of the news market. Without getting a special authorization we have removed the stamp "For special use" from all our "closed" bulletins that were circulated among the officials in the CPSU Central Committee, the Ministry of Foreign Affairs, the State Security Committee and other government departments, but not available to "common Soviet people". For the first time in Soviet history TASS offers a free subscription to these bulletins.
>
> For example, subscription has been opened to the daily bulletin "The World and the USSR", which was the direct successor to the highly secret "White TASS", which was regarded as "strawberry" government quarters. The bulletin contains translations of the deepest and most acute foreign publications on all aspects of life in the USSR—from its foreign policy to culture.
>
> We send seven daily regional bulletins on problems of America, Western and Eastern Europe, Asia, Africa and the Middle East to professionals in the sphere of business and international affairs, not to activists of political parties and the working-class movement. These bulletins familiarize specialists with the latest economic experience, stock exchange statistics, the organization of work of state services, the local self-government bodies and give recommendations regarding the conclusion of business contracts with foreign partners.
>
> Analytical materials on foreign topics—from economics to ecology—are published in the bulletin "Dossier of International Problems", that is issued five times a week. By the way, the former closed bulletin for the top leadership that was printed in 205 copies was incorporated in this "Dossier".
>
> But the most operative source of information is the tape of foreign news, which TASS issues round-the-clock since January 1, 1991. So far only newspapers, television and radio are its main consumers. However, these mass media had time to digest only the insignificant portion of news—from the latest decisions of the White House to the recommendations of the Common market experts regarding the convertibility of the Soviet ruble.
>
> We also offer the tape of business news; serious communications plus daily reviews of the press and TV news from the major cities of the world (without political editing, of course). We prepare a short digest of the most acute and essential materials—the so called Planet Service - which give a full idea of the situation in the world for 24 hours.

In short, we produce a large set of information taken from secret dossiers and offered for the free market. We warn our consumers that our bulletins are intended for professionals and some cost hundreds of rubles and more.

In 1989 EkoTASS bulletin of commercial information celebrated its 25th anniversary. This information service issues several publications exclusively for experts in various sectors of the economy, such as banking or foreign trade. For them EkoTASS publishes information on business talks taking place in this country and abroad, on import and export contracts concluded by Soviet organizations with foreign firms, some details of market trends, foreign-currency exchange rates, and so on. Under the heading "Business Dialogue—Partners Sought" it carries announcements by foreign firms and Soviet organizations and businesses of their desire to set up partnerships in the USSR or other countries or establish a joint venture in whatever sector of the economy.

In the TASS agency everything looks fine to the uninitiated—hundreds of rooms, thousands of employees, millions of words published every day.

However, one essential thing is lacking. One does not trust TASS information. For decades the agency has been juggling the facts, telling lies under Stalin, under Gorbachev, during the August putsch and after it. This is only natural because by Gorbachev's decree of August 28, 1991, his press secretary Vitaly Ignatenko, who had misinformed journalists about the January 1991 events in Lithuania, was appointed its General Director. Was Ignatenko's position in any way different from those of Kryuchkov, Pugo and Yazov? Did he have the moral authority to complete the reform declared by him and to turn the heavily subsidized colossus, the Kremlin's information ministry into an economically and politically independent news corporation? TASS prepared and spread information, and hundreds of people from the propaganda department of the CPSU Central Committee controlled the implementation of TASS orders by the local press. That was hard to change. In autumn of 1991 the Moscow press wrote that "the revolution in TASS had failed." Their verdict was pronounced by the Russian TV news program.

What do our TV announcers read in the evening? TASS reports. Relinquishing television, Gorbachev kept an equally important information citadel for himself.

Although the Soviet Union is no more, the Soviet News Agency is still alive. In September 1991 it turned out that TASS had three huge transmitting centers. The one which is known to all is situated in Nikitskiye Vorota, the second, under one of the Moscow railway terminals, and the third, in a village near Moscow. The second and third centers are reserves. They have life-support systems and 336 telegraphic and 180 telephone communication channels connecting TASS with the rest of the country and the world. TASS's Moscow underground center, which was opened in 1959, is subordinate to TASS and the USSR Ministry of Communications. Imagine a 53-meter-deep elevator shaft and a 100-meter horizontal tunnel with editors' rooms and communication halls built like defense installations.

The TASS computer and satellite communications are the object of lust for all the incipient market structures in the country. It is quite possible that in the not too distant future TASS will realize its pet idea of leasing its own technical systems of communication to the Moscow Commodity Exchange and of granting this institution the right to use TASS correspondent networks inside and beyond Russia.

Not only TASS staffers are compelled to seek jobs elsewhere. In the conditions of the impending market and serious economic difficulties, the Novosti Agency lets its premises for hard currency to all those interested, explaining this by the need to establish close cooperation with domestic and foreign companies dealing in marketing, advertisement, tourism and mass communication.

Under the Cover of APN

In addition to TASS, one more Soviet information agency—APN (Novosti Press Agency) renamed IAN (Novosti Information Agency)—had an exceedingly ramified network of correspondents and other representatives in this country and abroad. APN had different assets: a huge publishing house in Moscow, one of the biggest buildings in the capital for its editorial office, its own TV service, a network of correspondents in 120 countries, and domestic bureaux in almost twenty locations.

The well-known TV commentator Vladimir Tsvetov wrote the following in the August, 1991 issue (before the putsch) of the magazine *Zhurnalist* :

> The entire edifice of our international affairs journalism was founded on lies—and I was part of it too. Upon graduation from Moscow University's Institute of Oriental Languages, I found myself in Sovinformburo, which later came to be called APN. I started on the lowest rung and gradually "climbed up" to become editor of a Japan-based magazine. I then realized that APN was a big hat intended to hide our ears worldwide. Since no foreign periodicals published the nonsense brought out by APN, we had to contrive our own inventions to rationalize our presence abroad. I did that as well. In Japan there were a lot of specialized bulletins which didn't care much about what they published, so sometimes they would accept our information. Once a correspondent from Kalinin sent in a phony report about a wallpaper factory in that city which had allegedly invented heat-generating wallpaper which could replace radiators. A tiny specialized wallpaper bulletin with a circulation of two hundred published that information. The title of the bulletin did not disclose its true identity. Thus I reported that a piece of information was published in a foreign periodical. All such reports would be summed up by the party Central Committee like this: "Over this month APN has promoted 5,000 propaganda materials to the foreign press!" They all knew that was not true, but such were the rules.

Tsvetov left APN in 1964. The rules however never changed. After the coup attempt failed, Russian authorities started something long overdue: reorganization of that propaganda arm of the CPSU Central Committee. Its two latest bosses were high-ranking party officials Valentin Falin and Albert Vlasov, each taking powerful deputies from the KGB, Generals Fedyashin and Babushkin. A special propaganda department, one of the main ones at APN, was almost completely staffed by KGB people. The same security agency was amply represented in APN bureaux abroad.

On August 20, 1991, the second day of the coup attempt, IAN used all its channels to distribute around the world a commentary by its leading political affairs writer Vladimir Simonov. Although the commentary cannot be described as outright praise for the junta, it was clearly intended to lend it legitimacy in the eyes of the world public. One phrase ran as follows: "Gennady Yanayev and his colleagues on the State Emergency Committee have voluntarily made a great sacrifice by shouldering the formidable burden of Gorbachev's problems." Even threatened with dismissal, one translator refused to work on the text.

Incidentally, the bosses of Novosti Information Agency (IAN) fell for the charms of the State Emergency Committee even earlier, on August 19, when they banned the release of books by Alexander Yakovlev and Raisa Gorbachev, although these had already been printed.

On August 29, the Russian Minister for the Press Mikhail Poltoranin introduced the new general director Andrei Vinogradov to a meeting of IAN's board of directors. The agency itself changed status from a union to a republican one. Before his new appointment, Vinogradov was the head of the Russian Information Agency (RIA) which he organized after a long service record with Novosti. He had served as a special correspondent for APN in Czechoslovakia and later held the office of European department head.

In the summer of 1991, the APN-IAN flashed press and Soviet democratic publications all over the world in connection with the scandalous behavior of the Agency leaders towards its own photographer Vardan Oganesyan. The 23 year-old correspondent was arrested by the Azerbaijanian OMON (a militia squad for special purposes) in the Armenian village of Getashen on the territory of Azerbaijan. The militiamen took away his film and the journalist's identity card, and put him behind bars. Having learned about this incident, the APN leadership in Moscow informed by telegraph the Azerbaijanian authorities about the cancellation of the contract concluded with this supernumerary journalist. Oganesyan as an unwelcome witness of the outrages of the Azerbaijanian Ministry of Internal Affairs against the local Armenians would hardly have been set free, had it not been for a very active intercession and a stir caused in the Moscow and foreign press by the Bulgarian TV journalist Tsvetana Paskaleva, who turned out to be by chance in Azerbaijan in May that year and who also by chance learned about this story. In reply to this hue-and-cry Oganesyan was taken under the protection of the newly set-up Committee to Protect Glasnost under the Journalists' Union of the USSR and the Fund to Protect Glasnost. Was it by chance that the APN-IAN betrayed its journalist and gave him up by condemning the captive to the inevitable destruction in the zone of hostilities?

Perhaps his employers remembered only too well that when in January 1991 there had been a bloodshed in Baltic republics, the photographer Oganesyan immediately left by air for Riga, where he worked in the shooting group of Podnieks and Slapins. In July 1991, he was released from prison and took the floor at a press-conference in the permanent representation of Armenia in Moscow.

The items "People and Events" in the APN publications impressed the audiences with the news of a more pleasant nature. In early 1991, Valery Kuznetsov became Vice-Chairman of the IAN after he had quitted the post of assistant of Alexander Yakovlev, the then member of the Presidential Council. Journalists, writers and publishers remember Kuznetsov as one of the most liberal Soviet censors. In the early 1980s, he held the post of Deputy Chairman of the Central Board of State Secrets Protection in the Press. When he subsequently worked in the press section of the CPSU Central Committee, he looked after the paper *Argumenty i Fakty* and made it possible for it to become the most popular edition in the country. But this service record was not typical of the APN functionaries.

Meanwhile we can find among the latter some of the well-known progressive journalists, as, for example, Mikhail Poltoranin who worked for some time in the APN, Algimantas Cekuolis, the press-attache of the present Lithuanian Government, a good hand at writing and speaking, who had a perfect command of Lithuanian, Russian and English, and Gennady Gerasimov, who until recently was the Kremlin's official public relations officer and also a brilliant journalist, no less democratic and liberal than his aforementioned colleagues.

The activities of the organization known for the past 50 years as first the Soviet Information Bureau, then Novosti Press Agency, later Novosti Information Agency and now Russian Information Agency "Novosti" represent an iceberg with a small Information Agency "Novosti" represent an iceberg with a small part visible above the surface to Soviet taxpayers. The latest renaming of this Soviet equivalent of the United States Information Agency (USIA) took place recently following half-hearted attempts by many members of the USSR and Russian Federation Supreme Soviets to call into doubt its continued existence. This agency probably employs more people abroad than the Soviet foreign ministry. What does it not publish for the foreign reader, moreover usually for free? We can boldly say—not much that is worthwhile, if the foreign-language pamphlets that grace all railway and airport facilities for foreigners in the USSR are anything to judge by. Nobody takes them, even when they're free. And what about the magazines covering the delights of life in the Soviet Union, which are printed for foreigners in their own countries and in their own languages? They have never enjoyed any demand in either Sophia or Paris, due to their glaringly mendacious contents. If we had sufficient resources to financially support this or that communist party in the world (the print runs of their booklets and newspapers were bought up for hard currency, personnel were trained, leaders were feted and took their holidays in the Kremlin's special hospitals and health resorts, weapons were supplied to them, they were put into power and kept there), then of course there were no problems in paying for the upkeep of several dozen (or hundred) foreign journalists eager to support in print any action by the Soviet Union, not entirely out of altruism, of course. And how APN would welcome hordes of "friends of the Soviet Union", who would frequently and willingly arrive, at our expense naturally, and take the opportunity to spend their generous APN royalties in special shops with sumptuous selections of the best Western goods! These ladies and gentleman were so well looked after that they were not even requested to sign their payment documents—the accompanying Soviet journalist was supposed to do that. And then there were all the tours around the country by these foreigners with their offspring and various kin. Not a single Western travel firm could offer such a luxurious range of services. Much of this is now in the past, but not all. For many years the APN-IAN board has been populated by the same people, and in essence little has changed.

This is a description of the agency provided by a highly competent man, a former APN political columnist and now Russian minister for the press and information, Mikhail Poltoranin (as quoted in the Moscow newspaper *Menedzher* (Manager), issue 11 of 1990):

> The creation of a Russian information agency is especially complex. The Russian government thought it could be done using APN as a basis. We don't know how permissible this would be from the legal viewpoint, but there's certainly much sense in the idea. Suffice it to recall that APN was set up when the Cold War was in full swing, to counter Western propaganda. This purpose is now defunct, and nothing remotely similar has emerged to take its place. So why shouldn't this semi-official arm of the KGB begin to perform its true function, and become a real INFORMATION agency? However, the President of the USSR obviously didn't share this opinion, because he issued a decree turning APN into NIA—the Novosti Information Agency, under state ownership. The decree doesn't fit in very well with the law, since officially APN was considered a public organization and turning it into a state-owned one with the flourish of a pen is the same as turning some political party, for example, into a state ministry. The question of an information agency, and also of a television service, for the Russian Federation remains undecided. The situation regarding the press is better—more and more new publications are being registered.

Since its establishment in 1961, APN has been termed a "public" organization, formed by other "public" organizations such as the USSR Journalists' Union, Writers' Union, the All-Union Znaniye (Knowledge) Society, the Soviet Women's Committee, the Union of Soviet Societies for Friendship and Cultural Links with Foreign Countries, and others. But all of these were merely covers, or "umbrella organizations", to use the mild expression of Mr. Albert Ivanovich Vlasov, who for many years has been the chief of APN. For a quarter of a century, this gentleman moved from one top post to another, be it that of APN, or of a special and vast Communist Party Central Committee department coordinating the activities of APN with other equally heavyweight establishments, such as the foreign and defense ministries and the KGB. A mountain of articles and even books has been written in the West about the clandestine and strictly unofficial activities of numerous APN employees abroad.

If Vlasov were to be made to stand for endorsement in his post by federal or Russian parliamentary commissions, he would most likely be rejected. Not at all by virtue of his personal qualities; alongside his predecessors such as B. Burkov, L. Tolkunov and V. Falin, he has been a reasonably outspoken figure. But the problem is that the agency has engaged in numerous goings-on far removed from the journalists' profession.

It was a correct move to rename APN. As of July 27 1990, by presidential decree, it became IAN—the Novosti Information Agency—and a state-sector organization, with Mr. Vlasov confirmed in charge by the same decree. Removal of the agency from under the wing of the Party Central Committee and transfer to the sphere of influence of the Presidential Council can be called perestroika in action. But with the same management and functions? It looks like it. In any event, the very few and very brief interviews that Vlasov has been forced to give to the central Soviet newspapers display no sign of regret (not to mention repentance) for past sins. This is what Albert Vlasov stated in his interview to *Izvestia* (August 1, 1990):

> To our traditional publishing activities (newspapers and magazines in numerous languages around the world) have been added video, radio and TV channels, global computer communication systems, all, incidentally, for specific clients. For example, Stanislav Polzikov's TV group films in practically all the country's "hot spots" to order for American, German, Japanese and Italian TV stations. Our photo-journalists can send color pictures to any newspaper in the world from any part of the USSR within 17 minutes, using satellite and computer comms. The IAN headquarters in Moscow has a radio station that is carried by major foreign stations (incidentally, during the 28th Party Congress over 100 broadcasts were transmitted abroad via this channel).
>
> Our budget, as endorsed by the USSR Supreme Soviet, is about 100 million rubles a year. This is a lot, if you take into account the money spent in the past on

ineffective propaganda campaigns. But today we don't ask for anything more than we need. Information is a highly valuable commodity throughout the world. Some of our departments, for example, the Western Europe office, are already showing a profit, in hard currency included. A good source of income is helping foreign journalists on visits to or accredited in the USSR (over the past year there were more than 4,000 of them).

The official point of view of Mr. Vlasov and his cronies in the Party machinery and the KGB, which was on numerous occasions stated in public, is that East and West are equally to blame for the onset and conduct of the Cold War, all the way up to 1990. Three or four years ago these very same people were laying all the blame on the West's aggressive policies. In a few years' time, of course, when they have retired and publish their reminiscences or give interviews, they will be forced to admit through clenched teeth that the overall assessment by Western politicians of communist theory and practice has remained virtually unchanged for 50 years or more. It is we, and not they in the West, who have been standing on our heads for 70 years. It is we who by the beginning of the 1990s began to gingerly move away from dangerous utopianism towards political realism.

APN-IAN occupies hundreds of rooms in several large buildings. The main one, a vast edifice that looms above the Garden Ring Road, a central Moscow thoroughfare, is well-known to foreign journalists because it stands alongside the foreign ministry press center, the venue of most major press conferences by top Soviet and foreign politicians and heads of state.

There are several reasons for the rather low professionalism of most of APN's output. The agency's best writers do not hang around there for long, not wishing to become obscure bureaucrats organizing the transmission abroad of others' works, where such material is unwanted even when it's free. The intelligence service employees who are APN representatives abroad and even members of its board stand out like sore thumbs among the vast number of wives and offspring of Moscow bureaucrats who make up the agency's staff. The absence of contemporary library, archive, analytical and reference services is illustrated by the fact that for all of APN there is only one room with a photocopier, to which access is strictly controlled, plus a special reading room ["spetskhran"] with 30-50 Western periodical publications. Some of these, such as *Russkaya Mysl* and *Novoye Russkoye Slovo* (The Russian Thought and The New Russian Word, published in Paris and New York respectively) are available only to the chairman or his deputies. The agency receives only two copies of *Time, Paris-Match, Newsweek*, etc, from which, during the Brezhnev-Andropov epoch, anything concerning these leaders and their policies was cut out in advance, as well as any mention of the KGB, dissidents and the activities of Russian and Soviet emigres in the West. Only in such a truncated and castrated form could these "examples of putrid imperialist ideology" fall into the hands of the agency's most curious members...

One does not need to be very sophisticated or informed to be able to conjure up massive lies of a Stalin or Brezhnev type, as did APN and its successor IAN.

Addressing IAN's board of directors, Vinogradov admitted that he had no clear idea of how the agency should further operate. Again, the person at the helm did not have a conception. The numerous staff of the agency know all too well what that means. For four years they had been waiting for IAN's former chairman Vlasov to produce some general plan (in the meantime they bought big batches of consumer goods abroad, attempted to sell rubles for hard currency and engaged in a lot of other non-journalistic activities). The chairman changed editors for directors, and reduced personnel by thirty percent, but that was all. So what does the new leader have to offer? Apparently, he has one big idea: to cut and slash to the limit, since RIA, and Russia for that matter, does not want to have this big monster by its side. But so many hopes are now pinned on great Russia. If it ever emerges from the debris, it will need IAN with all its costly equipment, photo archives and skilled personnel. Some people may argue that a similar thing could be created anew, once Russia comes to might. But there had already been the sad experience of 1976, when the agency was nearly destroyed and it took fifteen years and hundreds of millions of dollars to bring it back to life. Isn't it wiser to preserve at least part of what we have? After all, that will take only worthless rubles. As for a concept, ask USIA, it has a wealth of experience.

Thankfully, in Moscow there are now other news agencies in addition to APN-IAN and TASS. Most of them harbor no dreams of even one ruble from the state budget, not to mention 100 million of them. All they want is no interference. In 1990 Soviet newspapers began to widely use news items from small information agencies such as Interfax, Postfactum, SibIA, Severo-Zapad, KAS-KOR and Dlya Vsekh (For Everyone). This has enabled newspapers to provide readers with an unorthodox view of events taking place in the country.

The Unsinkable

Interfax, all of which at first took up a few offices in the Radio Moscow building, is with increasing frequency being quoted by major media outlets. Initially TASS pointedly ignored its potential competitor, then tried to silence it. Later on it offered to buy up Interfax reports for hard currency, and after being turned down switched to rebutting individual items. This most likely merely increased the independent agency's popularity—fully in keeping with the laws of competition.

Interfax's credo is that information should be released as quickly as possible, and without any comment—let the reader draw his own conclusions. It was set up in September, 1989 by Radio Moscow and the Soviet-French-Italian business Interquadro, which put up the initial capital. At first, Interfax targeted foreign correspondents accredited in Moscow, and on a daily basis despatched by fax a few news round-ups in Russian, English and Spanish, and also 3 weekly compendia of items on important events in the USSR plus exclusive interviews with prominent state and public personalities. Censorship had not yet been abolished, but Interfax from the very beginning refused to have its material vetted in advance.

Its subscribers are steadily increasing in number. "We are always willing to use Interfax reports, which are up to international standards", said Alexei Mayorov, a BBC employee.

In an interview with *Argumenty i Fakty* (No 30 1990), M. Komissar, whose name in today's political climate is slightly unfortunate, said the following about his agency:

Question: The establishment of Interfax was in effect a challenge to the news agencies to which we have become so accustomed, such as APN and TASS. It must have taken a lot of confidence to decide to compete commercially with such monopolies.

Answer: The idea of Interfax arose because foreign diplomats and specialists were constantly complaining of the lack of reliable information on things happening in the Soviet Union. They were not happy with TASS, whose reports are tendentious, politicized, slow to arrive, and so on. The same criticisms also applied to APN. So we decided to set up a new agency that would promptly and objectively report events.

Question: The first Interfax reports appeared in September last year...

Answer: We recouped the initial outlay literally within two months, and now are in effect paying our own way. We have over 100 correspondents in various cities of the Soviet Union and use facsimile machines, which allow us to rapidly send to our clients large amounts of information.

Question: But we've already been able to read or hear rebuttals of your reports...

Answer: We always check up on news when in doubt, either by enlisting the help of other correspondents or turning to official quarters. And virtually every day we turn down several reports that don't stand up to scrutiny.

Regarding rebuttals, there have been just two, both of them via TASS, whose working practices have somewhat surprised us. Its staff made no attempt to approach us or find out what facts we had at our disposal. Incidentally, in at least one instance we had irrefutable proof that we were right. However, we decided not to enter into a slanging match and start "rebutting rebuttals".

By the way, the international practice is that one media outlet does not refute what's said by another; it simply gives its own information on an event. This is a kind of professional ethics.

Question: You have to be given your due in that domestic news is usually released by your agency ahead of even the West's radio stations...

Answer: But in theory that's the way it should be: Soviet reporters should be the first to know of events in their own country, American reporters in theirs, German in theirs, and so on. That this was not so in the past was the result of our deformed system. I think that the operations of Interfax have set things to rights.

On January 11 1991 the management of Gosteleradio, with chairman Leonid Kravchenko at the helm, decided to stop the Interfax news agency from working out of its premises in the Gosteleradio building. Kravchenko ordered the seizure of all assets legally belonging to Interfax at Gosteleradio. That same day, Interfax was offered a new home in the buildings of the RSFSR Supreme Soviet and the USSR Science and Technology Union. The Gosteleradio management never concealed the fact that Interfax's reports were at variance with their politics. The conflict was widely covered in the Soviet press, and in fact became a powerful and free advertising campaign for Interfax.

Moscow correspondents of the American newspaper *Novoye Russkoye Slovo* Oleg Kupriyanov and Alexander Kan described the position of Interfax Agency in its issue of January 15, 1991 in the following words:

> On January 11, the morning block of information of the Interfax Agency was devoted to the situation in Lithuania and the other Baltic Republics. As usual, the Agency's information greatly differed from the version of developments set forth by Soviet official sources--TASS, radio and television, and the Party press.
>
> On that very day the morning session of the USSR Supreme Soviet began with Anatoly Lukyanov's statement that despite the closed work of the session in the last days information was being leaked through Interfax Agency and other channels.
>
> The same morning the Board of the State Committee for Radio and Television met to discuss the question about the Interfax Agency. By 4 o'clock p.m. the workers of this independent agency began to save their equipment and belongings by carrying them out of the rooms of the State Committee on the Pyatnitskaya Street. By decision taken by the Committee's Board, headed by the recently appointed Leonid Kravchenko, the activity of the Agency was terminated and a distress warrant was issued.
>
> Telephones and telefaxes were switched off two hours after the decision had been taken by the Board. Having withdrawn the regular block of information, the Interfax Agency succeeded in transmitting to its subscribers: SOS! "We are convinced", the Agency transmitted, "that not financial or property claims are the causes of today's conflict with the State Committee for Radio and Television. Interfax regards this action of the Committee's leadership as a logical development of Leonid Kravchenko's course of abolishing independent information structures. The recent prohibition of the most popular Soviet TV program Vzglyad and the disappearance from the screen of acute publicistic broadcasts of the ATV program are the links in the same chain. The Radio and Television State Committee does not conceal that

Interfax's information does not meet its political conception... This action may only be prevented by the person who had appointed Kravchenko to his post--the President of the USSR--Mikhail Gorbachev."

The news about the closing down of Interfax was broadcast from the Soviet Union by the leading information agencies in second place after the information about the situation in Lithuania. By the way, Interfax reports about the situation in the Baltic Republics were widely used by many foreign mass media. According to the information received from one of the Interfax workers, the formal pretext for closing down the Agency was its transmission of the communication that the Latvian Minister of Culture Raimond Pauls had described the coverage of events in his Republic by Central TV as 'remote from the reality'.

The Interfax manager Mikhail Komissar was more diplomatic in his evaluation. In his interview, given to the correspondents of the *Novoye Russkoye Slovo* immediately after the State Committee's Board, he pointed out two causes for the conflict. First, it was the scramble between several groups of employees inside the Radio and Television State Committee where the extreme rightist Leonid Kravchenko made his appearance against a background of the quite conservative leadership. Second, Kravchenko was inimical towards Interfax. Before his recent appointment he had been the head of TASS, the agency which was not in the style of Interfax by its status and possibilities but could not compete with the latter by its professional qualities--objectivity, operativeness and independence.

However, Mikhail Komissar has appraised the situation in an optimistic way. "We shall resume our work in a few days, when the premises now under repairs are ready for our occupation. These premises were given to us by the Moscow Soviet," he said. Interfax workers who have recovered from the natural shock are not inclined to dramatize the situation. The commission members appointed by the Committee's Board to supervise the eviction did not remind anybody of the Chekamen of the period of repression, who even helped their colleagues in a comradley way to take belongings out of the rooms. Journalists jested that they were moved either to "the Butyrskaya or the Lefortovo Prison". "Sooner or later our rupture with the Radio and Television State Committee was inevitable, but from now on we shall be independent."

But the latest practice shows that there is a cat for every mouse. Interfax developments blend with the general campaign of repression against the independent mass media in the USSR. The source of free thought has been removed from the State Committee's premises, and the authorities, of course, have much more means and ways of dealing with the unruly.

Interfax took off before our very eyes, and is already an impressive success story. It proves that honesty and professionalism are still the qualities that make journalism work. In October 1991, Moscow-based researchers from the National Center for Public Opinion conducted a poll among 150 foreign journalists stationed in Moscow, learning that Interfax was their most preferred and reliable source of information compared with all other Soviet agencies.

That is easy to believe after hearing so much about the dishonest practices of its gigantic competitors TASS and APN. Here is what Mikhail Berger had to say about Interfax in an article published by *Izvestia* (August 31, 1991):

> "The office of Interfax has been taken by armed men. For reasons beyond our control we are suspending our work for an indefinite period of time".
>
> That report was prepared only hours after the State Emergency Committee seized power and one Interfax journalist was ready to release it if anybody came to arrest them. They even arranged with their Western recipients for a special code to signal that Interfax was operating under control should they be forced to convey biased information. Fortunately that did not happen. Along with Radio of Russia, Echo of Moscow radio station and Postfactum news agency, Interfax disseminated objective information on what was happening in the country during the coup attempt, and the responses to it at home and abroad.
>
> It is still anyone's guess why the "Soviet leadership" did not shut down independent news agencies or block the offices of the newspapers which it did shut down. That mistake allowed the former to cable their information, and the latter, to put out underground issues and leaflets.
>
> The Russian White House was constantly in contact with Interfax, and its reports helped the defenders to take decisions. The heroic Echo of Moscow, on the air despite official suspension, relayed Interfax information also.
>
> Interfax should be given much of the credit for the world being aware of what happened in this country starting from the first hours of the coup. Practically all Western news agencies and other mass media are subscribers to Interfax. More than forty countries receive its information. When communications channels with Moscow were overloaded on Monday August 19, journalists from NBC came to Interfax representatives in the USA and read out Interfax reports live.
>
> Interfax received a lot of letters of gratitude from its foreign colleagues for its coverage during those days. But the general director of the agency M.Komissar says he was especially pleased by a message from the public relations center of the Ministry of the Interior. The message said that the staff of the center had not been misled by the official information from their former bosses, because they trusted Interfax.
>
> It all started in September 1989, when editorial boards of Moscow periodicals first received fax messages from the hitherto unknown news agency Interfax. They had their doubts concerning the independent status of the agency, since it had sprung up in the bosom of Gosteleradio. But those were quality reports which arrived even faster than those from TASS, the state-run news monopoly. Thus the agency was gradually accepted. Official recognition came when the government newspaper *Izvestia* started publishing its materials.
>
> Former Gosteleradio chairman Leonid Kravchenko caused a lot of trouble as soon as he was appointed to the office. He even expelled the agency from the Gosteleradio building, but Interfax managed to survive thanks to the Russian authorities and the Scientific and Industrial Union. That confrontation only added to the prestige of the agency and eventually made its materials more versatile, because it started putting out business news in addition to political news. Interfax was the first to deliver regular

news from stock exchanges. It became so fast that it reported Gorbachev's resignation as General Secretary of the Communist Party five hours before his official statement.

The events during the coup attempt have shown that the society cannot exist without independent news media. Today there are many independent ones, but those which were independent before the putsch helped stop it.

The Russian Information Agency was another organization that fully supported the democrats and legal authorities during the coup attempt. Among other things, it transmitted a statement by the USSR Journalists' Union brought in by Eduard Sagalayev. (One passage in that statement read as follows: "There may be people of different orientations and political convictions among us, but there may be no liars or rascals"). RIA came into being in 1991. As opposed to TASS and APN, it was housed in a few rooms and produced ten pages of written text daily, increasing the output to 28-30 pages during the putsch. In September 1991 RIA changed its status: it moved to occupy one floor in the IAN building and practically merged with it.

The Postfactum Agency, whose reports now appear with increasing frequency in the Soviet press, is also a child of perestroika. This is what it says about itself (taken from *Trud*, September 18 1990):

> Postfactum was the first independent agency to be set up in the country that reflects not the official but its own viewpoint on events. It was established about a year ago. Every day, including weekends and holidays, at 12.00, 18.00 and 24.00 hours it sends to its subscribers its "USSR Today" round-up of current events by fax, telex and teletype. This bulletin includes on-site reporting by its own correspondents and reviews of the official (central and local) press and alternative press.
>
> Postfactum's round-ups are used by federal and republican state authorities, television and radio, newspapers, foreign correspondents, embassies and the offices of foreign firms. Its information is distributed by communications networks of Europe and the USA. In addition, Postfactum issues a weekly compendium of analytical and expert articles on the main political and economic issues in the USSR, containing data, research results and other materials previously unpublished.

Honest Journalism Takes a Stout Heart

To complete this section on the press agencies, here is a phenomenon quite unusual on our contemporary political scene: a detailed description of the work of the independent Siberian Information Agency (SibIA) by the monthly publication *Zhurnalist* (No 9 1990), which is put out by the USSR Journalists' Union, and of the agency's editor-in-chief Alexei Manannikov, who is also a Russian Federation People's Deputy. I think that if Sergei Grigoryants, the well-known editor of the most illustrious samizdat dissident newspaper in the USSR, *Glasnost*, were to become a member of the Russian or federal parliament, interviews with him would be printed not only by the foreign but Soviet press as well. The previously obscure Manannikov has now gone completely legal. Below is an interview with him by *Zhurnalist*'s Yelena Korolkova, which was titled "*Believe nothing, fear nothing, ask for nothing*":

Question: Mr. Manannikov, the newspaper *Sovietskaya Rossiya* ' in its article "*Saddling up the Free thinkers*", called you "simply the idol" of the independents and radicals and claimed you are a member of the Democratic Union. Is this true?

Answer: It's nonsense. I try as a matter of principle to be politically independent and not identify myself with any party, at least not officially. No employee of our agency belongs to the Democratic Union. We've even put out several anti-DU reports, after which it refused point-blank to distribute our publications. In general lumping opponents in with the Democratic Union is one of the central press's tricks, especially in the provinces: everyone who doesn't suit the ruling ideologists is labelled in this way.

Question: Your position—simultaneously an independent editor and a representative of the highest authority of the republic—to me personally seems a little unnatural. You're an "unofficial" in a highly official system. How did this come about?

Answer: Firstly, about how I ended up in journalism, since involvement with the press helped me get elected to the Supreme Soviet. I did not voluntarily become a journalist. By training I'm an economist. I taught political economy and for a time was a postgraduate student. After being arrested in 1982 and spending 3 years in prison I was excluded from my main profession.

Question: What were you convicted of?

Answer: For breach of article 190-1 of the Russian Federation Criminal Code: "distribution of deliberate falsehoods slandering the Soviet state and social system". Specifically, for speaking up in support of the Polish union Solidarity. Particularly incriminating were such expressions as "totalitarian regime", "partocracy", some unorthodox comments on the war in Afghanistan and on how the Soviet press was mendacious, which was considered the greatest "deliberate falsehood" of all.

For quite a long time I had to work however I could—as a rigger, warehouseman, and stoker. Once reform began in earnest I tried to get myself rehabilitated. After being turned down I declared a hunger strike in protest. I had to turn to the media and got in touch with *Glasnost*, which supported me. In the end I realized people who had gone through experiences similar to my own were engaged in a specific pursuit. They weren't out to get something for themselves, but had carved out such a niche in society as the independent press. I started to work on the paper, and later ran the "Chronicle" section. At the beginning of last year I returned to Novosibirsk and tried to set up an information agency.

Question: Why an agency?

Answer: I wanted to cover the entire area. I've always believed in the idea of Siberian independence. It's not a new idea and long before the Revolution it had its advocates, who, incidentally, at one time were deputies to the State Duma. During the 1930s supporters of independence for the regions of Siberia were physically exterminated as enemies of the Revolution. With them disappeared also the pan-Siberian publications, of which there was a large number before 1917 and even in the 1920s. After that the entire area was represented solely by the magazine *Sibirskiye Ogni* (Siberian Lights), which only came out monthly. So a huge information vacuum was formed, and we tried to fill it. Thanks to the contacts I'd established while working on *Glasnost* and *Ekspress-Khronika* I was immediately able to set up an office and a network of information sources. SibIA tapped into all the provincial and district centers and other major cities, about twenty of them. From reports received we compile a weekly press bulletin, "the first pan-Siberian information publication", as it says on the cover. We used to write "the only", but recently—and after us, let me stress—the *Sibirskaya Gazeta* (Siberian Gazette) and Radio Novosibirsk appeared, also aiming to serve the area that goes by the name of Siberia. We also issue *Severny Telegraf* (Northern Telegraph), which is a journal carrying independent views, similar to Referendum. Everything that won't fit into the bulletin goes into it. So far there's been five issues but now we're on a pause of several months: to print some major articles we need big money, which will make it expensive for the readers.

Question: A samizdat bibliographical handbook lists the typed bulletin *Svobodnoye Obshchestvo* (Free Society), which is published by the Irkutsk branch of the Democratic Union and of SibIA.

Answer: This is the first time I've heard of this bulletin. We are in constant contact with Radio Liberty and transmit the latest news to it. Liberty and the offices of *Russkaya Mysl* receive the full text of the bulletin by fax. We have occasional contacts with the Voice of America and the BBC.

Question: So it was circumstance that forced you into SibIA. But how did you become a People's Deputy?

Answer: This was largely thanks to my journalistic activities. I'm known in Siberia due to Radio Liberty broadcasts and what we put out ourselves. That's on the one hand. On the other, I was greatly helped by the hard line taken by the Party authorities. The entire election campaign added up to a direct confrontation: the Novosibirsk regional Party committee vs me. The kind of situation when if you're "against" you're actually "for".

Question: Could you please set out your political position in greater detail?

Answer: My program boils down to two main features: firstly, to implement the political legacy of Andrei Sakharov and to decolonize Siberia and, secondly, as a step towards accomplishing this—change the political and economic system in this country. As an economist, my views are close to those of the so-called right wing in Western political vocabulary—the Republicans in the USA, Conservatives in the UK, Christian Democrats in Germany and Liberals in Japan. So far Russia has nothing similar, and there can't be free people where everything depends on the state.

Question: You mentioned Radio Liberty. Did it help establish SibIA?

Answer: It pays us only royalty fees, we put the agency on its feet by ourselves. Liberty doesn't employ Soviet citizens as a matter of principle, which is set out in its statutes. Meanwhile, it discriminates strongly against our correspondents. As far as I know, Soviets are paid 12—13 marks for a minute's worth of airtime, while Western correspondents get not less than 30. Liberty is liberty, but as far as justice is concerned... Everything that we send them is thus a gift, a kind of act of charity. But we have to circulate our stories throughout the world. The SibIA bulletin is distributed mainly in Novosibirsk and other Russian cities. We have some regular subscribers, about 500 of them, in Moscow and Leningrad, virtually all the major libraries, including the Lenin Library, numerous newspapers, such as *Atmoda* for example, and unofficial papers. Reprints from our bulletin appear in the youth press in Siberia, and in Baltic and Moldavian papers. The Party press also uses our texts, but in its own way: we're quoted and referred to, but only in a critical fashion. But I have to give newspapers such as *Altaiskaya Pravda* and *Krasnoyarskii Rabochii* their due: they've been better advertisers for us than anyone else.

Question: Do you still consider the Soviet press to be full of falsehoods?

Answer: Not now, no. New publications with different viewpoints have appeared, and coverage of news is varied. For example, when I open *Argumenty i Fakty* or *Komsomolskaya Pravda* I find a mass of information that I want to believe. However, where are the guarantees that given the current structure of the mass media, this situation will continue? There's no withholding the credit that's due to the unofficial press, which was first to open up many taboo topics and forced the official publications to follow suit. The main achievement of our agency, in my opinion, was to break through the information blockade of the strikes in the Kuzbass coalfield. The central newspapers and TV only mentioned them a week afterwards; the local ones even in areas adjacent to the Kuzbass, were silent right until September and October even. We spoke out right from the very beginning of the strikes, via Western radio stations. The first video report from the Kuzbass got to CBS from us; we filmed it in Prokopievsk and Novokuznetsk.

Question: Does the agency have a large staff?

Answer: Five people.

Question: Is that all?

Answer: That's all. Typical of samizdat.
Question: **Then you must have recruited some big names to your agency.** *Sovetskaya Rossia* **paid you an unexpected compliment. I quote: "There is no reason to doubt the professionalism of the people working at SibIA".**
Answer: Wrong again: there's not one professional in the agency. Simply like-minded people formed an organizational nucleus, around which everything else revolves. Three of us do the writing, the others handle technical matters. We do have some professional journalists among our sources. For example, Marina Salnikova has been working with us for a long time. She reports for *Tyumenskii Komsomolets* (Tyumen Young Communist), but feeds material to us as well. Sasha Lavrova, who is virtually editor of the bulletin and also *Severny Telegraf*, is a philologist. In general we draw little official distinction between duties. Not only that, but the staff line-up is constantly changing, and there is a natural personnel turnover.
Question: **Does that disappoint you?**
Answer: The line-up has been constant for the past few months, which does disappoint me. There's no injection of fresh minds.
Question: **Tell us something about the material basis and financial resources of the agency.**
Answer: We have just one computer, which threatens to break down. The first two bulletins were typewritten, xeroxed and simply handed out. But we were lucky in that almost straight away we struck a deal with a printing works in the Baltic region, the press bulletin came out with a decent print run and for the first press bulletin came out with a decent print run and for the first time we sold it, at 50 kopecks a copy. We still maintain this original price, although it's low for an independent publication and we have problems with distribution, since others pay better. We currently have a circulation of 15,000, and are able to support an editorial team. Our people receive 50 rubles a week, and we have enough to pay fees only to graphic designers and artists. We had an emergency when we printed our 12th issue, the first one to come out with a large run, and we had to tighten our belts and take out a bridging loan to see us through. The print run was confiscated even before leaving the airport. Our distributors declared a hunger strike, led by our courier who was supposed to bring all the copies back from Vilnius. They all sat down under a monument to Lenin, where a crowd soon gathered. They passed a hat round and received 1,000 rubles, exactly what the printing costs were.
Question: **Is your publication often subjected to harassment?**
Answer: Last December, in the latest flat where the editorial team was working, a search was carried out in an attempt to detect drugs. They didn't find any, but did turn up some tear-gas canisters, ordinary things that are on open sale in West Germany—a good defense against criminals. The owner of the flat got three days inside. But drugs and tear-gas canisters were only a pretext, of course. In fact, we fully expected something to

	happen: the previous evening a special issue of the bulletin had gone out, devoted to the local security bodies and titled "*The Mafia upholding the law*".
Question:	But as far as I understand you are well-inclined towards the Law on the Press, although it lays down laws and standards that you, even though you're an unofficial agency, still have to observe. Despite the abolition of censorship.
Answer:	Until now, censorship hasn't bothered us. What does bother us is something else entirely: access to printing facilities. The Law on the Press should enter into force simultaneously with a market economy. If we have a real chance to look for paper at market prices, while the boss of a Party-run printworks starts keeping an eye on what's being printed, then there can be no free press. I proceed from the three principles of an arrested man: believe nothing, fear nothing, ask for nothing.

In early January 1991, in Moscow, the newly-established Christian Information Agency started work, releasing its own information bulletin, *Khristianskiye Novosti* (Christian News), and the periodical compendium *Khristianskii Arkhiv* (Christian Archive). The new agency is based on the Protestant independent publishing house (belonging to the Evangelical Christian Baptists), which already distributes its eponymous newspaper via Soyuzpechat, and also the journal *Khristianin* (Christian), revived after a 70-year break.

CHAPTER III

VETERAN POLITICAL PUBLICATIONS

What Was Interesting in *Pravda*

Eight papers, such as *Pravda, Izvestia, Rabochaya Tribuna, Komsomolskaya Pravda, Trud, Krasnaya Zvezda, Selskaya Zhizn* and *Gudok*, were financed by the USSR Cabinet of Ministers on March 28, 1991 and supplied with hard currency for their quick dispatch by air to foreign subscribers. All in all, there were 17,000 subscribers abroad. Foreign subscribers to other Soviet periodicals, whose number is much greater indeed, were to be content with their supply either by train (Europe) or by sea in 1990-1991. Moreover, they did not receive a large number of these editions in general. The putschists declared in August 1991 the cessation of the issue of all Moscow newspapers and magazines with the exception of those eight editions cited above (on the list of the State Emergency Committee the papers *Gudok* and *Komsomolskaya Pravda* were replaced by newspaper *Glasnost*, published by the CPSU Central Committee.

"*Will There Be a Pravda In 1991?*" Under this headline *Argumenty i Fakty* (No. 41 1990) carried a story setting out the situation that has evolved at *Pravda*, the Communist Party Central Committee's flagship. The words belong to V. Yegorov, deputy secretary of the newspaper's Party bureau:

> The situation is truly extraordinary, which is why the question "Will there be a *Pravda* in 1991?" was put on the agenda of an office Party gathering. The very wording of it testifies to the depth of the crisis. The paper is losing its authority and readers' support. It is late to react to the most newsworthy of events and is at times clumsy in its attempts to engage in debate with its political opponents. It ignores or hushes up trends that require immediate response or analysis.
>
> The majority of our journalists know this full well, but the bureaucratic hierarchy in existence at the paper prevents the staff from making the most of their creative abilities and has brought about an atmosphere of nervousness and estrangement. The conflict that has arisen can in no way be reduced simply to personality clashes. One of the key issues at the Party gathering was that the current management of *Pravda* (meaning the editorial board and the editor-in-chief) is incapable of leading the newspaper out of the crisis. A no-confidence motion failed to make it onto the agenda due solely to an announcement by the editor-in-chief: "In the

very near future I shall inform the Central Committee and Politburo that I cannot and do not want to work here".

The editorial staff hope that the Central Committee plenum scheduled for October 8-9 will take a very serious look at the Party newspaper's problems. There is no longer any time for "reviewing" or "coordinating". If the current situation remains unchanged, the newspaper will simply die. As an example, here is one of the latest figures (as of October 1) regarding subscription to *Pravda*: only 92,000 for all of the Ukraine. At the same time last year, there were 140,000 in the city of Dniepropetrovsk alone. There are whole areas where subscribers are in single figures.

The new Moscow newspaper *Kuranty* (November 1 1990) ran an article by *Pravda* journalist Vladimir Somov and given the voluminous headline "For many years journalism was a tool in the hands of a totalitarian system. The majority of newsmen, not even suspecting it themselves, have been involved in ideologically hoodwinking the public. And today one such speaks out in repentance, bitterly realizing that THEY HAVE STOLEN OUR LIVES":

Today we often laugh through our tears, because we are laughing at ourselves. This story, told to me by a friend, initially cheered us both up. But then after a minute we just sat in silence, sighing and thinking our own thoughts. This is the essence of it. A woman sharing my friend's communal flat went off to visit an acquaintance in West Germany for a week. It was the first time she had been abroad in the putrescent West. She came back miserable and withdrawn. To everything she simply replies, as if in a trance, "they've stolen our lives!". Weeks and months have passed, yet all she can say is, "They've stolen our lives!"

Virtually every Soviet citizen who breaks out of the cordon goes into deep shock. The abundance of food and clothes, their amazing cheapness and complete availability, good-natured service and friendly people—all these everyday realities of normal life could make even the most iron-willed lose his mind. The absurdity and inhumanity of the Bolshevik experiment is now clear to probably everyone. Except the Bolsheviks themselves, who are still hung up on the Party's vanguard role.

They have stolen the lives of hundreds of millions of people, of several generations, future included, since it will take time for us to come to our senses. They have stolen the lives not only of those who rotted in the dungeons of the Lubyanka, of those whose bones line the bottom of the White Sea Canal and other great construction projects of communism. They have stolen the life of everyone who stands in the never-ending queues, clutching in his sweaty palm his soap or sugar coupons. They have stolen the life of my 80-year-old mother, whose own state pays her a pension of 39 rubles a month. They have stolen the life of my 11-year-old son, who has not seen sweets for several months and dreams of owning his own football, something you cannot buy for neither love nor money.

They have also stolen my life. I am not going to complain about my frugal living conditions, although by all civilized standards I, like the absolute majority of my fellow-countrymen, am poor. My monthly wage, converted into dollars at the free-market rate, is less than the daily earnings of a Negro dustman. True, by our standards I have all the basic essentials. A 40-m^2 three-roomed rabbit hutch in the concrete jungle of Moscow's Bibiriev suburb, and a pair of shiny suits. Neither have I been deprived of a prestigious post: for many years I was the deputy editor of *Pravda*.

But away with the mercenary side of life! From childhood they try to drum it into us that this is not the most important. And they succeed. When I say that they have stolen my life, I have something entirely different in mind.

The totalitarian state has never allowed anyone to live the way that they want. Scientists, engineers, performers, carpenters, peasants—have they ever been able to make the most of their potential? Of course not. Our economy continues to stagger onwards like a half-dead nag, while our culture is in its death throes.

Let us be optimists: people will acquire property, and with it freedom, and begin to live like human beings. They will not be weighed down by guilt for the past. And what about me, a journalist, who was not only smothered by ideological dogmas but also did all he could to ensure that these dogmas bloomed in all their splendor?

Let us face it, it is not easy to admit even to oneself at the age of 45 that one's life has been in vain. For 25 years I worked in the Party press, faithfully and truly serving the idol of communism, now toppled by the people from its pedestal. For a quarter of a century I was a tool in the hands of a command and totalitarian system and, as the current in-phrase has it, brainwashed the public, pulled the wool over their eyes. This assessment of the journalist's trade cannot be too far from the truth.

I was, of course, only an unwitting party to such brainwashing, which is at least some consolation. It would be easiest of all to portray myself now as a victim. But while I was zealously depicting the enthusiasm of Soviet workers clocking on shift in honor of the definitive, decisive or final year of the latest 5-year plan, true patriots were being poisoned by degree or expelled from their native land for telling the truth about developed socialism.

Could I at that time have become involved in the human-rights movement? The paradox is that I also took a highly critical view of the regime, and did not hide this from my friends and acquaintances. Yet I never matured sufficiently to enter the organized struggle against The System. I was sympathetic towards dissidents, believing them hapless souls who did not understand that they were banging their heads against a brick wall. I was deluded.

Communism is an extremely successful attempt at mass hypnosis. Today it has been convincingly demonstrated that those in whose interests it was implemented were power-hungry and foolish maniacs, concealing their true intentions with the fig leaf of the dictatorship of the proletariat. The hypnotists managed to convince the people, in the most bigoted of ways, that Soviet power is as strong as granite and steel.

And I believed in communism as in the textbooks. I sincerely believed that the current generation of Soviet people would simply walk into a bright future.

When I started working for a district newspaper as an 18-year-old boy, I felt no pangs of conscience as I selflessly composed, every day, stories, reports and items for the next issue.

Both then and later, when I was working for a provincial paper, I would be out visiting factories and standing in farmers' fields almost every day. The editors liked criticism, and I served it up to them, with neither a thought nor care rubbishing those who were late to sow or harvest the hay, or lose so much as one ear of corn during the harvest. I soon convinced myself that I was more of an expert on farming than any agronomist or husbander. And (shameful now to recall), I would teach them how to do their job. Like a district instructor or public inspector come to life, whose examples were there a-plenty to be followed, I would shower rebukes upon a chairman or anyone else for slips and wastefulness. And they, just imagine, would humbly take it all in.

An old friend of mine, the free-spirited Volodya Polyanchev, more than once asked with a hint of sarcasm: "Still waving your sword about, then?" I would answer in the affirmative and with pride. As time went by I even began to feel like one of the bosses, albeit not very high-up, but first at district and then regional level. Responses to my critical writings would arrive, stating how the culprits had been either punished or even occasionally sacked. In the newspaper world this is the greatest honor of all—to get someone thrown out of their post.

Try to picture the people living in any of the "rotting" (capitalist) countries. It is not easy, but try. And now look at our country. And you will see ... a concentration camp. To this day it is surrounded by rows of barbed wire. To this day every citizen is tied to his barrack-block. Poverty-stricken, he returns to his doss-house with the day's meagre haul, begins to share it out, gets into bloody fights: Karabakh, Sumgait, Fergana, Osh... By somewhat simplifying the situation in these regions I mean no disrespect to anyone's national sensibilities.

Why do I say all this? To prove that there cannot be a free press in a concentration camp. The problem lies not only in the official censorship that is now adapting itself to the new environment. There is also the inner censor that the Party has placed inside the soul of every journalist. Newsmen very quickly develop a sense of what is permissible, and what is not. Curse a street-sweeper, even the administrator of a neighborhood, criticize a Party boss, if he is criticized by the bosses above him. But God help you if you touch someone who is in favor, and never, ever and in no circumstances cast aspersions upon the pillars of The System. These rules never existed in writing, but every journalist knew them off by heart and obeyed them. For all of us somewhere in the background was the conviction that this was right and proper in the name of the Party's highest interests.

The inner censor is more terrible than the official one, with whom you can argue, prove your point, strike a compromise or appeal to a higher authority. Although all these moves were usually in vain. The inner censor are your own convictions, cultivated within you by The System itself. I shall quote just one example, although for nearly 25 years I toiled under the unblinking gaze of my inner censor, and in fact so well that I do not remember a single run-in with the official censor.

This example, then. In the spring of 1982 I was sent to Uzbekistan as a *Pravda* special correspondent, immediately after Brezhnev had paid a visit there. My task was to relate how the cotton workers were doubling and redoubling their efforts to carry out the instructions of Leonid Ilyich. From Mukimov and Gladdov, *Pravda*'s own correspondents there at the time, I got the details of our leader's travels. The living mummy was carted around Tashkent with the utmost care. Delivered, let us say, to a lemon plantation, and thence to his residence. The next trip would be to an aircraft factory, but under the weight of onlookers a gallery in one of the workshops collapsed, and the mortally-terrified General Secretary was hurriedly packed off back to Moscow. But the thought of using these facts in my reports never even entered my head.

Despite this, perhaps I did provide a more-or-less accurate portrayal of the state of affairs in the cotton industry? Of, for example, the slave labor and total lack of rights of the peasants there? Nothing of the sort. During the entire week I managed only once to get anywhere near a field and for a couple of minutes speak with some machine operators. And that was thanks only to my own persistence. My minders did all they could to keep me away from people. I was wined and dined all over the place (thank God I hardly drink), and led from one Party dacha to the next. Yet for any report you need facts, figures and names. Obtaining them on such an "excursion" was extremely difficult. And when the story was published I was truly proud of myself and of my "professionalism", for I had nonetheless overcome the "difficulties" and written what the editors required—about the enthusiasm of the cotton workers.

Of course, I realized that I had entered a mediaeval princedom, where the Party bosses lounged in luxury while the simple ones existed in adobe shacks. My meetings with Rashidov, two Karimovs—the first secretaries of the Bukhara and Surkhandarye regions—and with Gaipov—first secretary of the Kashkadarye region—left me in no doubt as the existence of the well-organized mafia which I had previously merely suspected. Drunken orgies were arranged at palatial Party dachas (the Emir of Bukhara lived in more modest style). Tables groaned under the weight of drinks and delicacies. Toasts were proposed, eloquent speeches delivered. At the table was the entire ruling class of the region.

I told friends and colleagues in detail about this eye-opening trip, but naturally had no intention of writing anything similar for *Pravda*. The inner censor was right—nobody would have published it. Even after both the Karimovs were put behind bars for the rest of their lives, and after Gaipov committed suicide as they came to arrest him. How can you program a journalist to such an extent that he reconciles himself to his inner censor, regards it as his alter ego?...

For 73 years we have had the wool pulled over our eyes. Not only that, but an aura of profound and indescribable profundity and meaningfulness was constructed around primitive communist demagogy. Let us merely recall the semi-literate speeches of Stalin, pronounced with such gravity, feeling and pauses for effect. Or take *Pravda* leading articles. Apparatchiks would go through them with a fine toothcomb, believing them to be calls for action from the upper reaches of the Party leadership.

Having written seven or eight dozen *Pravda* leaders, I found it amusing that these worthy Party instructions were received with such seriousness out in the localities. Virtually everyone in the office took it in turns to write them, sometimes together with some run-of-the-mill bureaucrats from the Central Committee who, for some reason, were never too keen to advertise their co-authorship to their bosses.

The deep meaningfulness was achieved by way of banal and cliched summings-up of the latest Central Committee resolutions. It took no particular skill to learn to write a lead. I arrived too late to meet one member of staff who to this day is legendary. He would write lead within two hours and, according to the stories, only after consuming a liberal quantity of liquid to ease his thought processes. His was a harsh fate. He was found dead alongside an uncorked bottle of cheap wine, slumped over a desk on which lay an unfinished lead article.

But for me, assimilating the required style proved difficult. My first attempt, in which I tried to set out some thoughts and ideas, was returned with numerous comments in the margins. I took note of them. The second version also came back to me. A friend witnessing my creative pains read what I had wrote and laughed:

"Listen, nobody needs your artistic writings. There's a set way of doing this. A *Pravda* leader has eleven paragraphs, although there might sometimes be exceptions. The first paragraph is the introduction to the theme, and second must have some quote from our ruler. Previously they quoted Stalin, apparently because he ordered that paragraph two must have some wise saying of his. Now you have to quote Brezhnev. One paragraph, preferably the one before last—should be on the role of Party organizations".

I followed my friend's advice, and immediately joined the valiant ranks of *Pravda* lead writers. Thinking back, I feel bad about all this. But then not so long ago, already during what we call "perestroika", no sooner had *Pravda* stopped publishing leaders than high-ranking apparatchiks and regional bosses at Central Committee plenums started nostalgically wailing about how tough it was for them without guidance from above. And Afanasyev reinstated them for a while.

Mine was no siren voice. Of my own experience I wrote almost nothing. Most of my articles dealt with problems and were critical, even highly critical. It is a different matter that I did not dig down to the roots of vices, since to cast doubt upon the veracity of Marxist teachings or advocate private property was equal to insanity. Today it has become obvious that it is the lack of owners of factories, fields and farms that has led the country into the jaws of economic collapse. And a mere 5-10 years ago we sought specific culprits—those unable to mobilize and organize the workers in the name of glorious causes.

Almost any boss could be criticized over piddling matters. In the environment of a totalitarian System, this amounted merely to a pretence of democracy. Serious critical articles needed a "licence" from the Central Committee. For example, in 1983, I was given one to attack the Voronezh regional Party committee. Who issued it I do not know, but the editor of my department showed a rough copy to some mandarin in the Central Committee who even asked for it to be toughened up in places. In those days such criticism was devastating, and with hindsight to a large degree justified. But today, I myself cannot agree with the conclusions of the article, "Disrespect for economics": the regional committee and its secretaries were ticked off for insufficient intervention in agriculture.

Licences were handed out at the very highest level. This was flattering, and tickled one's vanity. I would be told, "Gorbachev (who was then a Politburo member) wants...", or "Ligachev has instructed..." And without a second thought I would rush to carry out these "valued" instructions.

What if there was no licence? Then freedom of the press and glasnost Party-style was displayed in all its splendor. For example, I never did find out at whose behest I flew to Volgograd in 1986, when in the article "The illusion of acceleration" the management methods of Kalashnikov were subjected to the description they deserved. My guess now is that there was no licence at all, and that the story was written, most likely, on the initiative of Afanasyev, then editor-in-chief. But is it not strange when a writer does not know whose orders he is executing? Much at *Pravda* lay under a smokescreen of secrecy.

The article came out on a Sunday and on Monday morning, before I had hardly had time to unlock my office door, Afanasyev's PA was on the phone calling me in for a carpeting. Afanasyev told me that the Party General Secretary, who was far from pleased, had phoned him twice and told him off for the article. "And what about glasnost and breaking down 'no-go areas'?", I asked in my naivete. He smirked as if I were an idiot and with a wave of his hand signalled that the audience was over.

Earlier, Kalashnikov had worked in Stavropol under Gorbachev's leadership. The entire editorial staff held its breath, waiting for the outcome of one of the first tests for Gorbachev and his perestroika. Will he stand up for "his own" man or really confirm that nothing and nobody could be exempt from criticism? Nikonov, a Central Committee secretary, was sent off to a Volgograd committee meeting. And with his blessing, clearly enough, the *Pravda* story was subjected to ridicule. However, not a single fact was refuted, which would have been impossible anyway because all the figures had been taken from the official statistics.

I expected to be moved on somewhere else. But it was my co-author, *Pravda*'s Volgograd correspondent V. Stepanov, who took the brunt of the onslaught. I was not touched. Yet for a few years all mention of the Volgograd region was purged from *Pravda* leads and reviews. Kalashnikov won the day; never had a Party regional secretary scored such a victory over our newspaper. He remained victorious until the day he was forced to resign by his public due to the collapsing economy. And he must have been very well-liked by the country's top leadership if until the very last minute he was marked down as a future first deputy chairmen of the USSR Council of Ministers. Only the good sense of the parliament prevented this move.

New times? And is it worth recalling all this in any event? But what am I supposed to do with my wasted life? With a quarter of a century of deception and self-deception? Perhaps by repenting I shall find consolation, in order to make a fresh start from scratch?

A truly new era has not been ushered in for the press. The Party monopoly has wobbled a little, but remains in place. Unofficial publications are unprofessional and have a tiny print run. Paper, printworks and everything else are still in the hands of the vanguard Party. The cosmetic changes made so far have not changed the essence of the matter: the central newspapers, including the "non-Party" ones like *Trud* and *Izvestia*—remain the propaganda mouthpieces and advocates of communist ideology.

But a new and free press is being born before our eyes. The labor pains are accompanied by a pitched battle against demagogy. Yet journalism has shown little remorse, has still not purged its sins against the people. And I do not think that it will do so soon.

The Moscow newspaper *Kuranty* continued its series of articles in which journalists from central publications repented for their past work during routine and special assignments. On December 20, 1990 it was the turn of Vyacheslav Goncharov, a correspondent for the Moscow trade-union paper *Trud* (Labor) to recount the tos and fros of his conflict with the powers that be, or rather the Party leadership of the Donetsk region (this was back in 1975). They put

Agatha Christie novels or the Sicilian mafia in the shade. According to Goncharov, by a coincidence of circumstances in the corridors of power of Kiev and Moscow, he managed to force the first secretary of the regional Party organization in question to resign. To be more precise, someone on high sacked him, citing "muckraking" articles by Goncharov. In 99 percent of such cases, such intrepid hacks could expect a bullet from a hired killer, a staged car crash, prison, a psychiatric ward or, at best, the sack. On February 1, 1991 *Kuranty* carried similar reminiscences by prominent Soviet journalist Ilya Shatunovsky about how, during the reign of Party ideologue Suslov, as a young trainee at *Pravda* he had to write an article on behalf of a supporter of the famous fraud scientist Lysenko, and then discuss with the senior editors a list of trustworthy possible authors who could then sign this ready-made piece.

And what about foreign policy issues? I've always been under the impression that the editors of *Pravda*, TASS and Novosti Press Agency and five other national Moscow-based publications have been exerting a minimal influence on their own correspondents abroad. They were appointed by a corresponding sector of the Communist Party Central Committee, their reports to Moscow were always agreed with the point of view of the Soviet embassy in the given country. And Soviet embassies are run by various departments—the Communist Party Central Committee, KGB, GRU (the Main Intelligence Agency), Ministry of Foreign Affairs and other agencies, KGB being the supreme and cruelest boss.

Here is what New York-based *Novoye Russkoye Slovo* (February 2, 1991) wrote about it when it carried a complete text of a letter sent to it by ten young Soviet employees of the UN Secretariat. The letter said in part:

> What Kalugin has said about the unlawful KGB activities is not all. He could have said, and now he simply must say, the whole truth about it. Kalugin, as he put it, worked as a correspondent in New York, and has to know that most soviet journalists in New York (and in Washington, of course) are regular KGB employees. These secret service agents disguised as journalists have actually become a free complement to those permanent KGB people in the UN. In other words, KGB illegal services are paid for from our national budget by Soviet newspapers and magazines.
>
> It stands to reason that it is due to such pseudo-journalists that Soviet press readers lack a genuine look at the United States—the way to it is tightly blocked by those grim and vigilant KGB people whose colleagues are trying to put General Kalugin—and the truth itself—on his knees.
>
> If we are to believe what is said in our "colony", professional KGB employees among journalists are the UN TASS employees Maslov and Menkes, a correspondent of *New Times* Andrianov, a correspondent of *Moscow News* Lukasevicius, a correspondent of *Komsomolskaya Pravda* Ovcharenko, TASS correspondents Kikilo, Bilorusov, Titov, Makurin and Babichev, TV correspondents Levskoi and Gerasychev, correspondents of *Literaturnaya Gazeta* Simonov and Ognev, a correspondent of *Izvestia* Shalnev, a correspondent of *Pravda* Sukhoi. All the rest, without exception, are paid agents of the KGB.

Does this sound like a revelation to the Soviet man in the street? Hardly.

Whose agents are national newspapers' own correspondents? For decades they represented the interests of the party apparatus in their localities or, at least, the Communist party Central Committee viewpoint. A *Pravda*'s own correspondent was traditionally always a sort of 'doyen' of the correspondents in this or that republican or regional center, and he was the only one of them who entered a narrow circle of the Party local buro, regional committee, etc. In the nomenclature of Party posts a post of a national newspaper's own correspondent was always a very desirable one and it was given only to trusted and obedient persons. *Pravda, Trud, Rabochaya Gazeta, Selskaya Zhizn, Sovetskaya Kultura, Uchitelskaya Gazeta* own correspondents got apartments, direct dial lines, country cottages, special foodstuffs, Volga cars and prestigious offices from local Party authorities. No wonder, none of them ever wanted to write truth about the situation in his region. For if he did he would be instantly dismissed. Of course, much has changed but in Uzbekistan, Azerbaijan, Tataria and Bashkiria the "Party guidance of the press" was practised till September 1991.

Reading the six pages of *Pravda* (on Sunday, eight) in the years of perestroika, always forced one to wonder—who is the intended target of this propaganda that strikes a chord in neither the heart nor mind. The low level of *Pravda* journalists' professionalism is compounded by the constant attempts not to write anything out of turn. Everything is like it was during the bad old days of Stalin and Brezhnev. During the 1920s and early 1930s, it has to be said, Soviet newspapers were extremely interesting and could be read from start to finish, since they were turned out by talented and educated people rather than Party hacks.

The manipulative nature of Party propaganda, of which *Pravda* has always been the best example, never stopped, however, this newspaper and the like from having millions of subscribers. Our communist leaders were no fools; they thought up and organized various forms of forcing people to subscribe. Once a year, in autumn, the local Party cell's public distribution officer would approach rank-and-file Party members at the place of work (an establishment, military unit, collective farm, etc), and suggest (ie., demand) that they subscribe next year to *Pravda* and some other local rag, or a journal such as *Politicheskoye Samoobrazovanniye* (Political Self-Education). If you didn't subscribe, your career would suffer. Even very recently not a single Party committee, be it at district, city or regional level, and not a single Party bureau experienced any difficulties in organizing and carrying out subscription campaigns for Party publications.

After all, you subscribe but once a year. But what if the Soviet press were to be sold via retail outlets, as is the case throughout the civilized world? The same unsavory scene would unfold every day, throughout the entire year and at every kiosk. Party publications were the last to sell, often for use as hard-to-get wrapping paper and often with other desirable products in short supply 'tacked on', such as soap or the even harder-to-get *Moscow News*. Even recently *Pravda* was compulsory reading for all Soviet managers at all levels wishing to glean from it, even by reading between the lines, any tidbits useful for one's career or about impending changes.

In summer 1991 certain Party committees continued in their old zealous ways, forcing enterprises and other committees to subsidize it, ie., pay the subscription fee for whoever wanted to receive it. *Pravda* had in effect become the Soviet Union's first freesheet. This is especially so when one recalls how just some time ago it was given away free to aircraft passengers, hotel guests, Party members and ordinary non-Party workers.

The current editor-in-chief, Ivan Frolov (who, like his predecessor V. Afanasyev is a full member of the USSR Academy of Sciences, from which the greater part of the ideological hierarchy come) has on numerous occasions called upon his colleagues to at last start doing their jobs properly and make the newspaper interesting, otherwise bankruptcy and unemployment beckon. But not everyone at *Pravda* is an academician or Ph.D.

Pravda was dying of natural causes. The majority of Party publications were undergoing changes of a different nature—moving from Party control to that of local Soviets, changing titles that are too 'communist' to something more innocuous, becoming independent, merging or joining together in associations, searching for sponsors and advertisers.

The winds of change swept the whole of the country, including *Pravda*, as I have written at the beginning of this chapter.

Onto the scene have burst new publications, the unofficial press of yesterday. The Law on the Press has legalized them and paved the way for a real newspaper market. The competitiveness of the Party's central and local publications—and the political competitiveness of the Party itself—is coming under serious and, alas, merciless scrutiny.

It would appear that nobody properly analyzed the consequences of abolition of Article 6 of the Constitution for the Communist Party press in our country. The 28th Congress resolution on the Party's media took insufficient account, in my opinion, of the fact that the main job of its press was to hand out instructions. Paradoxically enough, this was exactly why it was an interesting read. People wanted to know what the 'leadership' wanted of them and preferred to receive this information, so to speak, straight from the horse's mouth. *Pravda* was needed by those who cravenly served the totalitarian authorities, and those who secretly or openly opposed them.

The journalists who worked for this paper were the creme de la creme, elite writers who considered it an honor to work there. Of course, I mean those who believed they could afford to play according to the Kremlin rules. K. Simonov, Ye. Yevtushenko, G. Ratiani, V. Ovchinnikov, V. Gubarev, Yu. Chernichenko,

M. Poltoranin—this list of well-known journalists who often wrote for the newspaper *Pravda* is far from complete. In 1990 however, most of them thought better of it. They knew only too well that the paper had nothing in common with its name ["Truth" in English]. In the past, the more disinformation one produced, the higher one was paid. The only difference was that, unlike in the perestroika years, it had all been done professionally.

In recent years *Pravda*'s staff bent over backwards to turn the Communist Party into a laughing stock. But it always failed to keep up with *Sovetskaya Rossia*, headed by V. Chikin. Here is how Vladimir Volin, journalist, war and labor veteran, and member of the CPSU since 1944 described his "Farewell to *Pravda* (A Subscriber's Confession)" in *Ogonyok* magazine (No. 42, 1991):

> It's decided—starting in 1992 I'm leaving the close ranks of subscribers to *Pravda*, which I have been reading for over fifty years (except for during the war years). For half a century I have grown used to taking that paper out of my postbox. *Pravda* is a publication of the Communist Party, of which I have been member for almost half a century as well.
>
> I understand well that in our turbulent times when there is nothing one can be certain of, my decision will not be of crucial importance. Remember Chekhov: "One baron more, one less—who cares?"
>
> I don't want to seem presumptuous when I say that I have taken up writing these bitter words in hopes making the respectful *Pravda* people ponder the matter.
>
> I'm not talking about the years when lying was something natural for our press, when everyone did so. That was a time of lies about cosmopolitans, doctors accused of killings, Sakharov and dissidents, Solzhenitsyn and Pasternak. *Pravda* led the way, being the "best disciple". "Such was the time," they say.
>
> But in recent years, when there seemed to be no use for showing loyalty, *Pravda* carried a number of articles that hurt its subscribers deeply.
>
> It must have begun when Algirdas Zuraitis, an orchestra conductor, wrote about a foreign staging of Chaikovsky's opera "The Queen of Spades". The author was rude, slandering artists of international acclaim: stage director Yuri Lyubimov, conductor Gennady Rozhdestvensky, and composer Alfred Shnitke. He called the latter "a pygmy of a composer". *Pravda* published such words about a man of whom Soviet culture can be proud, a man who has won international acclaim as a genius of contemporary music!
>
> There were three more bitter incidents. In the "best" traditions of 1946-48, three writers—Yuri Bondarev, Vasily Belov, and Valentin Rasputin—used *Pravda* to give vent to their hatred towards rock musicians.
>
> Later there was one more letter to *Pravda* about *Ogonyok* magazine, signed by M. Alexeyev, V. Astafyev, V. Belov, S. Bondarchuk, S. Vikulov, P. Proskurin, and V. Rasputin, know as "the letter of the seven". (To Astafyev's credit, and to the delight of those who like his books, it should be said that he later thought better of this, inciting anger on the part of the "patriots".) In days of old such a publication would have spelled an end to *Ogonyok*, as had been the case with such literary journals as *Zvezda*, *Leningrad*, and later the editorial board of *Novy Mir*. "An unprecedented distortion of history", "people's achievements revised", "our spiritual

values being spat on"—we are only too familiar with this language of delations. Why did *Pravda* have to publish this "letter from five angry men", which was obviously far from being fair.

The newspaper had never before noticed TV journalist Alexander Nevzorov as he severely criticized party bosses. But after the January events in Lithuania, and his odious reports for the "600 Seconds" program, the latter having been proved fake by professional cameramen, *Pravda* wrote a eulogy under the catchy title "*The Truth From Under the Gunfire*": "We are talking about a splendid professional and intrepid person—the TV reporter of the Leningrad-based program "600 Seconds", Alexander Nevzorov. In order to give us information, he has once again ignored danger..." But was this true? The prodigal son was forgiven for his rough criticism of the party and the system (which he had called a "pitiful, cruel, and stupid power). He was also forgiven for his denunciations of the big bosses (which, to his credit, were done very professionally).

I feel sorry to have to mention Roy Medvedev's articles carried by *Pravda*. They were about "*The GULAG Archipelago*". I don't think he should have taken up writing about Solzhenitsyn, after TV had shown the entire nation Medvedev's true face at congresses and sessions. And he shouldn't have been the one to defend Sakharov from the democrats (in *Sovetskaya Rossia*). Yelena Bonner has written about this convincingly in *Demokraticheskaya Rossia*).

I will not elaborate on the most disgraceful publication of all—a reprint of an article by *La Repubblica*, an Italian newspaper, about Yeltsin. This time *Pravda* found itself in an ill-smelling swamp.

After that monstrous publication *Pravda* didn't publish any more outrageous lies, passing over the task to its smaller sister *Sovetskaya Rossia*. Just before the elections, the latter published absurd material about Yeltsin's ties with the Italian mafia.

Now we see a new *Pravda*. In the past it had its own face, whether one liked it or not. Now it is a spineless creature. Maybe I'm being rude, but let's compare it to *Nezavisimaya Gazeta*, and we'll see how far apart they stand. It is easier to have a clear-cut position with the motto "Sine ira et studio". But how about *Pravda*?

With its record described above, I think it'll find it hard to win authentic affection on the part of its readers.

It was amusing to read *Pravda, Sovetskaya Rossia, Glasnost, Rabochaya Tribuna, Moskovskaya Pravda,* and *Leninskoye Znamya*—all newspapers published under the auspices of the Communist Party Central Committee. It was no less amusing to hear nothing from such giants as TASS and Novosti Press Agency. This thousands-strong corps of journalists suddenly forgot their duty, and many started pulling down Gorbachev's portraits from the walls of their offices. They never mentioned their General Secretary in public though. When Gorbachev was released from his Foros dacha, he was a little angry, so he didn't stand in the way of Boris Yeltsin, who sealed the buildings of the CPSU in Moscow on August 22, 1991, and cancelled the publication of all the party papers mentioned above. But this process—call it denazification, destalinization, or departization—failed. Communists wreaked havoc, saying they were being accused without trial, and called it "neo-bolshevism". The Russian authorities had to cancel their decision on September 11, and find a slower way of stamping out the communist press. The notorious newspapers came back to life.

No profound change has taken place in the communist press as yet, only some cosmetic ones. In full compliance with party tradition—to repent after sinning—the revived papers ask their readership to forgive them, and assured them that they were loyal to the legally elected authorities. *Pravda* promised to become "a newspaper of civil accord", and *Rabochaya Tribuna*—"a truly national tribune". The words "Proletarians of all countries, unite!" were removed from the top of their first pages, and the papers refused to have anything to do with the Central Committee.

As usual, *Pravda* led the renovation process: an issue is now five kopecks more expensive, the paper now has a new editor-in-chief, and Lenin's profile is missing on the front page. In its first post-coup issue, *Pravda* called the USSR Supreme Soviet "an obedient Lukyanovite body". *Pravda*'s new editor-in-chief, Gennady Seleznev, is a former member of the Central Committee of the party, former editor-in-chief of *Uchitelskaya Gazeta*, and former first deputy editor-in-chief of *Pravda*. In his words, the situation with the newspaper is deplorable, and he even had to ask God to send him "strength and wisdom".

What was once the party press turned into "independent publications" overnight, which had no property, which was nationalized as party property. It happened on August 22, 1991. *Pravda* was deprived of the two apartment buildings which still under construction, together with the recreation sites used by its staff. A big overhaul was due in the paper's luxury building on Pravda Street: with the Communist Party providing no more money, eighty percent of the staff had to go.

And does *Pravda* really need the building it has occupied in the recent years? The twelve floors of the giant building would have been more than enough for the editorial offices of all the democratic press. It had not been by chance that the *Pravda* bosses used some of their offices for purposes other than journalism. Almost every staffer had his or her own office. There were libraries, lounges, swimming pools, restaurants, cafes. There was even a diamond-processing workshop. Why not, if in the Central Committee building they found a laboratory for making counterfeit documents, directly subordinate to the Central Committee's department for international affairs?

It reminds me of the situation which existed, for example, in industry. If workers wanted to eat pork, they had to set up their own small-holding to breed hogs. The same happened to the apparatchiks: instead of asking the KGB to stamp a counterfeit Polish or American passport, the Central Committee preferred to have its own stamps. Academician Viktor Afanasyev, editor-in-chief of *Pravda* until 1989, for seven years headed a group of enthusiasts who decided to create a center for cutting Soviet diamonds, instead of selling them for a nominal price to the "De Biers" company from South Africa. The international mass media devoted a lot of attention to room 626 in *Pravda*'s building. The first to mention this secret room, which had been visited by Politburo members Y.K. Ligachev and L.N. Zaikov, was *Moskovsky Komsomolets* (October 26, 1991). The article was called "*A Secret Laboratory in the Cradle of the Party Press. Diamonds for the Dictatorship of the Nomenklatura.*" On October 28, 1991 Viktor Afanasyev wrote a reply article in *Pravda*—"*The Diamonds of Room 626 Were Meant for the People, not the Nomenklatura*". The author claimed that he had managed to gather the ten best Soviet diamond cutters in Moscow, but after seven years the laboratory ceased to exist in 1989, without having cut a single diamond. What did they do during those seven years? The article by Afanasyev was not a bad one, but it lacked conviction, quite in the traditions of all *Pravda* publications.

This newspaper would like to hold on to its "socialist choice". Together with the Communist Party, it would like to avoid penance for the millions of lives sacrificed for the idea of communism. The anthology of *Pravda* will remain forever in the history of humankind. It will be studied by generations as an example of the blatant lie. Hitler's minister of information couldn't hold a candle to *Pravda*.

The latest ideological target of *Pravda* was announced after the coup (October 8, 1991): "Decisively Freeing Lenin's Name From the Stalinist Weeds That Have Clung to It". The Kremlin bad boys made the world tremble for over half a century using armies of mercenary killers, communist bureaucrats and senators. It won't be long before we see the real Lenin on screens and bookshelves, not the idol we're used to.

Then there are overtly fascist, or Stalinist, publications like *Sovetskaya Rossia*, *Dyen* (Day), *Glasnost*, to name but a few. Is it even conceivable that some day those who back them will run out of money? Even if Gorbachev, speaking at a political trial, tells the jury and the world all he knows (which he said he would never do), a dozen or so dummy companies will always remain afloat, having laundered—home or abroad—the big money stolen from rank-and-file party members and the state. In 1989-91, when USSR Vneshekonombank had no money to pay its clients any more, Gorbachev, as the General Secretary of the party, did all he could so that "friendly companies" got all that was allegedly due to them. I only hope that the era of forced subscriptions has ended, and that now *Sovetskaya Rossia* and the like will lose not communists alone as its subscribers, but also servicemen, peasants, and other subjugated strata of the population.

There is no doubt that *Sovetskaya Rossia* was the ideological headquarters of the coup staged by the Communist Party and the KGB in August 1991. This mouthpiece of the conservative, Stalinist forces in the USSR carried long excerpts from speeches by Kryuchkov, Pugo, and Yazov. It also let Vladimir

Zhirinovsky, a man who balances on the verge of fascism, air his views on its pages.

Before the coup, the newspaper consistently and uncompromisingly opposed private property, only to make a U-turn later, when, all of a sudden, the "Zavidiya" firm, together with the *Sovetskaya Rossia* labor union, became a co-founder of the paper. Andrei Fedorovich Zavidiya, who is a multi-millionaire, has this to say: "I am a future candidate for president of the USSR... I haven't spent a kopeck on *Sovetskaya Rossia* yet, and I never will if I see it's unprofitable... I take the losers' side. I will also draw support from millions of rank-and-file communists and non-party members, from Cossacks and the private business... I side with the military-industrial complex, the KGB and militia. In a nutshell, I side with all those who don't fare well now... I believe that if most cooperatives, private firms, and joint ventures will be headed by communists, the situation will change for the better." This view was published in *Komsomolskaya Pravda* on September 28, 1991.

In the words of *Nezavisimaya Gazeta* (August 31, 1991), "the personnel of the right-wing conservative body [*Sovetskaya Rossia*] have no doubt that this noble action may be explained very simply: the newspaper's former bosses managed to transfer part of their money to "Galant's" account, with strict instructions on how to use it.

Zavidiya turned out to be founder not only of *Sovetskaya Rossia*, but of the *Dyen* newspaper, which is very similar to the former. The staff of this body of the Union of Writers of the Russian Federation started its work in 1991, and before the coup they had worked on the territory of a military unit. The newspaper has as many pages as *Literaturnaya Gazeta*. It is headed by Alexander Prokhanov. Like *Sovetskaya Rossia's*", its circulation has never exceeded 100,000—neither before the coup, nor after.

When such names as Chikin, Prokhanov, Bondarev, and those of less educated men—Yazov and Zavidiya—come to my mind, I always remember of another person worth mentioning: Saddam Hussein. A friend of the Soviet Union, and a very interesting person. Our "patriots" talked a lot about him, both before and after the January 1991 events in Lithuania. If Bush hadn't thrown Hussein out of Kuwait, the national-liberation movement in Lithuania would have surely been drowned in blood by the Soviet Army.

Sovetskaya Rossia (February 2, 1991) recorded its firm support for ... Saddam Hussein, the Palestinians and various other such fighters for freedom and justice. "Being taught how to kill Arabs. As the Palestinian uprising fails to die down, in Israel there is a full-scale weapons-handling program". This was the caption to a photograph of an Israeli woman holding a pistol and standing alongside a range target. And this when Israel was counting the victims of Iraq's missile attacks. On the same page there was an interview with the Iraqi ambassador to Moscow; in the questions put to him there was not even a hint at the aggression committed against Kuwait. The impression was that the ambassador had been given carte blanche to use *Sovetskaya Rossia* as an outlet for propaganda about uniting forces against American imperialism and Zionism. I thought that over the past five years we had more or less managed to wean ourselves off such terminology.

By August 19, the CPSU had an overwhelming control of the printing capacities to issue newspapers and magazines. But everything was changing, even in this. The Young Communist League was openly disintegrating, independent trade unions and strike committees were being organized and many newspaper editorial boards had stopped printing on the front page the formerly obligatory motto: "Workers of all countries, unite". A regular theme of the Soviet press society news column and court-room chronicle was devoted to articles on how editorial boards of small Party newspapers in localities struggle to achieve independence from their founders--Party committees.

On August 22, 1991 the nightmare of 1917 was over. By the end of the putsch, the CPSU Plenum had spent three days deliberating over whether they should react publicly to the capture in the Crimea of their General Secretary. The forces of democratic Russia, with President Boris Yeltsin at its helm, suspended the activities of the CPSU on the territory of the Russian Federation and nationalized Party property. This property is enormous--hundreds of buildings and publishing combines. Denazification in Germany and Italy, the expulsion of collaborators in France required just a few months, whereas de-Stalinization in the USSR took decades to be carried out. Boris Yeltsin did for perestroika during 2 days no less than Gorbachev had achieved over 6 years.

On August 22, 1991 the propaganda empire, a relic of the past subsidized by the CPSU, virtually ceased to exist and became just like Goebbels' machinery of total propaganda.

In Moscow there three big printing newspaper and magazine combines: *Pravda, Moskovskaya Pravda* and *Izvestia* which issued not only the big newspapers of the CC CPSU, or Moscow City Committee of CPSU, but also a lot of periodicals attached to various party departments. Only a few newspapers (e.g., *Literaturnaya Gazeta, Krasnaya Zvezda*) had their own small printing-houses in Moscow. The overwhelming majority of periodicals were printed by "alien" printing-houses, which had, prior to August 22, 1991 belonged, in legal terms, to CC CPSU Management Department. The *Izvestia* combine is an exception as it used to belong to the USSR Supreme Soviet.

From Alexei Adzhubei to Igor Golembiovsky

Izvestia was lucky, incidentally, to have such editors-in-chief as A. Adzhubei, L. Tolkunov, I. Laptev, personalities recognized in the Soviet public opinion for their attempts to observe some rules of decency and make, with some success, the newspaper interesting enough during all seasons (as compared with the tongue-tied *Pravda*). *Izvestia*'s journalists, as employees of the main newspaper of the USSR Supreme Soviet, have until recently been receiving instructions from the ideological departments of the CPSU. But be it as it may, they respected their readers, just as the *Komsomolskaya Pravda*, *Trud*, *Moskovsky Komsomolets* tried to do.

On January 1991, Igor Golembiovsky, *Izvestia*'s first deputy editor-in-chief, was summoned by Anatoly Lukyanov, Chairman of the USSR Supreme Soviet, who suggested that he should be relieved of his post and go to Spain as *Izvestia*'s own correspondent. The name of Golembiovsky is associated, without any exaggeration, to all the democratic traditions and undertakings of the latter-day *Izvestia*. In the opinion of the *Nezavisimaya Gazeta* (January 31, 1991) "the attempt to remove him from his post should be considered in the context of the general offensive on glasnost, initiated in our country by the official mass media. Besides, Golembiovsky is one of the co-authors to the letter of the founders of the *Moscow News*, which directly accuses the present regime of a crime against the Lithuanian people."

On January 30, 1991 at a general meeting of the employees of the *Izvestia* and its *Nedelya* and *Soyuz* weekly supplements, the journalists expressed their firm determination to defend their "first deputy" and were even ready to call a strike. The confrontation was aggravated between *Izvestia* and the paper's Editor-in-Chief, who had been appointed in 1990 by the Presidium of the USSR Supreme Soviet against the desires of the *Izvestia* collective, which had unanimously nominated Igor Golembiovsky. A comparatively young journalist, N. Yefimov, had occupied high posts over the past 10-15 years, had been deputy chief of the Novosti Press Agency Board, Editor-in-Chief of *Moscow News*, Chairman of the USSR State Committee for Publishing, Printing and Book Distribution and displayed everywhere the qualities of an official obedient to those at the top and a conscientious censor. The former *Izvestia* Editor-in-Chief (before N. Yefimov took over) Ivan Laptev, Chairman of the Soviet of the Union of the USSR Supreme Soviet, expressed in an open letter his disagreement with Igor Golembiovsky's resignation. Political 'corrections' of *Izvestia* articles and the removal of "hot" material from current issues of the newspaper by N. Yefimov became especially frequent after the January 1991 events in the Baltics.

There was not one single big newspaper in the USSR, and perhaps in the world, which did not debate the issue concerning the *Izvestia* conflict in the first half of 1991. This has nothing to do with Nikolai Yefimov's personality. In the opinion of his colleagues his days in the newspaper were numbered anyway. Many years ago he had occupied the post of *Izvestia*'s deputy Editor-in-Chief and later became its Editor-in-Chief. Whatever he did, whatever personnel reshuffling he invented, would always lead to a national scandal, although his first deputies Mamleyev and Sevruk were authorized to their posts through Lukyanov and Gorbachev and so by-passed the paper's editorial board. "Yefimov is letting the boss down, another, even smarter servant will be found. So much worse for the newspaper," penned Ed. Polyanovsky, special correspondent to *Izvestia*, in *Literaturnaya Gazeta* (July 17, 1991). "The authorities so undermined the reputation (prestige, authority, trust) of *Pravda*, *Sovetskaya Rossia*, TASS and national TV that now they are clinging to *Izvestia*, the last half-democratic bridgehead in the official propaganda" (in the words of Polyanovsky).

This idea was corroborated by Ilya Mahlstein in the *Ogonyok* (July 27, 1991):

> The newspaper *Izvestia* is dying. *Moscow News, Ogonyok, Znamya, Kommersant* and their like were given up as lost long ago--let them print everything they wish. They can be removed at any moment merely by denying them paper! But it's dangerous to let *Izvestia* free even for a day! It is the only Center-oriented national daily, and its one, even timid, step to the left (*Izvestia* has already made quite enough decisive steps) threatens the authorities. There are different ways of approaching genuine freedom. The *Izvestia* people had attained more than a little.

The main thing is that this newspaper, as, in principle, any traditional Soviet publication, depended little on personal opinions, honesty and the competence of its staff. If they possessed all the aforementioned virtues, they would immediately leave the paper. For example: Shevardnadze left. Soviet policy in the US-Iran crisis had undergone considerable changes by mid-February 1991. Gorbachev stated that, in his opinion, the USA had in its actions overstepped the framework of the powers conferred on it by the UN Security Council. And how did *Izvestia* react? Like the majority of the orthodox and even perestroika publications, the whole Soviet press began to wail unanimously that the US was waging an imperialist war in Iran, striking blows at civilian targets.

Izvestia's political analyst Stanislav Kondrashov wrote then in black and white that the US military operation in the Middle East "should be called not a storm but a murder in the desert. Our conscience cannot be reconciled with the fact that in this war we sided with the murderers, acting under the guise of nobly striving to stop the aggression." Kondrashov went on to compare the actions of US aircraft in Iraq with the atomic bombing of Hiroshima, after adding that the USA had always been prone to employ a weapon of mass destruction to save the lives of its own soldiers.

Another *Izvestia* political analyst Maxim Yuzin also sided with Saddam Hussein. "Whatever the military outcome of the present crisis may be," Yuzin wrote, "we can now predict a deterioration in US-Arab relations... In this situation we can enhance our influence in a strategically vital area, and therefore, in the heat of the war, we should not cut our ties with Baghdad and should distance ourselves from the actions undertaken by Washington."

I am a regular reader of *Izvestia*. But why should I delve into an article on a topic not that familiar to me ("*The Western Ukraine: New People in Power*"; August 2, 1991) if I have no guarantee of the quality of either the article or any other published item in this newspaper in general? Tons of printing paper have been used to expose N. Yefimov, an ordinary executor. But we'd better look at his superiors. Take, for instance, A. Lukyanov's interview accorded to *Komsomolskaya Pravda* (March 13, 1991). Save us from such champions of democracy! Who was "in charge of ideology" after M. Suslov? V. Medvedev, E. Ligachev--bright personalities! And here is a portrait of one more boss, a bit lower in rank who, after being N. Yefimov's curator from CC CPSU, suddenly became not his first deputy but rather *Nedelya*'s editor (*Nedelya* is *Izvestia*'s supplement). The portrait (with a photo) of the former big official was drawn by a very spiteful and sly writer Andrei Nuikin (*Moscow News*, June 6, 1991):

> Rumors that Vladimir Sevruk is a new rising star have been confirmed. Our top authorities, the Presidium of the USSR Supreme Soviet and Anatoly Lukyanov in person, have given him full control of the *Nedelya* weekly.
>
> What is so sensational about this? In a feudal society posts and titles are always granted like this. Why should journalists get into such a state about it?
>
> The new Editor-in-Chief of one of our most popular and respectable weeklies was notorious because of the way in what he stifled free thinking during the years of stagnation.
>
> Sevruk is no ministerial bureaucrat. He is a messenger from the other more sombre world ruled by Brezhnev's propaganda chief, Suslov. There was no mystery about this product of the Stalinist and Brezhnevite system; he was as straight forward and simple as the galoshes he is said to have put in the fridge shortly before his death. He was a dogmatic ignoramus brought by chance into the upper reaches of the party quagmire. Sevruk, on the other hand, is no ignoramus. He is a Candidate of Philology. And he is not dogmatic, but full of official romanticism and bureaucratic mystique.
>
> I must admit that I had a hand, along with a group of post-graduates of the Academy of Social Sciences of the CPSU Central Committee, in promoting Sevruk's career. We heard our fellow student singing praises to Vasil Bykov's *The Dead Feel No Pain* for weeks, and then read Sevruk's ideological denunciation of it in *Pravda*. We called a party meeting and condemned Sevruk for his duplicity and hypocrisy: our main objective was to bar such a man from a post on the Central Committee staff.
>
> How naive we were! Our condemnations brought Sevruk the publicity he needed to be noticed by the Central Committee and to be promoted even more quickly. He never appreciated the good services we did him. For two decades he methodically stifled all those, who had unwittingly helped him climb up the ladder. As a Central Committee staff member, first a common political instructor, and subsequently first deputy chief of the ideological department in charge of personnel and all censorship, he had unlimited opportunities to do so.
>
> What do you think are the favorite ideological methods of the party apparatus? They avoid all commotion violence, rudeness or bad language. A quiet word over the

telephone is sufficient for a victim to die of suffocation, totally unable to understand what's happening. No fingerprints, no eyewitnesses, no evidence for the prosecution.

Sevruk for one was particularly fond of the following technique. He would ask the editor to send him an article by so-and-so--and then get snowed under with other urgent work. The editor would wait for the article to be returned for months, and after a time would understand--not so much about the article, as about the author. The author himself would never know to his dying day why the editor had cooled off all of a sudden.

Another technique was to wait for the victim's book to be ready for the press and then instruct the publishers, over the phone, to delete a certain objectionable passage or episode from it. In one of my books, for example, Sevruk ordered that a page be removed (from a print-run of 100,000 copies) on which a nameless careerist was mentioned as being the aide of a certain regional boss. 'Don't you know,' Sevruk told the publisher sternly, 'that only first secretaries of regional party committees are entitled to personal aides?'

The cutting was done manually, and I never had my books published by that publisher again.

A similar thing happened to V.Oskotsky's postscript to a one-volume *Selections* by Vasil Bykov (also printed in 100,000 copies), simply because the critic mentioned the story *The Dead Feel No Pain.*

The Jesuit Sevruk is persecuting a writer of world renown! The desperate Byelorussian publisher cabled Suslov and Zimyanin. He might just as well have sent the cable to Sevruk himself. They cracked down on the publishing house, and the publisher died of a heart attack. You will note that neither dagger nor poison was used. Nothing but a few hints on the phone and the will of the party was exempted and its prestige soared ever higher.

On behalf of our writers, Ales Adamovich has often told Mikhail Gorbachev that as long as ideology in this country is supervised by Sevruk, not a single serious person will believe that perestroika has begun.

Justice for *Izvestia*'s staff and all its readers triumphed on August 23, 1991 when after N. Yefimov's sacking, who had been supported by the Ministry for the Press and Information, the paper's collective elected and appointed Igor Golembiovsky (the newspaper's journalists became its founder instead of the former founder in the person of the Presidium of the USSR Supreme Soviet). A happy end? Nothing of the kind. The *Izvestia* people have committed no less sins than the *Pravda* people. The reader believed the latter less than the former. That is why the effect of *Izvestia*'s poisonous misinformation was always much stronger than that of the rest of the Party press.

To be fair, in the three days of the August putsch each issue of *Izvestia* carried information about the work of Boris Yeltsin and Anatoly Sobchak, and thousands of their supporters in Moscow and Leningrad. Its Moscow evening issue No. 198 of August 20, 1991 frontpaged two large photographs of demonstrations of protest against the dictatorship held on the demonstrations of protest against the dictatorship held on the evening of August 19 near the

White House in Moscow and in Leningrad. Although issue No. 197 was totally devoted to the official materials of the Emergency Committee for the State of Emergency and Yanayev's press conference, the newspaper found space for a couple of articles which showed that Boris Yeltsin had not joined the Committee but had called for opposing the dictatorship and the impostors. On August 22, 1991, I. Ovchinnikova, one of *Izvestia*'s most honest workers, described the situation in the newspaper and compared it with that of 1964. She described how Aleksei Adzhubei, the most famous and truly the best central newspaper editor, left *Izvestia* after the October 1964 coup and Khrushchev's resignation. Khrushchev's son-in-law, he had the right to his own opinion and besides, he was very talented:

> In those days each and all took a test for journalist's responsibility, young ones for the first time.
> As for older workers like myself, we remembered that long day in October 1964 when our respected editor-in-chief, Aleksei Adzhubei, slowly descended the marble stairs of *Izvestia*'s office. We clenched our fists and did not hide our tears when we saw him off, but in the evening of the same day we published a newspaper which was quite different from what we had published with him only the day before.
> Those who wanted to keep the huge country in their dirty hands were sure that everything would go on smoothly according to the same scenario. However, they miscalculated the situation, ignoring what could not be measured or felt—the degree to which the people's conscience has been aroused over the past six years. They could not possibly have expected *Izvestia* printers to declare at 1 p.m. on August 19 that the newspaper would not be published without Boris Yeltsin's appeal to the nation. At 3 p.m. the editors headed by acting editor-in-chief Mamleyev unanimously decided to publish the appeal. At 3:40 p.m., when the pages were ready for print, editor-in-chief Yefimov returned from his vacation unexpectedly and told us to remove Yeltsin's address from the issue.
> Should it have happened five years ago, we would have obediently removed the material because our superiors know better, but things have changed greatly since then. Those of us who found themselves in the type-setting shop by accident or on purpose, saw proud workers rather than meek and humble servants. They truly defended the pages to the last and they won.
> In spite of the manipulation, threats of cutting wages and depriving them of the opportunity to get new flats, and the reasoning that the newspaper's content was none of their business, the workers would not give up: either they would publish Yeltsin's appeal or the newspaper would not come out at all.
> *Izvestia* did not come out that evening. The next morning it carried a slightly abridged version of the appeal which the whole country read. Even before that they had printed it by hand and a few minutes later Muscovites could see the leaflets in the hands of soldiers sitting in armored cars in Pushkin Square and still later, the same leaflets pasted to the tank sides. People read them and decided on whose side they were and what they should do next, but none of them knew what dramatic developments had preceded the printing of the text which was becoming a material force under our very eyes.

Hundreds of journalists work in *Izvestia*, which occupies a whole block of spacious buildings in Pushkin Square, in the heart of Moscow. It is a whole legion of black limousines, policemen guarding all hallways, long corridors, sumptuous rooms of the numerous bosses, the aura of prestige and power of the country's main daily. All that is in striking contrast with Ovchinnikova's bitter confession that *Izvestia* managed to save face only thanks to the unknown selfless people from its printing shop. Today, after the abortive putsch, the inflexible N. Yefimov is the scapegoat, but what about the rest? Are Bovin, Kondrashov, Illesh and Shalnev free journalists? (I named *Izvestia*'s best writers.) Let's be honest—all of them are loyal Leninists who treasured their party cards just as their parents had treasured their bread rationing cards during the war!

Collusion on Silence

At the beginning of 1991 the withering CPSU press obtained, as it were, a second lease on life. It began to be bought just like other traditional official publications. *Komsomolskaya Pravda* became the record-selling newspaper in January. *Moskovsky Komsomolets, Vechernaya Moskva, Moskovskaya Pravda* were sold like hot cakes. *Izvestia* and *Trud* sold fairly well. Curiously, *Pravda* began to sell better. Newsstall-keepers explained the growth of interest to the "have-beens" by their moderate price, though it, as compared with 1990, rose from 3-5 kopecks to 10-12 kopecks. The leap in the popularity of these papers was also caused by the reader's striving for daily news which the majority of alternative publications (weeklies and monthlies) could not provide. The growth of interest in the traditional publications sold at retail is also explained by the constantly deteriorating work of the postal service in the country.

By autumn 1990 when the Law on the Press came into force a really unusual situation had shaped up in the country. An enterprising person wishing to make money has no right, without using ploys (a document from a collective farm, and so on), to buy a truck load of tangerines in the south of the country and take it to sell to Poland, saying nothing of even Siberia. But he can start publishing a newspaper, a magazine (or set a radio station) without any red tape--just get it registered, pay some hundred rubles and you may publish it. But the Kremlin easily found an antidote against this orgy of glasnost.

The Law on the Press is rather good; however shortly after its adoption newsprint began to disappear. Central papers failed to appear for days on end in many Soviet cities. There were regular editorial apologies to readers in various parts of the country, although the subscription fee, naturally, was not returned. Only *Pravda* came out regularly, immune from any shortage of paper. In fact, for Party publications there was an excess of it. Even new stablemates have appeared, for example, the weekly *Glasnost* (not to be confused with the magazine of the same name, with a total print run in Moscow and Paris of 30,000, of well-known human-rights activist human-rights activist Sergei Grigoryants, 49 years old, 9 of which have been spent in prisons and camps under Brezhnev). This is the underhand method resorted to by the powers-that-be to somehow muzzle the country's best-known dissident publication of many years that is under no government control whatsoever, although for the time being both *Glasnost* and *Yezhednevnaya Glasnost* (Daily Glasnost), which is published in Moscow, had been by that time officially registered by the Oktyabrskii district executive committee of the capital. Perhaps Grigoryants, a graduate in journalism from Moscow University was unheard-of in the state publishing committee, where they registered the new Central Committee's Glasnost, or even in the Kremlin?

Could we imagine that we would live to see the day when there wouldn't be enough paper for *Pravda* or the recently-founded monthly journal *Izvestia TsK KPSS* (not to be confused with the eponymous newspaper)? Or that the monument to the butcher Dzerzhinsky will be removed from Lubyanka? On September 5, 1990 the State Publishing Committee, in accordance with the press law requirement for registration and levy of a small one-off tax, issued certificates to the Party's central publications. The list makes impressive reading: the newspapers *Pravda, Rabochaya Tribuna, Selskaya Zhizn, Ekonomika i Zhizn, Sovetskaya Kultura* and *Uchitelskaya Gazeta*; the magazines *Izvestia TsK KPSS, Kommunist, Partiinaya Zhizn, Voprosy Istorii KPSS, Dialog*; and the weeklies *Glasnost* and *Voskresenye*. It sometimes began to seem that all these little-read and unloved publications existed solely to make others look more presentable, such as *Izvestia, Literaturnaya Gazeta, Moscow News, Komsomolskaya Pravda, Trud,* and the magazines *Krestyanka* and *Rabotnitsa*.

The analogy is thus: against the Leningrad Stalinist and humble college lecturer Nina Andreyeva, Politburo member Yegor Ligachev and Russian Federation Party boss Ivan Polozkov looked quite harmless. And in comparison to them, Gorbachev is a liberal. Meanwhile, the fence-sitting and dilatoriness of the latter give Boris Yeltsin the aura of a defender of the people and almost a dissident. After reading a few editions of *Pravda*, the clear style and abundance of information in *Izvestia* come as a great relief. This is the Soviet *Le Monde* or *Times*, although in fact *Izvestia* scrupulously observes the limits of glasnost handed down from above. We still have a long way to go to freedom of the press.

The reader of Georgian or central newspapers living in Tbilisi (the Georgian capital) knows almost nothing of what is happening almost alongside in the neighboring republics of Armenia and Azerbaijan. The Paris-published *Le Monde* or *Russkaya Mysl*, the Munich-based Radio Liberty and the Moscow dissident *Ekspress-Khronika* and *Glasnost*, much unloved by the official authorities, continue to provide reasonably full information on events in all the republics. Of course, the local independent papers in Armenia and the Baltic republics, for example, will cover local events best. Newspapers from the republics, even the most important and until yesterday published by the Communist Party, have virtually never been on sale either in Moscow or outside their own areas.

A Muscovite can subscribe to the official Georgian press. But in the summer of 1991 through retail outlets he could buy only a host of research-type journals and weeklies (including the weekly digest of sanitized translations from the foreign press called *Za Rubezhom* (Abroad), and also the labored weekly *Novoye Vremya* (New Times), plus the turgid monthly journal *Mezhdunarodniye Otnosheniya* (International Relations) and some other publications. Yet neither *Pravda* nor *Izvestia*, neither central television nor the *Literaturnaya Gazeta* would tell the Muscovite much or in detail about events in Georgia or Armenia, despite the fact that they had their own permanent correspondents with their offices, communications facilities, transport, considerable budget and staff of writers and technicians in Tbilisi and Yerevan. Of all the traditional central newspapers only *Moscow News* has managed throughout the years of perestroika to cover the situation in Tbilisi (Yerevan, Riga, Tallin) in such a way as not to cause outbursts of anger in these cities. Millions of Soviet readers of newspapers and journals are much better informed about what is going on in the White House in Washington than in the parliaments of the union republics; interviews with Bush or Mitterrand are printed by the official press after being received from TASS.

And this communist press strictly observed its vow of silence regarding political sayings by former Soviet political prisoners and now leading players on the scene as Z. Gamsakhurdia, L. Ter-Petrosyan, V. Novodvorskaya and P. Airikan. Yet first-hand information can be highly interesting. Most fantastic of all here is that these politicians had something to say. If they had an open forum in the federal press rather than megaphones at street rallies for their words to be published subsequently in small-circulation local papers, less blood would have been spilt in Transcaucasia, there would be fewer refugees in Moscow and the threat of civil war in the USSR would not arise.

The Cold War relocated itself from Soviet foreign to domestic policy. The Party has long given us to understand that when we are numb from hunger, cold and bloodshed, it will once again give us our crust of bread, install iron discipline and force us to fulfil the norms of communist labor. In the evening we shall, as we did before, read *Pravda* and watch the TV news bulletin Vremya. This, of course, is an extremely pessimistic viewpoint. Things might be even worse if we sink into the chaos of civil war and ruin. A less pessimistic forecast is also possible. The partocracy and generals will partly go in for legalized private business and partly take over the seats of state administrators, permit private ownership of land and of small-and medium-sized factories and thus rescue themselves from the jaws of economic crisis and leave the nucleus of their power and their principal personnel untouched. The writer Yuri Nagibin and political activist Valeriya Novodvorskaya believed that in such a scenario the Kremlin's domestic policies will be reminiscent less of the Stalin-Brezhnev style of socialism than of Hitler's national socialism. Also an interesting point of view.

Memories of Komsomol

"The Party and the Komsomol are ready to give up their principles, but for a good price." These ironical remark by Alexander Popov, chairman of the Moscow City Council Subcommission on Press Freedom, was used as the headline of an interesting article in the Moscow newspaper *Megapolis-Express*, August 30, 1990:

> The leaders of the Moscow Komsomol have learned a great deal from the sad experience of their Leningrad counterparts, who recently underwent an operation which involved the removal of an organ and proved rather painful to their self-esteem. The staff of the local magazine *Smena* said good-bye to their Komsomol bosses and had themselves registered as an independent publication. On hearing the news, the senior Komsomol functionaries in Moscow realized that the situation brooked no delay. Without waiting for their own paper, *Moskovsky Komsomolets*, to follow suit, they offered to help it with the intricate legal formalities and to act as full-fledged founders of the paper, holding the controlling interest, of course. This sparked off a storm of protests from *Moskovsky Komsomolets*.
>
> "In allowing the Komsomol to keep control of our newspaper, we shore up the finances of the teetering Party and Komsomol structures," argues Alexander Popov, People's Deputy, chairman of the Moscow City Council Subcommission on Press Freedom, and a *Moskovsky Komsomolets* correspondent. "The power of ideological dogmas is waning, but the power of money remains. We are witnessing a curious process: The CPSU and the Komsomol are doing their utmost to put their activities on a commercial basis. Forgetting the Communist ideals, which I am sure many functionaries have never believed in, they are looking to invest at a profit in order to survive and retain power under new conditions. Relinquishing ideological control of the paper, our Party bosses are going to pump money out of us continuously."
>
> The situation seems paradoxical. Indeed, who of the *Moskovsky Komsomolets* subscribers would have thought that the rubles they paid for reading scathing articles in this paper went to strengthen the financial standing of the CPSU, the very party the criticism of which gained Moskovsky Komsomolets such popularity in the first place.
>
> "To the best of my knowledge, annual revenues from the paper's publication run into millions of rubles," says Alexander Popov. "The lion's share of it did not end up in the Komsomol coffers nor even in the treasury of the City Party Committee; rather, it went directly to the Managing Department of the CPSU Central Committee. This is because the newspaper comes out in the Party-owned Moskovskaya Pravda Publishers. Now the Komsomol is after our money."

Well, all things considered, it becomes clear why both the Moscow Region and Moscow City Komsomol leaders think is so important to keep control of its newspaper—popular with the readers and, in consequence, profitable, even if not ideologically orthodox. On the one hand, the thrust of the paper must most certainly embarrass the apparatchiks holding traditional beliefs. On the other, principles can be abandoned, especially if this "abandonment" of principles is backed with the Komsomol's swelling bank accounts.

Curiously, the rapid commercialization of the traditional ideological structures of the Soviet Union is evident not only in news media but also in other serious areas of activity. On August 16, Kompartbank, one of the three banks which the CPSU has co-founded or where it holds large interest, applied for registration with Gosbank (the USSR State Bank). The chief Party newspaper, *Pravda*, has openly stated its readiness to publish advertisements, saying, not without pride, that it will charge more than any other Soviet paper. As far as the Komsomol is concerned, it seems to have plunged into business wholly and entirely. Looks like the current commercial drive of Party ideologists is not a joking matter.

Pavel Gusev, editor-in-chief of Moscow's most popular newspaper, *Moskovsky Komsomolets*, on January 3 published a profile of himself and an anxious appeal to readers. For a long time this paper has been striving to be as honest as possible, and Gusev is known in the capital as a man of utmost honor. In 1990 he became chairman of the Moscow Journalists' Union (he was elected, not appointed from above).

On August 19, 1991 *Moskovsky Komsomolets* was banned, together with other Moscow and central press. The Emergency Committee's Decree No. 2 "temporarily limited" socio-political periodicals published in Moscow to the following list: *Trud' Rabochaya Tribuna, Izvestia, Pravda, Krasnaya Zvezda, Sovetskaya Rossia, Moskovskaya Pravda, Leninskoye Znamya* (Lenin's Banner), and *Selskaya Zhizn*.

Many papers mentioned above didn't live up to the hopes of Mr. Yanayev, the so-called "acting president of the USSR". None of *Trud*'s own correspondents supported the coup: there were photographs showing the disturbances, the protest of Russian trade-unions, reports from the hot spots. *Moskovskaya Pravda*, published by the Moscow City Committee of the Soviet Communist Party, couldn't turn down its publishers, but its editorial board had enough courage to state that it didn't agree with all the preventive measures taken by the Emergency Committee. Here is what Viktor Loshak wrote in *Moscow News* (August 22, 1991): "We had this lesson already: an illusion of a nice person who has to carry out dirty duties".

The first to throw themselves into the junta's arms were—guess who?— *Sovetskaya Rossia* and *Pravda*, representing the "mind, honor, and conscience of our epoch", as Lenin once called the Communist Party. We do have many journalists ready to fight for the party.

There turned out to be many of those who managed to make their choice of conscience. Among them were journalists working for a newspaper with a weird name, *Moskovsky Komsomolets*. Can you imagine a newspaper called something like Berlin Hitler-Jugend? Sounds absurd today. Though banned by the junta, *Moskovsky Komsomolets* worked on for three days and nights running. Several issues came out every day, with hourly reports of the Moscow Resistance and decrees, President Yeltsin's addresses to the people, various documents adopted by the Russian government, speeches by Yeltsin, Shevardnadze, Leningrad's Mayor Sobchak, Moscow's Mayor Popov, reports from public rallies.

Thanks to the initiative displayed by *Rossiiskiye Vesti* (Russian News, No. 19, 1991), which polled Moscow's eleven editors-in-chief of the democratic press in September, we have a chance to present the answers given by *Moskovsky Komsomolets* editor-in-chief, Pavel Gusev, to the basic questions on how democracy, the press and power structures may develop today in post-communist Russia:

1. "Soviet democracy" is not quite the happiest word combination. For decades totalitarianism has been forced into the combination. For decades totalitarianism has been forced into the minds of people as a society and as individuals, transforming the human psyche one way or another. I'm deeply convinced that today an overwhelming majority of "Soviet democrats", unfortunately, can assume another role, i.e. become dictators of the Bolshevik type. They have been brought up to destroy any adversary not by legal, constitutional ways, but through violence. Many recent events point to this: the way the monuments have been pulled down, the search for someone to blame for the coup, and others.

   Soviet democracy, born out of the totalitarian system, may, unfortunately, lead to dictatorship of democracy today. This causes alarm.

   We can hardly hope for drastic economic changes to take place; neither America, nor Europe is going to feed us for nothing. They will not carry this burden—feeding us every year, sending us food all the time.

   After more than seventy years [of communism] people have forgotten how to work. They don't want to understand that work can bring benefits, give a chance to lead a free and happy life.

2. I am dead set against the word "glasnost". It's a word invented by Gorbachev and the Communist Party to make the international public believe that something is changing here. But in fact glasnost is what Gorbachev likes to hear. I am for freedom of speech within the framework of the state's legal system. Freedom of speech is something the whole world lives on. Way back before the coup it was clear that our society was isolated in terms of information. It was the party that decided if the people have to know something or not. As a result, the provinces hardly understood what was going on. People there didn't know anything; they only somehow felt that something was going on. It took some time for the whole thing to start

working. Lack of information and lack of a system for spreading out information should be overcome. What the Ministry of Communication was doing together with the Communist Party, providing sieved or even distorted information, was a crime. Today we should start with the Ministry of Communication by completely destroying the machine engaged in spreading information.
3. Extremely complicated election campaigns lay ahead of us. I can't rule out that parties and groups which do not at all represent the democratic public or the people who defended the Russian Parliament [during the coup] may again come onto the political scene. Democratic forces must unite to win the elections.

The Komsomol apparatchiks have changed tack much quicker than their senior colleagues and teachers from the CPSU. The journal *Molodoy Kommunist* (Young Communist) was renamed *Perspektivy* (Outlook) back in mid-1990, and the boring *Komsomolskaya Zhizn* (Komsomol Life), once concerned with narrow departmental interests, is now advertising itself under the name of *Puls* (Pulse).

Since perestroika started, the Soviet Komsomol newspapers have shown much more common sense than the Party press.

The world's biggest daily *Komsomolskaya Pravda* (Komsomolka, for short) is much more popular in this country than *Pravda*. Even convicts prefer it to other newspapers and spend their hard-earned rubles on it. Convicts serving their terms in the Trans-Baikal region unanimously say that they like this newspaper for its truthfulness, original language, attention to the rights of millions of people serving their terms and for hot information about the life of their "colleagues" at large.

The growing competition on the Soviet press market is being successfully sustained by Komsomolka and by the illustrated weekly *Sobesednik* (Interlocutor), Komsomolka's ex-supplement which detached itself from the parent newspaper in October 1990 and became independent. The degree of this newspaper's independence is discussed in its last year's issue No. 41, in an interview with its former editor-in-chief and the newly-appointed Editor-in-Chief of Komsomolka, Vladislav Fronin:

> We met a few hours after Vladislav Fronin ceased to be our boss. In fact, I don't think our interview would have taken place if he had not. Really, there is some awkwardness in the situation whereby the editor-in-chief grants an interview to his own correspondent in his own newspaper or in its supplement. But last week was quite remarkable for *Sobesednik*: it stopped being a supplement to *Komsomolka* and became independent.
>
> Fronin: Congratulations!
> **Corr.:** **The same to you!**
> Fronin: Thank you. The somewhat artificial 'supplementary' period in *Sobesednik*'s life is over. In fact, financially, it has always been

independent of *Komsomolka*. Eventually, as it stood firmly on its feet, it became independent intellectually, as well. Now everything has straightened out and *Sobesednik* has two founders—not bosses, but founders. You yourselves have chosen them—*Komsomolskaya Pravda* and your own editorial board. We agreed, although it's strange that *Komsomolka* should receive its 'birth certificate' at the age of nearly 65 and *Sobesednik*—at nearly 7. Well, it's a sign of our times.

I'm *Komsomolka*'s 17th editor-in-chief, but, perhaps, the only one who has not been confirmed by the Secretariat of the Komsomol's Central Committee. Why? The moment I was appointed, one of our materials angered a top-ranking Party boss.

Corr.: **Which article?**

Fronin: If I start retelling it, some may accuse me of attempting to gain cheap popularity. Okay, it was an interview with the then disgraced Boris Yeltsin, prepared by our correspondents before my appointment. Imagine me, the newly-appointed editor-in-chief, removing the interview from the issue. But then I couldn't do this in any case. The next morning, there was a call from a Party chief. 'All right,' he said, 'we shall not upset you on the New Year's Eve, but on January 2, drop in for a talk.' Then there were other controversial publications, among them 'Novocherkassk. 1962', an interview with Oleg Kalugin and Alexander Solzhenitsyn's booklet. At one of the party conferences Vadim Medvedev remarked: 'You're a communist, but your work is actually counterproductive to the Party.' The Bureau of the Komsomol's Central Committee must have been instructed to discuss *Komsomolka*'s conduct, but Viktor Mironenko, who was the Komsomol's First Secretary then, and my Party colleagues must be given credit for not yielding to the pressure.

Approaching this dialectically one must admit, though, that there were times in the *Komsomolka*'s history when the Communist Party's Central Committee had to defend the newspaper from overly-zealous Komsomol leaders.

...Vladislav Fronin was 'appointed' *Komsomolka*'s Editor-in-Chief for the first time on May 24, 1975, at the celebrations of the newspaper's 50th birthday which was attended by all of its ex-editors-in-chief. Introducing the then young journalist in training from the Department of Young Workers' Affairs to one of them, Boris Pankin, someone said: 'Here is he, our future editor-in-chief.' 'Very nice, glad to meet you,' Pankin said, responding to a joke with a joke. (Pankin ' too, began his career as a trainee journalist.) [Boris Pankin, appointed Soviet Ambassador to Czechoslovakia in early August 1991, was one of the few senior officials in the Soviet Foreign Ministry to correctly assess the usurpation of power in Moscow and Gorbachev's arrest.—G.V.]

Corr.: **Vladislav, we've been talking about the past, not so distant though. How do you get along with the Komsomol's Central Committee now?**

Fronin: Our relationships have changed. We must cease to be anyone's press organ, rid ourselves of anyone's control and build our relationships on a mutually advantageous basis. I think Vladimir Zyukin, the Komsomol's First Secretary, as well as the members of the Bureau are well aware of this. But who can guarantee that the leading post in the Komsomol will not be occupied by some young assistant-professor from Gorky with his rigid 'communist initiative', and that he will not remove *Komsomolka*'s editor-in-chief and replace the whole of the editorial board? Judging from the speeches made at the constituent congress of the Russian Federation's Communist Party, zeal is there in abundance. Therefore, we and our young readers must have guarantees that whatever turns the situation takes, we remain what we are now.

Corr.: Generally speaking, I think that property is the key issue in the Komsomol. An organization which is falling apart (I can see you are ready to object, but this is my own, or if you want, a long thought-out opinion) and is facing the prospect of split is trying to save as much money as possible. I think that at the forthcoming plenary meeting of the Komsomol's Central Committee, the chief argument will flare up over property. By the way, the agenda of the plenary meeting includes the mass media, doesn't it?

Fronin: Here again, property is the central issue. Yes, the current developments in the Komsomol and in the country as a whole arouse concern about the future of our newspaper. Therefore, by having two founders we are creating definite financial and political guarantees of *Komsomolka*'s further existence whatever the circumstances. I've said already that we need political guarantees. But we are in need of financial guarantees, too. We must keep in mind that there are 19 subjects of the federation in the Komsomol. Undoubtedly, they have the right to their share of the income which the newspaper will transfer to the Central Committee's budget. But our newspaper cannot belong to each of the 19 subjects. If it does, it will be torn into pieces and cease to exist as a national newspaper. Really, *Komsomolka* is not a news bulletin highlighting what is happening in the youth union. It has never been and, I'm convinced, will never be. The Central Committee has other publications reserved for this particular purpose.

Corr.: Why then is the Central Committee among your founders? Why don't you proclaim yourselves an independent newspaper? This would be quite logical.

Fronin: You know, I have my own attitude to the vogue of proclaiming all and sultry 'independent' and doing it emphatically. Will the quality of cognac change if you write 'good cognac' on the label? I don't know when truly independent newspapers will appear, but I do know for sure that they will not, if independent journalists do not walk out onto the scene. Incidentally, *Komsomolka*, too, lacks such journalists. I dare say we have become a truthful newspaper. But as to... Well, our newspaper

	has become much more independent, first of all in what concerns its principles and position. But historically, it is linked with the youth union. And that is why we have a co-founder.
Corr.:	**Does this mean that you will divide everything into two equal parts?**
Fronin:	Each of us will get a million and run away. Why are you smiling? There are people among the Komsomol workers who think this way, as if we were a sham cooperative and not a serious newspaper with long-established traditions. May be, we will increase not the journalists' salary rates, but our staffers' fees. You know, funny things happen sometimes. In some of the new newspapers and magazines the author's fee for one printed page may amount to 50 rubles. We pay only 6, given the print-run of 22 million copies.
	The newspaper needs this money, first, to develop. Our printing equipment has gone obsolete, so the world's biggest daily newspaper is published in antediluvian conditions. We are still insiders in the system of the Party's publishers and must invest our own income in our own printing facilities. Then again, one has to pay on one's own for everything—for the maintenance of our own correspondent bureaus and for the publishing house.
Corr.:	**But youth newspapers function at a loss, don't they? And then, do we really need so many provincial youth newspapers?**
Fronin:	What do you mean, at a loss? It's not true. There are 269 youth and children's newspapers and magazines in this country; 160 of them are printed in the Communist Party's publishing houses. About 62 per cent of them are unprofitable and function at an annual loss of 6 million rubles. However, *Komsomolka*'s profit is 10 times greater than this sum. And now about provincial newspapers. Can one describe Riga's *Sovetskaya Molodezh* (Soviet Youth) as a provincial newspaper? In *Naberezhniye Chelny* I could see that this newspaper is as popular as *Komsomolka*. Or take *Moskovsky Komsomolets*, or Leningrad's *Smena*? It's another thing that matters. Why do the national newspapers have more rights than local ones? Why is *Komsomolka* allowed to have its own correspondent in Kazan, and the Tatar youth newspaper cannot send its reporter to Moscow? What's the idea of such discrimination? Newspapers must be equal. If they are, their popularity will be measured by the professional skills of the staff alone.
Corr.:	**And the last thing. Why didn't you become a people's deputy? There are many people's deputies among the editors-in-chief of the national newspapers. The more so since *Komsomolka*'s authority is, I'm sure, the reflection of the authority of its editor-in-chief.**
Fronin:	I'm neither a speaker nor a political figure. I'm a reporter, and I do a job I'm interested in. And then, I don't think people know me well.

That's true. TV shows Fronin only occasionally. He gives virtually no interviews, but simply makes his newspaper, which takes all his time.

On January 5 the staff of *Komsomolskaya Pravda* declared a one-hour warning strike after the Pravda publishing house, citing "a shortage of paper", announced that they would in the future be limited to five issues a week instead of the traditional (and paid for by subscribers) six. This was followed by assurances on the pages of *Komsomolskaya Pravda* from almost everyone who is someone that there is no reason to worry, everything will be okay: deputy chairmen of the USSR Council of Ministers, and even the President himself. Evidently, nobody wants to get into a fight with the country's only major youth newspaper.

For many years it was Brezhnevite and recently (under new chief Vladislav Fronin) seems to have become more progressive, ie. democratic, while retaining its influence in all corners of Soviet officialdom. Few papers could have their editorial board, in its full line-up, meet with KGB chairman Vladimir Kryuchkov and then USSR defense minister Dmitry Yazov. (Only three newspapers—*Komsomolskaya Pravda*, *Pravda* and *Izvestia*—plus TASS and the Novosti Information Agency (former APN)—have extensive correspondent networks abroad. The fact that many of their bureaux are populated by KGB and military intelligence personnel, who prior to their postings had not spent a day working for these papers and agencies, is another story).

At a time when the central television refused to directly broadcast the statement of Boris Yeltsin, *Komsomolskaya Pravda* stated that readers would be able to put personal questions to him. On March 14, 1991, the questions and answers were published on the paper's full page, and this was a sizable action, if one takes into account its total print. Yeltsin answered to the questions precisely and clearly, shortly and intelligibly, honestly and competently, not in a spirit of endless and empty twaddle, reticences and excuses, hints and insinuations, falsehood and slander, with which Gorbachev and Lukyanov, Pugo and Kryuchkov, Yazov and Pavlov, Varennikov and Rodionov had distinguished themselves in their public speeches. It's a pity that *Komsomolskaya Pravda* had not been the speakers' platform for such leaders gradually falling into disgrace as A. Yakovlev and E. Shevardnadze, Bakatin and Yeltsin, Bonner and Sakharov, Popov and Sobchak. It had a liking for Roy Medvedev, Eduard Limonov and Valery Chalidze and gave them the floor on its pages, although their writings seemed to be drafted from the beginning to the end by the back-writers from the Lubyanka House which for several decades had a huge department of misinformation with its branches (for example, in the APN-IAN) and hundreds of paid plain-clothes men inside the country and beyond its borders.

Komsomolskaya Pravda managed to don liberal garments and began to look like a non-communist paper from afar as . Its staff workers began to lie to a lesser extent than their colleagues in *Pravda*. For example, on July 4, 1991, both papers carried almost a similar item of the Russian Information Agency about the collection of signatures in Vilnius in the defense of the Lithuanian OMON, but unlike *Pravda*, *Komsomolskaya Pravda* retained at the end of this communication a key phrase to the effect that only 100 signatures had been collected in Vilnius during two days. As for *Pravda*, it kept silent and, therefore, told a big lie.

Vladislav Fronin, *Komsomolskaya Pravda* editor-in-chief, was questioned by *Rossiiskiye Vesti* in September 1991. The questions pertained to three topics: 1) the situation in the country and the future of democracy; 2) the importance of the coming "fourth power"—the power of information and freedom of speech in the life of society; 3) your message to the people and those who are at the helm today.

Here are the answers:

1. When times were tough the democratic forces and democratic newspapers joined together, and now I'm worried that with the victory over, friction will start up within the, including the newspapers as well.

    We pinned great hopes on the writers realizing that now is not the time for having it out with each other, or for removing people from their staff. Therefore it is extremely important now to understand that although democracy has apparently gained the upper hand, serious trials are still ahead. If democratic forces don't unite, something more horrible than what happened in August might occur. The most horrible of all, a Yugoslav variant, shouldn't be dismissed.

    My hopes lie, first of all, with the Russian government. I hope it takes energetic action and unites reliable, thinking, and business-like professionals.

    I'm not an expert in concrete economic reforms, but I know that we can't do without them.

2. I think this process will take a long time. We lack a free and independent press; we have lots of independent newspapers, but I don't think they are as independent as they appear. By the way, we are perhaps the only publication at Pravda publishers which is still dependent and published together with the Young Communist League. The paper hasn't removed its orders yet; nor has it been renamed. I don't think names here are really important. We are fond of renaming our cities, providing mottos for our newspapers, but the most important thing is economic independence, which our editorial offices lack completely. I mean economic independence from every outside source.

3. In the forthcoming elections, the people shouldn't make the same mistakes as in the previous ones. The difficult days we had to live through in August may be explained in part by those mistakes. We would like to lay the blame on the President, but we elected the people's deputies ourselves, and they

obediently confirmed the appointment of those who surrounded Gorbachev, and who later betrayed him.

It is our duty to express public opinion. If the presidents make mistakes, we will criticize both of them. This is not an end in itself, of course, but the "fourth power" should be in some kind of opposition. We will remain in this opposition, no matter who comes to power—democrats or non-democrats.

The rather benevolent review of the main Soviet periodicals cannot conceal the main thing: even at the beginning of 1991, as the transition to market conditions continued, the Soviet press still remained the product of a military-ideological economy. This most profound observation was made by Academician Yuri Ryzhov, People's Deputy of the USSR and Rector of Moscow Institute of Aviation Engineering, in the newspaper *Sovetskaya Kultura* of the Communist Party's Central Committee.

Despite the press's inspiring breakthrough to openness, the absolute majority of our newspapers and magazines remain in a state that has been typical of Soviet intellectuals over the past 70 years, particularly of those specializing in the humanities. Our journalists, like our historians, philosophers, lawyers, economists and philologists were third-rate people. The label of the leader was on the working class which was exploited even more ruthlessly than under tsarism; its ally, according to the Communist Party, were the half-strangled and almost destroyed peasants, while educated people wearing spectacles were in the background. The top bureaucracy needed technical intelligentsia for work in the arms industries and in research centers, also controlled by the military. The rest of the intellectual layer was deliberately eliminated so that finally only a handful of intellectuals had survived. To this day, the regime has been dutifully implementing Lenin's well-known slogan that any housewife must be involved in running the state. The result was political reprisals and mottos similar to the "Get Down to Work, Comrades!". It is not surprising that now we badly lack professional parliamentarians, skilled school teachers and top-class journalists.

Meanwhile, the need for professional reporters is enormous and their rating on the present-day market is increasing while that of the party functionaries has dramatically fallen. Common sense prompted the Communist Party to set free the so-called thick magazines and newspapers with small print run, many of which were losing subscribers and income (if it does not, it will have to spend much money on keeping them alive), and tighten their mortal grip on the monthly *Chelovek i Zakon* which is still bringing in millions, and which is in stable demand among both law-obedient citizens and the rest of the population. It is pleasant, of course, to witness the journalist's prestige rising.

CHAPTER IV

THE NEW INDEPENDENTS

The Court Jesters of the Epoch of Perestroika

But there were some publications which the Ideological Department of the Communist Party Central Committee wanted to control at all costs. Yet it had to back out, because the prestige of these publications in this country and abroad was immense.

Who was better known—Yegor Yakovlev, Editor-in-Chief of the newspaper Moscow News, or Albert Vlasov, Chairman of the Board of the Novosti Press Agency (APN)? Novosti employed thousands of people, publishes dozens of newspapers and magazines abroad and, until September 1990, was the founder (publisher) of the newspaper *Moscow News* with a staff of just a few dozen people. Now *Moscow News* is independent and there are only two things standing over and above the staff's convictions—the law and the will of the founders—representatives of the democratic-minded public who have united into the society "*Moscow News*—Popular Newspaper".

Published in many Western European languages, *Moscow News* was a dull propaganda newspaper only 10 years ago, was circulated abroad mostly for free and was bought in this country by students of English, French, Spanish and Arabic, given the absence of foreign periodicals on the Soviet press market. It was never published in Russian during pre-Gorbachev years. From 1985, when Mikhail Gorbachev came to power till 1989 *Moscow News* was the only Soviet periodical published openly that enjoyed the luxury of having (and expressing) its own viewpoint which was much closer to the truth than the viewpoint of other Soviet newspapers. Of course, everyone knows that the king's fool is allowed to say sacramental things that would cost others their heads.

Inaccessible to the general reader, *Moscow News* (an "ersatz-newspaper", as the Politburo members, Vadim Medvedev and Yegor Ligachev, contemptuously described it) was to show the West the extent of glasnost in the USSR. Whatever foreign political scientists and Sovietologists thought about those twists in the democracy games, the sophisticated Soviet reader, grown wise with bitter experience, (*Moscow News* simply had no other readers) would eagerly await the continuation of every scandalous article to learn whether or not the editor-in-chief had been dismissed. During the first five years of perestroika, Yegor Yakovlev was in the focus of attention of the democratic-minded Soviet intellectuals who thought with every reason that his removal would signal the end of perestroika and the return of everything from where it had started. And even in 1990, the openness (sincerity and honesty) of all Soviet national newspapers taken together still lagged behind what *Moscow News* allowed itself in 1986. Although, of course, now as before, *Moscow News* was actively involved in the political battle on the Soviet political scene and for this reason alone sticks to the unwritten, but strictly observed rules (limits) of glasnost.

Izvestia congratulated its *Moscow News* colleagues on the occasion of the jubilee (September 13, 1990) and offered its readers the following interview with Yegor Yakovlev:

Yakovlev: There are three main principles by which our staff will continue to be guided: conscience, common sense and the readers' demands. The time now is different from what it was four years ago, when we realized that there were no and could be no forbidden topics. Now these principles have been upheld by many newspapers. Yes, we rejoice at the fact that our newspaper has been registered and that we have become independent and do not come under any political bias. I've been a journalist for 35 years and I thought that I would not live up to see the Law on the Press, promised by Lenin shortly after the revolution, to be adopted. We are also glad that subscription to the newspaper's Russian edition has been opened. Really, the fact that there was a newspaper which had to be obtained only by underhand means was nonsensical.

Much is becoming a thing of the past. But life has not become any better. Unfortunately, there's still a great deal of intolerance and enmity not only among the retrogrades, but also among those who think they serve democracy. We want to show people how conflicts can be settled in all spheres of life, whether in the economy or in politics. We want to assert human rights and dignity. We want to help revive a free, prosperous and civilized state. If we succeed, this newspaper will become a newspaper of democratic accord and democratic understanding on which we reckon.

Corr.: **Symbolically, the newspaper's renewal coincides with your anniversary. In October, *Moscow News* will be 60...**

Yakovlev: Well, that's right.

Corr.: **Do you know who your readers are?**

Yakovlev: Previously, I used to say that our readers were those who woke up early and who stood waiting at the kiosks at 6 a.m., when the newspaper was brought in. The Soviet readers had to put up with just 350,000 Russian-language copies. Now we'll have more exact information about our readers. In fact, this year's subscription is the first attempt to measure our popularity. The results are quite pleasing so far. But if the number of subscribers is too great, we'll have to suspend subscription. In this new economic setting, following our withdrawal from Novosti, we have been confronted with many problems, including the shortage of paper.

Corr.: How are you going to deal with your problems? Obviously in a market economy their number will increase...

Yakovlev: Indeed, so far, we have nothing at all at our disposal. We are establishing contacts with printing houses. And there are plans to make our publication a joint-stock venture and issue 25 million rubles worth of shares. There are Western businessmen who are ready to buy them, although they are entitled to the ruble income. Finally, we are setting up a Moscow News concern and are having talks with France on creating our own radio station, and with the Moscow City Council on establishing a *Moscow News*' international information center and a small book-publishing house. That's what we are planning to do. We hope we'll cope.

The 20 January issue of the newly-independent *Moscow News* was edged in black as a sign of mourning. Eight of the 16 pages were devoted to the tragedy in Vilnius. This was honest journalism, ie., the direct opposite of that carried by *Pravda, Sovetskaya Rossia* and *Krasnaya Zvezda* at the time, and also the daily Vremya news program. Thirty members of the *Moscow News* founders' council, known throughout the country, signed a declaration, "A crime by a regime unwilling to depart the stage", with a detailed analysis of Gorbachev's fateful mistakes.

Anatoly Sobchak did not have time to sign the letters of the founders, since he had gone away. For this reason he made a special statement in *Moscow News* on January 1, 1991. Sobchak said:

The most tragic mistake committed by Mikhail Gorbachev constituted his participation in effort to preserve the unity of the USSR via the use of force in the Baltic area, while I personally consider the refusal of the President--again and again-- to recognize his involvement in such methods of 'political dialogue' disgraceful. After the bloody night in Vilnius, after the storm of the Lithuanian television tower by commandoes and KGB-men, the President said that he personally had not known anything about this action. This statement of his and similar declarations by the Minister of Defense and the Minister of the Interior, as well as the TV statement of the KGB Chairman, where he justified the shooting of civilian people, produced a disturbing picture for the whole world.

The President was duty-bound to show fortitude and assume the burden of high responsibility for what had happened. This repelled not only democrats but also many of the military who had been sent by him to quell the independent Baltic republics and who only learnt the next morning that they had participated in the action on their own initiative.

The loss of trust is the most terrible thing for a political leader. But the loss may take place in different circumstances: a politician may lose the people's confidence but preserve his authority, if his retinue, that is, those on whom he relies (civil servants, police, the army, etc.), trust him. But if he loses both confidence and power, there's trouble ahead!

Our President did not manage to become a genuine president of his people and remained the Party's General Secretary. Whatever will happen to him later on, the peoples of our country will never forget either Tbilisi in 1989, Baku in 1990 or Vilnius in 1991.

As the commission elected by the Congress of People's Deputies of the USSR discovered, Gorbachev was not involved in the massacre in front of the Government House in Tbilisi. But he did nothing to punish the guilty parties. Up until now we have not been shown a TV film shot by KGB cameramen, although a decision to this effect was taken by the supreme organ of our country--the Congress of People's Deputies. If in April 1989 this man seemed to be the object of a reactionary coup, subsequently the situation in the country changed. In Baku the troops failed to take any action when there were pogroms of Armenians—it was after the pogroms had ceased and the first secretary of the Azerbaijanian Communist Party had fled the city and actual power had passed to the Popular Front, that the tanks began to storm the republican capital at night. This action was carried out by decision of the Chairman of the USSR Supreme Soviet, and those who were responsible for this action did everything to spill more blood in the city. Within a year the President had been made fully compliant to the forces of the past era, who had managed to fully compliant to the forces of the past era, who had managed to win him over to their side. He ceased to be a democrat and reformer. The General Secretary overpowered the President.

Tbilisi, Baku and the Baltic area are the three landmarks, which determined both the personal drama of Gorbachev and the fate of our perestroika which he initiated in the mid-80s in brilliant style.

Moscow News has always been and still is an interesting and original publication, where people's opinions dominate over fresh news. The history of any press organ may be told in an intelligible and interesting manner from the inside. This view from the editorial office of *Moscow News* was suggested by Radio Liberty, which broadcast in early March 1991 the story of a former contributor to the paper Andrei Vasiliyev (the text of the radio broadcast is quoted from the newspaper of the Democratic Party of Russia of March 17, 1991):

In mid-January, when the echo of tank motors died away in Russia, a report in small type published by *Moscow News* all of a sudden sounded very loud: Yegor Yakovlev had quit the ranks of the Communist Party.

By that time such action had become a daily occurrence and it became uncomfortable to boast of this action even before one's family members.

I admit that the readers of *Moscow News* were surprised to know that Yegor Yakovlev was still a party member.

But people who knew him personally (naturally, in Russia and abroad they numbered several tens of thousands of people) were shocked in a different manner.

Many people knew very well that Yegor Yakovlev was a convinced Bolshevik of the Leninist school. And this characterization meant that even five years ago he was a rebel, even a dissident.

In 1956, however, Yakovlev had already sensed that he was an inner dissident, for when he heard the report of the 20th Party Congress he could not believe Nikita Khrushchev. For the secretary of a district YCL committee that was an act of bravery.

One more landmark. The magazine *Novy Mir* was usually regarded as the last publication of the period of thaw. But there was also another magazine—*Zhurnalist*—remodelled by Yakovlev from a departmental bulletin The Soviet Press. He managed to issue 15 numbers before being summoned to the CPSU Central Committee. Yegor Yakovlev behaved himself as a champion of liberty. Accused of disobedience to the Party leadership of the press, he stated: "In this country there is no Party leadership of the press in Lenin's conception".

I think that at that time Lenin was considered a dubious figure. Naturally enough in 1970 Yakovlev's TV serial about Lenin had been forbidden for showing for 15 years.

Naturally, Yakovlev was dismissed from his magazine and sent to work at *Izvestia* as a rank-and-file journalist. This period is now omitted by me, since the legends about him are not very interesting, and moreover, as I was much younger than him, I had no personal impressions of him.

I came to work in *Moscow News* in 1986, two weeks after Yegor Yakovlev had become the paper's Editor-in-Chief. I joined the staff on the recommendation of his son and very soon realized that Soviet power had not given birth to such an Editor-in-Chief.

I was shown a made-up page with a detailed exposition of a meeting of journalists with the First Secretary of the Moscow City Committee of the CPSU, an alternate member of its Political Bureau Boris Yeltsin. At that time small TASS reports on such events were a regular feature in Soviet papers. But here I saw a whole page full of journalistic arguments.

"Who has given you the authorization?"

"Nobody would authorize this. But I did not ask anybody for permission to publish this article. For Yeltsin met journalists and not party functionaries. This means that this communication is 'fit for the press'."

The issue with this article was the first Russian-language one sold in Moscow down to the last copy. (Before that mainly English-language issues of *Moscow News* enjoyed popularity with pupils of English-spoken schools). Within three weeks it had enhanced its prestige and disappeared from the shop counters.

In *Moscow News* I was probably the fifth number in 'Yegor's team'. Before he came to the paper, its editorial office was some sort of Foreign Office department, for an honorary exile of exposed spies and unsuccessful diplomats. The 'new wave' greatly frightened them. The Yakovlev team was indeed exotic. He invited to work at the paper a political commentator without a higher education, a Jew without a registered passport in Moscow, an international analyst, who had slipped up, a reporter with a criminal record... I was considered an unrepentant hippy. At the beginning Yegor tried to persuade me to wear a dress suit at least one day a week. He in fact agreed with my objections, although on that very day I found myself in a sobering station. He recommended, although he did not persist in his suggestions, that I should join the Party ranks.

I enthusiastically told my friends about an Editor-in-Chief, who might come to office in a blue jeans coat and would drive his car.

By the way, Yegor Yakovlev exponded on his staffing policy at a meeting of Moscow intellectuals in the Central House of Writers. When asked why *Moscow News* contains so many Jewish names, he replied: "When I give somebody a job, I do not make him undo his trousers".

The staff of the paper was reinforced not only by non-Party Jews. There was a flow of APN journalists of proven reliability. Yegor pious to these cadres, something, which we as ordinary journalists did not understand. There was also a third invigorating source—perestroika supporters, people of the generation of the 1960s. Shmelyov, Nuikin, Afanasyev, Popov, Bunich and Bovin represented a gentlemanly set of prominent publicists. These powerful authors strengthened *Moscow News* as a speaker's platform and at the same time killed it as a regular paper. However, there was a social order for such a platform. For this reason the editorial board represented a thin layer of journalists between two thick layers of exposed spies (Yakovlev failed to sack them all) and exonerated dissidents. Although this was only garnish.

The paper was created by one man, who worked from dawn to dusk, without taking any days off. During Yegor's travels abroad it was unpleasant to pick up the paper, as all the controversial articles were held back by his deputies: 'the grand gentleman will come and judge between us.'

The grand gentleman used to come on Mondays, screamed into our ears and summoned journalists to his office for a grim talk and would even show us the door. On the whole, he adhered to a common Party style of management.

He was forgiven by his colleagues, who understood very well that without Yegor *Moscow News* was nothing. At his own risk he decided to reprint from the Paris *Le Figaro* a letter written by ten emigres entitled "*Let Gorbachev Submit Evidence to Us*". He thereby raised the paper to its Zenith but also began to trample on the reputation of those who signed the letter. He probably could not have acted differently at that time.

During the victimization of Yeltsin, Yakovlev spent a long time looking for an authoritative author, who would write an article commenting on the work of this 'man in the political vanguard'. He soon found such an author. This was Gavriil Popov, then professor of Moscow University. After the publication of his article, University students refused to attend his lectures.

It was an acute struggle, sometimes involving resignations, when Valentin Falin, the Chairman of the Novosti Press Agency, would read the paper before its publication, correct it or return it to the editorial office.

There were also general battles. When Yegor would send his resignation letter to Ligachev, Gorbachev would himself settle the matter amicably and his letter would be read out to the newspaper staff.

There were also some victories, when, for instance, Falin was removed from the Novosti Press Agency and Ligachev from the sphere of ideology.

With Lenin's quotation book in one hand and Gorbachev's letter in the other hand Yakovlev advanced perestroika and did not let his colleagues help him. Consequently he advanced perestroika so far forward that he ended up left behind.

His adherence to Lenin and Gorbachev reflected in his interviews, and indicative of the explicable complex nature of the great man, became a professional disease for all *Moscow News* staff workers. But the collective complex cannot be either exquisite or explicable given the background of the incipient new press, devoid of any complexes. This press was sold out by declasse elements, as if derisively, near to the entrance of the paper's editorial office. Here the news would be regularly discussed by people at round-the-clock meetings. This phenomenon was often the 'hero' of all Moscow TV reports.

Yegor, by the way, did not like these political meetings and, as a serious politician, repeatedly ordered his business manager to disperse the crowds. Then, he dismissed the manager, as he failed to cope with this task.

Soon the newspaper was called the organ of the left wing of the CPSU Central Committee and then the accidental coincidence of the 'Right' name Yegor [the first name of Ligachev as well] with the "Left" name of Yakovlev [the first name of Alexander Yakovlev, the then adviser of Gorbachev]] began to evoke sad thoughts. Some journalists quit *Moscow News*. It was convenient for its Editor-in-Chief to present things in such a way that defectors had left in pursuit of higher wages.

It's interesting to note that Yegor Yakovlev who glorified private enterprise in his paper proved not capable of meeting the transition to market conditions. In one of his interviews, answering a question about his son's paper *Kommersant*, he replied that he could not accept the extremely high earnings of the competing firm. Practically the same statement was simultaneously made in *Pravda* by Ivan Polozkov, the First Secretary of the Communist Party of the RSFSR.

Meanwhile commercially the paper was not doing very well, although this was seen only inside the editorial office. The first subscription campaign brought in two odd million subscribers as an aftermath of the overall deficiency. Copies sold out in retail within a week, although earlier on they had sold out within the first few hours of its issue.

Moreover, the British publisher R. Maxwell refused to cooperate with *Moscow News*. Other foreign-language publications also went bankrupt.

Yakovlev understood this but could not put up with the change in the social order. Readers need information and not glasnost. It's time for publicists supporting perestroika to write books and not small articles or notes.

The cosmetic repairs--the appearance of the word 'independent' on the front page and the election of a board of founders--did not salvage the situation. Yegor stated at one of the meeting of the editorial board, attended by all the workers that he did not intent to cooperate with them any longer and left the room. The collective did not understand the situation, because they never cooperated properly with the Editor-in-Chief and only obeyed his instructions.

There was another extremity in Yakovlev's behavior. He said that he would create the paper for the older generation, for those who were accustomed to old journalism and accepted perestroika at its outburst. This splendid idea led to a sharp decline in total circulation and therefore remained as a pure idea.

Yegor invited young journalists from *Moskovsky Komsomolets* and *Komsomolskaya Pravda*. This time he made another mistake. The young people changed their attitudes and methods and grew in status to reach the level needed by *Moscow News*, while the deputy chief who came from *Komsomolskaya Pravda* failed to do so and, therefore, still enjoys the glory of a 'local fool'.

After failing to set up his new team, Yakovlev began feeling uncomfortable in Gorbachev's team. The first symptom followed the prohibition of the bulletin *The 13th Mike*, issued by him during the 28th CPSU Congress for its delegates. I had written about this in *Kommersant*, but now I had no sympathy for the former Editor-in-Chief, who had taken up with Bolsheviks.

The resignation of Alexander Yakovlev from the Presidential Council and the resignation of Eduard Shevardnadze from the post of the USSR Foreign Minister sapped the spirits of Yegor Yakovlev. I think that he will not forgive Gorbachev for this, although the President came to his 'rescue' again by sending tanks to Lithuania.

The night of January 11 witnessed the events in Vilnius and a merry evening party in the Moscow Cinema House devoted to the 60th birthday of *Moscow News*. The day before a narrow meeting of specially invited colleagues had taken place to decide whether to hold this party or not.

Yegor assumed responsibility for this soiree once again. The audience of 1,500 guests heard before drinking free champagne, a brief brilliant speech by Yakovlev. He said: "Of course, this is not the time to enjoy ourselves. But, who knows, maybe we shall be on a spree for the last time".

Next morning we worked over the special issue dealing with Lithuanian events. We prepared this issue in a purely journalistic style, more professional and interesting than previous numbers.

The next day Gorbachev, who was introducing a new foreign minister to the ministry collegium, said with resentment, brandishing the last issue of *Moscow News* that 'somebody' regarded him as a criminal. He referred to the letter, written by the newspaper founders, where it was said: "All of us have become the victims of our criminal regime". The founders had worked over this letter for almost 24 hours, although some of them had refused to include their signatures.

For example, Yury Afanasyev refused to sign, as in his view, the letter was not sufficiently harsh, while Stanislav Kondrashov did so due to its excessive harshness.

The same issue of the newspaper carried a report that the remaining Party members had quit the ranks of the local branch. Yakovlev said: Why do you look at me? I'm leaving the Party, and you may act as you please."

Soon *Moscow News* disappeared from the shop counters. Yakovlev stopped shouting and twitching. He raised author's fees and workers' wages. he managed to strengthen production discipline in the newspaper office.

We had the impression that Yakovlev had come back to life and regained his sight by relieving himself of the Party burden. Consequently he said quite recently to one of his favorites: "It seems to me that I'm interfering with the paper".

Western non-governmental organizations closely follow the developments in the Soviet Union and applaud the most stubborn and valiant journalists. Every year Italians grant dozens of literary and journalistic awards. One of the most authoritative prizes, initiated in Milan 30 years ago, the European

Journalist Prize, was for the first time, in 1990, awarded to a foreigner. It was awarded to Yegor Yakovlev, Editor-in-Chief of *Moscow News*. After the August putsch he became Chairman of the All-Union TV and Radio Broadcasting Company.

Although banned by the junta, *Moscow News* continued to be published during the coup. Special issues were prepared by the Moscow editorial board of the newspaper, while the basic (regular) issue dated August 21, 1991, was printed in Tallinn (in Russian for Moscow and the rest of the country), Cologne (in German for Germany, Austria and Switzerland) and Paris (in French). The aforementioned actions were spontaneous and required the selfless, round-the-clock work of translators and printing workers. The French government started to create groups of specialists to publish the best Soviet democratic newspapers and magazines (*Ogonyok, Moscow News* and *Nezavisimaya Gazeta*) in Russian and French. Thankfully, it was not needed.

Moscow News No. 261 (September 8, 1991), signed by Yegor Yakovlev, reported that it was "YEGOR'S LAST ISSUE". This was the heading of the following article:

> The experience of dealing with that person—and not necessarily for a long time, or for even that many years—prompted me to conclude that our shattered lives wiped out completely the best of the species. Yegor Yakovlev became chief three times, owing to his energetic and honest attempts to improve the system. And three times he was ousted from the nomenklatura because his attempts betrayed too much talent.
>
> There is a tale about the Soviet editorial genius, who would faultlessly find and cross out the best lines. Yegor was the best line in Soviet journalism at a time when there was no other journalism here. He was appointed for the fourth time editor-in-chief of the newspaper which pioneered the movement from the camp of "agitators, propagandists and organizers" into the camp of mass media. And he led *Moscow News* along this road for five years, turning the "Welcome-to-the-Soviet-Paradise" propagandist-cum-advertising publication into a symbol of glasnost, that is, freedom of the press Soviet style.
>
> How could Yegor Yakovlev emerge out of this totalitarian monster?
>
> There is as yet no answer to this question; it's akin to the question: How can life be borne from inorganic matter? Dead totalitarian molecules can give birth to an organism, which comprises quite different properties, a thing which starts moving, tearing apart and breaking up the surrounding monolith.
>
> Many of us, that is the majority, thought differently. He acted differently.
>
> Yet the molecules he was made of influenced him. The totalitarian foundation was transformed by his talent into authoritarianism. Only such an organism could, it seems, stand firm against the powers that be. The wall can be broken through only by a ram, which is also a sufficiently firm object.
>
> We—those of us who were attracted to *Moscow News* by the fire of his talent—felt that firmness every day. And we fire of his talent—felt that firmness every day. And we put up with it, because there is nothing more attractive for ordinary people

than talent. By the way, he is able to value other people's talent nobly and selflessly. So, is it surprising that we did not want to leave him for somebody less firm?

When the ram broke through the wall, new people rushed into the gap. They were initially different, and they probably thought that they were born free. But in actual fact they emerged into freedom owing to the sound of the breaking wall, a noise which conceals the development of a new psychology.

The appointment of Yegor Yakovlev as head of Central TV led to personnel changes in *Moscow News*. Here is an interview with Len Karpinsky, the new editor-in-chief of *Moscow News* (October 17, 1991), to show you the way new leaders of Soviet journalism differed:

On August 28, 1991 Len Karpinsky, political analyst of *Moscow News*, was unanimously elected the weekly's editor-in-chief.

Question: Will the concept of the weekly change now that you've become its head?
Answer: Yakovlev's departure is not important now, as I believe that the August developments placed society in a qualitatively new situation. This does not mean that it has changed; it is still a post-totalitarian society. And we shall have to clear away the dirt and build a new democracy for Russia for a long time to come. But, owing to the victory of the democrat-oriented forces, society is confronted with new tasks. We shall have to change as part of these transformations.

Question: Much is being said now about a crisis in the mass media. What should newspapers do to attract readers?
Answer: That's a difficult question. I think that newspapers should be different. Readers have a wide range of interests. Consequently the idea of the common denominator is not valid. Every newspaper should have its own image and voice.

For example, we shall try to maintain our materials at the highest possible analytical and intellectual level.

We cannot report immediate news, as we are a weekly. Consequently our main task is to offer readers a politological, philosophical and psychological interpretation of developments. Consequently I am greatly interested in regaining some of our authors from the clan of the 1960s. But our main task is to attract new intellects, that is people who think differently. We need new ideas and brains which constantly generate them.

Question: Do you mean that this will be a newspaper for the elite?
Answer: I don't like that word. As Solzhenitsyn says, there are 40 million ragamuffins in this country. If these ragamuffins (people with university diplomas) so desire, they can evolve into an intelligentsia. In addition, there are quite a few people without a higher education who are prepared to work with their brains. In short, we shall work for that sector of the population who want to think and discard the ideological

cliches of the past, people who want to sense the independent nature of their thoughts.

Question: I know that much of your earlier writing before has not been published and that you were even regarded as a dissident. Have you ever clashed with the KGB?

Answer: Yes. I remember Fillip Denisovich Bobkov, until recently first deputy of Kryuchkov. He retired before the coup. Maybe this was the reason why he retired. He was a super professional, an intelligent man, even though he was employed by the KGB. He worked mostly in suppressing dissent.

After the 20th Congress, when I was secretary of the Komsomol Central Committee, he would frequently come to see us and say what he thought about the first dissidents of that time over a cup of tea. He denounced mostly poets, especially Yevtushenko.

Many years later, in 1975, we met again. I had to visit him in his office and to explain certain things. We talked for a long time, this time without tea—which offended me most of all. At that time I started accumulating a so-called library of unpublished manuscripts. It wasn't in actual fact samizdat, but rather merely a collection of explosive material. The KGB learned about my designs and I was firmly reprimanded.

There were different things. External shadowing is when they follow you without even trying to conceal it, in order to put pressure on you. But I don't consider myself a dissident. I'm too insignificant for this role. I was afraid to take part I'm too insignificant for this role. I was afraid to take part in any direct action. So my dissent was rather relative.

Question: And yet how did this transformation—from the upper sections of the Komsomol Central Committee to relative dissent—come about?

Answer: I'll begin with the general condition: if the totalitarian monolith as represented by the apparatus was indeed monolithic, there would have been no perestroika. Not even in the form it took until recently. Perestroika was conceived in the upper quarters and clearly shows that there existed and developed two poles within the apparatus, the pole of inflexible, conformist thinking, and the pole of critical thinking. The motives differ depending on the individual. Yet even in that absurd situation some people realized that life was passing them by and being squandered on a farce. And believe me, there were quite a few such people. Gorbachev is one of them. In general, he walked along a parallel road, only that he was more integrated with the nomenklatura. He grew up via the party-determined direct line. But when I recall him telling me what he thought when he was 26... Already then he could see the absurdity of the existing mechanism. Not completely, perhaps, but partially.

Question: You had quite a few meetings with Gorbachev. Can you recall the most striking of them?

Answer:		From the Komsomol he moved on to work in agriculture in Stavropol Region, as secretary of the party committee of a directorate. By that time I had already started to work for *Pravda*. Once we talked with him for nearly two hours. Gorbachev spoke indignantly about the figures set for farmers, when the final result was calculated on the basis of the kilometers they covered, rather than on the products they produced. I think that the idea of market prices had already come to him even then. The pole of protest evolved on the basis of this background.
Question:		In that case I cannot understand his fanatical loyalty to the Communist Party, which he maintained until recently. He even tried to bring the party together after the Foros events.
Answer:		The point is not the party. The Communist Party of the Soviet Union could be only called a political party in the early days. Then it became a holy union of superiors, including those working for the national economy. It was a power structure cemented by the ideology and apparatus of the CPSU. It is not a party, it is the ruling class.

In 1990, *Guinness Book of Records* registered the record printing of the Soviet weekly *Argumenty i Fakty* - 33,392,200 copies. In March of that year, Vladislav Starkov, Editor-in-Chief of the weekly, received in London from the Speaker of the British House of Commons the prize "The Newspaper of the Year". At the traditional ceremony that gathered the flower of British journalism it was declared that this Soviet paper had become the first prize winner for 33 years of the existence of the BBC prize.

At the end of 1989 the name of Vladislav Starkov spread through the world press like wildfire in connection with the campaign launched in the USSR to remove him from the post of the Editor-in-Chief of the paper he had founded. The paper *Argumenty i Fakty* is a very popular weekly in the country and reflected perestroika in the press perhaps more than any other edition. To obtain independence from the insidious planning bodies and state producers of newsprint, its editorial office issued an appeal to the people about the collection of money for setting up a People's Enterprise for Processing Waste Paper, announced the number of its settlement account in the bank. And the readers' money flew. Moreover, the editorial office had promised to refund their contributions out of the profit of the future enterprise.

Already in 1990, the journalist team of the paper announced the dissolution of their Communist Party branch and thus succeeded in releasing from the ideological control of two Communist parties—that of the Soviet Union and that of the Russian Federation, of Gorbachev and Polozkov.

On June 30, 1990, the editorial office of the paper published a special item: "We would like to inform our readers that in recent months the number of 'valuable instructions' from the CPSU Central Committee has dwindled sharply. True, we still do receive requests from it but they are not in a compulsory nature. Sometimes motorcars with special messengers bring in 'secret' packets, in which, as is the usual case, there are no secrets at all." There are no longer summons of journalists to the Old Square [Staraya Square the place where the CPSU Central Committee had its seat--G.V.], which fact had been widely known to the Soviet readers in the early stages of perestroika.

Since the end of 1990 the weekly has ceased to be a departmental publication of the ideological and propagandistic organization—the Znaniye Society—and had become a fully independent edition. But as before the newspaper has no guaranteed supplies of newsprint. Now in an effort to survive it is meeting in single combat the economic and not the ideological *diktat* of those who control the stocks of newsprint, printing works, post offices, banks, uninhabited premises, and information into the bargain.

A month after the August coup the newspaper *Rossiiskiye Vesti* (No. 19, 1991) asked Vladislav Starkov, editor-in-chief of the weekly *Argumenty i Fakty*, to speak out on the problems of democracy, press and power today. Here are his answers:

1. Life has become far more difficult, at least for my newspaper. Prior to the coup we knew what we could not write about, for there was a kind of inner censorship. Today it is obvious that we can write about anything we want, competing with TV and radio, which have become much more interesting and informative.

   As for the country as a whole, we are not witnessing peace, but rather a civil war, raging on the outskirts of Russia in the republics bordering it. It is clear that society cannot move on along a straight line and consequently I think that the near future will be a time to establish democratic foundations throughout the territory of the former Soviet Union. I believe in this.

   History is rolling towards democracy, but the situation in the economy is not so good. There are no answers here. Maybe they will be supplied tomorrow or the day after tomorrow. The avalanche of economic freedom did not affect Moscow and Russia. Meanwhile, our economic problems must be resolved by a real avalanche. This is due primarily to conservative thinking. For 74 years the people were browbeaten with socialist and communist ideals, and one August cannot eliminate this. The problems are to be found within ourselves. We need an economic avalanche, but what should we do not to sink under it? I think that we should display wonders of political manoeuvre, in comparison to which all Gorbachev's manoeuvres will look like child's play.

2. This "fourth power" already exists. During the coup silence fought glasnost, and society, which had tasted glasnost, did not give the coup any chance to succeed. And the press should be given great merit for this.

3. To put it in a high-flown way, the people must be vigilant and must not allow any interruption to ongoing democratic processes. We must bring the cause of the revolution to its logical end.

   And one more thing. It is vital that young people are given power in all structures. So far I don't see that this process is developing enough. Today it is especially important to take collective decisions, which are rational and analyzed by the team to be selected not on grounds of personal loyalty, but on grounds of wisdom, a talent for analysis and a critical outlook.

The Time of "Heavy-Weight" Literary Magazines is Up

In 1990 a dozen or so major Moscow publications have managed to cast off their shackles, after a protracted fight and months of argument in the corridors of their founding bodies and every conceivable state institution. So who has won freedom from whom? *Ogonyok, Znamya* and *Literaturnaya Gazeta* have struggled free from the iron embrace of the CPSU Central Committee and its close relative, the USSR Writers' Union, that vigilant overseer of the belletristes. The unfolding drama took pride of place within all three publications, and in fact the entire country looked on avidly. Is it truly possible to lock horns with such omnipotent organizations, and especially over such fundamental questions? Not so long ago a single misprint or unfortunate expression that found its way into a text would lead to the hapless editor responsible being ejected onto the street to seek alternative employment, while the editor-in-chief would receive a flea in his ear from the entire Central Committee and Writers' Union hierarchy.

A series of articles in the most respectable of all Soviet dailies, *Izvestia*, under headlines such as *"Clash of the Titans"* and *"Clash of the Titans Continues"* was typical. Meanwhile, these publications, headed by such "star" writers as V. Korotich, G. Baklanov and F. Burlatsky, are already losing their readers. They would, of course, be snapped up from any kiosk in an instant, but they hit the newsstands in exactly that quantity required to ensure that they remain in short supply and available only under the counter (and to the vendor's acquaintances). As throughout the state-run trading system in this country, vendors in kiosks receive a fixed salary rather than a percentage of sales revenues. Thus rather than "trade" they create artificial shortages of whatever they can.

Also interesting is the fact that products like *Ogonyok, Znamya* and *Literaturnaya Gazeta* in any normal society would simply not be able to exist, let alone rake in vast profits. *Ogonyok* is a lightweight black-and-white magazine. It is produced by journalists and writer-historians in Moscow who on very rare occasions venture further afield on fact-finding missions. Exposes of the excesses of Stalin's days have won it millions of readers. Eventually they started criticizing the whole of the pre-Gorbachev era. But the general details of such events are well-known, and all these discoveries and goings-on belong to the past. Given the lack of normal school textbooks in the country, *Ogonyok* makes ideal reading for students (and teachers) of history, sociology and literature.

Znamya, Novy Mir, Moskva, Oktyabr (October), *Druzhba Narodov* (Friendship among Peoples), *Inostrannaya Literatura* (Foreign Literature), *Yunost* (Youth), *Neva, Ogni Sibiri, Prostor* (Expanses) and dozens similar in all regions of Russia and the union republics are virtually without Western equivalents. These are highbrow 200-page monthly journals devoted to literature and available under limited subscription—a purely Soviet phenomenon. It should be added that prior to October 1917 there were no subscription ceilings. Under the Soviet regime such journals belonged completely and in full to writers and their central and local organizations. Reflecting on why a novel (short story, poem, etc.) had to be published first in a journal and later in book form, the only feasible answer that comes to mind is that it served the interests of our eternally half-starved writers themselves, who would thus receive royalties twice. It was also to readers' benefit, however—on occasion something actually deserving wider attention (for whatever reason) would emerge, and immediately catch the eyes of the intelligentsia, especially in outlying areas far removed from any significant cultural events, given the absence in this country of a normal book market. Ideological dictatorship of the CPSU dissolved into glasnost and subsequently a truly free press (in a free market, of course) it was not difficult to predict a decline in demand for the heavyweight literary journals. Publications dealing solely with literary criticism and helping the reader select from among the mass of works that will grace the shelves of the book shops of the future will appear and be in hot demand.

A good idea of the Soviet periodicals may be given by a long and tough article written by the Moscow author Nikolai Klimontovich, entitled "*The Danger for Literature*" and published in the American paper *Novoye Russkoye Slovo* on June 29, 1990:

> For the last 70 years people in Russia cry: "For the last 70 years people in Russia cry: "Our literature is in danger!" Pretexts for this have been appearing every day, but paradoxically enough it is today, when the Bolshevik empire has adopted for the first time the Law on the Press, that the collapse of the Russian literary process has become a flagrant reality. Literature has stopped and now it is no more.
>
> Such a result for the most participants in this process has probably proved to be unexpected. Meanwhile, three years back it was clear that the main literary trains of the Moscow thick journals had stopped on the track leading to a gulf.
>
> We remember the desperate shout of the Stalinist writer Pyotr Proskurin in *Pravda* at the address of the zealous publishers of the works by Nabokov and Pasternak: "Necrophiles!" Even his supporters of like mind dropped their eyes, whereas the liberal 'gendarmery' trampled the simpleton under foot in the same instant. Even today nothing is heard of him. Yet this can be interpreted not as a hardly appetizing excess but as a shrewd warning. The attempt undertaken three years ago to limit the subscription to periodicals seems to be a reasonable measure, but at the time a veritable popular revolution took place, in which 'everybody to whom the

fate of perestroika is dear' participated, being led by the unquenchable *Ogonyok*. However, it is now clear that while swearing and having a good time, being accompanied by the fanfare of trumpets and pipes, looking for ever new icons and stopping to glorify themselves for a bold overthrow of the hated censorship, the motley band of national literature set off not for the Promised Land, but, as always, for the Chevengur kingdom.

Passion for self-education. One of the first to demonstrate this passion was the moss-covered Mikhail Alexeyev, who until recently was the editor of the *Moskva* journal (incidentally, he published Bulgakov's "*The Master and Margarita*" with the aid of Simonov) and who read four years ago Nabokov's prewar novel "*Luzhin's Defense*". Perhaps he said on this point: "There is nothing anti-Soviet in the novel. Now it's possible to pull it." And "*Luzhin's Defense*" was printed. This seems to be a signal. We can only guess how the brains of the Editors-in-Chief of Moscow journals were being rammed during the years of servicing Brezhnev's court. Among these editors we find Ananyev (*Oktyabr*), Baruzdin (*Druzhba Narodov*), Dementyev (*Yunost*), Ivanov (*Molodaya Gvardiya*) and Vikulov (*Nash Sovremennik*). One thing is known to us: The journals' pages were now flooded with the fine literature of yesterday pouring from all crevices.

The 'liberals' mobilized by the Secretariat of the Union of Writers for rendering assistance to them, including Baklanov (*Znamya*) and Zalygin (*Novy Mir*), energetically joined the race. The editors snatched from each other Nabokov's novels they had read.

It gets more and more. Nabokov was only a touchstone, the censorship kept mum, which meant: "Enjoy yourselves, lads!" And the lads began snatching up any *samizdat* as we could see what happened in Voinovich's well-known episode near a rural shop when the war was declared, and gradually moving towards the brink, beyond which there were wares belonging to living owners. Having reprinted the most striking novels from Nabokov's legacy, they proceeded to squander what the Russian writers now living abroad had managed to write and get published.

Substitution in functions. The reader abides by the simple rule: give and take. It's difficult to buy new books and one may see the same "*Chevengur*", the works by Grossman, Nabokov and Dombrovsky taken from the magazine, bound an arranged on the book shelf. They comprise a whole home library. The thick journals that had assumed the publishing functions (the books they printed during the last years had been published abroad in Russian and the total reprinting of books by journals is without any precedent) had a large army of subscribers. Moreover, the subscription to all "necrophile" journals had increased many-fold.

The appetite of the readers provoked the publishers. The volume of print media continued to rise. Suffice it to say that the total print of *Novy Mir* exceeded the 3 million mark and this was unheard-of. It would be a different matter, if they published doctor's pieces of advice or culinary recipes. But we cannot say that this was the success of the journals. What matters is the satisfaction of the book hunger, and the journals made themselves the hostages of the shortage of books.

It's good that the journals had acquired new readers and a new circulation. But what did they lose? They lost all the rest, namely: the perspective.

In reality the tradition of Russian literature was as follows: the literary forces had always concentrated and crystallized around thick journals. The latter made up a vast kaleidoscope of everyday literary activities.

The famous magazines of the past—*Sovremennik, Otechestvennye Zapiski* or Katkov's *Russky Vestnik*--sought to rally around themselves as constellation of prominent journalists and writers and when they succeeded in this, they acted effectively in literary battles. Not so long ago, in the 1960s, our journals, from *Oktyabr* edited by Kochetov to *Yunost* edited by Katayev sought to attract public attention and traversed precisely the same path. New young contributors of like mind, brilliant individual writers attached to definite editions, created the necessary nimbus of literature in the eyes of the reader and the latter hunted for new works by Russian authors that were printed in definite journals. In a certain sense this has always been the Russian literary process, if we add to it effective aesthetic criticism and professionally managed publishing business. It would be much easier for Tvardovsky to fill in the pages of *Novy Mir* with unpublished works of Bunin, Shmelyov or Aldanov or to win back from censorship the stories by the late Platonov or Bulgakov, than to put his head under the axe and get in touch with the unpredictable author of "*One Day of Ivan Denisovich*". But Tvardovsky was a true publisher, a reckless, efficient and risky manager, and not a dividend recipient from archive publications. It must be noted here that the path of using archives leads to nowhere.

The fate of *Novy Mir*, the brainchild of Tvardovsky, that was seized by a mediocre, is an unnecessary illustration. For *Novy Mir* is no longer with us!

Of course, it is still registered in the list of subscribed editions. And its plate can be seen on the Pushkin Square. And its editors puff away at their cigarettes as before. And gloomy and downtrodden authors with beards and without them continue to camp on the doorstep of the journal. And the editorial office continues to deceive them diligently: leave your manuscript, we shall read it (of course, nobody will do this), a final decision has not yet been adopted (but in reality it has been adopted for good: the journal will never publish any of these authors). In other words, the overall situation outwardly does not change, but the journal no longer exists physically. Practically it is impossible to keep a copy in one's own hands. The subscribers have received only half the February printing. The March, April, May and June issues are not available. What sort of devilry is this? Who is guilty of this devilry?

The liberals of the editorial office, no doubt, see the KGB's hand behind this picture. The Editor-in-Chief Zalygin succeeded in getting the mandate for personal immortality after the heaviest battles waged by him in the dizzy upper strata with the use of the threat of throwing a Party card at the table. It was he who, being included into a Soviet delegation to visit China, pressed Gorbachev to the Great Wall: let us publish Solzhenitsyn! It was he who defeated Medvedev the obscurantist, responsible for Party propaganda. He revealed in his triumph at a meeting of the Secretariat of the Union of Writers, when Mikhalkov punched in his chest and cried that he had always been in favor of publishing "*The GULAG Archipelago*", while Verchenko, former KGB General and a secretary of the Union of Writers, promised to obtain paper for printing the complete works of Solzhenitsyn. He sent messengers across the Atlantic. Consequently he has become the holder of shares of the entire Russian literature (and may be world literature), when he got the exclusive rights to Solzhenitsyn's legacy on the Soviet territory. And now when the enemies have been defeated and the riff-raff has been sweeped aside, while Solzhenitsyn's books have been distributed for publication purposes among the issues of the journal for three years ahead, *Novy Mir* has turned out to be without paper. We know why this has happened. With the permission of the authorities the selfless fighter for truth Zalygin contrived to include in the April issue the work by Avtorkhanov. His motto is to do everything for Russia and then die.

Meanwhile it has never occurred to the editorial office workers that they themselves have ruined the journal by means of the endless reprinting of books published abroad long ago, by fully ignoring the real needs of our current literature, by pandering to the avid reader who wants to acquire *The GULAG Archipelago* and *In the First Circle*, and thus by the artificial increase of the journal's circulation up to three million copies.

To put it short, *Novy Mir* has gone up and overtaxed its strength by printing Solzhenitsyn's works.

Liberals of average abilities. Solzhenitsyn's works did not fall to the lot of all magazines. Some crumbs from the lordly table of *Novy Mir* fell to the share of other journals, but *Yunost*, *Znamya*, *Oktyabr* and *Volga* had to look for other reserves. But it is ridiculous to believe that these journals will provide themselves with their own contributors and will look for new authors, because their Editors-in-Chief lack the energy. Therefore, they embarked on the well-tried path: having printed books from the archives, they began to reprint *samizdat*, that is the books written by the authors living abroad and being in good health. The readers have seen on the pages of the journals the names of such authors as Aksenov, Voinovich, Sasha Sokolov, Dovlatov and even Limonov. For fairness' sake it must be said that the works of the two last authors have proved useful. For instance, Dovlatov's *Foreign Woman* has become a best-seller: the story was unknown in the country, while its author was only mentioned in the radioscripts of the Radio Liberty. Limonov's works also sounded fresh. And, of course, Sasha Sokolov. But Aksenov's *The Small Golden Piece of Iron*, *The Island of the Crimea* and even hilarious *Chonkin* by Voinovich proved to be the dishes heated up the day before yesterday. The same happened to Andrei Bitov's *Pushkin House* and to Fasil Iskander's chapters from his *Sandro from Chegem*. All these works had been printed abroad and widely circulated in the country. Therefore, they cannot be called 'recent publications'. It's difficult to say about the effect that was expected by the journals which printed these works with a delay of ten to fifteen years. They could only count on the good name of liberal editions or on a small row. But nothing happened, and all these shots proved to be blank.

Meanwhile the slowed down literary process in the country has stopped altogether. The paradox of the situation was also redoubled by the fact that literary criticism had quit the journals, being ousted by political and economic publicism. The danger to literature came from those magazines on which the readers had recently pinned their hopes. The conservative tastes of the writers of the 1960s like Lakshin, who assisted Baklanov in *Znamya* (under Tvardovsky he was one of the leading critics in *Novy Mir*) and ruined the journal for the second time, Zalygin or the Komsomol poet Dementyev from *Yunost*, their full inability to engage in creative publishing activity and their striving to compensate their inconsistency by printing *samizdat* of their youth days, and the strong politization of these editions--all this has put up a powerful dam on the way of the new literature of today, with which no Brezhnev's censorship could compare.

Conservatives in opposition. Strange though it may seem, the 'conservative', 'soil' journals, such as *Nash Sovremennik* and *Molodaya Gvardiya*, have held up on the rails of the current literary process in an attempt to use the form given to them by 'liberal magazines'. Each issue contains circumstantial critical reviews, chiefly using the abusive language against the left cosmopolitan editions and the glorification of their idols and prophets led by Vasily Belov and Valentin Rasputin. Refusing to publish the works by Kestler or Orwell, to reprint the books of the American Ardis or the West German Posev publishing houses, the 'soilers' are forced to look for national poetry and prose and thereby to rally the literary camp of the seekers of patriotic and popular values and denunciators of 'Russophobians'. How much they succeeded in this organization is evident from the well-known plenary meeting of the writers of Russia. Yet the quality of their literary production leaves much to be desired, to put it mildly. According to an apt expression uttered in the Central House of Writers the authors fight for the right to write badly and in this sphere the contributors of these journals, 'the rocks', as they like to call themselves, may not fear the competition. The experienced readers of the times of Kochetov's or Ivan Shevtsov's novels did not have for a long time to digest something similar to delirium in Belov's novel *Everything in Store* or the late senile prose of Bondarev, who is very active today.

But let us show objectivity: several names emerge among the young and consistent authors of this wing of our national literature. No doubt, Lichutin's works are good as are also several wonderful stories by Vladimir Krupin, who has become the Editor-in-Chief of the magazine *Moskva*. Among the more young writers we can single out Pyotr Palamarchuk, who wrote the story *Derzhavin* about the last days of this great Russian poet. We cannot deny to Kozhinov his competence in literary criticism, although sometimes he sticks to obscurantist positions.

What matters is the fact that the literary process on the 'right' flank is gasping and glimmering and this intensifies disorder and stagnation from the left.

This 'liberal conspiracy' on the part of the thick journals against today's living literature is broken through on rare and sporadic occasions.

Logical also is the fact that Literaturnaya Gazeta is losing its readers. The weekly *Literaturnaya Gazeta* has 16 pages, the first 8 of which are devoted to the purely internal affairs of the USSR Writers' Union, its publisher and founder. Home and foreign news reports are more detailed and written in less turgid language than in the dailies, often with human-interest stories.

Ogonyok, Znamya and *Literaturnaya Gazeta* have won their reputations against the background of a throng of purely Party papers and magazines (although, of course, until 1989 they also received their orders from the same Party mandarins in the Central Committee's ideology department). In Brezhnev's day, and during the first years of perestroika up to 1989, these publications, the flagship of them being *Novy Mir* (and in more recent years *Moscow News*), were allowed by the authorities only so that they could then show the West the successes of "detente", the "new thinking" and "perestroika" and various other surrogate democratic freedoms.

On September 14, 1990 the staff of *Ogonyok* received their registration certificate, naming them as the magazine's founders. Their battle against the giant *Pravda* publishing concern (belonging, like all publishers until August 22, 1991, to the CPSU Central Committee, and not to be confused with the eponymous newspaper) was prolonged and tense right to the end. For example, on September 3, 1990 at the Central Committee's ideology department they were informed that the publishers' director, Vyacheslav Leontyev, had been instructed by the State Committee for Printing to rescind all claims to the magazine. However, even by September 11 no written confirmation that they were pulling out had been received.

After this *Ogonyok*, on the basis of article 14 of the Law on the Press, sued the Committee at a Moscow district court for its failure to observe the one-month time limit for registration, and published a photocopy of the writ in its next issue.

On September 12 Leontyev sent to the State Committee for Printing confirmation that his publishing house had no claim to founders' rights, and on September 13 *Ogonyok* was duly registered in the name of its editorial staff.

The magazine submitted to the publishers for consideration the draft of a new agreement, drawn up by independent lawyers.

This long-awaited freedom was celebrated at *Ogonyok* with 4 bottles of champagne for 100 invited guests.

Later that year the International Editor of the Year Prize of the US monthly *World Press Review* was awarded to Vitaly Korotich, editor-in-chief of Ogonyok, in the UN headquarters in New York.

Is it not absurd and sad that Vitaly Korotich, our famous author, *Ogonyok* chief editor and People's Deputy of the USSR, was compelled to issue his 180-page "*Waiting-Room*" (in Russian) in New York instead of Moscow? It goes without saying that this did not affect the quality of the book which was published by American "Liberty" Publishers. True, it is rather costly and thus hardly accessible for us. The *Nezavisimaya Gazeta* carried an excerpt from this book (June 5, 1991) under the title "*I've Never Feared Gorbachev*"—an instructive essay on Soviet ideological life:

> I've never feared him, even when he yelled at me, because it has never been the yell of a cruel and powerful man. I always tried to understand what was behind the yell and why he should yell at that particular moment according to the scenario.
> Once he shouted at me in his office, on February 2, 1988 between 1 and 3 p.m. in the presence of Frolov who was a Gorbachev aide at the time, and A. Yakovlev. I had no idea about Frolov's attitude to me, nor did I care. But Yakovlev's attitude has always been an important indicator to me, as the man's intelligence and integrity were beyond question. The first thing I did as I entered Gorbachev's office on the fifth floor of the Central Committee building, was to glance at Yakovlev. But he didn't

return my glance because he and Frolov were looking at Gorbachev and waiting for him to speak.

Gorbachev swore. I have always taken men's swearing calmly. I was not impressed with the past-masters of foul language in the belief that a person may give vent to his emotions as he sees fit. However it was the first time I saw the head of my own state cursing like a stevedore. I was not dumbfounded but I startled. Possibly, that was the purpose of Gorbachev's introduction—to strike me dumb. Suddenly—and very keenly—I realized that the man was pretending to be a churl but in real fact he was polite and that the talk with me was a part of something more important than I could fathom.

Gorbachev banged his fist on a thick file lying on his desk and reverted to a more civilized.

"What did you drivel in Leningrad about the USSR Defense Minister? In this file I have a shorthand record interpreted for me. The man's honestly working at the most difficult sector and you are attacking him for no good reason..."

Two days earlier poet Yevtushenko and I appeared in Leningrad's vast Yubileiny palace. In answer to the question about my reaction to Defense Minister Yazov's statement, who had cast aspersions on me and *Ogonyok*, I said something like this: "I hope that before long our army will be rid of the biggest missiles and the biggest fools. This'll do it nothing but good." That was taken down in shorthand, interpreted and reported to the head of state—and how quickly!

Gorbachev went on, almost making no pauses:

"Who are you with? In what team are you? Do you imagine you're the perestroika leader?"

"Why, no! I am in your team," I replied.

I was on a more familiar ground now—the country's first person always these and thus everybody, irrespective of age and the degree of intimacy.

"There you are!"—said Gorbachev. "Alexander here is defending you but I don't know if I should believe him or not..."

I didn't realize at first that Alexander stood for Yakovlev. When I did I looked in his direction and saw his smiling, intelligent face. So it wasn't that bad. Frolov sat next to me on the same left side of Gorbachev's desk. He kept silent and I had no way of knowing what he was after. I glanced up at the smiling Yakovlev and looked aside, because Gorbachev started shouting again:

"What do you have against Ligachev and Chebrikov? I work with them and I know better what kind of people they are. Are you going to teach me who's my friend and who's an enemy?! Ligachev's been 17 years on the Central Committee and you'll teach me, what?"

"No," I said, "I won't teach you."

"Now you are talking," Gorbachev summed up and pushed up one of the two saucers with cocktail sandwiches to me. "I have no time for dinner, this is my dinner. Have some!"

I took one sandwich. I didn't like it. Moreover, I had the impression, which was intensifying, that this wasn't for real, but I couldn't make out what it was all about. Gorbachev was talking in a loud voice and distinctly articulating words as if he were in a recording studio and he had to polish his monologues without heeding the cues of the other actors in a play. After a pause he expounded his thoughts on the need for transformations in the country and how important it was for those backing him not to make hasty and rash steps. He did so for a long time, as was his wont. His speech was quite literary again, even with a tinge of oratory. Only his face had not changed—the same intense, kind and very tired man preoccupied with important matters. As he talked, he modulated his voice and varied his intonation, got up and approached his desk, pronouncing words loudly and very distinctly.

Our conversation lasted long. We discussed the alignment of forces in the country, the position of the intelligentsia and its difficulties. Wishing to throw Gorbachev out of time and unsettle him in order to better understand what was going on, I said:

"The intelligentsia has recognized you as the leader. There are no offending anecdotes about you. And who makes up anecdotes? Exclusively vicious intellectuals..."

"It's a lie," said Gorbachev with a clear articulation. "Want me to tell you one? There's a line for vodka and the last guy in the line says: 'I can't stand anymore. What a shame! I'll go to Gorbachev and hit his muzzle for such orders!' He was absent for a long time. At last he returned. 'Well,' those standing in line rushed to him, 'did you hit him?' 'No, there's an even bigger line there'..."

"Who tells you such things?"—I asked.

"Some people do," Gorbachev drawled and all of a sudden he worked himself in to a frenzy and cried, reverting to the earlier adopted lexicon and temperament:

"Do you think those who were in power before are all enemies? You can't stomach Ligachev and Chebrikov, but we all used to lick Brezhnev's ass. All of us! It was in the past, and today we must unite all who are for perestroika. Don't forget we are members of the same party and each who is with us today must remain with us!"

I helped myself to another sausage sandwich, got up and thanked him.

"Alexander will see you off," said Gorbachev and Yakovlev went with me, limping a bit. Frolov, who never said a word, nodded farewell to me.

"Is it clear to you that he stood by you," Yakovlev told me when we were in a small lobby separating the first and the second door of Gorbachev's office. "Is it clear?"

Nothing was really clear to me. Later I hated admitting to myself that the head of our state, the man I respected sincerely and profoundly, had to recite for the public to placate his powerful opponents and demonstrate to them that he held those bloody liberals in his fist.

No, I couldn't take that.

It could be just a figment of my imagination running wild. I guess it wasn't that. Our conversation simply took such a turn.

Anyway, I have never taken this man's actions at face value, wondering at the accuracy of his combinations. Like a grand-master, he contrived many moves ahead and effected them on the brink of the impossible. He is paying, and will pay, with his own immortal soul for many things. However, we have been able to advance and Eastern Europe has acquired freedom precisely because he has proved to be a good and sensible strategist in a society not trained to think in realistic terms. Surrounded on all sides by the old party guard, stool pigeon and martinets, he has been constantly devising how to advance without antagonizing them. He has been acting as if to say:

here I am with you and I am holding all those pen-pushers—reformers—in my party fist.

I well remember another meeting in the personnel department on the same fifth floor where Gorbachev's office is. It was an enigmatic meeting which began at noon, when he again yelled not so much at me as to me, and not just at me. And again I had no fear of him. Nor did the others even though he tried hard to accentuate the image of a stern leader. I couldn't get rid of the sensation of unreality and see through Gorbachev's long-range design.

To begin with, he didn't look his own self: gloomy and with knitted brows. For a start he said how important it was to synchronize our watches in the struggle for the common cause.

The common cause, indeed... I can't believe that Gorbachev had no way of knowing that he and his opponents did not share any common cause. But he kept on invoking it and I felt that, like in a good play, there must be the second, hidden and crucial meaning beyond the upper layer of the theses which were neat to the point of banality.

Each year, nay, month of his tenure has seen his Komsomol plush-like ways and affected exaltation going. In their place his anguish surged forth, rendering Gorbachev tough. He, it seemed, felt like a big-time athlete thinking out how to advance as far as possible. Thus, the halfback in American football is tearing at full speed knowing in advance that he'll be halted by the rival back and maybe even knock down...

Then, on October 13 Gorbachev was yelling at us. He charged the media with irresponsibility, leftist excesses and lip service to the party cause. Then he started shouting at Starkov, chief editor of the already popular but not yet renowned paper *Argumenty i Fakty*, whom he spotted in the auditorium. I remember the dead silence and amidst it Gorbachev, his glasses in a thin frame glistening, pointing an accusing finger at Starkov and saying that if he were in Starkov's shoes, he'd tender his resignation and leave.

The spark that set the forest on fire was the statistics published in the newspaper. According to it, Gorbachev hasn't always topped the popularity list, while Ligachev has been somewhere at the bottom. Gorbachev was raging against the editor as if he had divulged the secret of bomb making or something on which our might hinged.

Gorbachev was yelling but I didn't fear him, I was sorry for the yelling leader. I cast a glance at Yakovlev, with whom we were on good terms, and on Medvedev whom I didn't stand and it was mutual. The central committee secretaries were impassive as if they were watching a match over TV whose outcome they already knew.

Gorbachev was on a talking spree. He regretted the fact that the US Secretary of State, Baker, was more optimistic about perestroika than the Soviet economist Shmelev. He scolded another economist, Popov, and demanded that the editors follow the party course strictly. He spoke sternly like a teacher who had just been assigned to the most unruly class in the school. The politburo members turned to stone.

Gorbachev broke off almost like Khrushchev who had promised to give it to us hot, and rose up—unsmiling and grim. I came up to him. Our eyes met and suddenly I saw a different man. That man, outwardly looking like Gorbachev, sideways like a crab, edged himself through the presidium and, poking his finger at me, cried:

"You haven't kept your word, you haven't! You're still indulging in literary disputes and bickering!"

That was indeed very strange. I was bickering with chauvinistic monthlies like *Molodaya Gvardya* or *Nash Sovremennik*. But in doing so, I tried to defend Gorbachev and the theses he enthusiastically put forward from time to time. After all, it is not so much me as Gorbachev that the chauvinists attacked, clamoring that the leaders are selling the country (mostly to Jews) and socialism (I wonder, who'd buy it). But then central committee secretary Medvedev described the view permeating the quasi-patriotic publications as pluralistic, and attempts to rebuff it as the fanning of passions in society. Another central committee secretary, Ligachev, has seen to it that arch-patriots would be regularly decorated with orders and medals by the grateful Fatherland. But why should Gorbachev pose as their advocate?

The perestroika leader edging himself through the door and angrily poking his finger at me, was the last impression I have of the October conference in the Central Committee (it was really the last impression for after he was elected President, Gorbachev suspended such meetings).

I looked round. Never before had I seen the old-regime editors's mugs beaming so smugly—all those Alexeyevs, Gribachevs, etc.—their name is legion. They were grinning from ear to ear, spread their shoulders and were gazing at me victoriously. I couldn't so much as return a stare for stare.

I went for lunch with the *Krokodil* editor Pyanov. We tried to sort things out and guess whence that aimed volley had been fired at us, who were 'ours'. But perhaps now Gorbachev had confused the notions 'ours' and 'theirs'. That was not very likely, but still...

Next morning I felt dead sure I'd be summoned to the personnel department. In the USSR, there are rituals for everything. The central committee, for one, exists for interpreting for us mortals the lofty thoughts of leaders. I squinted my eyes at the telephone with the coat-of-arms on the dial (it connected me with the government), but the telephone was dead. Later *Argumenty i Fakty* editor Starkov said he was expecting a call too and his nerves were on edge. He received a call from a party boss who told him, Starkov, to relax and work calmly. That was something the frustrated editor expected least of all.

Right after noon my telephone rang too. A friend of mine from *Pravda* was awfully excited. "Our chief Afanasyev's been relieved of his duties!"—he said breathlessly. Twenty four hours later the East German dictator Honecker resigned.

The 'explanatory' conference in the central committee never took place. There have been no conferences at all since then. We have been summoned there occasionally—separately. Once I was invited by Medvedev. I gasped with surprise when I saw biscuits, a coffee-pot and small coffee cups on his desk in the office.

"Help yourself", the Central Committee secretary said. Leafing through the latest number of *Ogonyok*, he added after a pause: "Vitaly Alexeyevich, reading your magazine people stop believing in socialism."

I crunched a biscuit, sipped my coffee and answered:

"People going to your shops stop believing in socialism."

"This talk will lead us nowhere," Medvedev said.

I was under the same impression.

On August 28, 1991, *Izvestia* reported that Vitaly Korotich was no longer *Ogonyok* chief editor. His first deputy, Lev Gushchin, succeeded him: he was elected to this post by the staff. On the eve of the event Korotich faxed a letter from New York requesting resignation. The motives were his failing health and his intention to devote himself to lecturing in US universities. At the *Ogonyok* general meeting Lev Gushchin said that the magazine would continue its course to the left of the center.

Gushchin will not go down in history as an active fighter of the citadel of Stalinism and the GULAG, but Vitaly Korotich will. This man from Kiev who has had a brilliant career in Moscow is well known across the ocean. And consequently, he is presented not only with flowers during his public appearances. The emigre Russian-language newspaper *Novoye Russkoye Slovo* twice (issues of April 7 and June 2, 1991) cited Korotich as saying that Gorbachev has no other sins other than the fact that the "he studies the works of Brezhnev." According to Korotich, the leaders of the KGB should be trusted and supported because the KGB chief Kryuchkov "is a man who believes in Gorbachev and supports him."

To understand the phenomenon of Korotich, the Soviet democratic press and Soviet political life in general, we should again read what the ex-chief of *Ogonyok* said in an interview to Yevgeny Dodolev, published in *Moskovsky Komsomolets* (September 21, 1991) under the headline, "The Sad Attempts of Vitaly Korotich. Requiem for the Young Men of the 1960s?".

> "I would not like to give you a forwarding address. From time to time everybody should have a desire to change his or her life dramatically," Vitaly Korotich smiled. "I changed my profession several times, consciously and dramatically. In 1965, after working as a doctor for six years, I became a full-time writer, discarding my dissertation. I was a freelancer and editor...
>
> "*Ogonyok* was another sharp turn in my biography. From the very beginning of my work in the magazine I saw its future boundaries. The past few years have marked the finishing line, the end of an era, which my generation began in the 1960s, thirty years ago. It's funny that my generation still regards itself as the salt of the earth, the core of a universe that occupies one sixth of the world's dry land. And the young people of the 1960s are still bearing on their shoulders the cause called Perestroika, like tired atlantes.
>
> "When I was offered a good contract in the USA, I thought the proposal over for a very long time. But I am not leaving for good. In December I want to hold a conference in Moscow under the tentative name "End of the Era of Enmity." The era of enmity engendered by the ideology of communism is over; it gave way to the era of enmity induced by nationalism and religious conflicts.
>
> **Question:** You probably know the Lefevre theory, whereby Western society is based on the idea of compromise, while Soviet society is based on the idea of confrontation. It is profitable to be in confrontation here. Yeltsin, TV

program Vzglyad and *Ogonyok* all scored points on that very confrontation.

Answer: After the bonds of discipline were removed from this country, born of enmity, it produced unprecedented streams of enmity. This proves the theory whereby three totalitarian empires appeared in the world over the past 100 years—Germany, Japan and Russia. These structures presented a serious threat to humanity. Two of them were reformed with the help of foreign investment.

Question: Will your December conference become another attempt to squeeze from the West more money for our expiring economy?

Answer: Unless Russia abandons its attempts to carry out reforms single-handed, it is doomed. I came to an agreement with Henry Kissinger and Helmut Schmidt that the conference will be held in Moscow on December 15-17, whatever happens. I discussed this question with Sobchak, Popov and Yakovlev.

Question: Couldn't you do the same while living here?

Answer: Nobody offered me anything here. I think that perestroika represents the sad attempt of the Soviet Union to rediscover the norms. What I am doing is only a sad attempt to lead a normal life. Usually, I am not understood. It was quite normal that I dropped the medical profession, although I was a qualified specialist, I think. The current situation is comparable. I headed a respectable magazine; the bird in the hand is better than two in the bush, as they say.

When I was editor-in-chief, many people asked me indignantly, "What do you need this for? Why do you stick out?" Now they ask, "Why are you leaving?" I am leaving because I want to work in normal conditions. In this country nobody wants anything. Take my book, for example. Not a single publishing house wanted to print it here (a cooperative company undertook to publish it, but then thought better of the idea, although they had already paid me some money in advance). The Americans have already published it! What should I do, call Soviet universities and offer my services, remembering that I am a representative of the second oldest profession? Why should I do this if the magazine's fax pumped throughout the past year printing offers from across the ocean?

Question: In the magazine's "oral items" you often addressed young people. What can you say about the difference between the Soviet and the American audiences?

Answer: Our people are more realistic than Americans. Not long ago I was in Aberlin College. The people asked me, "How can you abandon the wonderful ideas of Marxism-Leninism? How can you turn away from the legacy of Lenin? Why is your country destroying the powerful system created by generations of people?" This is what interests the well-fed and well-clad American students who never tasted the fruits of this system. Perhaps it would be good if I spoke to our students. I may be wrong, but I believe that our students are less politically-minded than their American counterparts: they are tired and do not look like the students of the era of great reforms.

Question: **This country is an example of a society without a system of coordinates, either religious or state-imposed. Do you feel this gap when you deal with young people?**

Answer: Yes, our young people are kind of wild. They might know the dates of party congresses by heart, but they have no notion of elementary things. All the current attempts to revive religion look like profanity to me. In the Ukraine young people are arguing on whether to become Catholics or simply Christians.

I do, however, believe in our young people. They did not absorb the gallant example of Pavlik Morozov. When I came to *Ogonyok*, its personnel comprised mostly middle-aged men and seniors older than me. I then decided to choose young people, the younger the better. I resigned because I was afraid of impeding the new wave of *Ogonyok* journalists. Not long ago I gave an interview to the Moscow correspondent of the *Los Angeles Times*. She is around thirty. Can you imagine a Soviet correspondent of her age in the capital of the largest Western state? A rhetorical question, of course. We must give way to young people. The young people of the 1960s should remain as their mentors, but they will not be able to become the catalyst of this onward-moving train. This also concerns *Ogonyok*: the magazine must be overhauled.

Question: **In this case you remind me of a captain who is the first to leave his sinking ship.**

Answer: No, *Ogonyok* will remain afloat. But it must change course. We began by fighting on behalf of the general tenets of democracy. If I published an article about a general building a dacha for himself with his department's money, or about rampant corruption in the upper echelons of the Communist Party Central Committee, I would lose my readers. That's for starters. Second, today there is no such notion as the Soviet reader. The Baltics have left, and the Caucasian republics are leaving. Today Ogonyok should become a Russian magazine.

Question: **Your resignation seems strange because it is not considered normal in this country to resign from high posts voluntarily.**

Answer: Indeed. Take the Kremlin, which there was only one exit from, to the cemetery. Apart from the toppled Khrushchev, all other leaders left their Kremlin throne for the better world. But I decided to leave *Ogonyok* because I understood that in several years I will be liked less, so to speak. Last year I was happy to hear the Mexican President tell me that in his country you cannot be President for more than six years. The limit in the USA is two terms of four years each. All medical postulates say that six or seven years of exhausting work is the human limit. This is the first. Second, in another six years you get bogged down in the net of stereotypes, and consequently lose flexibility.

Question: **Do you mean Gorbachev when you talk about the six-year limit? He's been in power since the spring of 1985.**

Answer: Yes, I think that everybody should leave: Gorbachev, Yeltsin, Shevardnadze, Yakovlev. They should remain, but not in the leading roles.

Question: **When did you last talk with the President?**

Answer: Long ago, when Sakharov died. After that Gorbachev started distancing himself from us all. His political resources were spent. I know few people who Gorbachev has deigned to talk to of late. He was separated from the world by his team.

Question: **Which members of the State of Emergency Committee did you know well?**

Answer: I once dreamed of interviewing CIA director Webster and KGB chairman Kryuchkov simultaneously. I bombarded them with letters, but could not get them to agree to give an interview to me simultaneously. But I have met Kryuchkov. He reprimanded me very harshly twice.

He summoned me to his office and told me than he was talking on behalf of Mikhail Sergeyevich. The first time he claimed that I was friendly with too many foreign diplomats. I tried to convince him that I did not know any state secrets. But Kryuchkov was adamant: all foreign ambassadors are bad guys. He uttered a telling phrase that time. "Tell me," exclaimed the chief of our secret police, "why doesn't the liberal intelligentsia want to work with us? Why do we have better relations with US intelligence than with our own intelligentsia?"

The other time we talked he said, looking closely at me: "You understand that you are pushing me into a situation where more people would suffer than in the repressions of the 1920s?" He implied that hard labor camps were awaiting us all. And then there were reprimands concerning the Gdlyan-Ivanov case. You probably remember that *Ogonyok* defended these two investigators. Kryuchkov came down on me very heavily then.

Question: **And Yanayev?**

Answer: I am usually quiet as a mouse during Supreme Soviet sessions. But last December was an exception. Shevardnadze resigned, Vzglyad was closed down, and it was clear that something was going to happen. When Yanayev was suggested as a Vice-presidential candidate, I was totally stunned. I ran around gathering signatures against his election. I recall that when I went to the ballot box, I saw Yanayev standing at it. Honestly, I crossed his name out in front of him.

Question: **Oleg Kalugin once told me in an interview that you refused to publish his first revelations, and that it was Yakovlev who told you to turn him down. It this true?**

Answer: You see, Yakovlev and Kalugin studied in the University of Columbia in the 1950s. At the beginning, some people believed that Kalugin acted at Yakovlev's prompting. Yakovlev was accused of encouraging his old pal to blow up the KGB. At the same time, there were quite a few people in the upper echelons of power who wanted to compromise Yakovlev. I was afraid that if I published Kalugin's revelations I would harm Yakovlev. The general was not eager to reveal the secrets of the power struggle in the KGB. If Kalugin put on my table some clear-cut proof of the evil deeds of the KGB, I would have convinced Yakovlev that *Ogonyok* should publish Kalugin. But Kalugin restricted himself to some general accusations of the organization which had made him a general. I remember how I drove Yulian Semenov crazy by asking him which atrocities Stirlitz, the Soviet spy in Semenov's novel, should have committed to become a colonel in the German secret police under Hitler? The same question could be asked of Kalugin: What did he do to become a general when a comparatively young man?

Question: That might be a state secret. As far as I know, Oleg Danilovich has had enough trouble for his revelation of secrets. I can understand that you tried to keep as far from Yakovlev as possible in order to protect him. Did he sponsor you for your tact and understanding of the situation?

Answer: He greatly helped my magazine. Thanks to his assistance, *Ogonyok* was able to maintain its neutrality, swinging back and forth between the hammer and the anvil. We did not allow ourselves to be drawn into the anti-Yeltsin campaign. On the other hand, when Yumashev, head of the letter department, ghost-wrote Yeltsin's book, we did not publish anti-Gorbachev excerpts from it. I am not sure that the magazine will keep its neutral position now.

Ogonyok has published a multitude of absorbing features which left no stone unturned from our Leninists, militarists, Cheka men and other dangerous characters. Take the interview with former dissident Vladimir Bukovsky (*Ogonyok* No. 18, April 1991). In the USSR this man spent 12 years in psychiatric hospitals, jails and prison camps. He would have died there if some people had not advised Pinochet and Brezhnev to exchange this 'loony' for Luis Corvalan, the great friend of the USSR and the general secretary of the Chilean communist party. Fourteen years have elapsed since that time, but the verdicts meted out to Bukovsky have not been revoked, nor have the ridiculous charges lifted, nor citizenship returned. Thanks to Yeltsin and the British government, he was reluctantly granted a 5-day stay in the USSR. Bukovsky has met and talked with the leaders of practically all major countries of the world.

For a title *Ogonyok* used Bukovsky's words: "As long as you have no courage, you'll have no sausage." General strike as the sole chance to avoid hunger and bloodshed, the dismantling of the CPSU and the KGB, a guarantee of peaceful life for all, and voluntary renunciation of the empire's "superfluous" territories—such was the range of advice of that well-known physiologist and public figure and a confirmed anti-communist. That was what happened in August 1991, when Muscovites took to the streets and sealed the CPSU-owned buildings and "disturbed" the Cheka men.

With such authors and such a chief editor *Ogonyok* was destined to a sovereign (from the CPSU) existence one year back.

Of course, the controversies involving *Ogonyok, Literaturnaya Gazeta,* and the *Znamya* journal, among others have all ended happily. However, no one knew that in August of 1990.

A conflict seemed also likely to erupt over the registration of the *Yunost* and *Neva* magazines, to which the same bureaucrats from the Writers Union lay claims. Indeed, no one could ever accuse its staff secretaries of liberalism. Admittedly, none of them has ever become classics, but there is one thing in which they have outdone all of the world's modern classics put together: the huge press-runs of their own nauseatingly boring and ideologically perfect works done in the Stalinist-Brezhnevist style. As the secretaries had everything to lose, the grip of their stiffening hands was deadly, the more so that they had no dearth of high-placed backers who played their cards so that the controversy would drag on, which was to their advantage for many reasons. In this unsophisticated way, the upcoming subscription was being put at risk. Indeed, who would choose to pay in advance two or three times the usual rate for a magazine that may not come out at all,

It is "secretaries' literature" that litters the shops, book depositories, and publishing houses. In the thick literary journals, words of praise for the "guiding" men of letters and their cohorts was not very noticeable amid the mass of new works by talented writers.

On January 9, 1991 the authoritative *Literaturnaya Gazeta* headlined an article "*The journal boom is over*", something that has become evident. The reference, of course, is to our heavyweight literary journals. They have become pricey, are irregularly delivered to subscribers, and have difficulty finding printing facilities. And in any case the days when the choice of literature was forced upon us are receding into the past. Current-affairs and political writings should, and already have, move to respectable and (partially) independent newspapers, while deserving works of literature should come out as separate books so that the reading public can vote with the ruble, ie., buy and read them. Why should I buy an issue of a journal in a kiosk, or even subscribe to it for a year, simply in order to enjoy what little there is inside that is worth reading, or that I want to read? Merab Mamardashvili, one of our renowned unpublished philosophers, was buried in Tbilisi in November 1990. And the very next month the journal *Znaniye—Sila* (Knowledge is Strength) printed one of his last works, "Calling things by their true names", on ethnic relations. But his books, articles and interviews are yet to appear in Russia.

In legal terms, *Literaturnaya Gazeta,* the literary journals *Znamya, Novy Mir, Yunost, Druzhba Narodov, Oktyabr,* and *Inostrannaya Literatura* have stopped being "all-Union" publications; they are now under Russian Federation jurisdiction. All of them are registered with the Ministry for the Press and Information of the Russian Federation as publications independent of the

Soviet Writers' Union. Defending its status as founder of a number of Lithuanian papers, the Communist Party Central Committee used army units in an attempt to keep control of the Party printing facilities. As the Soviet Writers' Union has no army of its own, it took court action against the *Znamya* journal, *Goskompechat*, and the Ministry for the Press and Information of the Russian Federation. The plaintiff was a First Secretary of the Writers' Union Board, V. Karpov, who demanded the following: first, that the registration of the journal as independent by the Russian Federation ministry be ruled illegal; second, that Goskompechat register *Znamya* as an organ of the Writers' Union; and third, that "the bank accounts opened by *Znamya* be frozen pending the court ruling."

The law-suit was filed with the Moscow City Court in late September, 1990. The plaintiff was even ready to prevent the publication of the journal. It is anyone's guess what the Writers' Union, "left out in the cold" all of a sudden, will achieve following months of litigation. Logically, the final outcome should have a bearing on the future of the Soviet press as a whole and, indeed, on the climate in the Writers' Union itself. To a certain extent, I would go along with Karpov's demand to close down the *Znamya* journal. Indeed, we don't have surplus paper. A literary monthly coming out in 100,000 or even million copies under a fixed annual plan equalizes the degree of publicity received by each contributor. Surely, no one reads all the ten literary monthlies from cover to cover. The *Oktyabr* journal was in demand in 1991 because it was publishing the memoirs by General Denikin. But then, the memoirs of one of the famous generals who led their armies against the Bolsheviks in the Civil War which followed the 1917 Revolution account for just a small portion of the journal's annual volume. For example, in 1990 it offered its readers long excerpts from Boris Yeltsin's "*Confession on the Given Subject*" (it was published in Great Britain under the title "*Against the Grain*"), alongside dozens of other authors I am not interested in.

For the time being, though, one would be better-advised to read the free *Literaturnaya Gazeta*, *Oktyabr*, *Yunost* and *Inostrannaya Literatura* and take pleasure in what is offered by *Novy Mir* than to have nothing besides *Pravda* and *Izvestia* and buy books at inflated black market prices. Looks like even the journal *Literaturnaya Uchoba* (Literary Education) may well become an attractive buy thanks to *The Gospels* it is publishing. Its monthly circulation is up from 25,000 to 900,000 copies.

How *Literaturnaya Gazeta* Passed Away

As it was already mentioned, *Literaturnaya Gazeta* traditionally devoted eight of its 16 pages to literary criticism and writers' life. The rest of the paper was prepared under the watchful eye of senior Party apparatchiks. The quirks and severe nature of ideological censorship were compounded by constant intrigues between various groups of the more than 12,000-strong body of Soviet writers, half of them old-age pensioners. So, *Literaturnaya Gazeta*, in double dependence and considerably faded over the perestroika years, happened to have no way to survive other than get rid of the dictatorial writ exercised by the ideological departments of the Party Central Committee and the Secretaries of the Writers' Union Board. Following unsuccessful attempts to crush the defenses put up by Goskompechat, the newspaper still managed to win the battle and have itself registered—albeit not by a central body, under the auspices of Gorbachev and Ryzhkov, but by a Russian Federation body, under the wing of Yeltsin and Silayev. It would be interesting to learn how it all happened from the original source, the anonymous editorial in *Literaturnaya Gazeta* (Sept. 18, 1990) titled *"Free Forum for Writers. The Necessary Explanation to the Readers"*:

> Today moves are afoot to lead the writers' community to believe that *Literaturnaya Gazeta* has been "stolen, kidnapped" and that in becoming free and independent it "parts company" with the writers. The time is ripe for an open explanation and a candid answer to the question of who *Literaturnaya Gazeta* is about to abandon and where it goes.
>
> This brings us to look at its history. It came into being in 1929 as Writers' Forum, but shortly afterwards a series of arbitrary decisions placed it under the control of arbitrary decisions placed it under the control of the salaried bureaucrats who ran the Soviet Writers' Union formed in 1934. A detailed account of the implications is hardly worthwhile. All manner of purges and dressings-down, harassment of the best writers who were the pride of national culture, and the heaping of unjustified praise on the so-called "secretaries'" and other time-serving literature, among many other tragic and disgraceful practices are all on the conscience of the Writers' Union bureaucracy and the publications it controlled, something we are sorry and ashamed to confess. It is only the current wind of change in Soviet society that offers a chance to shake off the fetters clamped on by the bureaucrats and gain freedom and independence, which has been the dream of two or three generations of upright writers and *Literaturnaya Gazeta* workers.
>
> For decades the Writers' Union bureaucracy has zealously upheld the interests of the totalitarian state, unswervingly enforcing its policy in the sphere of literary endeavor and demanding unflagging compliance from all publications under its control. Today it's painful to remember how many pages of *Literaturnaya Gazeta* have been marred by scathing articles about literary "renegades", reports on political trials of dissident writers, and disgraceful eulogies to those who managed to join the league of "modern classics" thanks to someone's ambition and self-interest. In fact, the whole point of directing the literary process in the country was to ensure that writers felt constantly watched by the higher political supervisor and guided by a strong hand lying on their shoulder to warn against "wrong moves."
>
> That said, it's no wonder that even the first years of the reform effort, which melted the ice-like "monolithic unity" of the writers' ranks, laid bare the long-suppressed differences of opinion, giving rise to conflicting attitudes to current issues. Polarized views were clearly in evidence not only in the Writers' Union but

also in literary publications, which, in the best traditions of world journalism, began to rally and rely on forces expressing and reflecting the objective differences of opinion on the processes taking place in society and ethical preferences.

Like all other papers, and indeed the country as a whole, we are bracing ourselves up for work in a market environment. It is a matter of certainty that our profits will not be the same, what with the higher cost of paper, printers' services and delivery, and a possible drop in subscription. We will have to count every ruble rather than millions as previously. If we are to keep *Literaturnaya Gazeta* going, we must do the counting ourselves. The Law on the Press gives us this right.

Having become the de jure founder under this legislation, we *Literaturnaya Gazeta* staff gain the status of a legal entity -- for the first time since the newspaper began more than 60 years ago. For the first time ever, we will have our own settlement account in a bank, and subscription fees will go right there. Our incomes will no longer be end up within vaguely-defined jurisdiction, and items of expenditure will be clearly specified.

Contrary to occasional allegations, the editorial staff is not trying to rob the writers of financial support. As well as further financing the Litfond (Literary Fund), we are considering new ways of assistance, including extra pensions for the older generation and grants for young writers. We are hoping to increase fees for contributed articles, to subsidize work on large books, to cover travelling expenses, etc. The size and purpose of this aid will fall within the jurisdiction of Literaturnaya Gazeta Writers' and Readers' Editorial Council.

To find the wherewithal for all this is also our concern of the moment. Amid current market reforms nothing short of a new economic arrangement can help us sort out our problems. We will try to set up a joint-stock company which will most likely involve foreign capital and where the Writers' Union will hold an interest at our expense. We proposed this right at the start of talks with the Union's Working Secretariat. Under this arrangement, the Union would have a guaranteed income. Writers themselves would be able to become shareholders too, thus sharing the work and profits of the newspaper. We will offer the printers and other services shares on credit, which will allow them to participate in the management of the company.

In closing, we would like to say that we do not consider the current controversy with the Writers' Union to be a fatal one. Much the same is happening throughout the country—between ministries and producers, between agro-industrial committees and farmers, in short, between the old and the new forms of economic and, indeed, social relationships. It is our firm belief that passions will subside eventually, reason will prevail over emotions, and every one of us will find our niche in the writing business.

The readers could not have overlooked the words "The Free Forum of Writers" which appear in the titled of the paper. Our basic aim is to make *Literaturnaya Gazeta* free and thereby help every individual to live a free life in a free society.

Miracles do not happen. Such fiery statements from *Literaturnaya Gazeta* staff became possible in the wake of change in its management. Left without the Editor, the staff of the paper decided in early 1990 to find the right candidate on their own—breaking the tradition of bureaucratic games played by functionaries from the Secretariat of the CPSU Central Committee and the Writers' Union. The latter had to climb down and endorse the opinion of the paper's 240-strong staff, who chose Fyodor Burlatsky, a political analyst and People's Deputy of the USSR. He was to run the newspaper which in the Brezhnev era served as a safety valve for the pent-up anger of the intellectuals, who saw it as a guide. In 1990, with perestroika in its sixth year, the number of its subscribers was down by 1.5 million. Of course, about five million are still there (the year 1991 saw a further steep drop in circulation). That Burlatsky took over the paper not in the best of times is obvious to journalists and readers alike. To top it all, *Literaturnaya Gazeta* strongly displeased even those it was supposed to serve, the literary community itself.

The heyday of this weekly is past; it can no longer compete amid the fresh air of glasnost. The centrist stand of the newspaper is no longer to readers' liking, neither the reformists nor those who side with the top army generals and die-hard apparatchiks. From the Western point of view, *Literaturnaya Gazeta*, which appears to be a quality paper, is unprofessional, for the degree of honesty and competence it offers is no longer sufficient. But, surely, a person like the late Andrei Sakharov, Sergei Grigoryants or Yelena Bonner would not take the job of *Literaturnaya Gazeta* editor. It is not by chance that I mentioned these world-famous human rights activists. I mean that Burlatsky was the main official human rights activist, as chairman and board member of a multitude of corresponding national and international commissions for many years. Yet he did not give a helping hand to imprisoned dissidents and never attended political trials of human rights activists. Dissidents and like-minded people came to power in the Baltic region, Armenia, Georgia, and some countries of Eastern Europe. By contrast, the Moscow political landscape has so far been dominated by Communist party leaders who, in terms of their moral and intellectual qualities, have always been a step ahead of other apparatchiks and, for this reason, have been generally seen as prominent and fairly progressive, malcontent figures. The only fault of these people is that they, in fact, have managed to get on well with any regime. Fyodor Burlatsky is one of them.

The newspaper *Moscow News*, April 15, 1990, profiles him in the following way:

> At 63, he is a leading Soviet writer on political affairs, a Doctor of Philosophy, has the same first name and patronymic as Dostoyevsky, is a former advisor to Khrushchev, and the author of a book about him. His face often appears on the television screen: he is a member of parliament and the chairman of the Deputies' Club and Subcommittee for Humanitarian, Cultural, and Scientific Relations. Dr. Burlatsky is fond of emphasizing his anti-Stalinist stand. He was admitted to the Writers' Union long ago for his books about Machiavelli, Mao Tse Tung, Hitler, and Franco, as well as for "*The Tzar's Counsellor*" and other plays. Since 1967 he lost his job three times for "publishing the wrong stuff." "Dr. Burlatsky does not side

with any of the existing factions," says a letter from *Literaturnaya Gazeta* staff. "I have always been interested in the problems of authoritarian and totalitarian power," the man says about himself. At one time Burlatsky walked out of an important job as head of a sub-division at the CPSU Central Committee, but not until Khrushchev had been deposed, and decided never again to be part of power structures. Asked whether he then saw the danger of being close to the top echelon of power, Burlatsky said that "we have always felt it," meaning Georgy Shakhnazarov, Alexander Bovin, Georgy Arbatov, Oleg Bogomolov, and Fyodor Petrenko—the people he brought together and worked with, the people who have remained his friends to this day.

Literaturnaya Gazeta has Yuri Rost on its staff, the man who became a national hero in Georgia. He was the only professional news photographer who, despite beatings, searches, and harassment by army and KGB officers, managed to capture on film the tragic events in Tbilisi on April 9, 1989, when special troops broke up a peaceful protest using spades and war gases, which left 20 people dead. *Literaturnaya Gazeta* refused to carry the pictures and reports send by its special correspondent. The only publication which did was the *Molodyozh Gruzii* newspaper in Tbilisi. The military reacted by impounding and destroying the best part of that edition. Two months later the Georgian Journalists Union gave Yuri Rost a special prize for his civic courage, promptness and talent.

And so, has the newspaper changed in the last two years? Outwardly, yes, but the abolition of censorship has not affected it in any meaningful way. It appears that real communists have stronger inner brakes than the shackles of the main literary censorship department were.

> ...The left-wing press is split. True, on the surface everything is all right. There are no trenches or barbed wire. There are two houses, that is, two editorial offices. Working in one of them are good and honest people hating the existing order from the bottom of their hearts; the same is true of the other office. But they live, as it were, in different states. There is a frontier between them—ethical, political or some other. Let me explain.
>
> Our President let slip the words that the law on the press should be suspended. As the saying goes, better the foot slip than the tongue trip. That might mean trouble. What did the chief editor of a perestroika magazine do? He deleted the most polemical and interesting items from the forthcoming issue. What did the editor of a perestroika newspaper do? He devoted a whole spread to that ominous slip of the tongue—and thus gave the President his due. See the difference? Two friendly periodicals came out that week. One raised a hue and cry and there was peace and harmony in the other...
>
> If you are subscribed to *Moscow News* (or can get it in some other way), you are sure to see how much the newspaper has changed since the Lithuanian events. A man of sterling qualities, Yegor Yakovlev it seems discarded as it were the yoke and Truth has streamed in torrents from its pages, having broken the dam of prejudices and the intellectuals' naive hopes for the coming of a good tsar. I well remember the not-so-

distant past when Yegor Yakovlev guarded Mikhail Gorbachev against his young and cocky journalists. Today... the newspaper has acquired a new lease on life and the readers are keenly aware of this, especially now when glasnost is being ruthlessly and brazenly attacked. Yegor Yakovlev did not allow the relations between him and Gorbachev develop the way they did between Gorbachev and *Argumenty i Fakty* editor Starkov, when Mikhail Sergeyevich shouted and stamped his foot at Starkov. But it's obvious that they have fallen apart.

What about the chief editors of some other perestroika periodicals? (I hate naming them.) Did they get cold feet? They did! Honest journalists groaned and started quitting the most prestigious periodicals in bunches—*Ogonyok* and *Literaturnaya Gazeta*, let alone radio and TV services. We can't work in such a stifling atmosphere, they said. Our superiors have clamped down on us, screening every word.

At this junction I would like to speak about the *Literaturnaya Gazeta*. The matter is I worked for it for four years some time ago. In subsequent years I have tried not to pass judgement on it, but now I'll break this rule since there's a good pretext for this.

Our leaders, beginning from Stalin, used this newspaper for letting out steam. It had such a reputation up until perestroika. It used to publish tale-telling court reports, fiercely attack the authorities who could not cope with the ice-crusted pavement in the streets, and send correspondents to cover Brigitte Bardot's private life! Ministries and departments constantly trembled with fear, while those on the very top were quite well off for the paper let them be.

And it never occurred to the ordinary Soviet reader that the *Literaturnaya Gazeta* outspoken editors brought every single 'bold' article to the central committee and the KGB for endorsement. And there every single line was scrutinized and sifted and the verdict passed as to the percentage of the truth to be allowed to appear. The *Literaturnaya Gazeta* was permitted to do a lot but not everything. Its editors were aware of that and they knew their place.

I can't tell you how sadistically they in the *Literaturnaya Gazeta* adjusted my reports. If my target was a right-wing author, they demanded that I bite a leftist one "for balance". If an Armenian was mentioned I had to add an Azerbaijani, and so on and so forth. In this way, it was believed, impartiality was achieved.

Yevgeny Alexeyevich Krivitsky and Yuri Petrovich Izyumov (the latter now heads an out-and-out CC newspaper *Glasnost* and he clean forgot about the 'struggle for objectivity') were notorious in their struggle for 'objectivity' and a 'balanced approach'.

Then I got involved with *NEDELYA* and contributed to my *alma mater* less and less. When I chanced upon my ex-colleagues I'd hear stories about their struggle for every good paragraph. Perestroika came—but they were still struggling. New and independent periodicals mushroomed and the oil ones were thriving—but the *Literaturnaya Gazeta* journalists were struggling. They are struggling until today. For the same specialists in cutting out and censoring, in balancing and adjusting have not slackened their efforts. I wonder why the journalists, which once ranked among the best, couldn't muster their courage and leave the sinking ship.

And now I shall explain what has inspired these pessimistic thoughts on the border of Switzerland and France. Before leaving for the Leninist State, I was stupid enough to place a *Stolitsa* ad in the *Literaturnaya Gazeta*. They demanded an exorbitant price of eight thousand rubles. I agreed, and signed a guarantee letter. We discussed in what issue the ad would be featured, and I left them. Then we in *Stolitsa* started thinking about the themes from the forthcoming issues to be announced in the advertisement. We decided as follows: 1) Lenin fulfilled the German government's assignments not only before the revolution but after it too. Intriguing? I guess it is. 2) Did M.S. Gorbachev as a student collaborate with the KGB? (We naturally put a question mark here, despite the fact that the article which was being prepared for publication explained it in so many words.) 3) Scenarios for inter-ethnic conflicts are written in Staraya Square (i.e. in the Communist Party Central Committee). Opinions differed on this score. Should this statement be announced? It is indubitable as it is, for everybody realizes that none other than communists are interested in whipping up ethnic conflicts. But after all was said and done, we decided to leave that phrase. Then the usual text followed: our index is such and such, subscription can be obtained in all post offices at such and such a price, it is not yet late to subscribe to the second quarter. Our designers stepped in and after that we sent it to the *Literaturnaya Gazeta*.

Oh Lord, that started a whole string of telephone calls! Bosses—big and small—called. Some demanded that we put a question mark at the end of the first item (about Lenin), others insisted that the KGB be not mentioned, still others wanted the verbs to be used in the past tense. In a word, the same rigmarole began, which was customary for the *Literaturnaya Gazeta* but not for me any longer. I cast prudence to the winds and paid a visit to the acting chief editor. I said: "My dear comrade, I've bought some space in your newspaper for my advertisement and I am free to use it as I see fit. You bear no responsibility for this. Even if an ass is depicted there."

"Please yourself as far as the ass goes," answered the acting boss, "but will you please not mention Gorbachev." And the boss showered me with compliments, filled me with tasty coffee to the brim. We made a compromise, shook hands and I parted. On the next morning it began all over again—persuasions, censorship, introduction of question marks and crossing out of names.

After that I broke all relations with that paper. Can the leopard change its spots? What is bred in the bone will not get out of the flesh. But frankly, I was eager to ask them get out of the flesh. But frankly, I was eager to ask them a sacramental question: 'With whom are you, cultural workers?'

I can tell the inquisitive people that the negotiator was Yuri Dmitriyevich Poroikov, first deputy chief editor who succeeded Izyumov (who left for *Glasnost*, but not Grigoryan's one). Prior to that Poroikov was chief editor of the magazine *Molodoy Kommunist*. By the by, I am surprised at the ease with which our liberals travel from communist publications and back. I feel that had Burlatsky (*LG* chief editor) been in Moscow at that time (he was in the United States), the result would have been the same.

To be sure, a great many penetrating and topical features see light in *Literaturnaya Gazeta*, but this is only true of themes which simply cannot be left without comment (practically the entire central and Moscow press has been "screaming" on this score). Besides, authors from the "Left" are published, who cannot very well be rejected. Thus, A. Sobchak in early April and Yu.

Shchekochikhin in early July, 1991, told the world in the pages of *LG* about arbitrary acts perpetrated by the USSR Procurator-General, the chairman of the KGB, the USSR Minister of Defense, the CC CPSU General Secretary and the USSR Minister of the Interior.

The five of them did all they could to drown the national liberation movement in Georgia in blood and justify the butchers of April, 1989 in Tbilisi (People's Deputy of the USSR Sobchak protested against this). People's Deputy of the USSR Yu. Shchekochikhin documented and exposed the above mentioned persons' actions in Lithuania in January 1991. Sobchak also well documented his case, as he headed the ad hoc committee of USSR People's Deputies that was mandated by the congress to investigate the Tbilisi events. Burlatsky, Sobchak and Shchekochikhin realize full well that should the ultra-left seize power, the three of them would be incarcerated in the first place.

The trouble is, however, that during the coup Sobchak, the Mayor of St. Petersburg, not only understood what should be done, but did it by organizing total resistance to the coup in his city. None of the putschists' designs materialized in the city on the Neva. Yuri Shchekochikhin of *Literaturnaya Gazeta* (without getting the permission of his superiors, as Fyodor Burlatsky wrote in *Nezavisimaya Gazeta* on September 19, 1991) invited the democratic press to hold a meeting in the building of his newspaper in the morning of August 21. On August 20 Shchekochikhin spoke at the White House, while Burlatsky (see *NG* of September 19, 1991) phoned his newspaper from the resort in the Crimea on August 19-21 and "several times asked the resort administration to help him buy tickets to Moscow."

The reader might say that this is more than strange, because in such cases any normal person just hops into his car and rushes to the airport. *Literaturnaya Gazeta* thought so, too. But when the journalists read the text of Burlatsky's statement, issued on August 21 (when the fate of the coup was sealed), they passed a vote of no-confidence in him. For a month the office of the chief of *Literaturnaya Gazeta* remained empty, but on 23 September Burlatsky's deputy, Arkady Udaltsov, was elected editor-in-chief.

CHAPTER V

THE PRESS THAT EARLIER WAS NOT

Vitaly Tretyakov, a Friend of M.S. Gorbachev

During those days of trial and tribulation in 1991—on the other hand, every day is a day of trial and tribulation in this country, the residents of the Soviet Union's two capitals (St. Petersburg and Moscow) could choose between listening to all kinds of radio voices and reading *Nezavisimaya Gazeta*. The fledgling newspaper clearly published the best Soviet information, but its distribution throughout the country was hindered by the general chaos in the Soviet postal service and stubborn resistance of bureaucrats in the provinces.

On August 24, 1991 I bought *Nezavisimaya Gazeta* from a street vendor and read the headline, running all across the page:

"THE FAILURE OF THE COUP DOES NOT MEAN VICTORY. ONLY ON EXPERIENCING A PERSONAL TRAGEDY DID MIKHAIL GORBACHEV UNDERSTAND WHAT TENS OF MILLIONS OF PEOPLE HAD KNOWN FOR A LONG TIME, WHICH HAD BEEN WRITTEN ABOUT LONG AGO BY THE DEMOCRATIC PRESS, WHICH THE PRESIDENT, FREED BY DEMOCRATS, CRITICIZED AT HIS PRESS CONFERENCE IN MOSCOW. PRESIDENTIAL PRESS SECRETARY IGNATENKO DID NOT ALLOW A SINGLE JOURNALIST FROM NEWSPAPERS BANNED BY THE JUNTA TO ASK A SINGLE QUESTION."

Do you see now? Vitaly Tretyakov, editor-in-chief of *Nezavisimaya Gazeta* wrote, under the photo which showed the monument dedicated to Iron Felix raised into the air by a crane (the point at issue is not the butcher Dzerzhinsky—there are more than enough live KGB men around):

I would not like to sing praises to yet another victory of perestroika, or join the applause of Western journalists for the first public appearance of the USSR President after Foros. He appeared not before the people, but before journalists, and mostly Western ones. It was to these journalists that Ignatenko, the press secretary of the President who was nowhere to be seen during the three fatal days, gave the floor in that clearly well-orchestrated reappearance of the President.

Ignatenko did not seem to notice the hands of journalists from Soviet newspapers which had been banned by the junta, including *Nezavisimaya*. Although Tatiana Malkina of this newspaper was the only one of Soviet and foreign journalists to ask the puppet dictator Yanayev on August 19, at a press conference beamed throughout the country: "Do you understand that this is a coup?"

Both Gorbachev and Ignatenko revealed a good knowledge of the individuals who had asked questions at the Yanayev-Pugo-Starodubtsev press conference, and who had answered them and what they had said. For example, Gorbachev commended the correspondent of the Italian newspaper *Stampa*, recalled the trembling hands of "Gorbachev's friend", etc. And what a fantastic advertisement for BBC radio! It's a good radio station, of course, and worth listening to, when there is no other source of information. But why search for its correspondent so fussily, staring with unseeing eyes at the Soviet journalists?

THE SHOCK OF GORBACHEV OR FROM GORBACHEV? And, of course, the correspondent of the banned Russian newspaper *Vesti* was allowed to ask a question. This was a must, because, after all, Gorbachev was saved by Yeltsin. More gratitude to the correspondent of *Rodina*, the magazine of the Russian Supreme Soviet. But she broke the routine of gratitude by asking a question about mysterious satellites which nobody—including Gorbachev and probably she herself—understood. Then a miracle happened: Viktor Lyubovtsev, presenter of Central TV, was given the floor. But it was Central TV and the seven newspapers of the Communist Party Central Committee which for two and a half days, like a cheap pro, did everything the putschists demanded and popularized their information swill!

Did this merely reflect the personal taste of the President's press secretary? Why then did Mikhail Gorbachev, while lauding mostly the Western press and finding barely a few words for the Soviet democratic press, criticize the latter? He seemed to be asserting that the irreconcilable position of the democratic press had led the right-wingers to engineer the coup. He said this about the press, which, although banned, had protected him, Gorbachev, throughout those three days in August. He said this about the press which had many times raised the question, carefully glossed over by Gorbachev himself and Lukyanov, about falsifications during the election of Yanayev to the post of Vice-President. He said this about the press which had openly warned him of the danger from the right, and had given names to this danger: Yanayev, Lukyanov, Pavlov, Pugo and Kryuchkov!

Indeed, it was a personal tragedy for Mikhail Gorbachev. Forced into a corner, he understood what the democrats had been trying to tell him a thousand times, what millions of Soviet people had understood long ago, what Yuri Karyakin had said openly at the press conference—and received a reprimand for from the President.

In his official address in Vremya TV program, Mikhail Gorbachev, keeping to his text, said everything he was supposed to say. Speaking at his press conference, he did not have a text and spoke off the cuff, especially when he answered questions. At that press conference he did not say a word about the victims of the coup in Moscow. Instead, he criticized Yakovlev for leaving the party, mumbled a few strange words about Shevardnadze, and lastly, lauded the CPSU, whose channels were used to guide the coup.

I was shocked by that first press conference. The President did not lose his sense of humor, but we did not hear direct answers to direct questions. The West was appeased, of course—but not completely, I think.

Many people asked why Gorbachev didn't meet the people as soon as he returned to Moscow. Why didn't he go to the democrats who were holding a meeting at the scene of their victory, Russia's White House? The answer should be sought in the question. What would he have heard there? Would it only have been shouts of jubilation at his release? Or something else? Wouldn't it have been a gesture of genuine gratitude to stand side by side with his liberator, Yeltsin? Risky and painful for Gorbachev's ego, but a necessary gesture. It was not made. Gorbachev has never attended a single democratic meeting. Neither did he come to the meeting on August 22, the day when the democratic forces of Moscow celebrated at the White House the victory over the junta, which had arrested not only Gorbachev but also his entire family.

The point is not only the personal tragedy. The matter concerns politics. The political struggle is not over yet. And in this struggle Gorbachev still represents the center and Yeltsin a republic. Yeltsin was defended in the White house not by the center but by the people. And the people know that some smaller figures, which did not get caught out openly supporting the putschists, will try to hide behind Gorbachev's back. If the President was greatly mistaken in his Prime Minister, Vice-President, Defense Minister, Interior Minister, the KGB chief and chairman of his Parliament, who can guarantee that their deputies, assistants, business managers and other small fry do not smell as bad as their superiors, who rose up against two presidents simultaneously?

Let's be honest, although this might mar the euphoria of "everybody's" victory. The Center is closer to losing power than ever before. This means that Gorbachev, General Secretary and President, can lose power, too. But the Center is not only Gorbachev, but also the small fry with big teeth. Gorbachev for them is the only potential defender. They will flock around him even though they might hate him. And he will need them, too, in order to balance the dramatically grown political weight of sovereign Russia and its sovereign President.

On August 25, the *Vzglyad* program showed a USSR People's Deputy and a staffer on the Presidential team who had stayed with the latter in Foros during the dramatic events. This elderly Russian who could hardly speak proper Russian, was telling TV viewers in a live program about the villains from the KGB and the CC CPSU who were responsible for information supplied to the President. They fed him distorted information about the situation in Baltia and Transcaucasia, in this way prodding him to take stringent measures.

I have no doubt that that's really how it was.

But what would the American President do in such a situation? In addition to intelligence dispatches he would watch CNN and other TV programs, read newspapers and magazines. The French *Figaro* allotted from eight to eleven pages a day during that August week, and the other French political weeklies did the same. The Baltic events (January, 1991 in Tallinn and Riga) were covered by the Western media dozens of times more fully and objectively than in our central press. One may argue that our President does not know foreign languages and that the TASS and KGB services issue incomplete and sample information. There is only one way out of the predicament, namely, an independent, honest and professional national press should be created—and everything will be okay. This is feasible today: after all, hasn't V. Tretyakov fulfilled his promise to launch a daily *Nezavisimaya Gazeta* in January 1992?

On January 21, 1991, in the Moscow Cinema House there was a presentation of the *Nezavisimaya Gazeta*, a 12-page newspaper issued three times a week by very brainy and very young Vitaly Tretyakov, formerly deputy chief editor of the *Moscow News*. As V. Tretyakov noted in January, "it is interesting to make the newspaper, each issue of which may be the last one." His paper was supported by the Moscow Soviet, but unfortunately not the USSR Ministry of Communications. That was why it was distributed solely in Moscow for many months. In terms of quality, *NG* ranks with such new Soviet periodicals as *Kommersant, Kuranty, Stolitsa* and *Megapolis-Express* hallmarked by high journalistic standards. Their par value being far lower, readers can obtain them for one or two rubles. In 1991, subscription could only be made to *Kommersant*.

The Moscow Soviet was the founder of *NG*. It also granted an interest-free loan of 300 thousand rubles, mainly to cover the expenses involved in printing the pilot issue. It was put up for sale on December 22, 1990. Provision of subsidies by the USSR State Planning Committee and favorable rates (i.e. fixed state prices) offered by the *Izvestia* publishing house, enabled them, Tretyakov remarked in the December 24, 1990 issue of *Kommersant*, to print his newspaper using the profit from marketing the first issue and publishing advertisements there. The French weekly, *Courier International*, printed 100,000 copies of the newspaper in French, as a free advertising supplement of a regular issue. It was then, Tretyakov admits, that the *Nezavisimaya Gazeta* received a great variety of tenders from major advertising firms and potential partners in the publishing and trading business. As its staffers say, some part of the profits accruing from commercial activity will be funneled for the publication of the *Nezavisimaya Gazetta* and for building their own printing facilities. In particular, there is an idea of establishing a commercial publishing house that would issue socio-political literature.

When the subscription campaign began on August 1, 1991, *NG* declared that its avowed principle was not glasnost but freedom of speech; that *NG* is the first Soviet newspaper being published in the USA since June 1990 (its format is different and it comes out more seldom than in Moscow); that no party will ever control *NG*; that the paper provides the most complete and honest information about developments in the republics, the USSR and the world. Those were not just empty and meaningless words but the summing up of the newspaper's six-month activity.

Moscow's *Nezavisimaya Gazeta* is being published in the USA in English (from April 1991) and in Georgia in Russian.

NG chief editor Vitaly Tretyakov addressed readers in the Republic of Georgia (11.4.1991). It amounted to a political program—something inconceivable for the other central newspapers that have been published in Georgia for decades.

> In launching the publication of *NG* in Tbilisi, our staff journalists first of all would like to congratulate the republic's citizens on their adoption of the Act on Restoring Independence, and point out that the gory date of April 9 will always remind us of the crimes perpetrated by the totalitarian regime that was in power in both Russia and Georgia.
>
> The *NG* is extensively covering developments in the republics formerly incorporated in the USSR. Most of these republics are now seeking their own path for integrating into world civilization. The process is going on not without errors, conflicts or bloody clashes. *NG* journalists will honestly report about all this, from different sources and points of view.
>
> The latest events in Georgia have been the focus of *NG* attention. We wish happiness, prosperity and accord to all peoples living on the territory of your wonderful republic. We shall facilitate the achievement of these goals as best we can—by honestly discharging our duty as journalists: the *NG* readers must know the truth about the state of affairs in your republic, even if this truth is complex and involved.
>
> Hopefully, those who will read our Russian newspaper in Georgia will be able to appreciate its impartiality. Our sole wish is not to be hampered in our effort to be impartial. The democratic media is one of the few avenues of trust between nations having a common destiny however tragic. It is not given to anybody to question a people's right to independence and self-determination. Nor is it given to anybody to question the principle of freedom of the press. One does not exist without the other.
>
> We thank Samshoblo Publishers for assistance in printing NG in Georgia. We are confident of the success of our joint undertaking."

This cooperation was very important for Georgia. "Information Blockade Is Raised"—was the title in *Svobodnaya Gruzia* (Free Georgia, April 12, 1991) of a commentary on the event. It read in part: "Truth is needed everywhere, especially at times of trial. For Georgia, which has found itself in an emergency situation and information blockade where the central mass media are heaping misinformation, the unbiased and complete truth about what is really going on here, is a vital as the fresh air. Understandably, we link with the *NG* our hopes that the wall of alienation raised around Georgia will be breached... The people of Georgia are now waging a struggle to return to the world community. And we think there is no need to repeat the truism that the world should know that it is straight dealing on our part." In the same feature Vakhtang Esvandjia, director of Samshoblo Publishers, pointed out that throughout its existence (more than three months) *NG* publications concerning Georgia had been very unbiased; all reports dispatched by republican journalists or forwarded through official channels to NG had been published undistorted.

Remember these meaningful words, reader! 'The global theme of the *Nezanisimaya Gazeta* is the rational man in the flood of irresponsibility'. The author, Lev Anninsky (*NG* of June 13, 1991) goes on to say: 'The logic of independence in a chaos of unpredictability. Under our feet is not the terra firma but an abyss, a precipice, a gulf. Just try and maintain your composure in an atmosphere of overall madness.' Even the democrats are fighting one another, Anninsky notes annoyingly in his 'Profiles of the New Press'.

NG often uses information rejected by other newspapers they either don't like the text or have no room, etc.). Thus *NG* (of the entire Moscow press!) published the full text of Elena Bonner's speech at the opening ceremony, on May 21, 1991, in Moscow, of the First International Sakharov Congress. She delivered it in the presence of Mikhail Gorbachev, President of the USSR (*NG* of June 8, 1991). For the second time Bonner and Gorbachev used the same rostrum during the funeral of three young men who had died defending the White House during the August putsch in Moscow). The motto of the Sakharov congress was "Peace, Progress, Human Rights". Independent periodicals—*Argumenty i Fakty*, *Ogonyok* and *Moscow News*—subsidized it. But it was only NG that published Bonner's brilliant speech.

The same newspaper was the only one in Moscow to publish (March 9, 1991) the Memorandum of USSR Procurator-General N.S. Trubin that was circulated among the People's Deputies of the USSR. The document made it abundantly clear that the servicemen were not to blame for the bloody events in Tbilisi of April 8-9, 1989.

The *NG* has a famous reporter on its staff—Andrei Karaulov. On March 7, 1991, *NG* carried his interview with Zviad Gamsakhurdia. When people read the full texts of the statements by Bonner, Trubin and Gamsakhurdia, rather than curtailed excerpts or summary, they came to understand who is who and no comment was necessary.

NG analysts are not of the worst grade either. Thus, Pavel Felgenhauer noted that according to the 1926 census there were 194 peoples and nationalities in the USSR; in 1959 the figure was 109, in 1970—104 and in 1979—101. He cited these statistics in his article "*South Ossetia: Is the Outcome Predetermined? The Rules of Survival for National Minorities in the Transition Period*". The South Ossetian communist leadership, seeking to preserve their own privileges with the help of the government troops, is forgetting, or prefers not to think about one thing, namely, when the Russian troops and the Ossetian commandoes pull out from the north and go home, local Ossetians will be banished from Tskhinvali across the pass in the north. There are not my words, nor the Georgians' but Felgenhauer's. And indeed, have the communists ever thought about anything but their power?

In completing our brief review of *NG* we shall again have recourse to its chief Vitaly Tretyakov. In the April 4, 1991, issue he depicted a portrait of his brain child (on the last, eighth page) under the title *"Independence is our style, including independence from folly, backstage games and a desire to backheel our rival"*:

> In the first issue of *NG*—precisely on this page—as the chief editor I was so bold as to state some principles of independent journalism to be espoused by our newspaper. More than three months have elapsed since then. NG has grown into one of the most popular Soviet papers being quoted widely both inside and outside the country.
>
> We are trying not to miss the critical remarks our colleagues may make about our paper. And we can't say that they are 'inattentive' to us. However, we never fight back at the mere mention of *NG*. To begin with, it's impossible. Second, the editors have definite principles on this score. The main one is not to engage in polemics with traditional publications. I have always tried to impress on the *NG* journalists that it is indecent for a new newspaper to teach others how to write. The best thing is to write the way we deem necessary.
>
> Yet we haven't pledged not to answer criticisms, especially untenable ones, when our professional honor is at stake. And on certain occasions we hit back, warning at the same time that this or that periodical should think twice before launching critical articles. For in the absolute majority of cases the denounciators of *NG* have not been able to prove their point, but it was a good advertisement for our newspaper which, for reasons, not depending on us, has still a 'small' circulation. And they did it for free. Many heeded our advice, among them the Vremya program. But there are some that still take the risk and embark on this unsavory path.
>
> I mean, among others, *Ekonomika i Zhizn*—a little known newspaper. In one of its latest issues it mentioned *NG* three times, in a hostile manner to be sure. Tastes differ: some like the priest and others like his daughter. However, I'd like to clarify one thing. *Ekonomika i Zhizn* wrote: 'the dependent *Independent Gazette*'. We admit it's a fine pun, though lying on the surface. Did the *Ekonomika i Zhizn* bother to substantiate its charge? Not really. We'd like to say a few words about this paper which is decorated with the 'motto': 'The founder—the CC CPSU'. Its fairly large (for a specialized paper) circulation is due to the fact that it has the right of 'first night' in publishing normative economic documents issued in the USSR. It is clear that such documents are badly needed by managers of numerous enterprises and they (i.e. the managers) have to subscribe to *Ekonomika i Zhizn* in order to obtain the required documents as quickly as possible. The question arises: Why is it that not being a USSR government publication, *Ekonomika i Zhizn* enjoys this privilege, which, by the way, is commercially profitable? Is not this an illegal monopolization of state economic and juridical information by the mouthpiece of one party, namely, the CPSU? What will happen when *Ekonomika i Zhizn* will be deprived of such a privilege? Will it still bother about *NG* or try to find sponsors other than the USSR government and engage in an honest competitive struggle with other economic weeklies, for example, with *Kommersant*?

Or take another paper partial to *NG—Rabochaya Tribuna*, intended to uphold working people's rights in the social sphere, as specified on its first page, and founded by the same CC CPSU, as written on its last page. Its chief method is hurling remarks at *NG*, but they are so incoherent, unfounded and absurd that our conscience forbids us retorting in the same vein, while to take it seriously is not to respect oneself.

Generally speaking, the communist (the CPSU-owned) newspapers are disputing with us in a strange way. They are not so much against the *Independent Gazette* or its authors' words as its name. Some of them, such as the *Ekonomika i Zhizn*, have not gone farther than the pun ('the dependent *Independent Gazette*), while others are intimating we are dependent on the Moscow Soviet. Thus V. Trushkov, Ph.D., is right when referring to *NG* as 'founded by the Moscow Soviet' in *Moskovskaya Pravda*. But he ends up writing 'the Moscow Soviet's publication'—which are different things (see the Law on the Press). The *NG* Charter has recorded the independence of the newspaper, founded by the Moscow Soviet, from the founder. Over the three months of our existence, *NG* has published no more than two or three articles by Mossoviet deputies. We are far behind *Moskovskaya Pravda* in this respect. For example, the Mossoviet chairman, Gavril Popov, hasn't been given the floor in *NG*—not even once! Meanwhile, we interviewed the leader of the Moscow communists, Yuri Prokofyev, and published the interview.

NG makes a point of giving a wide variety of opinion, without, however, making an absurd reservation each time—'the author's opinion may not coincide with that of the editors.' Those debating with *NG* are free to use the phraseology they like. Thus, *Krasnaya Zvezda* used to describe us as 'the so-called democratic paper'. When we published an article by L. Sigal, a *Kommersant* observer, where he criticized the democrats' stand regarding the referendum, *Krasnaya Zvezda* quoted his statement, but 'forgot' to mention the author's place of work (although this was pointed out in *NG*).

Many people do not believe in our independence. They are free to do so. We are not going to give them a lie. For a slave will never understand that a person can be free. Independence arouses the suspicion of dependent people, or even malice and the desire to expropriate this independence for their master.

This is human folly and we are trying to be independent of it too. The best attitude here is not to argue with fools.

There is a delicate aspect to the talk about the *NG* stand. It has to do with the state of affairs in the democratic press. Right-wing newspapers never attack one another—such is their present-day principle. And a very good one.

The left democratic periodicals would like to agree on unity, but they can't. And they will never be able to. For on the one hand, this unity would be the end of the left democratic press—it would cease to be both left and democratic. On the other hand, competition is in the way of unity—real-life competition with the CPSU as the monopolist of all printing facilities.

Not all means are good for a democratic edition in competition. It is clear why the democratic press did not enthuse over the rise of *NG*. If my memory serves me right, only *Vechernaya Moskva* and *Moscow News* hailed the *Independent Gazette* when its first issue came out. But as *NG* was gaining in strength and popularity, some democratic periodicals felt apprehensions. I repeat: there's competition. The *Moskovsky Komsomolets* published a report about the sale of Moscow and central periodicals in Moscow, at the end of March. It cited the statistics for January (when *NG* was founded), ignoring the latest statistics for February. Worse still, it overstated the number of unsold copies of *NG* and did not say a word about the system of distribution through Soyuzpechat which gave advantages to the traditional (first of all, party) newspapers including the democratically-oriented *Moscow News*. *NG* is not included in the list. Further, *Moskovsky Komsomolets* said nothing about how often each newspaper came out, thus concealing the main thing from its readers. The matter is that at the time of publication of this information (but in reality a month prior to it) *NG* was in the lead in terms of distribution through Soyuzpechat.

There is no doubt that the right-wing press is overjoyed with the 'bickering' in the democratic press. I don't care. I want to declare that never and under no circumstances will the *Nezavisimaya Gazeta* step onto the path of struggle either with the rightists or the leftists, even those leftists who in their time campaigned for the abolition of censorship in the USSR but now have censors in their office 'just in case'.

I can understand the zeal with which many democrats plunge into the struggle against the right-wingers, the conservatives who, in their view, restrict freedom of information in this country. However, if you haven't won, lay the blame on yourselves, not others, notably on the *Nezavisimaya Gazeta*.

Honestly, I like the straightforward ways of many conservatives. For example, NG allotted a page and a half to the strange—to put it mildly—ties linking Kurguinian's corporation 'The Experimental Artistic Center' and the Prime Minister of the USSR and the first secretary of the CPSU Moscow city committee. Both pretended nothing had happened. *Moskovskaya Pravda* which scolded our newspaper occasionally, kept silent. So did the USSR People's Deputies—both on the right and the left. I can see through this. Kurguinian in the Vremya program is teaching us to live—everybody keeps silent, including the Moscow Union of Journalists. But then the latter didn't utter a word when *NG* called on Moscow journalists to stage a protest action against the Law on the Press being suspended. Meanwhile, many provincial papers supported us—like in *NG*, there was a blank spot on their front page. One can see that they do not view backstage stratagems as the method of struggle against political censorship.

The other day the publishers in many Trans-Urals cities suspended negotiations with us, concerning printing *NG* in local print shops. This change of heart came all of a sudden. We were told, however, that the CC CPSU management department forwarded to them the list of newspapers not to be printed in print shops belonging to the communists (read: the whole country). According to our information, *NG* is first in that list. Alas, it can't be helped. As long as the Journalists Union and People's Deputies craving glasnost are waging a backstage struggle against Kravchenko, instead of openly campaigning against the monopoly use by the communist party of the national printing facilities, which belong to the people, this list will have a stronger effect that "Faust"—even if Goethe was at the head of the Journalists Union of the USSR or its Moscow organization.

As for *NG*, we will remain independent. And there will be no censor in our midst 'just in case'. And we have no privileges in distributing our paper, like those enjoyed by the party press. And the Journalists Union never sends us on missions abroad. Our sole stake is on our honest, responsible and independent work—without folly, backstage intrigues and backheeling our brothers-democrats.

Till we meet at the newstand!

The Power of the Democrats Has Newspapers on Their Own

At the end of January 1990 subscription was announced to the newly founded *Rossiiskaya Gazeta* - the mouthpiece of the RSFSR Supreme Soviet. In November 1990 this paper appeared in Soyuzpechat news-stands in Moscow. In January its circulation reached 200 thousand and the paper began to be distributed in all republics, territories and regions of the Russian Federation. It is the only daily of the Russian Parliament (unlike *Rossia*—the new daily of the Presidium of the RSFSR Supreme Soviet). Since June 1991 *Rossiiskaya Gazeta* has been published not only in Moscow, but in Volgograd, Kazan, Krasnodar, Mineralnye Vody, Nizhny Novgorod, Novosibirsk, Sverdlovsk and Uzh, and a little bit later in Leningrad, Irkutsk, Omsk and Saratov. In the summer of 1991 the newspaper's daily circulation (5 times a week, 4-8 pages) reached 560 thousand copies. Practically all of them got to the readers on the day of issue. It's a good paper of the not so good Supreme Soviet of Russia. It actively campaigned against the Vilnius events to be repeated in Moscow. It is not accidental that the communist leadership of Tatarstan (*Rossiyskaya Gazeta* had been published there since July 3, 1991) disrupted the long-term agreement and banned the paper.

The political line of the newspaper *Rossiiskaya Gazeta* is clearly reflected in the answers of its editor-in-chief Valentin Logunov to questions about democracy, the press and the powers that be (*Rossiiskiye Vesti* No. 19. September 1991):

1. I think that the situation in the country is critical. The coup was engineered owing to the transition of society from one state into an opposing one. The forces which engineered the coup have a vast social basis.
Take the lumpens. They exist in all countries, but there are a great deal of them in our distorted society. These are the unskilled people with a low level of social conscience, who have simple demands: a bottle of vodka and liver sausage every evening. I think that there are about 20 million of them in this country. Apart from this section, which is impeding our progress, there is also the state, governmental and party apparata. They are also very numerous, especially if we take them together with their servants, which keep close to them and sometimes get a bite from the master's table. In all, half the country is resisting change, consciously or subconsciously.
I myself don't want to offend one-fifth of the people—I mean pensioners, but they have instead been offended by the times. Offence is their objective state. For decades they lived a painful life, and the current changes are painful reminders that their lives were in vain. They lived and worked, but they did not

earn anything. And in the nearby flat lives someone who runs a cooperative, 25 years old, who has a car, champagne and 5,000 rubles a month.

Society has been divided and the gap will grow. A society which would be so fair socially as to provide everything to everybody, is an illusion. This means that we should, when implementing our reforms, seek support. We could rely on the weak, underdeveloped, nascent middle class of businessmen, farmers, specialists and cooperators. Yes, they will become richer, but a part of their profits will be used, through taxes, to increase pensions, grants, etc.

2. The mass media is the indisputable sphere where we have scored practical achievements. Before creating *Rossiiskaya Gazeta* I worked as Russian Deputy Minister of the Press for half a year. Our provincial newspapers, as you know, were subordinate to the propaganda departments of regional and city party committees. Their material basis and nearly all printing shops belonged to the party.

    In trying to destroy this monopoly, we assisted in the birth of new inter-regional newspapers, and helped them obtain newsprint. We have helped dozens of newspapers throughout the country to appear. We often underestimate the role of provincial newspapers, although there are more than 2,000 of them in Russia. They are not printed in many copies, but their influence is very strong, which was seen especially clearly during the coup. And Russian TV and Radio Russia! And they all had to be rescued from the teeth of the party monster.

    I think that the current authorities, from President Gorbachev to the local Soviets, respect this "fourth power", and this is a great achievement.

3. We in Russia have grown used to living in smelly, rotten and dilapidated houses. We tolerated this life for centuries. I pray that we have the patience to build a new, comfortable and sunny house. This task will require patience, as well as skill and persistence.

    I have this to say to the powers-that-be: Never underestimate the people. I would even say: Don't flirt with the people. You should be absolutely sober in your assessments, you should try to rise to the top in order to see the whole of the country. And you should be wise and honest in your relations with the people, and take its troubles to heart.

Rossiiskiye Vesti quoted above is a new phenomenon in our life. It was one of the eleven Moscow newspapers, banned by the junta, which pooled their efforts and published the *Collective Newspaper*, a joint publication of democratic press registered (to spite the putschists) on the special decision of the Russian Ministry for the Press and Information on August 20, 1991 (registration number 1054). The list of founders, published on the first page of the newspaper, included famous periodicals, such as *Megapolis-Express, Moskovsky Komsomolets, Rossiiskiye Vesti, Rossiiskaya Gazeta, Stolitsa, Kuranty, Argumenty i Fakty, Nezavisimaya Gazeta, Komsomolskaya Pravda, Kommersant, Moscow News*.

The coup failed but the newspaper *Rossiiskiye Vesti* decided to continue that congress of 11 periodicals and asked their editors-in-chief to speak out about democracy, the press and the powers-that-be. The column is called "The

11 Club. The Fourth Power in the Fourth [Russian—G.V.] Revolution. Editors-in-chief of the *Obshchaya Gazeta* (Collective Newspaper), Issued During the Coup, in Our Newspaper. Valery Kucher's Article, From Glasnost to the Freedom of Speech":

> Historians claim that the methods used to suppress dissent have been tried and tested and are neutral. Consequently, they can be used for a very long time by any power. Although we are witnessing structural changes in society, there are too many elements which lead to centralism, bureaucracy and stagnation. Newspapers constitute, of course, a great force, but also a very fragile one, as the basis of that "fourth power" is the same as before, that is, state property. The time for spiritual unity and economic fraternity of journalists, that is, genuine freedom of speech, will only come when many different "collective" newspapers of the joint stock communities of journalistic collectives are published.

The first issue of *Rossiiskiye Vesti*, the weekly of the Russian government, saw the light of day in May 1991. *Rossiiskaya Gazeta*, *Rossiiskiye Vesti* and *Rossia* are the three main democratic newspapers of Russia, and none of them is over a year old. *Rossia* is the only "thick" newspaper of the above three, published on eight and sometimes 16 large-size pages and designed for the emerging middle class.

Moscow's new (not traditional) newspapers are astounding. Where and when was it possible in the USSR to read the Pope's encyclics in Russian? *Rossia* made this possible. It assigned one page to a feature "Man Is Created for Freedom" with the Editor's short introduction:

> In 1891, when the Pope Leo XIII issued an encyclic which gave rise to the Church's social doctrine, the spectre of communism was only making its first, trial steps in Europe and was relatively new. The encyclic was entitled *Rerum Novarum* (*On New Things*). One hundred years have passed. Can we say that the specter has reached its destination? Today's Pope John Paul II in his encyclic *Centecimus Annus* (*Centenary*) written for the jubilee of *Rerum Novarum*, recommends abstaining from hasty conclusions. Anyway, for us who were raised on the 'spectral' principles, the ideas underlying the above mentioned papal encyclics, as well as the Church's social doctrine with its understanding of the human essence and the fundamentals of social organization, remain totally unknown.
>
> Published below are excerpts from the first encyclic and an abridged version of *Centesimus Annus*.

Lenin and Stalin, Suslov and Fedoseyev would have punished those who would dare to discuss in their kitchen, let alone print, what's written in these papal encyclicals. Yet we ought to teach our schoolchildren those texts which, even though written in the lofty style, are understandable for all. For it is not a matter of religion, but a matter of our hard life. Those Popes were indeed very wise and the latter even brought his native country, Poland, to freedom.

'Noteworthy is the fact,' writes John Paul II, 'that nearly everywhere the rule of Marxism was toppled peacefully, using the weapon of justice and truth!"

The daily *Kuranty* is one more new periodical in Moscow that is independent from political parties. It was founded by the Moscow Soviet. Its staff are working in substandard conditions—there are 190 square meters of floor space for 90 people. Unlike the antediluvian linotypes of *Pravda* and *Izvestia*, *Kuranty* is set right in the office using Western computers which sometimes rebel refusing to suffer the stuffy air and static electricity. That is why misprints occur, thank God, not political slips. But then there are no censors in *Kuranty*.

In the Moscow 'Soyuzpechat' news-stands one can see not only new dailies and weeklies.

The magazine *Stolitsa* has easily won popularity among the Muscovites.

The newspaper *Vechernyaya Moskva* of August 1, 1990, published an interview with the chief editor of the new magazine:

> A literary commentator of Radio Liberty called him the "leader of the left literary youth." Vladimir Karpov, the leader of Soviet writers, called him "a born critic." However, since then Andrei Malgin has developed into a political critic. He won at the elections to the city Soviet and became the head of the Moscow City Council's new weekly, *Stolitsa*.

Question: Andrei Viktorovich, it is rumored that you intend to publish a sensation every week. Where will you get them from?

Answer: So far there are enough of them, and enough personnel and writers willing to contribute.

Question: Will you have to fight for readers, now that new newspapers are appearing like mushrooms after rain?

Answer: It's certainly true that the number of newspapers has been multiplying. But ours is not a newspaper and hence we won't be involved in this rat race. Regrettably, there are few weekly magazines in this country. Outwardly ours will we similar to *Time* (meaning a color cover with newsprint inside) or the Soviet *Novoye Vremya* (New Times). But it will be thicker and more interesting because we shall write mostly about domestic matters.

Question: You are a famous fighter against the evil past. You have been revealing the privileged "special conservatives" and plagiarists, like Lebedev-Kumach. Do you think that when (and if) your movement wins and we live in an era of stability passions will fade, circulation will fall and you, being a literary critic, will no longer get elected to local government?

Answer: I hope that I was elected not as a literary critic but as a public figure who voiced his opinions at meetings with the voters and in my articles, which have little in common with literature. And I do not intend to deal

Question: **Who is on your team?**
Answer: My deputies Valery Kichin, a commentator from *Sovetskaya Kultura*, Vladislav Starchevsky, who worked for *Nedelya*, and Vladimir Tsibulsky, who wrote for *Megapolis-Express* and *Karetny Ryad*. They are talented and experienced journalists.

with literary affairs in the new weekly. We have a special column for this purpose.
I even think that our literature and our writers are not up to the mark today, and hence they do not interest me much.

In the summer of 1980, when Solidarity was making its first steps in the awakened Poland, Andrei Malgin, a Soviet student at Warsaw University, was speedily sent home "for anti-socialist opinions", as KGB men told him. Ten years later he was elected a People's Deputy to the Moscow City Council for those opinions, winning two times more votes than his rival, head of the regional KGB department. He also became the editor of *Stolitsa*, the Council's first independent magazine.

He is 32 and has worked for four years as a columnist at *Literaturnaya Gazeta* and for four years as head of the literary department of the weekly *Nedelya*. When Malgin was a young journalist his articles were published in *Pravda*, but later his scathing commentaries could be heard more often over Radio Liberty. Another noticeable metamorphosis: having become famous as a literary critic who authored four books of literary criticism, Malgin has changed dramatically by engaging in politics.

In one of his televised addresses he described the main feature of his magazine in the following way: "It will give the leaders of the new generation, who managed to overcome the limitations of the generation of the 1960s—the latter are trying to take revenge for the losses of the past decades—an opportunity to speak up. We are the first perestroika publication which has no taboos and no indestructible authorities."

Judging by its first issue, one could believe that *Stolitsa* would become one of the most radical Soviet publications. The editorial board includes Galina Starovoitova, Arkady Murashev, Sergei Stankevich, Ilya Zaslavsky, Alexander Tsipko, Tatiana Tolstaya and Vladimir Voinovich. It is true that the weekly has a clear-cut position: the cover of the first issue carried the photo of people's deputy Yuri Afanasyev and his words: "Perestroika designed by the party apparat is a success." It will clearly become the mouthpiece of democratic forces.

Here is what Andrei Malgin, editor of *Stolitsa* and Deputy of the Moscow City Council Soviet, wrote in *Argumenty i Fakty* No. 40, 1990:

> When the Moscow Soyuzpechat received the first issue of *Stolitsa* for distribution, it started acting strangely. The magazine was delivered in small amounts throughout a month (some newsstands received the magazine only in October).

Moreover, sellers more than once complained to us that they were ordered to return the magazine to the warehouse even before they received the magazine itself.

On September 7 the Proletarsky inter-district department of Soyuzpechat received 15,120 copies of the magazine from the warehouse, but on September 9 it received an order to stop selling *Stolitsa* and a number of other publications, such as *Demokraticheskaya Rossia, Kommersant, Megapolis-Express* and *Moscow News*.

And lastly, a few words about subscription. Since we were registered as a national publication, we announced subscription throughout the country. But the Ministry of Communications "did not manage" to include the magazine in the national catalogue. I visited Y. Manyakin, Deputy Ministry of Communications, and he assured me that information about subscription to *Stolitsa* (index 73746) was sent out to all post offices. However, this information has not reached many cities and towns.

To understand the meaning (the exploit, to be more exact) of private publishing business in the country, it is suffice to read what Malgin writes in his magazine in the sixth year of Perestroika, when censorship has been repealed and the policy of glasnost has triumphed (with bitter tears). Andrei Malgin offered an article entitled "*Let Us Cherish the Hope*" and placed it under the magazine's heading of the Editor's Page. He wrote:

You keep in your hands the first issue of the magazine *Stolitsa* for 1991. We have been already in existence for six months and issued six issues. Now we are going to put out weeklies on a regular basis.

These six months were not simple for our magazine. The latter proved to be too radical for the publishing house of the paper *Moskovskaya Pravda*, which had started the issue of our magazine. At the beginning this publishing house of the Moscow City CPSU Committee set up a boycott to the issue of the first number of *Stolitsa* and later refused to publish it. We made our rounds of all the Moscow printing houses and discovered that all the large printing establishments that could print our weekly had been in the hands of the Communist Party, while the non-Party printing houses were too weak, and their obsolete equipment was at death's door. It was a paradoxical situation: the organ of the Moscow Soviet could not be printed in Moscow.

The second number of our magazine was issued in Chernigov (the Ukraine). As soon as we brought some printing paper for its subsequent numbers, the director of the printing house received a telephone call from Kiev, from the Central Committee of the Communist Party of the Ukraine, which prohibited the printing of *Stolitsa*. A similar thing happened in Odessa, but now the ban was imposed by the command of the Odessa Military Area. Nizhny Novgorod, Rostov-on-Don and Chekhov represented the geography of our further ordeals. And if we add to this the facts that our workers were given a terrible beating, that railway trucks with our paper were lost en route, that the Moscow Press Distribution Agency tried to write off the fresh print run of our magazine, it will be clear why we failed to set the issue of *Stolitsa* going in 1990.

Not all problems have been settled to this day. Now we have numerous subscribers who expect to receive the magazine on a regular basis. We are determined to discharge our obligations by issuing 52 numbers this year. And this is despite the fact that the printing and publishing industry was in the hands of the discredited Communist Party, that the Moscow Soviet was in fact deprived of real power in the city, and that the secret political police which was very strong and ubiquitous had devoted a great deal of attention to our magazine since the first day of its existence. We shall do everything in our power to issue all the numbers of our weekly on time. Should interruptions take place in the smooth issue, we shall inform our readers about those persons who bear responsibility for them.

What are the most interesting features to be published this year? Our principal theme is the political condition of our society. The reader will meet on our pages with positive and negative heroes of the day. We shall narrate about the role played by Communists in the country, about their attempts to destabilize the situation, to throw our society back, and to protect the ruling class of the *nomenklatura* top officials and bureaucrats. Another constant 'anti-hero' of our publications is the USSR State Security Committee. We shall continue the publication of a series of features about this body that still puts terror into our citizens.

The materials on economic matters will show to the reader not only the present situation (to see this, it will be suffice to drop into any shop), but also the way out of the crisis which had struck us. We shall continue the publication of historical materials and take particular interest in V.I. Lenin, one of the greatest adventurists in world history, who succeeded in plunging the vast country into the abyss of misfortune and misery. The available documents and eyewitness evidence make it possible to get a clearer idea of the stages of the great path to coercion and poverty.

At the same time we are afraid of making our magazine 'too serious'. We want to get the features the reader likes published in our magazine. We are going to print literary works, art book notices, notes about municipal life and even society news. And although there are no comic section in our weekly, the reader will have to smile while reading our materials.

In short, we hope that our magazine will be a really democratic publication expressing the interests of the popular masses and fighting for their aspirations.

In conclusion, I would like to wish you a happy New Year. The year of 1991 will be difficult, but let it bring to you some happiness. Let us cherish the hope that at long last a normal civilized life will begin in our country.

Andrei Malgin is a selfless person and his magazine, *Stolitsa* is the most radical of all Moscow's publications. *Stolitsa* employs top-class journalists, true professionals, who possess a well-developed sense of proportion and tact and profess uncompromising anti-Communism. The magazine's credo is that Lenin and his teachings, as well as all his followers, are criminals, although the magazine also publishes articles on topics other than politics and Soviet history.

Understandably the CPSU did everything it could to stop Malgin and his team, and would have succeeded if it had not died first. But who could know all this before August 1991? It's all the more interesting to read the interview

Andrey Malgin gave to the New York-based newspaper *Novoye Russkoye Slovo* (April 22, 1991), headlined "Stolitsa Is Not Published in the Capital".

Andrei Malgin's articles and reports were first published in *Novoye Russkoye Slovo* two years ago. Last year Malgin became editor-in-chief of the weekly magazine *Stolitsa*. Here is an interview he granted to our correspondent A. Viktorov.

Question: Last summer you were in New York, already as editor-in-chief of *Stolitsa*, although the first issue of the magazine had not come off the press then. You had great plans. Did some of them materialize?

Answer: Yes, in general, although we only managed to get the magazine out regularly later than I had anticipated. The first issue was signed for publication on August 1, the day when the Law on the Press, removing censorship, came into force. In early August the first issue was published and caused the first problems.

Question: Does this mean that the lack of censorship did not help you?

Answer: The lack of censorship and any other control of the contents of the magazine helped us make our articles more profound and critical. Our magazine has never been afraid to state the fact that the Communist regime is rotten to the core and breathing its last breath, that Communist ideology is clearly inhuman, and that the KGB is trying to push the country back to its horrible past and is fighting its own people. We proclaimed all this in our first issue.

Question: How many issues have you published?

Answer: Sixteen, six last year (one a month), and ten this year, one every week. We felt relief on one problem, but immediately came under fire from many sides.

We were offered newsprint at 1,500 rubles per ton (the price was less than 300 rubles last year). The rent of our building was increased over twenty times owing to party pressure and amounted to more than 70,000 rubles a year, the price of hired cars tripled and additional taxes were levied on our profits. More than half the nominal price of the magazine goes to pay for its delivery to subscribers. It would be all right if the magazine was delivered on good time, but whole cities and regions have not received a single issue of the magazine this year, although it's already late March. The issues get held up somewhere. Even in Moscow we cannot expect the issue to be delivered right from the printing shop to kiosks and subscribers. The post starts sending our magazine to subscribers only when the next issue is off the press. Other "left-wing" publications have the same problems, while the party press faces no such headaches.

Question: Your magazine seems to differ from other so-called "pro-perestroika" publications.

Answer: But of course! We don't recognize Gorbachev's bastardized word "glasnost". We decided once and for all that we are working in conditions where freedom of speech exists. That is probably the reason why the magazine has enjoyed a certain success. *Stolitsa* is issued in 300,000 copies, but this doesn't seem to be enough. Many "pro-perestroika" publications are issued by young people of the 1960s, whose political thinking is, to say nothing of their aesthetic values, rather limited. They have had their say.

We are making a new magazine with the help of fresh new forces, and the reader is bound to notice that. For example, not one other pro-perestroika publication has spoken out so harshly about Lenin. But we are not simply "harsh", for we want to say as much as possible.

We devoted several issues to articles about the relationship between Lenin and German intelligence, closely analyzed the question of the finances of the Bolshevik party, while the article "Red Hangover" cast a fresh look on the October 1917 revolt, carried out by drunken seamen and soldiers.

Now we publish articles by the most radical figures, such as Yuri Afanasyev, Valeria Novodvorskaya, Ilya Zaslavsky and Galina Starovoitova. We wrote in detail about Nagorny Karabakh, the Georgia-Ossetia conflict and the Lithuanian tragedy, and, regrettably, our journalists discovered "the hand of Moscow" in all those developments. If a miracle were to happen and the Communists ceded their power, ethnic conflicts would be a thing of the past, the economies would flourish (even if not immediately) and the living standards of common people would improve. But these are only pipe dreams, which we must fight for in the press and elsewhere.

Question: You said that the post office and Soyuzpechat are putting spokes in your wheels and that printing shops refuse to print your magazine. Wouldn't it be better, in these circumstances, to create an alternative distribution service (possibly in cooperation with other publications) and construct your own printing shop? *Stolitsa* was founded by the Moscow City Soviet. Can't it construct a printing shop in a city where it is the master?

Answer: You can judge who is the master of the capital by the fact that our "Moscow-based" magazine is not published in Moscow. Every week the new issue is brought to Moscow in lorries. We are concluding talks with a prestigious Western partner and have started equipping a new printing shop where the Moscow Soviet's publications—*Stolitsa*, *Kuranty* and *Nezavisimaya Gazeta*—would be published. It will also print *Stolitsa*'s advertisement supplement (the first issue will roll off the press in the next few days).

It is even more difficult to establish an alternative distribution service. To do this, we would have to double the 700 post offices in Moscow. However, we could sell our magazine independently. At the beginning of this year we sent more than 200,000 copies to Soyuzpechat kiosks; since then the figure more than halved. The rest is sold by several scores of private distributors. Soyuzpechat staff often hide our magazine from readers and then return them en masse claiming that it does not sell. They simply do not want to work, as their pay does not depend on how many magazines and newspapers they sell. Our alternative distributors get a percentage from what they sell, and hence they work like madmen and know what time of day and which part of the city the magazine will sell in larger quantities.

In principle, monopolistic structures must be destroyed wherever possible. Only then will we obtain genuine independence. Let me cite one example. Mezhdunarodnaya Kniga is the official distributor of the Soviet press abroad. Subscribers to Soviet newspapers and magazines who are resident abroad know, firstly, that it is expensive, and secondly, that they will get them too late, when news become old news and it is no longer worthwhile reading the newspaper or magazine in question. Readers might not know, so I will inform them now that Soviet publications don't want to have anything to do with that organization.

Late last year Mezhdunarodnaya Kniga offered to organize the subscription for *Stolitsa* abroad, as it had received requests from the USA, Australia, Israel and Europe. We asked them to send us a draft contract, and they complied. Under the contract, we should pledge to send free as many copies of the magazine to Mezhdunarodnaya Kniga as it asks in 1991, with the monetary issues settled in April 1992, and the bulk of profits in rubles, rather than hard currency. We could not satisfied with such a contract and consequently asked Mezhdunarodnaya Kniga to review it or at least discuss it. But they refused to amend a single letter in the contract and said that we must sign the contract. We replied that we do not owe them anything and would not use their services. More than that, we prohibited them from distributing our magazine.

What do you think happened next? Mezhdunarodnaya Kniga announced subscription for our magazine and obtained a certain amount of hard currency. It turned out that the organization intended to buy our magazine from Soyuzpechat and send it abroad without even informing us of its intentions and without paying us a single dollar. Or even rubles.

Question: **But is there a way out? After your conflict with that monopoly organization, you left foreign readers with no recourse to your magazine.**

Answer: Why? We have analyzed the offers of our foreign partners and chose the Swiss agency Econews, which is organizing subscription for our magazine throughout the world. The readers are satisfied, because first of all this is cheaper than obtaining our magazine through Soviet agents (one issue costs less than three dollars in the USA, including postage). Secondly, we are probably the only Soviet magazine today which is delivered all over the world on the same day as to Soviet subscribers (in fact, sooner, because the Soviet postal service is the slowest in the world).

We take the section of the issue designed for foreign subscribers from the printing shop directly to the agency of the Swiss air line company in Moscow. Two hours later the issue is on its way to Zurich, where it is sorted out and sent to subscribers throughout the world.

Question: **That's fantastic!**
Answer: It is, indeed, for Soviet readers. But that's how it is done the world over. Newspapers and magazines are perishable goods. By the way, after hearing about our experience, other Soviet publications intend to break their links with Mezhdunarodnaya Kniga and seek the assistance of foreign companies. *Argumenty i Fakty*, for example, which has more than 50,000 foreign subscribers, broke its links with that organization. When I was in Switzerland I learned that our Swiss partner was negotiating foreign subscription with *Argumenty i Fakty*. These talks must have been concluded already.

Question: **Where should those who want to subscribe to *Stolitsa* turn to?**
Answer: It would be simpler to write directly to Econews, Box 535, Lausanne 1001, Switzerland.

Question: **A few words about your plans, please.**
Answer: We shall not change our stance. Our agenda for the future includes a great deal of interesting articles—some of them, I'm sure, cannot appear in other Soviet publications today. There will be several sensations. I am responding to your question in such general terms on purpose, because declassified information ceases to be a sensation. We shall publish an advertisement supplement, called *Chastnaya Zhizn* (Private Life), which shall have not only interesting information, but a great number of advertisements as well as . Today it is difficult to publish an obituary in Moscow. The only newspaper, which does this regularly, is *Vechernaya Moskva*, but it publishes obituaries approved by the district party committee. Marriage notes and congratulations on jubilees are not published at all. Our newspaper will also publish advertisements of private doctors and businessmen, and run a lonely hearts section.

All our plans, concerning both the magazine and the newspaper, will be implemented only if the country continues its movement towards democracy. They will fail if Gorbachev moves more to the right tomorrow. In the past few issues we published critical material about such President's men as Roy Medvedev, Vadim Andreyevich Medvedev, Anatoly Lukyanov, Nikolai Gubenko and Vadim Pavlov. Here are the headlines of some articles about the President himself: "*He Lied to Us Again*", "*The President Is Becoming Dangerous*", "*Don't Light Up Gorbachev*". We were told that the ruling elite was annoyed. So, if the time comes when newspapers and magazines are closed down, we shall be the first victims. But we have an emergency plan for this possibility, a very unpleasant one for the authorities. In a word, the magazine will be published anyway, even if banned.

Question: **I would like very much to share your optimism.**

After the failure of the coup and the victory of the democrats, the situation of Stolitsa improved radically. At the same time, it became more difficult to make an interesting magazine. It is much easier to accuse and denounce, rather than take part in the creative process. This requires quite a different tone. Andrei Malgin put forth his program in his short address at "The 11 Club" (*Rossiiskiye Vesti* No. 19, September 1991). Once more about democracy, the press and the powers that be:

1. We have only recently awoken from a deep, lethargic sleep, from that horror which we lived under for more than 70 years, and there is no genuine democracy in sight yet. Democracy is reflected above all by the protection of the interests of the individual, while the individual has been, and remains, defenseless in this country. I hope that we shall manage to create some time in the future a normal Western-style democracy.
Our democrats must above all preserve the people's trust. Yeltsin and his team have received a carte blanche, a breathing space. Today nobody would dare come up to them and ask where food, etc., is. But they will within half a year.
2. Today the word of a journalist sometimes weighs more than the word of a politician. The fourth power is developing and exerting the most decisive influence on all evolving processes. The so-called democratic press is changing. Major liberal publications are sinking. At the same time, a lot of new populist and genuinely democratic publications have appeared on the scene. This puts forth the danger of neo-Bolshevism, which is much talked about and which I also see. There are quite a few publications, which have not determined their policy yet, but they will have to do this in the very near future.
Our magazine intends to steer the same policy which it followed prior to the coup: our task is to inform our readers. But, there will be some changes. We'll see what turn developments take, but we reserve the right to regard even the most serious figures of current political life ironically.
3. Those who stand above the people must not demonstrate all the time that they are the winners. This is over. They should use the power they acquired cleverly. It is trivial, but there is only one step between people's love and hate. I don't know how to maintain a healthy balance between the desire to keep the people's trust and the need to carry out reforms, which will force living standards down. Our magazine pledges to honestly follow these processes and to tell our thinking readers about them.

Kuranty, a very young and small newspaper of the Moscow Soviet, cannot be as free as *Stolitsa*. Here is how its editor-in-chief Anatoly Pankov spoke on the same issues (*Rossiiskiye Vesti* No. 19, September 1991):

1. Democracy is both strong and weak. It is strong owing to its spontaneity and the general spirit of its meetings. This is its external strength. But democracy is very weak geographically; it is divided and disorganized. In addition, democrats are fighting each other.

At the same time, the most reasonable people in the democratic movement did not miss the chance to settle the question of generally elected power. They elected Soviets in major cities, as well as the mayor of Moscow. This provides a certain firm basis in a dangerous power vacuum.

And yet I don't know who the democrats are. After all, we are all offspring of the Communist Party. Bolshevik thinking is still very strong in us, and we need to know how far each of us has moved away from the party and its slogans.

I think that the democracy of existing power is based on the fact that it is being pressed from below. Our task is to encourage the people to continue putting pressure on the authorities, however good they might look today.

This also concerns Yeltsin. I have no illusions and am not euphoric, but I pin my hopes on his government. There is nobody else to pin one's hopes on; his is the only more or less democratic government. But I think that Yeltsin will act on behalf of the people as long as the people force him to do so. The main thing now is for the people to exert pressure and for the press to be independent.

2. Any founder would very much like to control the press. I, for one, have been experiencing such influence from certain deputies of the Moscow Soviet. We are prepared to depict different opinions, but we shall not be the mouthpiece of any faction. The newspaper must oppose all kinds of power. We must honestly tell the people about the opinions and activities of the "leaders". Only then will the newspaper become interesting reading.

3. I believe that the authorities should be able to combine decisiveness, to attain their goals, and tolerance. The current authorities should propel us more energetically towards the market, rapidly remove barriers from the path leading to private property and entrepreneurship, especially in agriculture.

Let's stop telling all those horrible tales about capitalism—that part of the world is populated by clever people used to high living standards. When I hear some people say that our newspaper is popularizing capitalism, I want to reply: "Down with ideologies! Long live common sense!"

In the Spirit of Sergei Grigoryant's "*Glasnost*"

I don't grudge Malgin his success. His magazine in its issue No. 17 for 1991 told us a different story, which extends our knowledge about the journalistic process in this country. It published the interview with Sergei Grigoryants, the editor of the genuine journal *Glasnost*. Its major heading was entitled "*Paradoxes of glasnost*".

Question: Sergei Ivanovich, you had the peaceful profession of a specialist in literature and the interesting job of investigating the literature of the Russian emigration. You studied not the Moscow classics who built the broad-based image of a positive hero. One time you worked in the decent magazine *Yunost* and your articles were published in *The Great Soviet Encyclopaedia*. And suddenly...

Answer: For the first time I was arrested in 1975. Formally, I was accused of spreading anti-Soviet literature under Article 190 prim of the RSFSR Criminal Code and of exchanging pictures from my collection for a tape-recorder, which fact was qualified as a speculation on a large scale. In reality, however, I was not engaged at that time in any political activity, having the naive faith that literary men may stand aside from public life. I kept up a large correspondence with the Russian writers who lived in Paris and received from them books that at the end of the 1960s still reached the Soviet Union by mail. Moreover, my grandfather was a well-known figure in the emigres' quarters: before the war he was an operatic producer in La Scala and after the war in the Paris Grand Opera. The KGB wanted very much to make use of me in their activity. They went as far as to say that there are many Armenians in its apparatus: After a two-year long persuasion they decided to frighten me. They were sure that when I faced the choice (the more so that I was an absolutely apolitical person)--either to be imprisoned or to collaborate with the KGB, everything would be perfectly clear to me. Already in the prison they continued to prevail upon me to write an article for *Literaturnaya Gazeta* and to show what kind of person Sinyavsky was and to describe the role played by Viktor Nekrasov... I was offered a country house in Krasnogorsk (where premier Kosygin lived at that time) and held out lucrative earnings through the Moscow Philharmonic Society by writing little verses for holiday concerts... Perhaps, these were wonderful proposals, but I did not take interest in them. This being the case, the KGB investigation began to frame up the accusation against me. After all I was convicted for five years. Nevertheless the KGB-men continued to visit me in a corrective-labor camp.

At the beginning I was put in a reformatory near Moscow, for it was more convenient to pay me visits. Soon I was offered a job in the Tretyakov Art Gallery and when I asked with some interest: 'Oh yes, do all employees work in the Gallery upon your recommendation?', I was told that this was not the case but the offer should be of interest to me. Nevertheless I was not tempted with easy wages and a cushy job. The matter ended in my transfer first to the Chistopol Prison, where they found that its regime was not sufficiently severe for me, and then to the Verkhneuralsk prison. That was one of the most terrible Soviet prisons, which in Russian history before the Revolution was known as a political central prison. In 1980, when my term was over, I was released.

They have explained an important thing to me: perhaps you want to keep aloof from politics and intend to hold that it is pernicious literature. To make you consider that this is so, we shall poke your nose into all this dirt.

In 1982 and 1983, after the arrests of Ivan Kovalev and Alexei Smirnov and the exile of Valery Tolts, I was already the editor of the information bulletin B, which was put out three times a month. It told the readers about what we call the infringement of human rights in the Soviet Union, that is, about arrests and interrogations, prisons and labor-corrective camps, psychiatric clinics, etc. At that time I lived in the small town of Borovsk and was arrested by chance, almost three years after my first term of imprisonment had been over. At first, the investigators could not understand the meaning of my occupation. But soon it transpired and I got seven years of imprisonment plus three years of exile under Article 70 of the Criminal Code. So I found myself in Chistopol again...

Question: Sergei Ivanovich, tell us how the *Glasnost* journal was set up.

Answer: Its first issue appeared in June 1987.

The editorial board of the magazine consisted for the most part of the people who published the bulletin B. All of us feel that under new conditions the role of the independent press was increasing. Since in the early 80s we had issued the information bulletin, the *Glasnost* journal was also called a bulletin. We had planned to publish it three times a month. But very soon we realized that we needed a broader audience, a wider range of authors and eventually the coverage not only of the problems of protecting human rights, but also of many other problems, such as ecology and the status of small nationalities. It turned out that we must start an edition that would carry both information and analytical materials. Therefore, *Glasnost* began to feature serious investigatory articles, say, of Selyunin and Strelyany, on the one hand, and of Voslensky and Geller, on the other hand... Our monthly journal had 300-odd pages and was absolutely independent. During the so-called party boom it continued to be independent.

Since 1988 we have been busy with the shooting.

In conditions when the democratic movement was inspired by the powers that be (the government and the KGB), as many people believed, we saw no opportunity for cooperation with "government democrats", as we used to say at that time. We had no confidence in both the left and the right wings of the Soviet leadership. But now, when our leaders have ceased to talk about democracy, we have no grounds to be fenced from the millions upon millions of people. We see their visible movement to meet half-way. This precisely concerns the registration of our journal and the general rapprochement with those democratic forces who have taken part in the officially recognized structures but are now quickly turning into an opposition. On the one hand, there is "International" radio, and the "Echo of Moscow", on the other hand. So we are building up a joint radio station. We have pooled our efforts with the program of the author's television with some other official and non-official groups in drawing up a project of cable television. There are other directions in our work.

Question: Not so long ago the newspaper *Glasnost* has appeared in Moscow. It is being published by the CPSU Central Committee. How do you treat this plagiarism?

Answer: The reputation of our *Glasnost* journal is quite definite. But some people try to speculate on it or to stick to it.
"Certain quarters tried to put to use the popularity of our journal in the USA by setting up a base newspaper *Glasnost*. Originally it was put out once in three months but later on it languished. The same thing happened in Britain and elsewhere.
At long last this piratic technique was repeated by the CPSU Central Committee, which founded its own Glasnost, now in Moscow, the capital of the country. This step is marked by cynicism and elementary gangsterism.
In Poland the Deputy Minister of Culture said to me with indignation: "I have paid a lot of money for subscription but instead of your journal a nasty thing was palmed off on me.' Quite recently I have received a letter in which a certain man demanded that his subscription should be registered anew, because he wanted to subscribe to Grigoryants' *Glasnost* but in fact received something opposite...
In my opinion, the paper of the CPSU Central Committee is doomed and will perish in and of itself, although for purely pedagogically purposes we are going to bring the case of the CPSU Central Committee before the court in conformity with the 1928 Law on Companies. This, by the way, was one of the reasons that prompted us to have our journal registered. This Law provides for the punishment for the theft of trademarks and names and for the payment of compensation for the material and moral damage inflicted on us. Any attempt to affirm that we engage in disgraceful things which the CPSU paper does is quite serious moral damage to us. Any comparison with this paper is an insult to us.

Question: **Your activities during the so-called perestroika have repeatedly caused the exasperation of the Soviet authorities.**

Answer: During the perestroika years I was arrested three times, and in the early 1928 the editorial office of the journal was simply routed.
This oddly enough story is, by the way, characteristic of the perestroika period of democracy. We have threaded on the then premier Ryzhkov's pet corn and to some extent on that of the entire Soviet leadership. Nikolai Ryzhkov travelled on business about Western Europe and Scandinavia and assured their governments and business circles that literally in two or three months the Soviet Union would enter the period of prosperity. We had published in our *Glasnost* two articles which were reprinted by Scandinavian papers with great pleasure. My article dealt with the keen territorial dispute between Norway and the Soviet Union regarding the shelf in the Barents Sea. Since there are grounds to believe that there are oil fields there, this question is not simple, it is very dangerous. Had the Soviet Union with its old-fashioned equipment started its workings at great depths, in horrible climatic conditions, all the sea-side would have been ruined.

But the second article, the one written by Vasily Selyunin, proved to be much more important. In analyzing the economic plans of Ryzhkov, the author came to the conclusion that they might bring about nothing but disaster. At press-conferences and perhaps at other official meetings Ryzhkov was quite often asked: 'Why do you assure people that the Soviet Union has scored unusual and quick achievements, whereas your economists and journalists think differently? I was told later that Ryzhkov phoned to Moscow, to Talyzin, the then Chairman of the State Planning Committee, and demanded that Selyunin's article should be refuted. Talyzin issued pertinent instructions to the staff workers of the State Committee's Scientific Research Institute. On the next day they came to him and explained that Selyunin's article could not be refuted scientifically?

It was decided then to refute it by Soviet methods. As I was told, several members of the Politbureau and the Central Committee Secretaries had discussed this question and came to the conclusion: it should be put into Grigoryants' head that he should behave himself quietly. For this purpose 160 militiamen and also KGB-men and procurators were sent from Moscow to a country-house in Kratovo where the journal's editorial office was located at the time. This wretched dacha was actually routed without any legal grounds, even without any search warrant...

No inventory was drawn up. Nothing legal was done! Our equipment and other things were stolen. That was a normal Soviet robbery, in which a Moscow procurator had taken part. Among the stolen things there was a computer, archives and personal belongings... Four workers of the editorial office were at once arrested, being accused of beating up some little old women. It is noteworthy that the TASS communication about our arrests had appeared before our arrests were made!...

But the most terrible thing lay ahead.

I am not going to assert that the authorities have not limited themselves to this rout. There are essential suspicions that other operations were undertaken at that time. A week later, the person who had xeroxed *Glasnost* drowned in queer circumstances.

I have already said that our journal was and is published chiefly by people who had been under arrest and spent their time in Soviet reformatories and prisons. In our daily life we keep our camp traditions, chief among them being the following: nobody should know the details that do not concern him directly. I myself did not know who prints the journal, despite the fact that I was its editor-in-chief. The man who xeroxed *Glasnost* drowned at a time when our editorial office was being raided. This coincidence had looked rather suspicious especially after his partner was visited by the KGB-men, who, while hunting at this fate, ordered the *Glasnost* weekly to leave at once his place of work unless he wanted to face big troubles... The result of all this was the unwillingness of people to print the journal. For three or four months we could not find people who wished to do the job. I and Andrei

Shelkov was told by Xerox-operators that it was not dangerous to print the works by Solzhenitsyn but it was perilous to issue *Glasnost*. Yet the time of total mortal fear had passed not to return!..

Question: **And do you feel now the "paternal concern" for you?**

Answer: Periodically I have problems with travels abroad. Two years ago I was let out of the country for the first time to get the prize of the International Federation of Publishers "The Gold Pen of Freedom' and since that time I spend much time abroad. In some cases it was not so simple to go abroad: once I was disembarked from a plane, next time the booked tickets were returned as "unpaid" allegedly because of an error in a computer... There were incredible situations I got in. For example, at the end of March I would receive an invitation sent in last September. As a rule, all invitations reach the addressee after this or that congress or conference I was to attend is over...

Sometimes much more unpleasant things happen. Last autumn two distributors of *Glasnost* had been beaten up ferociously and found themselves in a city hospital. Both were given a terrible beating by militiamen, one was beaten up by staff workers from the second militia station and the other--by officers from the Moscow City Administration of Internal Affairs on the Petrovka Street. Both peddlers sold *Glasnost* with an official authorization and stood among other independent press distributors, but militiamen picked up precisely them. Generally speaking, we can't complain of the authorities' lack of consideration...

Question: **What, in your view, are the prospects for the *Glasnost* journal and for glasnost in general?**

Answer: The prospects of our journal are indeed the prospects of the democratic movement in the country. The prospects of the journal are directly associated with armored carriers and OMON in the streets, with the possibility of bursting into office premises in full conformity with the President's decrees. Unfortunately, we largely return to the situation of the early 1980s at the best and to the situation of the 1930s at the worst. We can't remain indifferent towards what is being done with glasnost in our country and with the nation itself. The prospects for our editorial office imply a changeover in its composition. One of the staff workers of *Glasnost* told me the other day that his relations are terrified and want to leave the country for abroad. Just the other way around, a few persons who do not work in the journal now phoned and asked: was it not the time to return and work on the journal?

They held that in such an atmosphere in the country (its character is clear to everybody) our journal is for many people the most natural place in public life. I repeat, today *Glasnost* is not only a journal, but also a fund that works in all directions of information. Time will show the path."

The editorial office of the weekly *Demokraticheskaya Rossia* called its interview with Vladimir Bukovsky in its issue of April 26, 1991 "the time of the democratic press". Together with Yury Afanasyev, Yelena Bonner, Garry

Kasparov, Lev Kopelev, Vasily Selyunin and Vladimir Tikhonov. Bukovsky is on the list of the members of the editorial board of this popular paper in Moscow. Yury Burtin and Igor Klyamkin are the Editors-in-Chief of the 16 page weekly of a small size. In this interview Bukovsky underscored two things: the paper must promote the safe opposition structures in the army and among the youth, and also create a situation in which Communists will not fear to abandon the reigns of government in all totalitarian structures.

Here is an excerpt from the interview:

Corr.: To make Communists sure, they must be given a guarantee that nothing will happen to them in the process of the further movement. There will be no Nuremberg for the Communist Party and its rank-and-file members.

Bukovsky: You see, a la guerre comme a la guerre. Take, for example, the war in the Persian Gulf. The first thing the Allies did was the scattering of leaflets addressed to Kurdish and Iraqi soldiers: "Come to us with this leaflet and nothing will happen to you." As for me, I propose the same thing: "Come and join our side and nothing will happen to you and no more."

Corr: And what about those who have not sided with us?

Bukovsky: They will have to surrender or to die from hunger.

These words of the people from *Demokraticheskaya Rossia* are just. For we know that our perestroika has slowed down with the fall of communist regimes in Eastern Europe. Our party and military leaders, including collective-farm and defense-complex leaders, have lost all desire for living by begging or even for finding themselves in the dock (Zhivkov, Ceausescu and Honecker). It would be more profitable for our society to increase wages for those whom we want to get rid of and to pension them off with equal amounts of money. In no case I would admit the shooting of the participants in the August putsch.

The editorial offices of *Demokraticheskaya Rossia*, *Stolitsa*, *Ekspress Khronika* and *Glasnost* of Grigoryan have similar problems. The Press Distribution Agency and its bodies in Republics, regions, cities and districts do not wish to sell these publications or take from the printing houses an insignificant number of copies. The most unpleasant thing is the return by the Agency of unsold copies. For this reason the Soviet democratic press have to rely not in the Agency, but on voluntary peddlers. It is unnecessary to mention that *Demokraticheskaya Rossia* has not announced the subscription to this paper.

Today Soviet publicists Malgin and Grigoryants, Burtin and Klyamkin are regarded by Russian national-patriots as much more dangerous figures than our compatriots living abroad. In March 1991, the Moscow publishing consortium Avers put out the first 100,000 copies of the journal Continent (issue No. 66).

Since 1973 it has been published in Paris by the writer Vladimir Maximov. A few years ago, before he died this journal was assisted by Axel Springer, a magnate from the Federal Republic of Germany, whom we had preferred to kick for his "yellow press". Now we try to save Maximov, our recent enemy, although some time ago the curious reader could be put under arrest or sent to a reformatory for the mere reading of this quarterly journal of 400 pages each. as distinct from the dull thick journals, Continent prints small topical works never published before.

As I have said earlier, Malgin is younger than Maximov but is more sharp-tongued than the latter. Maximov calls upon Soviet people to put an end to the communist experiment but highly values Gorbachev and believes that the West will not let Russia go to rack and ruin.

In most big cities of the country, one may buy on the market or in the street at high prices both fruits from the South and Baltic papers issued in Russian. The left press of Lithuania, Latvia and Estonia unlike that of the former Union republics has reached the nation-wide audience. The Kremlin seems to have done everything to change this tendency. The editorial office of the American paper *Novoye Russkoye Slovo* devoted a whole page in its issue of February 23, 1991 to the talk with Alexei Grigoriev, Editor-in-Chief of the Riga paper *Baltiiskoye Vremya*, a deputy to the Latvian Parliament. The New York paper preceded the interview with the headline "*Ambivalent Democracy*":

> Today the spectrum of the Latvian press is quite motley, although the papers are highly politicized in terms of ideological convictions. After the failure of the November holidays in Latvia the newspaper *Yedinstvo* (Unity), the press organ of the Latvian Interfront, kept publishing from issue to issue the lists of the managers of factories and establishments who wanted, contrary to the law, to deprive their workers of the possibility to celebrate the coming anniversary of the Great October Revolution. They intended to take this prohibitive measure either for the edification of the non-Latvian posterity or for the sake of future arrests and reprisals.
>
> The Riga fortnightly paper *Yeshche* (Some More) holds that the world may be saved by imparting sexuality to politics. Were are some of the headlines of the newspaper articles: "*Women in the Life of Lenin*", "*Four Thousand FIM for a Night in Brezhnev's Bed*", "*She Wont Sleep Even with Yeltsin, Though He Is Better Than Others*", "*Nothing Human is Alien to the Nobel Prize Winner*" (the reference is to Mikhail Gorbachev, who is alleged to have a reckless love-affair with the 19-year-old 'Miss Moscow' Maria Kalinina under his wife's very eyes)... Generally speaking, this perspective edition is not serious enough.

But we can see other news and a different editorial point of view:

> "At the current session of the USSR Supreme Soviet the Government at long last has openly announced the budgetary expenses for the maintenance of the KGB in the amount of 4.9 billion rubles..."

"According to Boris Yeltsin, the latest events in three Baltic states testify to the fact Gorbachev has lost common sense. Perestroika is over and communism has died..."

"Soviet troops are being brought up to Lithuania. These include the regiments from Rostov and Transcaucasia and have a sizable experience of operation during a curfew."

These lines are taken from the issues of the newspaper *Baltiiyskoye Vremya*, a Russian variant of *Atmoda*, the press organ of the Latvian Popular Front. This paper has been put out twice a week since June 1990. Its editor Alexei Grigoryev was on a tour of the USA at the invitation of a college whose students wanted to listen to the eyewitness and participant in recent developments in the Baltic area. When he was in New York, he paid a visit to the editorial office of *Novoye Russkoye Slovo*, where he was plied with the following questions.

Question: What is your newspaper today? How does the present right orientation of Gorbachev's laws on glasnost affect the fate of your paper?"

Answer: Gorbachev's laws do not worry us in a special way, because we in Latvia still observe our laws and not the Union laws. But the seizure of the Riga Press House by Communists has affected us. Now we have to go to a printing house for a distance of over 100 kilometers. The circulation of our paper is not large, it is below one million copies issued by our neighboring paper *Sovetskaya Molodezh*. But to print our paper, the small printing house needs 8 hours, or a full working shift, to do the job.

Take into account our concern for urgent materials, difficulties connected with the delivery and transportation of the paper. In principle nothing has changed, but we have to work much more now.

Question: Is any other paper in such trouble? Very likely the seizure of the Press House affected the editorial offices of other independent editions.

Answer: Our editorial office is not in the Press House and other independent papers are not there either. The trouble is that our printing house, the most powerful in Latvia, has been captured by Communists. The fact of its putting out of action affected not only independent papers. Many journals and magazines have ceased to be published. Even the large newspapers have found themselves in danger of closing down. They cannot be printed anywhere. It's practically impossible to print over 50,000 copies in a small printing office. The independent paper *Atmoda*, the press organ of the Latvian Popular Front, has the heaviest load of cares, for it has to move from the Riga Press House to the town of Siauliai.

Question: The old prescription of a Bolshevik coup is to capture the banks, post offices, printing houses in the first place... Was the seizure of the Press House by OMON soldiers a point in their great strategic plan or a simple tactical move made by local right-wing authorities?

Answer: I think that this operation was, of course, a part of their strategic design, but it was not obligatory to capture the Press House. The central authorities had planned a number of provocations in order to create tensions in the Baltic Republics. Their ultimate purpose is to prove with the aid of Denisov, the head of the USSR Supreme Soviet Commission, who is now in Geneva, that in Latvia, Lithuania and Estonia there are two roughly equivalent extremist groups that fight each other, that the people there are dissatisfied with this struggle, that they have to work now and there will be no order unless the strong central authority interferes in the present situation.

Question: To what extent does this correspond to the true state of affairs?

Answer: This is a pure invention; it is a fragment of the scenario now being translated into life. To make this invention look more plausible, a series of explosions was arranged by the military. At first they exploded some monuments or, to be more exact, the crosses on the graves of Latvian legionaries...

Question: Moreover, the remains of the fuses that had been found in the places of sabotage were identified as the army ammunition possessed by the Soviet Army units stationed in the region.

Answer: This is true. The Minister of Defense Yazov recognizes that the first explosions were the handiwork of Soviet soldiers but keeps silence about other explosions. So the seizure of the Press House is one of the points in the artificial escalation of tension.

Question: In the United States you have faced the keen interest of the American public in the events taking place in the Baltic states. Do we understand in a proper way what is taking place in your country or did you create a certain myth about actual events?

Answer: Of course, you do not understand the situation to the last. But today the picture of what is going on in Latvia is much more plausible. When I was here a year ago, Americans were intoxicated with Gorbimania. This is a children's disease like measles, through which the world had to go. We had run into Gorbachev and his political methods earlier and seen things clearly more quickly. You will have to go through this.

Question: Which Baltic Republic do you put in the first place as regards the striving to independence and the difficulties it has to overcome in this process?

Answer: In terms of real accomplishments in the struggle for independence Lithuania is ahead of the other two republics. But in terms of difficulties in the struggle Latvia is ahead of the other republics. To be more exact, it is left behind as a result of these difficulties. Although the relations between the three republics are not so close as we wished, some joint actions are nevertheless taken by them. The duties were approximately divided among them as follows: Lithuania is breaching, while Estonia is building bridges with the West. Thereupon both of them are bringing up Latvia.

We have to carry out democratic transformations with great care, thinking out every step to be taken by the Latvian population. The point to note is that the overwhelming majority of Letts, Lithuanians and Estonians argue in favor of independence of Moscow, independence at any price. If they are given a choice--either the Kremlin's dictatorship or their own dictatorship, they will prefer without any hesitation the latter in the hope of normalizing the situation in the future.

Our paper is published in Russian and is intended for Latvia's Russian population. It seems to me, it is good to do everything gradually and carefully, by enabling both the Lettish and Russian communities to check up every new bill.

Question: **Has Latvia full parted with the communist myth of its 'proletarian reliability' as a mercenary of the world revolution? I bear in mind the history of the Lettish riflemen, who were alleged to incessantly save the young Soviet state and later made up the state security bodies to strength.**

Answer: I think that the myth about the Lettish riflemen in Latvia has died together with the last rifleman. Today their activities are interpreted not as an object of national pride but as a complex of national fault. Earlier this question was hushed up, but now it is widely debated.

Question: **In the very near future, perhaps the most authoritative delegation of US legislators is going to visit the Baltic states. It includes the Republican senator from the New York State Alphons d'Amato, who last year tried to get into Lithuania from Poland illegally.**

Answer: I belong to those people who do not insist on 'special relations' of the American legislators with the Baltic republican authorities. The disintegration of the Soviet empire must attract the attention of the West in all regions, whether it is the Baltic area, the Ukraine, Byelorussia, Transcaucasia or Central Asia. Although, of course, it is impossible to ignore the fact that almost the entire civilized world recognizes our republics as independent and illegally occupied countries. I speak out for the most active participation of Western MPs in the expert examination of our reforms. By far not everything is ideal in our country, but today our difficulties are those of the democratic process. It is very important that the Western governments should understand this, because our opponents--the central authorities--try to liquidate the democratic process with the aid of these difficulties.

Question: **Recently I had the occasion to take part in a meeting with US Congressmen. A senator from Virginia (Dem.) was asked, why the American Congressmen did not regard the Baltic problem on a par with the problem of Kuwait or with the problem of Palestinians living on the Israel-**

controlled territories. How do you treat the question of recognizing Latvia, Lithuania and Estonia as the equally illegally occupied lands like Kuwait captured by Saddam Hussein?

Answer: We do recognize this fact. As for the Palestinian problem, the comparison here with the Baltic states implies a strained legal interpretation, since the territories occupied or controlled by Israel have not represented a sovereign state.

Question: Kuwait had been captured according to a traditionally Soviet scenario performed in their time in the Baltic area, Czechoslovakia and Afghanistan. At first troops were brought in and then puppet governments were installed, supported by 'the entire people'. Hussein is not averse to hold a 'national referendum' by changing the demographic situation in Kuwait. Why did this scenario fall short of the Soviet Government's expectations in January 1991 in Lithuania, Latvia and Estonia? Was the resistance here too strong?

Answer: The matter was sealed not by our resistance, but by our self-control. What kind of resistance? People barred the way to tanks, showing that they were ready to die. No other resistance could be put up. But the response that was aroused throughout the world by our determination to resist frightened the Kremlin leadership. Now it tries to conceal all traces of its actions and for this reason it has sent Denisov's team to Geneva.

Question: How would you describe this man?

Answer: Denisov is a typical Soviet politician of the Gorbachev era. As for the main traits of this figure, they are marked by the greater degree of hypocrisy and mendacity as compared with his predecessors. If the diplomats of the Brezhnev era were upset by the fact whether they lied for two days in succession in the same vein or contradicted to themselves, the Soviet leaders of today feel no anxiety about this. They act within the framework of one situation. Consistency in uttering lies does not worry them.

Some time ago Denisov asserted over the Riga TV that there were no grounds whatsoever for inter-national conflicts in Latvia and that the OMON actions were the only hotbed of tensions in the republic. But as soon as he returned to Moscow and received appropriate instructions, he began to say quite the opposite things. I think that this is not surprising: throughout his career in science he sought to prove the inconsistency of Einstein's 'bourgeois' theory and now he may act in the political field in the same spirit.

Question: You have mentioned tanks and OMON-men. Let us clarify what armed forces took part in the January operation ' the Baltic area--91'. On the one hand, they included the OMON, the detachments of militiamen of special designation, subordinate directly to the city or regional administrations of internal affairs. On the other hand, they included the air-borne or internal troops subordinate to the USSR Ministry of the Interior. In addition to this the Minister of Defense Yazov brought the commandoes in the Baltic area under the command of the Ministry of Defense.

Most likely American correspondents had no time to look at tab emblems or identify the color of shoulder-straps. Moreover, the landing variants of the Soviet commandoes' Kalashnikov submachine-guns are similar. Who, then, stormed the Riga Press House?

Answer: In Latvia, the Soviet command have used all the time one and the same detachment of militiamen of special designation, which in November 1990 stated that it had ceased to be subordinate to the city and republican authorities. In fact it obeyed Moscow, although the latter did not mention this fact anywhere.

Question: Is it a rebellion? Is it an orgy of anarchy? Why did not the Latvian Minister of the Interior disband this militia unit at once?

Answer: Such attempts were undertaken. On January 20, all the Latvian police were mobilized to dislodge the OMON-men from their military base in Vezmiligravis near Riga.

But Moscow warned us that such actions might cause undesirable consequences...

Question: There was a traditional threatening shout: 'Don't break playthings!"

Answer: The degree of mendacity and duplicity of today's Moscow leadership is much higher than it was before. Earlier they said 'Don't touch, this is our property'. Now they say simply: 'Don't touch'. In my opinion, very soon Moscow will announce to the Riga OMON that the latter is 'alien to the Soviets', will acknowledge its culpability and take it to court. Developments in Poland gained pace in the same manner following the murder of the Catholic priest Popeluszko.

In the Baltic area Gorbachev makes use of the means that come to hand. In Lithuania there is also a unit of OMON which is not subordinate to the Lithuanian government, but this unit is very small. Therefore, the Soviet authorities sent their commandoes there. It is a tell-tale fact that the troops of the Baltic Military Area whose garrisons are scattered all over these republics were not used at all. Gorbachev and Yazov could not rely on these troops. No matter how the officers and men were irritated and annoyed, they understood perfectly well that the story about the seizure of power by fascists and nationalists had been faked.

Question: Some people hold that according to Gorbachev's strategic design the suppression of the democratic movement in the Baltic area was synchronized with the military operations of Americans and their allies against Iraq. Garry Kasparov, for instance, admits the possibility of a

	collusion between Gorbachev and Bush. What do you think about this?
Answer:	Of course, there was no collusion. But the fact that Moscow actions in the Baltic area were timed beforehand to the war waged by Americans in Iraq is beyond all manner of doubt. The Moscow leadership had planned its actions and suppressed the Hungarian revolution in 1956 in the same manner and this was done when the world was infatuated with the Suez crisis.
Question:	Recent events in the Baltic republics have attracted the attention of the West to such an extent that certain political analysts began to speak about "Euroracism", that is, the preference given by the free world to Latvia, Lithuania and Estonia to the detriment of Soviet republics where the struggle for independence caused a greater bloodshed. Your anguish is regarded as a pain in the European organism, while the suffering of Armenians, Georgians or Moldova Gagauzes as outlays of great power Byzantism.
Answer:	I agree that this is unjust but it is a fact. In reality we have always been a part of the all-European house. But our republics were wrested from this house by force, while the West had forgotten and even betrayed us. Hence the inevitable complex of guilt in our relations today.
Question:	Do you bear in mind a moral betrayal?
Answer:	Not only. It's a fact that Britons returned Latvian gold to Premier Kosygin and settled at our expense their property disputes with the Soviets. But, of course, we have always been backed by the refusal of the West to recognize the legality of the occupation of the Baltic states. By no means unimportant is the fact that we have proved to be the last victims in a series of acts of state violence perpetrated by Gorbachev. If in the cases of Nagorny Karabakh or Tbilisi it was possible to believe that Gorbachev had not known anything or there had been an unexpected hitch, then in the Baltic area everything is plainly visible.
Question:	How do you envision the future of the Baltic republics, say, in twenty years' time?
Answer:	In twenty years the three republics will continue to be independent states united into a compact Baltic Union with sufficiently close ties with today's fellow-sufferers—independent Russia, Belarus and other former Soviet republics."

The Massacre in Vilnius Finished Off the Idea of the Soviet Union

February 1 and 2, 1991 saw the All-Russia Conference of the Newspaper Editors, the first meeting of this kind in Moscow with the participation of representatives of the Soviet and independent press. They discussed the problem of holding out against the information blockade of the Russian Federation, the attempts to strangle the existing islands of democracy and glasnost in the Republic. It was stated at the Conference that CPSU functionaries dissolve the refractory collectives of the local newspapers. In addition they conceal newsprint reserves, sell their premises by auction and transfer printing houses to third persons. The RSFSR Minister for the Press and Information Mikhail Poltoranin said at this Conference that the Ministry would render assistance to the Russian press in remote districts, in all big and small cities, and thus promote its revival. He added that three new republican papers (*Rossia*, *Rossiiskiye Vesti* and *Rossiiskaya Gazeta*) had already appeared in Moscow and they were now maintaining a safe feedback with the Russian Information Agency. The Conference participants demanded that the illegal decision taken by the USSR Radio and Television State Committee to close down the Russian radio channel (Radio of Russia) and should be revoked and that Russia should receive information sovereignty. They also appealed to all journalists of the Russian Federation to support the principle of activity formulated by the staff members of *Moscow News*: *to speak and write the whole truth, and if there is no such possibility, to keep silence*. This was reported by the paper *Moskovsky Komsomolets* in its issue of February 5, 1991.

In terms of public passions the year of 1991 has proved to be similar to the year of 1917. The CPSU dictatorship that usurped state power 74 years ago is at an end and the Party apparatus structures have been disbanded. Yet at the beginning of 1991 the severe political frost threatened to bind the incipient thaw. The events in the Baltic republics resounded as a funeral knell for glasnost in the Moscow democratic press. The horrors of hostilities and blood dictatorship in Stepanakert, Tskhinvali and Baku were feebly perceived by the Moscow public opinion and, moreover, in a distorted interpretation, as was the case in the areas which were unsuitable for living but where unfortunate people suffered from radiation for five years. But later the victims of Vilnius and Riga downright started the democratic forces of the capital of the disintegrating empire.

Moscow News arranged a round-table conference with the invitation of prominent Soviet journalists and editors. Taking part in the discussion were first deputy editor of *Izvestia* Igor Golembiovsky, editor of *Komsomolskaya Pravda* Vladislav Fronin, editor of *Argumenty i Fakty* Vladislav Starkov, editor of *Ogonyok* Vitaly Korotich, editor of *Moskovsky Komsomolets* Pavel Gusev, editor of *Kommersant* Vladimir Yakovlev, editor of *Chas Pik* Natalya Chaplina, executive manager of *Rossia* Alexander Drozdov, director of the TV and Radio Company Radio of Russia Sergei Davydov, host of the TV program "Pyatoye Koleso" Bella Kurkova, host of the TV program "Do I Posle Polunochi" Vladimir Molchanov, Chairman of the Russian Supreme Soviet Committee for the Mass Media and Relations with Public Organizations, Citizens' Mass Movements and Studies of Public Opinion, Viktor Yugin, and *Moscow News* political analyst Len Karpinsky. The discussion was chaired by the editor of *Moscow News* Yegor Yakovlev.

At that time the total circulation of socio-political dailies and weeklies amounted to some 87 million copies. The printing of the newspapers and magazines whose editors took part in the round-table conference exceeded 60 per cent of the total circulation. All the above-mentioned editions have long been defending the ideas of perestroika. They also were the target of the fierce attacks by the CPSU mafia, which did not want to follow the path of reforms and to lose their power. All these editors are very clever people. Therefore, their appraisal of their own positions are of great interest. The putsch began actually not in August, but in early January 1991, when a real information war was launched and in all border regions of the Russian-Soviet empire many people died. Below we cite the excerpts from the verbatim report of the discussion and reproduce the sub-titles given by *Moscow News*:

Glasnost In Opposition. Yegor Yakovlev: The fuss kicked up by the President's suggestion to amend the Law on the Press has led nowhere so far. Glasnost in its present form will disappear along with the reforms. *Nezavisimaya Gazeta* would be closed if the present Moscow City Council and its Chairman Popov were removed. *Chas Pik* (Rush Hour) would cease to exist if the Leningrad City Council led by Sobchak were disbanded. Moscow News would also be eliminated. But glasnost itself can't be eliminated without a direct coup, which is hardly possible. So far the democratic press can make use of what possibilities it has to shore up its positions. It is, of course, clear that no favors can be expected any longer. The latest remarks by the President show that he has made his choice by saying that the democratic forces are in opposition to him.

Pavel Gusev: The very term "glasnost" was introduced by Gorbachev and his team. But glasnost has since turned into freedom of expression, whether the authorities like it or not. And this is our main weapon. Glasnost is a fine word to advertise Gorbachev's course in the West. Thus glasnost will be preserved, while freedom of expression will continue to receive hard knocks from various quarters.

Igor Golembiovsky: You can't say that the buck stops with the President, that he has cooled toward the democratic press. There are wider implications than that. A new generation of party functionaries has emerged on the scene who realize that they are too late. The cake has been already carved up. Unlike the previous generation, they will act more vigorously and show more ingenuity. *Izvestia*, a rather moderate newspaper, is already under attack from several quarters. *Izvestia*'s position in the Soviet press is also unique. It still remains the only paper trying to bridge the chasm between the right-wing and left-wing press. If it moves to the right that would put many publications in jeopardy. And it's evident that we are being attacked from every quarter. Deputies of the current session of the Supreme Soviet have been given lists of "extremist" publications, one of which is *Izvestia*, I don't know why. There are suggestions that *Izvestia* be overhauled constructively. How constructively? By printing more speeches by people's deputies.

Vladislav Fronin: Journalists at all publications have changed their attitudes radically in recent years. They have developed a taste for freedom of expression. Their readers have as well. For this reason, no return to non-glasnost is possible, despite all the attempts to turn things back.

Vitaly Korotich: The newspapers *Pravda* and *Sovetskaya Rossia* use the word 'democrat' as if it meant 'class enemy'. The system is trying to connect in mass consciousness "democracy" and 'economic hardships', 'free press' and 'anarchy'. The system is setting the people against the very idea of reforms and scares lumpens with prospects of competition which would end their status as state dependents. What is happening is a dangerous fusion of the parasitic top echelons and members of the demoralized but obedient groups of people at the bottom. From their point of view, neither those on the top nor those at the bottom need information. Or better: the former get information, while the latter have never wanted it. They are satisfied with regurgitated information, like they are now getting from TV courtesy of Kravchenko.

Alexander Drozdov: What puts me on guard is when I hear the word 'pluralism' being used instead of 'glasnost'. It is patent that pluralism is impossible in one newspaper, because a newspaper cannot be a mishmash of assorted views. Our opponents see 'pluralism' first and foremost as a way to preserve party influence not only in their own newspapers but also on publications that have never had anything to do with the party.

Vladimir Molchanov: The idea of smothering glasnost is supported by more than just the CPSU Central Committee. It is sadly shared by some of our colleagues. Of late at the Central Television I've been constantly finding myself in an atmosphere where my professional duties are in conflict with my sense of morality. If the evening news program 'Vremya' coincides with your moral choice, what kind of professional duty is it that allows information to get so monstrously butchered. If you make another moral choice, your program may be axed as was the 'Vzglyad' program. People whose moral choice coincides with 'Vremya' are quite numerous. There is no official censorship on Central Television. All censorship is done by those who run the station or a particular program. When I first started to work for 'Vremya' (I officially quit on January 14) we had no problems as to what news went on the air. Fifteen minutes before air time, Ligachev phoned to give his instructions, ten minutes before air time another high official phoned to give his own instructions. Then that stopped. Now the practice is coming back, and instructions from secretaries and other highwings in the CPSU Central Committee (who are also members of the Supreme Soviet) are becoming the usual practice.

Vladislav Starkov: Unlike those who work for TV, I will not dramatize things. We have at long last entered a normal political struggle. We should have expected it. Fear of censorship? I don't think it does anybody any good, including Gorbachev. As soon as censorship returns, *Argumenty i Fakty*, for example, would either go or we would have to have a commissar in our office to watch over every word we print. There would be an underground press again, and people would listen again to foreign radio. People won't remain uninformed.

A War Without Rules. Yegor Yakovlev: We can make a list of the ways used to strangle the democratic press. One device is to constantly stress that whatever is done by the democratic press has allegedly been planned in advance. Then there is the use of imprecise or misleading facts. Let's say we write 'the crime of a regime that wouldn't quit the stage'. Clearly what is meant is the still lingering Stalin regime, the punitive regime, the regime that committed a crime in Vilnius. Our opponents give the phrase a little twist saying that the democratic press works against the Soviet system, against the constitutional regime, etc.

Len Karpinsky: The opponents of the democratic press have vast experience in organization. If the President drops a word about possibly suspending the Law on the Press and then retreats then and there, it does not in the least mean that nothing is being done to suspend the Law. I believe that party functionaries have been dispatched to the provinces to drum up support for the newspapers *Sovetskaya Rossia* and *Krasnaya Zvezda* and against *Komsomolskaya Pravda*, *Moscow News*, etc., and to persuade the workers to urge that the Supreme Soviet investigate the latter newspapers' activities. We are fighting for our existence honorably, while they are trying to destroy us through subterfuge.

Vladimir Molchanov: As for discrediting the mass media, there could be no greater damage than that done by Central Television. It pains me to see some TV programs becoming anonymous, like the one about Lithuania made by a studio referred to only as Absolyut. This is like the base propaganda of fifty years ago. Central Television discredits itself by making no attempt whatever to bring together the facts. It showed only one of the three recent public rallies held in Moscow. There were no attempts to discredit my program 'Do i Posle Polunochi' (Before and After Midnight) until the January program went on the air. Then things changed. While my program is not interfered with directly, we are being made to toe the line in a variety of ways.

Vitaly Korotich: Here are more examples. Marshal Yazov has declared that I was bribed by Western intelligence services. General Filatov has announced that I'm doubtful character, appointed editor of *Ogonyok* by the Americans. The "patriotic" rags like *Puls Tushina* and *Literaturnaya Rossia* denounce me as part of the Jewish Masonic conspiracy. *Molodaya Gvardiya* at times becomes apoplectic, even mentioning my name dozens of times in an issue. Their strategy is not to argue the issues but to smear their opponent.

Bella Kurkova: Many a plenum of the Leningrad Regional Party Committee has discussed the mass media. My program 'Pyatoye Koleso' (The Fifth Wheel) figured there as the main cause for all the country's troubles. The latest plenum also devoted much time to us, but they toned down their accusations and abuse, sticking to the published press reports. The obvious reason was: anyone persecuted in this country finds sympathy among the people. Then the newspaper *Leningradsky Rabochy* carried a big theoretical article by the Regional Party Secretary Belov. There is a remarkable passage about intellectuals who must be looked after so they don't get run over by

'The Fifth Wheel'. Comrade Belov followed this up by a series of meetings with workers, and every such meeting invariably had a speaker who asked: "How much longer do we have to put up with 'The Fifth Wheel?' The answer was: 'The Fifth Wheel' would stop turning soon.

New Pressures Replace Censorship. Natalya Chaplina: An attack against our newspapers is proceeding right before our very eyes. Relatively not long ago *Leningradsky Rabochy* used to be a good newspaper with a democratic orientation and a handsome circulation. But when new papers were allowed to form, the journalists at *Leningradsky Rabochy* were unable to come together and nominate a competent editor. Like an overripe pear the paper fell into the hands of the Regional Party Committee. And now from a moderately liberal publication it has gone extremely rightist. A former party functionary was appointed as its editor, and all its decent journalists have left for other publications.

Pavel Gusev: Whenever it is difficult to combat freedom of speech by means of ideological censorship, use is made of other methods of pressure: organizational and economic. First and foremost, there's the paper problem. I don't even rule out that there will be new attempts to block the production of larger supplies of newsprint. And the distribution of newspapers is completely controlled by the Ministry of Communications. This monopoly can simply mow us down; after all, if a daily newspaper reaches readers three days later the latter will drop all interest in it. *Moskovsky Komsomolets* is experiencing blatant economic pressure. In effect, subscriptions to our paper have been closed: the printshop has refused to bring out the general printing. On the other hand, the *Moskovskaya Pravda* Publishing House is still soliciting orders from other newspapers. Beginning this year, the distribution of *Moscow News* in other cities has been discontinued altogether.

Vitaly Korotich: Freedom of information can be suppressed in many ways, specifically by raising the prices of paper and polygraphic services, and deliberately disorganizing the Soyuzpechat distribution agency. There are numerous ways, and we are experiencing them (rather they are being tested on us). The liberal press is poorly protected in every respect. Just try and touch *Sovetskaya Rossia*, and you'll see what a hue and cry will be raised. Yet whatever they print has, on more than one occasion, insulted the good name of our Soviet land and the intentions of its leadership (as in the case of publications in support of Saddam Hussein and his war).

Igor Golembiovsky: One shouldn't oversimplify the situation. Earlier than the other media, the press has found itself tied in on market relations. This process will continue to develop. And there is a need to think of what to undertake on that strategic plane. The real economy beckons its own. For instance, beginning with January the *Izvestia* Publishing House has been under pressure to stop publishing the *Nezavisimaya Gazeta*. But the publishing House has an objective stake in extracting profits from its capacities.

Bella Kurkova: Radio and TV broadcasters have found themselves in a very horrendous situation. After all, we've not been protected even by the Law on the

Press, for it's almost impossible to apply it to the electronic mass media. Gosteleradio, the Soviet agency in charge of Radio and TV, in league with members of the Supreme Soviet, has been working to prepare a Law on TV and Radio. A special law. The provision on the All-Union TV and Radio Broadcasting Company, secretly set up within the depths of Gosteleradio, tells us that a monstrous supermonopoly is in the making. This document contains points which will deprive everyone of the possibility of speaking differently than the CPSU. Here there is a need to have a clear view of the situation. The TV program 'Vzglyad' has already been silenced. Another one, 'Before and After Midnight', can also be silenced. Our staff passed a decision on the independent status for a Leningrad TV and Radio, whose founders could be the Lensoviet, the Regional Soviet, the work collective and Russia's Ministry for the Press. However, three or four days after a presidential Decree appeared and all of our attempts were reduced to nil. It is not ruled out that tomorrow Leningrad TV will be controlled by the Central TV and Radio Broadcasting Company. All the more so since we don't have many people who are prepared to work according to democratic principles. And it's easy to guess what will happen if both the broadcasting network and the programs are dictated by Moscow.

Sergei Davydov: An alternative radio network appeared at the close of last year, perhaps for the first time in our country. How can it be stifled? With technology alone. Because given the hard currency hunger experienced both by the country as a whole and all the more so by Russia, we are totally dependent on Gosteleradio's equipment. Thus they are free to do whatever they like to us.

Bracing for Resistance. Igor Golembiovsky: We need to protect the character of our periodicals. And we can do this, primarily through the Law on the Press. Regrettably, our legislators don't understand this law very well. For that reason journalists have had to learn it by heart, and have had to fight for every letter in that law. We need to form a solid economic basis, without which we're done for--all of us. This can be achieved using our own incomes and not only them. Not long ago, the Union of Cinematographers decided to set up a fund to protect glasnost. If this fund were to expand on a large scale, we would have substantial means to support those periodicals, radio stations and television programs which come under attack. Next, we have our absurd Journalists Union. I don't believe that the change in leadership will bring about any tangible results. Yet the Union continues to receive a certain percentage of the periodicals' income. Why not transfer this money to the fund to protect glasnost? But in the future, we should work to create an independent journalists union.

Vladislav Fronin: I agree. The protection of the Law on the Press is a priority today. We should make sure that no destructive amendments are introduced into it. Say, if they adopt a time on protecting publishers' rights (publishers here are still monopolists, while independent periodicals are dependent on them, because they don't have their own printing facilities), then we'll have to say good-bye to freedom of speech.

Natalya Chaplina: We need the fund to protect glasnost not only to support independent newspapers, but also official ones, which are having their arms twisted particularly roughly of late. They are stifled by their official founders who use entirely legal means. Thereas the periodicals can do nothing about it. For example, why can't *Komsomolskaya Pravda* break off with its founder? Because it has neither paper nor printing facilities. Let me stress it again: we need a fund that can provide for paper and printing facilities.

Alexander Drozdov: We'd rather think not about a fund, but a bank that would finance independent printing houses, radio and television. An independent journalists trade union backed by this kind of bank could serve as a firm basis for an independent democratic press. It would be good if something could be undertaken very soon, preferably before March 17.

Vladislav Starkov: With Prime Minister Pavlov issuing more and more decrees every day, even our highly efficient *Argumenty i Fakty* can come to ruin. We've run out of time. *Argumenty i Fakty* is ready to make an immediate and substantial contribution to the fund in question. Besides, we also promise to take under our wing any periodical however small or television or radio stations that need assistance. We can help them get paper and money. One of our other concerns is that our periodicals should have a stable readership. Once there are readers, then there is a stable economic basis. We don't have to coordinate our efforts from the point of view of the content of our periodicals. But we have to work together to cope with problems concerning publishing and distribution. We won't gain much if we act separately.

Vitaly Tretyakov: I'm all for creating a bank and for a common trade union that unites the electronic press and newsmen. Perhaps there should be a common trade union for journalists and printers. Their interests may not coincide in full, but it's important that today they have a common trade union. Printers are on our side. In fact, they've always been in the vanguard of the Russian revolutionary movement, and we should be together with them.

Viktor Yugin: To create a fund to protect glasnost, we can hold an international lottery. We've already held one before--it was a success. Part of the revenues from this lottery could be used to set up a bank to promote the mass media in Russia. The Unions of Leaseholders, Entrepreneurs and Coop members could take part in that fund.

Vladimir Yakovlev: We have two strong points: money and readers' respect. Money is what particularly counts, since we are a commercial structure. The question is, how to use it. To put it in the fund, in my view, is not very promising. I can assume that in the long run there will emerge a person or even a whole group who will launch a business within the framework of the fund to take advantage of reduced taxes. There are two spheres in which I think, we can and should direct our investments: publishing and distribution. Particularly the second one. There are so many publishers one can choose from. As for us, we don't have problems with our publishers, *Krasnaya Zvezda*. Under contract, we pay bonuses to the workers there, and that suits them very well. Things are worse with distribution, since there is only our organization dealing with it. I think we have to encourage new distributors. Say, the distributing company Chelovek in Leningrad. Investing money in it, we could turn it into a nationwide distributor. As for creating banks, I don't see it as a worthwhile undertaking. It would be much more promising to form a joint-stock company involving democratic publications.

Vitaly Korotich: We have to defend each other's ideas, and encourage enthusiasm among the reform-minded democratic forces. When I say 'our ideas', I do not mean to say 'back-scratching'. I value too much the independence of every one of us, the independence of our positions. If someone defames principles that are close to you-- you should stand up and defend them. We'd rather organize more 'round tables' or anything like them. *Moscow News* is setting a good example in this. Take the leaders of the non-aligned countries: they meet to form a very strong union, yet they don't lose any of their positions. The entire conservative Soviet press enjoys strong support from above. But there is nobody to back us, except our readers. So let's unite them and help ourselves."

CHAPTER VI

THE PRESS FOR BUSINESS PEOPLE

Tough Guys From *Kommersant*

The soporific and propaganda-laden *Ekonomicheskaya Gazeta* and a few other government journals on various branches of the "people's economy" were all we had until recently. Having said that, the entire Soviet daily press, without exception, used to give front-page coverage to the exploits of our workers, the wisdom of the Party and its grandiose plans to build communism. In all higher education establishments students examined the "political economy of socialism" and "political economy of capitalism". Only now have they admitted that there is no point in examining contemporary capitalism according to Marx's Das Kapital, that our socialism was the final phase of feudalism, and that communism is not only a myth, but a highly dangerous theory, to say nothing of political economy and the economics journals.

This brings to mind an old joke from school: Lenin and some comrades are in a train which suddenly comes to a stop—because the line goes no further. Lenin proposes organizing voluntary work on Saturday to quickly lay some rails. And that is what they do.

The same train, but this time with Stalin. End of the line, and the train stops. Stalin orders rails to be brought immediately, otherwise everyone will be shot. This does the trick, and everything is done.

The same train, but with Khrushchev. It stops in the middle of a field, because someone has dismantled the track. Khrushchev proposes ripping up the rails behind, and laying them in front. Off they go again.

Brezhnev and his hangers-on are now in the train, which comes to a stop when the line ends. The adjutants and other assistants jump out and with shouts of "we're going again" they start rocking the immobile carriages from side to side.

And now perestroika and glasnost have been ushered in. Gorbachev's train, after gathering speed, has stopped because the rails and sleepers ahead have all been lifted. Gorbachev orders the windows and doors to be opened wide and everyone to shout at the top of their voices: no rails! no sleepers!

These, in a nutshell, were the economic models of socialism that we had.

But gradually businessmen have started coming in from the cold and going public, and openly discussing their needs. And for them have at last appeared new papers and magazines.

The weekly *Kommersant* prints the black-market exchange rates of foreign currencies for various Soviet cities, and of the ruble in Western capitals. It also predicts the cost of a dollar from Soviet and foreign currency speculators. Only recently for such activities people were picked up on the street and got if not the firing squad then a hefty prison term. The articles of the criminal code dealing with illegal currency transactions in Russia have not yet been repealed, which is why such interesting accounts in *Kommersant* are always anonymous. The paper reports regularly on the black-market price of all kinds of Western electronic goods and clothing in numerous cities and gives details on how much they cost in various Western countries. The end result is a profiteer's handbook. Neither have the criminal code's articles on speculation (ie., direct trading at all kinds of flea markets, with no tax going to the state) been repealed. Russia is preparing to enter an era of "primitive capitalism", the first stage of accumulating capital.

In 1989 the Soviet Union launched a process comparable to what happened in Poland ten years before. Opposition to the Communist regime spread to the sphere of business and management. The most active social forces came to power in the mayor's offices of Moscow and Leningrad (now St. Petersburg), Lvov and the Baltics, united in cooperatives in cities and villages. They attracted foreign capital and started creating cooperative and state joint ventures, newspapers, magazines, news agencies, data banks and financial and crediting establishments.

The weekly *Kommersant*, a 24-page small-size newspaper publishing top-standard information, became the best Soviet newspaper in a matter of several months. On the other hand, it can hardly be called a Soviet newspaper, for it has never published lies and propaganda and never overlooked crises. It carries articles by parliamentary, government, party, economic and military analysts, who write about everything that happened in the past week and offer believable forecasts for the future. We have not had such a humane and businesslike newspaper since the 1910-20s. Other newspapers tried to emulate the heartfelt style of *Kommersant* in their desire to flirt with the readers. It is admissible, but far from all newspapers manage to do this in style.

The Soviet press market is undergoing changes. It is interesting to see how this is interpreted by *Kommersant* (July 23, 1990) in a professionally-written article called "*The Publishing Business: Small and Expensive Will Be Most Viable*":

> The Law on the Press, which comes into force on August 1, finally puts an end to political censorship in the newspaper and publishing businesses and brings publishers' economic problems to the fore.

Although on the whole the Soviet newspaper market is far from one of plenty, in certain sectors of it tough competition is already underway—for example, between business publications.

However, in addition to this competition, the mechanisms for which are fairly well-developed in the civilized world, the main battle between publications will evidently take place within the purely Soviet confines of market shortages: of paper and printing and distribution services. So far there are no signs that these shortages might be eradicated within the coming year.

In such an environment, viable will be those publications able form commercial strategies most suited to the specific features of the market. Moreover, subject matter should be considered as part of such strategy.

Preliminary analysis of the commercial and organizational strategies of recently-emerged independent publications shows that the following option can be viewed as optimum: a small print run and high price, with a narrow circle of directly-interested readers targetted.

During the year preceding the enactment of the Law on the Press, the State Committee for Printing, in keeping with temporary procedures, registered 90 newspapers and magazines that are independent of parties or the state. Another announced their establishment or appeared in print in July.

So far, most of the independents have been set up in a similar and somewhat traditional for the USSR fashion: financially-powerful founders (usually a whole array of them) and an editorial team that does not view itself as an independent commercial player, although in theory it is just that. It is also interesting that virtually all founders in one way or another have access to supplies of paper or can provide printing works with much sought-after services or pay in hard currency.

It can be confidently predicted that many new socio-political publications will not survive for long.

There are numerous readerships that, albeit small, would be extremely interested in "their own" publication dealing with, for example, religion, certain pastimes, specific aspects of business, psychology. Also, expensive but entertaining magazines writing in various ways on sexual issues. Also worth considering are digests—reprints or summaries of articles from other publications. People who don't have the time to read everything else will probably pay well for them, and such products also have the advantage of lower direct overheads.

Neither will a small print run frighten off advertisers. On the contrary, the makers of specialized products should seek to promote them in publications with narrow but specific readerships consisting of likely consumers (thus better targetting promotional campaigns).

Particular attention should be paid to the market for expensive and glossy color journals, of which there are almost none in Russia (although a few such have appeared lately with foreign backing, such as *Moscow Magazine* and *Delovye Ludi* (Business in Russia), or *Menedzher* and *Megapolis International*, which came out in July). These are a separate category and exist mainly on advertising revenues, since overheads are huge and frequently not recouped by sales alone.

Such publications might be guaranteed a future due to market openings, the prosperity of potential buyers and also the (so far) relative abundance of high-quality paper, plus the possibility of attracting foreign firms seeking eye-catching advertisements. Not only that, but advertisements can be paid for in kind with foreign paper.

It is especially worth mentioning publications aimed right from the start not only at Soviet but also foreign readers, which should find it much easier to recruit foreign backers and advertising for hard currency.

Despite the fact that there are some ways of setting up one's own publishing business and surviving (without relying on wealthy founders), the situation in this sector, which has to fight against every conceivable kind of shortage, is far from normal. Yet for businessmen—and not only those active in publishing—there is a positive side to things. The fact that paper, printing facilities and distribution network are so hard to come by means that there is a huge market for investing to provide them.

True, progress in this respect is so far being held back by the absence of Soviet entrepreneurs with sufficient capital (in addition to political reasons, which are gradually disappearing).

According to an unofficial but well-informed source, in July 1991 *Pravda* lost 7% of its subscribers (158,000), *Izvestia*, 9% (359,000), *Trud*, 4% (791,000), *Rabochaya Tribuna*, 5% (32,000), *Sovetskaya Rossia*, 6% (92,000), and *Krasnaya Zvezda*, 6% (39,000), compared to the previous month.

The same concerns the democratic press: *Moscow News* lost 14% of its subscribers (180,000), *Megapolis Express*, 14% (12,500), and *Argumenty i Fakty*, 11% (378,000).

On the other hand, business publications gained more readers: *Kommersant*, 3% (4,000) and the weekly *Ekonomika i Zhizn*, 1% (6,000), while *Delovoy Mir* (Business World) neither lost nor gained readers; its readership remained a stable 18,500.

In May 1991 *Kommersant* signed a contract on the sale of a part of its shares to Euroexpansion, thus becoming a part of its European network of business and financial publications.

It sold Euroexpansion 20% of its shares and gave it an option to purchase another 20% of shares before the end of 1991. The auditing of the contract and the draft cooperation agreement was done by the US company Ernst & Young.

In selling its shares, *Kommersant* was guided by business considerations: new investment will enable the board to make the newspaper more interesting and attractive. In addition, as member of the European network of business and financial publications, it will gain access to the veritable well of economic information and the possibility to implement "transnational" information and publishing projects.

Euroexpansion is no fool either: its president Jean-Louis Servan-Schreiber said that "though there is an inevitable element of risk in investing into East European companies, the time is ripe for securing oneself a place in the most promising markets." Speaking at the presentation of the contract, Mr. Servan-Schreiber stressed that he always pays attention to the arguments that "exceed the traditional business concerns, such as the role of the press in democratic states."

Kommersant, very popular among Soviet businessmen, has changed beyond recognition since early October 1991. To begin with, it has become twice as thick and changed its columns, layout and print—to say nothing of the content.

Kommersant's spotlight still focuses on home-made commerce, which 70% of material is devoted to, but also writes about other issues.

The newspaper will not disappoint its readers. "They have changed," editor-in-chief Vladimir Yakovlev says. "Now that the frenzied period of activity when the Russian entrepreneurial spirit emerged, is over, our businessmen want to have both the information they need for transactions, as well as everything else one wants to read in a newspaper."

Considerable space in *Kommersant* will be given to news about foreign business.

After the failure of the coup, the famous father and son Yegor and Vladimir Yakovlev relaxed and published their dialogues in *Moscow News* (September 8, 1991). It was the last issue edited by Yegor Yakovlev before he took the chair of the head of the All-Union TV and Radio Broadcasting Company. At 61, Yegor Yakovlev was still a "playing coach", that is he both supervises and also frequently writes articles which as always to the point. His son, 31 years old, airs his views very rarely; he is a businessman and publisher, rather than a journalist.

Vladimir Yakovlev started working for the magazine *Rabotnitsa*, and then moved on to *Sobesednik* and *Ogonyok*. Here are some excerpts from the talk between father and son:

Yegor: I look at you as at a new man. You had barely 500 rubles when you established the cooperative Fakt and then the newspaper *Kommersant* and the Postfactum agency. In five years you created the structure which you are now heading. How many staff do you have?
Vladimir: More than 1,500, to judge by the payment sheets.
Yegor: And how much money has Fakt accumulated?
Vladimir: It's hard to say. I think that the aggregate capital of all branches, including the market cost of property and shares, amounts to some 300 million rubles. I don't own all this money; I only own some shares.
Yegor: What led you to drop everything and set up a cooperative?
Vladimir: Pure chance. A friend of mine decided to earn some money and set up a cooperative to knit sweaters or something like that. He asked me to help him register the cooperative. At that time it was a very complicated task, and we agreed that we would conduct a kind of experiment which I as a correspondent of *Ogonyok* would try to fulfill. Nobody in the magazine knew about this. I fought Moscow Soviet and tried to push the registration papers through bureaucratic barriers. I soon realized that I enjoyed doing this. It was a kind of creation, a

practical possibility to do good—something I lacked while working for newspapers.

We managed to register the cooperative and it started functioning. After its registration I had nothing more to do. I don't remember what prompted me to set up a business of my own. But I recall that when my friend and I went to Moscow Soviet I saw lots of people there, who all dreamed of setting up a cooperative of their own. They queued patiently in order to ask questions which we already knew the answers to. Our sweater-knitting cooperative was the second or third registered in Moscow. That's what prompted the idea of Fakt, which provided information for cooperative owners. Today Fakt has nothing to do with this, but that's how it began.

Yegor: How did you move on from Fakt to *Kommersant*?

Vladimir: Also quite by chance. Cooperatives mushroomed, leading to the emergence of a Union of Cooperative Owners, partly in response to social pressure but more in response to the attempts of different groups to influence cooperative owners. They convened a congress and Artyom Tarasov announced that it was attended by Academician Vladimir Tikhonov. Everybody rejoiced, because Tikhonov was also a people's deputy of the USSR. At that time cooperative owners suffered from a social inferiority complex; now they have got rid of all kinds of complexes. Tarasov suggested electing Tikhonov as Chairman of the union, and everybody voted for him. To be honest, I was bored and returned to my office. Soon Tarasov came to me: he had already been elected Vice-President of the Union, and started settling outstanding problems facing the union. He thought that the first thing to be done was to establish a newspaper. That task was entrusted to me. At first I shrugged my shoulders: I thought it would be a soap bubble. Yet they wrote a document and I started fighting for the registration of the newspaper.

It transpired in the summer of 1988 that nobody knew how a newspaper could be registered. I learned in the Committee for the Press that they could not register my newspaper without the permission of the Communist Party Central Committee. In the Central Committee they told me that they don't register newspapers and that I should go to the Committee for the Press. And so I shuttled between Pushkinskaya and Staraya squares. Eventually I convinced the Central Committee department which supervised the development of the cooperative to grant permission. I talked nineteen to the dozen, convincing them that we should educate cooperative owners in the proper way. In fact, they could do nothing.

While they procrastinated, I openly hired staff and spent money. We published two advertisement issues—which they in Staraya Square did not expect at all—and took them to the Glavlit censorship department. At that time advertisements could be published without censorship. It's not an advertisement, it's a newspaper, they told me. No, I replied, it's an advertisement. And so we wrangled on. It's an advertisement, I told them, but it looks very much like a newspaper because its an advertisement of a new newspaper. Eventually, they gave in. *Kommersant* was registered in late December 1988, three days before the publication of the first issue.

Then father and son talked about Gorbachev, types of property, their attitude to foreigners, other countries, big money, etc. In the course of that long talk Yegor Yakovlev expressed his admiration for his son more than once, and recalled parental worries. But the son never mentioned the fact that he had exploited all through his new career his position as the son of Yegor Yakovlev. Gorbachev was given large credits in the West for "glasnost", that is, *Moscow News*. That newspaper hardly ever reached common Soviet people, but was translated into foreign languages and became a symbol of perestroika in the West.

At that time Vladimir Yakovlev could do anything with impunity. As long as his father was in the good graces of the Kremlin, Vladimir Yakovlev was regarded as untouchable and could do well-nigh anything he pleased. Some 20 years ago, when I lived in the high-rise hostel of Moscow University in Leninskiye Gory, the black market (clothes from West Berlin and hard currency) was commanded by the student children of general secretaries of foreign communist parties (the off-spring of home-made boyars did not engage in business then), and the KGB and militia did not dare touch them.

Hundreds of young people, who had powerful family connections and consequently had no need to fear arrest by a militiaman engaged in business under perestroika. Today, in early 1992, a.) thousands of people were languishing behind bars for economic crimes, although in any other civilized country their actions would not be considered crimes at all; b.) the militia might enter without even knocking or showing a search warrant and confiscate any economic documentation they desired from anyone; c.) the privatization of land and state property has not even been initiated.

Meanwhile, the editor-in-chief of *Kommersant* writes with enviable youthful optimism in "The 11 Club" (*Rossiiskiye Vesti* No. 19 September 1991) about democracy, the press and the powers that be:

1. We needn't do anything in particular, we should just live normally. We must live. We are witnessing a process of normalization of life, which began, in actual fact, prior to the coup, and I think that the period of political campaigns is over.
Reforms? I don't see any difficulties which require any special reforms. I think that we have the normal legislative spirit to back the development of private enterprise. We have managed to interest Western investors, an interest which may become stronger with time, when they realize that the situation in this country has stabilized. The only thing we need now is time and normal working conditions, without hysteria and attempts to settle all

problems overnight. The economy merely needs an impetus, because the freedom is here.

Why don't we see any changes? Because of the 70 years of chaos and destruction of the national economy. This is reality. Consequently time presents the only solution. Time and work. The collective and state farms may be a thing of the past, but it would be sheer idiocy to dissolve them, as established economic forms cannot be destroyed by government orders; they should develop into a different form of economic management. The state can and must create the requisite conditions for this, which it has been doing, by and large. It is silly to talk about government decisions which will improve the economy overnight. It has been allowed to do everything permissible for a long time now. Everything. All we have to do now is live and work.

2. The way to the "fourth estate" goes through politics, which should allow for freedom of speech, only at the initial period. Then the way to the "fourth estate" will go via commerce. There are quite a few people who can create a newspaper or a TV program in Russia. Regrettably, there are fewer people who can make a newspaper profitable, working without state subsidies, etc. A ministerial decision is needed to establish a newspaper. Not much else is needed to make a newspaper which acts as the mouthpiece of the ideology of its editor-in-chief or its staff. But in order to be profitable, this newspaper should cater to the interests of those who buy it. The bulk of newspapers have not yet resolved this key problem. The "fourth power" will develop when they find a way to solve this problem.

3. What can I tell the powers that be? To remember that the people have changed.

USSR Prime Minister Valentin Pavlov Used to be a Journalist Too

Delovoy Mir, *Delovoy Ludi*, *Delovoy Chelovek* (Businessman) and other publications with titles similarly enticing and unusual to the Soviet public have been on sale since summer and autumn 1990.

The Moscow weekly *Nedelya* had this to say about *Delovoy Mir* (October 22, 1990):

Much has been achieved over the past six months. Five issues of *Delovoy Mir* have come out, with high-quality material and printing. As of the new year the paper will become an 8-page daily, 16-page on Sundays. One issue has been brought out in Armenian and distributed throughout the diaspora worldwide. Two weekly supplements—*Radikal* and *Rynok* (Market)—have appeared, a third, Avtorevu, is almost ready and next year a fourth (jointly with the state environmental protection agency and called *Ekologicheskaya Gazeta* (Ecological Gazette)) should join them. Also in the pipeline is *Nachala* (Beginnings), dealing with economic affairs and aimed at children.

Despite its relative youth, the consortium is already a powerful economic player. Its strength can be judged by the following fact: it is completely modernizing one production line at the Kondopoga paper works to meet its own newsprint requirements. Machinery and labor will cost nearly 100 million pounds, and the new line is due to come on stream in only two years' time.

The consortium currently has a mixed capital of over 15 million rubles, although at a press conference accompanying the launch journalists persistently named a figure ten times that. It's difficult to say whether they're right. Let us note straight away that top on the list of founders is the USSR Finance Ministry. After it come the USSR state committees for supply and science and technology, the USSR communications ministry, the Vozdushny Transport central publishing house, the AvtoVAZ amalgamation, Gazprom concern, foreign trade research institute, three commercial banks, the Znaniye society, USSR League of Designers and even the publishing unit of the Moscow Patriarchate. In addition there are another 7 associated members, among whom are such solid organizations as the AvtoVAZ vehicle service network and AvtoVAZbank. Last on the list is an associate member with special rights—the Maxwell Communications Corporation. For those who haven't heard of it, this is a major transnational business.

Chairman of the Board is Valentin Sergeyevich Pavlov—who is also the USSR finance minister.

As soon as Valentin Pavlov became the Prime Minister, *Delovoy Mir* stopped writing his name in the list of founders. In civilized countries, ministers do not publish newspapers or engage in business.

Delovye Ludi has attracted considerable attention. The press-release of this respectable publication described it as "an independent Soviet business weekly that aims to play the role of information bridge between new-generation Soviet managers and the Western business community". As regards the quality of its layout and illustrations, it gives nothing away to established international publications.

This is both surprising and somewhat characteristic. *Delovye Ludi* received a good promotional plug in *Pravda* (May 22, 1990), and not merely in the form of a paid advertisement, when its deputy editor-in-chief was interviewed. Even such new weeklies as *Rynok* and *Kommersant*, which focus on financial and economic affairs and take an interesting political line, have been accorded such a far from dubious honor. *Pravda*'s article accorded such a far from dubious honor. *Pravda*'s article was headlined "*For people of initiative and enterprise*":

Delovye Ludi is the name of a new international magazine, to be released by the Soviet-French joint venture Press-Kontakt, specially set up for this purpose by a Moscow joint-stock innovatory bank, Progress publishers and the French company Sokpress.

The variety of economics publications in our country is deceptive. In fact, the current situation is akin to one in which family problems can be solved only by reading the lonely-hearts columns or something like "Gynecology and Obstetrics". The press is entirely justified in focussing on the mechanism of economic reform, but overlooks the people capable of constructing it and getting it to work.

Meanwhile, society should actively support people of initiative and enterprise and help them discover their potential to benefit themselves and others. It is important for all of us that businessmen should fully recover their self-respect. We still suffer from the belief, which dates back to the era of "stagnation", that business means rip-offs and other dishonest dealings. And this is not by chance—the command system has a habit of condemning or punishing any initiative that goes beyond the prescribed limits. Independent people are a thorn in its side.

Delovye Ludi is a wide-ranging journal for business people, managers of industrial and agricultural enterprises and state businesses. The magazine will feature the greatest possible variety of themes, approached from an economic and business point of view. From liquidity difficulties to sport and leisure. Each issue will have numerous illustrations and advertisements by major firms from all over the world.

Delovye Ludi will be published in Russian and English. Every issue will be prepared entirely in Moscow, with only the printing to be done in Paris. Unfortunately, Soviet coverage of business affairs is inferior to that in the West—it's like comparing a Moskvich to a Mercedes. We're used to writing long and slow articles, and it's not easy to find eye-catching and expressive photographs, even for increased royalties. Only a small number of copies will be on sale via Soyuzpechat. The rest will be by subscription. We're not trying to become ultra-popular.

The creation of the magazine was inspired by Robert Hersant, president of Sokpress, famous in France and the rest of the world as the owner of some 30 newspapers and magazines published all over the world. In the spring of 1990 Hersant opened a radio station "Malopolska" in Krakow. He has newspapers in Poland, Czechoslovakia and Romania. To publish the magazine *Delovye Ludi*, Hersant established a joint venture, in which he owns 55% of shares, the rest belonging to the Soviet partner.

Moscow Magazine and *Burda*

In 1990 a new monthly appeared- *Moscow Magazine*, costing 7 rubles a copy and with a print of 60,000, two thirds of which is distributed abroad. It charges $6,000 for a full-page advertisement.

Moscow Magazine is a Soviet-Dutch joint venture set up by United Dutch Publishers, the Moscow Journalists' Union and the Interbranch Commercial Bank for Development of Wholesale Trade.

The nucleus of the magazine, according to a press release for the Moscow media, will be a business section with articles written by prominent Western and Soviet economists, comprehensive information and news, advice for foreign businessmen, interviews with and features on those of them working in Russia, and also the very latest news on legislation in this field.

In addition, there will be detailed coverage of social, political and cultural events in Russia. The main themes will be current events, social trends, essays, book reviews, what to see and where in Moscow, how to obtain everyday services, and other information that foreigners need about our capital city: taxis, theatres, restaurants...

This 100-page lavishly illustrated magazine comes out in English with a Russian translation.

The Soviet editor-in-chief is Gennady Musaelyan, who was previously in charge of the Journalists' Union international department, and the Dutch—Dirk Sauer, a journalist and winner of the Netherlands' Editor of the Year prize for 1989. "A blend of Western technical capabilities with Soviet journalistic talent", was how Sauer described the magazine.

Similar magazines are available in the world's major cities. *Moscow Magazine* is evidently not hard-up if it could afford to send out, free of charge, 4,000 copies of each issue to various Soviet recipients—libraries, government institutions, ministries and similar bodies, banks, and joint ventures. In the second most prestigious venue of all (after the halls of the Kremlin), the Moscow International Trade Center concert hall, a copy of the first issue was presented to Ria Lubbers, the wife of the Dutch prime minister, and G. Jeller, deputy chairman of the board of the Philips concern. Yet from the Soviet side powerful forces have also been recruited. No, not various members of the CPSU Central Committee or their relatives. There were often organizations whose favors were sought with equal assiduousness. Investors in this Soviet-Dutch joint venture include financiers from Tokobank, part of the wholesale development bank mentioned above (which itself was set up in 1989 with backing from such pillars of the Soviet establishment as the omnipotent State Committee for Supply and its regional branches, the USSR Insurance Society, administrative department of the Komsomol, USSR ministries of civil aviation, special construction projects and merchant shipping, the USSR Bank for Agriculture, USSR Savings Bank, commercial banks and a host of other major enterprises and cooperatives).

The *Megapolis* project turns out to have an even more impressive list of publishers. It was launched at the International Trade Center in July 1990, when the backers of *Megapolis International* were solemnly introduced to foreign journalists and business representatives. Among its founders are the Moscow City Council executive committee, the International Management Research Institute, TASS and APN.

The magazine is aimed at Soviet and foreign business circles requiring information on the economic, social, communications and cultural problems of Moscow and other major conurbations of the world.

At the moment, the *Megapolis* stable in Russia includes the popular weekly *Megapolis-Express* and the humorous newspaper *Utyug* (Iron). On July 3, 1991 the press center of The Ministry of Foreign Affairs of the USSR hosted the inauguration ceremony of *VIP* monthly, launched by the staff of the *Megapolis International* magazine. The Russian and English versions of the 96-page magazine had been priced at seven rubles and six dollars respectively. *VIP*, which focuses specifically on the leaders of the Soviet Union and countries of the former socialist block, was originally to be printed in 30,000 copies by the Moscow-based Pervaya Obraztsovaya Printing House.

Menedzher (Manager), a democratically-minded weekly (with the subtitle "An Independent Newspaper for Business people"), founded by the stock company Razvitie (Development), has been on sale at the newsstands in this country since May 1989. A paper under the same name, *Razvitiye*, with the subtitle "Building. Economy. Society."—an ideological successor of *Stroitelnaya Gazeta* and *Sotsialisticheskaya Industria*, which closed down on the instructions of the CPSU Central Committee—has been on sale since June 1991. The place of these Party rostrums, which employed over 400 journalists, has been occupied by the even more feeble, although slightly more independent and businesslike in all respects, *Karyera* and *Inzhenernaya Gazeta* (Engineer's Paper).

In July 1991 the Moscow-based *Sov-Econ* and the Siberian regional magazine *Direktor* (Director) emerged: the latter was priced at 4.5 rubles, while the former's price fluctuated from 50 to 65 rubles per copy (sic). In fact, *Sov-Econ* comprises two different magazines—a quarterly review and a monthly, to be subscribed separately. What is so good about *Sov-Econ* to demand such a sum? They say that it is extremely useful, as it aims to offer analytical and future-oriented business information on Russia based on the data, obtained from the most prestigious government agencies in Moscow. Well, it sounds reasonable. Very useful information costs far more than fifty rubles. Some people would be ready to spend even 50,000 rubles to get it. The only thing left to do is launch a magazine, published on a reader's request, whereby its economic and technological innovations would be printed in one only copy, which would go to the customer for quite a hefty sum of money. In fact, you wouldn't need tons of paper and a printing house to publish such a magazine!

The Mashinostroyeniye (Machine Building) Publishing House joined forces with the Eastern Economy Information Service from Germany and launched in April 1991 a 16-page Russian-language biweekly, entitled *Economika Zapada* (Western Economy), to be distributed in Russia for one ruble per copy with an initial 50,000 copy print run. The German co-founders expect to derive major revenues from ads placed in the paper by Western businesses (DM 2,500 per page). The partners in Germany intend to invest their share of profits in Soviet rubles into the creation of a correspondent network in the Soviet Union, designed to provide information for the West European *Eastern Economy* magazine.

Since April 1991 the British *Information Moscow* has been furnishing through its Data Press Service (DPS) international information agency some 150 English-language reports on political and economic news from Russia and elsewhere, data from world exchanges, as well as sports news and weather on all continents to any subscribers in the Soviet Union ready to pay 100 dollars a month. And what are other business people, who have failed so far to obtain intelligible and reliable information either from TASS' Economic Service with its thousands of correspondents in the country and abroad, or from *BIKI*, a heavy Russian-language bulletin of foreign commercial information, issued three times a week, supposed to do? *BIKI* with a mere 4,500 copy print run sells really well, and it would have been only natural to increase its run, but its editors still adhere to narrow departmental interests, contradicting the industrial, foreign economic and export-import interests of this country. Foreigners have to cope with this problem themselves to ensure that the exporters in this country do not die from information hunger. In this environment Data Process Service could think of nothing better than dispatch its own correspondents to various corners of the former Soviet Union and keep them there by paying them in hard currency.

By mid-1991 hopes were raised that an economic news agency—the biggest-ever independent organization, of prime importance for this country—would be created by the joint efforts of the Moscow Central Stock Exchange (MCSE) and Russian Commodity Exchange (RCE). It was announced that the Economic News Agency, a would-be joint stock company, would follow in the footsteps of Britain's Reuters, which had promised to provide consulting services. Russia's exchange executives—the most serious people in Moscow's economic structures—announced that the agency's statutory capital would amount to some 100-200 million rubles. It is common knowledge that the MCSE and RCE exchanges spare neither money nor effort for journalists or information, well aware that it repays a hundredfold. In April 1991, RCE in conjunction with a Canadian company spent as much as 150,000 rubles and 10,000 dollars to hold a three-day seminar on the fundamentals of exchanges' work for a hundred Soviet mass media people.

The issue of *Izvestia*, dated August 2, 1991, reported the registration of another business news agency, PAL Inform. Until quite recently, the Soviet Ministry of Foreign Economic Relations and Trade and Industry Chamber had enjoyed a monopoly on foreign economic information. A whole variety of publications—ranging from *Vneshnaya Torgovlya* (Foreign Trade) and *Sovetsky Eksport* (Soviet Export), extending to such luxury publications as *Aviaexport, Stankoimport Review, Elort Informs, Expocourier, Mercury, Pryamye Svyazi* (Direct Contacts) among others—were produced under their aegis. Meanwhile, the departmental All-Union R&D Conjuncture Institute [Russian acronym—VNIKI-Ed.], which runs the aforementioned *BIKI*, has retained its domination as a major information center, providing data on the world markets and foreign companies. Owing, however, to VNIKI's outdated storage and processing equipment and lack of computers and communication facilities it cannot process eighty per cent of up-to-date information on various aspects of the foreign trade it receives. VNIKI has commercial offices in the USA, France, India, Japan, Britain and Germany. The death of information has caused the majority of the 21,000 Soviet registered participants in foreign economic trade, who both enjoy the right to independent access to the world market and yet at the same time have a rather vague idea of the actual situation there, to suffer enormous losses, when they either trade their goods for next to nothing or pay threefold for goods purchased in foreign countries.

The first issue of the reborn 16-page *Moskovskiye Vedomosti* (Moscow Gazette) was dated July 31, 1990 and included a front-page declaration by its founders, including the ELEKS Association joint-stock company, the Kniga (Book) Publishing House, the Moscow Co-op Union and the Entire Moscow joint venture. *Moskovskiye Vedomosti*'s subtitle defines the paper as public, commercial, information-based and politically independent. Its editor-in-chief is *Moskovsky Komsomolets*' former satirist Leonid Krasner. *Moskovskiye Vedomosti*, the second oldest Russian paper after *Sankt-Peterburgskiye Vedomosti* (St. Petersburg Gazette) came out from 1756 to 1917.

In January 1991 one more publication appeared in Moscow—Moscow Observer—an English-language newspaper for foreign tourists, featuring city news and a whole range of useful business and entertainment information. Aeroflot runs a similar periodical—the *Leningrad News* English-language magazine, printed in Stockholm with a 250,000 copy print run and distributed among St. Petersburg-bound international passengers, as well as in travelling agencies in Europe and the USA.

Who could then dare assert that the Soviet Union has a lack of paper, given the abundance of newly-born and long-established periodicals? For the Communist party had enough, paying ten times less than the commercial price. It launched in its time the *Izvestia TsK KPSS* magazine, the *Glasnost* weekly, followed by another newspaper, *Uspekh* (Success), a 16-page, small-format "commercial weekly", published by the *Pravda* daily since December 1990 and priced at 30 copecks per copy, which is not much by modern standards. By January 1, 1991 the weekly was printed in 200,000 copies. You could distribute practically anything in this boundless empire and even in many more copies, provided that you gained the backing of the Soyuzpechat agency and the Ministry of Communications of the USSR. *Uspekh* used to carry pictures of nude beauties, although on newsprint and in black and white, recommendations on how to play roulette and bridge, reports by *Pravda* correspondents abroad, horoscopes, detective and adventure stories by foreign authors, ads, boring economic analytical reviews, in other words, the material which had been rejected by the *Pravda* daily for some reason or other. Both *Uspekh* and *Pravda* (the latter had been considered a serious paper at least three years ago, for each line reflected the unbiased view shared by the country's political bosses) were designed to cater to the tastes of the most ignorant and humble in this country's society. Hence, the "new style" of Party journalism—a minimum of theory and maximum of entertainment and pictures, brief news items instead of the former large articles, mottos and labels without any political argumentation whatsoever.

New popular magazines with the enthusiastic backing of Western investors have also appeared. The trendsetter is West Germany's *Burda Moden*, the Russian edition of which is printed and almost entirely imported into Russia. The October 1990 number was printed by the Germans on credit, while the Soviet side's debt already amounted to DM9 million. The entire project, called Russkaya Burda, was on the verge of collapse. The business knocked on the doors of the highest Soviet institutions, pleading for help. Yet it all started off so promisingly: the first issue was launched on March 3, 1987 not just anywhere but in the Hall of Columns at the House of the Union. The magazine had the enthusiastic support of Eduard Shevardnadze and Raisa Gorbachev, organized offices in Riga, St. Petersburg, Rostov-on-Don, Vladivostok and Nizhny Tagil, opened at the USSR Exhibition of Economic Achievements its own advice center, set up its own small experimental fashion bureau and even a national TV program, "Burda Moden Presents"; it was allocated a plot of land by the Moscow City Council for a printworks which it began building, and moved to luxurious new premises a stone's throw from Red Square on one of the capitals most prestigious streets. Mrs. Anne Burda also launched a Russian edition of another of her large stable of publications.

Journalist Svetlana Bulashova provided an account of the successes and failures of Burda in *Nedelya* (June 11, 1990), and also in the new "independent business newspaper" *Menedzher* (No. 9, July 1990). In the latter, under the headline "*Give me Burda*", this almost tragic and highly instructive story was told:

> The hall was filled by the fragrance of freshly-cut flowers. A wonderful carpet of carnations, poppies and roses descended from the ceiling onto the stage... The slender and regal models made no effort to conceal their pleasure at the surrounding scene—a summer fashion parade was being held at Burda Moden's impressive new premises.
>
> But this was happening not in Offenburg, but here in Moscow: the models were Soviet, and their clothes were Soviet-made. Everything was up to scratch, and even better. The Burda Moden joint venture was laying on the style.
>
> For three years, the venture has been supplying its Russian edition to Soviet readers (initially 300,000 copies each quarter, now 1,500,000 each month). It has experience of operating within our collapsing market and drawn-out economic crisis. But even stranger, Burda was an example of how to succeed in an unfavorable environment.
>
> This example might not be very typical for our time, yet I think it will be useful for those still wondering whether a market economy is a good or bad thing. To start off with, a brief explanation. The Burda Moden joint venture was set up to finance the Russian edition in hard currency, but sell it in the Soviet Union, as much as possible, for rubles. Initially, hard currency was prized out of the state, in the hope that in three years' time the business would build its own printworks and itself start earning greenbacks. To do this, the Soviet Burda Moden publishing house would

have to print a large range of magazines and journals and sell them abroad. Three years have passed. Good intentions remain nothing more than that, and the printing facilities still exist only on paper.

Then, for a year, the state refused to pay, while Burda continued to operate and finance its 1.5 million print run. How to earn some hard currency? Burda was one of the first joint ventures to propose to the government that it engage in foreign trade, selling waste metals and raw materials to the West and using the proceeds to pay for the magazine. (Naturally, nobody dropped the commitment to build the printworks).

Brokerage... To be honest, many think that this is an easy way to earn cash. We all remember the scandal that flared up around the ANT cooperative (which never did manage to sell those old tanks). And many to this day believe that something "not quite right" was going on. The general director of the Burda Russian edition thinks otherwise: there was no need for the scandal, and ANT earned the state some decent money. He clarified his views: his joint venture also engages in brokerage. "What's better?", he asked. "That waste copper and oil remain in this country, or that in return for them Soviet women can receive a glossy magazine and sew themselves fashionable outfits?"

The answer is obvious. But the Soviet bureaucrats in the foreign-trade authorities don't agree: better to have those waste products just lie there then let anyone other than them earn themselves some hard currency.

In May, Burda was rumored to be on the verge of being closed down (supposedly for being caught carrying out illegal foreign-trade deals). The rumors were believed, and even those in the know braced themselves for the worst.

Fortunately, the stories were untrue and the business's operations turned out to be perfectly legal; readers were treated to the next issue of *Burda*. Not only that, but Moscow journalists were invited by the directors to the launch of another magazine from Frau Burda's collection, *Verena*, a monthly costing 7 rubles 50 and specializing in knitting, needlework and, shall we say, particularly exotic fashion trends.

"So much for the rumors!", the reader will say, and rightly so. There were very good reasons for the rumors! The bones of contention were the superbly-equipped and luxurious offices in the center of the capital, and dozens of Western cars, computers, etc... When we're being exhorted to tighten our belts and prepare ourselves for hard times, the conditions in which Burda employees work and the opportunities at their fingertips will naturally cause nothing but irritation in those less fortunate.

But on the other hand, if there were no personal incentive for Burda's people, would they work so hard? Brokerage is not such an easy number.

From speaking with the venture's general director, I realized that neither he nor his staff suffer any pangs of conscience. The new offices have provided his firm with a respectable image, and Western partners with the confidence that they are dealing with serious people. Books are still judged by their covers.

Another question arises. How did the Western investors—publisher Anne Burda, her son Hubert, and director of the Ferastaal AG House of Trade Mr. Made—view this Russian "extravagance"?

"They thought it was normal", answered V Melentyev. "All our spending came from the venture's own profits. Not a single Mark from the initial capital was touched".

He went on to give some advice: over there prosperity is approved of, while here it attracts jealousy. Perhaps it's time to get used to the idea that in a market environment he who learns to work better will live better.

One may object, of course, that being allowed to operate on foreign markets, Burda Moden was in a more favorable situation than other Soviet enterprises. And it's quite possible that Anne Burda herself might have used its revenues differently. But let me have my say as a consumer. I don't care whether Burda has one, two or three offices. I care even less what makes of car are driven by its bosses. But if 1,500,000 Soviet women (the actual readership is much higher) are deprived of their favorite magazine, it will be a great shame—for all of us. The venture's success gives us hope that we'll also be able to buy *Anna*, *Karina*, *Bunte* and dozens more of Frau Burda's splendid magazines. The staff of the venture themselves probably want this to happen. And here the interests of the broker and the consumer coincide.

However, the Russian-language *Burda* overcame the crisis, reduced the output to one million copies a month and is still published in West Germany. Besides, there are now Burda Moden centers in Moscow, Tashkent, Orel, Nizhny Tagil and Vladivostok, where women can buy not only copies of *Burda* and *Verena*, but also foreign-made fabrics complete with buttons, zippers, etc. The centers have reading halls with copiers and consultants in sewing, hairdos and make-up.

In October 1990 10,000 copies of a 302-page one-off edition (in Russian) of the long-established American magazine *Ladies Home Journal* hit Moscow. In the States it comes out monthly with a print run of 5 million, and in order to make it available to Russian readers the editor-in-chief, Merne Blit, required the active assistance of APN board member Natalya Yakovleva and CPSU Politburo member Galina Semenova (who is also an elected People's Deputy). There has not been such a charming, cultured and educated lady in the Politburo for the last 50 years. For 10 years until July 1990, Semenova was editor-in-chief of *Krestyanka* (Peasant Woman), with a monthly print run of 21 million. We used to have just two large-circulation women's magazines. The other was *Rabotnitsa* (Working Woman). I cannot remember ever seeing either of them in the kiosks—they are available mainly on subscription, which itself is in hot demand.

Publishers in the Spheres of Culture and Charity

After Burda, probably the most significant Western project on the Soviet press market was that of the late Robert Maxwell. He didn't run into any scandals, since he was pumping money not out of but into the country. His charitable act was warmly greeted by the CPSU Central Committee's paper *Sovetskaya Kultura* (September 8, 1990):

Possibly no publication caused such a stir upon its announcement as *Nashe Naslediye* (Our Heritage). Its launch 3 years ago at the foreign ministry press center was attended by more journalists than many major political events. Today we can say that the early hopes have been justified. The magazine has won for itself a firm reputation for not only high quality printing, something to which we're not used, but also the depth of analysis in the articles it publishes.

Robert Maxwell, the British publisher, believes that it is the best-illustrated magazine on literature and the arts not only within his vast publishing empire but in its class as a whole.

A free press and market promise numerous problems for the world of newspapers and magazines. In any event, the battle for subscribers will get tougher. Therefore our first question to *Nashe Naslediye*'s editor-in-chief, Vladimir Yenisherlov, was not about the intended range of topics but what place he sees for the magazine in the new environment.

Answer: Nothing will change: the magazine has far-reaching aims, as defined by the notion of 'culture', and we shall continue to pursue them. We shall continue to carry quality articles on literature, and also the fine arts. For us the concept of form is not simply a word, a second-rate idea. The West German newspaper *Frankfurter Allgemeine Zeitung*, in a review of *Nashe Naslediye*, wrote: This excellently-produced magazine provides an opportunity to say: 'Things can be different!'. Also, *Nashe Naslediye* stands out from all other Western glossies, since it has its own refined culture". In my opinion, the reviewer correctly understood one of the ideas contributed to the journal by the Culture Fund.

Question: How do you regard the possible appearance of competitors?

Answer: The cultural scene in this country is so poor that this possibility to me seems remote. Dmitry Likhachev, the inspiration behind our magazine, was right when he said during the first Congress of People's Deputies that all our troubles stem from an absence of culture. One might expand upon this theme, but it's impossible to deny it. The more quality newspapers and magazines dealing with cultural affairs appear, the more books will be published and museums and theatres opened, etc., and the quicker our country will extricate itself from the horrendous crisis that it's been forced into. I would be pleased to have such competitors. We, that is, the Culture Fund, will do all we can to help them. But unfortunately, I don't see many people willing to set up a cultural journal. Everyone's gone for politics and commerce. In most magazines all I can see is the desire to carve out a market using any means—from exposes of KGB secrets to stories about Moscow nightlife. Nowhere do I see what Alexander Blok once called "the long idea", that is, the purpose of these publications, apart from to make money. Culture cannot be a self-financing business—it's not something you can earn from. Culture has to be helped. Currently our magazine is bringing in a decent income, but I don't exclude the possibility that at some time in the future we might start showing a loss. That would be quite normal.

Question: **You have one more indisputable advantage—your magazine was one of the first joint publishing projects.**

Answer: Everyone has some kind of advantage. I think it's extremely important that this has happened to a magazine writing on culture rather than business, many of which are cropping up now. But I think that they're in for big problems in our country. We, however, as Blok said, exist "under the sauce of eternity".

Question: **Are you sure of keeping your readers?**

Answer: I know that there are many more potential readers than the 200,000 that we can allow ourselves under the agreement with Robert Maxwell; as you know, he's publishing the magazine on a charitable basis. In fact, by investing so generously he's shown the correct attitude towards culture, even that of another country. And our millionaires and billionaires, and major enterprises, show no desire to sponsor the arts.

Question: **I'm told that you've resisted the temptation to raise the cover price of *Nashe Naslediye* for next year.**

Answer: There are several reasons for this. Although demand is outstripping supply (which is shown by the fact that on the black market copies go for 10-15 rubles), our aim is not to earn a vast income from our readers, who are mainly cultural workers. Secondly, for our magazine to be profitable, that is, operate without the patronage of Maxwell and other concessions, we would have to charge 25 rubles per copy or even more, which would be in keeping with world prices for similar publications. In Britain, for example, an annual subscription costs 52 pounds, or 80 dollars. Thirdly, we've found an alternative distribution channel, via Soyuzkniga, thus dropping the hopelessly inefficient postal ministry. We've been inundated with complaints from subscribers that receive their copies late or not at all. And this incapable ministry decided to demand three times as much for delivery.

It is difficult to overestimate what Anne Burda, Ted Turner (you will read about him in the chapter devoted to TV) and the late Robert Maxwell have done for the Russian people. They are guiding us to the civilized world. Thus, at the end of the 20th century we are beginning to see the emergence of normal mass media in this country—political, business, municipal, women's, entertainment and specialized. Every passing month convinces us more and more strongly that we cannot manage in this business without Western expertise and capital. Today, however, we can expect this help only from the very rich, and only from those who are ready to combat our inertia and red tape, risking their money, sustaining losses and persevering in their long pursuit of success. Those in the West who become friendly with us over the long years of close business cooperation, well versed in our political and administrative system, attain reliable partners, patrons and like-minded people in this country, manage to win ultimate recognition.

In July 1991, the first issue of the Russian-language edition of the American *Reader's Digest*, published by Progress Publishers and printed by Pervaya Obraztsovaya Printing House in Moscow saw the light. The event was extensively covered by the Moscow-based *Pravda, Moskovsky Komsomolets, Izvestia* and *Nezavisimaya Gazeta* newspapers. Over the 70 years of its existence *Reader's Digest* has become, alongside Coca-Cola, McDonald's, Marlboro and the Dallas serial, a symbol of the United States. Published in fifteen countries, it caters to an audience of 100,000,000 readers. The Russian edition is no different from the original—it goes out monthly too and has the same pocket size, the same text, even the same ads. Its format comes as a total shock to Soviet people—a minimum of politics and no ideology whatsoever. *Nezavisimaya Gazeta* was exactly right, when it defined *Reader's Digest* as a magazine "designed for a poor, but by all means free person, i.e. "private", uncommitted, stable and right-minded. How many of them do we have? Here we have a real chance to find out." Many are expected to subscribe, thanks to its relatively low price and the unheard-of promotion with a *Reader's Digest* balloon hovering over Moscow.

Former Soviet citizen and historian Alexander Gleizer, who now divides his time between New York and Paris, was able in July 1990 to get his independent weekly *Russky Kuryer* printed by Izvestia Publishing House in Moscow. On top of the 200,000 print run of the Russian edition, a monthly English-language digest for Western markets is also planned. Besides, there is a monthly supplement on literature and the arts. In the West the Russian weekly will be targetted mainly on Slavists, political analysts and emigres.

According to Gleizer, despite the newspaper's rather respectable line-up of founders, it is printed mainly at his own expense.

In 1990 a group of magazines whose importance to our society is hard to exaggerate appeared on the Soviet market, racked by social ills and the truly piteous plight of pensioners, the disabled and other deprived groups. This is where sponsors, patrons, philanthropists, simply decent creditors and managers are needed. Among these new magazines is the monthly *Sotsialnaya Zashchita* (Social Protection), published by the USSR State Committee for Employment. This is probably the only Soviet publication that promised not to increase its price in 1991. The result—Soyuzpechat didn't want to distribute it. It promises to become a bridge between those in need of help and those who can provide it; each issue carries a large number of short stories on specific people to whom life has been unkind, with appeals to assist them. The editorial staff is setting up a data bank for people who no longer wish to live alone. A lonely-hearts column? Not only that, but an organization actively providing relief for the less well-off: women, the ill, refugees, the elderly, orphans, widows. At the same time it gives advice on issues of employment, migration, various kinds of state benefits and payments, pension legislation and other rules and regulations. In a regular feature called Self-Help, readers are advised by experts on psychology, the problems of youth and old age and sex, and also on alternative medicine, extrasensory perception and astrology.

The USSR State Committee for Printing has received an application to register the magazine *Preodoleniye* (Overcoming), which is for disabled people. On October 2, 1990 newspaper *Vechernaya Moskva* provided a free platform to Moscow journalist Vladimir Kalinichev, the man behind this application:

> For many decades our society has tried not to notice that alongside healthy able-bodied people who, incidentally, also feel powerless in our system, there are others who find it much harder to achieve self-fulfillment. Not only are they defenseless in this state of ours but also estranged, they've lost all opportunity to communicate with each other. This is the difficulty of their fate. The magazine can to a certain extent protect and unite them, write about their cares, help them to overcome problems and return to active life. I want the magazine to become their friend, advisor and even mouthpiece. There are 30 million disabled people in our country, and they have not a single publication catering for their needs. There used to be one, called Russkii Invalid, but it disappeared together with the Tsar in 1917.
>
> *Preodoleniye* is aimed at the broad readership. Initially, we intend to issue it as a bi-monthly, with a print run of not less than 300,000. Its founder is the Eruditsiya-Sodeistviye-Prosveshcheniye (Erudition-Cooperation-Education) center of the Pushkin National Cultural Foundation.

Moscow's *Molodaya Gvardiya* (Young Guard) publishing and printing association sends out Sovetsky Shkolnik (Soviet Pupil) to subscribers. This is the only magazine in the world for children who are blind or have impaired sight. It is printed in braille, and contains stories, fairy tales and poems, 48 LPs by Soviet and foreign stars, old folk tales and current-events reporting, plus 12 sculptured drawings on a polymer surface as part of the annual subscription price for the complete set.

In September 1990 the 16-page weekly newspaper *Miloserdiye* (Compassion) was launched, as was the heavyweight literary and arts journal *Soglasiye* (Consent). The traditional Russian symbol of compassion—the camomile flower—has become that of these two new publications.

Miloserdiye is the first product of the editorial and publishing complex of the same name and recently established by a resolution of the USSR Council of Ministers. The public council of the complex is impressive: Patriarch of Moscow and All Russia Aleksii, prominent writers, public figures and journalists. Their aims are clear and noble, being to assist in reducing social tension and protect the more vulnerable groups within society. Their very first move—an 8-kopeck surcharge for charity to the newspaper's already low price (25 kopecks)—raised 1,000,000 rubles to build a home for single old people in the Taldom district of the Moscow region.

There is one more category of people in Russia who, at long last, have received a few depoliticized publications—for the first time our 14–18 year-olds can read *My* (We), printed in Finland and published by the Soviet Children's Foundation. Two million subscribed to the first issue in 1990. Another 2 million received *Tramvai* (Tram), also on glossy paper and also printed in Finland. The Russian version of Mickey Mouse, a collection of comics from the Soviet-Danish Egmont FIS business, has been coming out 4 times a year with 200,000 copies per issue since August 1990. Of course, all this spending hard currency, which will never be recouped by selling these three magazines for rubles, but at least they can take advertising.

Perhaps we really are ceasing to save money at the expense of children, and of people in general? Here is another achievement of 1990. An Australian firm began printing for us 200,000 copies each of two new monthly magazines of the Kniga publishing house, USSR State Committee for Radio and Television and USSR State Committee for Printing, called *On* (He) and *Ona* (She), and in Russian. "We're declaring war on the psychology of poverty": these words said by editor-in-chief Alexander Polyakov have been long awaited by the Soviet people.

There was much talk about *On* and *Ona* long before they hit the newsstands. No wonder. They stand out from the amorphous mass. Homo Sovieticus became simply Man and Woman. True, so far this applies only to the pages of the magazines, which few have been able to lay their hands on.

Perestroika has laid bare and aggravated for Soviet people the problems of politics, the spirit and morality, living standards and lifestyle. In the year 1990, so momentous for the Soviet press, the first Soviet environmental journal, *Ecos*, has begun to appear, so far with a miserly print run (only 15,000) and in English, German and Russian. Its publisher is the Novosti Information Agency, which prints all the copies in Finland and brings them to Moscow. Bearing in mind the dangerous state of the environment in our country, and that in the pursuit of hard currency it is willingly assuming the role of the world's rubbish tip, Ecos stands every chance of winning a large readership. Everyone wants to find out the reasons for the environmental genocide on the Yamal peninsula, doping in sport, the destructive effect on the ozone layer of the American shuttle compared to similar Soviet space systems. The magazine's editorial team has declared its intention to become an independent public supervisory body. Offers of cooperation from Greenpeace International and other such movements, and also research centers, have already been received. Ecos wants to be the mouthpiece of the 'Greens' in Russia. In search of sponsors to expand its print run, the editors have stated that the dirty money of such Soviet organizations as the ministries for the chemical industry and water management will not be accepted...

The pilot issue of the newspaper *Third Estate*, established by the National Conference of Trade Unions of Cooperative and Other Free Enterprise Workers and a group of journalists from *Izvestia*, came off the press in September 1991. It became a kind of a sensation, because its editor-in-chief is Aleksei Adzhubei, a patriarch of Soviet journalism and the famed editor-in-chief of *Izvestia* during Khrushchev's thaw. It's difficult to say if it will be a success; in free market conditions, three of the five businesses usually flunk, and publishing a newspaper in these troubled times is a risky business.

In late 1991 kiosks in the former Soviet Union sold all kinds of obscure business publications: *Makler* (an advertisement-cum-information newspaper of the publishing house Moskovskaya Pravda), *Birzheviye Vedomosti* (Stock Exchange News, a national newspaper with Arkady Maslennikov, ex-TASS journalist and head of the press center of the USSR Supreme Soviet, as board member), *Business, Banks, Exchanges* (an independent weekly of financial and economic information), all of them small and printed on bad paper.

There are few magazines published on good paper with color illustrations, and their number has been growing mostly owing to the appearance of publications in foreign languages. *Kommersant*, although it is not a magazine but a thick newspaper, appeared in English too. Here is what *Kommersant* itself (August 12, 1991) wrote about new business publications issued in 5,000 to 18,000 copies and sold at exorbitant prices of nine to 49 rubles per copy:

> Last week saw the appearance of three new business publications: the weekly *Anons* (Announcement), published by the Baltic News Agency, the monthly *Russian Trade Express* of the Leningrad company Russian trading company, and the *Leningrad Business Guide* of the publishing cooperative LIK.
>
> These are more or less traditional publications carrying business offers, exchange and bank reports, advertisement and presentation of companies. The most readable of them will be those that publish information materials about business activities in Leningrad Region (*Leningrad Business Guide* and *Russian Trade Express*) and the Baltics (*Anons*).
>
> The first issue of *Leningrad Business Guide* offers information about 140 largest Leningrad enterprises engaged in external economic relations, and 50 leading Leningrad businessmen. Apart from this publication, the cooperative LIK intends to put out weekly issues of *Leningrad Investors Guide* and *Leningrad Legal Guide*, at the request of foreign companies, to be sold through a network of distributors in the USA, Canada, Western Europe and South East Asia.
>
> *Kommersant* experts believe that the magazine *Russian Trade Express* is rather conventional for the Soviet market of business press, while *Anons* and *Leningrad Business Guide* are quite another matter. The Russian-language *Anons* represents commercial structures of the Baltics and Scandinavia, while the *Leningrad Business Guide* is the only of its kind published in this country.

We don't have the technology for color printing to speak of, either homemade or foreign. The construction of turn-key printing complex by foreign builders costs millions of dollars, which we do not have. That is the reason why the Americans have delivered information materials on business, address and telephone books of major American cities, a number of laser video diskettes crammed with information and personal computers linked with Western data banks, to 8 Yaroslavskaya Street, block 3. This gave birth to the Moscow Business Library.

Since 1990 the Americans have been helping us to publish the Russian-language version of the magazine Interlink, a kind of an encyclopaedia of American business which offers a unique possibility of getting education in foreign economic operation.

The Soviet people are waking up to new forms of business operation, which has long since been adopted in other countries. In February 1991 St. Petersburg hosted this country's first TV auction, at which the right for a 15-year lease of a food store was sold for 470,000 rubles (if the future legislation permits, the shop can be bought after the expiry of the lease term). This tentative beginning soon developed into a major business. Leningrad has been re-named St. Petersburg and a TV exchange appeared there. Here is how *Kommersant* (September 30, 1991) described it:

> Igor Berezovsky, director general of the St. Petersburg company "Prostor Plus", one of the founders of the exchange, said that the TV Exchange of sovereign republics and states had been devised as a limited-liability company. It incorporates 26 broker companies members of the inter-regional association of TV exchanges operating practically throughout the USSR, as well as three broker companies from the USA, Germany and Bulgaria.
>
> A broker's office costs 500,000 rubles for Soviet participants and one million dollars for foreigners.
>
> Unlike conventional exchanges, the TV exchange can simultaneously hold sales and maintain broker contact with clients scattered over a vast territory, Berezovsky says.
>
> During the broadcasting of the sales, held by the regional broker companies on the local TV station, the clients regional broker companies on the local TV station, the clients get information about all sales of the TV exchange and the commodities which will be sold there. A digest of that information will be broadcast by the first channel of Central TV in the program "TV Exchange of Sovereign Republics and States" on Mondays and Thursdays, beginning on October 7.
>
> After watching the central or regional program, clients will have a right to inform local authorities that they had bought certain commodities. The dealings between regional broker companies shall be broadcast through a modem network twice a week for the duration of 24 hours.

TV exchanges and banks of business information are quite unusual for our people. If you want to exchange your flat, you have to type announcements and personally paste them to lamp posts, or else crowd for hours in a public garden where other people come for the same kind of information. That is the reason why our home-made "businessmen" are using the simplest possible methods of knocking money out of clients. One example is wall calendars showing nude beauties in elbow-high gloves. It is the sign of the times that successful crooks are reaping profits in the sphere of porno business, which is still new for us.

In April 1991, it was announced that the first-ever illustrated magazine for men in the Soviet Union, *Andrei*, would be published in Moscow in a 150,000 copy print run, priced at Rbls 9.95. When it was issued, however, the price for it on the black market reached 50 rubles. *Andrei*'s cover contained a warning by the Editorial Board: "Not for sale to persons under 18." Its editor-in-chief is Aleksei Veizler, 27, a former journalist, professional actor and good photographer. The American magazine *Time* reacted to this unprecedented Moscow event pinning an extensive article, which dubbed *Andrei* the Russian brother of the world-wide famous American magazine for men, *Playboy*. The Editorial Board is planning to stage Girls of the Year shows, festivals of erotic comics and cartoons, engage in book publishing and publish art and photo albums.

Andrei's amazingly high polygraphic quality by Soviet standards has been achieved in Tver. A page of advertising in *Andrei* fluctuates in cost from 15,000 to 40,000 rubles. The success attained by this type of Russian yellow press with its pornography (Veizler insists on the term "erotica"), political and scandalous stories, gossip and catastrophe columns, has inspired *Andrei*'s Editorial Board to extend its distribution to Russian communities abroad. One of the projects of this Russian lewd periodical envisages distribution of no less than 100,000 copies of each issue of the magazine in the USA and Israel at a price of three or four dollars.

I wonder if all periodicals in this country will sink to this level and start carrying pictures of nudes, or rather advocate the views of the left or right wing, those in favor of communism or against it? A porno-historic magazine is bound to appear, carrying pictures of all our political classics and General Secretaries, their wives and possibly lovers, today's orgies of their doubles, next to comics, dirty stories and tales on historical subjects. Or will the newspapers disappear in this country owing to the paper shortage?

Those familiar with Soviet life and Western reality unanimously predict that our "bulky" magazines will have to be considerably diminished or even disappear, whereas the papers will become less numerous, but more bulky. And, of course, popular illustrated weeklies, both political and specialized, are bound to sprout up like mushrooms after a good rain. Here is what our contemporary, Mikhail Epstein, said in an article, carried by *Novoye Russkoye Slovo*, dated January 18, 1991, and reprinted in an abridged version by the March 12, 1991 issue of *Nezavisimaya Gazeta*:

> First of all, the following change will predictably occur. Our papers will swiftly become more bulky, while the magazines will diminish in size. Foreigners have always been struck by the emaciated, unhealthy-looking appearance of our papers

with their customary four or six pages, and stout, almost apoplectic appearance of our magazines, such as *Novy Mir* (New World) with its 300 pages.

In the West, a daily on the contrary usually consists of fifty detached sections (Politics, Business, Sports, City News, Life-style, Science, etc.), comprising 100 pages at least. As for the Sunday issues, these bulky wads of paper are terrible to look at. It contains such an infinite amount of information that it's impossible to take it all in. Western magazines with their 80, well, 120, okay, 180, if it's a very specialized one, pages seem a bit slender compared to our magazines.

It's not just that volumes differ. In fact, it reflects a different public consciousness. History in the Soviet Union could be compared to a drying-out stream, whereby a thin two-page newspaper was quite large enough to be filled with acceptable news. Each day differed only by the thickness of our dailies.

As for the monthly magazines—oh, that's quite another matter! They subjected our reality to literary and socio-political comprehension. The thin lining of facts was covered by a thick fur-coat of myths. Where else would magazines offer their readers fresh news of a family, war, novel in production or many-volume epopee, extended over months and years? Days were trimmed and shortened in our curtailed papers to prolong the malleable contents of our months and years of magazine reading.

They were followed by books, usually hardcover which seemed to be canned, designed to preserve forever the powerful somnolence of the imperishable literary mind. Paperbacks were considered insulting, as it implied that the author was second-rate, and usually went to some hapless writers. Literature hid away in hardcovers as if in an armored personnel carrier and kept on its sights the passing reality, which ran by glancing around in fear, and abandoned the timid half-truths to the papers.

The magazines will change in appearance, as will their profile. Previously, literary magazines like *Znamya* and *Moskva* were considered popular, whereas theoretical ones, like *Voprosy Filosofii*, were specialized and printed in small editions. Just what they deserved, for easy reading blossomed in the former, and scholasticism in the latter. Art for a few and philosophy for all—nothing could be more awful. Everything was done to prevent philosophy and psychology from speaking a lively common language...

Today, we should expect literary magazines to become specialized, find a readership and, with an underground print run of 100-1,000 copies, involve it in exquisite literary and art experiments. Predictably, magazines specializing in philosophy, ethics, psychology, sociology, religion, esoterics will appear, printed in hundreds of thousands, if not millions of copies, and designed to attract theoretical thinking to actual life and the wealth of commonly used language. In other words, magazines will emerge for the art elite and thinking people.

CHAPTER VII

BOOK-PUBLISHING

Don't Burn Gorbachev!

A visit to a dozen or so bookstores in the summer of 1991 was enough to understand the crux of the problem. As in the past, there were no books in the bookstores other than the works of Lenin and Gorbachev and other such uninspiring publications, usually referred to as pulp literature, since no one wanted to buy them or even borrow such books from libraries. But it costs quite a lot of money to publish them and much more to translate them into other languages.

All this was to be published, sold, stored and...destroyed. *Literaturnaya Gazeta* (January 30, 1991) reported that the book trading association Moskniga notified the publishing house of the CPSU Central Committee, Politizdat, of the destruction of 50 publications of fairly new books, including a booklet by Gorbachev "*Acting Resolutely Without Wasting Time*", as well as some fifteen other works written by him. Not to mention the books by Ryzhkov, Sluynkov, Maslyukov, V. Medvedev, Razumovsky. The Moskniga Publishing House was thus hinting that from now on books by top party bosses should be issued in much more modest numbers. This action was indicative of the perestroika and glasnost period—until recently such "general purges" of official literature were carried out less frequently and were not mentioned in the press. Some wise individuals from the *Stolitsa* magazine (No. 5, 1991) appealed to the environmental conscience of Soviet bureaucrats requesting them not to incinerate the books by Lenin and his followers, as they had been instructed to do, but to send them for recycling. Our children will apparently have nothing to sell to second-hand bookshops. Today the collections of works by Stalin, Khrushchev, Trotsky and Suslov have become rare books and cost quite a lot of money. "Don't burn Gorbachev's books", said a headline in *Stolitsa*.

The CPSU had always forced on the peoples of the USSR and the rest of the world its false propagandist literature, created by writers and poets, publicists and representatives of other humanitarian professions. The best Soviet books, which constituted a mere drop in an ocean of mediocrity, were virtually never sold for rubles, but instead for hard currency and would also be found in the homes of Soviet party bosses. The major branches of normal literature—belles-letters, educational, reference and foreign—had virtually never been published in our country. The ratio here was similar to that between the sausage and cheese varieties in any supermarket in the West, and to be found not in an ordinary grocery in our country but rather in a special store for the elite: they had dozens of brand names, while we had only a few.

In our bookstores you could not buy good books, to say nothing of the works by Pasternak and Sakharov. In the shops of Tbilisi, for example, there was a chronic shortage of Shota Rustaveli's immortal poem "*The Knight in a Panther's Skin*"; there were no Georgian-language ABC's, teach-yourself or similar books for students and no dictionaries at all; there was a miserable selection of children's books, and so on. Absent also were the overwhelming majority of books turned out by the 300 Soviet publishing houses (there are 1,600 publishers in Italy, in Japan—4,500 and in the USA—7,000).

Why were there no books that anyone wanted to buy? Some of them ended up on the black market, the least in-demand went to the 300,000 school and other local libraries, and some managed to find their way to shops in villages or out-of-the-way provincial towns.

The result was that the majority of the Soviet people were unable to obtain virtually any school textbook or learning aid, or classical or contemporary work of literature, without a great deal of trouble. To prevent the education system from collapsing, the state was forced to place the production of textbooks under special control and ensure their distribution directly through schools.

For decades in the Soviet Union the number of copies of a book was determined not by readers' demand but by instructions from Party authorities. These authorities could have several hundred thousand copies for some "tame" writer's work printed whom nobody wanted to read. And this book would gather dust in the warehouses, shops and public libraries for months before being scapped and recycled. But in the Soviet Union authors received their royalties not on the basis of sales, but upon issue of their works. If an author died, his relatives received nothing; if he was published abroad, the Soviet Copyright Agency (the monopoly go-between that handled all such arrangements) paid him not more than 20% of the proceeds and that in rubles, too.

And another sad fact—there were virtually no foreign-published books in Soviet shops and no shops specializing in them, with the exception of a few showcases in Moscow and ten or so in other major cities. Some foreign publications were brought into the country, but only one or two copies for the largest national libraries.

Until recently, 1989, simply reading a Russian émigré newspaper or novel would get you into trouble. It was virtually impossible to obtain them officially. The likes of *Russkaya Mysl* or *Novoye Russkoye Slovo* were kept in the safes of not more than two or three Moscow establishments. Some new works of Western literature, especially the more scandalous political bestsellers, would be rapidly translated into Russian and printed, but only for distribution among the top 600 elite bureaucrats, and according to a confidential list. This went on for decades until early 1991. Only 20–30 good Western books on politics came out this way every year. For example, with Guiseppe Boffa's voluminous work *The History of the USSR*, a Party mogul could be sure that he was reading accurate research, and not mythical claims from an official Soviet textbook. Not only that, but if Signor Boffa were to commit a small factual error, the Russian editor would assiduously correct him: wrong, Maestro, in such-and-such a year the NKVD shot not 15 generals and marshals, but only 14.

Twenty years ago the USSR Academy of Sciences set up a unique establishment—the Social Science Scientific Information Institute, the purpose of which was to prepare for leading Soviet institutions reviews and surveys, for restricted viewing and stamped "For Office Use Only". They constructed a splendid glass and concrete building, gathered a fine library of foreign books and turned out several hundred annotations and opinions on the writings of foreign authors. But, as it transpired, all was in vain. Nobody would authorize a fair book review, and in any case nobody had the appropriate qualifications to do this; the reviewer is to possess qualifications at least equal to those of the author himself.

It is difficult for Western readers to comprehend that by the eighth decade of its existence, the Soviet regime had managed to completely eradicate the social sciences and all those capable of doing research in them. Scholars who can be considered specialists in, say, economics and jurisprudence, history and philosophy, philology and sociology look like relics against the overall backdrop of ignorance and disinformation. The exceptions were a few of the most renowned and popular writers and screen and stage actors, who had learned to use a kind of Aesopian language according to their creative abilities and personal conscience. The social sciences were utterly destroyed, and no perestroika will help them now. What is needed is time, new generations of properly-taught schoolchildren and university graduates, not to mention properly-taught and trained school and university teachers. This is where we need the West's help in the first place. Teach our children! Help us in our education and book publishing! And in our libraries as well!

Ninety-nine percent of the Soviet population could never find a popular book in a shop or library. Not a year would pass under Soviet power without a censor visiting libraries (city, village, school, institute, republican, national, or whatever) to tell the directors which books were to be removed from the shelves and recycled. At best, these books were transferred to the so-called spetskhran (secret archives), closed for most readers. As a result: one copy of Trotsky or Bakunin, Nietzsche or Djilas for each federal republic. For 70 years the few contemporary foreign political writings and books of fiction that did come into the country through international library exchanges were kept in the spetskhran archives. Soviet libraries contained no up-to-date foreign works on religion, religious and mystical philosophy, Sovietology, commerce, marketing, sexology, etc. Not only were the books in the spetskhran archives secret: so were the catalogues.

Nobody in the USSR could keep abreast of the latest publications abroad. Excerpts from selected works would sometimes be prepared for a few categories of interested people at the top of the hierarchy. Although, to be honest, nobody in our leadership ever read the latest foreign publications, or was even interested in them. But what about students, post-graduates or young researchers? What did, or do, they get? The best they can hope for is to gain entry to a library, where the selection even of home-produced works is inferior to that of Russian libraries at the turn of the century, when nobody purged books and the spetskhran archives did not even exist. The libraries of Moscow and St. Petersburg have never possessed computerized cataloguing information systems. Not only have these libraries come to a standstill in their development—they have deteriorated.

In this country's largest library—the Lenin State Library - the spetskhran was alive even in 1991, and one third of all the books in the archives did not appear in the reader's catalogue. Their existence simply had to be surmised. The Lenin Library had no intention of collecting (and worse still, preferred to ignore) everything written about Russia ("Rossica") or the Soviet Union ("Sovietica"), and did not receive samizdat. Quite possibly, the only place where you might find a more or less comprehensive selection of the Soviet Union's small and independent newspapers is the KGB, which collects them for purposes other than educational.

The 1990 budget for the US Congress library came to 300 million dollars; that for the "Leninka" was a mere 11 million (unconvertible) rubles. While the Soviet government was allocating 100 million rubles for reconstruction of the Lenin Library, the French were preparing to fork out 4,000 million francs for their national book archive. In all developed countries libraries have optical discs, electronic communications systems, computerized catalogues and strong research services. And what do we have? Technology from the 19th century, with the only difference that in this country there is no comprehensively-educated and cultured class. There are research institutes, but not enough good researchers. In an interview with *Literaturnaya Gazeta* on February 28 1990, Dr Billington, director of the US Congress library, spoke of the work of his 5,000-strong staff, and also of the Congressional Research Service (CRS): "During the Washington summit, Gorbachev requested material on Russia compiled by the CRS, while one of his advisors on arms control met with a CRS author in this field".

I believe that the Library of the US Congress would, if somebody made a serious request, agree to maintain our Lenin Library as its subsidiary. Does this seem absurd? Not in the least, if one considers that our most famous publications (museum values, archives, etc.) will simply perish in bad storage conditions. After the famous fire in the library of the Russian Academy of Sciences in St. Petersburg, the Library of the US Congress spent 135,000 dollars on aid—the US specialists who had come to our country took part in the restoration of damaged books and managed to freeze more than 200,000 rare books in order to halt the destruction process.

A prison, orphanage and library—the state of things in these institutions can vividly reveal the civic spirit of a country. Stalinist order still rules in such establishments in our country today. The memory of nations that inhabited Russia is preserved in the Lenin Library in proportion to the truth to be found in our history books. Is this an exaggeration? Hardly. During our perestroika days the Lenin Library contrived to destroy the vast catalogue of newspaper and magazine articles it had amassed over many years! "Why did they do this?— wrote A. Rubinov in *Literaturnaya Gazeta* (June 26, 1991).—They claim that there is little room left in the library. Is that the reason why the labor of several generations of bibliographers, who day by day, year by year, decade by decade, first by hand and then with the help of a typewriter, filled in every card for each publication in each edition, must be thrown out? Or maybe there is another reason? Many suspect that this infamous deed was done on the initiative of those who are afraid of secrets from their shady past..."

The Lenin Library has for many years been threatened with closure "for restoration'. Until recently it was virtually impossible for an ordinary individual—unless you were there for scientific research and had a reference from your place of work—to get into the library. Well, maybe it would be worthwhile to consider a transfer of our libraries to foreigners, together with museums and archives. For in that case they will be safer, or else everything will rot.

The All-Union Library of Foreign Literature transferred one of its reading halls in the summer of 1991 to the French Cultural Center, the first such center in the Soviet Union. In exchange the French Embassy will replenish the funds of this Moscow library with new French books and periodicals, help install modern equipment and organize the training of the library's personnel in Paris.

The Soviet reader has already forgotten how to use a public library. One in every three young men "does not like to read." One in every three does not know where to get a book. Best-sellers on the black market are beyond his means. We have also deprived our children of books and consequently have killed off our future.

The choice of writers for would-be best-sellers in Russia has always been under strict control. An author might be paid a royalty of between 100 and two thousand rubles per signature (approximately 16 pages of book text) depending on numerous classifications and tariffs. The publisher could even pay nothing, consider the text mere non-fiction stuff and set a small royalty rate, irrespective of the number of copies published. A well-disposed publisher could consider the same text a work of fiction and set not only the highest royalty rate, but also make additional payments in accordance with publication figures, which will multiply this royalty several times over. "I've received money for publication figures!" our Soviet author would rejoice and bend over backwards to please all those who had authorized this manna from heaven. In most cases the book would never sell out but the author no longer cared. And even the publisher would not suffer in any way. The book would be either written off or sent to libraries. In any other country a writer depends far less on the publisher and the success of the book is determined by consumer demand. Writers abroad receive their royalties not on the issue of the work by the printing house, but instead after it has been sold out in book stores—in the form of 8-12 per cent of the book's sales. As a rule writers in this country are poor like the majority of their readers.

The authors of scientific works virtually never received royalties. There are very few scientific publishing houses in our country and they depend on donations from the state, which barely cover costs. Scientific information in this country is stored in the form of monographs, providing the reader with 10 per cent of scientific information. Scientific journals provide this interested reader with a further 40 per cent. Another 40 per cent is obtained by a scientific worker from office scientific reports and seminar and conference materials, which have a very limited circulation. The remaining 10 per cent is made up by correspondence, oral reports and other sources. However monographs provide information after a time delay of 5-7 years, scientific journals 2-3 years, and extracts from scientific reports from six to twelve months. Given the poor state of our scientific libraries, the result of all this is very disheartening. According to the data of the All-Union Institute of Scientific and Technical Information of Russia (newspaper *Radikal*, April 4, 1991), our scientists are 100 times less well informed than scientists from the USA and other developed countries.

Most Soviet books have been written and published in such a form that hardly anyone would pick them up, let alone read them. *"Literature and pulp literature. The portrait of a reader in the face of the book collapse"*, was the headline under which one of the newly founded Moscow weeklies, *Megapolis-Express* (December 20, 1990) published the following short interview:

> From childhood we know that our metro is the best in the world, and are equally convinced that the Soviet people read more than any other. But how much do we actually read? How is the structure of book supply and demand changing as we move towards a a market economy? To find out, we interviewed Professor Anatoly Solovyov, director of the Moscow Institute of Books.
>
> **Question: Anatoly Ivanovich, is it true that we read more than anyone else?**

Book-Publishing

Answer: Unfortunately, it's far from true. According to one set of figures, in terms of printed product per head of the population we're in 42nd place, while another set puts us at 50th and just ahead of such countries as Benin and Zanzibar. Let me stress that this concerns printed products and all paper expended on printing purposes. Actually trying to find out how much we read is no easy matter. Just a few years ago we thought that there were more than 50,000 million books in people's private collections, while today this number has been revised downwards to about 14,000 million. This isn't much at all.

Question: Are there any other yardsticks to measure the level of book "consumption"?

Answer: Of course. For example, 8-9 books are issued per head of population in this country every year. This, incidentally, includes various pamphlets, manuals and school textbooks. Fiction and literature account for approximately one quarter of the total. However, elsewhere in the world the practice is to assess the book supply not in terms of the overall quantity printed, but the number of titles. In Russia each year we turn out 280-290 titles per million people, which shows that we are badly lagging behind other European countries, where the average is 700.

Question: And there are probably also people who don't read at all, but prefer to spend their spare time watching TV or dancing at discos?

Answer: According to the Institute of Books and the State Committee for Statistics, a total of 13.6 percent of the population, or about 40 million, don't read at all. Add to them the 92 million who read only occasionally, and the result is 132 million "non-reading" people, ie., almost half of the population.

Question: What's been the most popular book this year?

Answer: The Bible, which is quite understandable and correct, since many people are only now discovering this eternal book for themselves. In second place was "The GULAG Archipelago", by Alexander Solzhenitsyn.

Question: So according to answers given by readers, Solzhenitsyn is the year's top writer?

Answer: That's right, jointly with Andrei Sakharov. I think that this is due not only to the high literary value of their writings but also to the insatiable interest in these two outstanding personalities and human-rights campaigners.

Question: I would've thought that thrillers would be most popular of all today. Is there a reason for the interest in this genre?

Answer: Of course. I think, people are fed up with politics, their hungry and poverty-stricken lives, and our fearful history and hopeless present, and thus seek escapism.

Question: Perhaps the onset of a market economy will relieve us of the book famine and attract lots of new readers?

Answer: The problem is actually that the market (ie., high negotiated prices) is splitting society into a reading elite and the non-reading masses. It

> deprives 60 million pensioners, 30 million disabled people and 45 million children and students of books. This is a real tragedy. As a result, a whole generation is growing up detached from the world of books. Hence vandalism, growing aggression within society and lack of respect for the individual. There are of course many reasons for all this, but one of them is the dearth of books.
>
> Question: But surely the market isn't only bad news for the reader?
> Answer: I didn't say that. It will to a degree meet public demand, especially for works of fiction. If you recall, just five years ago it was impossible to get hold of Bulgakov, Grossman or Platonov, while now they're being published at the rate of 10-15 million copies a year, and their black-market prices are falling.

We just cannot do everything right, but some progress in this respect can now be seen. There was neither a journalists' trade union nor press research institute in Russia. Recently the human rights fighter Sergei Grigoryants set up an independent journalists' trade union. But we still do not have a research institute to study the mass media and communications.

We do have an institute to study books, recently set up under the State Committee for Printing, and referred to above. The interview by Professor Solovyov, director of the institute, is of interest to us because it provides first-hand information (*Sovetskaya Kultura*, June 9, 1990):

> One can quite often encounter educated people in the Soviet Union, members of the intelligentsia, who see no need to know and develop the ideas, principles and ideals set forth by Homer and Socrates, Solovyov, Florensky, Bekhterev, Bogdanov, Platonov, Bulgakov, Bukharin, Vavilov, Vernadsky, and so on. Newspapers and magazines today have to introduce their readers to such classics anew. An interesting fact is that of the 86 writers awarded the Nobel Prize for Literature, 25 have never been published in Russia (in separate editions). Of the 16 prizewinners from 1973 to 1987, 9 have not been published here, including Patrick White (Australia), Eyvind Johnson (Sweden), Saul Bellow (USA), Vicente Alexandre (Spain), Isaac Singer (USA), Odysseus Elytis (Greece), Czeslaw Milosz (USA), Claude Simon (France), and Joseph Brodsky.
>
> Question: Our understanding of the word "book" probably also differs from that in the West. How do you define it in your institute?
> Answer: There is a host of definitions of a book. Every set of statistics supplies its own. Some count the pages, others the words.
> To strengthen the myth, we tried to call everything a book. Two thousand million books a year. This included a mass of pamphlets, ministerial brochures and teaching aids, ie., publications with no cover price. And if there's no cover price, it isn't a book.
> Question: But it's thought that in this country there are vast state libraries and personal collections.

Answer: We can examine the problem from the viewpoint of the number of titles published. According to the statistics this operates like a mirror, reflecting cultural peaks and troughs in our history. During the NEP period, from 1925 to 1931, the number of titles rose from 32,300 to 54,600, and during the Khrushchev thaw of 1955—1962 from 54,700 to 79,100. There was a headlong decline as Stalin's tyranny gathered strength, from 54,600 in 1931 to 37,600 by 1937.

Question: **What about the years of perestroika?**

Answer: During the 1970s we were at best just marking time, although, to tell the truth, a small increase was recorded. After that a gradual inexorable decline set in, which continues to this day. These are the figures: 1985—84,000 titles a year, 1986—83,500, 1987—83,000, and 1988—81,600. I just can't understand how a society supposedly acclaimed "the best-read of all" can so meekly accept the miserable amount of reading matter that it's given and the pitiful state of the printing industry, all of which is the fault of the command system. To remind you, in terms of paper production our country, the largest in the world and possessing vast forestry reserves, is somewhere below 50th place. According to some figures, existing facilities in Russia can process only 12% of all timber supplied, while in developed countries in the West the percentage is up to 50 or even 70. We're planning 5% growth a year, which is completely unacceptable.

For the Soviet elite, one of the yardsticks of seniority of office and one of the most sought-after privileges has always been regular receipt of a book list. Moreover, chauffeur-driven office cars, free-of-charge state flats and free holidays for the whole family at top notch resorts have been handed out much more frequently than the envied monthly book list of the latest good books. All you had to do was tick the books you want, forward the list with the requisite symbolic sum to the proper person, and away you go.

Until summer 1991, every self-respecting ministry had its own way of obtaining books for its senior administrators. One list of the latest publications would go to the Central Committee and other Party bodies, others would go to the upper echelons of the USSR Council of Ministers, ministerial collegiums and state committees, People's Deputies, and so on. Regular and completely independent supplies of good books were also enjoyed by the generals, Russia Academy of Sciences, Writers' Union, the ruling cliques in the provinces and union and autonomous republics. Meanwhile, 350,000 libraries had to make do with what was left. And they were often given what they did not need.

The General Public Needs Not Just a Few Dozens of Books, but Thousands of Titles

The Russian translation of the *Guinness Book of Records* recently made its first appearance on the counters (or rather under them) of Moscow bookshops.

Until 1988 this ideologically innocuous encyclopedia had never been published in this country, while the occasional copy from the West was kept in the spetskhran archives of two or three national libraries. The reason? The powers-that-be did not like the specifically Russian "records" it contained.

You can, however, get by without the *Guinness Book*. The West helps us with the *Bible, Koran* and other religious literature—millions of copies of these works in Russian and other languages (sent to us free, although our believers have to buy them) manage to find their way into our country.

But how can one live in a multinational country without dictionaries? No *natsmen* [Russian slang for any member of a 'natsionalnoye menshinstvo', or national minority—G.V.] with a higher education would turn down the chance to acquire (even from higher education would turn down the chance to acquire even at an inflated price a much-needed bilingual dictionary. Here I mean not English-Russian, Russian-English or other such publications for those who know a foreign language; they can be found in the shops and are released fairly regularly. According to Vladimir Nazarov, director of the Moscow book publishers Russky Yazyk (Russian Language), as quoted in *Literaturnaya Gazeta* of October 10 1990, and data released by the All-Union Book Chamber, the dictionaries and phrasebooks that were occasionally brought out in the republics were usually meant for students of Russian. But what should the millions of Russian speakers living in other republics do? For decades the Soviet government wouldn't solve this problem and persistently and deliberately waged a policy of Russification, although in official pronouncements the opposite was touted and there was much talk of "flourishing national cultures", etc.

Alexander Solzhenitsyn by his own efforts compiled a dictionary of Russian that incorporated much that has been lost. The Armenian and Ukrainian diasporas throughout the world will, of course, make sure that their national cultures do not die out. There will be Armenian and Ukrainian, and also Baltic (Lithuanian, Latvian and Estonian) dictionaries. But who is going to worry about the Georgians? Or about the indigenous inhabitants of the dozens of Russian autonomous units who have ended up in a vacuum? Instead of a national culture, they have been subjected to comprehensive Russification.

It is of course a good thing that Solzhenitsyn's contribution will be used during the preparation of the 20-volume contribution dictionary of the Russian language, which is even now beginning to come off the presses. The USA is to help us implement a highly promising international project: the release of a Russian Encyclopedia. The USA and Solzhenitsyn helping us to publish something—the very thought of it is fantastic. Any Soviet citizen who might have dared propose this (except Andrei Sakharov) just 3 or 4 years ago would very rapidly have been found a place in a psychiatric ward, without any court order or investigation. He would have been picked up from work with no time to pack his bags.

The Soviet-American Foundation "Cultural Initiative" has set up a publishing company, which is planning to issue between 1996 and the year 2,000 a 50-volume Russian encyclopedia, with "interim" encyclopedias to come out from 1991; among them will be specialized (philosophy, economics, Russian saints, etc.) and regional (the Urals, Caucasus, Baikal, etc.) works.

There is, of course, a wide variety of information on Russians within the *Great Soviet Encyclopedia*, the latest 30-volume edition of which still fails to mention thousands and thousands of outstanding Russian people hounded during the 70 years of the Soviet regime, who have emigrated or died in obscurity in Russia. There is hope that one day the Russian people will have its past restored, that Russians who have achieved success in the West will be spoken of well here too. The fact is that here today nobody has heard of the works or even the names of those mentioned in such respectable tomes as the two-volume *Bibliography of Russian Emigre Literature* (American Ludmilla Foster published this book in the USA in 1970), and *Russian Emigration. Journals and Compendia in Russian. 1920-1980*, published in 1988 in Paris by the Slavonic Studies Institute.

To this day the best Encyclopedic Dictionary in this country remains that published 100 years ago, during the Tsarist era, by Brockhaus & Efron, the print quality of which astounds readers even now. In response to readers' demand, some enterprising businessmen at the end of 1990 issued a facsimile reprint of the first 10 of this work's 86 volumes. There were not many copies and they cost a fortune, but purchasers can always be found for a fashionable rarity.

Similar to works of art in the West, books have become a form of investment in the Soviet Union, not less worthwhile and much safer than buying gold. Valuables are, after all, hunted down by thieves, and cannot be placed for safe keeping in any bank in this country, while books are difficult to steal because of their weight. Or perhaps the criminal fraternity suspect that readers will soon cease to pay twice the official (state) price for the single-volume *Soviet Encyclopedic Dictionary* (SED), since even in the similar single-volume French equivalent *Quid* there is a lot of information on the Soviet Union that the *SED* lacks.

The *SED* has been published in Russia several times, in print runs of millions; it truly is an accessible and very useful work. The only pity is that many aspects of reality under perestroika were not included. Popular Fronts were active in all our Soviet republics, the newspapers wrote about strikes and accused the Leninist Communist Party of having organized mass starvation in the Volga region and the Ukraine (during the 1920s and 1930s). And here are three small entries from the 1989 edition of the *SED* gleefully reprinted by *Komsomolskaya Pravda* on March 10 1990 :

> "POPULAR FRONT, a form of organizing the masses ... to struggle against fascism and war, for democracy, national independence, and also to uphold the vital

economic interests of the working classes... In France in 1936-38, Spain in 1936–39, Chile in 1938–41, popular front governments were in power. In some countries they played an important role in the victory of national-democratic and socialist revolutions".

"STRIKE ... one of the principal forms of class struggle of the proletariat under capitalism... The strike is an important form of the struggle against the reactionary socio-economic policy of monopolies and the bourgeois state, against the arms race and a new war".

"FAMINE, a social tragedy manifesting itself in two forms: overt (absolute hunger) and covert (relative hunger, malnutrition, the absence of vital components in the diet). In the developed capitalist countries tens of millions of working people suffer from malnutrition... Starvation is conquered only as a result of a socialist restructuring of society".

Dozens of books, calendars and reference books, which had already appeared in late 1990, published by Politizdat, the CPSU Central Committee's publishing house, contained no fewer evident falsehoods. In 1989-1990, the same publishers literally filled the country's bookshops with a political economy textbook, with a print run of 1,000,000 copies and written by the CPSU Central Committee Secretary, "our ideologist" Vadim Medvedev. There were ideologist" Vadim Medvedev.

The lifting of censorship and the CPSU monopoly revived the publishing business. TERRA Publishers emerged, among many others. The July 23, 1991 issue of *Rossiiskaya Gazeta* carried a review of a book in its Sensation column under the headline *If Such Books Are Published, Then Perestroika Is Really Underway*:

TERRA Publishers have printed an essay on the political history of Russia, entitled *Our Motherland*, which is, in fact, the first educational publication of its kind in the Soviet era. The publication of this two-volume work reads like a detective story. Its authors include Yu. Afanasyev, N. Maslov, G. Ioffe, V. Lelchuk, Ye. Pivovar, M. Milyutin, V. Shostakovsky, O. Volobuyev, and Yuri Felshtinsky, representing foreign historians.

Our Motherland constitutes the first attempt to radically reevaluate Russia's history and consider the relations between society and the authorities in the light of society and the authorities in the light of the Russian political tradition. The book deals with the period from Kievan Rus up to perestroika and the elections of the first-ever Russian President. It includes unknown and little-known documents on the Civil and Great Patriotic wars, collectivization, Khrushchev's reforms and the period of stagnation. Separate chapters are devoted to the history of resistance and dissidence from Martov, Raskolnikov and Ryutin to the present, with essays on both prominent Communist and opposition political figures. And, finally, the history of perestroika, on which documents can still not be found in the archives.

Professor Sergei Kuleshov, who headed the corporate authorship of the book, still can't believe that the book has been published. He says that Robert Conquest, who read several chapters of the manuscript, specially translated for him, exclaimed: "If this is published, then perestroika is really underway in the Soviet Union."

"In fact, we are all Stalinists," says one of its authors, history professor V. Lelchuk. "Even the youth of today. This is Stalin's greatest "achievement." Some are aware of it, others are not, but all of us studied history through Stalin's textbooks and are tainted with the spirit of *History of the CPSU (B)—Short Course*. Thanks to its successful propaganda, millions of people today still hold the view that a socialist system is the only correct path. When Mikhail Gorbachev refers to the Soviet Union as a developed industrialised state, I realize that he, too, studied Stalin's textbooks and has no intention of changing his views. All our troubles come from the immoral party authority, whose leaders must be held responsible for what they have done to the Russian people. Today we urgently need to take a long-term view and reassess our own history (soberly and respectfully). Of course, we are conscious of our limitations, but we hope that the book will help people see things more clearly."

And it does offer interesting facts which could be news for many. For example, the fact that the powerful peasant riots of the 1930s were mercilessly suppressed by the army, reinforced by all sectors, including the artillery and air force on a secret decision of the Politburo. The book cites reports by NKVD-MGB-KGB on the feelings of workers and collective farmers, examples of disloyalty to the regime and strikes.

Despite its profound scientific approach to historical issues, the textbook is written in comprehensible language and caters for the tastes of the widest possible readership. S. Kondratov, TERRA Publishers' Director, promises a print run of 1,000,000 copies. So far, however, only 50,000 copies have been issued."

The time will come when not only collections of essays, but textbooks on the history of Bolshevism will be written and published in Moscow. Meanwhile, the broadly circulated *Rossiiskaya Gazeta* thinks that there are better things to do than carry stories by Agatha Christie, and are serializing extracts from the aforementioned *Our Motherland. Experience of Political History*. It is far better than the CPSU's Vadim Medvedev with his book or the USSR People's Deputy and the CPSU Central Committee Member with the same surname, Roy Medvedev, with his thirty anti-Stalinist and anti-Khrushchev works, published abroad under Brezhnev, by permission of the KGB, and subsequently in this country.

Honest and true dissidents have not been rehabilitated in this country to this day. Enthusiasts from the Russian-Lithuanian Joint-Stock Publishers *Vest* (Herald) promised in the May 7, 1991 issue of *Izvestia* that they would compile and print 50,000 copies of their 50-volume *History of Dissidence*, which would focus on the post-Stalin years and provide evidence that the resistance movement consisted not of a handful of courageous people, but tens of thousands of them from all parts of the boundless Soviet Union. Samizdat and dissident publications, published in their time in this country and abroad, are being officially reprinted in this country in luxury editions destined for antique collectors.

In order to obtain a more or less interesting book, Soviets of all ages would meticulously collect waste paper, queue for hours at waste collecting outlets, and then for months would try to exchange the coupons they got at waste collecting outlets for the necessary books in bookstores. It is an intolerable situation, further evidenced by the following official discovery. According to UNESCO, the Soviet Union—"the greatest book-loving nation in the world"—was ranked 43rd in 1988 in the world for the intellectual level of its young people.

But this country has seen better times. The American-based *Novoye Russkoye Slovo* wrote in its November 26, 1990 issue that not long ago UNESCO staged a contest for the best educational program of all times. Which program do you think won the contest? The one employed in its time by Lyceum at Tsarskoye Selo, where Alexander Pushkin studied in his younger days. It was distinguished for its individual approach to students and high standards of education. It is noteworthy that even daily routines included an individual element and depended on the individuality of each student. Surely this is the reason why the lyceum produced a whole constellation of outstanding writers, scientists and public figures, who constituted the pride of Russia. In the early 20th century Ivan Sytin published 25% of all books in Russia. Thanks to him, books in those days were available to a far greater number of readers than today. In September 1991 a hawker in Tbilisi demanded up to a hundred rubles from me for a good edition of *Bible Stories*, published in the same year by *Detskaya Literatura* (Children's Literature) Publishers and priced at 15 rubles, whereas my wife, who worked at Moscow State University's Faculty of Journalism Department as an education inspector, earned a salary of 140 rubles a month, working daily from 9.00 a.m. to 6.00 p.m. What is our son aged 7 supposed to read? And will he develop the habit of reading in his life?

We went on telling lies to our people, or to be more precise, did not provide them with enough information. Ninety-nine per cent of Soviet children have never seen comics in their lives. Permission to publish them was granted only recently. And the first to do so in 1990 were Panorama Publishers. The majority of children have never held full-color, quality children's books or children's encyclopedia in their hands. Such publications are published in meagre print runs (100,000 copies for 300,000,000 million in the Soviet Union) by only two publishing houses in Moscow and are either directly exported or appear on the black market, where they are sold at seven-or even ten times their cover price.

"What Price Do We Pay to Satisfy Book Hunger?"—leads the headline of A. Dobrov's article in the September 2, 1991, issue of *Komsomolskaya Pravda*:

> Walk out of any metro station and you are bound to run into stalls, piled with the most tempting publications in attractive, brightly-colored covers. Detective stories, mainly by James Chase and Agatha Christie, science fiction and what was previously referred to as low-taste romances and adventure stories about all types of

lascivious Angelicas and great, sturdy and kind Tarzans are predominant. They are followed by religious books ranging from the Bible, Koran and Talmud to renderings of the Gospels for children. Almost all books by Pikul and Solzhenitsyn, *Rose of Peace* by D. Andreyev (strangely enough, this is one of the bestsellers). Any book, which was unavailable earlier, has become almost available. I say almost, because I touch my virtually empty billfold.

Looking at this display of books, you still cannot believe that we have managed to quench the thirst for books, that we do not need to read Soviet reviews of works, unavailable in this country, by authors such as Hermann Hesse in order to get an idea of what they are all about.

So, what price have we paid to quench this thirst? To answer this question, all you have to do is look at the prices.

It is worth mentioning that serious books, previously distributed by Samizdat, are only in demand from those who could have already read them with the help of the same Samizdat. What does the saturation of the book market with previously forbidden books lead to? It narrows their distribution to a still greater extent, for those who found that obtaining and hiding *A Day in the Life of Ivan Denisovich* in a ventilation hatch provided some kind of thrill, or even a feat of civil gallantry and valor, will drop out. Just compare the prices in Sverdlovsk: five rubles for Sakharov's *Anxiety and Hope* and 35 rubles for a collection of American detective stories.

Megapolis Continent, dated July 24, 1991, frontpaged an article by its reviewer, O. Pravotorov, on our readership's change of preferences under the headline *Classics in the Market Environment*:

Classics are out of fashion today. Some editions cost no more than waste paper. Our contemporary derives spiritual food from other sources, such as detective stories by James Chase and the erotic adventures of Angelica who is unlucky in her relations with men. In fact, Chase at the book market in this country is something more that the pen name of the popular author. A Chase novel could be accepted as a standard of demand, used to measure any other publication from the Soviet consumer's point of view. How many Chases does it take a Soviet reader to buy a many-volume edition by any great master of national or foreign literature? Given that a Chase novel is worth roughly forty rubles, a complete eight-volume collection of works by another gifted Englishman, William Shakespeare, would cost no more than four Chases. A ten-volume edition by Johann Wolfgang von Goethe—three Chases, as much as ten volumes by Dostoyevsky or fifteen by Balzac. A twelve-volume edition of Anton Chekhov's works and twenty-two volumes of works by Leo Tolstoy, equal two and a half Chases, whereas an academic ten-volume edition of Alexander Pushkin's works would hardly reach two Chases in price. Four volumes by Mikhail Lermontov are priced as little as a half-Chase.

How did this devaluation of the great come about? Chekhov or Balzac did not seem to do anything wrong either in Stalin's era, or in the years of stagnation, which Soviet readers could blame them for. Or is it because "the greatest book-caring nation in the world" knows these classics by heart?

"People are tired of problems and would like to relax during the time they spend reading," says the manager of a Moscow-based book co-op. "That's why they prefer detective and adventure stories and erotic-flavoured novels. The more so since most books of this kind have only just appeared in this country. Hence the interest in them is only natural."

Well, it's something like the first fresh strawberries after winter. However, many of our great masters, who are pushed aside by detective stories and erotica today, were not any easier to obtain before. For example, the author of The Devils, Dostoyevsky, was not favored by Goskomizdat. And long ago labor collectives drew lots for the right to subscribe to this or that classic writer and could not do so without quarrelling. Why do they cost almost nothing today? According to world market traditions, a collection of works by a serious author has always been much more expensive than entertainment publications. From the economic point of view, such editions are a profitable investment, for their aesthetic value has been proved by time, and time also increases their value.

This rule seems to affect our book market as well, whereas our readers' aesthetic demands seem to have outgrown the world masterpiece boundaries.

"There was a time when multi-volume editions of the classics were actually eagerly sought after," an attendant at a second-hand bookstore recalls. "They were used to decorate the home. Nowadays, those people who can afford a wall unit, are no longer interested in classical literature, whereas those who have become interested in it, cannot even buy a bookshelf. Moreover, the young are less and less interested in books by Tolstoy or Alexander Blok. The new generation of readers has been practically lost. How can this have happened? I don't know."

Poet Nikolai Nekrasov's wonderful hopes that the day would come when, to paraphrase him, people would go to the shops and buy not worthless detective stories, but works by the critic Vissarion Belinsky and Nikolai Gogol, are unlikely to come true even in this century. Moreover, nobody buys books by Belinsky or by Nekrasov from the stores, nor is there any sense in taking them to the bazaars either. Neither state-owned bookstores, nor co-op bookshops accept, even second-hand, books by these two prominent representatives of Russian democratic thinking. And this is despite the fact that in 1989 Goskomizdat priced a three-volume edition by Belinsky at ten rubles and a four-volume edition by Nekrasov at Rbls 12.50. Alas, today the market refuses to rate them at even a quarter-Chase.

Chase himself, who considered his talented novels no more than entertainment reading, would probably not have been happy to be such a success on the Soviet book market. As a man of culture, he would have probably quoted a line from Goethe who is also under-appreciated in this country: "He who doesn't take heed of what poets say, is a barbarian, no matter who he may be."

I can only add to this that the same could be applied to those who are ready to trade true values of art for a literary ersatz in brightly-colored covers, like a savage trading gold for a necklace made out of glass.

Things will sort themselves out, of course, provided that there is a market environment. Thus, Moscow News carried in its July 7, 1991 issue a promising headline for an article by V. Gubarev and A. Kolesnikov: "*Detective Stories No*

Longer In Demand. A Saturated and Customer-Oriented Book Market Appeared in Moscow As If Out Of Thin Air."

-The streets of Moscow have become crammed with bookstalls. The average speed in the underground passage at Pushkinskaya Square has noticeably fallen, for here they sell books.

Initially, the underground passage predominantly offered erotic works, replaced later on by pornography. Today, textbooks on electrotechnics, road traffic tests, which are in high demand, philosophical works by Friedrich Nietzsche and Nikolai Berdyaev, memoirs by Alexander Vertinsky, and the inevitable detective stories by Chase are on a par with pornography.

Some twelve months ago the publishing business in this country underwent tremendous changes, with new names—Prometei, Orbita, Interbook—emerging on the scene. The new businesses are dominated by the TERRA Publishing Center, which is already capable of challenging some state-owned publishing houses. Here is its service record.

During the twelve months of its existence, the center has brought out over fifty publications with a total print run of 6,000,000 copies. It has reprinted a four-volume edition of *Ahasverus* by Eugene Sue and Leon Trotsky's unique archives in four volumes, and published books by Russian émigré writers, Felix Roziner, Boris Nikolayevsky, Yuri Felshtinsky, and Valery Chalidze. An edition of works by Vladimir Maximov in eight volumes will soon see the light of day. The *Bible Encyclopedia* and the *Gospels* have been published on the order of the Russian Orthodox Church in a big print run. A reprint of *Encyclopedic Dictionary* by Brockhaus & Efron in 86 volumes is at the printing presses, as are *The Archives of the Russian Revolution* and the 16-volume *Jewish Encyclopedia*.

The office occupied today by the Publishers' Director, Sergei Kondratov, features a portrait of Peter the Great in a gilded frame, hanging on the wall behind his table, and a bust gilded frame, hanging on the wall behind his table, and a bust of Peter the Great on it. So far, he has no faith in new distributors. According to him, no publishing house which takes itself seriously, would trust them. Of course, the old state distribution system works badly, but it still works. That's why TERRA is doing business with it.

"But why do you ignore new businesses—co-ops, and small shops—which are ready to distribute your products at minimum interest?"

"Well, yes, some of them are ready to agree to as little as five or even 3%, compared to the fixed 20% in the case of Soyuzkniga, but in my opinion, there are few newcomers to the book trading business, who are really competent. Almost all of them try to derive a maximum profit from anything they get. That's why books get covered with dust, which brings our business to a standstill as well. In fact, there is no real rivalry between distributors, as there is already between publishers. It might appear when the entire book trade becomes private. This is the only path towards a real market economy."

The Soviet book market was distinguished by the fact that publishers and merchants preferred to deal with products, which sell like hot cakes. In 1991 publishing houses agreed to publish only those book, which people were prepared to queue for. *The Kremlin Empire* by A. Avtorkhanov, *I Hope* by Raisa Gorbachev, *The Window of Opportunity* by Grigory Yavlinsky, *In Places of Power* by Anatoly Sobchak, *Against the Grain* by Boris Yeltsin, *Without the Right-Wing or Left-Wing* by Nursultan Nazarbayev, *My Choice* by Eduard Shevardnadze, *The Wind of Change* and *Letters By a Russian Traveller* by Vladimir Bukovsky—these were the books which sold. Memoirs, promised by Yegor Ligachev and Dinmohammed Kunayev will sell too, whereas books by Anatoly Rybakov, Vladimir Dudintsev and Daniil Granin have left the bestseller lists. The market for thrillers, sci-fi and erotica will also soon be saturated.

Yet society needs not a few dozen book titles, but thousands of them. People who desire to read books rather than just acquire them will be glad to see the end—forever—of the concept of "book shortages". Like medicine, books should always be available in the widest possible variety and range. In our country shortages of everything reign supreme: of intelligence, honor, conscience, goods and services. The party elite and black marketeers line their pockets from the book shortage. The former foisted upon the market not only products that sell well, of course, but also of a clear ideological slant. For example, on orders from above a pile of works by compatriots of Lenin were issued, after gathering dust in the spetskhran archives for decades. Trotsky, Zinovyev, Rykov and Bukharin died in the dungeons of communism, but had they been able to outwit Stalin they would have done exactly the same as he did. The entire cohort of "Leninist Bolsheviks" had unleashed rivers of blood, and, instead of children's books, we were offered the scribblings of these sadistic utopists. The state did not stint newsprint, but not many buyers could be found.

Under Suslov Censors Wouldn't Take Bribes

What would we really like to read? It is not hard to guess. Just take a list of new Russian-language books released over the past five years by any publisher in the West. Here I do not mean bestsellers written by Western authors—for decades we were treated to novels by "progressive" writers from Asia, Africa and Latin America, and also the opuses of the leaders of the writers' unions in the "fraternal socialist countries". Before we turn to the West's experts, we should listen to our own. Mariya Shneerson, a contributor to the US-based newspaper *Novoye Russkoye Slovo* wrote the following in the October 15, 1990 edition:

> This year contains several anniversaries in the life and fate of Vassily Semyonovich Grossman. In 1990 he would have celebrated his 80th birthday. 1990 marks the 40th year after he embarked on the creation of his novel *Life and Fate*; it is 35 years since he began writing his story *Everything Flows*; 30 years since the novel

was completed; 20 years since publication of *Everything Flows* in the West (by Possev); 20 years since *Life and Fate* was first published, in Geneva.

In 1990 this novel at last came out without cuts, as it exists in the manuscript that contains the author's final corrections (Moscow, Knizhnaya Palata). This is the fourth edition of the novel in the writer's native country, if we count the one carried by the literary journal *Oktyabr* and considerably shortened by the censor (some time later, *Oktyabr* also published *Everything Flows*).

The dates enumerated above say much in themselves: of the fearsome times in which the writer commenced his life's main work; that simultaneously he was writing the story *Everything Flows*, in which his historical, philosophical and artistic views are laid bare with utter sincerity; that both these works spent long years in hiding and were harbored by the writer's friends before appearing in the West. They could be published in Grossman's own country only as part of the general flow of rehabilitated books.

The fate of Grossman's major work is as unique as the work itself. When he was finishing it, the author wrote to a friend, the poet Semyon Lipkin and one of the people who saved the manuscript: "It exists alongside me, apart from me, and will do so when I am no more".

In February 1961 Grossman's flat was searched and the novel's manuscript confiscated. A year later, evidently under the influence of the 22nd Party congress, Grossman wrote a letter to Khrushchev containing the following superb phrase: "There is no sense, and no truth in (...) my physical freedom while the book to which I have devoted my life is in prison. It is I that wrote it, I have not disowned, and do not disown, it (...) I consider as before that I have written the truth, that I wrote it out of love and pity for people, out of faith in people. I request that my book be set free".

The response to the letter was a meeting with Suslov, who told him: "... the publication of this work will inflict harm on communism, Soviet power and the Soviet people". He considered it dangerous to even return the manuscript to the author. This novel, he concluded, will only be published, if it is at all, in 200-300 years' time and no earlier. Suslov imagined that the authorities he embodied would remain in place for centuries!

By an irony of fate, a few years later, Brezhnev's minions confiscated Khrushchev's memoires: the persecutor of Grossman had to experience what he had inflicted on one of his victims (although, of course, on an infinitely lesser scale!)

The tragic fate of the novel of the century, which *Life and Fate* truly is, became not only the personal tragedy of the author. After reading it in October 1960, Alexander Tvardovsky was deeply shaken by the "unusual strength of its sincerity and truthfulness". He wrote in his diary: "The publication of this book (...) would represent a new phase in literature, the return to it of the true meaning of faithful depiction of life; it would represent a major move away from the preconditioned and hidebound literature that has led us into only God knows what a wasteland of lies. But this is virtually inconceivable".

It would be naive today to attempt to guess the possible influence of *Life and Fate* on the development of literature. Its publication was absolutely impossible. For it deals not only with the concentration camps and mass purges but draws an open comparison between the national-socialist and communist versions of fascism;

it lays bare the vices of totalitarianism, the very essence of which is hostile to the human individual. Grossman draws a portrait of a putrescent society paralyzed by fear: representatives of the "new class" are nailed to a post of shame, dramatic scenes of the destruction of the peasantry during collectivization are depicted. This great book raises fundamental philosophical questions, and their resolution can have nothing in common with Marxist ideology. *Life and Fate* is the creation of a master of genius, of a thinker, researcher and prophet. Suslov was right: it inflicts a crushing blow upon the Soviet system.

"This is one of those books", wrote Tvardovsky, "that, after reading it, you feel (with each passing day) that something serious has taken place within you, that this is a new phase in the development of your awareness..." Yet the novel saw the light of day in Grossman's own country only when much had already been discovered and experienced. The reader of the 1980s, upon first acquaintance with it, can not experience the same feelings as Tvardovsky in 1960.

Does this mean that Grossman's novel has appeared too late and has become obsolete as regards our times? By no means! There are one-day-wonders, books that reflect merely the ills of their day. They cease to affect subsequent generations, even if well-written. And there are books created for the ages to come, for within them, alongside the ills of their day, are timeless and universal human themes, within them live immortal characters created by master writers. It is to the latter category of works of art that *Life and Fate* belongs.

Reflecting upon this novel, one should not forget the environment in which it was created. Its very creation is in itself a feat, which only a man of rare spiritual power could perform.

Reflecting upon Grossman's feat, one involuntarily recalls that of Solzhenitsyn. Whose genius is greater, and whose feat is more impressive, is irrelevant here. Grossman was not fated to play the role that Solzhenitsyn played and continues to play on the literary and social stage of our time. Both writers sought the truth in different ways. Yet to an extent their lives and works overlap.

When Grossman was engaged with *Life and Fate*, the "underground writer" Solzhenitsyn had begun *The First Circle*, and had written *A Day in the Life of Ivan Denisovich*; during those same years *Cancer Ward* and *The GULAG Archipelago* were conceived. If we take a close look at the work created by both writers at the same time, we will notice the amazing similarity of subject matter and of interpretation of events, notwithstanding the profound difference between their creative individuality, world outlook and social temperament.

The life and fate of both writers followed different paths. Solzhenitsyn, who at the outset of his work as an "underground writer" consigned himself to "lifelong silence", was soon to speak in a voice of thunder and be heard throughout the world. Grossman was fated to long years of even posthumous silence. Yet his life forces us to recall the words of Solzhenitsyn. Even underground, the latter was convinced that he was not laboring alone, "that there are several dozen others like us—secluded and persevering individuals, scattered throughout Russia, each writing according to his honor and conscience what he knows about our era and what is the fundamental truth (...) And yet the time will come when we shall all emerge as one from the depths of the sea, like the Thirty Three Warriors of legend, and thus our great literature will be restored". Solzhenitsyn, however, believed that "this shall be merely a posthumous symbol, (...) this will be merely our books, perpetuated by the faithfulness and guile of our friends; it will not be us, not our bodies: we shall die prior to this". So fortunately for us, as regards himself, Solzhenitsyn was mistaken. But as regards Grossman, his prophecy came true...

The books of Grossman and Solzhenitsyn, Sakharov and Pasternak should be studied in schools. There is little chance of this happening for the time being, since the writings of these great sons of our country are as inaccessible to the public as the Bible. They cost a fortune on the black market, while the Bible cost the equivalent of not less than two weeks' average pension. This does not apply to Andrei Sakharov, a Nobel Peace Prize winner, whose major works, including memoires, published worldwide, have not been brought out in separate editions in his homeland. For three or four years following his release from a 7-year exile in Gorky, there was a tacit ban on any mention of his name in the press or on television. Only after his death in December 1989 did the Soviet newspapers enthusiastically begin to quote and discuss him; during his lifetime not once was he considered worthy of a major interview in the official Soviet press, not to mention on national television.

"There's not enough paper", was the answer cheerfully repeated by every Soviet government official to the curious journalist who, in the spirit of our glasnost, took an interest in publishing plans in this country. If forced to do so in order to save face, the authorities would release something juicy, but in abbreviated form and with a small print run. For example, in 1990 the Moscow Nauka publishing house began preparing a truncated version of the five-volume" A Diary of Russian Sedition (first published abroad) by one of the most active members of the White movement in the Civil War, general Anton Ivanovich Denikin.

A history of the Soviet state has yet to be published in Russia, meaning a history that is honest and devoid of deliberate falsifications. There are plenty of surrogates; each new General Secretary of the CPSU ordered a "new history" to be written in his own image, so to speak. The first historical account of the Second World War was created, naturally enough, to glorify the role of the "leader of genius and father of the peoples, comrade Stalin". The second was ... better to listen to the highly popular Polish science fiction and fantasy writer Stanislaw Lem, as quoted in *Literaturnaya Gazeta* of November 14 1990:

> Once, back in the 1950s, I subscribed to the Great Soviet Encyclopedia. When the volume dealing with "B" arrived, it was accompanied by a request that I cut out the entry on Beria and replace it with The Bering Strait. I took the encyclopedia off to a second-hand bookshop. Let the publishers themselves do the scissor-work. Then the 6-volume "The Great Patriotic War of the Soviet Union" was published. You should've seen the fairy tales about Khrushchev... Once again, to the second-hand shop. As a keepsake I kept only the 6th volume. Then there was a 12-volume history of the war, in which Brezhnev was the military chief.

Now I am discovering for myself an entirely new history of the war! In both your country and mine schoolchildren and students are in a dreadful position. Real history books just can't be written and published for them quickly enough.

We were promised yet another, now a 10-volume, history of the war to mark the 50th anniversary of the victory over Hitler's fascism. It will not, of course, concentrate on lauding the military genius of Stalin, Khrushchev or Brezhnev. But neither is it likely to be of any value, since the greater part of the archives in the Soviet Union remain classified and, therefore, out of reach. Consequently, *Izvestia* (November 19, 1990) suggested calling a halt to this latest (fourth already?) rewrite and begin instead releasing for scholars and researchers unseen documents of that period, and writing a couple of honest textbooks on the Second World War for students still deprived of them (in 1989-1990 all history exams in schools and colleges throughout the country were cancelled).

In the summer of 1991, when the first book of the ten-volume edition of the *History of Great Patriotic War*, written by a group of authors, headed by Dmitry Volkogonov, was ready, it produced a real scandal. Colonel-General Volkogonov, Doctor of Philosophy and History, a historian renowned nation-wide and a prominent Liberal Centrist MP, who had held high posts in the Soviet Army, was dismissed on short notice from both his posts, at the head of the Institute of Military History under the Ministry of Defense of the USSR, and head of the group of authors, who were working on the next ten-volume edition of the history of the latest Patriotic war. The Marshals, these "true Leninists", or to be more precise, Stalinists, went out of their way to vilify their colleague only for the fact that the first volume, comprising the period of our history up to June 22, 1941, was sincere. One of the few or maybe even the only one of the Soviet historians, Volkogonov, had access to the requisite archives and made use of many unknown documents from them, when compiling the first volume. Unlike his colleagues, Volkogonov sees the evil not in Stalin, but in the system, instituted by Lenin. I wonder, if the first volume will still see the light of day, given that the military and fascist putsch of August 1991 failed?

In June 1991 the first serious book on the war in Afghanistan - *Intrusion. Unknown Pages from the Undeclared War*—was published in the Soviet Union. Its authors, the famous journalists David Gai and Vladimir Snegirev, had had the chance to see with their own eyes that Soviet aggression in Afghanistan was both a crime and a political mistake and published this honest book. And this can still be regarded as an event for this country. Voyenizdat (Military Publishers), for example, has nothing of interest to offer except a diary by a participant in the 1905 Port-Artur Defense, notes and letters by Russian Marshals Mikhail Kutuzov, Alexander Suvorov and Pyotr Rumyantsev. In May, 1991, Voyenizdat put to press a book of reminiscences by the 40th Army's Commander in Afghanistan Boris Gromov...

Moscow News of August 18, 1991, issued several hours before the putsch, carried an appeal on the issue of a disgusting book, published by Voyenizdat in a print run of 1,000,000 copies. Only Sakharov and Solzhenitsyn had been honored with such a massive attack, although theirs was during in the period of stagnation:

> A booklet by V. Ostretsov, entitled *The Black Cossack Squadron and the Red Cossack Squadron*, was published by Moscow-based Voyenizdat. Its contents are all designed to praise the Union of Russian People and the Russian Assembly among other right-wing Black Cossack parties and societies, which were active in Russia in the early 20th century. These organizations are characterized by the author as truly popular. They had supposedly emerged "in a burst of national consciousness" and consolidated the "best intellectuals in the country."
>
> We are compelled to declare that the publishing house, attached to the Ministry of Defense of the USSR, has issued in a mass edition (1,000,000 copies) of a publication containing overt propaganda of national discord in the form of anti-Semitism. Here are some examples. The author asserts that the "particular alienation from Russian people's roots," inherent in Jews, had produced "cruelty even in their theories." The book ignores the historical truth, depicting the pogroms of Jews by Black Cossacks as clashes between the "left-wing Radicals" and the "Bund commandos" on the one side and the "indignant Russian people" on the other, as the "Russian people defending their national statehood." The infamous Belostok pogrom of 1906 is specifically interpreted in this spirit.
>
> We think that this publication only adds to the aggravation of ethnic tension in this country and outflow of immigrants, who do not feel safe here any more. In our view, V. Ostretsov's book is a slur on the prestige of the Soviet Ministry of Defense, whereas publications of such a kind disorientate the Soviet and international public as to the aims and content of political instruction in the Soviet Army.
>
> We suggest that the Soviet Ministry of Defense clarify the circumstances which made it possible for V. Ostretsov's publication to see the light of day and make it public. We also suggest that the Procurator's Office decide whether this publication complies with the existing legislation.
>
> We have sent our Deputy's requests to the Minister of Defense of the USSR Dmitry Yazov and the Procurator General of the USSR Nikolai Trubin.
>
> > People's Deputies of the Russian Federation: Oleg Basilashvili, Anatoly Belyaev, Sergei Kovalev, Mikhail Molostvov, Galina Starovoitova, Mikhail Tolstoy."

In December 1990, the sumptuous headquarters of the Novosti Press Agency in Moscow hosted a presentation party for a book by the secret police chief of what used to be the German Democratic Republic, Markus Wolf, who for thirty-three years stirred fear in his fellow-countrymen. Born and bred in Moscow, on the Arbat, the aging Markus once again found himself living in this country until September 1991. And all of this long after a warrant for his arrest had been issued in West Germany. As we see, there was enough paper to publish Markus' opus.

Few would venture to seek paper for certain books in Russia at that time. Neither Khrushchev's, nor Sakharov's memoirs have appeared in this country in separate editions. Works by such sovietologists as Zbigniew Brzezinsky, Richard Pipes, or Helene Carrere D'Encausse haven't yet been published officially.

At least books are now being mentioned which were published in the West by former Soviet citizens who had been sentenced to death in the USSR for high treason: V. Kravchenko, V. Krivitsky, Y. Nosenko, N. Khokhlov, O. Penkovsky, A. Shevchenko, O. Gordievsky, S. Levchenko and many others. As a rule, such books are very informative and instructive to Soviet readers.

In 1990, this country mustered enough courage to publish a book written by a certain B. Nosik about Viktor Andreevich Kravchenko. This was done instead of publishing Kravchenko's book "*I Have Chosen Freedom*". Kravchenko was a Soviet engineer who defected to the USA in 1944 when he was there on an official trip. In addition to writing the famous book which sold 4 million copies in the United States, Kravchenko won a suit against the Paris-based communist newspaper *Letters Francaises* which accused him of plagiarism. Interestingly, the newspaper was supported by people like Pierre Courtaud, Andre Wurmser, the famous Joliot-Curie, Roger Garodit, d'Astier de la Vizheri. To help the newspaper Stalin sent a bunch of "witnesses" to Paris, but it proved to be a wasted trip. After the court proceedings Kravchenko's book was translated into twenty languages and sold 400,000 copies in France alone.

In 1990-91, a thick documentary book titled "*KGB. The Inside Story*" and co-written by former Soviet spy, KGB Colonel and defector Oleg Gordievsky and Englishman Christopher Andrew was a best-seller everywhere in the West. There was hardly a newspaper or a magazine in the West which failed to quote from Gordievsky's book or recount some of the KGB's deeds of the past three decades. The list of names of the Soviet station chiefs currently based in foreign countries is a breakthrough in itself. It doesn't look as if we are going to see the book in Russian just yet.

The newspaper *Vecherny Tbilisi* said on January 31 of this year that the Soviet-American publishing house Sprint had refused to print a Russian edition (after a contract had been signed and the book was type-set) of a 200-page account of the Tbilisi tragedy of April 9, 1989. The story of the bloody dispersion of demonstrators was written by the Georgian newsman Irakli Gotsiridze after a thorough investigation which included interviews with Shevardnadze, Yazov, Yakovlev and Ligachev. Gotsiridze published his version of the events in Georgian. Many Moscow-based publishers offered to print a Russian edition but then suddenly changed their minds. Things became even more difficult after the resignation of Shevardnadze who had been officially supporting Gotsiridze. Gotsiridze, an editor with the Tbilisi film studios and a journalist of some renown in the past has gone down in history as the man who conducted the USSR's first ever independent journalistic investigation into a major political crime which was committed with the approval of top-level government officials.

The USSR never printed mass editions of "*The Yawning Heights*" by A. Zinovyev and "*The Island of the Crimea*" by V. Aksyonov. What has been published so far is being offered at almost unaffordable prices. For instance, late in 1990 street book-peddlers and kiosks in Moscow were selling books by Avtorkhanov, Alliluyeva and Topol. Avtorkhanov is known for his brilliant history publications, Stalin's daughter Alliluyeva wrote a rather dull book of recollections about her father. E. Topol and F. Neznansky co-wrote a book entitled "*Journalist for Brezhnev*" which was released by completely unknown publishers with an amazing print run of 500,000 and was available for fifteen rubles a copy (the price was fifteen to twenty-five times greater than the standard price of a book of that size according to regulations in effect till 1991). However the book was worth it in the sense that there were no falsehoods, exaggerations, concoctions, improbabilities or the grotesque in it. It was full of truth, pure and simple, about the morals in our press industry, censorship, police, the KGB, psychiatric clinics, prisons, everyday life, party agencies and the underworld.

In February 1991, the half a million print run of the reasonably-priced Vladimir Voinovich's "*Moscow in 2042*" sold in no time at all. Ten years ago Voinovich set the action in his book in a period sixty years ahead. He based his story on realities of the Brezhnev era, but who could have known that his forecast would come true so soon and that the evil reality of his novel would almost be seen by today's reader as a story of his own life?

According to *Literaturnaya Gazeta* (January 9 1991), 86% of the Soviet public, if they read anything at all, opted for newspapers and "lightweight" magazines such as *Rabotnitsa* or *Krokodil*. Two criteria accepted in international statistics were cited. The first was the number of titles of books and booklets published per year in the language of the majority nationality within a given area, per 1 million of the indigenous population (without this it is difficult to compare the publishing capacities of large and small countries). The second was the number of books published in the indigenous language per head of the population. The first criterion points to the degree of cultural diversity and the ease with which new thoughts can reach readers; the second illustrates the accessibility of printed ideas and texts.

For the period 1966-1988, the first figure for Estonian came to 1,322 (one of the highest in the world; in this respect the Scandinavian countries come top). For Lithuanian it came to 769.5; for Latvian 690.9; Russian—331.8 in the Russian Federation and 454.9 for the USSR as a whole; Georgian—443.6; Kirghizian—201.5; Moldovan—181.6; Armenian—161; Azerbaijani—148.5;

Turkmenian—141.5; Tadjik—128.7; Uzbek—113.4; Byelorussian—42.7; Ukrainian—42.0.

In terms of the number of books (copies) published, for each Russian in the Russian Federation there were 12.7, and in the USSR as a whole—14.4); for each Estonian there are 12.2; Latvian—8.7; Lithuanian—7.5; Georgian—5.4; Moldovan—2.8; Uzbek—2.8; Turkmen—2.2; Kazakh—2.1; Tadjik—2.1; Azerbaijani—2; Armenian 1.9; Ukrainian—1.9; Kirghizian—1.7' Byelorussian—0.8.

Such dry statistics for book publishing by nationality can reveal to the trained eye forced assimilation and Russification or, conversely, national renaissance.

It was no surprise to see, therefore, that the strongest resistance to totalitarianism was in the Baltic republics, where the overall level of cultural and material prosperity was considerably higher than in the USSR as a whole. Correspondingly, they had more periodical publications and twice the level of subscriptions.

The conclusion is disturbing: it will take another generation, better educated and less cowed than the current one, to drag the country out of the mire. We need to take a deep breath.

In the West, Russia is sometimes referred to as a country of failed modernization, implying its spasmodic attempts to become one of the world's most civilized lands. Six years of perestroika and plans for reform show that democracy is simply poorly understood and being absorbed with difficulty because of the impoverishment and exhaustion of the cultured sections of society. We are the "country of back-bench school kids" and, should the hardliners stage a coup, we risk becoming a "country of fools".

The USSR was the home of a hundred and fifty ethnic groups. Books were, however, only published in seventy-three languages, including nine languages of twenty-two small ethnic groups. The reason was simple: it was not profitable. Government policy never encouraged the publishing industry in any way. For instance, the Kremlin even thought of making Ukraine a Russian-speaking territory and banning the Ukrainian language altogether. Imagine what might have happened to smaller nations.

There is yet another problem which has been mentioned before. The newspaper *Pravitelstvenny Vestnik* (Government Bulletin) referred, in its issue No. 6 (1991), to the Institute of Books of the USSR State Committee for Printing, to point out that one out of six Soviets was forced to use the services of the book black market. The libraries' funds remain unchanged while even official prices of books have grown fourfold over the past decade. Ordinary libraries receive a mere eight per cent of published titles. Only one third of libraries' requests for fiction and children's literature are catered for, the figure for books in high demand standing at a catered for, the figure for books in high demand standing at a miserable 7-10%. Hence, the sad result: there is an increasing percentage of young people who don't read.

One thing escapes my understanding. When will it finally dawn on people who should have understood it a long time ago, that our children are becoming a generation which doesn't enjoy reading, is unable to read and won't read? If children in the West don't do much reading either, they at least have a multi-channel TV, video and entertainment industry available to them. At least they have toys to play with. Our children don't have anything at all. Even children's books, plain and unpretentious as they were, have vanished. In November 1990 the Kiev administration of the Russian Orthodox Church announced the beginning of a subscription campaign to a twelve-volume series entitled "*Monuments of Theological Thought*". The international Christian charity-educational group "Path to Truth" charged Orthodox believers a hundred and thirty rubles for the 6,000-page edition (in advance). Subscribers may or may not get their twelve-volume series in a year's time as the church publishers have promised. In 1990, the same year, the thin "*Bible for Children*" (published abroad and beautifully illustrated) was available for no less than eighty-five rubles from Moscow's black marketeers.

We should all thank the People's Deputy of the USSR, Father Pitirim who is the long-standing chairman of the Publishing Department at Moscow's Patriarchate. He has arranged for the publishing of a host of titles (on the church's peace-making efforts, the activities of the Soviet Peace Committee and various foundations). However he has never published religious literature in mass editions. The Russian-language bibles which are available for handsome prices in all Russian churches have been printed either in Brussels, Paris or Stockholm. The books were sent to this country as donations. They are even stamped "not for sale" on the title page. Is there anyone to argue that Father Pitirim's activities ever disappointed the leaders of the CPSU and the KGB? The archbishop was more of a loyal son to the party than our spiritual father.

Soviet children have never had interesting school books. This is due to the fact that such books (appearing in multi-million editions) were not composed by authors or scientists but by bureaucrats. Consequently the texts are boring or at times crude, the language is bureaucratic red-tape, illustrations are blurred and it all appears on yellow newsprint. The books are full of lies and banalities and cover history, geography, literature, natural sciences and foreign languages in such a way as to kill any interest in humanities. We have learned to put up with it, just as we have been putting up with the fact that the average Soviet (Russian) class consists of 30-40 pupils.

The Education Publishing-House in Moscow (the largest producer of school books in the Russian Federation) has been undergoing renovation since 1988. In compliance with a contract signed at top level, the US company Interconcepts began supplying computers and training personnel at the Education publishers.

Consequently the time needed to bring a school book from the author's desktop to the classroom was reduced many times over. All of a sudden the USSR Vneshekonombank refused to follow instructions from the USSR State Planning Committee, whereby it was to pay the US company close to a million dollars for delivered equipment. Reportedly the bank had hijacked in a similar manner a contract signed by the Education publishers with the German firm Zimeks and approved by the authorities at all levels. The bank ignored three instructions from the government over six months and refused to pay for books which had already been printed in West Germany. The Germans suspended deliveries, and it took lengthy negotiations and complaints about our problems to persuade them to write off the debt as humanitarian aid.

Even today we live in a looking-glass world, a wonderland. Our books are not sold, published or read, but rather obtained, resold, confiscated, hidden away, banned or invested in. They are also ... put on display, which is then reported by all the newspapers, while a few covers are shown on TV. Yet by repeating the word "sugar" to oneself over and over again, life does not become sweeter.

YMCA-Press is known throughout the world as the oldest Russian publishing house abroad. It was founded in 1921 in Prague, and in 1925 moved to Paris. In September 1990 it managed to arrange an exhibition of its books at the All-Union State Library of Foreign Literature, at the initiative of the USSR Book Chamber and with the participation of the Khudozhestvennaya Literatura (Fiction) publishers. The exhibitors were permitted to import into Russia about 40,000 copies of various YMCA-Press works, in Russian, which were sold to visitors or presented to libraries after the show.

In December 1989, at the same library, there was a public exhibition of 250 examples of religious literature in Russian, and in February 1990 one could admire 300 volumes of Jewish religious writings, also in Russian. In both cases no books were put on sale and visitors were not allowed to touch, but a promise was made to open at some time in the future (in the foreign-literature library) a religious literature reading room, the first in the Soviet Union. But how the press carried on about this fleeting glimpse of forbidden fruit. As Izvestia admitted on April 2 1990, in an article on yet another exhibition of foreign publishers' Russian-language books and magazines in St. Petersburg, "the majority of works by Voinovich, Zinovyev, Kluchevsky, Kopelev, Berdyaev and several dozen other 'undesirable' authors have still not been removed from the spetskhran archives". Meanwhile, these very same foreign publishers were labelled as centers of "imperialist, hostile propaganda undermining the tenets of socialism" in speeches by the then KGB leader V. Kryuchkov.

What clever people we had at the very top, occupying key posts in the defense of communist ideology. By way of simple machinations they managed to get something decent shown on TV, and then ensure that some controversial Valentin Pikul or the unmatched Mikhail Bulgakov, Solzhenitsyn and various pornographic newspapers were sold off on the black market. The newspapers printed interviews (and fairly long ones, albeit carefully balanced) with members of the editorial boards of such anti-Soviet and world-renowned publications as *Russkaya Mysl* in Paris, the journal *Grani* (published by Posev in West Germany and distributed on subscription in the USSR; the few hundred copies were regularly detained for months on end by the customs) and even the weighty English-language monthly *Problems of Communism*, published by the US government.

And why not. After all, in 1990 a collection of official speeches by Ronald Reagan was released in this country, as was the autobiography of George Bush (the fine cover of which flashed across our screens and then vanished, not even hitting the black market). From time to time even in the years of stagnation *Pravda* and *Izvestia* would print the after-dinner speeches of foreign politicians at official receptions in Moscow.

The reformers of Soviet socialism were quick to take credit for the fact that Sakharov supported Gorbachev and Solzhenitsyn gave permission in autumn 1990 to print his letter "*What Should Russia Be Like*?" in the leading Soviet newspapers. So why not score points with Western public opinion and, when it comes down to it, with one's own educated classes?

The main thing is that this controversial topic has been raised, discussed and even flogged to death. Mandelshtam, Gumilyov, Akhmatova and once again Mandelshtam, Gumilyov, Akhmatova plus Tsvetayeva and Pasternak. Thirty to fifty years ago, despite the mass destruction and expulsion of the educated classes, there were many more Soviet people than today able and willing to listen to their great compatriots. There are now fewer cultured people in this country than before. The inclination to the godly, or even just to the good, is less visible today. Many rejoice at the current, latest, thaw. Who could ask for more?

There are some interesting thoughts in this connection in an article by a prominent Soviet dissident (who was in the GULAG as late as 1987 for his political beliefs) in *Literaturnaya Gazeta* (May 23, 1990). This article caught the attention of all the main world media organizations, because for the first time, the official Moscow press was being allowed to name Felix Svetov and quote him saying that dawn has barely begun and the first rays of the sun are providing light but little warmth, that freedom is still distant, that thousands of dissidents have been pardoned but not rehabilitated (ie., to this day remain criminals in the eyes of the authorities), that the state has begun to support not so much the Church as its servile hierarchy. Svetov on the whole was little impressed by perestroika, since progress towards true liberty was too halting. Here is an excerpt from his "*Freedom for the Free*":

> And, finally, literature, the most visible "success" of perestroika. What is our literature today? One can only rejoice at seeing previously banned books being

printed in their millions, because they were written to be read in this country. But neither should we forget that they are well-known in the West, have as a rule been translated into many languages, and have acquired a fate of their own. I believe that publication 20, 30, 50 and sometimes even 70 years after their creation gives such books an existence that is complex and at times unnatural. In no way can they integrate themselves into the present literary process. They remain alien to it, while vociferous rhetorical proclamations on the unity of Russian culture "over there" and "over here" on occasion lead to absurdities: Platonov and Trifonov, M. Koltsov and Mandelshtam, Akhmatova and Sinyavsky, Voinovich and Zamyatin, Pasternak and Rybakov... By passing all these incompatible works through one big "mincer" and printing vast quantities of the resulting "sausagemeat", glasnost is transforming the literary process into something unfathomable: how can the journal *Oktyabr* print Akhmatova's *"Requiem"* in the same edition as the latest libelous scribblings of N.N. Yakovlev? But it did, side by side, in one cover! The shameful attempt to include classics of 20th-century Russian culture and the fates of their authors into Soviet literature, and their forced integration into the official culture, bear witness to today's ugly and unnatural literary process. Culture persecuted only yesterday and now thrown onto the market of perestroika is paradoxically becoming "reduced to clear", a museum exhibit, and ceasing to influence minds.

In this respect as, incidentally, in all others, most interesting of all remains Solzhenitsyn. There can be no doubt that the attempt to turn his books into mincemeat, *"The GULAG Archipelago"* included, into some kind of "historical work" or a tale of events of the distant past, and the very fact of their publication, are witnesses to the "new thinking". But behind GULAG lurk realities, the still existing psychiatric wards, the camps, the unrehabilitated prisoners of conscience, articles 64 and 70, the flourishing organs of repression and their "spotless hands"... But *"The GULAG Archipelago"* is not one of the books that can be simply thrown out onto the market, in the hope of some kind of gain. It is our shared fate, it is a sentence delivered upon the regime.

After the war, Thomas Mann wrote from California to a correspondent or a colleague in Germany, who had invited him to participate in their "perestroika" of those days, and confessed that he was unable to grasp how in those years splendid musicians in the Berlin concert halls could perform Wagner, and how music lovers could listen. And to this day I cannot help thinking: the books published in this country during the past decades, irrespective of when they were written, have certain things in common—they are either overtly fallacious, or full of subtle hints, or silent about things the Russian writer should not hush up. I cannot tell them apart.

Several years ago samizdat, which began in the 1960s with Solzhenitsyn's novels, printed and reprinted *"Requiem"*, *"The Heart of the Dog"*, Platonov, Voloshin, Shalamov and Mandelshtam. It was a drop in the ocean compared to the 100,000 copies and more printed of Trifonov and Aitmatov, immediately translated for an admiring West. It was also absurd—its royalties were in the form of camp sentences from three to ten years. This disinterestedness of samizdat is today called vanity: instead of talent, it prefers the shocking and sensational. Vanity, of course, is self-interest. But, I think, this is said only by those who do not know what prison is.

True literature is detached from political intrigue, it is incapable of joining forces with it. The dead cannot join forces with the living. Or, in tougher terms, the night after the battle belongs to the pillagers.

Svetov's article is an appeal to the human conscience. Morality should be accorded priority, in politics and all other spheres of human activity. Our awakening after the hibernation of our conscience has been painful.

The Last Keep of GULAG in the USSR Writers' Union

The reader probably has already guessed that this description of reality in the Soviet Union is somewhat simplified. The books and magazines coming out between 1988 and 1991 in Estonian, Latvian, Lithuanian, Moldavian, Georgian and Armenian, unlike those in the rest of the Soviet Union, were openly anti-Soviet and anti-communist. The same can be said of Russian-language publications from the same period in the Baltic republics, Moldavia and Transcaucasia.

But what about Moscow, which is home to most of Russian-language publishing houses? As *Literaturnaya Gazeta* modestly noted in passing on December 26 1990, the USSR Writers' Union was doing nothing to even begin publishing persecuted writers whose works have yet to appear in print in either this country or abroad. There are hundreds of them, including talented people who rotted in the camps both in the 1920s and more recently. This work was begun and successfully continued in all former Soviet republics, but not in Moscow (they said there was no paper).

The Moscow-based magazine *Stolitsa* employed even more precise phraseology in its issue No. 1 in January of 1991: *"The writers' department is the last keep of the GULAG"*. It was the title of an article by Vladimir Lazarev, a poet and critic, concerning moral standards and regulations in the USSR Writers' Union. Most of the leaders of that artistic group had as much to do with literature as the personnel of the Fifth Chief Department of the USSR KGB or the Agitation and Propaganda Department at the CPSU Central Committee. They all kept vigil together, fought free thinking, threw the unruly into prisons or psychiatric clinics and used the USSR Literary Fund to encourage the obedient. In late August 1991 the party-KGB alliance, obsessed with its "socialist option", was thrown out of the USSR Writers' Union. It is all the more interesting to read the testimony of V. Lazarev published as early as at the beginning of 1991:

> "For a long time I have wanted to report about the "secret library" at the Central House of Writers. This is not one of those elite distribution outlets, a treasury of literary rarities where only lifetime masters are allowed to work. After one of my speeches, a commission was set up to "correctly assess Lazarev's activities", something which had happened many times before. A member of the commission

told me in a fit of candidness that for this purpose the thick folders had been brought to the commission, which contained shorthand records of all of my previous public statements and all my personal and open letters. Certain paragraphs in them had been carefully underlined.

It wasn't very difficult to find out that, as it transpired, the Writers' Union ran a huge library which consisted of volumes providing accounts of the literary, public and personal lives of all those people who had, in various degrees, attempted to uphold the values of truth and justice. This "comradely", "family" type of surveillance was provided as well as KGB files and investigating agencies' information (the latter in certain cases). Where is the library now? Is it where it used to be in the past? Has it been transferred somewhere? These highly valuable archives must be preserved. The Central State Archives of Literature and Art could be the right place. Otherwise somebody might tear out sheets from the volumes, given the lack of order during this transitional period.

The reader will guess that writers, too, have their bosses. The reader might think that they should be the best bosses in the world. The leading bodies of the Writers' Union have been formed in a very subtle way: on the board there would be several big names, a few people of certain renown, and a few unknowns. The latter are the ones who set the tone. They are the so-called working secretaries (full time paid positions, and the salaries are by no means small). Some of them are artistic failures or skillful literary time-servers. They are bureaucrats who have nothing to do with literature and yet have the strongest positions in that organization. They organized and managed the "monkey trials" and the dishonest "disciplining sessions", which still painfully stick out in our memories. So what has happened to them now? They are still doing very well, quietly taking key positions in neighboring offices. As comrade Stalin used to say, "I don't have other people". As the "working secretaries" have ironically described their current situation, they are indulging in their old benefits as they master elements of new thinking. Previously allocated from the Staraya Square (the Central Committee of the CPSU), zones of influence are now assigned by other quarters which are just as powerful.

The "working secretaries" are the ringleaders, the actual bosses in the Writers' Union. All intrigues start from their desktops, and they have total control over the distribution of material benefits. The process deals not so much with general edicts but rather daily work, flexibility and quick reactions. The secretaries work a lot. They invite "reliable authors" on hunting and fishing parties and help them deal with the difficulties of "daily life". They become insiders in what was a new environment for them only a short time ago. They drink and sing together (the organizing secretary of the Moscow branch, V.P. Kobenko "studied singing"). In a year's time they already sit on literary commissions and in three years they are referred to as authors. They sign contracts on cooperation with foreigners, devise "codes" for the literary community (they may argue themselves hoarse, while they polish the wordings, working on their style as it were). They are the first to be rewarded. The Organizing Secretary of the USSR Writers' Union Yu.N. Verchenko has been lavishly decorated with orders and medals for his "outstanding services to Soviet literature". I still remember the ugly campaign against Lidia Chukovskaya and attempts to "evict" from K.I. Chukovsky's house in Peredelkino. The idea was to renovate the house, "bring it up to the standard" for a new high-ranking lord. There were attempts to do a similar thing to Pasternak's house. However museums were not enough for comrade Verchenko and his like, and they have made quite a few living authors suffer. They are not to be forgiven.

However, Yuri Nikolayevich Verchenko did more than just get away with it. He abandoned his previous position for the post of Executive Secretary of the Committee for Lenin Prizes and State Prizes of the USSR. In addition, he was decorated with yet another order, for promoting "Friendship Among Peoples". Officially he received an award for his active contribution to friendship among nations during the war in Afghanistan. A vehement advocate of official opinion in poetic and other forms, L. Shchipakhina, was awarded the same order. The lady and the gentleman have made several trips to Afghanistan where they made inspiring speeches before the Soviet troops and would then come back with suitcases full of Oriental souvenirs. They catered to their ambition and promoted their careers on the bones of sufferers. I wonder if they ever suffer pangs of conscience.

The clan of organizing secretaries and their servants is the first and far from the only barrier in the way of change for the better in the writers' organization. A group which should be providing an example of restructuring its activities (remarkably, the policy of glasnost began exactly with literary publications), the Writers' Union has in a mysterious way preserved all its departmental features intact and is as an organization acting as one of the more stubborn strongholds of resistance to the winds of change.

The totalitarian machine has failed to grind the truth-seeking author into dust but has over the years been able to breed the author as would-be boss. While it took the destruction of a gifted writer to do this in the 1930s or in the 1950s (Fadeyev is an example), things changed during the Brezhnev era when born bureaucrats began to work their way into the writing community. Verchenko knocked together a volume of selected speeches. His beloved boss G.M. Markov or the latest First Secretary of the Writers' Union V.V. Karpov have been showered with all kinds of distinctions, and their works have been translated into a number of languages! Meanwhile they were perfect species of the organizing secretary-cum-writer breed. Once a Komsomol functionary, Markov was made an aide to Konstantin Fedin, and ended up as the author of multi-volume novels on the unity of the party and the people. Karpov used to be a bureaucrat in the literary and the people. Karpov used to be a bureaucrat in the literary department in Uzbekistan, Rashidov's domain (interestingly, Rashidov, too, was a member of the Writers' Union and a big fan of celebrations).

Without going into details on the literary efforts of Vladimir Karpov, I would merely like to note that he, obviously, didn't have the potential to be the intellectual leader of a writers' organization. However Karpov was also the Chairman of the Board of Founders of the All-Union Copyright Agency. Until recently works by Karpov and his like, as well as Karpov's books used, in some miraculous way, to be published in dozens of countries. Who would care, in England or in Japan, to read a novel on the secretary of a regional party committee when such novels don't interest anyone in this country? Nevertheless hard currency flowed in like a river to the "executive writers". I think the flow is still continuing unabated.

The system of self-fertilization of literary generals includes a number of driving mechanisms, from the International Book agency to the Main Political Department of the Armed Forces. As a result of the smooth operation of such mechanisms, the villas of the leaders of the Writers' Union can be seen anywhere from the Baltics to the Black Sea coasts, while heaps of their opuses are to be found on the shelves of Russian book-stores in Mongolia or Ethiopia and in the libraries of military units inside the Polar circle.

I am positive that the current litigations started by the "executive writers" against publishers who have cast aside the humiliating supervision were not prompted by any concern humiliating supervision were not prompted by any concern for their older or younger colleagues. This is merely an early warning sign that the "executive writers" will not miss their chance to settle scores with editors who step out of line and justify themselves before their high-placed handlers for the serious mistakes in organizational work.

Incidentally, only recently there were portraits of the "pace-setters" of the army of "engineers of humans souls" hung on the walls in the hallways of the headquarters of the Board of the Writers' Union: Sholokhov, Simonov, Shaginyan, Markov, Verchenko and, unexpectedly, KGB General Tsvigun, then First Deputy to Andropov. With a little help from his friends from the apparatus of the USSR Writers' Union, the General became overnight a novelist and script-writer and was even awarded the State Prize of the Russian Federation! His wife (oh, what a talent!), too, was quickly admitted to the Children's Section of the Writers' Union. Whether or not the poet Brodsky has enough talent is still unclear, but Tsvigun's wife was obviously talented enough to be admitted. Some people would ask cautiously if Tsvigun was Verchenko's cousin because the two men bore some facial resemblance. What a naive question! Everything was so much more simple.

The Writers' Union maintained a good tradition of swelling their "first ranks" with members of friendly organizations. High-ranking officials from the Defense Ministry, the Foreign Ministry, the Academy of Sciences, the Public Health Ministry, the KGB, the Interior Ministry, even some of the cosmonauts and apparatchiks from the CPSU Central Committee were admitted almost unanimously as soon as they applied for membership.

It is quite possible that the young poet Bobkov is very talented. Alas, it was not, however, due to his literary talent that he published several books of poetry within a short period of time, some of which appeared in the same format as classics and literary prize-winners. Bobkov was awarded a literary prize and elected Secretary for International Contacts at the Russian Union of Writers. As things were happening for the son of the current First Deputy to the KGB Chairman, many of his coevals were waiting for years to be admitted to the writers' organization.

A lot but not everything depends on the moral code (or rather lack of any) of the temporary rulers. Their presence and impunity has contaminated the very atmosphere of the writers' organization.

Maybe there is no reason to make any effort to destroy the dilapidated windmill? Why not just wait till it collapses? Because it won't. For it isn't as defenseless and harmless as it may seem.

The former leader of the Moscow branch of the Writers' Union, Al. Mikhailov has conducted a restructuring program of his own. He has replaced the obsolete Secretariat of the Board with a Council (is it because of the emergence of the Presidential Council?) and replaced the Admission Commission with an Admission Collegium.

Who, I wonder, conceived and finalized such "historic" decisions? Neither I, nor my colleagues have been consulted. The trouble is not that the term "collegium" is no better than "commission", but that, once again, a new coat of make-up on the face of the Literary Camp (one of the few remaining divisions of Stalin's GULAG) is being presented as a revolutionary approach. But the face is degenerate and no make-up can disguise it as intelligent, good-natured or sincere. The question is natural: are they leaders at all? After the theatre, film-makers, architects and composers have provided answers to the same question, the writers are the only ones in the artistic world still clinging to the old dogmas. Is this merely a habit or a sign of impotence?

The Literary Fund's original prestige should be restored. It is no secret that people now join the Writers' Union mostly because they want to be entitled to a pension, paid sick-leave, accommodation at health-centers and artistic retreats. All the "working secretaries", in the first place the "organizing secretaries", are unnecessary. All of them, both good and bad, intelligent and stupid, writers and illiterates should go. There is no need for them, no matter where they come from, the Poetry Section or the KGB! We are sick and tired of them.

There is one vital precondition however: the understanding that the Writers' Union is a UNION, a partnership of professional literary workers, which can only be headed by indisputable leaders. By people who have the talent, rather than the authorization, to lead.

For the time being, the same old pack of cards is being reshuffled at the Writers' Union.

In July 1990 the weekly *Knizhnoye Obozreniye* (Book Review) summed up the results of a readers' poll and named the 100 most popular books of the previous year. The late announcement was caused by resistance from the management of the Kniga national association, which found it unacceptable that the top award should go to Alexander Solzhenitsyn for "*The GULAG Archipelago. 1918-1956*".

In first place was "*Poetry and Prose*", by popular singer-songwriter, poet and actor Vladimir Vysotsky. In second—"*Vladimir, or the Interrupted Flight*", by French actress Marina Vlady about Vysotsky. It is, of course, a pity that both these works were published in abridged form. Vysotsky is popular throughout the land. His songs, slating mendacity and hypocrisy and poking fun at the high-ups of this world who crush freedom of thought, calling unpleasant things by their true names, have become youth anthems and won recognition from the intelligentsia and working class alike. Since Stalin's death, no funeral processions in Moscow have attracted such vast crowds as those of Vysotsky in 1980 and Andrei Sakharov in 1989. Both were cruelly hounded by the Soviet authorities; both remained unpublished in their own lifetimes.

Of Russian writers alive and well, only one makes the top ten—Solzhenitsyn, in 5th place for "The GULAG Archipelago". In 3rd place is R Shtilmark, for "The Heir from Calcutta", which has achieved widespread popularity. Then come Alexander Dumas ("The Count of Monte Cristo"),

Valentin Pikul ("The Unclean Force"), Pikul again ("The Favorite"), Charlotte Bronte ("Jane Eyre"), Vassily Grossman ("Life and Fate"), and Boris Pasternak ("Doctor Zhivago").

In quantitative terms, best-represented in the top 100 is the recently-deceased Valentin Pikul with six mentions (6th, 7th, 17th, 38th, 56th and 98th places). After him comes Alexander Dumas with five (4th, 15th, 24th, 75th and 87th). "Children of the Arbat" by Anatoly Rybakov, which came top in the previous year's poll, took 13th place.

Among the authors of these 100 books there is not one from Latin America, Asia or Africa. Not even Garcia Marquez, who seemed so popular in the Soviet Union, is on the list. Neither is Kafka, whose works on the black market are astoundingly expensive. Evidently the rank-and-file reader does not value avant garde writing. I don't know about Kafka, but the works of another prematurely-departed philosopher, Merab Mamardashvili (unrecognized and persecuted by the authorities for his cultured yet outspoken thoughts and conscience) would have been read by many, had they been published. (Alexander Yakovlev, adviser to President Gorbachev, said of Mamardashvili that "in his lifetime he was an inconvenience to many, especially during the decades of misguided morality").

Soviet readers never had a choice and, naturally, opted for what was regarded by the party bosses to be the most interesting, fascinating and thought-provoking writings, to what they genuinely wanted to read. Yet even today the selection on offer is not wide. We need good writers. But where can they be found, when the best have departed from the Soviet Union, the majority involuntarily? The works of former Moscow University professor Alexander Zinovyev, who now lives in Germany, are unknown to Soviet readers. So far in the USSR this outstanding satirist (on a par with Zoshchenko and Saltykov-Shchedrin) has surfaced only in an interview with *Pravda*. His *"The Yawning Heights"*, were it to be published here (not in a literary journal as is usually done, but in a separate edition with a print run matching demand), would easily achieve astronomical popularity and profitability.

The best part of 20th-century Russian literature has been published abroad, and to this day remains unknown in its authors' own land. The same applies to works on history, philosophy, sociology, economics, literary and arts criticism, etc. Were the authorities to display the slightest flicker of interest, Western authorities to display the slightest flicker of interest, Western publishers would enlist public and government support to rapidly make the book—the staple diet of culture—available to the Soviet people. This would entail a minimum of outlay. Not even translation into Russian is required, and our readers would cheerfully part with a lot of money in return for the right to acquaint themselves with the creative output of writers rather than nomenklatura stooges of the authorities.

How did these people manage to get themselves into print?

By way of mutual back-scratching. For example, let us suppose that I am the director of one of the fewer than ten Georgian publishing houses. What did I do? Published my own voluminous novel in a Georgian literary journal, and then in a major Russian one. Then I put it out in a separate edition via my own publishing house in Georgian, and via a Moscow one in Russian, plus via publishers in all the union republics and "fraternal socialist countries" (as they once were). Naturally, at the same time I had to print all my colleagues from the two journals and the twenty or so above-mentioned publishers. The end result was a mass of mediocre books, friendship among peoples and, of course, royalties so fat for my own book that Alexander Dumas would envy me.

Our publishers loved printing classic foreign writers of the 19th century, because there are no royalties to be paid, and in any case such authors are unable to join the ranks of their present-day Western colleagues willing to voice their thoughts on democracy Kremlin-style.

Our government or rather the Communist Party Central Committee's ideological department (each director of which would command his own "personal" ministry, be it central television, printing or any Soviet newspaper or publishing house) traditionally favored only communists or a dozen or so other "faithful friends" of the Soviet Union from among the entire plethora of living foreign authors. As for the thousands of others, as soon as the question of publishing one of them in the USSR arose, publishing house directors would recall the dour faces of their bosses and in turn grimace and begin complaining about their inability to pay royalties in hard currency.

I believe that foreign authors could, in order to help the countries of Eastern Europe, waive their hard-currency royalties for a few years from the printing and reprinting of their works behind the former iron curtain. I am sure that publishers in this country, would immediately begin churning out what we so desperately need: Western textbooks and fiction. For this the West's goodwill is essential, especially since only small sums will be involved.

True, there is another obstacle. The 114 best Soviet publishing houses and 81 printing shops, with a staff of 80,000, were officially on the payroll of the Communist Party Central Committee. That publishing and printing empire robbed those whose works it published, by transferring all profits to the Central Committee. For many years the so-called party press got rich by using its monopoly on the production of books on which it did not pay royalties (for example, Mayne Reid and Charles Dickens).

Either by design or accident, the greater part of the USSR had no large printing complexes. Virtually all of them are in Moscow or nearby (Chekhov, Mozhaisk, Smolensk, Tver). Belorussia and Moldavia have one large printing house each, the Ukraine has a couple. Printing capacities in all the remaining ex-union republics and regions are small and intended mainly for turning out school textbooks and small-circulation books. Here it should be noted that in the USSR a small print run was anything under 100,000. The central authorities bothered merely to make sure the republics and vast expanses of Russia had plenty of printing facilities to reproduce what they receive over the wires from Moscow on the pages of vast quantities of national and other newspapers and magazines.

Moscow is able to print 200,000 copies of a book weighing a Moscow is able to print 200,000 copies of a book weighing a kilogram, have them bound and sent to the shops within a couple of weeks; in Tbilisi the whole process can drag on for several months or more. The issue of an ordinary book in the USSR was a rigmarole that could last several years, if it was not one of the publishers' priority projects, which went through without hold-ups within a matter of days. But the only books to get this treatment were speeches by our Party secretaries and a very limited number of high-demand political or anniversary publications.

As a rule, our book-publishing process resembled a theatrical farce, completely incomprehensible and illogical to foreigners. An author took his idea to a publishing house and submitted the mandatory outline, list of contents and even a trial chapter. Should the publishing house and the powers that be look favorably upon him, his application would embark upon a lengthy journey through the managers' offices of the publishing house and the printing committee. Even if all this took place in one of the union republics the text would all the same be sent to the USSR committee on printing for its consent. After all this to-ing and fro-ing, the publishers included the list of contents of the forthcoming book in the *thematic plan* for the next year published every spring. The central bookselling businesses circulated these thematic plans among their subordinate retail outlets, for the latter to collect orders for each of the books advertised.

However, before August 1991 the manager of any local bookshop knew that nobody need order propaganda publications. And that he would end up all the same with the political literature output of the Communist Party Central Committee. Even the most run-down village shop, where books are sold alongside all the everyday goods, had a separate shelf for the works of Vladimir Lenin. A bookshop manager in the Republic of Georgia might order 10,000 or 25,000 copies of Vysotsky's book, or that by his wife Marina Vlady about him, but these books would still come out with print runs of 50,000 and not more, of which a hundred or so would go to Georgia for the benefit of the local elite and black-marketeers. A "modern-day classic"—whom nobody reads—by one of the USSR Writers' Union leaders would be shifted in Georgia only if packaged with, for example, a good health food book. The former gathered dust on the shelves at the state price, while the latter would go at three times its cover price, from under the counter.

Any intelligent bookseller knew that the vast majority of books advertised were wanted neither by him nor by readers; he knew that volumes printed and bound in most of the union republics and Russian regions were shoddily made and would fall apart as soon as touched. He also knows that in the provinces the only bestsellers you could bank on getting were detective stories by Agatha Christie and other adventure novels.

Readers' demand had no relation at all to book-publishing policy in the Soviet Union. Readers' opinions were taken into account at every step, but in actual fact readers did not matter at all, as any Western specialist would put it.

Let us return to our author. You will recall that in spring he rejoiced as his book was included in the glossily-produced thematic plan. By autumn orders for his work were taken, the future of the book was determined and the manuscript was included in the editorial and next year's release schedule (it might come out in January, or December). The manuscript was then read by an editor, by a department head, the publishing house's editor-in-chief, the censor and a couple of outside reviewers. All of these readers would try to draw attention to any possible deviation from the Party's ideological line at the time, analyze any possible hint at the miserable reality surrounding us, and so forth. In this the opinion of the author was practically ignored, and everyone made what they consider to be essential corrections to the manuscript. Then it was dispatched to be typeset and the lengthy process (several months) of producing the book started. Two or three years could separate the day that a publishing house commenced work on a manuscript from that of its release in print.

Naturally, "perestroika" made its own adjustments to this time-honored ritual. In August 1990 preliminary censorship was repealed, and publishers were able to include manuscripts that they liked in their plans without the consent of higher-ranking printing committees. But other difficulties have cropped up. Previously, there were no problems with selling the printed product. Everything followed a well-oiled procedure: required reading was published and sold, while surplus stock lay on shop and library shelves for years and was then quietly written off.

In 1991 the official book trade, in the person of the Soyuzkniga association, was even more needed by the center than before. The situation was this: Gorbachev's books were on sale for a token state-fixed price in all bookshops up and down the country, while Yeltsin's memoires were also on sale throughout the land but for a fortune on the black market. Meanwhile, the writings of top politicians of, say, Lithuania, Armenia or Georgia, even when translated into Russian, hardly ever got any further than their home republics.

Vaclav Havel, when he was still a dissident and not president of Czechoslovakia received the West German publishers' and booksellers' peace prize in 1989, but his books have not appeared in Russia—neither on nor under the counter. I would greatly like to read Pope John Paul II, Lech Walesa and Mother Theresa, whose books are issued simultaneously in numerous languages of the civilized world by Western publishers and booksellers.

We do have special publishing houses, Progress and Raduga, issuing literature in translation from foreign languages. But what kind of progress can there be when most of the originals had come out 5 or 10 years before? The mammoth Moscow publishing house Mir (Peace) specializes in translations of works by Western authors in all spheres of technology. Development of the natural sciences, which is of importance for our military-industrial complex, was accorded great attention here. Anything of the slightest interest was translated and published immediately, and the publishing process allowed it to hit the bookshelves within a year or so of publication in the West. The best-known technical journals of leading NATO countries were also translated into Russian, published and circulated among the appropriate permanent subscribers. Technical bookshops (ie., those dealing with the natural sciences) in the major cities throughout the Soviet Union deserved their popularity. In any of them one could find, for example, up to a hundred or more book titles in Russian on computer technology, written by both Soviet and foreign authors. At the same time in even the largest general bookshops one might discover not more than two or three translated Western works on economics. The same applied to all the other humanitarian sciences.

Perhaps we might see one day in Moscow or St. Petersburg shops selling books reduced to clear by Western publishers. They might even be a year old, but they will be inexpensive, even in hard currency. Those wishing to study foreign languages here would eagerly buy hundreds of different Western illustrated magazines from those left over by the Western reading public. But perhaps I am deluding myself here. The newspapers here in 1990–1991 were overflowing with advertisements offering everything under the sun, at exorbitant prices, except Western books.

This, evidently, marked one of the invisible boundaries of perestroika and glasnost. Photocopiers, computers, Mercedes cars or Nissans, tourist trips abroad, food and medicines—a wide range of western goods and services could be acquired in the ex-USSR at commercial, that is, free prices (which, of course, are beyond the pockets of most working people). But for some reason, western books were absent from this list; as far as the Soviet customs offices are concerned, they continued to be like a red rag to a bull. In the majority of cases customs duties did not come into it. They simply pronounced the famous Russian "Niet" ["No" in English-translation], with no further explanation required.

Western booksellers in such circumstances preferred to remain optimistic and await better days. In your country, they told their Soviet colleagues, even cooperative and independent publishers began to emerge. But even this undeniably pleasant fact has done little to change the actual status quo, that is, the state monopoly over book publishing remains virtually untouched. Instead of the censor or Party bureaucrat it is the state that controls everything, keeping a tight hold on major printing capacities, paper combines and all tax and financial policy as regards the publication and sale of books.

The new command mechanism is as straightforward in operation as the old. If you want to have your own private publishing house, go ahead and register it. To found it you have to pay a small fee to the state, and if you want you can start work at home—all you need is a chair, table and telephone. Bring in from abroad a desktop publisher, and you can run off a couple of hundred copies. But the major printing facilities (entire factories) and paper combines (factories large enough to house a couple of jumbo jets) are not yet up for sale. They belong to the state.

PART II

CHAPTER VIII

RADIO

Radio Russia vs. the Politbureau of the CPSU Central Committee

Radio has played a major role in mass communications in the Soviet Union. An insignificant number of families in the ex-USSR have telephones; as to radios, most have a one-channel, and some two-or three-channel radios in their homes. From the thirties until the fifties, Soviet villages would have a loudspeaker on a lamp post somewhere in the central square. All day long peasants could hear party slogans and *Pravda* editorials, with propaganda songs in between. Up to this day, when people move into a multi-story building they find running water, electricity and a radio socket. And yet it would be a mistake to say that all Russia's citizens today have a radio, as there are only 65m radio outlets for 150m people.

After censorship was lifted in August 1990, Soviet radio changed: there were less lies and propaganda, and more information, comment and entertainment. Announcers have more personality, and there are more reporters and radio hosts. The information reaches audiences uncensored. Things have changed drastically. Radiojournalists have actually for the first time received a chance to make live reports on a regular basis, ie. they have given up the services of readers and the preliminary taping of their material, which was to be edited, endorsed and censored.

Yet there had been no decentralization or privatization of Soviet radio by the end of 1991. There is the First Soviet radio by the end of 1991. There is the *First All-Union Radio Program* and the news-and-entertainment program *Mayak*, another all-union program, recently taken over by *Radio Russia*, and one or two local radio programs in republics and regions. Then there is the World news service of Moscow Radio in Russian.

In some republics pirate stations sometimes started broadcasting without license from the local authorities.

Since September 1990, one such has been *Nadezhda* (Hope), operating in Russian, clearly hostile to the Estonian government, and broadcasting two or three hours a day from a naval base in the very center of Tallinn, a stone's throw from the republic's governmental and parliamentary buildings. When asked what he intended to do about this, premier Edgar Savisaar simply shrugged his shoulders. The federal interior and foreign ministries, the KGB and the defense and civil aviation ministries had their own radio frequencies and did what they wanted with them, beyond the control of the state electronics and telecommunications inspectorate...

The Gosteleradio management would say that journalists working for most of the republican radio stations were unambiguously nationalistic; others would say that they were patriotic, upholding their national interests. Journalism has always been a political and highly risky profession in this country. A sacked reporter could expect no help from the trade unions or courts. Today anyone who shows up on the streets of our cities with his microphone, tape recorder or camera during skirmishes between opposing groups of demonstrators is taking a big chance. And the job of editorial teams is now more complex than before.

The weekly *Argumenty i Fakty* touched upon one aspect of the journalist's work in an interview called "Perestroika at Gosteleradio?" in No. 30, July 1990:

> In February last year the then chairman of Gosteleradio, A. Aksyonov, decreed that two journalists, A. Zhetvin and S. Fonton, be removed from live broadcasting and for three months transferred to lower-paid duties. This was a punishment for having quoted during a *Mayak* news bulletin an article on the Katyn tragedy taken from the Polish magazine *Odrodzenie*. In the words of the decree, this "inflicted harm on the interests of our country" and was "a gross political error".
>
> Yet just over a year later, in an announcement carried by TASS, the USSR expressed to the Poles its deep regret over Katyn and called it one of Stalinism's gravest crimes. The two journalists appealed to the new chairman of Gosteleradio, M. Nenashev, to anull the decree that had accused them of irresponsibility and political immaturity. An *Argumenty i Fakty* correspondent went to meet them.
>
> "Only after three months did Nenashev inform us via his assistants that he would not be annulling the decree, even though he recognized it was unjust", Zhetvin said. "His explanation was that he did not want to establish a precedent that would lead to a flood of appeals from others who had been unfairly treated. We viewed this as perpetuation of the system that existed at Gosteleradio under Aksyonov. In our opinion, such a precedent is essential so that people can believe that perestroika has at last reached Gosteleradio and that justice will triumph".
>
> —Was the actual form your dismissal took proper?
>
> Of course not, since you can be excluded from broadcasting on only two grounds: violation of constitutional norms, which means advocating violence or war or inciting ethnic hatred, or if your professionalism is in question. Unfortunately, the practice of taking people off the air has become common in both radio and television. For example, over the past few months I've been taken off several times. In February for a report from a pro-democracy demonstration on Manezhnaya Square. In June for a report on the chaos at our airports, which was part of a *Mayak Panorama* program. I started getting interested in how our top leaders travel about the country. And finally

because in the same program during the CPSU 28th Congress I started an argument with some Party functionary.

What's really surprising is that today removal from live broadcasting is not noted down anywhere and no political assessments are given. They simply summon you and say that you're not working professionally.

—A presidential decree on democratization and development of Soviet radio and TV came out recently. What did TV and radio staff think of it?

On the whole it's something to welcome, but in places it begs a lot of questions. Nenashev commented on it on TV, and missed out a number of important provisions, probably on purpose. For example, he didn't say a word about the clause saying that it is prohibited to turn 'state-run television and radio into a mouthpiece for the personal political views of its workers'. But this clause contravenes the Law on the Press and Other Mass Media, which forbids such discrimination even when a journalist's personal opinion doesn't coincide with that of the organization for which he works.

The current Gosteleradio chairman talked about the need to make TV and radio more orientated to the people, and acknowledged that the Party used to dictate to them. But that raises the question who stopped us from shaking it off as soon as clause 6 clause 6 of the Soviet Constitution, about the Party's leading role, was repealed.

There are 86 broadcasting buildings and 199 city broadcasting units in the Russian Federation. After the Communist Party lost power in August 1991, all this was appropriated by the Russian government. But if one remembers the very beginning of hostilities between the Kremlin and the "White House" (Russian parliament), *Radio Russia* couldn't hope for any improvement. It could never get a chance to use the radio broadcasting network to broadcast all over the country. The very emergence of *Radio Russia* was a compromise on the part of Gorbachev towards Yeltsin, the ongoing game called "glasnost and perestroika".

In 1991 the All-Union Radio changed the names of most of its channels. The former *Channel 1* became *Radio-1*; the Mayak news-and-entertainment channel remained as it was; *Channel 3* became *Radio-2*, and *Channel 4* was named *Orpheus*.

Radio Russia was included in the newly-formed Russian independent TV and radio company headed by Oleg Poptsov. The morning programs (*Radio-1*, 6.30 a.m.—9.00 a.m.) were to create—if possible—a good mood. The "meet-an-interesting-person" type of program would be in the afternoon (*Mayak*, 2 p.m.—4 p.m.), with a hotline in the studio. Finally, the evening programs (*Radio-2*, 10.15 p.m. till midnight) were taken up by cultural events.

It was not long before *Radio Russia* was practically closed down. It stopped broadcasting on the first channel of the All-Union Radio and *Mayak*, which reduced its audience by one third. On February 5 1991 the government of the Russian Federation declared that it was ready to undertake extraordinary measures if the government of the Soviet Union did not cancel all restrictions with respect to the work of *Radio Russia*. The government of the Russian Federation demanded control of one main TV and one main radio channel, barring which it would use its sovereign right and constitutional duty to provide news for the republic's population. The first days of February saw a drastic cut in the number of frequencies for use by *Radio Russia*—but *Radio Russia* was a rostrum for Boris Yeltsin. The cuts followed the events in Vilnius and Riga, about which *Radio Russia* was sharply critical of the central authorities. It was *Radio Russia* that made a breakthrough (on a union scale) in the information blockade on Lithuania. Its journalists were among the first to make a live report from the heart of the events, and thus put their colleagues from the *Mayak* channel on the spot: *Mayak* came next after *Radio Russia*, on the same frequencies and from the same studios, but having TASS disinformation. To their credit, they added a lot of comment to that, which also became a turning point in the current history of Soviet broadcasting. Since that time, various communist editions stepped up their criticism of *Radio of Russia*. Leonid Kravchenko, who headed Gosteleradio, called the station "hostile" and said he knew no enemy worse than the one in broadcasting.

After the bloody events of January 1991 in Vilnius, their instigators—the Bolsheviks—started to clamp down, trying to do away with the glasnost they hate so much and with the newly-created Russian Broadcasting Company. There was an interesting article by Oleg Kupriyanov, written specially for the New York-based newspaper *Novoye Russkoye Slovo* (February 12 1991):

> On February 4 in Moscow, at the first press conference of the Russian Broadcasting Company, we were informed of a new step by the central government against glasnost. In the words of the company's chairman, USSR People's Deputy Oleg Poptsov, in the evening of February 1, the chairman of USSR Gosteleradio Leonid Kravchenko had told him that Radio of Russia would no longer be allowed to use the all-union Channel 1, despite the agreement between Gorbachev and Yeltsin.
>
> It was announced that Radio of Russia could only broadcast on Channel 3, whose audiences are limited to big cities. About forty per cent of Russia's population, in the North and in rural areas especially, was cut off from broadcasts of their national broadcasting company.
>
> Oleg Poptsov told the audiences how the "bosses" justified such a decision. They said that the broadcasting station established on December 10 1990 had been critical of the central government, didn't agree with some of the decrees of the Soviet President, and provided information which "nonplussed the government" (such as information on the forthcoming price rises). Which means that opposing the policy of the central authorities is tantamount to taking an anti-government stand; to criticize the drawbacks of the political system means to be anti-socialist; and to talk in favor of a multi-party system means to be against the Communist Party.
>
> The leadership of the Russian Broadcasting Company was going to sue Gosteleradio. The situation was seen as extraordinary. Ivan Silayev, the Russian Premier, was expected to make a statement in this connection. The broadcasting company's leaders were resolute: if the confrontation continued, they were ready to set

up an independent broadcasting network, and also place *Radio Russia* transmitters abroad. Oleg Poptsov was already discussing with specialists the question of possible jamming of Russian radio. "Such a measure, of course, would seem absurd," he said, "because we are talking about a sovereign republic broadcasting on its own territory."

Nevertheless, Russia is the only republic that barely has any of its own broadcasting time. For the sake of comparison, the total volume of national radio broadcasting in Kazakhstan was 28 hours a day, and in Russia only 6. Armenian TV has 22.3 hours on the air every day, and Russia only 3 hours a week.

What happened to *Radio Russia* has triggered discussion of the repressions by the central government towards independent mass media and possibilities of the consolidation of the democratic forces. Not so long ago 116 actors, film directors and writers had declared that they refused to cooperate with Gosteleradio as a protest against the policy of Kravchenko. Film directors Elem Klimov and Andrei Smirnov sent a letter to Gosteleradio demanding that their films not be shown on Central TV. Arkady Arkanov, a satirical writer, took off his program planned for Sunday, February 3. Moscow journalists are going to discuss further measures, to set up a support fund for glasnost, which, among other things, will provide money for journalists who have lost their jobs in the central broadcasting company.

It is yet unclear if there will be any proposals from Gorbachev—"Mr. Compromise"—on some kind of compromise. The situation is developing in such a way that the most popular and outlawed TV programs appear on other channels.

It is possible that a compromise will be offered to *Radio of Russia* when tempers have cooled and the official statements are made. On the other hand, the repression towards the radio station is quite in line with the policy of cutting off big cities from the provinces, where they have access to almost no printed matter but *Pravda*. It is noteworthy that after Oleg Poptsov learned the bad news about *Radio of Russia*, he received a call from the chief of Tyumen TV. The latter tried to encourage Poptsov by saying "we're on your side, so fight on, guys!" "It would be great if your hangers-on were with us, too," Poptsov replied.

Yuri Ryzhov, USSR People's Deputy, believed that if Gorbachev put the issue of suspending the Law on the Press to vote, he would get no less than 300 votes, which would be quite enough.

Not long previously—in the summer and autumn of 1990—it had seemed that the truth would be available on Soviet TV and radio and not only from abroad. Of course, Gosteleradio even then kept those whom it didn't like out of TV and radio. For example, the program *Auditoria* (Audience) was punished for reading excerpts from Yeltsin's book. As the Law on the Press came into force, the monopoly of state broadcasting came under attack.

"Echo of Moscow" Saved the Honor of the Nation

The Moscow City Council, the USSR State Committee for the Press (Goskompechat), Russia's Ministry for the Press and Information, and other agencies received dozens of applications from organizations and private citizens who wanted to establish their own radio and even TV stations. Many such applications were registered, but not many applicants got what they wanted. It may sound ridiculous, but the number of possible broadcasting frequencies is very small in this country because the standards for radio-signal transmission are the most outdated in the world. The range of our FM does not coincide with that in the rest of the world. That is why FM radio sets need to be adjusted to work in the Soviet Union. Finally, the most serious thing—the distribution of frequencies—was the monopoly of Gosteleradio and the USSR Ministry of Communication, which means total control by the KGB and the Ministry of Defense of the USSR—the loyal guardians of party totalitarianism.

Article 7 of the USSR Law on the Press reads, in particular: "There shall be no media monopoly of any kind (press, radio, television, etc.)". If we take this law, which was enacted on August 1 1990, into consideration, we will see that there August 1 1990, into consideration, we will see that there emerged a contradiction between it and the situation in broadcasting. What was the mechanism to be used to do away with that contradiction? First of all, radio stations fully independent from Gosteleradio should have been created. But was there a guarantee that independent broadcasting was possible after registration? According to the Law on the Press, "the right to start producing mass information is valid for a year after the licence is granted", but in fact, there are no "spare" frequencies. So all the new radio stations started working at the expense of the old ones, using the latter's frequencies.

Among the lucky people who were the first to break the monopoly of Gosteleradio was a group of young people from the *Ekho Moskvy* (Echo of Moscow) radio station. Since August 1990, *Ekho Moskvy* could always be tuned into from 7 till 10 p.m. in a radius of 200 km around Moscow. Its audience was approximately 20-30 million. There were plans for round-the-clock broadcasting, and also the use of FM bands, and purchase of a more powerful transmitter, which of course would have attracted advertising.

Sergei Korzun became chief editor of *Ekho Moskvy*, and Mikhail Rozenblat was its director general. Radio M employed many talented announcers who, at one time or another, had been expelled from Gosteleradio for "excessive boldness" and "rash assessments". It would hardly be right to call *Ekho Moskvy* an independent radio station, because among its founders we find the Moscow City Council, the editorial board of the magazine *Ogonyok*, the journalism department of Moscow State University, the former Novosti Press Agency, and the Radio association under the USSR Ministry of Communication. It was this association that once succeeded in cutting off a "piece" of air-time, and now turned it over to Korzun. Gosteleradio refused to provide *Ekho Moskvy* with a frequency of its own, considering the existence of that station "inexpedient". A monopoly will never produce its own competitors. Neither will it ever self-disband.

At the end of January 1991 the Moscow City Council allotted 250,000 rubles to the radio station for building a 150-meter high radio mast. It was worth the money. As *Nezavisimaya Gazeta* justly remarked on February 5 1991, "this radio station saved Moscow's face on January 13 with its reports on the events in Lithuania".

Here is what *Literaturnaya Gazeta* wrote about that radio station on January 16 1991, in the tragic days of carnage carried out by the Soviet Army around the TV center and TV tower in the capital of Lithuania:

> "*Gun fire and Ekho Moskvy.*" As in Brezhnev's time, people were tuning in to Western stations to learn the news from Vilnius. And in Moscow, the news spread immediately that on wave-length 250 and frequency 1,205 kHz, *Ekho Moskvy* was broadcasting.
>
> Moscow tuned in. For 13 hours running, one after another, young journalists of a radio station independent from Gosteleradio told their audiences the truth in agitated voices. They were busy doing what real journalists should.
>
> Few people had known their names before that Sunday, but after it hundreds of thousands learned them.

There were only five journalists and a dozen technicians working at *Ekho Moskvy*. In the summer of 1991 they occupied two small rooms in a lane behind the GUM department store, and broadcast eight hours a day. Those were always live broadcasts, without any texts written beforehand, and without any permission from above. There was a lot of information and music, all this non-stop, very fast, in an understandable language, sincere, warm and amusing. The station asked for no subsidies from its founders, making its way thanks to those who placed their ads with it. Though, to restore the worn-out equipment it needed $60,000 to buy from abroad. According to polls, *Ekho Moskvy* has a permanent audience of one to two million.

Here are some expressive Moscow press headlines about the station: "*An Island in the Ocean*" (*Zhurnalist* magazine No. 7, 1991)—this probably meant the ocean of lies by party propaganda; "*An Echo of the Truth*" (*Argumenty i Fakty* No. 3, 1991, the first post-coup issue). This latter article is worth quoting in full:

> To think that the journalist profession is a comfortable one is a grave mistake. In the time of a coup it becomes the most dangerous occupation. Any junta closes down the radio and press right after seizing bridges and the telegraph. The recent events were no exception.
>
> In the early morning of August 19, the premises of *Ekho Moskvy* in 7 Nikolskaya St. were visited by eight people in plain clothes. They produced their KGB ID and ordered broadcasting to be stopped. The chief editor S. Korzun refused. After which the "guests" themselves cut off the line and sealed the transmitter. Yet the journalists didn't stop gathering information, preparing to go on the air as soon as possible.

> *Ekho Moskvy* went on the air again at 1:40 p.m. on August 20. The decision not to comply with the order of the new authorities was made by the journalists together with the people's deputies of Russia and Moscow, and the staff of the ministry of communications of Russia.
>
> The radio station was cut off twice during the night. It had three offices on different floors of the building of the Supreme Soviet of the Russian Federation, and one in the building of the Moscow City Council. When the tanks and APCs started crushing the barricades at the approaches to the "White House", it seemed that this was the end. People would come up to the journalists who were reporting live and say good-bye to their families... But they were lucky, and the nightmare ended.
>
> In the morning of August 21 the authorities confiscated the transmitter for the second time. On an order from the commandant of Moscow, Col. Gen. Kalinin, the building where the transmitter was working was occupied by an airborne unit with Lt. Col. Zakharov at its head. In the afternoon it became clear that the coup had failed, and the "warriors" quietly left...
>
> *Ekho Moskvy* resumed its broadcasts at 3:40 p.m. At approximately the same time a special militia detachment offered its services, but the need was already over."

What are the other radio stations that would not lie to people? Valdas Analauskas wrote about another in the newspaper *Novoye Russkoye Slovo* on March 19, 1991:

> "Every evening at eight o'clock sharp I switch on my short wave radio and, like the hearts of thousands of other Lithuanians scattered all over the world, mine misses a beat while I wait impatiently for the signature tune of *Kalba Vilnius* (This Is Vilnius), the tune of my motherland. In the past I often spent the night trying to tune in to *The Voice of America* or *Radio Liberty*. Some twist of fate... Many ethnic Lithuanians now living in the West have short-wave radio sets, which, in general, are not popular here. To us *Vilnius Radio* with its half-hour broadcast abroad is the live voice of the besieged homeland, our Lithuania, which is being tortured by a cruel enemy. It was a daily confirmation that our motherland was alive and struggling, that its spirit hadn't been broken... And every time I turn on the radio my heart skips a beat: will I hear the words "Kalba Vilnius" this time? This feeling is especially intense now, after the bloody Sunday, when there was silence on the radio instead of the familiar tune of the Lithuanian psaltery. I didn't know in my New Jersey seclusion that exactly at that moment Gorbachev's warriors were attacking the Vilnius radio station. When it's 8 p.m. here on America's east coast, it's already 2 in the morning in Vilnius. That was the hour at which the radio station was stormed. In January Vilnius Radio went silent for almost two weeks. Now it's on the air again, though the communists are still calling the shots while hiding behind the backs of airborne troops. Now the broadcasting company of independent Lithuania is literally working behind barricades. So we may say that the signature tune of *Kalba Vilnius* gets here from the barricades...

It is useful to become better acquainted with Lithuanian Radio: many people in the Soviet Union expressed their admiration for the courage and perseverance of Vilnius. It was national resistance of the Lithuanians against communism, and they were the first to win independence in August 1991. The Paris-based newspaper *Russkaya Mysl* of April 16, 1991 carried an interview with Nerijus Malukevicius:

Question: Some days ago we marked a tragic date—three months since the Soviet troops had seized *Lithuanian Radio* and TV, and the TV tower in Vilnius. Is it possible to believe that those buildings haven't yet been returned to their legal owners?

Answer: Unfortunately they haven't, though this has been going on for over three months already, despite protests and appeals to the highest authorities of the Soviet Union, including the Soviet President. All the appeals meet with a wall of silence. Neither has the Supreme Soviet of the USSR given an answer to that signed by the 1,200-strong staff of the Lithuanian broadcasting company. I believe that one of the reasons why Mikhail Gorbachev is not solving this problem is his complacency because of the lack of international publicity for the fact that those buildings are still being held by Soviet troops. In Germany, which I have recently visited, and in Belgium, too, journalists know very well that there was an attempted coup, and that people were killed during the attack on the building. And they are very much surprised to learn that those buildings still remain the barracks for the soldiers who guard them, and that the personnel of the Lithuanian broadcasting company has to work in rooms not suited for that kind of work, that the captured buildings are being used for slandering the lawful parliament and government. This is something a civilized person would find hard to understand, but these are the facts. In protest, the people working for the broadcasting company have been on a hunger strike taking turns, replacing each other every three, six, and ten days. A campaign for collecting signatures to the UN is under way now, as radio and TV are the property of the people, and to take them away from them by force is a crime before these people, before common human values in whose favor the USSR President has spoken so much. Such a measure was not used even against the criminal Saddam Hussein by the allied forces: Iraq's radio and television were never bombarded or otherwise destroyed. A government of a country where journalists are despised, where TV programs can be closed down arbitrarily the way one closes a finished book, and where tanks have the right to crush people who gather to defend their radio and television—and all this done in a foreign state—can't exist for long.

Question: So how do your radio and television work under such conditions?

Answer: We have regained the former volume of broadcasting. For example, we have two republican programs with a total volume of 38 hours a day. We continue to relay the religious program *Blagovest*, which we started in August 1990. Speaking of the content, all the programs have regained their power, but the working conditions are terrible: we don't even have professional equipment. So Western journalists may find it amusing to visit us and see that Europe has television completely equipped with household appliances, using VHS videotapes, etc. Yet we haven't lost our optimism, and we are not going to return to the past, no matter what difficulties we come across in post-communist society. All the more so since some new laws are starting to work, among them laws on the economy, such as the law on privatization. This law came into force on April 10. Banks are becoming more active, the ruble-dollar exchange rate becoming more stable, which consequently hits the black market. There is no way back. But we still believe that radio and television will come back to our old building some day. Before that happens we will not give in.

The nightmare of the Baltics is over. It has taken the Baltic states less than half a century to win independence. When the Soviet Army left the buildings of the TV center, they turned out to be practically empty. One may come across the equipment missing from there on the black markets of Pskov, where the Chernigov airborne division and the Vitebsk air force division, which took Vilnius in January 1991, have now been redeployed. The looters caused damage of millions upon millions of rubles to the Vilnius broadcasting company. They destroyed what they couldn't take away. The local communists had to buy the most necessary equipment and work day and night for a whole month to assemble it to resume their broadcasting. This went on till the end of February 1991. It took twelve electronics specialists to do the job.

The Gosteleradio monopoly was broken not only by *Ekho Moskvy*, and not only by the military announcers who read their reports from written texts to the Lithuanian audiences, but also by the French, no matter how strange this may seem.

Foreign Radio Stations Broadcast in Russian

"Name your advertising agent, and I'll tell you who you are." This turns out to be quite true for another new Moscow-based radio station, *Europe Plus Moscow*, whose advertisements with a silhouette of the Eiffel Tower were to be found in every periodical issued from mid-1990 by the Central Committee of the Communist Party. This joint Soviet-French radio station became, in fact, a subsidiary of Gosteleradio, fully controlled by it and following one principle: no politics. When its regular broadcasts for St. Petersburg started in February 1991, it gathered an audience of 20 million. The collection of Western pop that *Europe Plus* has of 20 million. The collection of Western pop that Europe Plus has numbers a thousand CDs, with its studios packed with state-of-the-art computer equipment. The suspended broadcasts on the medium waves have been resumed. There have been serious attempts to establish broadcasting via subsidiaries on the entire territory of Russia. Several Soviet radio-producers have received a contract for putting out cheap car radios tuned to *Europe Plus*.

Channel 1 of Central TV also enthusiastically advertised the first musical radio program in Russia.

The announcers there never read from script, they improvise. The daily musical program is compiled by a computer, fed in by the French once a month, when they bring out new CDs. There are different categories of songs. "A"—hits of the month, European Top Twenty; "B"—less popular songs, etc. The "A" songs may be broadcast several times a day. The announcer doesn't have the right either to replace songs, or to change their order, and the French partners keep a strict eye on that.

In May 1990, Muscovites started listening to broadcasts of *Radio Nostalgie*. This new Moscow station uses the musical part of the Paris version, relayed via satellite, and adds Russian music and newscasts in Moscow.

During perestroika *Radio Moscow*'s world service has switched from cold-war propaganda clichés to more balanced and objective information, and has even begun regular cooperation with the world's major radio corporations. *Radio Nostalgie-Moscou*, a Soviet-French music and news station working in Russian for Soviet listeners, is based at the world service studios and for six hours a day on short wave (and in the future on VHF) it pours out French and European music plus, of course, commercial breaks and news bulletins. In response to this the French host Moscow music editors and other staff in Paris for practical training.

The newspaper *Moskovskaya Pravda* gave the following account of the run-up to the establishment of *Radio Nostalgie-Moscou* (April 29, 1990):

> A pleasantly smiling couple, not in their first flush of youth, on the publicity brochure announce: "This is something different"; such is the image selected by the Paris radio station *Nostalgie*, which today is one of France's biggest.
>
> "This is something different"—meaning first of all a different audience. Unlike most Western VHF stations, *Nostalgie* targets not the teenagers but the "golden oldies", the 30-50 age bracket. It does of course have fans both younger and older, but in any event these are people who have left their childhood hard-rock and heavy-metal inclinations behind and now want to listen to ... music.
>
> "Bearing in mind the traditional Soviet interest in French culture, I'm sure that our program will win listeners. Not only that, but it gives French businessmen a 'radio window' onto Moscow. Because of perestroika there are hopes to expand contacts, and this attracts the business community", said Coste.
>
> Curiously enough, the project, even the technological part of it, became possible due to conversion of the Soviet defense industry. Broadcasting will be from premises that previously housed transmitters jamming Western broadcasts to Russia."

Other achievements of our radio are also linked to foreign broadcasting.

In terms of quantity of broadcasting to other countries, not so long ago *Radio Moscow* was top of the list: 2,257 hours per week, in 80 languages. According to a special report by the British parliamentary foreign affairs committee, the world's largest audience is enjoyed by the BBC (120 million listeners a year). Then came *Voice of America* (85 million), *Radio Liberty* and *Radio Free Europe* (55 million), *Deutsche Welle* (30 million), *Radio Moscow* (15 million), *Radio France* (10 million), and *Radio Peking* (5 million). For 60 years, *Radio Moscow* was the mouthpiece of socialism Stalin-and Khrushchev-style. Then the management of Gosteleradio has agreed in theory that there is no point in spending 150 million rubles annually on filling the airwaves, and that it is better to try to sell or simply give its frequencies to Western studios to use.

In Moscow and its environs, as on the Russian shores of the Pacific, *Radio Moscow* and foreign stations, including Russian-language ones, were always present. But where are broadcasts from the republics? Siberia and the Far East are full of construction workers, military men, former convicts and other people of various nationalities, who would enjoy listening to radio programs from their native lands in their native tongues—from Kiev, Tashkent, Tbilisi, Yerevan, Baku, Vilnius, and so on. This kind of non-Russian broadcasting has already appeared in Central Russia.

"There's no paper, er sorry, no money", smoothly answers the practiced Moscow bureaucrat, able to handle any inconvenient enquiry. *Radio Moscow*'s foreign service had studios and transmitters not only in the capital but in numerous cities along the country's borders close to the target countries, and the Soviet government was always able to find the cash for them even when it was glaringly obvious that nobody bothered to tune in. And how could anyone pick up Moscow's English-language broadcasts on short wave in the United States, where the majority of receivers do not have short wave? However, for decades the Chinese were broadcasting to Russia, from morning to night. Nobody jammed them, but neither did anyone listen, even though in most parts of the country reception of Chinese Russian-language programs was often better than that of Soviet ones.

Soviet diplomats abroad would use their powerful short-wave receivers to regularly tune into *Radio Moscow* in the appropriate languages, and then give a favorable report back to the center. Gosteleradio correspondents abroad found it easy to organize, via local associations for friendship with our country, a dozen or so tributes from *Radio Moscow* listeners; these would be lovingly translated and published in special bulletins "for official use only" and thus serve as grounds for the good work to be continued. Ever-increasing state finance was guaranteed, since the Soviet parliament never used to debate it as a separate item of expenditure. We still do not know whether People's Deputies have agreed to dip into the taxpayer's torn pocket to finance "Radio Moscow listeners' clubs abroad" (the cash went not to the clubs, of course, but simply to the foreign broadcasting service, whose budget has never been made public). In the USSR Supreme Soviet they did, after all, read the new government weekly *Pravitelstvenny Vestnik*, issue No. 25 of which for June 1990 carried a report on the effectiveness of *Radio Moscow*'s broadcasts to foreign countries: "Our transmitters are geared to short wave, which is an ever less popular band in the West, where either VHF or medium wave are used for listening in the car or at home. Thus much of what we would like to tell people in the West does not get through to them purely because of our poor technology".

Here is how Ivan Liprandi described the political cuisine of *Radio Moscow World Service* in *Novoye Russkoye Slovo* of January 7, 1991:

> Some ten years ago, Danchev, an announcer in the English section of *Radio Moscow World Service*, worked a night shift in live broadcasting. Instead of reading out a centrally-distributed text, he made a personal statement denouncing Soviet aggression in Afghanistan. Next came his public punishment orchestrated by Alexander Plevako, the then secretary of *Radio Moscow*'s communist party committee. Danchev was fired, declared insane and put into a mental institution. Later he was saved by a campaign in his defense which swept the West—eventually he was released. Despite that incident, Plevako continued to climb: in 1988 he was appointed deputy chairman of Gosteleradio, and head of *Radio Moscow*.
>
> It's hard to find any other institution which has seen as little change in the past ten years as the broadcasting-house on Moscow's Pyatnitskaya street. The world's biggest radio station in number of languages, countries broadcast to, and hours on the air, *Radio Moscow* also led the world in terms of independence. It was absolutely independent of its listeners. Nobody ever raised the question of what to report, why and to whom. The thinking was as follows: since radio was invented for all, it should be used to make soundtracks in all the many languages of TASS and newspaper reports.
>
> Nobody ventured to emulate the Danchev deed and there was no room for compromise, since every report was written and had to be signed by a colleague, then it moved on for approval by department head and then editor-in-chief or his deputy. That system worked well to sift out any dissident thought and sometimes common sense, too—but nobody cared.
>
> Staff writers were prolific, since writing earned them fees in addition to basic salary. Motivated in that way, each produced in excess of ten pages daily. They drummed like mad on their typewriters, a particular obsession being with phrases containing the words "progressive", "socialist", "effective" and the like. That drumbeat was echoed in translators' rooms, with the same result: new combinations of old words. Journalists also copied their materials, crossed out lines like "This is *Radio Moscow*" or "Dear listeners", put them into envelopes and sent them by official mail to the Novosti Press Agency (APN), which also paid fees.
>
> Conversely, APN staff writers sent in their materials to *Radio Moscow*. These were eagerly accepted, because that greased the mutually-beneficial business and complied with a rule under which forty percent of the materials were supposed to be generated by staff writers, and sixty percent, by non-staffers. Some people trace back this rule to Lenin, who had ordered that more than fifty percent of newspaper space should be given to articles from "hammer-and-sickle" people. This, he thought, would bar professional journalists inherited from the old regime from a monopoly on the printed word. Since then, non-professionalism has established itself as an absolute principle.

International affairs analysts would start their day by browsing through newspapers and wire service offerings, looking for evidence of vicious imperialist misdeeds. A black person hanged or shot dead was special luck: to write a commentary about the eternal topic of bad, ugly racism needed less ingenuity than that of a robot. Racist material was in special demand with sections broadcasting to conflict-ridden multi-ethnic countries, their obvious intention being to incite an explosion that would solve the ethnic problem "once and for all"—as in Russia.

Home affairs writers would read *Selskaya Zhizn* and reproduce in their own words new progressive farming methods described there. Given some experience, one could easily conjure up an interview with some head shepherd of a sheep-breeding team in Kirghizia. (Don't leave your office and finish before lunch. Ask your neighbors for a recording).

One very special department was that dealing with China. Over the years of confrontation with the PRC ("the period of mutual abuse" as the department insiders flatly called it), the staffers were instructed to "unmask the misdeeds of Mao's criminal clique". But the face of China at that time strikingly resembled our own past, if not present—with its own oriental tinge, of course. That gave journalists a unique opportunity to speak their mind on a totalitarian communist regime and try their hand at describing how the people were coming to resent that unpopular regime more and more. That was only part of the fun. The other part was to look through the reports of foreign news agencies some time later and see those which swallowed the bait. When the times of mutual abuse came to an end, the bosses started complaining that previously their young subordinates had demonstrated quicker professional progress. Ironically, that conventional criticism of the young struck home: after the period of mutual abuse was over, journalists were advised to write stories about the charms of Soviet life—which anything but inspired young talent. Meanwhile, the Chinese reform was progressing at a staggering pace. Against that backdrop, any stories by *Radio Moscow* about the advantages of "team contract" work in the Soviet Union could deliver only one message to a Chinese farmer: good riddance.

But again, *Radio Moscow* was least interested in how it was accepted by the audience. Appeals to improve broadcasting quality would only be born out of a fight for lucrative vacancies. Otherwise, nobody cared about making radio propaganda more efficient. One proof of that came in 1986, when a new boss Kezbers was appointed to head *Radio Moscow*. Coming from the Baltics, Kezbers had had a somewhat variegated experience of serving with different Soviet embassies. As a young, energetic European cosmopolitan, Kezbers decided to find out how Radio Moscow was coming through abroad—a task never set by any of his predecessors. It turned out that inside the Soviet Union it was coming through all right, but abroad there were problems. Outside, broadcasting quality depended on the weather, much the same as Soviet agriculture did. The USSR Ministry of Communication had long and successfully saved money at the expense of Radio Moscow. Kezbers started "perestroika". He decided to move the Cuban section from the department of Latin America to the department of socialist countries, and the Turkish section, from the European department to the Asian-Pacific department. Kezbers had offered some more or less constructive ideas, but after a year in office suddenly disappeared. Later he was spotted by some of his former colleagues in the secretariat of the CC of the

Communist party of Latvia. He was the only man who managed to combine the functions of a high-ranking communist party official with leadership in the Latvian Popular Front.

There was a long-standing policy to use *Radio Moscow* as a temporary stop for those aspiring to the top or a dead-end for those sentenced to life-long exile. Frequent references and recollections of Paris, London and Singapore could be heard in the smoking rooms of the *Radio Moscow* building, but the number of the smoking rooms of the *Radio Moscow* building, but the number of staff correspondents the station maintained abroad was next to none. Those wistful recollections came from the unlucky: former foreign ministry officials, exposed spies or ungainly diplomats.

Kezbers' office was inherited by the above-mentioned Alexander Plevako. The latter proclaimed that *Radio Moscow* would become the mouthpiece of perestroika. Several senior editors were forced to retire, several departments reshuffled and all journalists told that they should have an opinion of their own on any matter. It was clear though what kind of "opinion" they should have-- after all, *Radio Moscow* was no toddler, it was almost sixty years old. Wage rises were promised and additional bonuses paid out. To respond to the challenge of improving the quality of its programs, *Radio Moscow* played music between news items, which made the programs less boring. With perestroika still on the rise, official material broadcast from the building on Pyatnitskaya street was undergoing change too. Ironically that resulted in *Radio Moscow* losing what it had of the few listeners abroad, the people who watched from afar how a fair society was being built in the Soviet Union. Loyalists were few: radio fans ready to tune in to anything that produced coherent sound; freedom fighters, who got their instructions from Moscow; and editors of puppet newspapers who reprinted our materials. But professionally nothing has changed at *Radio Moscow* during perestroika.

Once a small airplane hovering in the evening skies above Red Square was spotted from the *Radio Moscow* building. Several enterprising correspondents hastened to the square and scooped an interview from Mathias Rust. But it was too late to get approval to air the news. Nobody gave clearance the next morning either. The morning after though, Alexander Plevako denounced those "wise-fools" who rushed to Red Square, and even wrote reports. Of course, he said, the reports never went on the air, but the journalists showed immaturity and sheer lack of responsibility.

Beginning in 1988, foreign radio stations started using information supplied by an independent Moscow-based news agency Interfax. The agency distributed topical and objective information about political parties in Russia, demonstrations and public statements. It was truly quick and competent. But few people knew that Interfax was situated on the seventh floor of the building on Pyatnitskaya street, the place where news and so-called basic materials were prepared for all departments. That news was a minimum of information and a maximum of opinion and propaganda. So how could Interfax emerge in *Radio Moscow*? Here is the opinion of Alexander Nekhoroshev, who occupied the office of *Radio Moscow Russian Service* chief, next door to Interfax:

"It's strange how Interfax came into being and how it continues its existence. Neither TASS nor *Radio Moscow* nor any other agency is allowed to present controversial facts—but not Interfax. The agency is supervised by *Radio Moscow*'s director. The boss of Interfax is a staffer of *Radio Moscow* who arrived recently and has conspicuous gaps in his working record..."

It is understandable why Nekhoroshev should be bitter about that. His Russian World Service started its broadcasts in January 1989, and many journalists from *Radio Moscow* were attracted by its promise of professional and interesting work. Step by step, Nekhoroshev brought together a good team, and its materials were reaching a decent level in terms of efficiency and objectivity. The Russian Service alone reported on the alternative May 1 demonstrations (which nearly cost Nekhoroshev his job).

At a party conference of the entire Gosteleradio the head of the official TV news program *Vremya*, Eduard Sagalaev said: "We'll put out *Vremya*—that's the program of the Politburo. But we'll also put out the Television News Service—for people to know what's really happening in the world."

"The Russian Service", continues Alexander Nekhoroshev, "is the first attempt by Radio Moscow to set up a channel which would inform the public of what is truly taking place. Plevako wanted to correct us but failed. So they "corrected" me: in November I was replaced by a former communist party secretary of *Radio Moscow*."

Where does *Radio Moscow* get its ideological guidelines from? Its staff renounce party membership, as elsewhere. What is its ideologist then, *Pravda*?

"*Radio Moscow World Service* is oriented toward the person of the president," explains Nekhoroshev. "Plevako has declared he will always belong to the party of Mr. Gorbachev. But the awkward thing is that we don't know what Gorbachev really told our bosses and what their own interpretation is. A recent article by Gosteleradio chairman Kravchenko is entitled "I Came To Fulfil the Will of the President". One of his first orders was to stop showing sex and violence on TV."

"What is the will of the President?"

"Here is his recent decree "On Democratizing Television and Radio". Among other things, it sets a shocking demand that a journalist should not maintain an independent opinion! As far as I know, the president is very concerned about the fact that the mass media have taken a wrong turn and are defying central authorities. To put everything under control he is creating a ministry of information. It will control the press (a challenging job, now that we have the Law on the Press), television and radio. The latter are very important. Television and radio will gain in importance as the price of periodicals has rocketed since January 1, while living standards have fallen. People will not be able to read as many newspapers and magazines as they used to."

"Where's the silver lining then?"

"Last week I witnessed the inauguration ceremony of the Russian State TV and Radio Company. Its chairman is Mr. Poptsov, an author and former editor of *Selskaya Molodezh* (Rural Youth) weekly; general director Mr. Lysenko, creator and former boss of the popular *Vzglyad* (Viewpoint) popular talk show. Doubtlessly, the appearance of the TV\Radio company is connected with the line followed by Boris Yeltsin."

January 1991 put a damper on the democratic thrust of Soviet journalism. The ultra-reactionary forces of the CPSU managed to reanimate the practice of cold war in propaganda. In its issue of January 24, 1991 the newspaper *Glasnost* resentfully reported that Munich-based American *Radio Liberty* was increasing its broadcasting time in the three languages of the Soviet Baltic region. The station had been transmitting for an hour every day to each of the republics, but after the Soviet army captured the Press House in Riga and the tragic events erupted in Vilnius, it increased the time to three hours.

In its next issue January 31, the communist *Glasnost* came out with an editorial whose title, "*Fidgety Radio Liberty*", reminded one of older, harder times. Those older times, when radio could be enforced upon all people of the vast empire, remain a pipe dream for older hardline ideologists. It's not a plug-in radio which we now have in our hotels, hostels, houses, etc. That was compulsory radio, a radio which could not be switched off and was transmitted at will to the squares of dozens of thousands of Soviet towns and villages. Radio listening en masse from 6 a.m. till midnight was a kind of fashion in our country, which lingered on until the late 1980s.

The fashion of making sweeping accusations of the West came back this year. Here are two headlines from this year's issues No. 17 and 27 of the newspaper *Pravitelstvenny Vestnik*: "*Foreign Nationalist Centers Operating in USSR Without Camouflage*"; "*Grimaces of Radio Liberty*". The USSR central television reciprocated by issuing a prime-time show featuring KGB agent O. Tumanov—that program was reviewed in the *Rossiyskaya Gazeta* on April 13, 1991 under the title "*Their*" and "*Our*" *Voices in Radio Broadcasting*". On April 7, Channel 1 of the central television put out a program called *Alien Voices*, devoted to *Radio Liberty*: it was too primitive to analyze professionally, but gave a clear impression that Kravchenko and Co. were taking us back to the times of cold war.

-More heartening was that the weekly *Sobesednik* (No. 4 1991) thought it possible to carry a full-page interview with Savik Shuster, chief editor of *Radio Liberty*'s program "In the country and the world". *Sobesednik* is closely linked to *Komsomolskaya Pravda* and to the Komsomol Central Committee. During the interview it commented that the USSR has admitted that the invasion of Afghanistan was a major political mistake. But the leaders who made it not only did not even dream of repenting but for many years blithely continued to justify themselves and hold back the truth. Not only did 15,000 Soviet soldiers die, but a million Afghans as well. And who is to blame for the appearance in our society of hundreds of thousands of Afghan war veterans, embittered and morally and physically crippled. Nothing has yet been written about the atrocities committed as a matter of course by the occupying forces. The Americans, because of systematic violence within their own forces, pulled out of Vietnam, and wrote copiously about this. We have yet to follow suit. In the interview, Shuster mentioned one detail about which we know little. The escalation of violence, extreme cruelty and maximum intensity of military operations took place in 1985 and 1986. If the mujahedeen had not obtained Stingers and thus reliable anti-aircraft defenses, the Politburo would have won the war. The Soviet army has quit Afghanistan, but our vast arms and food deliveries to our puppets there continue, to an extent that is ruinous to ourselves.

From the beginning of the 1950s foreign radio stations could be received by the Soviet people. It is difficult to say why in this country following Stalin's death short-wave receivers came onto the market. Possibly the Party leadership, not wishing and unable to tell its people the truth about the Soviet regime, thought it a good idea for the middle-ranking administrators to have at least some access to accurate information on the world situation. To this end lengthy transcripts, dozens of pages, of Western broadcasts in Russian and other languages of the Soviet Union would land daily on the desks of several hundred members of the privilegentsia. Billions and billions of rubles were spent on jamming "Western anti-Soviet radio stations" in the cities. Jamming was prohibited several times, but receipt of transcripts of intercepted broadcasts, stamped "secret" till 1990, is still viewed as one of the perks of high rank (granted, for example, to chiefs of federal ministries, republican and regional Party secretaries, etc).

One day in the future many Western presenters broadcasting in Russian, as well as in other languages of the former USSR will become national heroes in the states that once composed the Soviet Union. This will be done officially, since already for decades Soviet youngsters and the educated classes have been gratefully tuning in to hear the truth. Certain themes have been taboo for the Soviet and Russian press; although their number is decreasing, they still exist. The only way to receive full and objective information is to listen to the West.

If it had not been for Russian-language broadcasting from abroad, the Soviet public would have found out about Chernobyl not several days but long after the event. The *Voice of America*, *BBC*, *Deutsche Welle* and *Radio Liberty* provided non-stop coverage, due to which the Soviet authorities four years later reluctantly confessed that 1) the nuclear-accident public warning system was not put into operation, 2) on May 1 1986 columns of schoolchildren were marched out in radioactive Kiev to take part in the festivities, 3) new settlements were built for the people of Chernobyl in contaminated zones unfit for habitation, 4) to this day hundreds of thousands of people live on land where all agricultural output is unfit for consumption, but despite radiation levels they continue to grow and process it and, at best, send it to other parts of the country: thus radioactive meat is used in sausages somewhere in Siberia, contaminated powdered milk ends up on tables in Central Asia, and so on (there is no end to the list of such crimes, which for years the censored Soviet press was forced to keep quiet about), 5) to this day supplies of uncontaminated food and the required medical treatment have not been organized, compensatory payments to the victims of radiation have not been agreed (only those who persist receive a monthly allowance of 15 rubles). Only in 1990 we found out officially that a vast tract of the Ukraine, central Russia and Byelorussia, about half the area of Western Europe, was affected by radiation.

I repeat—were it not for the efforts of the West's Russian-language broadcasts, our government would have been able to keep this horrifying information under its hat for many years to come. We have only just been told officially that millions of people will die from radiation-related illnesses, even if they were comparatively lightly contaminated at the time. And we still refuse the generous aid offered to us by the international community, the Japanese especially. What we should have done—was sign a peace treaty with them, give them back the Kurile Islands and accept in return a major aid program for the victims of Chernobyl. Instead of this our military, with the Communist Party Central Committee's blessing, has set about building itself three aircraft carriers. Simply operating them, as publicly announced by USSR Supreme Soviet deputy and academician Georgy Arbatov, will set our taxpayers back 54,000 billion rubles a year in terms of the 1990 prices.

In 1989 the Soviet Union seemed to stop jamming the US station Radio Liberty. The central press began for the first time station Radio Liberty. The central press began for the first time to carry unbiassed reports written in the stations's HQ in Munich and even detailed and approving interviews with staff members. The *Voice of America* has a correspondent officially based in Moscow.

Another new happening would have been inconceivable in the old days— the central Soviet newspaper *Izvestia* (August 14, 1990) published the terms of a literary competition for Soviet listeners, launched by the Russian department of the ... *Deutsche Welle* station. There is a Soviet representative on the jury and the competition involved, in addition to *Deutsche Welle* people, the German embassy in Moscow and consulates in St. Petersburg and Kiev and the Goethe Institute. The latter contributed two fully paid-up places for two one-month German-language courses in Germany, to be added to the two prizes of DM5,000 each for the best radio play and radio story.

The competition was just part of a larger event.

On August 7 1990 something rather unusual happened in Moscow: a partnership agreement was signed between *Gosteleradio* and *Deutsche Welle*.

Here is how Yelena Tumolskaya described her visit to the *Deutsche Welle* office in the weekly *Kuranty* (July 31, 1991):

> Our vigilant propaganda portrayed *Deutsche Welle* as something closely guarded and top secret. You won't even find its office, it said. But I found it. As it turned out, that was not hard to do, since the three tall buildings of the radio station can easily be seen from downtown Cologne, looming like a lighthouse to the Southwest. My German guide joked that *Deutsche Welle* is like the Ostankino tower, only cut into three. That was right in a way: each of the office buildings is 138 meters high. Strangely for me, the Russian service was not its core element. At first I felt I was back in my country, for everybody spoke fluent Russian. It was a real island of Russian culture in Germany, for most of its employees were former USSR citizens. Editor of the Russian Service Nelli Kossko, with whom I talked there, comes from

Moldavia. Since there are no comrades there, she'd been called Frau Kossko for the past sixteen years. German by nationality, Frau Kossko moved to the country of her ancestors in 1975. She got a job with Deutsche Welle by chance. She first came into contact with the radio station when its correspondent had an interview with her. Similar paths led many other Soviet emigrants to the station. Of course, the new generation of emigrants finds it much harder to get employment.

"*Deutsche Welle* is considered a punctilious radio station," said Frau Kossko. "We are not as quick as the BBC or some other stations in reacting to political events, nor do we rush to praise or criticize. That's a reflection of the German character: we are meticulous and reserved. We broadcast less material from our own writers and more translations from the German press. That's one of the explanations why we don't have such recognized stars as Seva Novgorotsev at the BBC. I think he wouldn't be able to make a name for himself at our radio station at all, since we pursue a different style in presentation."

"Does that mean you prefer a go-slow approach and avoid sensationalism?"

"Well, at least we double-check any sensational news before putting it on the air, even if that takes time. My Russian department sometimes uses the services of correspondents in the USSR to get more reliable information. But in this case I often have to interfere, since your journalists present their materials differently from the way we are accustomed to in the West. In Russia, you give preference to emotions over hard facts. I remember an incident with one young journalist from Moscow. He prepared material for us about the events in Lithuania and had a lot of interesting information at his disposal. But he laid emphasis on the description of... winter, dreamy trees, grey skies—trying to draw parallels between the political situation in the Baltics and the weather. Consequently, his report looked more like a weather forecast.

There are thirty-four language departments in *Deutsche Welle*. So there is nothing strange about the fact that Arabic, English, Portuguese as well as Russian should be heard in its corridors.

The German department is doubtlessly the main one. It does not only radio, but also television broadcasts, primarily news programs. In this respect, DW is No. 1 in Germany."

"Does the government control the programs of DW?"

"There is no censorship like that in the Soviet Union. But the radio station is legally responsible for authenticity and correctness of its information.

Deutsche Welle is free and has the status of an independent public organization. It's financed by the federal government of Germany.

We no longer regard *Deutsche Welle* as an "enemy voice". The DW treats the Soviet Union objectively and amicably. Recently, on the initiative of some of its employees, the editors sent several consignments of free gifts for distribution in Moscow's orphanages and old-age homes in Latvia. I believe that the Germans are sincere in their desire to help us through our times of trouble.

In September 1990 many Soviet newspapers took advantage of a lack of censorship to report on an unusual public meeting held by *Radio Liberty*'s editorial board.

Among the speakers in Kiev were editor of the program Human Rights and member of the Ukrainian Helsinki group, Vladimir Malenkovich, regular RL contributor Davy Arkadiev and numerous other writers well-known from afar to grateful Soviet "midnight listeners", whose number is estimated by RL to exceed 50 million.

As it turned out, glasnost is in slightly short supply in the Ukraine: what the Western stations say remains highly topical. People were falling over each other to get into the meeting. Everyone wanted to hear the unofficial version of Sakharov's death, find out about what Vladimir Ivashko, the then CPSU Central Committee deputy general secretary and former Ukrainian prime minister, got up to when he was a military advisor in Afghanistan, and so on...

Asked about RL's future, Malenkovich replied: "There is much more strident criticism in your media now than in our broadcasts. But the view from outside, so far, continues to justify itself. When all the barriers disappear, every Soviet citizen will be able to travel abroad and see with his own eyes. Then, possibly, the need for *Radio Liberty* might disappear. But there's still a long way to go".

For years, people in the USSR went without sleep at night, in order to catch, between bursts of jamming, snatches of Western "radio voices", to use the Soviet term for them, with news of events in their and other countries. Under Stalin anyone caught doing so was thrown into jail, under Khrushchev and Brezhnev it was forbidden to discuss what you had heard, and the authorities dealt ruthlessly with all who distributed information gleaned from foreign radio and actively hunted the original sources. Nonetheless, Western taxpayers' money was not spent in vain—any politically-active Soviet listener knew that he would be kept in touch with the international political and musical scene by the "voice" from London, that he could pick up US news from Washington, in-depth coverage of German and Eastern European news from Cologne via *Deutsche Welle*, and especially detailed coverage of Soviet affairs from Munich via *Radio Liberty*.

The Soviet press, while maintaining a dutiful silence, closely followed all these broadcasts and tried to respond to them—without mentioning the radio stations themselves. They did all they could; sent spies to those stations, blew up their transmitters and published stories about the lack of morals of the emigres working for them; jammed the frequencies of "the enemy's programs" and produced useless receivers by the million and terrorized all who tuned in. To no avail. People would arrive at work in the morning and with trusted friends surreptitiously exchange views on what they had heard the night before. Meanwhile, in the Communist Party's higher educational establishments and in other "humanities" faculties hundreds of "scholars" and Party workers were laboring over a plethora of articles and pamphlets on "counter-propaganda" and "effective counteraction of bourgeois imperialist propaganda", on criticism of nationalism and popularization of "the ideals of communism". It was a flood of lies, which paid well, though.

For Soviet people, Western broadcasts were a ray of hope in this dark kingdom. Kremlin officialdom would use the information received for its own ends, while jammers howled ceaselessly (a very noisy motor would be placed in front of a microphone, and the resulting cacophany transmitted over the air). All Soviet cities, all the way down to district centers were "served" this way. Effective jamming, of course, is more expensive than broadcasting the target programs. For every dollar spent by *Voice of America*, hundreds more were spent on blocking it out.

But throughout the vast expanses of the Soviet Union there were plenty of places that were unaffected or simply left alone. The socialist countries of Eastern Europe, incidentally, never bothered to jam Western broadcasts because they knew it was pointless—the transmitters were too close to their borders. Somewhere in the countryside, say, near our western-most border, powerful receivers would pick up all radio broadcasts from the West in Russian and cable them to Moscow, to Pyatnitskaya Street and Gosteleradio's "radio interception" studios. A legion of transcribers, typists, editors and technicians would record it all on tape, decipher it and type it up in triplicate. A duty officer of the appropriate seniority would read all the news as it came in and report immediately to the Gosteleradio management, who would pass it on to the Party Central Committee and to the very top of the hierarchy. The directors of the Western stations, which were mostly run by governments or had extremely close links to the official establishments, knew perfectly well that any important announcement sent over the air in Russian would within minutes (at any time of day or night) end up on the desk of whoever in the Kremlin would find it particularly relevant and interesting at the given moment. This rapid-reaction system exists to this day.

A similar procedure to keep a written record of intercepted broadcasts in other languages of the Soviet Union was (and still is) followed in the republics. Only recently (in 1990) has Moscow begun to relay republican stations in other languages throughout the country. So far, the only language used in programs made in Moscow was Russian, no attempt was made to use the tongues of other nationalities. Yet the Americans broadcast to the USSR in twenty languages. Georgians, Armenians, Ukrainians, Balts and Central Asians listen carefully and with great interest to what their compatriots working for *Voice of America* and *Radio Liberty* have to say to them.

Russian-speaking Moscow journalists, when covering controversial and sometimes confusing aspects of the national-liberation movement in the former republics of the ex-USSR frequently misrepresent them due to ignorance of local conditions. There are vastly fewer such blunders with the Georgians (Uzbeks, etc) working for the appropriate services of *VOA* and *Radio Liberty*. While Moscow used its propaganda to impose its viewpoint and will on the republics, emigres in the USA simply informed their compatriots in the USSR, trying not to whip up events or provoke controversy.

Anybody in Georgia with even the slightest interest in politics has always known the names and voices of Marina Ellis (Ebralidze) at *VOA*'s Georgian service, and of Konstantin Nadirashvili at RL's Russian service. And now, in the newspapers *Vecherny Tbilisi* (Evening Tbilisi) (December 12, 1990) and *Molodyozh Gruzii* (Youth of Georgia) (August 31, 1990) he can see their photographs and read RFE (*Radio Free Europe*) special correspondent Vladimir Matusevich's reports from Oslo on the ceremonial presentation of Mikhail Gorbachev's 1990 Nobel Peace Prize. At times you feel you have to rub your eyes: *Vecherny Tbilisi*'s interview with Marina Ellis is accompanied on another page by a lengthy opinion column written by Matusevich. Neither I nor anyone else is in any doubt that the TASS report for the Soviet press of the same event in the Norwegian capital was brief, boring and uninformative. In any case, TASS will say nothing about how members of the Lithuanian, Latvian and Ukrainian Supreme Soviets and human rights activists from Russia and Moldova, speaking in Oslo, sharply criticized the choice of prizewinner.

President Yeltsin's Decree on Opening Bureaux of *Radio Liberty* in Russia

Of course we know that the Russian-language "imperialist" stations beaming their programs to us since the early 1950s, and the émigré journalists working for them uphold primarily the interests of the appropriate states, ie., their founders. He who pays the piper calls the tune. But we have no choice, we have to listen to the "enemy voices". And they, cunningly, strive to inform us about ourselves with as much objectivity as possible. They do their best. While our side has put out distorted half-truths. With the Communist Party press virtually destroyed, its place was filled by central (Moscow) radio and television up till September 1991. The audio-visual media, in the sixth year of perestroika, became the main buttress of presidential power, the voice of Moscow and all its centrist and hardline forces.

The émigré journalists of *RFE* were the voice of the opposition in Eastern Europe right until the complete rout of the communist parties there. The same is continuing here, in the Soviet Union; *Voice of America* and *Radio Liberty*, with support from others similar such as the *BBC* and *Deutsche Welle* were furthering and strengthening the influence of anti-communists, nationalists and other reformers, promptly providing them with a nationwide and, when necessary, a worldwide audience. If it were not for the efforts of *RFE* and *Radio Liberty* there would have been no Solidarity or Lech Walesa in Poland, nor Vaclav Havel nor even Boris Yeltsin. The communist parties that ruled nearly one third of the globe, from Eastern Europe to the Pacific, were faced in the second half of the 20th century with a powerful opposition in the form of anti-

Soviet and anti-communist radio stations in Munich and their no less competent colleagues at a good dozen or so other Western broadcasting centers.

We have more than enough transmitting stations. According to the *Pravitelstvenny Vestnik*, issue No. 1, January 1991, about 2000 Soviet jamming stations with a capacity from 5 to 200 kw each had been used to protect the air over the entire territory of the country from the "mischief" of foreign radio stations. Two hundred jammers were then converted to re-transmit programs from the union republics to Moscow, another two hundred to ensure short-wave communications for the military, navy, police, etc., and eighty more were put at the disposal of Radio Moscow world service. Five hundred stations were put in cold storage, and the rest scrapped.

In 1990, Russia lifted a ban on the production of radios with frequency bands below 25 meters. The prohibition had been dictated by economic reasons: the absence of receivers with a range from 13 to 25 meters allowed the jammers to save money by not needing to interfere with those wavelengths. But for all those positive developments, jamming continued, albeit in a modernized form. Instead of a harsh noise, jamming stations put music or some other less objectionable sounds on to interfere with western radio broadcasts. KGB agent Oleg Tumanov, who worked at a radio station for many years, used Orwellian newspeak to describe the jamming situation in a TV documentary broadcast on April 7, 1991 by USSR central television. He said: "Jamming practically stopped in 1988". Translation from newspeak: jamming continued.

We are aware of our radio problems. But what about "them"? At *Radio Liberty*, they are not absolutely free either. Here is what the director of *Radio Liberty*'s Russian Service, Vladimir Matusevich had to say when questioned by editor-in-chief of Moscow-based *Stolitsa* magazine, Andrei Malgin (*Stolitsa*, No. 24, June 24, 1991):

—Has anything changed at your station lately? Have you changed your orientation or tone?

—Of course we have. Until a few years ago, we had been virtually isolated from the Soviet Union. In three months, we would receive only one letter from a listener—usually an insulting one from the KGB. We did not know how many or what kind of people listened to us.

—Do you know that now?

—We do, more or less. Being a film critic, I used to attend a lot of film festivals. My former acquaintances from the Soviet Union would avoid meeting me at them at any cost. Should anybody start a conversation with me—someone like Georgy Kapralov or Rostislav Yurenev—I immediately felt who authorized the contact, and why they needed it.

—We heard little from our audience and that was very discouraging. That brought down our standards, because we did not feel answerable. Now that has changed. We know we have millions of listeners.

—When I took a job with the radio station, I found some of the people from the first generation of Russian emigre still working there. They were already old and were few. But Victor Frank, Vladimir Varshavski, Gaido Gazdanov and some others from the first wave set the tone. The majority came with the second wave of emigration, but there were people who came even later—during and after WWII. The third wave came in the mid-1970s to meet with a chilly reception from those of the second wave. Their hostility was justified, too, because our American bosses paid little attention to the professional standards of the new recruits. Newcomers were accepted on the principle "Profession: Russian", irrespective of their background before emigration. We had professional accountants, career military, engineers and what not. So many chance people without talent were taken on. Their incompetence and helplessness have been especially evident over the past few years of perestroika reforms. Fortunately, now we have many talented employees and people with natural journalistic skills.

—When perestroika came about and the jamming of *Radio Liberty* stopped, how were these events greeted by the staff? You said that a sense of responsibility had developed.

—That does not properly describe what happened. In fact, we were deeply shaken and launched our own reforms. Back then we operated alongside Soviet news media outlets and, like it or not, competition followed. It is widely held now that our audience is the largest in the USSR, even though we have never pandered to the listeners and have never tried to woo them the way *Voice of America* does, broadcasting youth programs hosted by a fake disc jockey, who in broken Russian reads the memoirs of Michael Jackson. We have not descended that low.

—How many letters does *Radio Liberty* receive from the Soviet Union?

—I don't know the exact figure, but I think about sixty a week. Unfortunately, we have no proper system for handling mail.

—Inconceivable. You do run a major research center, don't you?

—Yes, we do. But it's predominantly concerned with information from the Soviet press, monitoring and analyzing Soviet television and radio broadcasts, studying official statements, and news agency reports. The people there are doing a very good job.

—Do they read our magazine too?

—They give it very careful perusal. To return to correspondence, I'm glad to see many letters from young listeners—like students and ordinary workers from remote provinces. They have a clear understanding of everything and come up with very sound and interesting arguments.

—Can you identify the type of listener you cater for?

—No, I can't. We cater for all tastes. Admittedly, we do political programs, for the most part, and if a person has absolutely no interest in politics, he or she would hardly be our regular listener. But to the best of my knowledge, the number of such people in the Soviet Union is diminishing.

—For all that, your broadcasts are not all about politics. You broadcast many special programs on culture and politics. You broadcast many special programs on culture and produce a few regular ones on ethnic relations.

—When perestroika and glasnost started, we got worried. It seemed to us that the Soviet news media were breathing down our neck. But now we've calmed down, as the Soviet newspapers and magazines, as well as television and radio, steer clear of the more sensitive issues, such as race relations and related controversies. The weekly *Soyuz* is trying to do something in this respect, but it has a small circulation. Central Television simply lies about the events in the republics, whereas our aim is to provide full and unbiased coverage.

As far as culture is concerned, I was once at daggers drawn with many members of the Russian service staff who used to underrate the importance of the cultural dimension. Politics are organic to our cultural programs, but are regarded as being outside the primitively interpreted context of current events. I know for certain, for example, that the daily program *Poverkh baryerov* (Over the Barriers) has a large audience, and not only among intellectuals.

—Yet another merit of *Radio Liberty* is that it provides an insight into the events here from a different perspective. A detached view unaffected by any personal or group ambitions is very useful. Lately, you have been working with more and more contributors from the Soviet Union. Some programs—like *V strane i mire* (In the Country and the World) and *Aspekty* (Aspects)—consist entirely of telephone reports from Soviet correspondents. Of course, this makes broadcasting more lively. But isn't there a risk of losing the lively. But isn't there a risk of losing the advantages which I've just mentioned? You don't perceive the danger of turning into a mouthpiece of particular social forces in the Soviet Union, do you?

—This danger does exist. So we have to know where to stop. But we wouldn't be able to do without the help of our correspondents and contributors from around the Soviet Union. Normally we give them assignments, asking them to report on a particular issue. Some have failed to meet our expectations and we have parted company, but others have proved to be excellent reporters, participating in our programs day in, day out.

—Do you pay them for their services?

—We do, just as your magazine pays its contributors. It's common practice, isn't it?

—Just about every hour *Radio Liberty* reminds its listeners that it is funded by the Congress of the United States. As far as I can judge from our press, Congress, and indeed the American news media, occasionally question the need for a radio station telling the Russians about themselves at a time when their country enjoys freedom of speech and sees the appearance of new papers, magazines, and broadcasters. To keep a radio station broadcasting around the clock in Russian, plus other languages spoken in the USSR, is a rather costly affair for American taxpayers. Is it possible that you'll be closed?

—I have often been asked this question, and every time I answer no, we're not afraid of being closed. People in the US will not allow themselves to be misled about Soviet glasnost or openness. The USSR still has a very long way to go to achieve true freedom of expression. Any doubts that may have arisen center on *Radio Free Europe*, which broadcasts in the languages of the former socialist nations of Europe (and now also in the languages of the Baltic republics). But recently, the presidents of Czechoslovakia and Poland asked the US Congress to continue funding *Radio Free Europe*. What's more, local stations in Prague, Warsaw and Sofia now relay Free Europe programs. During Congressional hearings a few days ago on the question of funding Free Europe, no one questioned the need for our station.

—Incidentally, a year ago president Bush praised the work of both stations. So the American government seems to be spending a lot of money to promote the development of democracy in other countries, doesn't it?

—Yes, that seems to be the case.

—Can this activity be qualified as interference in the internal affairs of other countries, this country in particular? Who is in a position to decide what processes in the country are favorable and should be encouraged and what trends are adverse and should be reversed? All this is pretty uncertain, isn't it?

—*Radio Liberty* and *Radio Free Europe* have from the first been regarded as substitutes for the national mass media. The need for substitutes will disappear when the Soviet media reach maturity, which will take some time. Even in a favorable setting, the Soviet Union will take decades to see the triumph of civilized democratic principles.

—Have the Russian service staff ever happened to be at odds with the policy of the American Administration?

—These things do happen. But there is what we call editorial control, which is exercised to resolve any controversies. The editor has the right to clear programs for broadcasting or ban them, and decides what parts of them should be scrapped and what should remain.

—Aren't you annoyed by constant control on the part of the Americans?

—Americans? I am an American citizen.

—I mean editor's control, censorship.

—Let's specify: editor's control or censorship?

—O.K., censorship.

—We've got no preliminary censorship. What we have is common editor's control. For instance, today I ordered that all material on the Armenia-Azerbaijan conflict be heard by me before going on the air. The current period is very explosive and delicate, any careless word could have serious implications. And I don't want anybody to accuse us once more of siding with only one of the warring parties. In this case I'm the highest authority and there'll be no other Americans.

Compared to the *Voice of America* we are not obliged to reflect the US government's views. In some programs we even had to criticize the stand of the American administration, especially when covering the Gulf war. But these are rare cases. Our main topic is Soviet, not American problems.

But still, when the political situation in the Soviet Union is so tense and the confrontation of social forces is heating up, you just can't avoid taking sides. The position of the democrats is, probably, closer to you than that of Gen. Makashov.

—No doubt.

—So that means you take sides.

—Now I understand what you're driving at. Our Russian service has a very motley staff. Take Vladimir Malinkovich. He's in charge of the "Barometer" program. And he's a genuine Centrist, sceptical about so-called radical democrats, and is showered with letters from supporters of Yeltsin, Afanasyev and Murashev. In these letters people try to make it clear to him that he works for the KGB, being on the US Congress payroll. What we have is pluralism, to use a fashionable term.

Of course, it has its limits. If one of the Russian service personnel likes to use *Radio Liberty* broadcasts for developing national-patriotic ideas in the spirit of the Pamyat society, I would bar him from the air with my powers.

—But you allowed Polozkov and the leaders of the Baltic Communists...to speak...

—That's another cup of tea. And this list is far from being complete... We give them the opportunity to dwell on their positions.

—And then you add your comments?

—Not as a rule. When the "*In the Country and the World*" program features Polozkov and Dzasokhov we provide no comments. They may follow in a different program. It depends upon the genre and the host. For instance, not long ago Fatima Salkazanova interviewed Tchekhoev, one of the Soyuz leaders. She is by nature a very aggressive journalist. She practically wrenches out the answers from her interlocutor and makes no bones about showing her attitudes.

My temper is different. When I interviewed Zviad Gamsakhurdia, I was trying to demonstrate my respect in every way and it's not my fault that Gamsakhurdia did not come out very well in that interview. That's the way he could tell his story.

Hardly anybody has doubts about our dislike of either Polozkov, or Petrushenko, Alksnis or Shved. Nevertheless they want nothing better than to make speeches via *Radio Liberty*. The same can well be applied to nationalist and patriotic-minded writers. No matter how hard we come down on them they still keep on pressing for the *Radio Liberty* rostrum.

—In short, though *Radio Liberty* is trying to remain unbiased, it still has its own stand...

—Of course we have. You've just asked about American control. We're financed by the US Congress and it would be strange for us to propagate ideas at variance with the letter and spirit of the US Constitution, basic principles of American foreign and domestic policy and traditional values of a democratic state. If I were, say, an orthodox Communist and worshipped Polozkov and Nina Andreyeva, I would obviously be unable to work in this agency. But I feel no inner constraints because my convictions match the basic principles I've just mentioned. I am sure the bulk of *Radio Liberty*'s Russian service staff can say the same of themselves.

Radio Liberty proved it was indispensable during the coup. Its two correspondents, Andrei Babitsky, 27, and Mikhail Sokolov, 29, conducted live round-the-clock broadcasting from the White House's eleventh floor all three days of the coup. On the terrible night from August 20 to 21, when an assault seemed inevitable, *Radio Liberty* was the only national and international mass media body able to tell about what was going on around the Russian Parliament.

The victory of democratic forces and the Communist Party withdrawal from the political arena immediately changed *Radio Liberty*'s official status in Russia. For the first time in international journalism an opening of a bureau was decreed by a head of state. Below is the interview with Vladimir Matusevich carried by the Moscow-based *New Times* weekly (No. 36, 1991).

August 27, the President of Russia Boris Yeltsin signed Decree 93 which reads: 'Following the request by the Board of *Radio Liberty/Free Europe*, an independent radio station financed by the US Congress, and taking into account its role in providing unbiased information to the citizens of the Russian Federation and the world public about the progress of democratic reform in Russia, about the events in the country and the world and the activities of the legitimate Russian Federation authorities during the coup in the USSR, I hereby decree: 1. To permit the independent *Radio Liberty/Free Europe* Board to open a permanent bureau in Moscow and correspondents' points on the territory of the Russian Federation...'

Konstantin Isakov, a *New Times* correspondent, talked to the head of *Radio Liberty*'s Russian service Vladimir Matusevich.

Matusevich: The decree came out of the blue. We arrived in Moscow with Savik Shuster without visas. They stamped them right in Sheremetievo airport on instructions from the Russian Foreign Minister.

I had not been in Russia for twenty three years and never thought of coming back. A flight to the Moon seemed more probable.

Incidentally, this is what KGB head Vladimir Kryuchkov wrote two months before the coup to Yuri Ryzhov, chairman of the USSR Supreme Soviet science committee, in response to the latter's request about KGB black lists: S. Shuster, citizen of Canada, is denied permission to enter the USSR .... because since 1988 he has been a staff member of the *Radio Liberty* Russian service, which is aimed at disrupting the Soviet constitutional system, and which prepares and broadcasts programs intended to discredit our system and the Soviet President.

Question: How did you learn about the coup?
Answer: I woke up at 6 a.m. Munich time when the head of the Russian newsroom phoned me. I could well understand he was absolutely serious and it was not an April fools' joke. But I still couldn't believe it. I switched on the TV. Instead of *Utro* (Morning) program, a TV host was reading out the statements by the State Emergency Committee. I rushed through the radio station and it struck my mind that this just could not be quite unexpected. In my mind's eye I recalled some past events and wondered why nobody had taken overt appeals for a military coup seriously.

I thought dictatorship had come for good. Yet in the radio station I met a woman from our research section and she said in a calm, steady voice that the coup was a matter of days.

When I saw that Yeltsin and his team were prepared for a last-ditch struggle, that the people that gathered around the White House were ready to protect Parliament with a human shield I understood Gorbachev's effort was not in vain. That man nearly worked wonders for his country. The people there could feel they were individuals.

Question: Do you think it is thanks to him?
Answer: In my estimation he is one of the greatest and most tragic figures of the 20th century. Despite all the monstrous, absurd and evil things associated with Gorbachev's rule, if it were not for him, there would be neither Yeltsin, nor these people by the White House.

Question: How did work proceed at *Radio Liberty* during the coup?

Answer: There was no heroism at all: people came to their studios and worked for days on end. I think we shouldn't even mention that: there's nothing special about more or less professional and honest work in remote and safe Munich.

Question: But you should have understood that you were the only source of information that could tell the truth to the entire Soviet Union?

Answer: Yes, we were quite aware of this. I'm awfully proud that *Radio Liberty*, unlike *BBC*, did not broadcast any report of Gorbachev's death. It seemed to me inadmissible in an extremely tense situation to go on the air with such an item, (an unconfirmed one at that) just for the sake of being the first.

Question: Of late the only Soviet agency that has kept on depicting *Radio Liberty* as a nest of spies and speaking of its anti-Soviet activity is the KGB. How do you see your relations with this department in future?

Answer: I rejoiced at the news that its new chief Vadim Bakatin provided the new head of radio and television Yegor Yakovlev with the list of KGB agents in the Soviet radio and TV company. I believe this is not for the sake of revenge, humiliation or destruction. Any journalist working for a newspaper or radio feels disgusted to know that somebody is informing on you all the time.

The new Czechoslovak authorities have given *Free Europe* a list of Czechoslovak KGB moles working there. Hopefully Bakatin has enough common sense to help us get rid of Oleg Tumanov's successors.

Evidently, on a signal from Moscow a month before the coup they stepped up their effort and did everything possible to make us, if not paralyzed, then at least ineffective during the coup.

Question: How did this show up?

Answer: Sorry, but I can't tell you more yet.

Question: But *Radio Liberty* continued to be an American radio station. Speaking of the KGB you can't avoid mentioning the CIA influence.

Answer: There is no direct connection, as far as I can see. But I understand the need for intelligence is still there. The KGB will, obviously, build up its presence in the CIA, the Pentagon and electronics corporations. Well, an American radio station has no secrets for the KGB to find out for the sake of USSR national security. Why should the KGB keep agents there who endanger its reputation and fan internal strife?

Question: The USSR has now lifted all restrictions on the press. Are you afraid of competition?

Answer: Two or three years ago when we saw a breakthrough in publishing previously banned literature I had similar apprehensions. But in precisely those years our listeners grew in number. In my opinion, to compete in the level of professionalism is wonderful. Secondly, its a long way before the press stops "taking sides" or seeking firm support. I think the word "independent" should be more and more associated with *Radio Liberty*. That will be our trademark in the boundless sea of information.

CHAPTER IX

TV STARS

Eduard Sagalayev, Tatiana Mitkova, Yuri Rostov vs. President of the USSR

In 1989 presenters reading out TASS (governmental news agency) reports began to be replaced by commentators and anchors. The results of the change were not long in coming. A huge number of TV journalists became household names overnight... and won seats on the Soviet national parliament, republican parliaments and local power structures.

Channel 1 of Soviet Central TV covered virtually the whole country. Channel 2 reached a slightly lower number of viewers for technical reasons, and in 1989 and 1990 for the for technical reasons, and in 1989 and 1990 for the first time ever in Soviet history it covered live the many-day Congresses of People's Deputies, USSR Supreme Soviet sessions and national conferences and the Soviet Communist Party congress; Channel 3 broadcast only in Moscow and the Moscow Region and Channel 4 was educational.

An opinion poll conducted by Moscow's *Literaturnaya Gazeta* among its readership named Vladimir Molchanov the best 1989 anchorman on Soviet Central TV. And the second most-popular program of the year was live coverage from the Kremlin, according to the readers. I am quite sure that two or three political observers following the free-and-easy western news observer style could be giving terse and equally interesting coverage of such parliamentary debates. But at that time, firstly, purely political TV programs continued to be plagued by the dreary style typical of newspapers such as *Pravda*, and secondly, many parliamentarians queued up in front of the mikes to tell home truths, and what they said was a cri-de-coeur, not just another propaganda play based on speeches prepared and approved by the Communist Party Central Committee.

It can be claimed that radical changes did not take place on Soviet TV— and in the Soviet Communist Party—before late August 1991. Both have been in disarray and losing prestige and authority—yet neither has really mended its ways, nor repented for the torrents of falsehood and the years of ideological terror they caused.

The powerful state machine having a monopoly on the sale of vodka, the issue of money and on TV and radio information did not intend to share this right with anyone else. I even can provide an illustration of this. Moscow's new mayor Gavriil Popov, a USSR Supreme Soviet's deputy whose vigor is now proverbial, was very eager to have the daily program Dobry Vecher, Moskva! reflect the new alignment of political forces. The administration of Moscow TV responded—on instructions from the Party—by taking off the program the most popular anchormen, including Georgi Kuznetsov, one of the Moscow TV audiences' favorites.

Urmas Ott with his brilliant interviews was a very rare guest on national TV. This show appeared only on red-letter days.

But the biggest scandal was when the Sunday news program *7 Days*, a universal favorite, was given the axe. Following is an excerpt from an item by Eduard Sagalayev, then editor-in-chief of the Main Department of Information of the USSR Central TV that appeared in No. 16, 1990, of the daily *Argumenty i Fakty*:

> TV program *7 Days* went on the air on November 12, 1989, and passed away on March 4, 1990. In its lifetime of less than 4 months the program received more than 20,000 supportive letters.
>
> The program was dropped by an order of the Soviet State Committee for Radio and Television that said: "In view of the growing volume of information on the home and foreign scene and a complex socio-political situation in the country", *Vremya* will again be on the air on Sundays, and the program *7 Days* will be broadcast at a different time.
>
> Our mail indicates that 99% of the writers of the letters disagreed with the sudden disappearance of the program. And for those wishing to be objective, below are the results of an opinion poll conducted by the National Center for the Study of Public Opinion (Russian acronym: VCIOM) under the All-Union Central Council of Trade Unions and the USSR State Committee for Labor: only 2% of TV viewers opposed the replacement of *Vremya* by *7 Days* on Sunday.
>
> Taking account of the public need for a Sunday program, we were willing to go on the air at a later time. But the administration of the State Committee for Radio and Television laid down one condition: the program was to broadcast without one of the anchormen, Tikhomirov. Given the situation, the program team regards the restoration of *7 Days* as unethical.
>
> Such is the situation today. We support *7 Days* going on the air as soon as possible again."

The TV program *Vremya* was again going on the air every day. It was always my impression that its announcers read out an issue of *Pravda* (or the French Communist "L'Humanité")—and one edited by Politburo member Yegor Ligachev at that or by the glorious General Rodionov (who massacred a peaceful demonstration in Tbilisi in April 1989 and bragged about the great victory in the USSR Supreme Soviet). And what I wished to see was a screen equivalent of *Ogonyok, Moscow News, The Times* or *The Washington Post*, not everyday lies about the developments in the Union republics.

"Alternative TV. Yes or No?" was the topic of a debate in the *Literaturnaya Gazeta* office on May 5, 1990, that attracted the most popular of the Soviet anchor people.

"**V. Tsvetov.** Never in its entire history has Soviet TV been run by people who rose through the ranks on TV itself. Nor is that much of a problem. In Japan a minister is never a professional: one is health minister today and foreign minister tomorrow. A minister is a politician who takes political decisions. But apart from the top slot, a ministry is staffed by professionals, while we have legions of amateurs at all levels of the power structure. Dmitry Zakharov presented in the magazine *Ogonyok* a vivid picture of a chief who confuses "a paragraph" with a "news item". A cameraman would prepare to shoot an art show and would say he needs an hour to position the lamps, and his chief asks, why when, a still photographer over there does the job in five minutes.

When the 2nd Congress of People's Deputies discussed the Tbilisi unrest on April 9, 1989, it decided against broadcasting the proceedings. However, TV cameramen were shooting the meeting. When the Georgian delegation was walking out of the hall in protest, the cameras showed close-ups of the faces of the delegates who stayed back in the hall, as if nothing was happening; that is, at the very moment when history was being made, it was being distorted!

In 10 or 20 years' time this moment may be considered a milestone in the history of relations between Georgia and the Soviet Union, but the lack of professionalism on TV has already buried the moment. An amateur is different from a professional in that the former is only a destroyer, whereas the latter first destroys and then creates. The second danger plaguing Soviet TV is its "Kashpirovization" (after Kashpirovsky, a popular faith healer). TV is beset with all sorts of magicians. I command, says Kashpirovsky, sit in front of the TV set, fold your arms and wait. I will save you from physical diseases, social crises, economic troubles. Don't move. Don't do anything. This is a Lysenko mentality of sorts (Lysenko was an quack agronomist in Stalin's and later Khrucshev's period), but in the field of human spirit, not agriculture. In contrast, *Vzglyad* and *Do i Posle Polunochi* urge people to be active: think, fight, they say, no one's going to save you except yourselves, so you must take action. And that's a position some people on TV dislike.

I. Fesunenko. Today TV must catch up with the level society is reaching. Until very recently we were in effect an organ of ideological structures that all too often supervise our work far more closely than we would want it to be supervised. Here's an example: On April 11, 1990, or two days after the troops broke up a mass demonstration, I flew to Tbilisi to cover the developments and, as my instructions went, "to try to calm things down". Even in the first interviews I took, people were asking bitterly: who ordered the use of gas against the demonstrators? And any mention of the use of gas in our coverage was cancelled in Moscow. As a result, when the Georgians watched the coverage in *Vremya*, passions flared up, rather than calming down. The "overly close" supervision by censors was counterproductive. The lesson is clear: journalists working in the epicenter of events must be trusted more. And another: TV must stop being the mouthpiece of apparatchiks. We should return to an idea expressed at the 1st Congress of People's Deputies: the State Committee for Radio and Television must be accountable to a parliament that expresses the whole spectrum of public opinion, at least theoretically.

V. Molchanov. What and how we can say is both an important and often insoluble question. For example, I'm horrified when I have to handle the whole program *Vremya* on my own. How can we comment on the Baltic developments? For example, I'm unable to make the kind of comments TASS wants me to make. If our journalists sent to the Baltics were given a free hand, they would make No coherent comments. And our directorate would not allow comments from local journalists. It would be far easier for me—I mean, for conscience' sake—to comment on the program's international news than to appear a fool who comments on the home scene but doesn't have the slightest idea of what's going on in the country.

V. Pozner. Once again, a professional approach is imperative. It's quite clear that any permanent program must be produced by a permanent team. The program *Vremya* must have permanent teams and this arrangement will provide for competition between them. What's the point in today's reshuffles of personnel? Or take *120 Minutes*—the program with the biggest audience, I believe. Everywhere—Britain, the US, Italy—such a program would be produced by a single crew. Its staff go to bed at 9:00 p.m. and wake up at 5:00 a.m. This is their way of life five days a week. But do you know what salaries they draw for their exhausting work? And how much are the makers of *120 Minutes* paid?

The State Committee for Radio and Television, the way it is structured now, is the product of a certain stage in the development of a society that is, basically speaking, not interested in professionals. And now, when this society seeks to change its face, professionalism is running foul of the huge rock of unprofessionalism. This is increasingly often the case on TV today."

There are honest journalists on TV who do not believe that "a clear conscience" is just an empty phrase, who are willing to stick to their opinion, no matter how hard their chiefs seek to break them (there was no alternative TV in existence at that time, and the central TV was at the beck and call of the ideology department of the Communist Party Central Committee). Below is the opinion of yet another well-known Soviet Central TV employee.

Eduard Sagalayev who was separated from his brainchildren on two occasions (*7 Days* and a year earlier, another of his programs, the very popular *12th Floor*, was closed down by the authorities) gave a magnificent interview to *Izvestia* on April 6, 1990.

Today the Central TV's Channel 1 has a potential audience of 96% of the national population, and Channel 2, 72.5%. And Channel 4, the only option for the alternative TV, can reach some 10% of the population. A meagre 10%! And now question No. 2, a far more important one. What will become of the other, the "main"

TV if alternative TV becomes the only vehicle of free expression? Following this logic, 10% of the audiences will watch a creative, intelligent and independent TV, and the rest of the Soviet people will have to make do with the dreary, drab, watered-down and bombastic official TV.

By the way, the chairman of the USSR State Committee for Radio and Television (Gostelradio) Nenashev also supports the idea of an "alternative" TV in the February 5, 1990, issue of *Pravda*. To be sure, he pursues a slightly different goal. He also agrees to the need "to allow the creation, alongside state TV, of an alternative TV reflecting the views and opinions of various public organizations and groups. It would be clear in this case who's who and who urges what. The stand of the Soviet Committee for Radio and Television would be better-defined and understandable."

I'm afraid that this project aimed at disowning those who "urge the wrong thing" will defeat, not promote, state TV which dozens of millions of people are forced to watch whether they desire it or not.

The selfsame article by the chairman of Gosteleradio calls into question the very possibility of reflecting on TV a wide spectrum of opinions. It says: "Many of our difficulties... stem from the fact that we seek to harmonize and reconcile within the state TV different social stances, views and approaches that exist now thanks to democracy and pluralism in society." This thesis implies a need for an alternative TV, which would force pluralism beyond the bounds of the state TV.

But is our country not embracing the principles of political pluralism and a multi-party system? If Soviet TV is indeed a people's TV in a people's country, it simply has to reflect the entire spectrum of public opinion.

But in actual fact, our policy is very often anti-popular and anti-state. You think I'm overstating the issue? As if it does not matter whether people see this or that particular news item. But when, for example, there are pogroms in Baku every day, and we keep silent, we do huge damage both to the Armenians and to the Azeris, and to all other nations in this country. I emphasize: I'm only speaking of straightforward information, not comment or opinion. People want Vremya to be a source of information about the country and the world, not the authorities' opinion about what they believe the country and the world should be like.

<u>The policy of silence and of covering up some facts and neglecting others robs everybody, from the man-in-the-street to the President, of objective information, and objective information is a reliable pillar of any power structure and any administrator. Using biassed information is tantamount to taking a road to behind the Looking-Glass.</u> [underlined by author–G.V.]

And yet, I'd also like to dream of what future TV will be like. I'm an educationalist, not a politician, by inclination, and I developed my ideas when I was under the influence of very interesting work on our educational TV program.

I see it as a TV college. I believe, it would be a noble mission for us to gradually expand our audience and produce cassette recordings of the most successful films. I hope that with time our people will have in their homes video libraries containing not only *Red Heat* but also English language courses, world cultural history, the best cinema and theatre productions... But all of this has to be collected and purchased, hard work is needed so that an individual can see it on screen and want to have it at home. This public channel should look into the future, even if not a too distant future.

In the 21st century an individual should have computer literacy, know what's what in business, master two foreign languages at least, know the *Bible*, myths, philosophy, i.e., a Soviet individual should be able to hold his own with nationals in any other country in intellectual, ethical, physical and other terms. I understand that TV alone is not up to this formidable task. Yet, it can also do its bit. How is this for an alternative to an alternative TV?"

Understandably enough, the new Chairman Kravchenko and Sagalayev clashed. Eduard Sagalayev was elected head of the Union of Journalists of the USSR in the first democratic elections, held in 1991. Shortly afterwards he quit his job in TV. In August 1991, when Kravchenko was forced to resign and the USSR President appointed Yegor Yakovlev of *Moscow News* as new Chairman of the All-Union TV & Radio Broadcasting Company, Sagalayev became his second in command. In order to understand this young man better, here is an interview with him, taken by Yelena Chekalova and published in *Moscow News* No. 29 (3484), 1991. It is called "*Godfather*" and includes a long insert listing all of Sagalayev's posts:

Eduard Sagalayev, now 45, Chairman of the Union of Journalists, former head of the youth editorial office of Central TV, former director of the *Vremya* news program, former Vice-Chairman of Russian State Committee for Radio and Television (Gosteleradio) and author of the abortive project TV-21st Century, was the "godfather" of many of Central TV's achievements in the 1980s: "*Veselye Rebyata*" (Jolly Fellows), "*12th Floor*", "*Vzglyad*", "*7 Days*" and "*TSN*" (televised news service). Now his name is associated with the newest TV sensation—a project run by the first private telecorporation.

Sagalayev is certainly the head of a TV clan. As soon as a new project appeared a new team had to be formed. The project could be one of Sagalayev's own ideas, or come "from below", with Sagalayev acting as sponsor. But his involvement always made the survivors rush to offer their services. And there are few such people in Central TV.

It's his calling to be a patron, as reflected in the nicknames he has been accorded at Ostankino studios: Saggy (after the pattern of Ronnie and Gorby, by the youth program's office), or simply Sam (Sagalayev Eduard Mikhailovich, by *Vremya* news program).

At a plenum of the Moscow City Party Committee, Sergei Tarasov, deputy secretary of the party committee at the State Company for Television and Radio Broadcasting, angrily remarked that Central TV was full of Sagalayev's anti-party personnel. The main "TV boss" of the late 1980s now occupies the well-appointed study of the head of our professional Union, who is busy "else where". Sagalayev has changed his establishment—style blue suit for striking casual outfits. The last time we met—about a year and a half ago—I came away deeply disappointed: he answered curtly on the reasons for the closure of the 7 Days program and then hysterically withdrew the material before publication.

"Why did you do this?" I felt obliged to start with something which had affected me personally.

Answer: At that time I still believed in the salutary nature of compromises and round tables. I also believed that one could in the long run come to terms with the leadership of Gosteleradio. For a very long time I clung to the hopes that party-and government-dominated TV could become state-owned and even people-owned. When I finally realized that Central TV belonged to the party apparatus I quit. It's a type of slavery which requires you to sacrifice everything—even your personal life. I remember one of my last talks with the first vice-chairman. I asked him where the order to conceal information about Chernobyl came from. His reply was: the party. And the lie about the miners' strike? I was told: that was the party, too. He proudly sacrificed even his own honor for the sake of party fraternity.

Question: Have you now left the party?
Answer: No, I haven't.
Question: Why not, if you're so disappointed in it?
Answer: I've never been satisfied with it, either. No one has—this is all rubbish. I don't see anything positive in simply leaving the party. Moreover, I can't rid myself of a feeling of guilt. For so many years I enjoyed privileges... Now I must help prevent any new destructive move made by the party apparatus.
Question: But what if you came to understand that this was yet another illusion?
Answer: All things considered, our whole life is spent parting with illusions. I once applauded "perestroika." I nearly worshipped Gorbachev. Now I know that no one is going to grant me freedom and independence. The road to freedom traverses all the paths we have endured—compromises with our conscience, prison camps and hatred. Tolstoy used to say that there had been several Tolstoys during his long life, but the real one only existed in his final years. This can be said of anyone. In the past two years I've become a different Sagalayev. Maybe not the one I'd like to be. But at any rate I seem to have discarded many character traits I'm ashamed of.
Question: For example?
Answer: Well, first and foremost, the readiness to compromise with my conscience. I don't do this so readily now.
Question: Are you quite sure that you've severed your links with the party?
Answer: I was recently asked: what would I do if I was offered Kravchenko's post? I can't, of course, provide a firm guarantee that I'd refuse it. Weakness forms part of human nature. But I still have plenty of ambition. I'm comforted by just one thing: "they" will Nolonger offer me this kind of temptation.
Question: Do you mean "they" are disappointed in you?

Answer: Absolutely. They see their kith and kin in anyone who says one thing in private, something else in public, and then acts altogether differently. Such are their corporate ethics. Unpredictability is the main vice for them. And they know that Sagalayev might come up with anything. He'll accept a top post with special privileges and suddenly imagine he's a free man. That he never sold himself.

Question: When did they lose faith in you?

Answer: It was gradual. The *12th Floor* program was discussed twice by the Politburo, and *7 Days* was actually taken off the air after a decision by the Politburo. When I was forced to leave my job at the youth editorial office and given the post of chief editor of the *Vremya* news program, it was a chance for me to strike roots in the system. After all, the system needs competent, professional people. And without undue modesty I'm fairly good at doing whatever I put my mind to.

Question: Does this explain the career of a boy from Samarkand?

Answer: Yes, it does. I got into the public eye and a role was allotted to me. The system has been built in accordance with biological laws. It requires not only executives and slaves, but also high priests, guardians and leaders. As well as people with ideas. I can soberly appraise my creative potential. And I'm aware of my limitations, too. There is one indisputable quality in me: I am able to recognize and value talented people.

Question: Yes, you discovered Lyubimov, Politkovsky and Listyev. You made a star out of modest behind-the-screen editor Tanya Mitkova. But why do all these talented people feel, as well as gratitude, that you abandoned them at the most difficult moment?

Answer: If they really think so, they are simply naive—in the best way, of course. Like everyone else, I'm involved in a constant struggle with myself. I also have the elementary desire to survive. The point is that people forgive weaknesses in themselves, but not in their leaders. What did they expect me to do? Go to the stake? Would they have followed me? Let them answer that one first. I'm not sure they would have done. But I've never demanded this of anyone. The demands were made solely of me.

Question: What do you mean by "go to the stake"?

Answer: In Soviet terms I mean being left without work and forfeiting the possibility of influencing social changes.

Question: And you could no longer conceive of yourself in a position of "No influence"? Would you be happy as a rank-and-file journalist?

Answer: I'm a fatalist. My destiny has probably taken its optimal shape. In my youth I worked in a city newspaper, wrote poems, even dreamed of becoming a writer. But my own taste ran into conflict with my creative efforts. In all probability, organizing creative processes—something I've been doing for most of my life—is what I do best.

Question: You've never suffered any real loss. Things have never been really that bad for you.
Answer: And you'd very much like me to be in a bad way, pass through a period of failure, or better still, tragedy, wouldn't you? External prosperity is always external. The most important things, as we all know, are tranquillity and freedom. And in this sense I'm less content than many others. I can't say I've suffered unduly. But there are things which it's impossible to change and which it's impossible to break free from.
Question: So perhaps it would be better if you forgave yourself for everything and started living a normal life—from scratch, as it were?
Answer: I've thought of this on more than one occasion. But I consider that one way of forgiving myself is fulfilled by doing something.
Question: What have you and your Union done for TV journalists who have lost the chance to work on the air owing to their convictions?
Answer: It has never been the purpose of the Union of Journalists to defend its members. We lodged an official protest in defense of Lithuania's TV journalists who had their place of work guarded by sub-machine guns—but what's the use? To become effective, the Union must be transformed into a trade union, which stands up for its members' interests vis-a-vis the employer. But this process will probably take some time before it actually bears fruit. I'm sick and tired of hitting my head against a brick wall. I've decided to try out a different method—to build something entirely new which will ultimately oust the old.
Question: The current project was ironically referred to as "private television named after Sagalayev" in the newspaper *Rabochaya Tribuna*.
Answer: Just imagine: even after this hostile article and similar rejoinders on radio and TV, I have been showered with proposals.
Question: But *Rabochaya Tribuna* believed that "private enterprise" would make the public indignant, didn't it?
Answer: Yes, it did, but things have turned out to be quite the opposite. I understand that something very serious has occurred in our society. People are tired of state monopolies—including the one on information. Today they are more willing to believe a private individual than a state which adapts TV to serve its own interests.
Question: So you're really opening up a private TV service?
Answer: No, of course not. I'm thinking of setting up the first TV corporation free of state ownership. The founders will, as a rule, invest not money but instead intellectual talents.
Question: And you will be the president?
Answer: Yes.
Question: Will you name the principal shareholders?
Answer: No one will have a controlling interest, not even foreign partners. Negotiations are underway with the scientific-industrial union headed by

Volsky, involving Moscow's mayor, Vladimir Pozner and Tatiana Mitkova. But it's still too early yet to publish the list of founders.

Question: What does the new creative concept mean?

Answer: This must be TV for viewers. Every program will be tested by its ratings. In actual fact the concept has been developed as part of the educational project TV-21st century, complemented by a news service which must be the main component of broadcasting. I would like to create TV with a high degree of spectator credibility, which can only be achieved in a non-governmental structure, as the desire to impose its own image is natural for any government, whether it be totalitarian or democratic.

Question: Sounds interesting. Incidentally, all your previous ideas were also attractive...

Answer: You know, every one of us still has opportunities ahead of him. In the past I rarely thought about death. Now I live with thoughts about it. And just imagine, I have become much happier—in the sense that I'm getting rid of unnecessary vanity. As long as you live there's opportunity. Every new day will become your past tomorrow.

After the tragic events in Lithuania in January 1991, intelligent (upright) people started leaving Central TV—some of them not of their own free will. Such men as Kravchenko and Reshetov, Kakuchaya and others, held on to their positions until late August. All professionals, who adhere to principles, were either sacked or escaped to the newly-established Russian TV. On March 19, 1991, *Nezavisimaya Gazeta* dedicated half of its front page to an interview with Tatiana Mitkova and Dmitry Kiselev from the TSN television news service, called *Farewell to Evening News. Popular TV Presenters Tatiana Mitkova, Yuri Rostov and Dmitry Kiselev Have Been Prohibited from Working. This Has Brought to an End the Best News Program on Central TV.*:

Question: Was TSN devised as an alternative news service? Or did it just happen that way?

Mitkova: The idea originated long ago. We have always believed that a news program was required which would differ from *Vremya* both in style and content. But the word "alternative" was not fashionable then. It only came in when Eduard Sagalayev was appointed chief editor. And his coming paved the way for the idea.

Question: Is it true that Alexander Gurnov was the founding father?

Mitkova: No, it would not be quite right to say so. The program was in fact created by many people, but Sasha was the first to present it to TV audiences. But, if we compare the first issues of TSN in the autumn of 1989 and those, for example, which were made last summer, you'll see that there is a truly amazing difference. You might remember that TSN was initially designed to satisfy common inquisitiveness, and hence offered scandals, sensations, criminal news, etcetera. But in January last year Yuri Rostov and I joined the program, each with our own individual style. Yet the general style remained unchanged. But gradually, month after month, TSN became a more and more serious program.

Question: Is it true that before the Lithuanian developments in January this year nobody controlled what you wanted to say on the air?

Mitkova: None of our superiors did. Yet we did not regard ourselves as partisans fighting the enemy. On the contrary, we felt an enormous responsibility, because we were trusted so much.

But one day last summer we suddenly sensed that TSN had reached a new class altogether, that news is a very serious business, and politics even more so. Before that we hardly had any idea of what televised news is.

Question: And what is it?

Mitkova: Frankly, I don't like definitions. But I think that televised news should be precise, specific and must always refer to sources. It should provide the maximum pictures with a minimum of "talking heads."

Question: Do you mean that TSN is what televised news should be?

Kiselev: We have not invented anything from the viewpoint of world journalism. It is just a professional news program, just like any other in the world. But it was a discovery for Soviet TV. We had the Main Department of Information, but we did not have a single news program.

Question: What about *Vremya*?

Kiselev: It's an ideological tumor.

Question: Are news and ideology incompatible?

Kiselev: It is only natural that the news program of the first state-owned channel should reflect the diversity of opinions and ideologies existing in society. Yet facts should take precedence over opinions. Although opinions themselves can sometimes be facts. When Yeltsin says that Gorbachev should resign, his opinion is a fact of political life, which deserves mention.

We should simply report things that influence people's lives. For example, they show the sowing campaign. First, the collective farm system will not feed us. Second, the sowing campaign does not mean that the harvests will be taken in and eventually reach the consumers. This piece of news does not influence our lives, you see? But when half a million people come to Manezhnaya Square to express their support for the republican authorities, this means that our life is changing and that if TV does not report it (*Vremya* did not), it is violating the principle of a news program and encroaching on the right of TV audiences to information.

Question: But isn't it true that sometimes it is better to keep silent than report the most precise information? In such an explosive situation as in this country? What happens if a fact which you report acts as a detonator?

Kiselev: I believe that the issue of expediency of freedom of speech was settled a long time ago in the world. I don't see any issue here. Freedom of

Mitkova: information in society is one of the necessary elements of its existence. And I cannot imagine a situation, where it would be better if we kept silent.

Mitkova: The lack of information can lead to unpredictable consequences, above all in the region which is not reported on. Embargoes on information—be it from Moldova last autumn or South Ossetia not long ago—did not help to alleviate the situation. On the contrary. But as soon as we started reporting from those regions, we sensed that the situation improved because the people felt better.

The same issue of *Nezavisimaya Gazeta* (March 19, 1991) carried a comment by its editor-in-chief, Vitaly Tretyakov, "*Finita la Commedia: Comedy with Glasnost at Central TV*". He wrote:

> When in the evening of January 13 Tatiana Mitkova told the people about the bloody developments in Vilnius, there were tears in her eyes. Today she was punished for these tears and for doing her job honestly and professionally: TSN has in fact been eliminated. It is reported that Bella Kurkova has been removed as head of *Pyatoye Koleso* (Fifth Wheel). What other honest programs have remained on Central TV? *Do i Poshe Polunochi*? Let's see if it is broadcast on March 30. Or will Vladimir Molchanov suffer the fate of his other honest colleagues?
>
> It is not strange that there is a struggle for control of the first—Presidential—channel of Central TV. This is normal. But it is strange that Presidential TV has No need for the most professional, intelligent, honest and popular journalists. They are being replaced. By people with different qualities. What kind of politics is served by this kind of propaganda?
>
> Several days before the referendum Central TV was more or less objective and displayed a certain readiness to allow a divergence of views. But on the eve of the referendum Central TV transgressed all boundaries. Presenters, who are employees of the state, took voting papers and showed the people what to cross out. *Vremya* broke its own records of bias—it tried to set railwaymen against the striking miners and accused the latter of "links with the USA". It invited first secretaries of regional party committees to assure the people that the "whole" of their region would vote for [the preservation of the Union. *Vremya* openly claimed that the people holding a different opinion of the referendum were trying to break up the Union and were leading the country into civil war. Every *Vremya* program was filled with lies—we in the offices of *Nezavisimaya Gazeta* have contacts with all the republics and can prove this with facts.
>
> What do we see on our TV today? Communist propaganda, which is very intolerant of dissenters. An abundance of erotic, extremely vulgar, programs. Unbridled propaganda on religion, mostly the Russian Orthodox Church. Endless rock concerts. And astrologers. So, Communism, Eros, Orthodoxy, astrology and musical kitsch. I think that Marx and Lenin would turn in their grave if they knew what their doctrine was being seasoned with on Central TV.
>
> A lid has been put on glasnost. But we already have the freedom of the press which cannot be shut up.

The editorial office of *Nezavisimaya Gazeta* is willing to hire all the TV journalists who find themselves unable to earn their living HONESTLY as a result of the "new TV thinking." This concerns above all journalists from TSN.

Nezavisimaya Gazeta is prepared to create an independent TV company "TSN" specially for Tatiana Mitkova, Yuri Rostov and Dmitry Kiselev, help this company financially, and find premises and equipment for it. The professional and political independence of this TV company would be guaranteed by the prestige of our newspaper and a corresponding memorandum of association.

The Russian President might have no need for such journalists, but TV audiences and readers need them. And they will work in this country—with or without our assistance.

First Interview with Academician A. Sakharov

The year 1989 found Academician Andrei Sakharov and many other Soviet political and public leaders, including former dissidents and Orthodox Church hierarchs, appear on Soviet TV for the first time ever. It was disclosed on TV in 1989 that we had more than a million orphans, more than after the WWII, that every year 45,000 babies with congenital heart disease are born in this country (and half of them die because of a shortage of facilities to have them operated on), that 400,000 Soviet children are ill with infantile cerebral paralysis, that 6000 Soviet children die yearly of cancer alone, that 24 babies per 1000 are born with diseases of the locomotor system, and 48 babies per 1000 births, with psychoneurological pathologies. Soviet health services and the pharmaceutical industry are as bad as any country's, including most of Africa, and all TV can do to help is organize a 24-hour TV marathon to raise funds for the Soviet Children's Fund. The fund raiser was suggested by well-known Leningrad journalists Tamara and Vladimir Maximov who were the event's anchors. The millions of rubles and dollars the event raised are important, and so is the fact that the fund raiser reminded the Soviet public of such concepts as honor, conscience, nobility, charity, alms-giving, honesty, help, support—concepts the Soviet authorities have been trying for decades to play down. For previously, to judge from Soviet press and TV, there were no beggars, homeless, handicapped, diseased, cripples, orphans, or even jobless people in this country.

In 1986 we had the Chernobyl nuclear accident. For several years vital information concerning the radioactive contamination was suppressed. In April 1990 the Maximovs held a second TV marathon, this time for the children and adults who had suffered from the Chernobyl fallout and from the criminal callousness of authorities in Byelorussia, the Ukraine and central Russia that had closed their eyes to the fact that millions lived in the contaminated zone for years. no one has been punished among the Communist Party leaders, ministers of the nuclear power sector, health services, defense, etc. who had suppressed data concerning the actual scale of the nuclear catastrophe for five years. It was not until 1990 that, under pressure from Soviet parliament, TV little by little began to claim that some interested public circles would favor the investigation of why people still continued to live in contaminated areas years after the accident. But the response on the part of TV to these demands was truly staggering. Did TV send crews to cover farming in the town of Narodichi, Zhitomir Region, where children die of radiation—and where farming still goes on, and where contaminated produce is still gathered from contaminated fields, to be sent to the neighboring areas? No, it did not. Nor did TV report that a trainload of radioactive meat had come to Georgia, was unloaded at the town of Gori, and the fact that it was contaminated only came to the surface accidentally, whereupon the meat was shipped back to the sender. Did Central TV report that Georgian tea was contaminated by the Chernobyl fallout in 1986? Some newspapers did, but Central TV did not. It is by means accidental that cars marked Vremya-CTV USSR are no longer visible in the Union republican capitals as they were attacked by irate TV viewers in 1988-89.

And administrators of the USSR Central TV and other ideological watchdogs realized that it was necessary to broadcast on Channel 1 in evening hours at least a fraction of the footage showing the sufferings of the population in the contaminated zone (spreading throughout the western part of the USSR, not just 30 km. from the epicenter). These films were sometimes mentioned by critics, but the population and TV audiences have never seen them in full, including a documentary by Georgy Shklyarevsky, *Micro-phone!*, or *Off-Scale*. In fact, the latter is the film Alla Yaroshinskaya, a people's deputy of the USSR from Zhitomir, handed over to Gorbachev. Below is the description of an episode from the film (produced in May 1989) in February 28, 1990, issue of *Literaturnaya Gazeta*:

"The camera shows children in a playground and a close-up of a Geiger counter, its pointer off-scale. These are our children, these are all our children! Tomorrow my son will marry that girl over there, and they will have children, and then grandchildren... But will they? Or are there people who believe that they will be able to build a Chinese wall between themselves and the world and that having access to uncontaminated foodstuffs, they will be able to live with their children in a special world off limits to others? And what do they think they are doing, those guys higher up?" *Literaturnaya Gazeta* noted that there had been no changes for the better even by February 1990. If we had a free television, all the principal ministers would have had to resign in disgrace.

Yet, there was a free television in the USSR, both in the republican capitals and in regional centers in the Russian hinterland. In 1990 TV centers in Tbilisi and Yerevan, Riga and Vilnius, Tallinn and Leningrad were different from the USSR Central TV as much as the large business newspaper *Kommersant* is different from the Communist Party's *Pravda*. The problem was that regional TV centers and central TV reached audiences of vastly different magnitude. Nor did they cooperate on an equitable basis. For example, one 1-2 hour program by Tbilisi TV would be broadcast by Central TV every three months, while the same Central TV occupied Georgian airwaves every day as Channel 1 was broadcast in its entirety, and the evening broadcast of *Vremya* went on the air in Tbilisi at 9:00 p.m., Moscow time, on Channel 1 (Moscow) and Channel 2 (local).

One exception to this rule was Leningrad television that could reach 50 mln. viewers in Leningrad and Moscow Regions, the Baltics and the neighboring areas. Leningrad TV journalists had much leeway, but there were limits to what they were allowed to do too. Leningrad TV was officially part of the USSR Central TV, i.e., Moscow had more control over its personnel, policies and programs than over Sverdlovsk, Tbilisi or Tallinn TV. In 1979 the USSR Council of Ministers passed a ruling on the establishment of Central TV pilot program No. 5 on the basis of Leningrad TV.

Leningrad's *Pyatoye Koleso* (The Fifth Wheel) became a new genre on Soviet TV—a video channel combining a variety of materials. But what principles does it follow? The answer is its ironic name: as the Russian saying has it, the fifth wheel is something that can be dispensed with. But what is it we have managed to dispense with for such a long time? A viable ideology, a real public life, sincere discussions—public discussions, I mean, not homely chats. This is what *Pyatoye Koleso* is all about.

To characterize the level of this video channel's materials, here are but some of the firsts in the history of Soviet TV that appeared on this Leningrad program. It broadcast the first interview with Sakharov on Soviet TV, the first recordings of rallies held by the chauvinist society Pamyat, the first showings of alternative movies, the first meetings in support of building a Memorial to the victims of Stalinism, the first talk with Veniamin Yerofeyev, a star of underground Soviet literature, and so on and so forth... Taking into account the thoroughness of discussions on *Pyatoye Koleso*, I believe that its best broadcasts are the greatest accomplishments of Soviet TV.

Izvestia observer Arseniev wrote in the March 23, 1990, issue:

> "*Pyatoye Koleso* has become a forum for the expression of the views that are diametrically opposed to those known as official in the city.
> This is the view of an outsider. But when I came to Leningrad and met the editor-in-chief of *Pyatoye Koleso* ' Bella Kurkova, many things I saw on TV were confirmed. For example, *Pyatoye Koleso* changed to assume its new identity on a November day when Bella Kurkova talked on the air with USSR people's deputy Anatoly Sobchak who described the developments in Tbilisi in April and the Leningrad region party boss with a frankness suggesting it was time to introduce a new glasnost measurement unit: "one wheel.".
> "Yes, that was a milestone broadcast," agrees Bella. "At least for me. I believe that even if I did nothing else as a journalist, that talk show alone would be enough to prove I have done something in life."

Is it because you share Sobchak's view on things in General? I ask. She replies:

"Yes, that's true. We have made clear what category of people we see eye to eye with. We wait for them to take part in our program. These are politicians. But for all our commitment to the revival of spirituality and culture we cannot remain apathetic to political situations—nor do we want to. Politics determines the state of culture too..."

Kurkova's opinion concerning whether one program can or should present different opinions is interesting and it provides a good insight into the structure and nature of *Pyatoye Koleso*. Quite unexpectedly, Kurkova is of the opinion that a program can only focus on one set of views, much the same as an individual cannot subscribe to conflicting opinions. The format of a program, if I understood her right, precludes juggling with a variety of opinions at the risk of cancelling out the authors' stand. A program must have an identity of its own, while presenting the whole spectrum of opinion is the responsibility of a bigger unit, the entire studio. The TV journalist and the audience must take sides as one does in a voting booth. 'One program—one vote' is her principle.

With the years we will probably have an alternative TV, a subject of heated debate today. It may be big stuff, with time. But its prototype is already here, at 6 Chapygin Street, Leningrad, where *Pyatoye Koleso* studio is located as a unit of Leningrad TV.

...March 4 Bella Kurkova was elected to the Leningrad City Soviet and to Russia's Supreme Soviet. This is a sign of public recognition."

The courage of Bella Kurkova as a journalist and politician gained her the respect and recognition of TV audiences. The weekly *Argumenty i Fakty* (No. 12, 1991) asked Bella: How did she manage to show on screen episodes with "unwanted" politicians, in particular, Yeltsin's address in the House of Cinematographers and talks with Yuri Afanasyev and Artyom Tarasov?

Question: After seeing the work of Leningrad TV journalists from our base in Moscow, we came to the conclusion that you had surpassed us from the viewpoint of glasnost in the use of the camera to show all the good and bad sides of our life. On the other hand, we also hear rumors that your life is not as cheerful as the one we tend to see when watching your work on TV.

Answer: In general, we owe our popularity more to the "written" media than TV journalists. If newspaper and magazine journalists had not written about us, the country would not even have known about the existence of our program. Leningrad TV has 70 million viewers, but our program begins very late at night. With the time difference, it begins at one in the morning in Sverdlovsk. I very much doubt that everybody who would like to watch our program does so, because everybody has to go to work in the morning.

Question: Why is your program put on at such a late hour then?

Answer: We created our program for the elite, that is for the intelligentsia. Previously there were no programs designed especially for the intelligentsia. We thought: actors end their performances by ten in the evening, and musicians return from their concerts, etc. But gradually our program was put out later and later. A presenter even read out a list of programs for the next day before the beginning of *Pyatoye Koleso*. Today our audience comprises all social groups.

Question: What is the basic principle behind your program?

Answer: The revival of spiritual elements, probably because St. Petersburg suffered more in this sense than any other city.

Question: What is the attitude to your program at Leningrad TV?

Answer: No sign of any goodwill whatsoever. Vladimir Molchanov said at a meeting at *Moscow News* that it is the most terrible experience when your colleagues try to "sink" you. The staff of our department, which I head, feel as if we have all been marked down for extermination. Just as in Vysotsky's song, "Hunting the Wolves".

Our department comprises 58 independent-minded journalists who do not want to quit the team despite our precarious situation. Our staff consists of people who have taken quite a few beatings and are consequently very difficult to deal with. I myself am no angel, far from it.

Question: Everybody knows about your democratic beliefs. But they say that you never invite people from the opposite "camp" on your program.

Answer: No, we don't. Never! That is another of our basic principles. We believe that if we invited such people onto our program, we would be providing free advertising for them. Let these people appear on other programs. We don't want to publicize them. Let them have air time on other programs.

Question: Let's talk about the Leningrad television company. Everybody wants to have their own company. Do you also want to have a company which would include *Pyatoye Koleso* and *Monitor*?

Answer: The situation is very complex. For some time we were left at peace—after all, I'm a people's deputy of Russia and the Leningrad City Soviet. In a way, this protected our department. In addition, we are good friends with courageous and respected people and many of them carry a certain political weight. We are proud of our friendship with Anatoly Sobchak and Yuri Afanasyev, who had no other chance of speaking on TV other than through our program, etc.

Leningrad TV as a phenomenon does not exist. It does employ many good journalists and directors, but, regrettably, I cannot say that we have whole departments where creative workers are united by common views. Quite often they hold opposing views. You can't watch every single program, and consequently it is generally assumed that Leningrad TV is permeated with a democratic spirit. This is not true. Consequently I fear that if we have a "Kravchenko era", nearly all departments will start working in his manner, doing whatever Kravchenko tells them to do. Only we and a small group of individuals from other departments will fight. This makes me wonder about our potential.

Question: It is rumored that something like a detective atmosphere surrounds the treatment of some issues on your program.

Answer: We have our own methods. I can tell you about one of them, because it can be used only once. I mean the program with Artyom Tarasov. If I had filed a script, as I must do according to instructions, and had written that Tarasov would take part in the program and say this and that, the program would not have been shown. Shortly prior to going on the air, a report about cinema workers who were protesting about the actions of Central TV had not been shown. So I had no other choice and was obliged to lie. As the episode with Tarasov was due to appear somewhere halfway through the program, I could easily camouflage it. We edited it at weekends, when our TV superiors were not working.

I managed to convince Anatoly Sobchak to appear live in the program which included the episode with Tarasov. Usually Sobchak leaves immediately after he has done his piece. But that evening he remained in the office of Petrov, the head of our TV, at my request, while other episodes were on the air. Consciously or unwittingly, he distracted the attention of Petrov by talking to him. As I expected, the episode with Tarasov went on air while Petrov was in his car, driving home. He would not have dared to try and stop the program after it had begun for such actions would have created a tremendous scandal.

A similar thing happened with the *Vzglyad* program. You cannot conceal the appearance of Lyubimov on our TV. At first we showed only a small part of their program, around five minutes. But they had given us a cassette containing the whole of their program. Once again we handed in a false script. I understood that the head of the TV committee would not allow us to show *Vzglyad*, if it were prohibited by the chairman of the state committee. The program director asked me where the program had been taped, in Moscow or Leningrad. I lied for the first time in my life. I told him that it had been taped in Leningrad, otherwise we would not have watched it. *Pyatoye Koleso* was preceded by a live address by V. Pravdyuk, who deals with problems of philosophy and literature. His appearance did not allude to the fact that our program would deal with politics. Then we showed the *Vzglyad* program. It was a fait accompli. It entailed victory for us, albeit a small one.

After the failure of the August coup, *Pyatoye Koleso* moved from Leningrad TV to Central TV. Bella Kurkova became head of the Leningrad Directorate of the Russian State TV and Radio Company. She was interviewed by *Uchitelskaya Gazeta* (September 1991):

Question: How did you appear in the White House?

Answer: I came to Moscow on business. On the morning of August 19 my husband phoned me from Leningrad: "Is it true that a coup has occurred?" "Don't be a fool," I replied. "I see the Kremlin from the window of my room. Everything is quiet, and the birds are singing as they should." But then I turned on the television and understood that this peace had been exploded. I called Sobchak in his Moscow flat. He told me to meet him in Yeltsin's reception room. When I came there, Yeltsin's secretary told me, proudly: "We have sent Sobchak to the dacha in Arkhangelskoye, to Boris Nikolayevich. Burbulis, Silayev and Khasbulatov are there, too. In short, all the Russian leaders are there." I was outraged: "What kind of conspiracy is this?! Have you decided to lose everybody at once?" It felt very scared until Yeltsin and Sobchak arrived at the White House.

Question: You spent all three days in the White House. Many people said that it was not women's business there.

Answer: They are completely wrong! Deputies cannot be divided into men and women. During the coup I was not just a deputy—I was also a journalist. I did my professional duty. And our women's TV brigades worked together with me. Two of our girls have small children and I demanded that they leave the White House. But they didn't. So much for "women's business".

Question: The Russian Parliament was first called The White House in your program a year ago, wasn't it?

Answer: Yes, the program was called "In Russia's White House." In fact, the White House is extremely uncomfortable. We equipped a radio room in the Parliament's ground floor. Oddly enough, before that there was not a single loud speaker which Yeltsin could use to address the people. This reflects our Russian thoughtlessness.

At 2:12 I brought the first speaker, Khasbulatov, into the radio room. He was going to address the people on the barricades. He was walking along the corridors, grumbling at deputy Lopatin, who offered to lead us to the radio room by the shortest route. We sat down at the microphone and I said: "Friends, we shall report to you every hour about the developments in the White House and Moscow. Relay everything you hear from us to your relatives, acquaintances, colleagues and diplomats. Moscow must get information." The first night of our work in the radio room was very difficult. Vladimir Molchanov and the boys from the *Parlamentsky Vestbiz* (Parliamentary Herald) and *Vzglyad* helped us.

Question: You are a courageous woman and are often involved in scandals. Have you ever been frightened?

Answer: No, although I have been through a lot. I have had crosses on my door, received threatening telephone calls, and been the subject of insults. Once my friends even "armed" me with a cosh. I have never had a car. I live far away from work and often return home late at night. My colleagues won't let me take a taxi alone; they always accompany me. If I return home by the metro, my husband meets me at the station. No,

> I'm not afraid. You only have to fight back the fear once, and then it is easier and easier to do it.
> I remember how I went out onto the roof of the White House on the night of August 20. It was raining and I could hear the thousands of defenders on the barricades, wet and cold, down below. The tank lights on Kutuzovsky Prospekt. And young people with sticks and stones on the barricades. What would happen if the tanks moved against them? It was frightening. I was not frightened for myself. I'm not sixteen; I have lived a difficult life. We had to stand firm at all costs. The people believe me.
>
> August 1991 toppled not only the coup leaders, but also their allies in the leadership of Leningrad TV (B. Petrov), including Alexander Nevzorov, the presenter of the 600 Seconds news program. Since the autumn of 1990 this "angry young man" has been transformed into a notorious feature of Soviet political life. He expresses the views of the most reactionary and ignorant part of Russian society.

"*600 seconds,*" for all its brevity, has proved equal to its more reputable counterparts and offers microthemes—reports by news agencies, the Leningrad criminal chronicle and other bits presented at a fantastic speed in a slightly ironical manner. Alexander Nevzorov, who handles this daily program almost entirely on his own, has become one of the most popular TV commentators.

Thus it has often happened that the Leningrad TV journalists offered solutions to problems their colleagues in Moscow and other cities and towns were grappling with. And if glasnost is the main result of the first five years of revolutionary perestroika, isn't what is going on in the Leningrad TV network a television revolution?

It is indeed a revolution. However, today, having learned a lesson from the bitter experience of the Greater October revolution, we are wary of even the most irreconcilable (!) enemies...of communism in our midst, especially of TV journalists and political figures. At the end of 1990, even those who by dint of remoteness from Leningrad, Moscow and other central zones, practically had not seen a Nevzorov on the screen, nevertheless knew him. On December 12, Nevzorov was shot in the heart on one of the Leningrad clearings. He had a narrow escape from death. Mikhail Gorbachev sent his condolences. The Leningrad police and KGB were sent out to apprehend the criminal. Still, Gorbachev's press secretary, Vitaly Ignatenko, did not link the President's condolences to his sympathy with Nevzorov's political stance. Personally, I (and many others) do not like Nevzorov with his nonacceptance of the Soviet establishment, criticism of all and sundry, monarchism and struggle to "save Russia" which he is prepared to wage "to the bitter one." Who is fond of the Emperor and the "strong hand" here? Who doesn't like Bolsheviks, cooperators and avant-gardists? Have you guessed? Members of the Pamyat society—serious, broad-shouldered, leather-clad, poorly educated and carrying black banners with a skull and cross-bones. We see such a flag in the photograph of Alexander Nevzorov's office published by the newspaper "*Kommersant*" (December 10, 1990). So the year is 1990; Nevzorov is 32 years old. He was born in Leningrad, sang in a church choir, was going to take monastic vows, applied for a job of stuntman. The last three years he has been hosting "600 seconds" on TV, showing burned CPSU cards with the picture of Lenin. Strangely, he getting away with it—his program wasn't banned. When I look at him—nervous, tough, forever exposing someone, intimidating and relishing in evil and human filth, I think: no, we don't want this commissar, this hungweiping, we've had the likes of him before.

We know that A. Nevzorov worked hand in hand with the Pugo-Yazvo-Kryuchkov clique and that several St. Petersburg psychiatrists, upon request from "*Nezavisimaya Gazeta*" (July 27, 1991), provided excerpts from Nevzorov's medical exam when he was drafted into the army.

His war record No. 613/683 dated 1975 on file at psychiatric hospital No. 3. The psychiatrists confirmed the earlier diagnosis watching their ex-patient on TV. However—let me repeat—the trouble is not that we have a crazy commentator on our TV, but that the struggling regime has chosen him as the spokesman for its criminal actions. Worse still, millions of Soviet people have made Nevzorov their idol in this new, semi-official capacity.

"The Nevzorov syndrome is one of the most dreadful problems in present-day Soviet society," Vladimir Matusevich, director of the Russian service at Radio Liberty, told Moscow journalist Andrei Babitsky (the weekly "*Golos*" of the USSR Journalists Union, No. 31, 1991).

Question: **Vladimir Borisovich, has your opinion of the Soviet Union changed over the past few years? Do you still think that there is an insurmountable barrier between the Soviet Union and the West?**
Answer: I saw this barrier twenty years and ten years ago, and nothing has changed my perception of the Soviet Union.
Question: **But you must admit that much has changed in the Soviet way of life and the thinking of the Soviet people during perestroika. As for social ideals, the Soviet Union has moved closer to Western ideas of freedom.**
Answer: This is a vast subject, but I would like to talk about one phenomenon, which I think points to the abyss which divided, divides and will divide the two worlds. I mean the phenomenon of Alexander Nevzorov. I could use other examples in our conversation, yet this phenomenon made the greatest impression on me. Why?
You see, I am not referring to the fact that Nevzorov is an indoctrinated puppet manipulated for certain ends. What is important is the medium, the conditions and social atmosphere which made his appearance possible. The notorious film about "ours" appeared. Nobody should

have any doubts that this man has committed a professional crime comparable to rape, murder preceded by torture. He has committed a professional crime which, if it were a criminal offence, would earn him a life sentence even in the most humane country. When making his documentary report about the horrible events, this man falsified it from beginning to end. That journalist committed a professional crime and afterwards he should not have been be allowed to work for any mass media, be it a newspaper, magazine or TV studio.

I know that a group of film-makers wrote about this in *Nezavisimaya Gazeta*. I know that a great many outraged articles were published, which exposed Nevzorov, etc. But they were dominated by emotions.

A society which allows Nevzorov to work for television is a society which knows no boundaries. Paradoxically, in some sense I liked the pre-Gorbachev society more, because in that society Nevzorov could not appear, although for considerations other than those of professional ethics. It's a paradoxical situation which I have not fully understood yet. In a sense, today's Soviet society is more horrifying, demonic and inhuman than the one existing prior to Gorbachev. It is one thing that the current pluralism of *Ogonyok* is countered by the magazine *Kuban*, which has published articles by a certain Tetenov, who describes Solzhenitsyn as a Zionist and a Mason. But the phenomenon of Nevzorov is quite another matter, because the worst thing is that there are people who continue working with him, shooting films and editing them for him, paying him his salary and working in the same building with him, despite the general outrage.

Question: Do you think that Nevzorov's appearance on the screen is partly due to the absence of proper legal relations in society? If lies and falsifications in the press or on TV automatically led to court hearings and punishment, publications of this kind would be much harder to get away with.

Answer: This is an interesting subject because I believe that this is indeed one of the worst problems of Soviet society which cannot be resolved today or tomorrow. Despite Gorbachev's incantations on the dire need to create a state ruled by law, the self-same Gorbachev and his team are doing everything they can to teach people to despise law from their very childhood. And this problem is much more important than all economic hardships. Maybe this is the reason why the Soviet Union was not and will not be a truly legal state. So, you are right to say that the phenomenon of Nevzorov is closely linked to this problem.

On the other hand, it is not that important if there are legal articles and norms whereby the leadership of Leningrad TV was bound to sack Nevzorov immediately. I am astonished that the medium—I mean TV, or on a broader level, the journalistic medium—did not oust Nevzorov. This is a moral and professional problem. The Union of Journalists seemed to have been reorganized and to have adopted a professional code. But this does not mean a thing as long as Nevzorov continues to work on TV. What he is doing provides an absolute, undeniable challenge to professional journalism.

Question: What you have said prompts me to come to a very simple conclusion: the consciousness of the Soviet people, freed from the totalitarian bonds which provided for a certain, perhaps only external, respect for appearances, has not become either civilized or free. It has become barbaric and self-willed, rejecting all norms whatsoever of civilized living. I would like to unite different forms to express this barbarism: Nevzorov's lies, the anti-Semitism of "patriotic" publications, and the current regime in Georgia. I believe that these constitute elements of the same order.

Answer: That's the interesting thing about Georgia. After his election victory, Gamsakhurdia, in reply to claims that he had been transformed into a big dictator of a small country, snorted: "Have you ever seen a dictator come to power democratically, through democratic elections?!" Regrettably, at that moment nobody reminded him that there were parallels, the most notorious of them being the example of Hitler, who came to power not by means of a coup or a bloody revolt, but by winning democratic elections (later on a lot was written about this in the US and West European press). Yet I don't regard everything that the monthly *Nash Sovremennik* (Our Contemporary) stands for and what Gamsakhurdia symbolizes as elements of the same order, although it is clear that developments in Georgia are largely a result of the 70-year-long Soviet history.

However, I can well imagine that processes similar to those underway in Georgia can happen in a small Latin American country.

Nash Sovremennik is a phenomenon of a different, much more frightening order. It transpired that the thin layer of civilized behavior existing in Soviet society before Gorbachev meant that common people in trams and queues could denounce Jews and "chachlik-makers" from the Caucasus, which was a taboo for the intelligentsia, at least in public, in the press. It was regarded as indecent as suffering from a venereal disease. But these limits disappeared with unbelievable ease. When *Nash Sovremennik* published the first part of Shafarevich's Russophobic creation, I was shocked. It seemed to me that the Russian soil would open up and that there would be an explosion. The explosion did happen, but in the West, leading to an avalanche of articles and critical essays. In the USSR, even *Moscow News* merely reprinted an item by two foreign authors.

I refuse to put Russian chauvinism and nationalism on the same plane as Georgian, Tartar or Lithuanian chauvinism and nationalism. Berdyayev wrote about this nearly a hundred years ago, when he noted the fundamental difference between the chauvinism of a big, oppressive nation and the nationalism of a small, oppressed one fighting for survival. Russian nationalists are outraged: why are the Ukrainians and

Lithuanians allowed to do what they can't do in Russia? This is not only completely incompetent and irresponsible; this is sheer demagogy. But, returning to the plague of Russian chauvinism, I am especially saddened that it is being popularized by those who are expected to be intelligent—writers and other literary workers.

In July 1991 Nevzorov accused presidents Gorbachev and Yeltsin of high treason in his show *Panopticon* on Leningrad TV. Valeriya Novodvorskaya was put away in the KGB Lefortovo prison for criticizing the USSR president at a meeting, while Nevzorov, who broadcast the same views over TV, remained unpunished.

According to the generally-accepted norms, Nevzorov can be called "brown", Kravchenko's TV and Communist Party Central Committee's *Pravda*, "red", and some the traditional and new periodicals, "pink". By the same classification, Sergi Grigoryants' newspaper *Glasnost* and the weekly *Ekspress-Khronika*, the emigre *Novoye Russkoye Slovo* and *Russkaya Mysl* can be regarded as the press for decent people, made by professionals free of the dogmas of Communist education. The Novodvorskaya case was hardly written about in the Soviet mass media or mentioned on TV. Only after the August coup had failed and the "human rights activist" Fyodor Burlatsky was sacked from *Literaturnaya Gazeta* did Novodvorskaya appear twice in *Literaturnaya Gazeta* in September 1991. But in the summer of the same year Nevzorov was very much alive and kicking, while Novodvorskaya languished behind prison bars. Malva Landa wrote in Ekspress-Khronika (No. 25, 1991):

> Valeria Novodvorskaya and Vladimir Danilov, members of the Democratic Union who signed the "Letter of the 12", have been arrested and accused of perpetrating crimes punishable under Article 70 of the revised Criminal Code ("calls for the violent removal or change of the Soviet state and public system").
>
> The "Letter of the 12", dated January 12-13, 1991, was a direct reaction to the attacks by Soviet troops on legal establishments and peaceful civilians in the Lithuanian republic—one of the Soviet republics which is trying, by peaceful means, through legislation, including international law, to become a sovereign republic which settles its internal problems independently.
>
> The instigators of that attack have not been called to account. On the contrary, the mass media, which are controlled by the Center, are putting the blame for the tragedy on the leaders of the republic, on citizens who are trying to defend their government, on republican establishments (the TV center), etc.
>
> A vivid example of this perversion is Alexander Nevzorov's pseudo-documentary, which has been shown more than once on Central TV.
>
> The Center is overindulgent of the leaders of the Communist parties of Latvia and Lithuania, who are calling for violent actions against the governments of these republics, or of the representatives of the military command, who are issuing similar appeals. The Center fails to denounce the creators of the so-called National Salvation

Committee in Lithuania, that is the committee which attempted to pull off a coup d'etat.

The actions of the Soviet Armed Forces against establishments in Lithuanian and other Baltic republics, who are defending their right to state sovereignty, continue, just like the corresponding disinformation, to make attempts to fan the dislike or even hatred of the indigenous population of the Baltics.

One is led to assume that this is a gross breach of both international law and human rights, including the right to live, and Soviet legislation.

The General Secretary of the Soviet Communist Party and the USSR President, Gorbachev, is apparently supporting—if not inspiring—these actions. He has not denounced them publicly. The Soviet Armed Forces are directly controlled by the Defense Minister and the Interior Minister he appointed, who are subordinate to him. Central TV, ruled by a man who had been appointed by the President, is spreading biassed disinformation. This also applies to the Communist papers, of which millions of copies are published.

In such a situation the people's attitude to legality is easily deformed, giving rise to the idea of self-defense, armed resistance and a struggle against the enslavers.

I don't support those who are calling for armed resistance. This can only lead to more bloodshed and new tragedies. But, from the viewpoint of legality and law, in their true sense free of party interpretations, it is above all the leaders of the USSR and those who collaborate with them, who they rely on in the perpetration of acts of violence against unyielding peoples, social groups and individuals, who are committing a gross violation of the law.

Of course, they can and will use their "might is right" position—demonstratively relying on law—to judge those who, in their naivete, blinded by outrages, are insisting that might be countered by might and violence by violence.

In the summer of 1991 the USSR Defense Minister Dmitry Yazov personally decorated the Leningrad reporter, Nevzorov, with a medal "For Strengthening Combat Comradeship", not awarded to other journalists who wrote about the participation of the Soviet Armed Forces in many other "ethnic conflicts" in the Baltics, Central Asia and the Caucasus. The Soviet press dedicated dozens, even hundreds of articles to the phenomenon of Nevzorov, a TV fascist. This is what Alexander Timofeyevsky wrote about Nevzorov in *Novoye Russkoye Slovo* (February 1, 1991):

> About two months ago I wrote ironically that the new signature tune of *Vremya* resembled that of the BBC. A week later Comrade Kravchenko was appointed the new TV Minister and by New Year's Day Shchedrin's new signature tune was replaced by the old Sviridov's "Move on, Time".
>
> I have to hand it to Comrade Kravchenko for his taste: at long last he harmonized *Vremya*'s form and content. The change of the signature tune symbolized the changing of the times, and the end of perestroika: our man-eating TV stopped pretending to be vegetarian and offered the people "move on time", meaning backwards. But it cannot go back. The period of stagnation, with its mediocre, feeble hostility will not return, but the feeble-minded perestroika will not survive either.

There will be something different, similar to what we saw in Nevzorov's Lithuanian report.

The most surprising thing is that this report actually surprised somebody. Nevzorov began his program by saying that it would probably cost him many of his friends and fans. But why? There was nothing fundamentally new in Nevzorov's report. He never tried to camouflage his love of a strong hand, order, the army and the KGB, "the Czar, religion and homeland", which adds up to an empire. Nevzorov's report was highly predictable from the ideological point of view. And it was interesting not because of its ideology. More than that, it was not the report that was interesting, but rather the situation on TV which accompanied it. As Kozma Prutkov said, it is not the medicine but the accompanying lotion that heals.

Immediately after the program was shown, Nevzorov was accused of many things. In particular, of being illogical. Indeed, there is no logic in that report. The author glorified the Russian army yet mumbled something about a "criminal government", which had sent in the troops. Then he said that the presence of these troops was necessary to protect the Russian-speaking population. Why should troops protect anybody from a legitimate government? To say nothing of the strange methods of protection which looked more like an attack? The program did not look into this and it cannot be explained by logic, because logic played no role in the show.

Nevzorov was accused of falsifying his report. His report was indeed incorrect, to put it mildly, from the point of view of documentary film-making. It is not life shown as it is, but rather life which was diligently but sloppily orchestrated. A life that was orchestrated apparently sloppily, daringly sloppily, in order not to camouflage it, but rather to show off. Yet accusations of the absence of "real life" in the report are as ungrounded as are accusations of the absence of logic, because neither were provided for in Nevzorov's rules of the game.

Nevzorov has been playing by these rules for several years now, inciting the admiration—more often than indignation—of the intelligentsia who have now recoiled from him. These rules are quite unusual for a reporter, who is expected to disappear and dissolve into his material. Nevzorov's style is quite the opposite: he dominates the information and pours it from the screen directly into people's ears.

His show—the embodiment of impersonal knowledge—has so little in common with simple reporting that it is surprising that even clever critics have called him a top-notch professional. He is not a professional, but a hero, an apostle, a sufferer, a Robin Hood who is fighting each and everyone of us single-handed—Bolsheviks and prostitutes, embezzlers and avant-gardists, democrats and cooperators, and despicable alimony evaders, who have settled in the Leningrad City Soviet. He alone stands his ground against everybody else, and he alone speaks the Truth.

Three elements—Confrontation, Defense and Exposition—determine everything in Nevzorov: his appearance—dramatically tired, with three-day stubble, his life—hounded by the enemies, he "took the bullet to heart" (an unmatched witticism coined by *Kommersant*), and the style of his program—loud music, a ring on fire, and the sign "600" coming upon you (why not 666?). All this prepares the audience for a mythological spectacle, something of the Pyriev-Chiaureli magnitude, a package of openly orchestrated information, affected phrases, head-on metaphors, and the inevitable Mother Russia, with her beggarly knapsack, at the end.

The disparity between common fact, which should be simply reported, and exposition, which Nevzorov is destined to pour over us, is so big that a sense of reality disappears altogether. Taking a child-like offence at the Leningrad City Soviet and its petty intelligentsia truth, he went to Lithuania in order to find his own, Higher Truth, which was maliciously concealed from us. He began by mixing the Red Army with the White Guards, even the Crusaders, and himself with Archangel Michael. Consequently, the question on his attitude to Gorbachev, Yeltsin and Gidaspov after the program sounded painfully tactless. Nevzorov shrugged it off: "What do I care for Gorbachev, Yeltsin and Gidaspov?", and he was right. Indeed, why should Archangel Michael care for all this insignificant nonsense?

His pronounced superiority complex no doubt conceals a no less pronounced inferiority complex. His Archangel Michael, who has no army of his own and most probably never served in the army, and his Lithuanian program seem to point to the existence of a big-headed, narrow-shouldered teenager who looks up at servicemen, begging, "Will you let me touch your gun please?" It is not my job, however, to root out the complexes discernible in his programs about raped children and old women; this should be dealt with by a psychiatrist.

His Lithuanian program can only evoke tears of compassion. Yes, compassion for Nevzorov. When listening to this popular leader, this feeble-minded victim of paranoia, who said, "What do I care for Gorbachev, Yeltsin and Gidaspov?", I had to stop myself from reaching out through the screen and patting him on the head, trying to soothe him with something like, "You are the bravest and the best looking guy. Why do you worry?"

I should have put a full stop here, yet I cannot. If the Lithuanian program had been shown only when it should have been shown, during *600 Seconds*, I wouldn't have minded. In actual fact, *600 Seconds* has become one of the colors of perestroika, its theme tune. The problem is not the medicine but rather the lotion accompanying it. Nevzorov's film was shown twice more on the decision of the USSR Supreme Soviet.

The trouble is that the program was presented as the official version of the Lithuanian developments. To top it all, the author was forgiven not only for swearing at Bolsheviks (who minds that now?), but also for accusing the "criminal government" of sending the troops in the first place. Nevzorov was forgiven because despite all these accusations, despite everything he had said in general, he had poured into the ears of our compatriots that impersonal Higher Truth which had been concealed maliciously by democrats. He was forgiven because the version of Pugo, Yazov and Gorbachev was based on the same old scheme, the same Higher Truth.

The people asked questions based on law and common sense: Why did the army carry out the orders of a criminal Salvation Committee and act against the legally-elected government? Because the Truth is on the side of the committee, was the actual reply. And this Truth is a hair-raising one.

The feeble lies of the Brezhnev era and the "Move on, Time" Vremya could be tolerated, when they did not terrorize us directly. One could hide from them behind closed doors, by reading Pushkin and listening to Britten, by looking at pictures of Milanese barocco—whatever you liked most. The silly Vremya of perestroika was funny and encouraged one to think, despite its ambivalence, eclecticism and tastelessness. But one cannot hide from Nevzorov's paranoia when it is elevated to the rank of state thinking, and this is not funny. All attempts to protest appear to be half-hearted, and worse still, pointless.

The Center is looking at the thousand-strong meetings, which demand the withdrawal of the troops and the resignation of the Center, as an elephant might look at a meddling Pekinese. The arguments of common sense and an appeal to law prove as helpless as moral denunciations, such as "Tanks Are Horrible" and "Nevzorov, You Are a Scoundrel". Even the telegram by prominent film directors denouncing Nevzorov's film as a fraud did not seem convincing.

All this professional mumbo-jumbo looks pathetic against the mutual protection of madness.

The following is an excerpt from a piece carried in No. 42, 1990, of *Ogonyok*; the piece is by journalist A. Terekhov who wrote it after a TV program covering the "criminal scene", on the national (or Moscow, Leningrad) TV that cater to the lowest of tastes:

"When the old light failed, and the new one has yet to dawn, the mob leaves the basement, twilight is their time, and the mob demands: give us what is our due!

And our sleazy television feeds the mob out of its hand with smut and songs mumbling "Russia, Russia" against the background of ruined churches, and our culture is crushed by the burden of the retching "wishes of the mob" that are not any better than the "wishes of the working people", and we do not have a single decent newspaper averse to prostituting its pages by pieces on "flying saucers", "poltergeist" and astrological drivel about the end of the world. Very often one would like to write as a footnote to this stream: things are not that simple! A crowd becomes a herd when there is no diversity of menu—we really should not oversimplify matters. We are too poor to permit the dictatorship of the mob.

Any revolution means changing levels, but, for mercy's sake, not levelling! There was a time when we hurled the lace and marble of the nobility into the mud and lifted the village, having thereby uprooted it—and we robbed ourselves both of the soil and the air.

We cannot give in to the mob that always wants to have its nerves set on edge, to sense its heart skip a beat and a shudder run up its spine before going to bed, we cannot casually sweep the camera over a line of corpses and to show people who are unmistakable mental patients. Pain must remain pain, and it cannot be allowed to be dulled because it floods the screen on a regular basis.

With time the mob will get its newspapers and magazines, TV channels and comic strips, but this does not mean that people will be free from their eternal moral duty of educating and uplifting; but for the time being, the mob must be beaten off. The mob despises convolutions, it favors short-cuts. Let's topple the czar, it says, and we'll live well. Let's exile the kulak, and we'll live well. Let's assemble a thick crowd, find a strong head, use it to ram through the Kremlin or Lubyanka door, drag out a couple of boyards by the hair, and we'll live well again.

By giving in to the mob, we are driving people from the country, we shorten the time of those who are still attempting to do something. We force people to believe that we are living on the eve of something terrible, on the eve of the explosion of the surrounding world. And people who are used to expecting "hot" events every day, may pine after such events and think them up. The mob is always dreaming of riots and impostors.

The most horrible thing is that we do not see any doubters or undecided people around of late: everybody is sure of everything.

But what I am afraid of is not even this wave, it is the absence of a counteraction, however half-hearted. I have long ago stopped dreaming of having aristocrats in this country or of a princess on the pea, and I have long ago given up hope of meeting at least one state figure who did not begin his career at 13 as a collective farm herdsman and who has not preserved the vocabulary and manners of that unforgettable period.

But where are, simply, the well-mannered people who would just switch off the TV after the anchor of *600 Seconds* asks the rapist what his victim defended with more energy, the wine bottle or her honor? Have long food lines and the power of illiterate morons demolished our university education, traditional folk ethics, lessons from our parents and great books? Have we ceased to tell between a truth that is a gold speck we find after long, back-breaking work and use for a spiritual revival and a search for a difficult, uphill road and a truth that a lout with dirty fingernails splashes into our plate?

I do not know how to answer, and it gives me pain just to think of this.

But I am convinced that the duty of writers and speakers today is the social rehabilitation of the people who have seen the moral fundamentals of their life collapse. People are like children in our tragic times. They must be told the truth, but they cannot be scared. If they get scared, they will want to go back.

The depoliticization of society begins with the destruction of the oppression of information-distributing structures seeking to hammer into every head one and the same message: it may be a good message, but the problem is, it never varies. Private life must become the centerpiece of a person's existence, not reports from elections, rallies or speculations about whether General Kalugin will win a seat in parliament and how an old woman had been raped in a public toilet.

It is a disgrace for people to discuss newspaper dirt, not themselves, when they meet.

Let people have pot flowers on the window sill, calm family evenings, a vegetable garden, eternal books, and rest after work. Let them attend fewer elections and rallies, let them see less and live more.

To wish to see the next morning as soon as possible, one must know that truth, honor, courage, conscience, kindness, altruism and love of country remain unfading values at the time of a universal collapse of values.

Life must bring joy no matter whether *Vzglyad* goes on the air tonight or not. After all, the President's statement is no better than a wet bench in the garden in autumn or autumn leaves falling.

Let people sleep peacefully."

Soviet TV avoided showing people who had something to say and who were nice to listen to. We wanted to see interesting people on TV, but they normally shunned the medium as they hated to lie and would not be allowed to be sincere on TV. Garry Kasparov would knit his brow over a chess game, and

Alla Pugacheva would sing her heart out, but they were not allowed to express their views on Central TV. Central TV showed decent people only after strict censorship. This long-drawn-out practice of pervasive falsehood spoilt both TV stars and the entire body of journalists, including many journalists who really sought to improve the quality of their programs. But all their attempts came to grief as we have distorted the natural criteria of good and evil, and even elementary integrity and manners. The following is a report by V. Solovyev, a journalist on the *Novoye Russkoye Slovo*, that appeared in the newspaper on July 24, 1990:

> "The first thing I noticed on my coming to Moscow is a great number of beggars in the streets, railway stations, metro and subterranean passages. Muscovites dislike but don't despise them; in fact, they are envied as people who have mastered a lifestyle still inaccessible to their critics. I was told that beggars hire children, and when I expressed doubts and asked about the source of the information, my question made the people angry.
>
> Some consider Moscow's beggars to be underground millionaires and even demand they be searched. Most of the TV viewers sided with a popular TV anchor in his conflict with an anonymous beggar woman.
>
> I had an argument on the matter with Alyosha, 14, an intelligent lad who was the first to tell me of the televised conflict.
>
> Towards the end of a work day the reporter and his team, with cameras and microphones, accosted a beggar woman and inquired how much she had earned during the day. The woman would not answer, and the reporter snatched her bag and counted the daily takings that ran into several hundred rubles (which does not mean of course that she had earned the entire sum in one day).
>
> Alyosha was delighted with the broadcast and retold the episode excitedly. According to him, the broadcast was hugely successful and much spoken about the next day; the resourceful reporter was applauded and the underground millionaire, denounced.
>
> "Do you have this kind of program?" asked Alyosha proudly.
>
> "They are impossible in my country. Firstly, the police would arrest the reporter for molesting the beggar, the scuffle he started and an attempt to appropriate her property. Secondly, he would have to quit his job as most TV viewers, in contrast to Soviets, would be harshly critical of the reporter's ugly behavior."
>
> Alyosha was staggered by the American attitudes as much as I was staggered by Soviet ones. Alyosha's father, my friend of long standing, and I managed to persuade him that the reporter had, to say the least, abused his powers, but is there any way to persuade the reporter himself and his numerous fans?
>
> Generally speaking, I noticed that my tastes as a TV viewer were by no means identical with ordinary Soviet tastes, but in that case it was a disagreement over ethics, not aesthetics."

For decades we watched on TV Soviet international news analysts, experts on the West—actually, people with double moral standards. Knowing full well what the "decadent West" was like, they talked rubbish on the screen, then wrote books in a similar vein, received academic degrees and taught public opinion manipulation techniques to their students. Characteristically, these professional liars were never invited to double as, say, councillors at the Foreign Ministry (Communist Party Central Committee, the Council of Ministers, etc.). The Soviet establishment has always drawn a distinction between mass propaganda stereotypes and real politics, but the distinction was never believed to be very important. In western countries talented journalists and sovietologists become respected political and academic figures. Richard Pipes and Zbigniew Brzezinski were so often criticized during the years of stagnation that today there is no need to present them to our audiences. But Hélène Carrère D'Encausse, a world-renowned sovietologist whom all the French know from her frequent TV appearances, became France's third woman to have been elected to the French academy in 1990.

Information War on the Air Ended on August 21,1991

Information means power. Information is a very important strategic commodity. A dictator who impedes the dissemination of information, which may do him harm stands to gain in the sense that he will retain his position. He also, however, transfers his nation into a fools' paradise. Within two or three generations the country is an intellectual desert.

It took Gamsakhurdia just one month(!) to overturn things in Georgia and to bring the republic onto the brink of civil war. As he began to lose ground because of the pressure of the democratic opposition he dissolved parliament in September 1991, jammed all television programming from Moscow and switched off the republic's TV, closed almost all the local papers and banned local printing and distribution in the republic of all Moscow-based newspapers and magazines. He also republic of all Moscow-based newspapers and magazines. He also cancelled for an indefinite period of time classes in schools and colleges, practically stopped paying salaries to the intelligentsia and in this manner punished it for its opposition. To complete the picture he brought in hundreds of buses full of his supporters from all over Georgia to Tbilisi where they staged an ongoing rally several weeks long in his support in front of his residence.

Prior to the events in Vilnius in January 1991 and subsequently, the Moscow communist forces acted more cautiously, as they were worried about the reaction of the West. Nevertheless the military-industrial complex, supported by the KGB and other party leaders, waged an ongoing information war against the democratic forces. At least the latter had something they could use to counter the attacks mounted by the orthodox communists. In 1991 the men with the best brains in the CPSU defected to the democrats' side, which constituted the main achievement in the democratic campaign to gain public sympathy. Television became the communists' last battlefield from which to fight for the power slipping through their hands.

"*The Main Intention Is To Prevent Russia's Information Independence*" was the title of an interview granted by the Chairman of Russian Television and Radio Company, Oleg Poptsov to *Nezavisimaya Gazeta*'s Sergei Fomin on March 21, 1991. The interview ran as follows:

Question: Leonid Kravchenko told a news conference, held upon his appointment as Chairman of the All-Union Television and Radio Broadcasting Company, that in terms of relations with Russian Television and Radio Company a "situation has emerged which cannot be dealt with quickly and painlessly.

Answer: As far as the All-Union Company is concerned, the Russian Radio and Television company is a competitor, and not a very agreeable competitor at that. It doesn't share the views of the Chairman of the All-Union company with respect to the mass media and the role played by them in the renovation of society. It is consequently an irritating competitor. On the other hand, I think that L.P. Kravchenko realizes that Russian television and radio has to exist.

Question: He emphasized that the idea of dividing the property of the former Gosteleradio was inadmissible as far as he was concerned, and that Russia was the only republic which had asserted that it should be done...

Answer: With a miserable five hours of airtime a day on the radio and seven and a half hours a week on television, Russia is the most unjustly treated republic in terms of the mass media. All the other republics own relay radio links from the capital cities to the regional centers. In Russia such links are the property of the Union. Why such injustice? For Russia the lack of a television and radio network means that it cannot manage its economy and culture.

Russia will have to sign the Union Treaty, and given the current situation is in an unequal position. There should be guarantees of equality, when a republic has the right to make economic claims on the Center when it encroaches on the republic's right to free information for its citizens. By the way, it is a constitutional obligation of both the parliament and the government.

The Russian parliament has been obstructed and is irritated by the fact that its laws are not being observed. Such irritation is only natural. The laws are being sabotaged by the conservative forces locally, but the citizens of the republic simply have no information about such laws. At the same time, the lack of unity and the Center's irritation with the uncompromising approach displayed by Russia and its leaders who refuse to disdain the principles of sovereignty, have led to an information blockade because the Central TV is opposed to the concept of independent Russia and makes no secret about it.

I am astonished at the amount of effort, which is being expended to prevent Russia from having its own radio and television. It is particularly annoying that the key figure behind this counter-action is the President. The President cannot see Russia behind Yeltsin's silhouette.

Question: **It was said at that news conference that seventy per cent of the programming on the Central TV was about Russia and for Russia...**

Answer: The seventy per cent mentioned by Kravchenko is the result of Gosteleradio's inability to portray each republic on the all-Union screen. For this reason the events and conflicts which take place in a republic, as a rule, take the viewer by surprise. Truth about the people is a portrait of the people.

The emergence of a Russian Television channel will allow the All-Union company to give more coverage to life in all republics, above all on the presidential channel. My understanding is that Kravchenko doesn't want to do it and that he is afraid of doing this. His main intention is obvious: to prevent Russia's information independence. One should not talk about internationalism, one should build it.

Given that the first channel is the presidential one, as the President himself has claimed, its most important objective should be to preserve the Union. It is natural that the function of the first channel should be to focus on inter-ethnic communication. The second channel has always been a kind of garbage dump where poor quality programming (as seen by the leadership) would be shown and where controversial programming would appear. For instance, the "*Avtorskoye Televideniye*" (Author's Television) program was put on the second channel. Why did it happen? Because the management of the All-Union company would have been so happy if those uncompromising and talented people had not formed a working relationship with the leaders of Russian Television.

Question: **It is unclear how local and republican radio and television committees in Russian territory can be independent when a presidential decree has passed all the property of former Gosteleradio to the All-Union company.**

Answer: This needs some clarification. Even before the decree was issued, we agreed together with Gosteleradio that local committees would be made the property of the republics. When almost everything was ready to enable us to receive the property directly from the hands of Gostel, out came the presidential decree. The USSR and the Russian government plunged into a lengthy period of correspondence. Delays and procrastination are the norm in the relationship with the former Gosteleradio. Astonishingly, the obstacles are being mounted by people who are not on the staff of the All-Union company. The only staff member of the company is the Chairman himself.

Every time L.P. Kravchenko and I meet to talk I have the impression that we have agreed on something. After all we are partners, albeit competitors. Kravchenko isn't having a very easy time either, and I sympathize with him. However the situation has been changing slowly. Kravchenko is not the only problem. Republican red-tape is a mature beast. The story about the decision on mass media organizations which was submitted to the Russian Supreme Soviet, is a subject for a separate conversation, but I should say a few words about it now. The decision was drafted by experts and had to do with equipment for mass media. It was discussed by politicians who basically didn't understand anything about radio, television or the printing industry. The adoption of the decision was frustrated by parliamentarians who thought of themselves as politicians. We are doomed unless we learn how to respect professional people.

We view our work at the second national channel as a transitional period. Our purpose remains the same: an independent Russian channel. The Russian Council of Ministers has allocated some funds for us, but Russia is having immense difficulties in terms of hard currency. Television isn't something that could be set up overnight from scratch. It would take a country with a perfectly-organized economy three years to build a television center. That is how long it took to create one in Catalonia. The project would take a country with a mid-level civilization five years. This country would need seven years in a normal situation, or ten in a crisis situation. How would Russia survive during this time?

By the way, even last year the President issued a decree on the democratization of television, wherein he said that Russia would build a television center of its own. The President sought to make the impression that he wasn't prejudiced against Russian television. It was only an impression though.

Question: As we know, Kravchenko "has come to perform the will of the President".

Answer: This could be the reason why he is preventing the creation of normally-functioning television and radio in Russia.

But Russia cannot look on calmly as decisions taken by a congress of Russian Deputies and by the Russian government are being trampled underfoot. An end must be put to it some day. I keep trying to explain the President's moves either by an information blockade or by the influence of his entourage. As I say this it immediately occurs to me that the President has all the power in his hands, that he has an overabundance of extraordinary powers. Consequently he could prevent any information blockade. If he hasn't been doing so, that means that he doesn't want to or that he only wants to hear information which suits his purpose. In plain language, this information blockade is the work of the President himself. I can draw no other conclusion from this.

Attempts are already being made to amend the Law on the Press which was passed less than six months ago, because it is a law and must be abided by.

This is the original cause of such questions as "How long will the independent press last?" and "Isn't it time to abolish *Vzglyad*?" I don't subscribe to such statements. One should never be in a hurry to give in. The conservatives are fighting hard because they have realized that the democrats have become a force to be reckoned with. The reactionaries display hatred for newspapers like *Kuranty*, *Moscow News* and your newspaper as well. I have never heard the President ever reproach *Sovetskaya Rossia*. Why not? Because this newspaper has been attacking the President's opponents. This makes the President close his eyes to everything else, things like vicious language, its evil, humiliating tone, hysteria and lies. It turns out that anything is fine with the President as long as it's in his favor. That's a great shame.

As a writer and citizen I was insulted by the President's address at a meeting with public prosecutors. His allegation that the press maintains contacts with the Mafia is too serious to be written off as an emotional outburst. It was a conscious step to provoke discord between the press on the one hand and society and the public prosecutors' offices on the other. He accused the press of bribery. If he has any proof, the President should submit it to the public prosecutor's office. The case will then be investigated according to the proper legal manner. If he hasn't any proof, then he should apologize. By setting the public prosecutors against the press, the President enables them to settle scores with the press for criticisms made two or three years ago. At that time the passions ran very high. This is the calculation behind such statements. While paying lip-service to the cause of harmony, the higher levels of authority have been sowing discord.

There is a presidential decree which has exempted artistic unions from taxes. This is merely an attempt to bribe them. Why has this been done? The intention is to suffocate the press because it has distanced itself from artistic unions and has shielded itself against authority. The presidential privileges haven't been extended to the press.

Question: What is your view of the future of the Russian Television and Radio Company?

Answer: In the first place there should be no monopoly. The local radio and television committees should have complete independence, both in economic and artistic terms. Should they need us they will come to us anyway. We are prepared to help them improve their standards on air. We are willing to teach them everything we know so that their standards will match those of Moscow and Leningrad. In terms of controversy and boldness many local studios, especially in larger cities, can do a lot better than the central studios. That is, of course, if some provincial redundancy is removed. Our main objective is to coordinate ideas and ensure that there is enough programming for Russia.

Several chairmen of the local committees will be put on the board of our company. It will make sense, and we need this ourselves. On the whole our relationships have only started to be formed.

Question: It has been alleged that people have been quitting their positions in mass numbers from the Central TV. Have they been applying for jobs at Russian Television?

Answer: I wouldn't speak of mass numbers. I can say though that people who have offered to work for us are not the worst you will find on TV.

Question: What do you think of the fact that both the Moscow and Leningrad television and radio committees will fall within the jurisdiction of the All-Union company?

Answer: I see it as another example of monopoly thinking which boils down to seizing, oppressing and ruling. Apparently, the President is confident that he knows better than anybody else what the viewers, listeners and readers need. At Leningrad TV, we have been setting up our own Directorate which we have the right to do. *Pyatoye Koleso* will be our program, this I'm positive about.

The battle is going at three levels, as it were: the army, the working class and the mass media. Open a newspaper or turn on your radio, and you will see it for yourself.

The individual should have the right to think and have his own thoughts. Unless there is such sovereignty there can be no individual, no state, no freedom.

May 13, 1991 was the first day that Russian Television went on air. Almost all Soviet television stars began to appear on it. It is true, many of them, no longer with Kravchenko's TV, refused to be on the staff of Russian Television.

Both companies, the Central TV and Russian TV, were government entities and went out of their way to demonstrate loyalty to "their" politicians and to abuse the "enemy" ones. Neither of the companies depended on the viewer. In the West advertisers pay television companies depending on viewing figures of their programs. This kind of responsibility is much more of a motivation than one's fear of the bosses.

Before the August coup the Central TV had at times been pathologically dishonest, but Russian Television never came up with intentional lies, nor did it ever hush things up. The former was luxuriously accommodated at Ostankino, the latter dragged out a miserable existence and struggled against equipment shortages in Yamskaya Street. While the former reigned over national air, the latter was only rarely given air time on the second channel which enjoyed only half the audience that the first channel reaches. Besides, in many regions and republics local programming would be put on air to jam when Russian Television.

On the eve of the coup (August 14, 1991) *Literaturnaya Gazeta* carried the following article by Yuri Bogomolov about the newly-emergent situation in television:

> In mid-May the long-expected split in television finally occurred. Ostankino now resembles the mountain Elbrus in the Caucasus with its two peaks.

One peak comprises the new version of the TSN news show and the well-known *Vremya*, the latter being the embodiment of the Central TV.

The other one is the program *Vesti* which the public associates with Russian Television.

By severing its ties with the Central TV, Russian Television has created an unprecedented situation where the two are fiercely competing for the attention of TV viewers.

In autumn last year L.P. Kravchenko made his comeback to Ostankino with the heroic and romantic intention of preserving the Fatherland's television, the most important mass media, which had almost been stolen by the democrats.

It is public knowledge why this was done. The diversity of opinions which had appeared on screen via such programs as "*Vzglyad*", "*Pyatoye Koleso*", the "*Do i Poshe Polunochi*", "TSN", was under various pretexts eliminated by the All-Union TV and Radio Broadcasting Company.

Kravchenko not only kept his promise (or was it an instruction from his bosses?) but went farther than that. He made an eccentric attempt to preserve a totalitarian regime in an individual government department. It turned out, however, that the restoration of a rigid hierarchy inside the agency was not enough. The TV viewer also had to be brought back into a subordinate position. Any autocratic organization runs on its own logic, one of command and enforcement.

Enforced television, as it were, is unaffordable in a situation where democratic mechanisms have started working, if even erratically. Obviously, it doesn't owe its bad name to comrade Kravchenko himself, but rather to the very nature of state television (it shouldn't be mistaken for Western type state television which provides a different degree of integration of the communications networks in government structures) which is corroborated by the experience of the newly-born Russian Television.

The question is not whether Russian Television is functioning better or worse than the Central TV. It is obvious that Russian Television is doing much better.

But then it is extremely easy for Russian Television to perform better, as it would be difficult to make a news show which could be worse than *Vremya*; to shoot a documentary which could be even less original than the film "*Byt Samin Soboi*" (To Be Oneself); to make a comment on public affairs which could be inferior to "*Pryamoi Razgovor*" (Speaking Frankly).

The only interesting things left in the stiff-necked *Vremya* today are the items the program keeps silent about. Being silent about something is a news technique in itself, but then if the Central TV makes more use of such techniques it will lose its battle against Russian Television, which has easily scored points by filling in the gaps in news. Where *Vremya* limits itself to announcing that Shevardnadze has made a sensational statement, *Vesti* informs the viewers of the actual content of the statement.

Russian Television, too, has done better in terms of documentary research. For instance the Central TV completely ignored the tragedies in Tbilisi and Novocherkassk. On the contrary, Russian Television has come up with films like "*Repetitsiya*" (Rehearsal) and "*Novocherkassky Albom*" (The Novocherkassk Album).

Both networks ran programming for the election. It turned out that the Central TV's "*Kto yest Kto*" (Who's Who) program had long since run its course. It also became clear that one can manipulate live almost as much as pre-recorded programming. Igor Fesunenko's shows are crammed with banal questions for which his interviewees have equally banal answers up their sleeves. Also, his shows are absolutely conflict-free.

From this perspective, Russian Television's approach to conducting political debate is much more fruitful. The hosts engage interviewees in live dialogue by asking them uncomfortable questions, which help reveal the politicians for what they are.

In terms of entertainment, Russian Television's more remarkable achievements are Andrei Bitov's non-political dialogue with Rezo Gabriadze about the poet Pushkin, and a film about Rostropovich called "*Fantaziya na Temu Rokoko*" (A Rococo Fantasy). Programming by the crew "*Kommanda-2*" (Command-2) is unusually mobile. The crew especially gained from this during the Moscow Film Festival, when it promptly screened cultural information and did so with a very personal touch.

These and other successes of Russian Television look all the more impressive when one considers its modest logistics and shortage of equipment.

The advocates of state television are scared to death by the prospects of a non-government television service. For some reason they tend to believe that such television should necessarily be anti-state.

It is interesting to note in this respect the role played by Mr. Turner's private company CNN during the Gulf War.

Had there been no television cameras on both sides of the front line the war would most likely have taken a different course. The Gulf War is the world's most thoroughly covered war so far which is one reason why it was so brief. The readily available news helped the belligerents adapt their moves.

If only the Afghan war and the Armenian-Azerbaijanian conflict had received as much coverage...

If television had acted as a mediator during the negotiations of the parties to the conflict in the Baltics...

These "ifs" are like last year's snow but then they are also last year's blood.

The real problem is that it is up to the government to provide for government-free television. Such television would act in the interests of the state, not a totalitarian and imperial state, but rather a free one.

Today non-government TV seems like a rather distant prospect. But then non-government press seemed impossible only a short time ago.

There are certain prerequisites for an independent television even now. "*Vzglyad*" is carrying on as a non-staff outfit. Vladimir Pozner and Vladimir Molchanov, too, have gone solo.

It all could be more than just an idea. What if it is public-private television in a condensed form?..

The stars on our television are a reflection of our own problems and poorly-organized life. Every day our television personalities appear on the silver screen, tired and worried as they are, as if they had just been put through the mill in a food line or reprimanded by their bosses. The Western commentators look so much different. Any TV viewer would be happy to invite them to his home. It's because what the Western TV viewer sees on the screen is decent people who are aware of their human dignity and are doing their best to keep up their reputation. It is a shame that even the more honest of Soviet broadcasters were unable to speak as frankly from the screen as they did in the democratic press. In this country a broadcaster depends on the bureaucrat more than he depends on the viewer. This was the case in the USSR Gosteleradio, in the All-Union State Television and Radio Broadcasting Company which replaced it on February 8, 1991.

CHAPTER X

TELEVISION FOR THE PRESIDENT

Earthquake in Georgia as the Fourteenth TV News Item from Moscow

Opposition politicians account for as much air time in Britain as the Prime Minister himself. Whenever he makes a political mistake they are there, after him. No television company can afford to make a secret of the Government's mistakes because it will at once start losing points to competitors and will itself become an object of scandal. In any Western country television is forced to work professionally, i.e. to abide by the *moral* and legal standards. In this country there has always been the monopoly of power which has corrupted all and sundry.

There can be no discussion of morals, honor, conscience or at least one's intention to abide by the Criminal Code when we assess the criminal activities of Kravchenko and his masters from the Politburo of the CPSU Central Committee. News was falsified in varying degrees in the *Vremya* night news shows. This is the opinion of Tatiana Ivanova from *New Times* (No. 19, 1991). The article is titled "*The Fourteenth News Item*".

> The earthquake in Georgia was the fourteenth (or maybe thirteenth) news item on *Vremya*. That means that *Vremya* had thirteen (twelve?) more important news items. Meanwhile Georgia has just experienced its largest catastrophe in eight hundred years. The earth has closed up on several villages literally swallowing all and sundry, the young and the old, the separatists and the communists, the right and the wrong, the lazy and the diligent, the beauties and the monsters, babies, cows, cats, the bosses and the subordinates.
> For decades we have lived together in one country. It was even claimed that we lived as "one family". But Moscow isn't in mourning; its television hasn't stopped entertaining people; demonstrations haven't been cancelled in the main square of this country; in honor of the tradition, the highest-level officials stood at the main tomb in this country to greet demonstrators but no one said, "Bend your heads, we have something to mourn".
> People were dying in two Armenian villages in Azerbaijan. Real people were dying. People were dying but no one from the leadership of this country appeared on the screen to say, "I will carry out an investigation immediately, to find out who is

to blame, the culprits shall all be punished, let's weep for the victims, I will do everything to ensure that no one else is killed in my country..."

What an inhuman, anti-human life we are living, I thought to myself. Where is the limit? Is it true that there are so many people in this country that our leaders don't feel sorry for us?

Are you hungry? You should work better. Is someone killing you? That's because you have been behaving badly. Okay now, somebody got killed in the earthquake, but others have survived, why should we upset everyone else, life goes on all the same.

The relationship which has taken shape in this country between the government and its people could be the most astonishing relationship of this kind in human history. The people and the government can't stand the sight of each other. It could be a relationship where the parties are not guided by mutual love. There are other motivations besides love, such as mutual respect, agreement, expediency, common interests. These and many others are also possible. What is happening in this country could not happen anywhere else. There is no respect, no agreement, no expedience, no interests—nothing.

The official newspapers, government television and government radio are exuding cosmic cold. So do the supreme rostrums. The word "democracy" is the number one swear word in this country. The runner-up is the word "populism".

As far as I understand, a populist is a person who talks to people about their concerns and promises as a politician to give priority to such concerns and do everything he can to remove anxiety, misunderstanding and pain. Populists seek popularity.

I wonder what the supreme bodies of authority in the USSR are seeking? I don't know the answer to this question. But I will never vote for someone who is seeking not popularity but who knows what. Let this "someone" vote for the person then.

Watch the television yourselves, a television which put "Watch the television yourselves, a television which put an earthquake in Georgia after thirteen other news items."

What do people who worked at the "Presidential" Central TV think of it? On April 27, 1991 *Nezavisimaya Gazeta*'s Sergei Fomin interviewed a well-known broadcaster whose name the newspaper decided not to disclose.

Question: Mikhail Nenashev once said that Gosteleradio was an unmanageable structure. However its course was transformed rather quickly after the arrival of Leonid Kravchenko. A series of scandalous bans and cancellations of programs has brought about a pacified television airtime. Some of the controversial programs are gone, others are on their way out. How is this done technically?

Answer: It is done in a rather banal and boring way. Every Monday there is a working conference which discusses the more important programs. The conference is attended by the Chairman or any of his deputies. During the conference comments are made on programs which have been put on the air and plans are made. The Departments' Editors then pass the information onto their staff.

Question: What if somebody disagrees with such decisions and wants to structure his program to his own liking? How can this be monitored? Is there anyone who watches all the programming before it goes on air?

Answer: The President of the All-Union Company has several deputies, who deal with different sections of the air time. The control is carried out by them and through them. They are people who can promote original ideas up to a certain extent, can act as an author's allies, but will all the same side with the leadership at the critical moments. For instance Valentin Lazutkin for a long time provided assistance in the setting up of Russian Television and in the search for compromise solutions with Union leaders. Recently he has become less active in this field, because it has become dangerous for his own position in the structure.

The more important programs and programs which gather large audiences are pre-viewed before screening. The main concern is to keep an eye on the people. There is less supervision with regard to people who have been very loyal. The removal of a program which has appeared in the listings is effected following instructions to the Main Programming Directorate, to the so-called chief control room. The program is removed from the air, and the announcer says that this has been done "for technical reasons."

For the key news shows, the text for the presenters is edited or sometimes even written by the Departments' Editors in close contact with the Deputy Chairmen. Pyotr Reshetov did it for *Vremya* during the Baltic events. By the way, *Vremya* has very rigid guidelines on what it can show on air, subject to approval by the leadership on a daily basis. Observance of the guidelines is ensured by a team of rather conservative editors. The guidelines may be subject to sudden changes. The initiative may come either from "above" or from "below". Those from "below" are mostly amendments of a non-political nature, which are suggested by the authors. The changes from above are done over the telephone. Everybody calls: Yazov, Lukyanov, Dzasokhov. Everyone who has a Kremlin telephone outlet.

All instructions are given by telephone. The written instructions issued by Reshetov to "suspend" work on *Vzglyad* provide a unique example in the history of Soviet television.

Question: How are live shows controlled?

Answer: There are the so-called tract rehearsals for live shows. This is when there are no audiences in the studio and the hosts say what they are due to say during the show. As it happens the show is watched by the Deputy Chairmen over the internal broadcasting system. In addition, live shows are viewed via the four Orbit systems. More often than not direct broadcasts are viewed. After that instructions are issued on which sequences need to be edited for subsequent showings. In principle, one could put a show on the air for the European part of the country with edited sequences and pretend that the show is coming live.

Question: The rumor is that live shows are put on the air with a 30-second gap during which things can be edited.

Answer: It doesn't seem to be the case. I have hosted live shows, and there would be a TV set in the studio which was connected to the external aerial. The pictures always fully coincided. However there is no need to "delay" the signal because the person who is monitoring on air can at any moment ring the control room or the program director. There are always presenters on the ready, the appropriate texts and reels with footage which may be used instead.

There are also some preliminary sanctions. For instance a studio may be simply locked. Or they can put up a police block in order to prevent the entrance of somebody who has been invited by the host. This is what they did when *Vzglyad* invited Andrei Sakharov for a live program. He never came but a police block was put up.

Question: Yeltsin said in his address at the Kirov works that the Central TV were under the auspices of the KGB.

Answer: I think he said it in a burst of passion. There is simply no need for the television to be controlled by the KGB. Kravchenko maintains personal contact with the highest-level authorities, but of course there are agents. The building in Ostankino is transparent.

Question: Are there any rigid criteria as to what can and cannot be shown and what can and what cannot be said?

Answer: They are difficult to put your finger on. In many ways the system of bans and permissions depends on taste. In a major way it is determined by the process of ongoing negotiations, the authors of programming being one party and the leaders of the organization being the other party. The negotiations are conducted either through the Editors or directly. The Chairman's personality plays an immensely important factor in this process. He provides the guidelines for what is allowed. This clearance is especially complicated, given the changing political situation.

Question: Several times programs announced in the listings have been replaced with films dealing with controversial political subjects. A few examples comprise the film "*Litso Ekstremizma*" (The Face of Extremism) which was shown instead of the last *Vzglyad*, "*Razmyshleniya na Baltiiskuyu Tema*" (Reflections on the Baltic Theme) and "*Chuzhiye Golosa*" (Alien Voices). These are strange films. The way they are shot is different from the usual manner of your correspondents. The films offer a comment which is biassed and one-sided. There are no credits to the authors, and there is no mention of the studios where they were shot. Where do such films come from?

Answer:	As a rule, they are made at the suggestion of the KGB which the latter clears with the top authorities. Besides, no secret is made of this. Teams of journalists and directors are then set up to make such films. The editing is done in Ostankino but the shooting is usually done previously by somebody in that government agency. It is obvious from the footage that either it was done using amateur equipment or on other systems and wasn't assembled on state television for this reason.
Question:	It is curious that while "*Vzglyad*" has been closed and "TSN" has been disciplined, "*Pyatoye Koleso*" is still putting its programming on air as if nothing had happened. How can you explain this?
Answer:	This could be due to the fact that the Leningrad TV doesn't cover the whole country. Or it could be that Bella Kurkova who is the Chief Editor of "*Pyatoye Koleso*" in Leningrad has more weight than the Chief Editors at the Central TV. There could be some kind of agreement between Sobchak and Gorbachev. The process of control is exactly what it is, a process, and as such it may have nuances and paradoxes.

Symbiosis of the Central TV and the KGB

President Gorbachev did not and could not carry on without an obedient national TV network. There were local TV networks, however, which have been Central TV's strong rivals. It looked like the Kremlin was ready to part with many things, including Pravda, plus the whole of the Central Committee's Politburo, for the sake of retaining on television its former monopoly on information in any form acceptable for the supreme leadership.

In the periods of sharp confrontation between the Kremlin and the republics' national liberation movements, the armed contingents of the KGB, of the Defense Ministry and of the Ministry of the Interior made attacks on the local TV centers. Since 1989, all of the TV centers in the Baltic and Transcaucasian republics, and in Moldova have gone through military sieges and even devastation. The TV centers of Lithuania, Latvia, Estonia, Moldova, Georgia and Armenia refused to follow the Kremlin's instructions, although for a long time the necessary minimum of proprieties was observed everywhere, and at the beginning of 1991, as before, all Soviet citizens watched the government-controlled program, "*Vremya*", broadcast from Moscow. The television networks of the Ukraine, Byelorussia, Azerbaijan and Kazakhstan, and of the three Central Asian republics (Turkmenia, Kirghizstan and Uzbekistan) angrily criticized the Union government's obvious reluctance to delegate considerable part of the demanded powers to the republics. As for the Russian Federation, the biggest republic of the USSR, it had no television network of its own. The Russian Federation and the USSR have one capital and, consequently, one television network. Despite that, Boris Yeltsin, then

Chairman of the Supreme Soviet of the Russian Federation, was very seldom given time on national TV.

On January 14, 1991, after a one-hour-long issue of the national TV program, "*Vremya*", which featured Mikhail Gorbachev and the Union ministers of defense and internal affairs, Dmitry Yazov and Boris Pugo, justifying the newly accomplished seizure of the Lithuanian TV center in Vilnius by the Soviet armed forces (the incident took 13 lives; hundreds of civilians were wounded; one serviceman was killed) the TV audience saw episodes from a film, shot in Riga in front of the Latvian TV center. In anticipation of an armed attack, the local population had encircled the building and blocked the approaches to it with prime-movers, tractors, lorries, concrete blocks and gravel. The next thirty seconds highlighted Boris Yeltsin's one-day visit to the Baltic republics and his press conference in Moscow. On the screen was Yeltsin, but the only thing the audience could hear was the remarks of a commentator who went silent just when Yeltsin was saying the following phrase: "I'm convinced that now Russia cannot do without an army of her own." Moreover, "*Vremya*'s" presenters contrived not to say that Yeltsin's visit to the Baltic republics had been crowned by the signing of one more joint document of the parliamentary leaders of the Russian Federation, Estonia, Latvia and Lithuania (the first one was signed in 1990), this time in protest against attempts to do away with the legitimately elected parliaments and governments by force of arms.

The way national TV, particularly the news program "*Vremya*", interpreted events in the union republics could disappoint hundreds of millions of spectators from Sofia to Kabul and from Berlin to the shores of Alaska. As for the TV viewers, who witnessed the key events of the liberation movement, silenced or distorted by "*Vremya*", they went hot and cold all over at the information broadcast from Moscow's TV center in Ostankino.

The thing is that in the autumn of 1990, the Communist Party lost the parliamentary elections in Georgia, as it had done earlier in Lithuania, Latvia, Estonia and Armenia. Even in the pre-perestroika times, national TV news did not enthuse TV audiences in the republics. That was mere brainwashing which kept the whole of the multi-national Soviet Union in a state of sleep. Really, who of the TV journalists or editors, speaking on "*Vremya*", would have ventured to offend same Georgia, whose boss, the then First Secretary of the Georgian Communist Party's Central Committee, Eduard Shevardnadze, was also an alternate member of the Communist Party's Central Committee's Politburo?

In the spring of 1989 after the tragedy of April 9, Central TV lashed out indiscriminately at all of the Georgian nationalists. Hence the letters coming to Moscow, to Central Television of the Soviet Union, some of which were published in the local press. Here is one of the most harmless letters, published in Tbilisi's Russian-language weekly *Narodnoye Obrazovaniye* (Public

Education), on October 12, 1990 and signed by Chairman of the Union of Georgian Christians V. Rtskhiladze.

On the night October 9, All-Union Central TV advertised the subscription campaign. The bit dealing with the magazine, *Sovetskaya Literatura*, showed one of the magazine's future authors, veteran of the Afghan war and "hero" of the Tbilisi tragedy of April 9, General Igor Rodionov, who smiled sweetly as he spoke about his plans. The magazine's Editor-in-Chief, Prokhanov, who sat next to him, said approximately the following: "There is much talk today about bad and Satanic Russia. But there is holy and mystical Russia, as well."

Then the audience saw masterpieces of church painting whose photos, they were told, will be published in this magazine.

Let me tell you that this letter is written by a Georgian, a believer, an Orthodox Christian, a former political prisoner who, in exile, where his heart was incessantly tormented by the clatter of the Russian soldiers' boots, watched with love and reverence holy mystical Russia, the Russia of Sergius of Radonezh and Serafim of Sarov, of Vladimir Solovyov and Leo Tolstoy.

Since my release, I have been translating into Georgian and also publishing gems of Russian religious philosophy, from Nikolai Berdyaev to Vladimir Losk. But your program showing the murderer of the Georgian people talking about the holy shrines of Russia, is super-blasphemy in my opinion. I am convinced that the same view is shared not only by Georgians, but by all honest and faithful Russians. Such programs and publications incite anti-Russian moods and Russophobia.

The next thing I would like to draw your attention to is the statements made in a Moscow court by anti-Semite, Smirnov-Ostashvili, shown in the same program, just a few minutes after Rodionov's speech. Your program introduced him to millions of TV viewers as Ostashvili, having edited out the Russian part of his name. I do not think that was accidental. Or are there no purely Russian names among the numerous Russian anti-Semites and supporters of the organization, Pamyat, that you chose Ostashvili? Or is the spreading of anti-Semitism in Russia is through the fault of Georgians, as well?

In the autumn of 1990 national TV began to drift towards the positions of "sound communist forces", as we used to say recently. The main national news program not only angered the ordinary viewer in the national republics, but depressed Russian intellectuals, as well.

In its second issue (September 1990), Moscow's new weekly, Kuranty, published the sensational results of an opinion poll in which the news program, "Vremya", was rated as the worst Soviet TV program, with an enormous gap down from the second worst program.

As long as there was only one news program, run by one department, we could not overcome its dull monotony and primitive bias. As in the Brezhnev era, it remained the voice of the state and a kind of illustration to TASS reports. Incidentally, whereas the essence of TASS aroused no doubts, "*Vremya*'s" illustrations could delude the viewer and create an illusion of plurality. Although it is clear that the diversity of illustrations cannot compensate for the monotony of the presented information.

The totality of this news program was conceived at the beginning. "Vremya" brazenly intervened in the evening prime time, splitting it into two unequal parts and devouring the best part of it. Moreover, all the channels were forced to show it, too: the official news was a must for all Soviet citizens. Only in the fifth year of perestroika did the ideological machine loosen its grip on television: depending on the day of the week, only three or four (!) out of the five channels received in Moscow showed "*Vremya.*"

The TV bosses used every chance to remind the audience that "*Vremya*" was the main program. It was the only program that knew no schedule. You might wait for a film, scheduled for 9:40 p.m. (i.e., after "*Vremya*") all evening and go to bed disappointed without seeing it. Almost daily this news program turned into a bulky and verbose account of some official event that in fact deserved just a couple of words. The rest might be presented in detail by newspapers.

"*Vremya*" announcers and commentators changed daily. Indeed, it is not that easy to pretend, in a live broadcast, that you are indignant over the actions of nationalists in Lithuania or Georgia when you know very well that foreign radio and half of the Soviet press cover the same events far more objectively. What a trial it must have been for the announcers of presidential TV (the TV channel expressing the President's will) to say in all earnest in "*Vremya*," on January 13 to 15, 1991, that the night assault on the Vilnius TV center by paratroopers, backed by tanks and by machine-gun fire against an unarmed crowd, had been sanctioned by the commander of the Vilnius military garrison without prior consultations with Moscow! Without suffering any pricks of conscience, "*Vremya*" assumed the functions of an exponent of the interests of those military-communist groups which did not conceal their plans to topple the legitimately elected governments in quite a few republics. Before perestroika, "*Vremya*" announcers would read what others had written for them. Under Leonid Kravchenko, "*Vremya*" commentators, gray-haired professional liars and fledglings alike, were involved in intensive subversive activity, doing their bets to fulfill the order of the outgoing communist forces in Moscow (Vilnius, Yerevan, Baku etc.).

By passing its own judgments on the events in the Baltic and Caucasian republics, the official news program "*Vremya*" acted as a detonator of a civil war, since it encouraged people of non-native nationalities to speak up. This is what analysts N. Koginova and L. Polskaya, specialists on TV, wrote in *Literaturnaya Gazeta's* article entitled *Vremya, Reverse!* (January 16, 1991):

> The position assumed by the leaders of the State Committee for Television and Radio (Gosteleradio) can only be described as information violence. The official news program <u>Vremya broadcasts biased, incomplete and often knowingly false</u>

information from Lithuania. In fact, the national TV channel has become a source of misinformation [underlined by me—G.V.]. Hundreds of millions of people get their scanty ration of truth from the TV News Service TSN, although even TSN reports have not escaped censorship.

In this crucial moment of our country's history, the role of objective information becomes well-nigh decisive. Given the fact that the Gosteleradio TV administration has taken the side of a certain political ideology, it can provoke events which may develop into a catastrophe.

In the same issue, *Literaturnaya Gazeta's* other famous reporter, Yuri Rost, appealed to his compatriots in his article *They Fired at You!*:

It was you, the reader, who was fired at in Vilnius. It was you who was killed in Tbilisi. And in Baku. And in Czechoslovakia, in Novocherkassk, in Afghanistan and Hungary.

You have not been killed not because you bent down. Simply, the burst of machine-gun fire, meant for you, is still to come. The neighbor's grandson is not grown-up enough yet to kill you, and your son—to kill the neighbor. But they are growing. They are brought up according to the laws of a dubious world, obediently fulfilling the orders of their chiefs, be they in military uniform or in civilian clothes, who implicated our children in their unseemly deeds, turning them from citizens into criminals. The older generation were children once, too, and were involved in a crime. Now they are indoctrinating the young.

A society based on the cover-up principle needs neither law nor freedom, and its ideologists implicate generation after generation in their crimes. They poison their minds, pushing them to crimes and covering them up from punishment.

Who has been punished for thousands of victims in Afghanistan?

Who has been punished for those killed in Tbilisi?

Who has been punished for bloodshed in Baku, Prague, Novocherkassk and Budapest?

No one.

Who will be punished for the bloody night in Vilnius?

This means that more children and adults will be caught in this horrible whirlwind, and that dozens and maybe hundreds of thousands of people with a conscience that was not freed by fair punishment will take the side of those who know about them being implicated in unseemly deeds. They will be bound by the common fear of exposure, which is, incidentally, indispensable for making a political career in our social system.

Oh God! How can one describe a state where you can climb the political ladder only if you have made a deal with your conscience and know that your fault is known to others.

Stop turning your citizens into accomplices~ Put away your machine-guns. Go out of Lithuania and never enter Leningrad, Moscow, Kiev or Vorkuta. The reader, look at your son. He will fire at you. Do not look away, but ward his arm off! No more victims and criminals!

Allow at least one generation of Soviet citizens to grow up to be honest, and they will save their country. Each one his own country.

I do not think we could ever live to see the emergence of an honest generation, if we have TV like ours. TV bosses have been replaced quite often in recent years. Indeed, it is not easy to popularize perestroika in a way that would not hurt the System, that would keep the "socialist values" intact as we move towards the market and preserve glasnost in iron rule.

On November 14, 1990, by the Soviet President's decree, the 52-year old People's Deputy of the USSR Leonid Kravchenko became the Gosteleradio boss, replacing M. Nenashev after his 18 months in office. All of the TV and radio headquarters in Pyatnitskaya and Shabolovka streets and in Ostankino are very well known to him. For four years prior to his brief performance as TASS Director General, he was Gosteleradio's First Deputy Chairman in charge of TV, which was a time of cardinal change on TV and the emergence of the most popular TV programs, "120 Minutes," Vzglyad and "Before and After Midnight." But people have a nasty habit of changing. At least this is what an extremely spiteful and experienced *Izvestia* correspondent, V. Arsenyev, meant when on December 4, 1990 he headlined his interview with the new TV boss "I Have Come to Fulfill the Will of the President—Leonid Kravchenko." The title was very much to the point, although I do not think the almost 90 staffers of Soviet TV would share this motto gladly.

Soviet television's new concept, as set forth by Leonid Kravchenko (shortly before, similar decisions made at the top were revealed by his predecessor, M. Nenashev), is based on the following postulate: the rule of the once omnipotent Department of Ideology of the Communist Party Central Committee is over. A new era is coming, Kravchenko said, whereby each of the four channels will receive relative commercial freedom and specialize in different subjects.

Channel 1, the new boss said, is the main channel broadcast throughout the country and subordinated to the President. Among its sponsors are also the Supreme Soviet of the USSR and the government. Channel 2, not received by the entire territory of the USSR, will be called "Sodruzhestvo" (Community) and run jointly with the newly-founded Russian TV. Channel 3 has been reserved for Moscow and Moscow Region and will be run jointly with the Moscow City Soviet and public organizations (the Communist Party one of them). Channel 4, so far dedicated to educational programs, is viewed as the 21st Century Television, which means that it will do what it is doing at the moment but still better.

The relation between Central TV and republican TV and radio committees, until recently rigidly subordinated to the former, are being put on the same footing as the relation between the central and republican press and book-printing organizations. The republics that will sign a cooperation agreement with Central TV, or rather with the Coordinating Council for TV and Radio which will replace the current Gosteleradio, will have an opportunity to buy, at more or less stable prices, TV equipment. The republics which do not sign such an agreement (for instance, the Baltics, Georgia and Moldavia) will not have such an opportunity. Perhaps they will buy it for hard currency or at an exorbitant price from Moscow.

In another interview (*Pravda*, November 27, 1990), Kravchenko said that every year TV is allotted 2.7 billion rubles, of which 2 million are immediately taken by the Ministry of Communications. The filming equipment, relay lines, space tele-communication satellites, land aerials, as well as time and frequencies are under the Ministry of Communications' control, and all parts of this sophisticated equipment are manufactured by defense enterprises. The conclusion is that neither the TV staff, not journalists will control it.

The title of the interview was not without a hint either, "Re-Distribution in Ostankino," suggesting that the forthcoming re-distribution of property will leave the disobedient with what they have at the moment at the best, or with nothing at all, at the worst. An original form of censorship, isn't it? Instead of the former Glavlit, every program will now be dealt with by generals, financiers and President's advisers.

The republican and regional TV programs are always alternated with programs broadcast from Moscow. But there is no "feedback." Muscovits can watch anything they like (even Western TV programs if they have expensive individual or collective aerials) except programs of republican TV centers. Leningrad has been given time on national TV as "one of us." TV has promised, however, to show bits made by republican TV studios on Channel 2, alongside programs of Russian TV. The parade of the republics on Channel 2 will be commanded by the Central TV bosses.

The schedule of TV innovations, to say nothing of the date of this TV monster's split into four independent TV companies, have not been given. In its present form, TV keeps its journalists safely on the lead. As to the public, TV is independent of it and is on the state budget. A few advertisements and the emergence of commercial bits, paid by outsiders, do not make any difference. Our much praised Central TV does not care how many people watch its programs. Those were the words, spoken by M. Nenashev at his last press conference on November 13, 1990, a few hours before his resignation. Many had criticized him, of course, but the few days following his resignation again showed to the world that the Kremlin was drifting to the right (Alexander Yakovlev, Vadim Bakatin and Eduard Shevardnadze left the political science one after another).

Today no one can watch the "Vzglyad" program which was described by TV reporter Yevgeni Dodolev in the popular newspaper *Moskovsky Komsomolets* (October 27, 1990) in an article entitled *Pamyat, KGB and "Vzglyad."*

Retired lieutenant-colonel of the KGB, Valentin Korolyov chose not to remain a pawn in somebody's hands. I do not think that act of repentance was easy form him to accomplish. Nevertheless, on October 19, accounts of this ex-counter-intelligence agent could be read in the magazine *Ogonyok* (No. 43, 1990), and heard on TV in the programs "Vzglyad" and VID.

Valentin Korolyov said that Pamyat, in its current role, is the brainchild of the KGB, conceived as an instrument of political and, subsequently, armed struggle against objectionable social trends. All of this organization's prominent figures are on the secret service's payroll, Valentin Korolyov said, and many of them believe that they, Russian nationalists, are guiding the KGB along. (When he proposed a parallel KGB department to recruit a Pamyat member, he was given to understand that the entire leadership of that organization was on the KGB payroll).

Thus, the KGB bosses think that Pamyat is under their control, while the godfathers of Soviet-made fascism believe, on the contrary, that the KGB is in their hands. All of the Pamyat members are ready to act when required. The mutual penetration of Pamyat and the KGB, Valentin Korolyov believes, has reached its highest point.

You might remember that Vzglyad as part of the Friday program VID was broadcast live to the Far East in the day time (and was subsequently repeated in Siberia and Central Asia via Orbita satellites), and in the evening, also live, to the European part of the USSR. The two versions usually differed.

The bits recorded on October 19 were not edited. However, unlike the recorded bits, the live ones differed from each other like "Vremya" differed from the program "Seven Days," pulled off the air by the Politburo. In all of the Orbita versions the interview with Valentin Korolyov was crowned with the following dialogue between the two hosts of the program:

DODOLEV: Back to the KGB, now. Since last spring Valentin Korolyov has been trying to get in touch with our popular deputies and with the most radical publications. It looks like the watchful KGB has its secret informers everywhere.

LYUBIMOV: "Assistants," using the KGB language.

DODOLEV: Besides paid ASSISTANTS, there are involuntary ones. Even the fearless *Ogonyok* officially refused to publish his article, titled "The Secrets of Secret Services." At the last moment, however, the editors decided to keep the manuscripts to themselves, so the author received the letter of refusal without his manuscript attached. time dots all the i's and crosses all the t's, however. *Ogonyok's* issue No. 43, which the readers will receive tomorrow, will carry Korolyov's article at last.

LYUBIMOV: Anticipating an attempt on his life, Valentin Korolyov had given a part of his archives to our program's archives. Incidentally, if any

	of the Pamyat leaders decide to refute their involvement in the KGB, we are ready to invite them to the studio for a discussion.
DODOLEV:	Many must have been amazed by the KGB's link with Pamyat. I, too, once wondered why the young thugs from Pamyat escaped punishment, how Pamyat managed to hold a meeting in Red Square and how Pamyat got into the Central House of Writers, when I and my colleagues were denied admission even though we showed our journalists' cards. I do not wonder any more. The state has the Party, and the KGB has Pamyat.
LYUBIMOV:	Perhaps otherwise: the party has a state? I doubt sometimes if the army or the super-syndicate, the KGB, are really subordinate to the president.
DODOLEV:	Most of the KGB leaders are not professional intelligence or counter-intelligence officers but ex-party officials. They are loyal to the caste principles which, as we know, they cannot betray. Many of the KGB leaders are... um... veterans, so to say. Among them is one Lt.-Gen. Tolkunov, who is in charge of the KGB's Inspection Department, no matter that he is 75 years old. When Gorbachev worked in Stavropol Region, Tolkunov was the head of the local KGB. General Kalugin believes this is an important fact. To whom do Tolkunov and the KGB report? To no one! The KGB may invent some paper threat (similar to General Kalugin), convince the supreme leadership that such a threat exists, sign a related document and act on it. It's a state within a state.
LYUBIMOV:	"Intelligence and counter-intelligence are not within the range of our inspection," Viktor Ilyukhin, Chief of the Procurator's Office's Department Monitoring the Implementation of the Law by the KGB, admitted in *Literaturnaya Gazeta* a few days ago. "It is impossible to regulate its activity with laws." Of course one could see that the Lefortovo prison is kept in order. Suppose the Procurator's Office exercises certain control over the KGB. But. In charge of this dubious inspection service is Deputy Procurator-General Abramov, who had previously worked for the KGB.
DODOLEV:	Incidentally, he worked in the 5th Department and was its chief. This department which, we are told, is busy safeguarding the constitution, once tackled the Solzhenitsyn and Sakharov cases.
LYUBIMOV:	Abramov worked under keen supervision of the current 2nd Deputy Chairman of the KGB, Bobkov, with whom Ivan Abramov maintains friendly relations to this day, in the spirit of cooperation between the incorruptible Procurator's Office and the magnificent KGB going back to the time of Vyshinsky and Beria. Dog does not eat dog.

At a brief conference after the Orbita broadcast, we decided to hold the Moscow issue still more rigidly and stake our all. But the KGB itself put the necessary accents.

As far as I know the Orbita variant is checked in at least three places in Moscow: the State Committee for Radio and Television, Staraya Square (the Central Committee's headquarters) and Lubyanka (the KGB). The program broadcast to the Far East ends at about 4 p.m. A couple of hours later telephone buzzed in the Vzglyad director's room No. 1231. By the time the program *Vremya* was to begin, two visitors—a colonel and a major—arrived at the Ostankino TV center. They said they would like to comment on the bit about the KGB, live.

It would have been inhospitable to deny such rare guests an opportunity to speak. The subject of the conversation was not known to us, but we guessed that Korolyov would be accused of a) having been recruited by the Israeli intelligence, b) being mentally unbalanced, c) having been bribed by Zionist cooperators and d) having been dismissed from the KGB for alcoholism. The same charges, with the exception of the last one, could be brought against Vzglyad.

The more so since when "Vzglyad" had been preparing an interview with a KGB veteran K., one of the visitors blackmailed the host, Artyom Borovik, and editor, Tatiana Dmitrakova.

"We keep files on all members of the `Vzglyad' team. If this bit is shown, we shall publish compromising material about you in all central publications.

"Let us have a look at what you have," the `Vzglyad' guys said. Unfortunately, K. did not appear on TV. The KGB put pressure on other people.

Last Friday passed without threats.

The officers proved to be excellent debaters, however, and managed to lead the discussion away from Pamyat and Korolyov. They told the audience politely that there are no basements in Lubyanka. They also spoke about Savinkov's suicide and new books.

At the end of December 1990, Soviet Foreign Minister Eduard Shevardnadze resigned. None of the supreme leaders ever resigned in this country over its history of 70 years. Shevardnadze announced his decision at a session of the Soviet Supreme Soviet, broadcast live. He resigned in protest against growing pressure put on him by the supporters of the oncoming military dictatorship. It is quite possible that Eduard Shevardnadze knew that he would have to go, but did not want to do so as obediently as the ex-minister of internal affairs Vadim Bakatin did. Central TV stopped mentioning Eduard Shevardnadze's name a few hours after he announced his resignation, although he continued to remain in office for another three weeks.

This is how *Komsomolskaya Pravda* (December 29, 1990) responded to the event in one of A. Vassilyev's notes, entitled *Out of Sight, Out of "Vzglyad."* Who and why banned the program with Shevardnadze's aides participating?

Yesterday, TV viewers did not see the program "Vzglyad" in which ex-Foreign Minister Eduard Shevardnadze's closest associates Teimuraz Stepanov, the ex-minister's aid, and Sergei Tarasenko, Chief of the Planning Department, were to speak. As we learned, Steanov and Tarasenko were the first people to learn about Shevardnadze's contemplated resignation.

"Moreover, a strange situation emerged after his resignation: the West was in turmoil and in this country there was total silence. Each new version concerning Shevardnadze's resignation was even more improbable than the next. Therefore, Tarasenko and I decided to appear in `Vzglyad.'"

"Why were you denied such an opportunity?"

"I don't know."

We got in touch with 'Vzglyad.'

"Yes, we wanted to invite Teimuraz Stepanov and Sergei Tarasenko," Alexander Lyubimov said. "But Gosteleradio's chairman and his deputies prohibited us to do so. Since Monday we've been trying to persuade them—all in vain. It is clear that it was a political decision.

"Without a story about Shevardnadze we could not go on air. We did not want to raise a ballyhoo over this and score points that way. But things took a different turn."

"I have information that Leonid Kravchenko discussed the matter with Mikhail Gorbachev."

"Most probably Leonid Kravchenko, just appointed to his new post, discussed the issue with the top leaders. By the way, on January 4 we are planning to show the film `The Team' about Eduard Shevardnadze and his colleagues, instead of the usual Vzglyad program. The film was banned as well."

So we phoned Leonid Kravchenko.

"The guys wanted to invite Shevardnadze. I told them not to do it, because I knew that Shevardnadze would not come all the same. In the evening I had a meeting with Alexander Lyubimov, who said they would not go on air. Next time they are ready to broadcast their program will be January 11. I suggested that they invite Yanayev. They refused."

"As far as we know, you banned the program with Shevardnadze's aids participating."

"I didn't... I don't know... It's games..."

We phoned Alexander Lyubimov again.

"For the first time over the past six months a ban was put not on a guest but on the subject itself. I can only guess that the standard card, confirming the inviolability of the hierarchal mentality is played. It's better to be closer to the top of the pyramid than to its bottom.

"The situation is more than strange. We have grown used to strange things happening to Vzglyad. But now in the focus of the argument is Eduard Shevardnadze, whose name seems to have been crossed out from all programs. Who will believe now in the statements concerning the inviolability of the Soviet foreign policy?"

At the beginning of 1991 TV's best political program "Vzglyad" kicked the bucket. The weekly *Argumenty i Fakty* (No. 2, January, 1991) front-paged the following account of this sad event:

> "Vzglyad's New Year issue did not go on air, and neither did the next issues. On January 4, the TV administration again did not allow `Vzglyad' to show the film `The Team' about Eduard Shevardnadze and his colleagues, and on January 8 Alexander Lyubimov, who was in charge of the program, was told by Gosteleradios' Deputy Chairman P. Reshetov that the program was indefinitely suspended. Our correspondent A. Binev interviewed this popular program's authors.

Question: Was the decision of the Gosterleradio administration final?

A. Lyubimov, head of the program: We were told that the program would not go on air until we formulate our concept. Our concept is put forth in corresponding documents, however, and our job is to spotlight social and political events in this country. I think Leonid Kravchenko did not like the way we did it.

Question: Or was it because you spotlighted reshuffles in the upper echelons of power, including the well-known statement by Shevardnadze?

A. Politkovsky, `Vzglyad' special correspondent: I think it was only a pretext designed to see what we were really after. By January 11, 1991 we had produced a plan of our program without bits about Shevardnadze. The program was not shown all the same.

Question: Why?

A. Lyubimov: We were told that the political views of the Gosteleradio's administration and of our program differed. That was the main reason.

Question: Isn't it the beginning of a crusade against the democratic media?

A. Shipilov, Director of TV company VID: No one authorized us to speak on behalf of all the democratic media, but what is going on worries us, as we consider this to be not merely a one-time attempt to close down `Vzglyad,' but the confirmation of certain political trends. I perceive this as a sign of political censorship which is banned by the law on the press and other media.

V. Listyev, `Vzglyad' observer: In the past two and a half years we had a chance to express different views on TV. And so we did. We fitted into the general trend and, moreover, were pioneers in this field. Now that a need has arisen to consolidate the centralized authority, the trend began to change. We are not wanted any more.

The weekly *Kommersant* (December 31, 1990) quoted a `Vzglyad' observer as saying the following: "Although party and ideological control has been removed, we have again found ourselves in a situation where the creative work is 80 percent a fight for getting our material accepted." At the end of 1990 and the beginning of 1991 the Yeltsin-Gorbachev confrontation, or rather the struggle between the divided democrats and the close ranks of the military-party oligarchy, became more acute. "Vzglyad" announcers were laid off on the day when the KGB elite spetsnaz troops started the shoot-out in Vilnius in preparation for a coup there and later in Latvia.

But "Vzglyad" did not die, as is proven by the article of Nikolai Kirillov, *Politkovsky's Kitchen: `Vzglyad' Underground*, published in the weekly *Golos* of the Russian Union of Journalists (No. 23, July 17, 1991):

One day the kitchen of Alexander Politkovsky turned into the "Vzglyad" studio. The equipment they use is not professional, although of high quality. they have shot already the third program in this way.

Journalists know very little about how the program is made, because it is very difficult to find its authors and coordinators, people's deputies of Russia Lyubimov and Politkovsky. And yet I found Politkovsky, the author of the first underground program, which has become a legend since.

Question: How much do underground "Vzglyad" programs cost?
Answer: Twenty-five to thirty thousand rubles each, and this is not much. A similar program will cost 75,000 rubles at the state television. We shoot our programs in the kitchen and don't have to pay for broadcasting them. We only spend money on trips and equipment.
Question: Where are your program shown?
Answer: We make video cassettes and send them to TV studios throughout the country. Not long ago a "Vzglyad" program was broadcast live from Riga for the Baltic republics. We will probably maintain relations with Leningrad TV.
Question: Why not accept the patronage of Russian TV, whose director general is the former head of your program?
Answer: Russian TV is a state structure just like Central TV, and like Kravchenko, its chairman has a direct telephone line to the Kremlin. Russian colleagues may be more democratic, but the situation there is not unlike that on Central TV.

When we started shooting underground "Vzglyad" programs, we knew the place it would take and the role it would play in society. The work of state-owned TV studios is unpredictable. If Ryzhkov wins the elections, we know whom Russian TV will serve. I don't think TV should try to pamper the ambitions of statesmen. That is why we have decided to establish an independent organization, the limited liability stock company Vzglyad.

We are turning into a kind of capitalists, but this is a guarantee against anybody trying to interfere with our business. Nobody can enter our premises without permission. We have no political censorship. I am both the owner and the censor of the program.

"Vzglyad" cannot be banned now, because we are independent financially and legally, and are operating in accordance with law. Experienced lawyers are helping "Vzglyad," and it is our financial principle never to engage in illicit machinations.

Question: Have you been offered to establish a joint venture with a U.S., West German or Italian company?

Answer: Of course we have, but I am against it. This would hinder us from attaining our main goal of creating a truthful information program, which the people need. Later on "Vzglyad" clips might be used by, say, Japan, but initially I don't want our association to be modeled after Hong Kong companies.

We have received an interesting proposal: to buy air time on Central TV, but this will cost 150 million rubles. We have only 20 million. A commercial agreement with Central TV seems like a good idea, if the sides keep to its conditions: the seller sells air time, the buyer pays for it. Nothing more.

Question: How much does a cassette with an Underground Vzglyad program cost?

Answer: Being a people's deputy, I have no moral right to raise the price from 200 to 1,200 rubles. Yet we manage somehow to keep our business profitable and to pay the team who works on the program.

Question: What subjects do you usually take on yourself?

Answer: I contributed to the first program material about the secret of the notorious room in the building of the Russian Parliament, the one owned by the KGB and allegedly stuffed with equipment needed to stop information leakage. I tried to make people understand that despite the new legislation the KGB and the Party Central Committee are still linked like the white and the yolk of an egg.

You want proof? The KGB is still prohibited to collect compromising materials about party leaders. Until this ban is not lifted, these two organizations will not be separated. I used the assistance of Yeltsin's guards, one-time KGB men. I have not revealed any state secrets, although I know some.

I am currently making two video programs about Yeltsin. The idea is to analyze not only his successes but also the reasons for his flops.

CHAPTER XI

TELEVISION TECHNOLOGY

The Kremlin Threatens to Shoot Down Russia's First Communication Satellite

When Lenin and his colleagues were scheming their coup in 1917, they decided to commence it by capturing the post office, telegraph and telephone facilities. In 1991 an abortive coup to overthrow the constitutional power in Lithuania began from an attack on the Vilnius TV center by airborne troops and KGB units supported by tanks. By that time the country had already enjoyed hard-core Leninist and liar Leonid Kravchenko, planted by the Communist party and KGB at the head of Central Television in Autumn 1990. Kravchenko betrayed his home country, compatriots and common sense in each instalment of the evening news program *Vremya*. In August 1991 he turned on President Gorbachev, though limited his betrayal to the three days of the putsch. He got away with it, although consequently lost his high post. Systematic deception is not yet considered a crime in this country, and therefore cannot be legally punished.

As for the television tower and center in Vilnius, destroyed by the Soviet Army, Lithuania presented as early as February 1991 a bill to Moscow, amounting to 18,000,000 rubles. With the inflated ruble and the fact that the occupied Vilnius television center was out of operation from January to September 1991 taken into account, the total damage jumps up to several hundred million rubles.

However the Communist Party and its Secretary General, concurrently President, lost their monopoly on television long before the August 1991 coup. TV centers in former Union republics, now sovereign states, had already been independent by that time. Today TV centers in almost all autonomous republics within the Russian Federation and in dozens of Russian cities follow their own broadcasting policy. The lifting of censorship in August 1990 gave rise to hundreds of cable television networks and commercial joint-stock and private TV studios, to say nothing of former Union republics, launching their own communications satellites.

St. Petersburg Television, catering to viewers in all of central Russia and Estonia, has a two-thousand-strong staff.

State-owned television in the Ukraine employs dozens of thousands in Kiev and in fourteen regional TV centers. Ten more local TV centers will soon enter into rivalry with the 15-hour-long daily TV broadcasts from Kiev. The Ukrainian Channel 1, covering the whole of the republic, has been in operation for forty years. A new 24-story TV center, as soon as it is built and equipped, will gear the Ukrainian information and commercial Channel 2. Bearing a strong resemblance to the Ostankino TV center in Moscow, this Kievan telegiant has already risen in the old town next to the 380-meter-high TV tower. Does it seem that Kiev will continue to finance Soviet Central TV? Hardly. Kiev is prepared to transmit Moscow television to the Ukraine, but it is not going to pay for it. Instead, it offers to telecast Ukrainian channels to Russia in exchange. With millions of Ukrainians resident on its territory, Russia would be happy to watch Ukrainian channels, the same way as half of Europe and a big portion of Asia would be happy to view Leningrad TV. To do so some of satellites, thousands of which have been launched by this country's military and paramilitary agencies, are required.

Twenty-one TV centers and the Alma-Ata-based national channel are on the air in the Kazakh steppes and deserts.

The Communist party in Russia fought tooth and nail to prevent democratically-minded people from appearing on the air. It took the democrats nine months of exhausting struggle to obtain at least part-time access to television facilities in Ostankino in Moscow, when journalist Tatiana Ivanova of the *New Times* weekly was able to entitle her notes in the magazine's issue No. 21, 1991, written on the occasion of Russian Television's first and long-awaited TV appearance, "*Russia On the Air!*":

> Shame on sceptics! Shame on those, who said that if we wanted to have Russian TV, first of all, we had to raise money, at least a ruble from each resident in Russia, and all of us build a TV tower, higher than the one in Ostankino. Secondly we had to launch another money-raising campaign, and exchange the collected money for hard currency at a flea market and a flea market rate. After that, they said, the exchanged currency had to be smuggled abroad to purchase TV equipment, which also had to be smuggled back. And that we should give it at least five years to assemble the equipment. And only when a tower, TV center and assembled equipment come together, would we be able to watch Russian TV. I confess that I was one of those sceptics and I am sorry for that.
>
> In fact, it took considerably less time for Russian TV to go on the air, for Russia was allowed to use the Ostankino TV Tower. Indeed, the generosity and kindness of Ostankino's legitimate and actual owners have no limits. The fact that they shared the most valuable thing, air time, deserves special mention, for Russian TV was apportioned a very convenient time indeed!

The first two portions (each two hours long) are during work hours, when people come to their work places, draw lots for food coupons and after that have nothing to do. And here it is, Russian TV.

The last two Russian TV hours come late at night. That is, instead of sleeping. If you don't feel like having bad dreams at night, don't go to bed. Rather sit down on a chair in front of your TV box and don't waste your time while you are waiting for Russian television to come. Darn your socks!

The date for Russian TV's inaugural appearance was also chosen with taste. Yes, Monday the 13th. That was a date indeed! Exactly four months since the TV center in Vilnius had been captured and guards with automatic rifles put on guard at its doors. It had been exactly four months since the whole country had got it clear that television was the Communist party's inviolable property and that this party even had the right to kill anyone who would dare touch it. Unfortunately, folks here are foolish, and those in Vilnius did dare. Naturally they had to be frightened off by tanks. People in Moscow thought better than to go to Ostankino. They rallied in Manezh Square, shouting that television was theirs, because the TV center had been built and its staff educated with their money, while they, the people, worked hard at factories. Russia, they demanded, should be let in, for it was also a state. Even Kirghizia, the shouts went, had its own TV and Russia didn't.

I think Russian Television's marvellous announcers should stop blushing and say frankly to televiewers why their video doesn't always coincide with the audio, and the picture is far from clear, and why something there cuts or switches off or on at from clear, and why something there cuts or switches off or on at the wrong moment.

I would advise them to make it a point and regularly remind the TV audience that Russian Television doesn't possess any TV equipment except a children's film projector, working on batteries, which are virtually unavailable, and if you are lucky to come across them, you can't afford them. And that you, televiewers, should be aware that the rest of the TV equipment in Ostankino belongs not to us, but Central Television, presented by a presidential decree to Comrade Kravchenko and turned by the latter in no time into Kravchenkovision. Well, being folks with manners, you never grab things which don't belong to you, do you? We don't either. So you'll have to be patient. Now look, we've managed to find a mike in the garbage. Do you hear any better? Good! Don't worry, we'll save money and build our own TV Tower, and things will be different some day. But you'll have to be patient enough.

If Russian TV's announcers follow my piece of advice, it will have a tremendous, even invaluable educational impact on televiewers, who will feel themselves ever more loyal to Kravchenko, Central TV, presidential decrees, party property and its inviolability. . .

Though I must admit, people are very fond of all these things already today. Very fond indeed.

As for me, I watched Russian TV's programs constantly with great pleasure on the first days after it appeared on the air. And I close my eyes to its blunders, for I never forget about the children's film projector and the mike from the garbage. What blunders can one speak of in such circumstances?

There is only one thing left I would like to say: Welcome! We've waited for you for so long. We are happy to meet you!

Tatiana Ivanova's point of view was presented in *New Times* in the Women's Logic column. What do you expect to hear from a woman, they would say. Let her say anything, even the real truth, but we (evidently, the editorial staff) wouldn't believe her. For what was considered to be truth in the Soviet Union? Any lie, provided it was uttered from the Kremlin rostrum or published in *Pravda*.

To make the reader of this book believe in what this honest journalist Ivanova says, I would like to confirm her words with the opinion of the no less honest Mikhail Poltoranin, Russian Minister for the Press and Information, who voiced it in the *Golos* (Voice) daily (No. 17, 1991), the organ of the USSR Journalists' Union.

> When President Gorbachev turned his back on Russia by issuing a decree on the creation of an All-Union State Television and Radio Broadcasting Company, our Ministry was confronted with the task of searching for other ways for Russia's independent television and radio to go on the air. Thanks to President Gorbachev (Kravchenko declared that he followed his instructions), many Russians were deprived of the chance to listen to their radio station, which had been pushed to some other frequency.
>
> According to this decree, Russia's property had to be transferred to Kravchenko, authorized to personally control it, which was a gross violation of the USSR Constitution. At a sitting of the USSR Supreme Soviet Committee on Glasnost, Rights and Appeals I exhaustively demonstrated which articles of the Constitution and how they had been violated by the President, giving evidence that his decree was juridically inconsistent. The President, sworn to comply with the Constitution, constantly infringes on it and, moreover, gets angry that he is not held in high esteem.
>
> So we took efforts to find a solution and discovered laid-up civil defense radio channels. It turned out that the satellite catering to Central TV had seven broadband channels, of which it employed only two, whereas five others were used by the military.
>
> We also found out that there was a TV center with a tower on the road to Noginsk in Moscow Region, built and reserved for potential military activity.
>
> Moreover, mobile printing shops with good equipment have been created and reserved for the same purpose. They also stay idle, and that at a time when there is a lack of facilities to print newspapers. The reserved printing shops should be urgently engaged, however Central authorities act like a dog in a manger. We'll investigate the case of the printing shops staying idle, but I would like my colleagues to know that we do have them in Russia.
>
> And now I would like to tell you how our quest for a communications channel for Russian Radio developed. The Council of Ministers of the Russian Federation adopted a decision, sealed by Silayev, whereby Russia could make use of a civil defense satcom channel. This decision fully complies with the law, for all civil defense communications lines on the territory of the Russian Federation belong to none other than Russia.

We just tried to put things in motion, and what a fuss it brought about! Informers hurried to Marshall Yazov (I know the name of a general who was in such a hurry), and he in turn to Gorbachev. Eventually the President issued a classified decree, declaring the Russian Council of Ministers' resolution null and void.

It's useful for my colleagues to know who stands so reliably on guard of the mass media facilities, belonging to Russia and its people. Why do they do that? Obviously, to be able to continue disinforming people by dosing in the best Bolshevik traditions the truth about national developments, and sieving away facts which the people should be spared of.

Our Ministry is busy today creating a material base for its own mass media. We've already launched a communications satellite, which cost us 20 million rubles. As soon as we manage to transfer Central TV's Channel 2 to Russian Television, we'll need two more satcoms to extend the Russian channel to the entire population.

We'll use another satellite channel to transmit coded 'matrixes' of Republican newspapers to local printing shops, enabling them to reach their readers in Siberia and the Far East the day they are issued.

The military demanded 40,000,000 rubles for the second satellite we would like to put into orbit. Consequently the USSR Communications Ministry laid their claims to these satellites. Does this imply we would have to ask permission from the USSR Communications Ministry to use the channel? I'm sure it won't give it, preferring to remain under the heel of the Center and Gorbachev.

We went out of our way, asserting Russia's rights to them, only to hear the following warning: 'If you don't give up your claims to the channels, we warn you that it's not that difficult to...shoot the satellite down...'

In a nutshell, the warning implied the following: Listen pals, you've gone too far, even daring to speak the truth to the President. Have you forgotten in whose hands the power, army and rockets are? We've had enough of you playing independence. That's all.

I'm afraid the threat is quite real, for there is a tough clash, or to be more exact a real war, between Russia and the Center for the right to inform the population. Russia doesn't have currency to create its own TV. What it has goes to purchase medicines and food, and it would have been immoral to demand even some of it to buy studio equipment.

Therefore I suggested another solution at the rally. I appealed to the people, saying that they themselves were capable of creating alternative TV, and suggested that those interested in it could help it by contributing, say, a half gram of gold, provided naturally that they had it, to the Russian Independent TV Fund, which would be used to buy equipment.

Besides, I made the warning to shoot down the satellite public at the March 28 rally. The next day the "*Vremya*" program blamed Poltoranin for misinforming the public. How do you like that?

Soviet press had been forbidden to make any references to the domination of the military industrial complex in the national economy. Five years of "glasnost and perestroika" had to pass before censorship was lifted. We learnt many curious things after August 1990...Another number of revelations reached us after August 1991. However even the first wave of exposures turned out to be too big a shock for the majority of us. It's one thing listening to what our defectors whisper on the air through the "enemy's voices. " Another thing is to hear it admitted by People's Deputies of the Supreme Soviet, and Ministers and journalists.

You never get bored listening to or reading Minister Poltoranin—the talented journalist and strong and not indifferent man in him show. Vladimir Bulgak, Russia's Minister of Communications, Information and Space, who had showed enough perseverance as the head of the new Ministry right from its first days, displayed emotion within reasonable limits in his interview, given to *Rossiiskaya Gazeta* (June 26, 1991). Here is what he said to Vladimir Fyodorov, a *Rossiiskaya Gazeta* correspondent, on the eve of the launching of Russia's second satcom to a geo-stationary orbit:

Bulgak: Russia hosts the world's biggest telecorporation, featuring 620 powerful transmitters, over 7,000 satellite receivers, and some 9,000 retransmitters, supported by a satellite network catering to five time zones. However three million people in Russia are deprived of the opportunity to watch TV. It sounds strange, but two dozen thousand cities and villages in Russia's European part are incapable of receiving TV. To put an end to this injustice, we launched Russia's first satellite in November 1990. Assisted by local bodies of power, we are now busy assembling ground stations to receive TV. Next year all people resident in the European part of Russia will be able to watch Central TV's Channels 1 and 2. Soon we will launch another satcom, and a third one by the end of the year. This means that Russian TV, like Central TV's Channel 1, will be available to 97 per cent of Russia's residents.

Corr.: **Yet two channels are not that much for such a large republic as Russia.**

Bulgak: We've submitted our further development program for the Council of Ministers' consideration, which envisages the introduction of another Russian channel by the end of 1995.

Corr.: **Is it profitable to invest in these projects?**

Bulgak: Speaking in modern language, we can make money even with the help of those outdated satcoms which we launch today. As soon as commercial TV takes ground, prospective advertisers will flood us with orders. This will enable us to return the invested money. It's quite realistic. We received over a hundred business proposals with regard to our first satellite, but were able to satisfy only thirty requests.

Corr.: **Russia was the first republic of the former Union to successfully challenge Glavkosmos' undivided monopoly. How did you manage it?**

Bulgak: We were the first in the country to buy a satellite. It was manufactured by the Applied Mechanics Association in Krasnoyarsk. The Missile Forces sold us a serial Proton rocket, capable of delivering five-ton payloads to a geo-stationary orbit. I would like to emphasize the fact

	that we didn't launch the satcom at the expense of the Union budget, which could have saved us the risk. We risked a lot. So to be on the safe side, we had to insure all stages of the launching. That came as a big surprise to all insurance companies in the country.
Corr.:	**I wonder, what was the insurance?**
Bulgak:	Among those who were the first to offer their services to us were the Vostok Bank and the USSR Ingosstrakh. We preferred the latter because people there managed to swiftly provide the requisite international documents regulating such things. We insured the first launching for seven per cent, having paid 650,000 rubles. Prices have gone up since then.
Corr.:	**Still, how did you manage to acquire a rocket? What was the sellers' initial reaction?**
Bulgak:	They were puzzled at first, but then got used to the idea: Russia buys, Russia risks.
Corr.:	**The Russian Federation allocates 23 billion rubles to the Union's budget to support Glavkosmos, among other things. That means you purchased something that has already been paid for by the tax-payers. That is, they have paid twice for one and the same spacecraft.**
Bulgak:	You're right. But we've won a stipulation, according to which the satellite's use will entirely be governed by the government of Russia, rather than those state agencies which could impose their veto on its use.
Corr.:	**You did this to acquire freedom?**
Bulgak:	Exactly. It had been our major precondition. Now we have certain rights. Why certain? We've acquired an orbit point which belongs, according to the world's division of space, to the Soviet Union. The Union had a satellite there, finished by now, and certain commitments before communications agencies of various countries. We've taken these commitments upon ourselves, but they demand a smaller part of the satellite's capacities.
Corr.:	**Does what you have said exhaust the idea behind the last word in the name of your Ministry?**
Bulgak:	Of course not. The idea is that the Ministry should provide expertise for the Union space programs, sponsored by Russia. In other words, we are to furnish data to the government, which would help it determine the expediency and amount of funds to be allocated by Russia to the Union budget. The second area is this country's existing and potential satellite groupings and their use in the interests of Russia. We are interested in these systems most of all. The majority of the republics mistrust the space programs and refuse to finance them.
	Our Ministry supervises some of the programs and determines the use of satellites in the republic's interests. We maintain contacts with chief designers of spaceships and ground accommodation facilities. In fact, a satellite is only part of the system. If you invest a ruble into a satellite, you have to invest ten rubles into ground facilities.

And finally, space communications systems, the biggest area.

Any satellite is really a communications one to some extent. We are about to commercialize space surveying in the interests of agriculture, geology, cartography and ecology in the nearest future. In other words, to open up shops where a farmer or entrepreneur may order space surveying, scanning or monitoring for money.

Corr.: A satellite is an expensive thing. That is why joint ownership of them is being practised more and more in the world. For example, there is a transnational corporation uniting 150 countries, with the United States receiving the lion's share of its profits. Will it bring Russia to such partnership as well?

Bulgak: The Soviet Union is already incorporated in Intersputnik, an organization providing services to 27 countries. We are making efforts to incorporate Russia with its several spacecraft to Intersputnik as well. As for Intelsat, the largest international space organization, the Union's government intends to join it. As a matter of fact, Western companies refuse to insure some of Soviet satellites, because they don't fully satisfy international requirements. Because of this we are negotiating with a number of Canadian companies, interested in the making and joint use of satellites.

Corr.: Do you think it's high time to think of Russians living beyond the republic's borders? Two dozen million people is quite a figure.

Bulgak: They are already on our minds. The satellite we are going to launch will service Kazakhstan's territory as well. Moreover, we invite all union republics to take part in our programs, and some of them have already displayed interest in them. Some of the broadband channels of Gals satellites to be launched in the future will be used to cover union republics and for multi-zone broadcasting to Russia. Broadcasting will be organized on a regional basis by 1994. That is, Bashkiria for example is ready to invest in the construction of an active transmitter in Ufa, which means we'll be able to provide a national channel to them in the Urals broadcasting zone.

Corr.: You can't help but enter into rivalry there with Glavkosmos.

Bulgak: Yes. Nevertheless, Russia is getting everything it would like to get despite the fact that the Union structures are doing their best to maintain a monopoly in this field and represent these issues internationally all by themselves. Unfortunately, this is stipulated by the law. Sometimes our dialogue with the Union structures assume a strenuous and unyielding character. Yet progress has been attained in favor of Russia. We have been allocated orbit points for our three satellites. We've been guaranteed that we'll be able to launch two more satcoms. We've already invested money in their creation. Despite the existence of two systems, Union and republican, the latter is on its way to finding a decent niche for itself.

"Vladimir Borisovich, first of all let's have it clear. Who do communications means located on Russia's territory belong to, the republic or the Union," asks of Minister Bulgak another journalist, the *Rossia* daily analyst Yu. Belyavsky, in its August 8, 1991 issue:

Bulgak: Predominantly to the republic, or to be absolutely exact, 75 per cent of them belong to the republic and 25 per cent to the Center. Out of a million of Russia's communications workers 900,000 work for the Russian Communications Ministry, and only 100,000 are subordinated to the Union Ministry.

Belyavsky: And how do your relations with the Union Ministry go?

Bulgak: Far from easily. The Union Ministry is a managerial body, and in the present environment they have almost nothing to manage. As for me, I'm sure that the Union Ministry shouldn't have communications equipment as its property. The republics should delegate it certain functions, say, those concerning the coordination of a single technological policy, research and development, and pay it for the fulfillment of them. The Union body, no matter how it is called, a ministry, committee or, say, association, should restrict its activities to coordination.

For example, all key cable lines and major networks on Russian territory are still in the hands of the Union Ministry, who reason that they are used to controlling the Army, which is run by the Center; therefore the communications means should remain under the Union's jurisdiction. That's right, though I don't understand why Russia cannot be entrusted with the lines' operation. OK, let's assume that our opponents are right. The Army's requirements constitute only a definite share of the powerful systems' capacity. But why should the profits accrued from commercial exploitation of the communications lines go to the Union pocket and not to the republican one? However, there is another cause- by retaining control over the communications systems the center will always be capable of closing down television channels covering 70 per cent of the Russian Federation's territory.

Belyavsky: That is evidently the major cause. The Union authorities don't want to let the tap, used to dose the information, slip out of their hands, do they?

Bulgak: That seems to be the case as well, although all of the 312 teletransmitting and 7,000 receiving stations on the territory of Russia have come under the jurisdiction of our Ministry, which means that there is some kind of a TV parity between Russia and the Center. To my mind, the point is that the Union Ministry is seeking to remain as a governing body, which is facilitated, by the way, by our own political disarray in Russia. When adopting a declaration on sovereignty, the First Congress of People's Deputies by someone's mistake put communications management under the center's jurisdiction. Of course, the Supreme Soviet has presently corrected the mistake. But a decision adopted by the Congress can be annulled only by the Congress. However, the Secretariat failed to put the issue on the agenda of the four Congress sessions which have passed since then.

A Gorizont communications satellite, the last of the three satcoms of this type purchased last year by Russia's Communications Ministry from the USSR Defense Ministry, was put into near-earth orbit on October 23, 1991. The pleasure of becoming a space power has cost Russia quite a hefty sum of money—7,000,000 rubles for each of the Gorizonts plus 10,000,000 rubles for their injection into orbit by a Proton carrier rocket.

Today Yeltsin's government has legal, juridically substantiated property in space, which cannot be said of anybody else in this country, no matter how strange that may sound.

Almost a hundred Soviet spacecraft spin around the Earth, but nobody can tell to whom they belong or who has the rights to them. The same applies to ground objects serving to accommodate Soviet spacecraft—launching pads, flight control and monitoring centers and points. This is fraught with unpredictable consequences in the uncontrolled privatization which has rocked what had been the Soviet Union like a natural disaster. Hosts of those willing to enter into "space property" rights have appeared in this country already now.

Here is what the *Megapolis-Express* weekly wrote on this score in its October 31, 1991 issue:

"Space privatization is something new to us,"—Yuri Semenov, General Designer of the Energiya R&P Association, one of the most renowned Soviet space exploration companies, says. Nevertheless, Energiya seems to be active enough in making its way through it. In September the leading information agencies reported a sensational sale by the Soviets of its unique Mir space station to the West for 600,000,000 to 800,000,000 dollars, adding that negotiations on the score were under way in New York and that from the Soviet side they were conducted by Energiya people. However the wide publicity prevented them from striking a deal. The reason was trivial enough: the space station simply did not belong to Semenov's firm.

What had turned out to be too a big chunk for an enterprise was easily coped with by the sovereign republics of the former Union. Kazakhstan proclaimed itself a space power by declaring its rights to Baikonur, the major Soviet spacedrome, and is already busy exploring and inspecting the Baikonur facilities.

Even if Kazakhstan does nationalize Baikonur's launching pads, it does not have anything to launch from them, for the republic has no space industry. The Ukraine, on the contrary, will have enough rockets as soon as it succeeds in placing the enterprises turning out Zenit and Cyclone space carriers under its own jurisdiction, but no spacedrome to launch them from. As a next step logic prompts the division of operational Soviet spacecraft between the sovereign republics—this satellite would go to Georgia, that one—to Yakutia, these two to Moldavia, the space station—to Uzbekistan. And no matter how absurd it sounds, it could be easily substantiated, for, actually, each republic of the former Union had financed Soviet space programs by making allocations to the Union budget.

However the most curious thing is that Soviet space facilities have always had an owner and only one at that! Though it had been strictly forbidden to disclose it. All space programs in the Soviet Union had been conducted exclusively by the USSR Defense Ministry's Space Forces. The Soviet Space Forces have played and go on playing the same role as NASA in the USA, the only difference being that the Soviet national space agency's staff are military and their American colleagues not.

"The Space Forces are designed to launch and maintain operational in space research, national economy and military spacecraft, interplanetary automatic stations, manned spaceships and orbiting laboratories. Organic to them are the Baikonur and Plesetsk spacedromes with their requisite spacecraft testing and check-out divisions, and the Major Command and Control Complex of the Defense Ministry. . . " Until quite recently this had been top classified information—a secret which could cost us the Soviet space program's breakdown or its splitting into tiny fractures of "space sovereignty," which actually makes no difference.

Having been faced with a powerful thrust by Russia's democratic figures—Boris Yeltsin, Mikhail Poltoranin and Vladimir Bulgak—the Soviet military-industrial complex, in the face of the former all-mighty Union Ministries, CPSU Central Committee, KGB and the Ministry of Defense, tried to seize the initiative and either sell out its entire (i. e. belonging to the people, of course) space equipment to Western companies or set up a network of joint ventures with the participation of Western capital. Being in a hurry, the Kremlin was ready to sell it even at a buyer's price, but in no way to let Yeltsin get hold of it. Let it go to the Germans and Americans, rather than our democrats, they said. It may sound appalling or even funny, but it's true. You can read about it in the April 1, 1991 issue of the *Novoye Russkoye Slovo*, a newspaper with a tendency to be serious even on such a funny day:

> Washington, March 31—The *Wall Street Journal* correspondent Bob Davis reports that the Soviet Union is making efforts to attract the attention of American companies in its new space project—huge satcoms capable of covering a vast area, including the territory of the USSR and many other countries with satellite television.
> Alexander Dunayev, Chairman of the USSR Glavkosmos, a space cooperation foreign trade organization, met with NASA representatives in Washington to declare that starting in 1994 the Soviet Union is planning to launch four 18-ton satellites with the help of a powerful Energiya carrier. Provided the project is successfully implemented, the satellites operating in space will find themselves in the company of satellites exceeding their weight five-fold, flying 40,000 km above the Earth.
> Dunayev reported, inter alia, that his organization is going to hit foreign markets with pictures of the Earth taken by the Almaz satellite, which had been established in orbit last week. These pictures are taken with the help of radar technology, which makes the planet visible even at night time or through thick clouds, owing to radar waves generated in space. It goes without saying that this type of earth survey from

space is especially useful to military reconnaissance. The Americans actively used radar survey from space during the Gulf War, with their Lacrosse satellites collecting info on the Iraqi troops' manoeuvring.

Rounding up his two-day negotiations, Dunayev gave an interview to the *Wall Street Journal*, in which he revealed Glavkosmos' perspective aims, saying that the organization is seeking both to promote the development of the Soviet space industry and establish ties with their counterparts in America.

It is of little doubt that Glavkosmos' major aim, which Dunayev preferred not to mention, is to earn as much hard currency as possible by expanding the Soviet presence on the world market for space services. Glavkosmos' desire to earn hard currency, the more the better, is so evident that experts do not rule out such commercial offers on its part as the sale of a full-scale Mir orbiting laboratory, to be displayed at an international aviation and space exhibition slated to be held next June in Paris.

The Soviet program to create and launch a direct satellite TV system, which cannot be described other than as gigantic, is considered by experts to be the most challenging, if not desperate, move by the Soviets. According to Dunayev and his aides, each of the system's satellites should be of such a size and power that would enable it to retransmit TV, phone and telecommunications signals. Dunayev made it known that the Soviets were assisted in their work on the project by German companies, which agreed not only to finance the program but help design and build the satellites.

According to the project, the new system will employ three satellites to provide telecommunications services to the larger part of the Soviet Union, and one more to cater to other countries of the world. The reception will be ensured by a dish antenna half-meter in diameter.

Having laid emphasis on the fact that Germany had already become interested in the project, Dunayev added that his organization would welcome the United Sates if it would like to join the program.

Edward Crowley, a leading American expert in the field of space technology and director of the Massachusetts Technological Institute's center for space research, was among the initiators and participants of the business meeting with Soviet representatives. He shared his thoughts on the Soviet space industry's potential, saying that in his view the Soviets were quite capable of designing and launching powerful large-size spacecraft, though they would find that hard to do without American electronics to ensure the work of their new telecommunications system both in space and on the Earth. Moreover, the Soviet Union, with its helplessly outdated telecommunications system, will need Western assistance to modernize its ground telecommunications facilities.

Mr. Crowley warned that the Soviet project to create a huge telecommunications system in space may turn out to be less cost-effective than a similar infrastructure created on the Earth.

Aleksei Radionov, head of the newly-established press center of the Defense Ministry's Space Forces, confirmed in the September 17, 1991 issue of *Nezavisimaya Gazeta* the opinion of Edward Crowley to the effect that Soviet space equipment is of extremely low quality:

The crackup of the Soviet Union will inevitably kill this country's space industry. In an effort to switch over to a market economy, our MPs raise their voices high for cuts in space programs, being unaware of the fact that this country has only half a dozen outmoded communications satellites compared to the United States' sixty high-tech satcoms. A Soviet-made Gorizont satcom is capable of servicing slightly more than 3,000 telephone subscribers and has a lifetime of three years, whereas a US-produced Intelsat can cater to up to 120,000 phone users and stay operational in orbit for ten to twelve years. The conversion of arms factories to civilian production, which is under way in this country, has brought about an unjustified curtailment of Soviet space programs. Highly skilled specialists of the space industry have preferred to go work for co-operative enterprises, rather than produce bicycles or saucepans instead of space equipment. However the conversion has not saturated the market with commodities, but rather lowered the quality of space equipment. In civilized countries the space industry yields profits but our country, more and more losses.

If we are to follow the arguments of the military, almost completely presented in Radionov's interview above, we should increase this country's military expenditures, since Soviet-made tanks proved their fighting inefficiency in Iraq. Who will explain to Radionov and his chiefs that a people without bicycles and saucepans, hungry and having no clothes to put on, cannot challenge the USA, Japan and West Germany in space research. The military, however, refuses to comprehend this, because in a socialist environment even a magic saucepan is of no use to them, whereas another military satellite produced by them yields also orders to decorate their chests, and give them larger flats to live in, academic degrees without the need to defend them and money rewards amounting to their annual salaries.

According to data from foreign sources, cited in the *Nachalo* weekly No. 13, 1991, a highly promising new newspaper based in Moscow, the Soviet Union spends as much as 1. 5 per cent of its GNP and employs over 600,000 people in its space industry, compared to the USA's one per cent and 250,000.

The interests of nine large departments (seven, after the last reorganization campaign) are focused in Soviet space industry,—continues V. Postyshev in his article in *Nachalo*. Over 1,000 establishments, R&D institutions, enterprises and firms are involved in its work. All of them have become accustomed to setting tasks for themselves and, having attained their financing, work on them without any proper control by the state or the public. The existing coordinating bodies (for example, the USSR Academy of Sciences' Inter-departmental Space Research Scientific Council) are virtually ineffective, as they don't have any real authority and are more of a representative nature.

Strictly speaking, such management with departmental alienation and monopolism in each sphere of the space industry could hardly be called a system. The Soviet space industry is being torn apart by this country's military and civil agencies, scientists and industrialists, each claiming their right to one and the same piece of the budget cake. None other than this sprawling monster, whose every part is striving for a monopoly, is inflicting the horrible economic, political and moral losses, which so heavily burden the Soviet space industry.

Here is a vivid example of this. The idea to render space services for hard currency was born in this country as early as twenty years ago, but was rejected outright under the pretext that state secrets had to be kept. However, the country desperately needed hard currency and in 1985 it tried to introduce some of its spaceship carriers to the international space market. Had it been done in the 1970s, the Soviet Union would have probably become a dominating power in this sphere. By 1985 the market for space services had changed tremendously with the USA, France, China and India emerging with their own highly-efficient carriers, far better than their Soviet-made analogues.

Still earlier, a global commercial satellite communications system, Intelsat, was created. The Soviet Union preferred to establish an alternative structure— Intersputnik. As a result, Intelsat enjoys the company of 120 countries and an annual profit of over 250,000,000 dollars, whereas Intersputnik managed to involve only fourteen member-states. As for its finances, no reports have been made as yet. The USSR has recently joined Intelsat, while the disintegration of SMEA puts the future if Intersputnik into question.

For fifteen years this country opposed free distribution of satellite pictures. As a result, the world's growing tendency to commercialize this sphere of space industry went unnoticed in this country. Today the French company Spot-Image earns as much as 30,000,000 dollars annually from the sale of distant probing of the Earth data. Here we have neither equipment to receive information from satellites, nor high-density recording tape, nor efficient specialists in satellite data processing.

The Soviet Union was the first to introduce satellite television in 1972. However, satellite TV antennas appeared on sale in this country only recently. Why? Because Soviet citizens were forbidden to view foreign TV channels by a secret government decree, which was in effect even two years ago. Who will be held responsible then for the backward state of an entire branch of space industry, which is, by world standards, one of the most profitable? A satellite telephone costs today five or six times less than the conventional cable communications. With us it is impossible to make a call from Moscow to Leningrad, though the country has a dozen of operational satellites. By the way, today the country is planning to invest big money in the development of communications, satellite included, and this is when the Defense Ministry's satellite communications systems are engaged to a mere five per cent of their aggregate capacity.

Our unparalleled generosity as regards the launching of cosmonauts from the former socialist and developing countries to space has become a notorious phenomenon. According to unconfirmed data, the Soviet Union bears 95 per cent of all expenditures on the Interkosmos program, whereas foreign countries finance almost 70 per cent of NASA's space cooperation programs.

"Better Fewer But Better. " However, the military in this country obviously found it difficult to comprehend these classic words by V. I. Lenin, for all we have now has been schemed and erected at our expense by none other than the military.

Georgi Kuznetsov: Yes, We Do Need 20 TV Channels

The paramilitary and para-party USSR Communications Ministry was headed until recently by V.A. Shamshin. Today his articles on our "multi-channel television" are frequently carried by this country's technical magazines. His competent view was carried also by the Moscow-based *Elektrosvyaz* (Electric Communications) monthly in its No. 5, 1991 issue:

> Today 98 per cent of the country's population is accessed by television, although only half of it has the capability of viewing three or more channels. To reach this coverage we had to erect some 600 powerful TV stations and over 10,000 TV low-capacity retransmitters, and connect them to central TV studios through radio-relay and satellite communications lines. The length of radio-relay lines alone exceeds 500,000 km, whereas satellite channels, operating through the Orbita, Ekran and Moskva communications systems, are of a far greater length. In the aggregate, these facilities ensure the distribution of two Union-level and a republican (Russian Federation) TV channels in five time zones over virtually the entire territory of the country, republican and regional channels within their corresponding limits, as well as the exchange of TV programs between republics and cities. The economical TV network structure is ensured by a single automated communications network, capable of distributing almost all TV channels. Judging by their performance, it seems preferable to use radio-relay channels at distances up to 1,5000-2,000 km and satellite channels for greater distances.
>
> Over 10 billion rubles have been invested in television in the Soviet Union, however the population has had to spend ten-fold on TV sets, which explains the notorious conservatism of approaches to the modernization of television in this country. This was taken into due account during the transition from black-and-white to color TV. During the transition the world's nations were to choose between the so called compatible TV systems—NTSC, PAL and SECAM, which is the case with our country, as it permitted them to keep their old TV sets and receive color television in black and white.
>
> I would like to remind you that color television was launched in the Soviet Union in the mid-1960s and covers by now the entire TV broadcasting zone, however more than fifty per cent of TV sets here are black and white. Apart from the fact that a TV set's average lifetime exceeds ten years, such "passivity" is also explained by the relation between the market price for a TV set and the average pay in this country. These considerations will dominate further development of television in this country, including high-definition TV.

V.A. Shamshin optimistically promises to "access up to 90 per cent of the USSR population with three-channel TV broadcasting from Moscow in the coming ten years. Eight thousand more retransmitters will be constructed." Cable networks in some cities can make it possible to receive ten and even twenty channels, writes Shamshin. But it's much too expensive, laments he, especially if you are going to watch foreign satellite channels with the help of dish antennas. Much too expensive.

Georgy Kuznetsov, head of Television and Radio Department of the Moscow University Faculty of Journalism and one of the most popular hosts of the "*Dobry Vecher, Moskva!*" (Good Evening, Moscow!) TV program, once remarked that our television and party leadership would favor only the kind of pluralism, where the announcer Igor Kirillov would read the daily *Pravda* on Channel 1 and Aza Likhitchenko sound the *Sovetskaya Rossia* daily on Channel 2. Not surprisingly, the Gosteleradio management got rid of this popular host. Kuznetsov decided together with his University colleagues to see what prospects television had in this country and partially tackled the problem in an article carried by the *Zhurnalist*, magazine (No. 7, 1991) under a rather long headline: "*Who Needs Twenty Channels? Twenty More Channels Is In No Way Different From Present Central TV? But Maybe This Is the Only Way to Get Rid of the Central TV We Enjoy Today*":

> The former Gosteleradio's engineers gathered to discuss the television development project suggested by journalists-theorists from Moscow State University. They looked through nine bulky files with the material collected by the journalists, appreciatively saying kind words about the huge amount of work done by them while studying world experience and conducting sociological surveys involving public figures and journalists. "Well, it sounds nice," the engineers went on, "but the idea of having eighteen to twenty channels in the Soviet Union by the year of 2015 is absolutely unreal. " After that the Gosteleradio engineers—and no other than they define our TV's technological policy—explained why the idea suggested by "dreamy theorists" is alien to them.
>
> First, the government has no money, whereas other sources of financing are unacceptable, because "television in this country cannot be for sale. " Secondly, it's impossible technically. Three channels are all we can have, as all the others are reserved by the military and security agencies. And, thirdly, do we need so many channels, if we have nothing to fill them with?
>
> Nevertheless, the faculty prepared, on the request of these honored customers, an outline to substantiate the idea that our viewers need twenty channels already today, not tomorrow.
>
> The opinion, voiced by Soviet TV's head of technical services in an interview with a *Zhurnalist* correspondent some fifteen years ago, came in handy. Excuse me for rather a long citation, but I think it is quite apropos here. Here is what H. Juskevicius, deputy chairman of USSR Gosteleradio, a Russian State Prize winner and Honored Technician of the Lithuanian SSR, said:
>
> "Unfortunately, our engineers for a long time dominated the editors and producers telling them what they were supposed to create within the potential of the equipment they had. As a materialist I have no doubt that ideas come first. I told the producers that they could use their imagination to the full when creating a program and demand whatever they considered expedient, and that it was not their headache how to achieve it technically.

-Didn't they request twenty channels? a correspondent asked. "

I'll intrude here into the citation to remark that the idea of twenty channels is far from being new, as it emerged in *Zhurnalist* as far back as 1975 and still earlier, in 1965, the first and the last conference on teleprogramming principles took place, where theorist R. A. Boretsky requested more than the would-be Ostankino TV center could give.

The percentage of those in the country who are happy to watch only one channel or, in other words, Moscow, the Kremlin, and consider it the manifestation of paternal care of the people on the part of the government, is far from small. However, there are other televiewers, those who became thoughtful after having acquainted themselves with the data from *Information in the USA*. A televiewer in the Boston area pays two dollars a month to watch 29 major channels or $12. 50 for 46 channels. There are other channels for the same $12. 50, which an average worker earns in one hour and a half. Maybe the free-of-charge care of the people by its state should really be confined to, even in the perspective, three channels, whereas we should pay for the rest?

Equipment mounted in the Ostankino TV Tower guaranteed the reception of CNN International throughout Moscow, initially without coding, which was done as advertisement. The plans for 1992 provide for settling the question of simultaneous translation and subscription payment. Two satellite antennas for receiving CNN broadcasts from the USA have been mounted in Ostankino.

CNN International has become a fact of Moscow life not only because its Moscow correspondents broadcast directly from Red Square, with the Kremlin and Lenin's mausoleum as the background. *Literaturnaya Gazeta* (July 25, 1990) announced the CNN competition for the best literary work. Over the next thirty years the Ted Turner Prize will be awarded annually. The topics should be survival of humanity and prosperous life on this planet. Several prizes will be awarded to authors from different countries for their creative quest for ways to settle global problems and for literary depiction of these problems. The first prize is 500,000 dollars, which is more than the Nobel Prize, and there are four 50,000-dollar prizes.

Here follows the text of the interview, titled "*CNN Comes to Moscow*", which the newspaper *Sovetskaya Kultura* published on November 21, 1989:

Prominent American journalist Stuart Loory, who had worked for the biggest newspapers of New York, Los Angeles and Chicago, was employed by CNN as director of its Washington bureau in 1980. In 1983 he opened a CNN bureau in Moscow, working as bureau head and correspondent for three years. On November 17, 1989 Stuart signed an agreement with Gosteleradio on behalf of TBS (CNN is a part of it), which provides for broadcasting CNN subscription programs in the Soviet Union.

We talked with him a day after the signing.

Question: TBS, like its subsidiary CNN, has long-standing and diverse links with this country, and a number of projects

are being worked on. Could you go into detail about some of them?

Answer: Sure. The most important of them, which we're now working on flat out, is the Goodwill Games, scheduled for July and August of next year in Seattle, Washington state. Within the next few months we expect to wrap up talks on new contracts between TBS on the one hand and Gosteleradio and the USSR State Committee for Sport on the other, concerning the Goodwill Games III, which are scheduled for 1994 in Moscow and Leningrad, and also on the Goodwill Games IV, which will be held in the USA again, in 1998.

There are a number of current projects. For example, we're discussing with Gosteleradio the broadcast on Soviet TV of a whole series of top-class feature films owned by TBS. The idea is to show 24 films over two years (one a month) from what is probably the world's richest cinema collection, which was bought by Ted Turner from MGM.

For example, we want to let Soviet viewers watch "*The Forsyte Saga*", which has already had one highly successful screening in this country, and also many other vintage classics. We're also holding negotiations on showing American cartoons.

Gosteleradio has proposed that we make a program called "*The World as seen by CNN*", which every day would be the start of a special advertising feature for Western businesses on your TV.

Now about agreements already reached. We recently signed up with Intersputnik (International Organization of Space Communications), which has its head office in Moscow. It's a 5-year deal, and we're really enthusiastic about it. The arrangement is that Intersputnik will transmit CNN programs to countries in the Indian Ocean region. It came into force on October 1 this year. The signal that comes off the satellite is so powerful that CNN goes out to a whole host of countries, from the northernmost point of Norway to the southernmost of New Zealand. The picture quality for this entire zone is extraordinarily high-quality.

Question: Unless I'm mistaken, in May 1988, during the Moscow summit meeting, journalists could watch CNN in international press centers. Recently on behalf of TBS you signed the agreement that I mentioned earlier with Gosteleradio for CNN broadcasts to be available in our country...

Answer: That's right. We think that this 5-year contract is historic—it gives our Soviet partners exclusive rights to broadcast CNN programs to the entire Soviet Union. They now have a licence from us, and are even entitled to pass on broadcasting rights to third parties. The contract provides for revenues to be shared 50-50. I imagine that initially CNN will be sold to people who can pay in hard currency. In certain circumstances it will also be sold for rubles, probably to various organizations and establishments. Our long-term goal is to make CNN available to everyone that wants it. But the problem is that your finance ministry for the time being will not allow TBS to receive rubles for the additional equipment needed to allow everyone that wants to watch our programs on their own TV.

One way or another, once the contract has been signed, the equipment should be installed. If, for example, this can be completed within the next 2-3 months, then CNN will be on the air in Moscow as early as the first quarter of 1990. Our experience shows that as soon as the first installations start operating, the rest follow suit fairly quickly.

As regards the 1988 summit, you're absolutely correct: all the 5,000 journalists accredited at the time in Moscow could watch our programs. This was a particular source of pride for us. Today, as far as I'm aware, CNN can be picked up in a number of Gosteleradio departments and also in the recently rebuilt and refurbished Hotel Savoy in central Moscow. This is a kind of test run, although things are going extremely successfully: the pictures being received here are no worse than those on my own television in Atlanta, Georgia, where the CNN and TBS head offices are located.

Question: How long were you working on this contract, and how did the signing go?

Answer: We began negotiations four years ago. Throughout this time both sides had large teams working on the contract. At first things moved fairly slowly, but as the situation in your country began to change signing the contract became an increasingly realistic proposition. We signed it with Vladimir Tavrin, the general director of Sovteleexport. After that I had an interesting meeting with the Gosteleradio chairman, Mikhail Nenashev. He proposed that 6 people from each side could spend a year working in each other's country, gaining experience and sharing their knowledge. We're now going to prepare for such exchanges.

Question: In the future are there going to be more conferences like the one held recently in Atlanta, in which you directly took part?

Answer: Without any doubt. We intend to hold the second CNN Global News Service conference in the first half of September 1990, in Moscow. Sponsoring it jointly with us will be Gosteleradio. We estimate that 200-300 television reporters from all over the world will come to Moscow, which is a good thing in itself. The theme will be "The role of TV news in the further improvement of human rights". As you can see, this is a wide-reaching and to a large degree philosophical topic, and we will, of course, be discussing ways to improve the CNN Global News Service. I think that now Soviet people can watch it, they also will have an interest in making it better. We're discussing with our Soviet partners the possibility of putting out special daily CNN bulletins before and during the conference. At the same time we could release the first-ever joint US-Soviet news broadcasts. What I have in mind is that these will be made entirely on a partnership basis: shared reports and choice of subject matter, joint editing and cutting. After the conference we intend to invite TV reporters from countries that participated to travel to various parts of Russia to make their own on-location reports. Later on we'll create a single wide-ranging program about the Soviet Union, made by a large group of foreign correspondents, on how they see your country today. We're really enthusiastic and excited about this project.

Technological progress in the West will probably enable this country also to enjoy "21st century television" in the foreseeable future, Vadim Kozyulin writes in the newspaper *Rossia*, October 9, 1991.

Imagine the following scene: a morning sky with a small lark under the clouds, a meadow filled with grasshoppers, a river nearby, and sunlight playing on the pebbles. All this, including the skylark, the grasshoppers, and the patches of sunlight on the pebbles by the river can be received with superb quality via high definition television (HDT) sets.

Work on HDT is now in its second decade. In addition to the superb picture it provides, HDT has a number of very promising merits—stereo sound plus flatter and larger screens. In the future, HDT will most likely become like a guardian angel in every home, a super television set capable of receiving pictures from anywhere.

Specialists consider this a revolution, a complete change of standards in television. This is of no minor importance, for it might do away with an unhappy outcome of the early television era, which is the parallel existence of three systems of color television: SECAM, PAL, and NTSC. Developed a few decades ago in different parts of the world, they brought about a wide variety of receiving, transmitting, viewing, and recording devices with three different "blood types. " Today sophisticated equipment is used to convert a program from one system into another. When television came into being, the developers on different continents failed to agree on a common approach. This time round the chance to standardize world television seems to have been missed as well.

The HDT race is in full swing, as the Japanese push ahead with the operational development of Hivision, the Europeans upgrade their HD-MAC system, and the Americans work on their own version. It's just a question of who will carry the day. Considering that the world as a whole now has 700 million television sets, by the turn of the century the TV market will most likely be worth tens of billions of dollars. The first to wield new technology will have a head start in producing television programs and the equipment to carry them—from video recorders all the way to video disk readers. Even the closest rivals will be hard put to catch up with the leader; for other countries, it will be simply impossible.

The stakes in the HDT game are high, which the Japanese were the first to realize. They first showed their HDT technology as early as 1983, and in 1985 even began to work with CBS and director Francis Coppola in a major promotional drive.

Industrial interests, the government and TV networks in Japan have long been working together, providing all-round support for their companies competing on the world market. In fact this approach has become official policy in Japan.

In American industry, high definition television has triggered nationalist feelings. On the one hand Congress must remain committed to the liberal principle of free competition; on the other US manufacturers can expect government-assisted credit facilities and an easing of antitrust laws when it comes to HDT. The Pentagon itself pays for research in this field.

At one point the Japanese electronics industry appeared far ahead of all its rivals. But Europe, long worried by the dominance of foreign programs, American first and foremost, found people who made the whole of Europe join the HDT race. In 1985, Francois Mitterrand, working closely with Helmut Kohl, managed to put together billions' worth of funds and went on to launch a wide-ranging European research program called Eureka. The Dutch electronic giant Philips, joining forces with the Thomson and Bosch concerns and a score of other European companies, led the work on high definition television under the Eureka program. Today Mitterrand is calling on Eastern Europe to help Western Europe beat the Japanese and Americans to it. And concerted efforts by the Europeans now seem to be bearing fruit. Recently Philips announced the intention to begin mass-producing HDT systems in early 1994, a year earlier than originally planned—proof positive that the Europeans are dead earnest in hoping to do their rivals one better.

Philips has managed to develop receiving units for the HD-MAC system more quickly than expected. To date Philips has succeeded in largely simplifying the previous designs so that now all the electronics of the TV set fits into a box the size of a small suitcase.

Although the Japanese have outdone their rivals in the production of HDT programs and have even been broadcasting a one-hour trial program via satellite for three years now, the big shortcoming of Hivision is that it is a system in its own right, and one will need a special Hivision set to receive HDT programs.

The compatibility of conventional television with HDT and evolution towards HDT through an interim standard are the trump cards of the Europeans. However if it is to achieve success, European television needs to progress beyond exhibition films and secure support from respected TV producers. Maybe this will happen at the Olympics, which will be relayed by Thomson. This will be only the first, yet very promising, "preview screening" of European high definition television. In fact, something like this has occurred before: the 1968 Winter Olympics at Grenoble marked a watershed in the development of color television in France.

Now what about the USSR? Are we likely to have a place in front of the European screen? In 1989 the Soviet Union and 25 other states took part in the European organization called Audiovisual Eureka. Having joined the work with enthusiasm, the USSR turned out to be the only major state which failed to pay its contribution—almost 100,000 ecus. If the secretariat in Brussels continues to receive nothing but promises from the Soviet Union, it will run the risk of being barred from the television technology of the 21st century, and barred from the television technology of the 21st century, and unable to make its own HD sets, just as today we have no fax and xerox machines of our own, let alone many other things.

Whatever the case may be, the future of world television can be seen today, not by lesser mortals though. HDT was demonstrated to the participants in the European Community meeting in Madrid, and Mikhail Gorbachev saw the new technology in Paris. But the top men failed to come to terms. So the question is, when will television be able to cut across borders?

Our chances to develop and mass-produce HDT sets are slim—about the same as in Eastern Europe. This is to be regretted, for we used to be in the lead before and made the whole world applaud our accomplishments. But that happened in the first half of the 20th century, when this country still had the people whom my grandmother called "Nicholas leftovers. " She meant the Russian czar Nicholas II, during whose rule or shortly afterwards, many people were lucky enough to receive truly good training in special fields. Then again, it was conscience rather than fear that made them work well.

In the closing decade of the 20th century, the people of what until recently was the Soviet Union are hardly less intelligent. On March 2, 1991, the American Academy of Motion Picture Arts and Sciences in Los Angeles gave its award to a fellow of the All-Union Cinematography and Photography Research Institute. The head of Institute's stereo cinematography laboratory, S. Rozhkov, brought to Moscow from the US a diploma with the Oscar and the Academy award for the constant improvement of technology and provision of stereo cinematography for Soviet viewers during the past 25 years.

The Americans have on more than one occasion conferred awards on Soviet specialists. H. Juskevicius, a deputy chairman of Gosteleradio for many years running and the strategic planner of Soviet television development, has been known as the right man in the right place by virtue of his competence and befitting personal qualities. On September 3, 1990, he was appointed Assistant Director-General of UNESCO. When already in Paris, he was awarded in 1990 the honorary prize of the American National Academy of Motion Picture Arts and Sciences for his effective work in promoting relations between the East and West. (The 1989 award went to Ted Turner, the founder and owner of the Atlanta-based CNN television network.) In his country, Juskevicius was known for being the Vice-President of the USSR Tennis Federation and a member of the USSR Olympic Committee. He began his career in 1958 as an engineer with Lithuanian television.

On July 13, 1990, *Izvestia* published an article by Gosteleradio's deputy chairman, Henrikas Juskevicius, on prospects for fitting out the national TV center with new equipment. The 124 Soviet TV centers broadcast their programs in 48 languages. "But where will the money to pay for this come from?" Henrikas Juskevicius asked. TV subscription was abolished in 1962 and replaced with a symbolic addition to the price of TV sets. Our shops are empty and there is no advertisement which can only be promoted by competition of consumer goods. Gosteleradio is a monopolist in everything and pays on its own for everything (naturally, from the tax-payer's pocket), including studio equipment which in this country is manufactured by defense-industry enterprises because of the West's embargo on sales of high-tech equipment to the Soviet Union. As a result, we are 5 to 10 years behind the West. Taking into account the grim prospects for the conversion of the defense industry, as well as our general crisis, the gap appears to be too wide. The Soviet Union has actually found itself on the sidelines of TV progress without which multi-channel TV is unthinkable, Juskevicius wrote.

In the opinion of leading Soviet economist Vasily Selyunin (see *Literaturnaya Gazeta*, July 31, 1991), defense orders account for up to eighty per cent of Soviet engineering products. That is why COCOM restrictions on exports to this country remain in place; in fact, the West has even increased the lists of telecommunication technology and state-of-the-art electronic equipment that cannot be sold to what used to be the Communist bloc under any pretext.

I will stress that the Soviet television industry has the technological capacity to widen its dimension to a considerable degree. Its capabilities have been proven in practice. Radio, of course, was invented at the end of the 19th century by Alexander Popov in Russia and Guiglielmo Marconi in Italy almost at the same time. One television pioneer was St. Petersburg Professor Boris Rosing, who in 1907 proposed using the cathode-ray tube for transmitting images over distances. He applied to register his invention in Russia on June 25, 1907, in Germany on November 26, 1907, and in Britain on December 13, 1907. Professor Rosing was arrested as "an enemy of the people" in the early 1930s and died in exile in 1933. Before the 1917 Revolution, he had a pupil, Vladimir Zvorykin, who later emigrated to the US, where he designed and built the world's first television studios in the 1930s. He even help the American firm RSA to sell the Soviet Union a set of studio equipment designed by him. From 1938 until the Nazi Germany attack on the Soviet Union in 1941, television programs were broadcast in Moscow with the help of Zvorykin technology. By 1943 Zvorykin had upgraded his television technology to the state in which it existed in the US up until now. He died in the US in 1982.

Soviet inventor V. A. Konstantinov once put forward a design for a TV tube superior to that of Zvorykin in the 1930s, but he too was soon arrested. Other Soviet television pioneers are S I Katayev, P V Shmakov, and P V Timofeyev. In September 1931, independently of Zvorykin, Katayev patented a particle tube, and in 1935 developed it into a 250-line electronic image-projection system. From the late 1940s onwards a fairly large team of Soviet scholars and engineers developed and put into operation a television system that in effect forms the basis of Soviet TV technology today.

And now, in 1990s, we have to decide which high-resolution TV system to opt for—the Western European (1,250-line), Japanese (1,125-line) or Soviet (1,375-line)? Without going into the technical details, if we go for the last one we shall have a realistic chance of ensuring high-resolution pictures to the standard currently enjoyed by viewers in Western Europe (with 625 lines). This means that following the introduction of high-resolution TV hundreds of millions of people owning old TV sets will be able to watch. In Russia alone there are 90 million.

The best option for us and the rest of the world, in the long run, is to adopt a single standard, so we and everyone else are going to have to take an important decision very soon. This applies to us in particular. To this day we are lumbered with the results of an arbitrary and technically foolish decision taken long ago by our leaders in the interests of Soviet-French relations, ie., we chose to use the French SECAM color TV system. This has cost us dear, and will continue to do so in the future. Our color television is of inferior quality, and equipment for it is priced 2-2.5 times higher than that for other systems.

The final decision should of course be left to the experts. High-resolution television for a fairly wide audience has been promised for 1995. But for this to come about a large amount of new TV technology needs to be produced, and possibly new-generation TV sets as well. We are still unable to turn out old-style sets in the required quantity and quality; every year we make only a few hundred (!) items as simple as dictaphones, walkmans and electronic typewriters with a 2-page memory. And another cry from the heart—our camera films are useless for professional photography, and our photocopying paper and typewriter ribbons are no better. The list is endless (pencils, glue, pens, etc.). Our military can make for themselves a couple of Buran space shuttles, which are the equal of their American competitors, for an astronomical price, while our industry cannot, and probably does not want to, make consumer goods like sports shoes, for example. Even nowadays our weapons factories turn out audio-visual electronics as spin-off products; television sets were of little importance to the careers of those who directed our military-industrial complex.

At the end of 1986 in the USA there were 813 TV sets and 2,126 radios per 1,000 persons; in the Federal Republic of Germany 379 and 439 respectively; in Britain 346 and 1,157 respectively. In the USSR in 1988—314 TV sets and 292 wireless radio sets, plus 394 wired loudspeakers.

In terms of production of radio receivers, Hong Kong is the world leader, turning out about 53 million a year. Then come China (15 million), Japan (14 million), South Korea (14 million), Singapore (13 million), and the USSR (8 million).

In 1989 China made 26 million TV sets, Japan 15 mln, the USA 14 mln, South Korea 10 mln, Russia 10 mln, the FRG 4 mln, Britain 3 mln and Poland 1 mln. Most of these countries hardly bother to produce black-and-while sets, which only in China and Russia account for over half the total.

Since the summer of 1990, Soviet shops selling household appliances, TVs, radios and cameras have been bare. Sales were on ration cards for some time, or at the place of work. Even that which used to remain untouched has disappeared from sale. The Soviet Union has never enjoyed an abundance of goods, and in the past people had to hunt from shop to shop, to stand in queues or to pay sales assistants or profiteers extra for a particular kind of television, or the latest make of refrigerator or vacuum cleaner.

This kind of market situation does not, of course, provide any incentive to improve the reliability and quality of one's products. In 1988, in the Russian

Federation alone, one TV set in four was returned for major repairs under warranty within 12 months of purchase. This included every third color TV set, not to mention every fifth tape recorder and every twelfth radio receiver.

The experts believe that in production of household appliances Russia is about 5-10 years behind the developed capitalist countries. The laymen (ie., consumers), think that the gap is much wider than that. To this day in our country a purely token quantity of photocopiers, video recorders, typewriters and PCs is produced, all of them of abysmal quality. What point is there in complaining about frequent breakdowns in VCRs, when they are vastly more complex to manufacture than ordinary TV sets.

Meanwhile, Soviet televisions catch fire (up to 7,000 officially-registered cases per year) and even explode; in 1988 271 people lost their lives as a result. And this happens even with the latest TVs, made in 1987-1990. Particularly dangerous are older sets, made 5, 10 or 12 years ago. Not for nothing do instruction manuals usually recommend purchasers not to leave such sets unattended while switched on, and even to unplug them from the mains whenever they leave the room. Even more infuriating for the Soviet consumer is that nobody pays compensation for the damage caused. Human rights and consumer rights go hand-in-hand, and are observed only in a law-based, ie. democratic, society. The well-to-do in the Soviet Union prefer to pay 5 or 10 times the price for a Japanese or South Korean set, so as to be sure that it will provide 15-20 years' safe and reliable viewing, and that there will be no hassles hunting for spare parts.

If our arms industries, run by the Communist Party's Central Committee, had shown enough will at one time, there would have been telephones in all homes today and every TV set would have received 20 to 30 programs. This was obviously not in the Central Committee's plans. Neither did the military bother to do anything in this area. What they did was to report about their space exploits on the eve of the national holidays and front-page the menu and biographies of Soviet cosmonauts. Space exploration i. e. virtually the entire hi-tech sphere, was an aspect of the campaign to praise the successes of socialism. As a result, our space vehicles's service life on orbit is never longer than 5 years (there is no talk about a service life of 10 to 20 years), and our TV sets never work even for 20 years.

In New York, a video cassette recorder is 300 times more expensive than a loaf of bread. In Moscow—10,000 to 20,000 times. This attests not so much to the cheapness of bread in the Soviet Union (the average wage of a Soviet worker is 10-15 times lower than that of his American counterpart) as to inaccessibility of video cassette recorders and other types of audio-visual equipment. According to the USSR Committee for Statistics, in the mid 1990s, despite the absence of goods in shops and rationed distribution of household appliances, the quality of the latter dropped dramatically (between 1989 and 1990, 20, 6 and 12 per cent of the Soviet-made tape-recorders, record-players and TV sets, sold to Soviet buyers, were rejected because their quality was no good). "Be careful, buyer," many of the Soviet newspapers warned. And yet, our stores remain empty even though the Russian Federation alone, in 1990 (against the previous year) manufactured 3. 6 times more video cassette recorders (0. 5 million), 14 per cent more tape-recorders (3. 4 million), 4 per cent more radio sets (5. 7 million), 25 per cent more leads (0. 8 million), and 5 per cent more TV sets (4. 7 million), including 11 per cent more color TV sets (2. 6 million).

Moscow's new newspaper, *Rynok* (Market), fairly remarked in its 2nd issue, put out in January 1991, that in the current year the Soviet trade's demand in household electric appliances and audio-visual equipment will be met only halfway. The title of the article very well reflected its content: "*Do Not Upset Yourself Dreaming About a New TV Set*".

To this day, the Soviet industry has not launched mass production of the long-promised multi-standard TV sets of the fifth generation—most of their stuffing is still foreign-made. The Lvov and Minsk TV plants have put off the production of such TV sets to 1992.

A sudden and sharp upsurge in Soviet—South Korean economic partnership has prompted South Korea to extend a 3-5 million-dollar credit to us. Obviously, 300 million dollars of the sum will be used to build assembly lines and organize supplies of spare parts for manufacturing TV sets (1. 5 million during 5 years) at the formerly defense enterprise, Gorizont, in Minsk. The new Soviet-Korean 40-channel TV monitor will be a product of Soviet conversion and of our diplomatic breakthrough into Southeast Asia. At the initial stage, to quote the newspaper *Kommersant* (issue 2, July, 1991), the stuffing will be Korean-made. In the middle of 1990, South Korea's biggest corporations opened their offices in Moscow and announced that they had reached agreements on supplying the Soviet Union with consumer goods worth hundreds of millions of dollars annually, partially on a barter basis.

The conference of the inter-governmental Soviet-French Commission for Economic, Industrial, Scientific and Technological Cooperation, held in Paris at the beginning of February, 1991, produced the decision to set up a plant in Moscow, jointly with the Thomson company which annually manufactures 600,000 color TV sets, and to build two enterprises manufacturing printed circuits, based on French know-how. The Paris conference also led to an agreement on laying the first ever fibre-optical communication line through Lake Baikal.

Now how about video cassette recorders? Prices on them continue to rise. Why? Because they are in short supply. The only enterprise manufacturing them, the one located in Voronezh, made only 250,000 video cassette recorders in 1990. Hopes for a breakthrough appeared when some of our plants (including steel-making) opened departments for assembling video-cassette recorders from foreign-made parts. The Voronezh plant received all the necessary parts from the South Korean company, Samsung, at the beginning of 1990; The Japanese company Funai is assembling Funai video cassette recorders not far from Voronezh, in a department of the Lipetsk steel mill, equipped by Danish specialists. The contract with the Japanese company is based on our metal exports.

In this Country You Can't Just Go to a Store and Buy a TV Set

Why is that? The newspaper *Argumenty i Fakty* attempted to answer this question in its No. 28 issue, 1991. It carried a letter from Lieutenant-Colonel V. Surikov, Chief Engineer of the Interior Ministry Department of the Smolensk Regional Executive Committee. Long live the GULAG Archipelago! It was never closed, to begin with. The Interior Ministry of the USSR continues using slave labor. Here is what Surikov writes:

> Our establishment is the country's only manufacturer of screen metal grid, with an annual production of 90,000km. Fifty per cent of its output is used to produce consumer durables (television and radio equipment) and is supplied to the radio industry of the USSR.
>
> Through your newspaper, which has a readership of millions, I would like to say that it's not our fault that production is being halted and that the Rubin, Rekord, Beryozka, Foton, Gorizont, and Elektron television sets, among other names, will not be available in the shops.
>
> The equipment we used in the production process came from what once was the German Democratic Republic, and Soviet industry cannot provide appropriate replacements. Before German reunification, the Interior Ministry of the USSR used to get funds for the renewal of such equipment and parts for it from Gosplan (the State Planning Committee) and Gossnab (the State Committee For Supplies). In 1990, the united Germany switched to convertible currency in dealing with the Soviet Union, but neither our establishment nor the Interior Ministry Department of the Smolensk Regional Executive Committee has hard currency at hand, and our repeated requests Committee has hard currency at hand, and our repeated requests to the bodies concerned—the users of screen grid, Gosplan, and the Councils of Ministers of the USSR and the Russian Federation—for the wherewithal to buy the requisite equipment and parts for it have reached no results.
>
> Of the 317 pieces of equipment now in use, 266 are completely worn out while the rest cannot be maintained in working order without spare parts.
>
> Now workers and management are facing the uphill task of turning over to the production of other types of products; in fact, this conversion is already in progress.

Not that anyone should be surprised by this. The whole country from the Dnieper Dam and the Belomor Canal all the way to the Baikal-Amur Railway has been built by prison labor. The best houses in Moscow were built by German POWs after the war. Their Japanese counterparts were felling trees in Siberian forests. But the labor of prisoners and army recruits cannot take us into the electronics era. Even the orthodox Communist newspaper *Pravitelstvenny*

Vestnik lamented (No. 11, 1991) the plight of the country's only manufacturer of video systems—the most sophisticated consumer products of Soviet industry:

> Even at this point, the Voronezh video equipment plant, which is planning to manufacture 150,000 video recorders this year, could double or even treble its output. The fine-tuned technology and the requisite capacities are all there. Yet the amount of resources allocated is not enough to hit even the plan targets.
> Here is one example. The Kuibyshev 4th State Ball-Bearing Plant promises to deliver 200,000 precision ball-bearings, whereas Voronezh needs almost four times as many. It is insufficient supplies that has made it impossible to produce as much equipment, components and materials as planned. Back in 1988 a new video recorder BM-18 was ready to go into production, but the absence of requisite chemicals delayed it for almost two years. By the end of this year, the Voronezh research institute is to develop yet another model, the VMT-22. But it's anyone's guess as to when this video recorder, which is well up to Western standards will become available to the consumer. Indeed, of the 36 new types of materials necessary for the new technology, only eight have been developed by the petrochemical industry, while the machine-tool builders have come up with only 15 of the 26 pieces of equipment required. Nor is the housing likely to arrive soon to the assembly line from the Ritm works. Its construction was to be completed this year, but the Belgorod Regional Executive Committee has put the project on ice.
> What about the video equipment plant already built in Voronezh? About a year ago, it opened up contacts with Samsung of South Korea, and two production lines bought from the new partners now operate at capacity in the final assembly bay. The result: an extra 250,000 modern video machines for Soviet consumers last year. They were assembled from Korean components.

On June 28, 1991, the newspaper *Delovoy Mir* carried a large front-page photograph of smiling young people holding a television set. They stood against a background of streamers and posters with triumphant slogans, reminiscent of enthusiastic labor-effort propaganda, *Pravda* style. The picture was taken in Kyrghyzstan on the day which marked the assembly of the first television set from components from the South Korean firm Goldstar. This kind of work could just as well have been done in Ethiopia or Bangladesh.

The fact is however that those first timid undertakings involving the assembly of audio, video and other electronic equipment from foreign-made components were effectively sabotaged by the Pavlov Cabinet. Here is what the newspaper *Kuranty* wrote in an article entitled "*Tax on Joint Ventures*" on June 28, 1991:

> The Varus Video joint venture, under a contract, was to produce the most up-to-date video recorders, video and audio cassettes, and cassettes with the best foreign films as early as last year. The right to duplicate 1,000 feature films in this country was bought for hard currency. But our socialist reality changed the plans. Even before

the builders left the factory, British technicians arrived and began to install state-of-the-art production equipment.

The General Director of the joint venture, Tamaz Topadze, is very enthusiastic, hoping that in August the factory will offer its first products to Muscovites. By that time, he will try to settle the issue of opening a Varus Video shop in Moscow, which may sell some 500,000 film cassettes, about a million audio cassettes, and at least 20,000 video recorders assembled from components produced by world leaders in the field. The shop will sell for rubles, not hard currency.

The example of Varus Video serves to show that many Western firms, despite a high risk profile, are still ready to invest in our economy. Ten million dollars has been invested in the factory to date. However while encouraging cooperation and investment, we in effect lure them into a bureaucratic cobweb, put insuperable obstacles in their way, and at times even set real traps for them. This involves more than construction delays.

When the joint venture was created, the business environment in the country was acceptable to Western partners; now the situation is different. Take the new, outrageous customs duties imposed in February this year on foreign goods being brought into the country by enterprises. The new tariffs cover video systems as well and come to 600 per cent of contract value, with the duty on video and audio cassettes fixed at 630 per cent. The tax also covers components. This means financial difficulties for the joint venture, and if it is to keep afloat, Varus Video will have to sell at higher prices. Such developments nullified the joint venture's original plans to help efforts to saturate our poor market and bring about lower commercial prices.

"Today we are setting all our hopes on the democratic Russian government," Tamaz Topadze said. "Those foreign partners who are ready to invest convertible currency in our economy and sell their products for rubles need to enjoy the most preferential treatment. And of course the tariffs on imported consumer durables and their parts and components should be reduced. "

After the August coup was put down many things began to move back to normal. In November 1991 the Soviet Customs abolished virtually all duties on imports. The general public has learned that, apart from room-sized television transmitters Voronezh factory can make TV transmitters that can fit in a travelling bag—using Soviet parts and components only. Exactly this kind of transmitter, called Sintez, and an antenna were installed by Voronezh technicians on the roof of the Russian parliament building in Moscow on August 20, 1991. The equipment worked without a hitch, and the government of Russia went on television to address the people at a time when the Ostankino television tower was in the hands of the coup leaders.

The country won freedom, and business people seemed to have gotten their second wind. In addition to its assembly plant project in the city of Saratov on the river Volga, the world-famous Xerox firm decided on a similar project in Chimkent, Kazakhstan. The autumn of 1991 saw the launch in Moscow of an International TV Industry Exchange (TVIN) with branches in Alma Ata, Barnaul, Perm, Nakhodka, and Novosibirsk. TVIN and all its branches began to offer air time for commercials on Central TV, Russian Television, and the Moscow TV Channel, as well as professional and home audio and video technology of various origin, video film production services, etc.

Hundreds of defense-related and other establishments all over the former Soviet Union, including leading Moscow enterprises like Proton, Skala, Kibernetika, Vympel, Almaz, and other producers controlled by what once was USSR Radio Industry Ministry came out of their seclusion into a wider world. Now they will have to compete with other entities in a tough and inspiring market environment.

Naturally, in addition to household appliances some items slightly more complex are made in the Soviet Union. The first man-made satellite was, after all, launched from the USSR, in 1957. The first man in space was from the USSR—Yuri Gagarin.

Since 1989 a similar system, called Moskva-Globalnaya, has been in operation, beaming Soviet television to the entire globe, except the north-west part of North America, via two satellites.

Since August 1983, a three-hour program called Moscow and produced by Soviet TV could be watched virtually anywhere in the world—just purchase a small aerial, tune it in to a Soviet satellite, and away you go. The majority of the population of the GDR, Poland, Hungary, Czechoslovakia, Romania and Bulgaria watched Soviet national Channel 1 in full, every day, on a special frequency and without the need for any additional aerials.

The Soviet Union always took seriously its monopoly on propaganda, especially via television. If you wanted to watch our TV abroad—you were more than welcome. But as little Western TV as possible was fed to the Soviet people. Only four years ago, if a cameraman were to film the shelves of a Western supermarket he would be sacked instantaneously, along with the editor who let it be shown on the air.

In 1990 the Soviet authorities permitted the use by private individuals of satellite TV aerials and photocopiers, plus communication devices such as walkie-talkies and fax machines. The problem is that none of these were put into mass production in the Soviet Union, and neither will they be in the near future. There are only imported ones and at breathtaking prices. The average 1989 wage in the USSR was 230 rubles per month. One dollar on the black market cost 18-20 rubles, while the cheapest xerox could be obtained for 17,000 rubles; a video player went for 5,000, and video recorder for 7,000. A satellite aerial cost 20,000 rubles upwards.

Before 1990, only two American satellite broadcasts could be picked up across much of the Soviet Union : the USA Information Agency, and CNN. The magnificent range of viewing at the disposal of all and sundry in any corner of Western Europe, including Scandinavia, can in theory be tuned into from Istanbul to Warsaw and in the Baltic republics as far as Leningrad. Deeper into the central part of the country and to the East, the signal from most Western television satellites fade out. If only we could watch, say, a TV equivalent of *Voice of America*, say, *Image of America*!

Academician Stanislav Shatalin, in an interview with *Ogonyok* (No 20, 1990), commented that the Soviet economy was run along the lines of a madhouse. Even at that time it was clear that we would not achieve radical changes in public opinion with the help of *Pravda* and Soviet central television alone. Equally true is that without the many years of hard work by Western radio we would still be sitting in the trees instead of getting on with perestroika.

The newspaper *Pravitelstvenny Vestnik* wrote in its 3rd issue, brought out in January 1991, that although the Soviet Union had allowed its citizens to watch programs, transmitted via satellites, it had not done the most important thing. It had not joined the Berne convention for the protection of copyrights. But we are very close to doing so and soon our numerous enterprising cable-television cooperatives, which make money by essentially piratical reception of Western TV programs via satellite parabolic aerials, will have to pay large hard-currency taxes to Western companies or...not to pay them.

However on the territory of the USSR, individual reception of Western TV programs, broadcast via satellite, is practically infeasible in this country because not a single western country broadcasts its programs to the USSR directly. Our vast territory receives only a weak signal from these western geostationary communication satellites which, to crown it all, are made to meet special TV standards our TV sets cannot handle. In Moscow, for instance, "our" standards allow us to receive only 10 out of 20 TV programs, necessarily via expensive and large aerials. To receive two programs from Germany and the US one needs an aerial 1. 5 meters in diameter, and CNN, and French and British entertainment or sports programs—an aerial 2. 5 meters in diameter. For the rest of the programs an aerial 4 meters in diameter is needed. Whatever the case, the satellite must be within the range of direct vision. At the Moscow latitude western satellites are usually seen at an angle of 10 to 20 degrees above horizon. The balcony and the roof must overlook the south and the horizon must be clear. The aerial, plus decoders and converters raise the price of Western TV entertainments to thousands of dollars which, in terms of Soviet rubles, is an exorbitant sum, inaccessible to individuals.

I do not think that the price of parabolic aerial will go down in the near future because they are produced in small lots and mostly by way of experiment. The plants manufacturing them are located in Krasnoyarsk, Moscow, Vitebsk, Lvov, Penza and Novgorod. Decoders (which cost from 350 dollars in the West), converters (devices used to transfer TV signals from the PAL to the SECAM system) and ordinary TV cable are practically not manufactured in large lots. In an attempt to solve these problems for Moscow, the Ostankino TV center announced at the beginning of 1991 its plans to set up a joint venture with the American company, ICI.

Cable TV

The first television cable was laid in Moscow before 1941. But only in 1988 did the Moscow City Council approve the "General Plan to Develop a System of Cable Television". The capital currently has over 1,000 "major collective viewing systems", which can pick up television broadcasts over the air from the 500-meter tall Ostankino tower and then transmit them via cable to various housing estates. The most powerful of them serves 10-13,000 subscribers, and in all they serve half the city. So far, such collective viewing systems are able only to provide better reception of central Soviet TV, but by the mid-90s Muscovites will have an additional 12 channels and also be able via their televisions to communicate with the emergency medical and fire services, receive information on the weather, etc. And without the help of a telephone line, but more about that later.

In Moscow it is planned to complete by as quickly as by 1995 the transfer of all reception to major collective viewing systems, and in a number of districts to cable. This means that a number of complex problems have to be sorted out. Whenever an aerial was broken or damaged by accident, for example when snow was being cleared up or the roof repaired, the result was the justified annoyance of just a few dozen viewers; similar damage to the aerial of a head station will affect several thousand. To ensure full reliability of a collective system, computer control of all its component links is needed, installed at the head station and monitoring the quality of each viewer's reception.

The technical complexity of equipment allowing several thousand TV sets to be linked into one aerial and a computerized monitoring system required major investment. Fifteen kopecks per month per viewer used to be enough to maintain an aerial for a block of flats, while the most conservative estimates for today are 10-20 times higher. This is only for the service itself, not to mention cost of the construction work, new equipment and expanding the network. No viewer is going to want to pay so much if all that is on offer are the same programs that were received before.

The answer is to significantly upgrade the system and make it more attractive to subscribers. Firstly, picture quality will be improved, and all fuzziness got rid of. Secondly, it will become possible to set up special fee-paying channels available only on cable. Such channels will be on a pay-as-you-watch basis, in the same way as you pay for length of your telephone conversations.

Cable TV provides opportunities that to many seem fantastic. Today in Moscow there are twice as many television sets as telephones, and virtually every flat has an input for TV, unlike for the telephone. Television, or more accurately coaxial, cable can firstly provide many more channels than can fit onto the airwaves, and secondly be used to transmit additional information. For example, with the aid of a simple adaptor every viewer can switch into various types of fire and other alarm systems, and also the emergency medical services, even if there is no telephone in the flat.

Additional finance for the establishment and operation of cable TV can be raised not only from TV set owners but also from other interested organizations. For example, the municipal utilities. Coupled up with simple sensors, the cable can be used to provide information from electricity, water, gas and heating meters, the state of non-residential premises (attics and cellars), serviceability of lifts and even security locks in hallways. All data received will be rapidly processed by computers located at the head station. Such a system would be highly reliable, since sections of cable fitted out with sensors or even simple microprocessors would immediately detect any fault on any section and inform the maintenance service with a provisional diagnosis, with a mobile repair being notified by radio.

The use of simple computer technology is a key feature of progress in cable television. By connecting a basic home computer to a TV receiving cable, a viewer will gain access to diverse sources of information, similar to the Teletext system employed in the West. But here there is a major difference: Moscow cable television system contains a special vacant channel for the transmission of additional information, which means it will have a greater capacity and thus operate quicker than Teletext. Viewers will be able to receive reference, educational and recreational information, which will be stored within the central computer's memory.

As is known, in the West fibre-optic cable is replacing coaxial, significantly expanding the range of frequencies and thus number of channels available. Another advantage of fibre-optic is its full immunity to electromagnetic interference, moreover it itself produces no fields that interfere with other devices. So far the Soviet Union is restricting itself to experimenting with fibre-optic, since it costs 10-20 times more than ordinary coaxial. Not only that, but it also requires new technology and new measuring instruments.

Widespread application of fibre-optic lines for cable television in the Soviet Union is considered economically infeasible. The only exception are trunk lines linking television centers with head stations; coaxial sub-trunk lines will be replaced with fibre-optics in the future.

In 1991, collective systems with built-in automatic monitoring appeared in Moscow. A number of cable TV trial zones are to be organized, and the first high-resolution broadcasts made. Once existing collective viewing facilities are upgraded, they will be able to carry up to 20 channels. Unfortunately, not one of them can be picked up by Soviet-made television sets, so it is already time to start thinking of making modified ones. Meanwhile, in Moscow alone the total number of TVs in flats is worth about 1 billion rubles in 1989 prices. It is obviously impossible to replace them all at once, so some kind of adaptor will have to be thought up.

The complete transfer of the Moscow television network to collective and cable systems will be completed in 1995. The volume of the work to be done is illustrated by the demand for coaxial cable—the capital alone will need about 10 million meters of it. Meanwhile, even home plants sell cable only for hard currency.

Another problem is that as soon as amplifying installations (which are essential in cable systems) started appearing in blocks of flats, they started being smashed up, as did lights in hallways or public telephones. This kind of vandalism testifies to a lack of culture. It looks as if not only contemporary technology but a degree of upbringing is needed to develop cable television.

Both Nenashev and Kravchenko believed (naturally, reflecting Gorbachev's opinion) that Soviet TV was overly politicized. All this caused an upsurge of cable television in this country. Foreign news, sex, music and other entertainment programs will help make our morbid life a little bit more attractive, lead people away from meetings and seat them in front of their TV sets, they think. Of course, there is something in it. In August 1990, long debates led to the decision to set up the USSR Union of Cable and Network TV Organizations. Eduard Sagalayev, Editor-in-Chief of Central TV's Department of Information, was elected its president. The organizers of this new Soviet association claimed then that they represented about 500 cable television studios, registered in this country (do not mix them with video bars which are a competing force), serving from 5 million to 15 million subscribers.

The conditions in which most of these studios work leave much to be desired. Then again, the TV equipment for cable TV networks is manufactured exclusively by one enterprise in Grodno (Byelorussia). Cable TV programs must be prepared and personnel—engineers and producers—trained. The professional standards of such studios must be enhanced, without lapsing into video piracy and with the rights to intellectual property respected.

The newspaper *Kommersant* wrote on December 31, 1990 that Moscow's hotel Ukraina has joined the pull of Moscow establishments and hotels, fitted out with equipment receiving foreign TV programs (in addition to CNN). This hotel has started commercial utilization of cable television. The system has been set up and operated by the joint Soviet-Austrian enterprise, Sovavstraltekhnika. The hotel's guests can now watch, besides CNN news programs, 4 Western European programs, and use satellite-broadcast information, Teletext, consisting of business, political, cultural and sports news. Moreover, this hotel will show licensed video-films specially purchased by this joint venture through the Soviet State Committee for Cinematography. Plus, of course, 4 Moscow channels and one St. Petersburg channel. The whole pleasure costs 3 rubles daily for a Soviet guest and 3 dollars for a foreigner.

The telecommunication system is autonomous, it is intended for 24 channels, receives coded signals of all kinds and is oriented to the all-European satellite, F-4. The control station and the aerials have been supplied by the Hungarian company, Hiradastechnika, and 1,000 40-channel TV sets have been bought from the South Korean company, Gold Star. The hotel's cable network has been fully changed to meet the highest technical standards. If necessary, it may cover 18,000 more subscribers in the neighboring district, for instance, the International Trade Center, Hotel Mir and apartment blocks. This system was much cheaper than similar foreign-made ones. This is because design and the assembly work are very expensive in the West. In Hotel Ukraina, all this work was done by Soviet experts.

There is always something that hinders us in our work. *Izvestia*'s V. Arsenyev, one of Moscow's best TV writers, brilliantly deals with the problem of "subjective difficulties" in his article "*Cable Television: A Few Steps Away From a Boom*" (*Izvestia*, June 11, 1991).

Cable television is gaining strength right before our very eyes. Enthusiasts in capital cities, regional centers and even townships are setting up TV studios. A cable television boom is about to come. What excited the US and Western Europe two decades ago is now upon us. Just as any new undertaking in this country, it is coming across numerous difficulties. The USSR Union of Cable and Network TV Organizations, established in August of last year, seemed to help the project. Alas, it turned out to be beset by problems also.

Why? With this question I began my talk with Tatiana Bolshakova, head of the Union's executive management.

"There are several reasons", believes Bolshakova. "Remember Woland in '*The Master and Margarita*'? 'You don't have what you need', he said. This is perhaps the main reason. The other reason lies, unfortunately, in people's psychology, which reflects the vices of our life.

Of the two hundred organizations which wished to unite only three remained loyal to the commitments taken at the founding congress. All the rest took a wait-and-see position and calculated profits. I think our public organization, called upon to develop cable television in this country, would have long ago ceased to exist were it not for the stubbornness of its president, Eduard Sagalayev, who did not let it die. "

Question: I'm not well versed in your sphere of activity. Still, I think that from the very outset we began to identify cable television with commercial, although there is a great difference between them.

Answer: Undoubtedly there is a difference between them. In the US, the first TV cable was laid in Pennsylvania in 1949 so that people could watch programs from major national TV companies without interference. Thanks to the cable network, people in Moscow got the opportunity to watch programs broadcast from St. Petersburg. If a cable is not laid, then you cannot watch TV even if you live near Ostankino Tower, due to strong interference.

Commercial television is quite another matter. It appeared in the same American state in 1972 thanks to cable television. Then for the first time for additional cost a private company began to show on a separate channel films which were not shown by either ABC, NBC, or CBS.

In this country, suffering from overall shortages and a lack of normal laws, commercial television took ugly forms from the very outset. Its ultimate goal is to make net profit without any spending. Studios make deals with residence-maintenance offices and occupy existing channels, often blocking other programs, and show films bought mostly on the black market: they have neither means nor equipment for the production of their own programs. Everything seems to indicate that this is an inevitable stage in the development of cable television in this country. Since we have neither laws nor mechanisms protecting intellectual property, we have no civilized cable television. As soon as we get all this, adventurism and piracy will disappear.

Question: As far as I understand, the union was established in August of last year precisely to make this sphere of activity develop in a civilized way.

Answer: You're quite right. The congress participants were unanimous that the union should coordinate the activities of all organizations concerned with the development of cable, network and satellite television. The main goal is to reach a high technological level and ensure the freedom of exchange of information and its selection.

Answer: Things are getting better now. I am grateful to our friends who believed in us. The Russian State TV and Radio Company provided us with premises. Still, we've got a lot to do. We have sent forms to both members and non-members of the union to form a data bank on cable networks and equipment manufacturers. We offer lists of video programs from among those available on the legal video market. We have become co-founders of the International TV Industry Exchange and help our members buy equipment through it. Under the American project "A Window on the World", the union is to receive gratis a hundred satellite TV antennas, which we would like to use to create regional cable television centers and, subsequently, a satellite channel to provide cable networks with additional programs in a truly civilized manner.

Question: Probably many people concerned about the problems of cable television will read your interview. You have far-reaching plans indeed. But will towns, settlements and outlying districts also have a window on the world?

Answer: We want to help all those who request it. The "Childhood" public organization asked us to help organize cable television in military settlements beyond the Polar Circle, where both adults and children have to make do with a single channel. It's clear that everything will depend on funds. The union would be only too glad to allocate the requisite funds, yet they aren't available at present. Perhaps the Defense Ministry will find the means for its own servicemen and their families?

Even so, we'll try to help the "Childhood" association: we've already found organizations which are prepared to take on the job.

Obviously, the union should determine its technical policy and deal with the legal, licensing and other problems of cable television. Let me remind you that we are hopelessly lagging behind in all these fields.

Question: **When do you think a cable television boom will come to this country?**

Answer: We are only a few steps away from that. One thing is not clear yet: when all restrictions imposed on the development of this news medium to promote the interests of television chiefs and other state structures will be lifted. And when will a law defining the status of cable television in this country and codifying viewers' natural right of choice be passed?

In the US, President Reagan lifted all restrictions in 1984. In France, President Mitterrand himself opened some municipal cable television studios. In Belgium, members of city councils are on the board of directors of the leading cable television companies. We have an advantage in a certain sense. We can draw on positive experience provided we are guided by common sense, of course.

Videomafia in Russia

In 1989 the Soviet Union produced 73,000 video cassette recorders (VCRs). Soviet people owned some 2.5 million VCRs, mostly of foreign make, in 1990, which is one per some 70 families. There are hardly any Soviet video cassettes made, either clean or master copies, and video cassettes sold at second-hand shops cost slightly less than a half of the average salary.

Prior to 1987 it was dangerous to watch video films, and even more dangerous to own a VCR, in this country. Catching the "criminals" red-handed was very easy. Electricity was turned off, the militia rang the bell and entered your flat, under a suitable pretext. And that was that: the cassette stuck in your VCR almost always had some nude shots, which was regarded as pornography punishable by several years in prison. Since the owners of the VCR usually watched films together with their friends, they were charged with popularization of pornography with the aim of making money, corrupting minors, etc.

Since then, the laws have hardly changed, yet fewer people are imprisoned on these charges now. But the unlucky ones who were imprisoned for owning a VCR and showing films to their friends are still sitting behind bars, while those who have been released have not been rehabilitated.

Three years ago many wealthy people in this country were afraid to buy a VCR, because the possession of one was fraught with trouble, if not imprisonment. Neighbors or workmates had only to drop a hint with the authorities, and the owner was bound to be persecuted by the vigilant party organization of his or her organization or enterprise. The rhetoric question could be read in the eyes of the "inspectors": "Where did you get so much money, for a VCR costs three yearly salaries?"

Yet no draconian measures could hinder the flourishing of the Soviet black market of video cassettes of Western films with simultaneous translation into Russian. It was done not too secretly, for video businessmen paid the militia off, in case of need. Now it is done quite openly in hundreds of thousands of video parlors across the country. Although until recently the customs arrested the bulk of foreign video films, they were still smuggled it, translated into Russian, copied and sold en masse. Understandably, no royalties were paid to foreign authors.

In December 1990, President Gorbachev responded to "the Soviet people's concern about the circulation of various porno and pseudo-medical books, and erotic films" by signing a decree on urgent measures to safeguard public morals.

The president said that he revolted against all that after he received a note from Yevgeny Primakov and Valentin Rasputin. The president did not say what exactly was written in the note. But observers were not surprised that the idea had appealed to the president. The newspaper *Dom Kino* (Cinema House) wrote at one time that Gorbachev walked out of the movie theatre during the review of the film "*Little Vera*" at the moment when Vera was having sex with her boyfriend.

The task of guarding the public morals was charged upon the USSR Minister of Culture, Nikolai Gubenko. However, he refused to tell journalists how exactly he was going to implement the President's decree.

Until recently, the moral health of the nation was guarded by the government's resolution on responsibility for popularizing violence and pornography, adopted in 1987. Guided by it, the Militia tried to define the standards of Soviet morals. The Ministry of Internal Affairs' black list began by Bertolucci's film "*The Last Tango in Paris*". The president's recent instruction proposes to "rebel" against pornography, taking foreign countries' experience into account.

Foreign experience, though, was once used by the Soviet Academy of Sciences which, in 1988, produced recommendations for carrying out artistic analysis of motion pictures and TV films. According to the Soviet Procurator's Office's figures, prior to the "recommendations'" entry into force, 200 people had been sent to prison for pornography and none—for popularizing violence. Following this document's entry into force, just about a dozen people were condemned.

Some of the Interior Ministry officials believe that the Academy of Sciences has legalized pornography. According to its recommendations, the video repertoire including films like "*Girls in Transparent Pants*" cannot be qualified as pornographic.

In 1990 the repertoire of the country's video clubs became 80 per cent erotic. Video clubs no longer show XXX-rated films, because the first wave of interest in hard porno rolled back a year and a half ago. The New York-based newspaper *Novoye Russkoye Slovo* (December 14, 1990) published an article by its Moscow correspondent, Alexander Vladykin, on the reasons for Gorbachev's decree on pornography. It runs as follows:

> During parliamentary debates on changes to the Constitution held on December 5, the issue of pornography came up. Mikhail Gorbachev, referring to coitus euphemistically as "certain relations," voiced his indignation with a television program about ancient Chinese painting where one print depicted erotic positions. That was his answer to a question from Deputy Vasilets as to whether the time was ripe to stop the "promotion of sex and violence" in video parlors. Gorbachev implied the time to act has come. The following day an announcement referring to "a presidential order" said that "in view of the Soviet people's concern" urgent measures needed to be taken to "protect social morality. The resolution was to be translated into practice by Culture Minister Nikolai Gubenko—obviously because Gorbachev had not yet set up a Ministry of Morality.
>
> Of course a political player of this rank does not do anything without a reason. Indeed, that parliamentary session was considering issues of major importance to him: the further concentration of power in his hands—in this particular case relating to the power to form a Cabinet at his own discretion—and the "Union Treaty", which is likewise cause for concern among the Soviet people since, incredibly for the Soviet empire, it is very liberal for the republics and, by all accounts, is in line with the accord reached with Yeltsin, the Russian and central government drafts differing only in certain details. Given this setting, to appease "the concerned"—by sacrificing the Kamasutra and sex primers—will seem no more than a wink.
>
> However a similar political exercise—when "the concerned" hardliners were given blessing to launch a nationwide anti-drinking campaign back at the start of the Gorbachev era—is still very much alive in people's memory. The impact of that gesture on society_was truly dramatic for the country.
>
> But then again, it was not merely a gesture. Demagogic concern over the "health of the nation" provided only the background for a tough political game—with immediate gain, on that occasion. The fact is that Gorbachev, a teetotaller by all accounts, thus acquired a foolproof weapon against the many inveterate drunkards among Party apparatchiks and Party appointees at all levels. One of Gorbachev's opponents, Romanov, lost his game through drink. When entertained by Kadar in Hungary, he drank so much that he was unable to proceed according to protocol, of which Moscow was informed. Dozens of secretaries of regional Party committees were removed from office on "drinking charges" or for insufficient zeal in the anti-alcohol campaign. Government departments from the foreign ministry on down were purged, let alone lesser mortals from some ministry of culture.
>
> But having won that round of the political game (and now saying that the prime mover of the campaign was Ligachev, who either through simple-heartedness, an ulterior motive or agreement, accepted full responsibility), Gorbachev presumably had already counted the costs of the reckless venture.
>
> First, inflation soared. The fact is that in a country where alcohol is accepted as payment for any services on a par with the ruble, its artificially created shortages are bound to send up prices. What's worse, in an attempt to remedy the situation at first,

Gorbachev raised the price of vodka, which marked the start of the disastrous fall of the inconvertible ruble. Secondly, the government saw its revenues dwindling fast, as more money remained in the hands of the people, which further whipped up inflation amid general consumer goods shortages. Thirdly, more money needed to be printed to pay wages and salaries. These factors combined to deal a powerful blow to the Soviet economy, sagging as it was. Finally, the country faced a new spate of organized crime. For it was alcohol shortages that helped various mafias develop efficient cross-regional ties, establish contacts with law-enforcement agencies, fine-tune security arrangements and communications, and store up money, so that today these are veritable armies that could easily take on even Afghan war veteran General Gromov, whose task now is to improve the efficiency of the Interior Ministry's top echelon. Having said that, the President's gesture pandering to the hardliners seeking protection for "the moral standards of the nation" against video films (all of Western make, of course) can be qualified only as another present to the mafias.

As far as moral standards are concerned, it is a difficult proposition to uphold them in what has now become of the USSR; witness venereal disease in schools and summer camps, an appalling divorce rate, widespread prostitution, the impending AIDS epidemic at a time when there are absolutely no condoms in the shops, an extremely low cultural level and a low sense of responsibility, plus a complete demoralization of the community—this is a background against which an Emanuel would look like a nun. In fact, it is prostitutes who will now be hunted by police and the KGB—a more pleasant job than fighting armed extortionists and racketeers.

What the President is about to crusade against now looks like this. Video parlors even in the most remote towns of the country now show erotic films—precisely innocent erotica, in most cases, not pornography. In fact, a whole department at a research establishment may well watch *Caligula* during working hours, and this is not a metaphor. Erotic films are watched by families and during parties, by kids and teenagers, who boo, demanding to be shown *Batman*. There is ongoing mass-production of Soviet films of very low quality which imitate Western thrillers with an overdose of extremely unappealing erotic scenes. So much for films.

In urban and rural areas street vendors offer poorly printed, often xeroxed copies, of books on sex and all manner of erotic bulletins, while some official magazines, such as *Smena*, the youth magazine once published by the Komsomol organization, carry illustrated cures for impotence. The standards of this kind of literature are very low, provincial hack work, in short, but quite reasonably priced—very much like on New York's 42th Street, and we can well imagine the implications of any taboos.

First, video parlors would most certainly go underground, and some movie houses would secretly show "the real thing" for ten times the normal price. The richer of such businesses might well start offering alcohol, drugs, and sex to their customers. The army recruits who have up until now quietly absorbed erotic production in video parlors would then constitute easy prey for hookers, with the prostitution business likely to prosper around illegal movie theatres. At a time of widespread hatred of the State and for want of more civilized forms of leisure, the success of such businesses is a foregone conclusion. This would mean a new kind of racket, the need for protection, and an upsurge in corruption, for it seems that not a single officer of the law in the USSR has ever rejected a bribe. Predictably, such black businesses would seek to diversify their operations to keep up a high rate of profitability. The drug business today sells sex as a sideline, while movie theatres can provide an excellent meeting place for various criminal groups.

Yet another aspect is printed matter. Now that home-made publications easily satisfy less refined tastes at every street corner, a crackdown would inevitably send the prices up, turning this business into a very profitable affair. Even now investment returns here come to 700 per cent. Since it is a costly and troublesome proposition to bring printed pornography from abroad, it would have to be produced locally, and at higher standards than now. This would call for more photographers and agents and a new market will come into being, setting off a new spate of crime and corruption.

Unarguably, some restrictions should have been placed on the erotica business long ago. Indeed, all countries take certain, quite effective measures in this sense. What is not clear, though, is why President Gorbachev should have brought the issue up in parliament and issued special orders. In short, why did he choose to inject such volatile material into the machinery of politics?

This question is rhetorical, of course, for no holds are barred in the cut-and-thrust of Soviet politics today.

The possible loot appeared so appealing and huge to people in authority and the police, that things went beyond the presidential order. The document which the USSR parliament adopted to bring back censorship came as a mockery at a time of economic chaos. That resolution proved to be the last in the 70-year history of ruling ideology.

RESOLUTION OF THE USSR SUPREME SOVIET
ON URGENT MEASURES AGAINST THE PROMOTION
OF PORNOGRAPHY AND THE CULTURE OF VIOLENCE

Acknowledging the right of each individual to creative freedom and satisfaction of cultural, emotional, and intellectual needs and being concerned over the wide distribution of films, publications, and other productions which glorify pornography and the culture of violence by depicting in certain television programs, theatres and leisure centers shows such scenes as are insulting to human dignity and ethnic and religious feelings and conducive to law-breaking and mental disorders among children and young people, the USSR Supreme Soviet hereby resolves that:

1. The Cabinet of Ministers of the USSR shall
   -set up within a month a State Expert Commission comprising highly qualified people to appraise theatre plays, public concert programs, television broadcasts, publications, films, audio, video and other products to determine whether the same contain elements of pornography or the culture of violence;
   -create a Cinema and Video Film and Program Register that shall classify such films and programs and issue licences;
   -draw up within two months and approve a Resolution on the public demonstration of audio and visual works, that shall set forth the terms and conditions for showing and otherwise using and importing and exporting the same, and the procedure for opening and registering businesses showing video

films and for obtaining licences for the showing of the said products, and specify the admittance age limit and other aspects of the operation of such businesses;

-set up within Interior Ministry bodies a specialized service to prevent and curb breaches of the law in the sphere of social morality;

-take extra measures to stop the movement across the State border of pornographic products and works glorifying the culture of violence.

2. Products with erotic content may be sold, distributed or advertised by organizations and individuals only in places specially designated by the executive bodies of local Soviets of People's Deputies.

3. It shall be recommended to the Supreme Soviets of the republics:

-to institute republican expert commissions and Cinema and Video Film and Program Registers;

-to establish such admittance age limits as would preclude the possibility of underage people being involved in the manufacture, distribution, advertising or sale of products with erotic content;

-to establish rules for the sale, distribution and advertising of erotic material;

-to establish administrative responsibility for breaches of the rules of sale, distribution and advertising of erotic material and set forth regulations on the public showing of films and audio-visual works.

4. The Supreme Court of the USSR shall study the practice of enforcement of legislation which punishes individuals for the manufacture, distribution, advertising or sale of pornographic objects and such objects as glorify the culture of violence, and shall give appropriate explanations to courts of law.

5. The USSR Cabinet of Ministers shall before November 1, 1991, apprise the Supreme Soviet of the USSR on the work in carrying out section 1 of this Resolution.

6. The USSR Supreme Soviet Committee for Culture and the USSR Supreme Soviet Committee for Legislation and Law-Enforcement shall monitor the execution of this Resolution and shall report thereon to the USSR Supreme Soviet at the end of 1991.

Chairman of the USSR Supreme Soviet
Anatoly Lukyanov
Moscow, Kremlin. April 12, 1991

To conscript 18-year-olds and send them to fight the war in Afghanistan or order them to shoot their compatriots is thought to be all right. To keep people rotting in prison camps (even today) is thought to be all right. To show films about the horrors of civil and other wars to foster patriotic feelings is thought to be all right. To cultivate class hatred, state-sponsored terrorism, and homosexual relationships in the army and prisons is thought to be all right. To starve the elderly and children and allow them to die of malnutrition, an unhealthy environment and lack of medicines is thought to be all right.

But to watch naked girls enjoying themselves against the background of Western luxury is considered wrong. This attitude is preposterous, as has been, and is, our entire miserable Soviet life.

At the very beginning of 1991, the Interior Ministry of the USSR was quick to react to President Gorbachev's rescript urging action to uphold "the moral purity of Soviet citizens. " The police saw the new measures as the start of an era of "sex for hard currency. " The methods employed to combat pornography and immoral attitudes included demands for round sums of money, partly in convertible currency, for the issue of licences allowing erotic films to be shown, fines for breaches of admittance age regulations, and trade in pornography outside designated areas. Dealing in open pornography will continue to carry a prison sentence under Article 228 of the Russian Federation Criminal Code.

Quite reasonable measures, really, but the question remains exactly what should be considered pornography and whether the USSR parliament ought to have wasted its efforts on introducing moral censorship and vice squad practices, queries Dmitry Starostin in the newspaper *Nezavisimaya Gazeta*, April 11, 1991.

As loud crowds in Tbilisi applauded the secession of a fourth republic from the Soviet Union, the USSR Supreme Soviet was deliberating on where to draw the line between pornography and erotic material. USSR Culture Minister Nikolai Gubenko interrupted his holiday in the Crimea to take part in the discussion of his draft resolution designed to protect the country's morals. Following three hours of debates, the resolution was adopted in principle on April 9.

"The important thing is to protect women against pornography," Deputy Boris Oleinik told parliament on April 9 in a speech setting out ways to do away with what he called "the pornographic occupation" of the Soviet Union. He came down hard on "so-called beauty contests" and proposed that the USSR president do something to combat pornography and extend his personal protection to the creative arts unions.

Valentin Rasputin took a less radical line, arguing that the statue of Venus de Milo was not pornography. The ex-member of the Presidential Council accused the Communist Youth League (Komsomol) of moral degradation, pointing out that about half of the 25,000 Soviet video parlors were run by the Komsomol. Heavy criticism was levelled at the recently formed Video Rental Association, headed by Ismail Tagi-zade, who, according to Rasputin, gets advice from the former Chairman of Goskino (the State committee concerned with the film industry) Filipp Yermash and the former USSR Prosecutor-General Alexander Sukharev.

Of course, on July 8, 1935, the Soviet Union acceded to the International Convention on the Suppression of the Circulation of Obscene Publications. Article 228 of the Russian Federation Criminal Code carries a prison sentence of up to three years for the production or sale of pornography, including the confiscation of pornographic objects and means of making them. Under Soviet law, the definition of pornography covers engravings, emblems and even tape recordings, as well as books, photographs, and drawings.

In 1989 and 1990, the Soviet customs impounded more than 350,000 copies of books, magazines, and audio-visual products qualified as pornographic. The border post on the highway linking Finland and St. Petersburg keeps a special person whose only duty is to run through the video material being brought into the Soviet Union.

In early 1980, some people were even arrested for watching pornographic films in their homes. As many as 300 persons were convicted under Article 228 in 1985, according to official sources. Protests from creative arts unions and widespread use of video equipment brought that figure down to 20 in 1990.

The relatively liberal resolution adopted on April 9 at the initiative of a commission headed by ex-actor Nikolai Gubenko was obviously not enough for the anti-pornography lobby of racy-of-the-soil writers. Vasily Belov, who had previously said that seeing a naked woman on the screen would make him want to smash the TV set with an axe, reserved comment, saying that *Nezavisimaya Gazeta* [the Russian for "independent newspaper"—Translator] was not independent.

There has never been any respect for the law in the USSR. In each particular case, the authorities made all decisions at their discretion, with a measure of stupid free-wheeling. Under Mikhail Suslov, the chief ideologist before Yegor Ligachev, the kind of public erotic entertainment we see today was out of the question, and we would not even steal foreign films on such a scale as we do now. When Gorbachev came about, the authorities were already unable to exercise much power on the ground, with video piracy in the Soviet Union taking on a total, absolute character.

A three-hour cassette with copies of porno films cost from 150 to 200 rubles (1990 prices). As the consumer is becoming more and more demanding, a need has arisen in simultaneous translation which is provided mostly by St. Petersburg women-translators. A translated variant is more expensive. In experts' estimate, the overall monthly profit, gained from piratical copying of videofilms in Moscow alone amounts to 6.5 million rubles. Porno films account for not more than 10 per cent of the profit.

American and other Western films are circulated in this country in great numbers no one controls. The state has turned a blind eye in this and only collects small taxes from private owners of video centers. If everything were run according to civilized laws, Spielberg and Bertolucci would have drowned in rubles, and any Soviet citizen would be able to buy or hire video films of superior quality out of a list of about 10,000 names suiting all tastes and ages. Meanwhile, the demand has narrowed the Soviet video market to about 200 Western erotic comedies and westerns. In the Soviet Union, the gap between video supply and the cultural standards is the greatest in the world and has become a means of squeezing money from the young folk with the exception perhaps of American and Japanese animated cartoons for children. Partially, the job of recording and circulating animated cartoons is done by official video clubs, attached to Goskino, although their share in the video business (the circulation and selling of video cassettes) is not greater than 1 per cent. The rest is piratic video.

Our press described as an important event the supply to Moscow shops last September of video cassettes with copies of 12 new full-length films made in Japan, the US, Italy and Spain, for the first time in many years. Can one take such reports seriously?

Only by chance, for a large sum and with a bit of luck can one get Soviet and foreign documentaries which are shot in our hot spots and shown in parts by some of the local TV networks and movie theatres and which millions of Soviet citizens would like to see. Georgians, for instance, would like to buy a copy of the video film, made by the KGB on the night April 8, 1989, in the square in front of the House of Government. The decision to show this film on TV, a film documenting the paratroopers' bloody pogrom against a peaceful sit-in in Tbilisi was taken at the highest possible level—at the Congress of People's Deputies of the USSR (an even higher instance than the Supreme Soviet of the USSR). It has not been shown to the public to this day. The film was being shot by a KGB cameraman for several hours running, and its characteristic feature was that cutting or editing was ruled out because the timer counting minutes and seconds could be seen by the viewer. One could see at what time the troops began to disperse the demonstration and all the details of the massacre which continued for 20 minutes, involving tanks and paratroopers carrying entrenching tools, going mad with their own cruelty. None of the servicemen was killed. Among the 20 people who were left lying dead on the ground were 2 young men. The rest of the victims were women of various ages.

In the middle of January, 1991, Moscow hosted a festival of masterpieces of European cinema unknown in the Soviet Union, organized by the Association of Soviet Cinema Initiatives. It was a great success. But those journalists who did not go to the French embassy to meet with French film-makers and gathered in the Moscow Cinema House to meet with Lithuanian documentary film-makers, could see a film, shot in Vilnius on the night January 12, during the assault of the city's TV center by the Soviet armed forces. On the night, January 17, the film was shown on Leningrad TV:

> Tanks clatter along Vilnius streets and trucks carrying soldiers are speeding along. The tanks are encircling the TV tower.
> The armored vehicles and sub-machine-gunners, clad in bullet-proof jackets, are separated from the TV center by a fence of humans, unprotected and unarmed.
> A sub-machine-gun burst is heard. "Don't be afraid! They are blank!" someone shouted. Meanwhile, the camera shows bullet holes left by "blank" shots on a concrete wall. The next moment one sees a guy with a hole on his cheek, also made by a "blank" shot, led to an ambulance. Shouts are heard: "That man shot! That man!" And the camera shows a big man wearing camouflage clothes. He is standing on the armored vehicle with a sub-machine-gun in his arms, high above the crowd—the conqueror.

The tank's turret begins to turn ominously, and the gun tube begins to seek the target.

On the screen there are cars smashed by the tanks, as well as a smashed lorry which carried toys.

The smashed cars remained in the street. The smashed people were carried away.

A hospital. The elderly driver of the lorry. His back was broken. But he can speak and recalls the year 1940 and the arrival of fascists.

And now the assault of the TV center. Shots are fired. Big guys strike people with butt-stocks, with all their strength. The victims are screaming. The soldiers' movements are perfect and they strike the victims without swinging their arms. There's just a short and crushing blow, a blow against which there is no protection.

A butt-stock end flies to the camera.

The picture wavers. Judging by the shouts and moans, the cameraman was wounded but saved the camera, and, falling, was still filming the events. The camera continues working and the film goes on and on.

The dawn. One can see soldiers wearing military uniforms, bullet-proof jackets and helmets, with sub-machine-guns clearly visible against the sky, walking slowly in the park, amid bushes and trees. The rhythm of their movement is reminiscent of the final episodes of American films about the Vietnam war. Tired but proud of having performed heir duty and happy to have gone through inferno without a single scratch the green berets (or Commandos, or whatever they are called) are returning to their garrison.

Suddenly a figure, impossible in the jungles—the silhouette of a large man wearing a coat and a hat, turns up between the tanks and the tankmen. But the silhouette of this civilian and the rhythm of his movements bring back to memory silhouettes familiar from childhood. They welcome parades and demonstrations, kiss children and cut ribbons at inauguration ceremonies.

What is he doing here, amid tanks and tankmen? Why is he not afraid? Why is his gait so confident? Is he checking on the work done? The only tranquil civilian among shouts for help and moans.

No, no. Here are thousands of tranquil civilians who stand in lines protecting the Lithuanian parliament with their bodies. They keep standing here the whole night. They hear shots and shouts, but do not go away. No one among them wears a hat. They are silent. But in a minute the square explodes with shouts: "Shame!" and "Fascists!".

The film is over—a hastily and badly made masterpiece. One could be sure that neither the movie theatres nor television in the regions still ruled by the communists would show either this or any other film under the pretext that it would not bring enough box office takings (previously, there was less cynicism and innuendo, and the authorities would have divided films into categories determining the scale and territory of their circulation. Our best films from among those which won awards at dozens of foreign film festivals, have never been shown in their homeland.)

In late 1990, Moscow film artists held a political meeting in the Dom Kino Center in Moscow. They supported a call from one of their colleagues that they should act like the Polish intelligentsia, who kept silent for years during the dictatorship of Wojciech Jaruzelski. Another proposal was to draw up a code of ethics for the cultural community to abide by in the period of what the filmmakers saw as an impending dictatorship. The boycott idea did not work, though, since with the exception of a dozen or so film artists (truly talented and conscientious) the vast Soviet film industry (producers, bureaucrats, distributors, and those who run movie theatres)—more than 300,000 people in all, excluding the semi-legal operators on the video market—look set to survive the current economic chaos, to survive by engaging in any business, which, whatever the efforts, is difficult to keep within a civilized framework, even with the full-scale participation of Western partners.

ASKIN (the newly-founded All-Union Film Distributors' Association which met for its second, three-day, congress in the Kremlin Palace of Congresses, of all places, in January 1991) recently announced that it had bought hundreds of American films and was going to put them on the Soviet market. That is not many. The country's movie houses play thousands of Western films of all times and of various origin, mostly American of course. Given the negative attitude to Western mores, Soviet laws have until recently simply ignored the problem of duplication of Western films on video cassettes. No one would even think of paying for copyrights, apart from the films officially purchased abroad and their showing in state-run movie houses. As for Soviet citizens found in breach of the letter of the law or simply behaving in an objectionable manner, they could always be sent to prison for "anti-Soviet propaganda," or "profiteering" or "private business activities," or fired from work for "immoral behavior," etc.

Brought together by ASKIN—led by Ismail Tagizade, an art historian with a Ph. D. and a successful businessman—Soviet movie and video distributors began doing well before long. They went to international film festivals in the US and France in the hundreds, which raised eyebrows in the US. How come, reasoned the Americans, they had the money to travel round the world, yet would hardly pay anything for American films? Home-grown "well-wishers" also did much to bring about a situation where the rightful wrath of American producers came down on the head of Tagizade. The fact is that people in this country dislike and envy the rich, as a result of Communist indoctrination.

In the early summer of 1991, the Americans announced they were not going to sell us films, would not attend the Moscow Film Festival, and were in fact breaking off relations with us altogether. As well as video parlors, they accused of piracy Soviet Central TV and the country's top echelons of the motion picture industry. In all likelihood, the American Film Association headed by Jack Valenti gave the issue careful consideration before sending a strongly-worded letter of protest to USSR Deputy Foreign Minister Vladimir Petrovsky. After all, US producers were still receiving one billion dollars in yearly dividends for their films shown in this country. Then again, we appeared useful in other dimensions of the movie industry.

The huge difference in the cost of producing films in the USSR and in the West accounts for foreigners' interest in partnerships with their Soviet counterparts in the movie and video business; witness the joint Soviet-French movie theatre opened on Moscow's Tsvetnoy Bulvar in late 1990. In another development, the Moscow City Soviet has approved a contract whereby Hollywood is to build six movie-playing complexes in Moscow based on American designs.

A major event happened in early 1990. The first 50,000 compact discs with 15 different programs of Russian classical music recorded in the USSR on West German equipment went on sale abroad and in Soviet hard currency shops. The rated capacity of Gramzapis, the Moscow experimental plant which produces the discs, is between three and five million CDs a year, but it will make only half a million.

Early January 1991 saw the establishment in the USSR of the first private business to emerge as a competitor to the All-Union Melodiya Label on the audio market. Called Erio, the firm is planning to conquer ten to fifteen per cent of the Melodia music market, and to manufacture and sell LPs, CDs, and cassettes featuring popular performers, in batches of no more than 20,000 copies. Erio is already selling its first products in its own special shops in Moscow, Leningrad, and the Baltic states.

CHAPTER XII

COMMUNICATION NETWORKS

Telephone from "the Big Brother"

In this underdeveloped country—with an inefficient economy and social policies far removed from true humanitarian values—communications are rightly considered one of the more backward sectors of the economy. What accounts for the plight of postal, telegraph and telephone services and the absence of public access to computerized communications facilities and data banks is an ingrained protective instinct and the peculiar mentality of Soviet totalitarian society.

Not very long ago, ordinary individuals could not even buy common typewriters. Seven years ago it was common practice to register all typewriters used in government offices with local Interior Ministry bodies, plus a print sample from each typewriter, and before days off all typewriters would be taken to one specially guarded room. Stalin, Khrushchev and Brezhnev ruled like their counterparts in Albania and China, rightly thinking that a poor and ill-informed population is easier to handle. Hence all manner of disincentives to private car ownership, the difficulties involved in getting a separate apartment or installing a home telephone, and the lack of press information—everything which makes an individual free and independent.

Up to one-third of urban families still live in kommunalki—apartments shared by two or more different families, with one kitchen, one toilet, and one bathroom for all. For decades, it has been common for up to ten families to live in one apartment, an arrangement which made it much easier for the Soviet Big Brother, the omnipresent KGB, to keep tabs on them. The result of this policy is well known. The people worked as they lived: doing neither well, they earned little and spent little, and they waited for decades for the state to give them a free room or apartment or to install a telephone in their home.

The housing situation is a little better in rural areas, but telephones are more of a problem. In fact, telephones can be found only in official institutions and the homes of local bosses. Even so, these are connected only to local telephone exchanges and it is a very difficult proposition to hook up to another city or district, with such calls being made through telephone operators in most cases.

An infinitesimal percentage of Soviet cities have international telephone codes. The result is that it is easy to call from Moscow to St. Petersburg by code, but next to impossible to get through from one village or town outside Moscow to a similarly remote place, even if the distance between them is only 100 to 1,000 kilometers. It goes without saying that the railways, aviation, Communist Party and government institutions, state security forces, the Interior Ministry departments, and the Ministry of Defense all have their own, autonomous and efficient nationwide telephone networks, while the general-purpose telephone exchanges handle international calls by official establishments, first and foremost, with their own order of priorities, and only then come private individuals with home telephones.

The state of international communications is even more lamentable. In January 1990 the country's first international pay phone was installed in the luxury hotel Savoy with the assistance of a British company, but the difficulty is that one needs a credit card, bought for hard currency, to use that phone. This is disgrace, if we stop and think that (a) it takes a few hours to several days to order and make an international call from Moscow or other large cities, (b) instant automatic telephone links with Western countries are available only in Moscow to foreigners, from special telephones paid for in advance with hard currency, and (c) as early as the 1970s everyone in Warsaw could call any place in Poland and dozens of other countries from any public phone.

In Moscow (but not other Soviet cities) you could dial a code on just about any home telephone and call people in Bulgaria, Romania, Hungary, Poland, Czechoslovakia, the German Democratic Republic, Mongolia, and even Cuba—evidence that until recently access to telephone communications largely depended on ideological preferences in what was then the USSR.

In October 1991, *Moscow Magazine* carried the following article about our telephone troubles:

> The Soviet approach to telecommunications has always been somewhat different from the Western one. The fact that a caller in the USSR has less difficulty getting through to a Cuban caller than the US, reveals the core of the problem. For years the telecommunications chiefs of the Western world have met regularly to discuss how best to promote the integration of world communications networks. Soviet experts have never been invited to attend such gatherings. Instead they would confer with their Communist bloc partners.
>
> If this scheme of things is to be changed, one old barrier needs to be removed, the COCOM agreement (the coordinating committee for export controls) which bans the sale to the USSR of equipment which may have military uses.
>
> "Our problems," says Pyotr Chachin of the Economics and Communications Research Institute, "can be ironed out with the help of foreign companies, which would enable our own potential to be turned to the best possible account. Yet

Western partners want something more than just to sell their products; they are looking to participate in the development of our system, to provide their own expertise for handling such a system, and to promote collaboration. "

One obstacle is the size of the USSR. Thus the strategic challenge now is to establish telephone communications with the most remote parts of the country. Currently there exist places hundreds of kilometers away from the nearest telephone.

Once the far-flung districts are hooked up, more lines between large cities will have to be provided. The answer here could be satellite technology. Furthermore, there is a need to expand networks in large population centers, as more than eighty percent of calls from cities are local). International lines will also have to be improved. In short, there is much work ahead.

Compare this situation with Iceland. If an Icelandic fisherman wants to call his nephew in the States, he will dial direct via one of a total of 1,500 channels connecting his small country to the US. By contrast, a giant superpower with a population of about 286 million has at its disposal only 2,600 channels connecting it to the outside world.

Paradoxically, the Soviet firm Dalnaya Svyaz (which means "telecommunications"), or Dals for short, manufactures in Leningrad (now St. Petersburg) the more important components banned by COCOM.

"This is third generation equipment for use in optical fibre networks," says Dals General Director Yuri Rudov. "The distance between regenerating stations is more than seventy kilometers. I think this is well up to world standards.

COCOM restrictions are only part of the problem. What came as a heavy blow was the dissolution of Comecon (the Council for Mutual Economic Assistance), since members of that trading group had provided the Soviet Union with fifteen thousand pieces of telex equipment a year.

The USSR is experiencing severe shortages of digital switchboards. The government's plan is to produce five million such switchboards over four years. For this purpose, several joint ventures were established—AT&T of the US, STET of Italy, and other Western firms. Siemens has come up with two plans to make switchboards in the USSR—in Kiev and at an Izhevsk factory which formerly catered to the defense sector. As we toured the factory museum, we learned that the plant had produced Kalashnikov automatic rifles. But information on other products is still kept under wraps. Siemens people were amazed to see that as far as attitudes to work and technological standards were concerned, the factory was no inferior to its successful Western counterparts. Here again, the problem is a shortage of Western components, which are available only for hard currency. The Soviet Union is hoping to receive a big aid package from the West.

There are few short cuts to the solution of the communications problem. Cellular radio and telephone networks can do much to help meet telephone needs in large cities, where people may wait for decades before they acquire a home telephone, and which account for the bulk of telephone calls.

Five years ago one would have been arrested for using walkie-talkie. Only Communist Party leaders, the KGB and the police were allowed to play with these toys. Today the business community in Moscow has its own radio and telephone network, created jointly with the Finnish firm Nokia Oy.

A year ago the commercial All-Union Telecommunications Association, known by its acronym, Vart, set up a number of joint ventures with foreign consortia. Vart is evidence of the reshuffle taking place in the industry. The telecommunications sector, once the province of bureaucratic government departments, is now hard at work to encourage private investment by principle users, such as a powerful industrial enterprises. One aim on Varta' priority list is to get joint ventures in large cities and free economics zones top join forces in developing cellular radio telephone communication systems. For many people, a radio telephone is a basic necessity, not a social status symbol. Soviet citizens may pay for these services in rubles. For those users who sill pay in hard currency, one minute on the radio phone will cost some twenty-five cents.

Some cellular radio telephone projects are being developed for Leningrad—at the cost of 6.7 million dollars and with the participation of American and other Western companies and the Leningrad City Telephone Network—and for Minsk.

Varta became possible in the wake of a shake-up in the Ministry of Communications. Today there is an independent organization called Telecom, concerned with equipment production. This separation of users and suppliers is intended to help the development of something like a market.

In all likelihood, the most significant trend today is the encouragement of private investment in space systems development. Previously only the military were in a position to carry out such projects, but no longer. Today the Soviet Union is coming to realize that it is high tie to make leading world technology yield prosaic capitalist profits, the more so that space technology in this country costs less than competing Western systems

But one can hardly reach the West from the USSR by phone from anywhere but Moscow or the capitals of the republics. The Tbilisi republican newspaper *Zarya Vostoka* (December 5, 1990) published a letter, without any commentaries, by a woman, E. Shamlitsi-Grammatikopulo, from Sukhumi. She writes that for two years already she has been unable to make a call to Salonika, Greece where her children live. The newspaper also published a response to her complaint by the republican communications ministry. It informed her that the republic, with its five million population, had only four long-distance phone channels with a capacity of no more than 320 calls a day. One can immediately reach any of two hundred settlements in the USSR and forty in Georgia from Tbilisi using codes for the automatic phone exchange without having to bother with telephone operators for advance orders. But those who don't live in Tbilisi, i. e. the rest of the Georgian population, are in a much worse position since their access to long-distance calls via codes is very restricted. (It was not accidental that there were several dozen degrees of access to national and international phone lines for Soviet nomenclature. This represented the actual position of a particular bureaucrat in society.)

By the end of 1990 Americans received consent from Soviet authorities to set up a direct-call system via the Inmarsat satellite. It should be noted here that making a phone call to the Soviet Union is a headache for American business people. Some of them argue that it's much easier to get by plane directly to the negotiating table than to spend hours on end to get a connection with a Soviet partner and then not even be put through. Try, for example, to call General Motors from the VAZ auto-making plant (Volga region). The experience would be frustrating even if you had a multi-billion contract in your pocket. In November 1990 General Motors incurred big expenses to bring to the Volga equipment for a satellite phone communications system from the New York-based firms Belka International and Ken Schaffer. A multi-billion contract is worth such expenses. "If the West wants to do business with the USSR, let it establish telephone connection with us itself". This is how Soviet bureaucrats respond to energetic steps taken by the Japanese, who have lost all patience and announced that in 1991 they will increase the number of telephone lines between Tokyo and Moscow from 24 to 60, and establish a direct telephone system with Leningrad. Annually there are seven international calls per person in the USSR, 66 in West Germany and 100 in the USA.

Several generations of automatic telephone exchanges are in operation in the Soviet Union at present—manual, built in the late 1930s, which are few in number today, and coordinate-grid ones, which constitute the majority (such exchanges have for a long time been obsolete in any technically developed country). Our country is only starting production of electronic automatic telephone exchanges—by 1990 the Soviet Union had launched the production of equipment for these exchanges with a capacity of only a million subscribers. However this equipment also needs to be assembled and installed.

In December 1990 a contract was concluded with the company IL SHIN (South Korea) for the delivery of semi-finished products, and assembly of 500,000 telephones at Soviet enterprises. In future South Korea will help the Soviet Union assemble technology lines for making telephones.

According to *Pravda* (February 6, 1989), only one quarter of Soviet families have telephones at home (22 mln. private telephones in all). The number of telephones for official use is twice as many if one takes into account departmental telephones and public networks. If one sets aside statistical levelling one can learn that 87 per cent of Moscow flats have telephones while in the Baltics the figure is 60, in Sverdlovsk, Gorky, Ashhabad and many other major cities—from 10 to 15 per cent. The figures for the countryside are far more frustrating: there are only six million telephones, with a little more than half of them home telephones. In Russia's Non-Black zone alone 20,000 settlements have neither telephones nor other communications means.

The newspaper *Sovetskaya Rossia* (October 13, 1990) reported that 126,000 families in Moscow were on the waiting list to have a telephone installed at home.

The pathological backwardness of the communications infrastructure in this country has an ideological basis. It is no accident that in the former GDR there are fewer telephones than there were before the war. In Hungary people have to wait for 10-15 years to install a telephone at home.

Bugged by Kryuchkov

In our country however money was always found for particular purposes. The newspaper *Komsomolskaya Pravda* (February 5, 1991) reported that telephone tapping equipment had been found in the Russian Federation White House (Krasnopresnenskaya embankment) in rooms 420 and 420-a, right above Yeltsin's office. The newspaper staff was informed that the decision to install this equipment was taken by the former manager of the Russian Federation Council of Ministers' affairs, who got a position in the KGB apparatus. Neither Yeltsin nor the Soviet press wanted to start a fight with the KGB and there were no further reports on this account.

In September 1991 the weekly *Argumenti i Fakty* placed a very interesting article, "*How Yanayev and Lukyanov were bugged by Kryuchkov*":

> The former KGB chief, V. Kryuchkov, as early as August 15 ordered the corresponding security services to tap telephone conversations of Yeltsin, Silayev, Khasbulatov and Burbulis, made via the government telephone network. No matter how strange it may seem this list also included Yanayev and Lukyanov. The latter two evidently aroused great suspicion on the part of Kryuchkov. One for being weak-willed, the other—because of the fear of his insidiousness.
>
> Some of the latest victims of Kryuchkov's telephone war were US President George Bush and French President Francois Mitterrand. Their conversations with B. Yeltsin were accurately recorded.

Argumenti i Fakty, whether under the strain of the subscription campaign or formal disbandment of the KGB, published a number of stunning materials after the coup about the omnipresent Soviet monster. "The Lopukhovs from Moscow," wrote the weekly (No. 34, August 1991), "ask: 'During the coup our telephone as well as telephones of our friends were suddenly disconnected, especially in conversations with other cities. Why?'" And here's what the weekly has to say:

> Many readers ask the same question. Our editorial board could not get any answer from official authorities. However, as became known to us from unofficial but well-informed sources, the KGB technical center (new building on the Lubyanka) maintains control of all communications means: telephone trunk-lines, radio communications, etc. Various devices have been developed which conduct round-the-clock monitoring without human intervention. There is a whole system of keywords, after the uttering of which by a potential telephone user, a recording of the conversation starts in order to determine the phone number of the calling person. For example, if one has to control "loyalty", these words may be "the Central Committee", "the party", or some concrete names.

On August 19-21 the key words ("tanks", "coup", etc.) were uttered so many times that even automatic systems could not control and record all this. Consequently conversations were merely cut off.

In issue No. 38, 1991 the weekly offered its readers a real masterpiece—an interview by its correspondent P. Lukyanchenko with KGB major I. Proskurin:

Question: Major, I know that you're eavesdropping on me and reporting to senior authorities. You know, I feel like spitting on you.
That is what Gdlyan would say during very important telephone conversations. Is it true that usually security men in the rank of major, like you, do the bugging?

Answer: Tapping telephones is a very qualified job. Not necessarily majors do it. I would say security officers from lieutenant to major are responsible for it. But in Gdlyan's case even a colonel could do the job.

Question: How does the KGB install bugging devices in the house of an 'interesting' person?

Answer: Usually three groups of security men are employed for this purpose. The first group blocks the place of work where the person is at the moment. The second group blocks the place of his wife's work.
The third group penetrates into the flat, leaving watch guards on the floors above and below.
About six men enter the room in soft slippers and move away, say, a furniture set from the wall, cut out a small square of wall paper, drill a hole in the wall, place a bug there and glue the wall paper back on. Then a painter from among them carefully retouches the spot—even at a close distance one would not notice anything. The furniture is moved back, the group leaves the flat and disappears. The whole operation takes only a few minutes.

Question: People say that at telephone exchanges virtually all telephone conversations are recorded and these recordings are kept at least three days. How is it possible to record such a great number of telephone talks? Surely this operation involves a great number of people?

Answer: Not necessarily. Nor is it necessary for security men to spend time at telephone exchanges—it's enough to get connected to the integrated system of the automatic telephone exchange. Moreover, it's not necessary to eavesdrop on all telephone conversations. Bugging is carried out selectively and only particular telephone numbers are tapped.
As for recording, it is done easily. There's a system which records telephone conversations on a slowly moving steel wire, which excels ordinary magnetic tape in reliability. Imagine two reels, from one of which several hundred meters of wire are rewound to the other one. The system records both the time of the rewound to the other one. The system records both the time of the talks and the phone numbers of the people between whom the talks were held.

Question: When one hears clicks during a conversation, is that the moment a bugging device is being switched on?
Answer: Not necessarily. Clicks may be heard for various reasons—maybe there are poor contacts somewhere or there's something wrong with the telephone set itself. Bugging devices never manifest themselves—they are made in such a way as to free an individual from suspicion that he is being listened to.
Question: Is it true that the KGB equipment can disconnect telephone conversations according to some keywords?
Answer: Yes, that's true. Until recently one such phrase was 'Down with the Communist Party'.
Question: I have a telephone set at my office which I don't use at the moment. How can one overhear our conversation with its help?
Answer: Special equipment makes it possible to read electromagnetic modes from the microphone capsule of your telephone set. Apart from that it's possible to set directional microphones, which will record our conversation from a relatively large distance, say 200 meters. It's natural that the farther the distance the worse the quality of the recording.

One can just as well do recording in the street. Suppose the KGB has gotten interested in some foreign diplomat. It wants to bug conversations he has with other persons while moving along his usual route. For this purpose "bugs" are installed in the facades of the buildings which the diplomat usually passes by, with an interval of three meters. Consequently all his conversations are recorded -even in a crowd of people shouting loudly. I don't exclude the possibility that many streets in downtown Moscow literally teem with bugging devices.
Question: For a whole year either a standard blue mail truck or a bus could be seen near Gdlyan's house. Gdlyan was sure that these were special vehicles fitted with bugging equipment in order to overhear what was going on in his apartment. It's rumored that the KGB has only three such vehicles because of the astronomical cost of the equipment installed in them. Some say that security officers call them "submarines".
Answer: I'm not sure that these were "submarines". It's more likely that it was checkpoint for watching people who came to see Gdlyan, the so-called open air surveillance vehicle. I'm not sure whether "submarines" were used in that case. It's much cheaper to install a bugging device in the flat.
Question: How much do these "bugs" cost?
Answer: From 100 to 200 rubles, occasionally up to a thousand.
Question: What's their size?

Answer: As a rule, they aren't big. In shape they may be square, round, in the form of a button, cuff-link, buckle, or flat—a little bit thicker than a sheet of paper. The smallest of them are of the size of a match head.
Question: **What's their power source?**
Answer: As a rule, a solar battery.
Question: Some people say there was a portrait of the American president in the study of the American ambassador to the USSR, given by the Soviet government. The Americans could not detect for a very long time the source of leakage of information about all conversations which were held in the study. One day one of the American staffers, while studying a picturesque layer of the portrait, discovered to his great surprise a bugging device inserted right into the eye of the president.
Answer: To insert a bug into the eye of the president is an easy job. But another thing is that it's without a doubt blasphemous.

The KGB always eavesdropped on Gorbachev and the president knew about it. This thought was substantiated by V. Korotich in his book published in the USA, which we dwelt on above, in the section about the magazine *Ogonyok*. In our country the KGB did not only eavesdrop but also took concrete actions, removing from power General Secretaries—as was the case with Stalin and Khrushchev, and appointing them—like Brezhnev, Andropov, Chernenko, and Gorbachev. The KGB decided to pin down the latter at his dacha in Foros but something did not work. Some security men turned out to be smarter than others, and some of the KGB generals were placed behind bars, others had to retire, and still others got a promotion. All the previous years Gorbachev himself had tried to strengthen the power of the security service in order to rely on it.

On June 12, 1990 Gorbachev legalized tapping of telephone conversations—on that day he signed a decree on amendments and changes to the USSR Criminal Code. Commenting on the presidential decree the Moscow newspaper *Megapolis-Express* noted that it contained subarticle 35 which legalized "tapping of telephone and other conversations" on USSR territory. The article says that tapping of a telephone conversation is an official investigative action, taken when instigating criminal proceedings for a concrete offence. "In this case", reads subarticle 35, "an investigative authority or investigator passes a resolution and applies to the procurator for the sanctioning of the tapping. " The resolution is officially sent to a corresponding communications office through which telephone conversations will be tapped.

Commenting on the new article deputy head of the department of supervision of legal activity of the USSR Interior Ministry forces, lieutenant-colonel Alexander Turbanov noted that it's not necessary to create some new and powerful technical centers for carrying out this article in practice. "Everything is much easier," noted Turbanov in an interview with a *Megapolis-Express* correspondent. "It will suffice to use those technical means which are available at present. A resolution sanctioned by the procurator, which we present to a particular communications office, must indicate: the conversations of which person are meant to be tapped and his phone number. The office workers carry out a purely technical operation—they connect a telephone to this phone number. No special premises are needed for this—there are telephone exchanges near which it is easy to make this connection."

However, as further noted Turbanov, apart from tapping phone calls as an official investigative act, unofficial operative work is also carried out which is "not regulated by the Criminal Code.

The KGB was always responsible for government communications, which allegedly existed for ensuring secrecy of government officials' talks. Such very popular periodicals as *Stolitsa, Nezavisimaya Gazeta, Argumenty i Fakty* and *Kuranty* had never had a special telephone line and consequently reported with great delight to their readers all information they managed to gather. However they didn't report how difficult it is to be a journalist or do some other public work in a country where there are no phone directories and it's impossible to reach an information service by phone. This could perhaps explain why offices of senior Soviet bureaucrats looked more like strong communications centers with dozens of telephones.

Argumenty i Fakty described the KGB phone communications network for the Moscow nomenclature elite in the following way:

> There are two automatic telephone exchanges (ATE-1 and ATE-2) which provide government phone connections. The rules on the use of a telephone of the ATE-1 government phone exchange indicate that this network is a self-contained government communications network in the city of Moscow, which makes it possible to hold secret talks.
>
> The list of the ATE-1 subscribers includes over 600 people, and that of ATE-2, over 6,000.
>
> * DOCUMENT. From a reply by Kryuchkov, the former KGB chief, to the USSR Supreme Soviet Commission on Benefits and Privileges:
>
> "According to Resolution No. 558-183 of June 13, 1979 and other regulatory acts now in force the costs of the KGB for maintaining government phone communications are not reimbursed by state, departmental or public organizations, including the Communist Party Central Committee.
>
> The costs for maintaining one telephone of the government long-distance phone exchange constitute 46,000 rubles a year, and one of the government city communications network (ATE-1, ATE-2), 16,000 rubles. Pensioners—former senior officials of the Communist Party Central Committee and of other state and public bodies of power, have 30 telephones of government communication. In 1988 61 telephones were removed, in 1989—42, in 1990—47, in 1991—18"
>
> * DOCUMENT. From the request by the USSR Supreme Soviet Commission on Benefits and Privileges to chairman of the USSR Supervisory Chamber, A. Orlov:
>
> "According to USSR Ministry of Finance data, the costs for using the government communications network of the USSR State Security Committee by top

officials of state bodies of power and public organizations constitute 500 million rubles a year."

At the expense of the USSR State Security Committee budget Moscow periodicals were provided with secret government communications. The list of such periodicals was cited by the newspaper *Nezavisimaya Gazeta* (July 4, 1991):

> "*Vechernaya Moskva, Za Rubezhom, Zemlya i Lyudi, Komsomolskaya Pravda, Krasnaya Zvezda, Leninskoye Znamya, Literaturnaya Gazeta, Pravitelstvenny Vestnik, Rabochaya Tribuna, Moscow News, Nedelya, Selskaya Zhizn, Sovetskaya Kultura, Sovetskaya Rossia, Sobesednik, Sovetsky Sport, Trud, Shchit i Mech*, and *Economika i Zhizn*.
> Almost all members of the editorial board of the newspapers Pravda and Izvestia have such telephones, although the latter is the newspaper of the USSR Supreme Soviet while the former is a newspaper of just one of the existing parties. However the KGB seems to be guided by other principles and its phone directory includes the following magazines: *Voprosy Istorii KPSS, Dialog, Zhurnalist, Glasnost, Znamya, Kommunist, Krestyanka, Mezhdunarodnaya Zhizn, Narodny Deputat, Novoye Vremya, Novy Mir, Oktyabr, Ogonyok, Rabotnitsa, Rodina, Sovetskaya Zhenshchina*, and *Sovetsky Soyuz*.
> The departure from communist ideals did not deprive such independent newspapers as *Vechernaya Moskva* and *Moscow News* of reliable, efficient and protected phone connection.

The KGB maintained such phone networks for top officials in the capitals of the union republics and in regional centers. These and even better systems were used by the military, the KGB and the interior ministry themselves. One could only wish that these billions of people's money could somehow contribute to expanding the telephone communications network in the country! But in reality everything was the other way around. Billions of rubles were spent uselessly: on constant clandestine tapping, and recording and protection of the telephone networks—from the Kremlin ATE-1 to urban, rural, factory, military, and fire-fighting ones, including even a confidential telephone for providing psychological help for potential suicides.

In this respect the Poles have done the right thing. From now on a business person must pay one thousand dollars a year if he wants to have access to an autonomous telephone network for business contacts, which is geared to two thousand subscribers (in comparison, one must pay 200 dollars a year for an ordinary telephone). With the departure of the communists from power the situation in Poland has changed drastically—almost all telephone lines built in the 30s have been replaced. In six months the Poles have done much more for upgrading communications than over the last fifty years: they bought 420 kilometers of fibre-optic cable and high-tech digital telephone equipment. This is because freedom and private capital came to Poland earlier than to us.

As *Pravda* wrote on February 6 1989, only one Soviet family in four has a telephone at home. There are currently 22 million phones for private use. For official use there are twice as many, if ministerial networks and general-access ones are taken into account. If we move away from the averaged-out picture supplied by the statistics, we discover that in Moscow 87 percent of all flats have a phone, in the Baltic republic cities 60 percent, and in such large cities as Sverdlovsk, Gorky, Ashkhabad and many others from 10 to 15 percent. The situation in rural areas is humiliating; there is a total of just 6 million phones, just over half of which are in homes. In the non-Black-Earth zone of Russia alone there are 20,000 communities without a telephone or any other kind of communication facilities.

The defense sector's space industry, faced with the prospect of its finance being limited, declares in the press that it could use a couple of orbiting platforms stuffed with electronic wizardry to solve the problem of telephone communications across the entire vast expanses of the Soviet Union, all the way to the Far East. The only drawback is the poor quality of Soviet electronics, which restricts our satellites to a service life of 3-5 years (while European and American ones work for 7-10 and in the near future will be usable for up to 15 years).

Where is the way out? In switching to fibre-optic cables. But we don't produce it in any amount yet, only in experimental batches. In the USSR the first fibre-optic telephone system using light conductors with low levels of quartz loss has been established in the town of Zelenograd, near Moscow. The academic institutes of general physics, chemistry and also the Institute of Radio Technology and Electronics made the necessary equipment in their laboratories and in the 1980s opened a number of telephone lines in Moscow, Leningrad and Gorky.

COCOM Refuses to Sell Us Fiber Optic Equipment

The problem is that the West, because of Cocom restrictions, refuses to sell or show Warsaw Pact members the latest in fibre-optic and electronic technology. A large contract with the Belgian subsidiary of the French firm Alcatel for telephone equipment was planned, but blocked by Cocom in September 1989. It envisaged the export to Russia of electronic telephone exchanges with a capacity of 500,000 numbers.

The Communications Ministry allowed part of a transcontinental fibre-optic communications cable to be laid across Soviet territory. As a result in about 1993 there will be a global communications network with a transmission speed of several billion dual units per second. Operating in conjunction with Intelsat and Intersputnik communications satellites, the network will be able to meet intercontinental and interstate requirements in telephone and fax calls, data transfer, computer links; it could allow millions of PC owners to use electronic mail and receive all types of information from national and international data banks.

The Trans-Soviet line is the most important segment of the system, and is fitted out with fibre optic to ensure a vast information exchange between Europe and Asia, with the countries of the Pacific basin, including Japan, other countries of South-East Asia, Oceania and also Australia.

The project is assessed in the West as a major late 20th-century undertaking. This applies also to the Trans-Soviet segment, which will be 17,000 km in length. The Trans-Soviet system will have three foreign sections. The northern one will link Copenhagen to Moscow; the southern will pass from Palermo to Sevastopol, and the eastern from Nakhodka to Yamada, in Japan.

The national system of the line, passing from the country's western to eastern reaches, will provide high-quality international communications to cities situated along it, and also improve contact between the West and this country's developing regions, such as Siberia and the Far East. All this is in the interest of the public, as well as of enterprises, organizations, cultural and scientific establishments, health care and management. The national system, like the international one, will contain about 8,000 digital telephone channels.

Existing international experience makes it possible to sell channels in advance, and use the revenue to create them. Approximately half the cost of the system on Soviet territory (several hundred million dollars) will be accounted for by equipment—optical cable, electronic information transfer systems—and the other half by construction. All equipment and cable for the both the international and national components of the system will be up-to-date and supplied by reputable foreign companies, on a competitive basis.

The US Department of Commerce has since May 1990 repeatedly expressed its unwillingness to allow deliveries to Russia of equipment by a number of Western companies for the construction of the Europe-Japan fiber-optics communications line. The firms assured the US that no risk was involved and that the Soviet side would receive earlier generation technology. The US as well as other COCOM members decided in 1990-1991 not to lift bans on the delivery of modern communications technology to Russia.

After the August coup we got a chance to be born again. And one wants to believe that post-communist Russia will be able to build not only the Trans-Soviet line (TSL) about which there is an article published in *Moscow Magazine* (August, 1991):

> Stan Crampton, vice-president of the largest subsidiary company of the Bell telephone corporation has become a legend for foreigners residing in Moscow. Having placed himself at the head of Russian Enterprises, a branch of the US-West company operating in the Soviet Union, he has managed to visit for business purposes Seoul, Tokyo, Copenhagen, Istanbul, Washington, Sofia and Moscow within just ten days.

A former semi-professional hockey player, 52 year-old Stan Crampton has been a "permanent" resident of Moscow since February 1991. He begins his working day at 7:30 a. m. with a business breakfast at the Savoy, which he considers his home. US-West has set up a joint venture with the USSR communications ministry. At present the major project of this new venture, which is called International Gateway Corporation, is the Trans-Soviet line (TSL), which will connect the Soviet Union with the rest of the world. According to this project U. S.-West is to lay a fibre-optics cable through the USSR and beyond it in order to connect Southeast Asia and Europe, using state-of-the-art communications technology for transmitting large volumes of information. TSL will cross eleven time zones of the Soviet Union and will extend over 12,000 kilometers from the Far Eastern port of Nakhodka to the Baltic Sea. Crampton believes that projects of such great dimensions have never been carried out in world practice.

Why did the Soviet Union invite namely US-West to work on this project? To some extent the firm must be grateful to Gary Hart for this. In 1988 when he had to withdraw from the presidential race because of his love affair with Donna Rice, Hart became engaged in international business and displayed particular interest in Eastern Europe. Pyotr Kurakov, head of the foreign relations department of the USSR Communications Ministry, was looking for a western partner for the TSL project, and turned to Gary Hart for help. The latter, like a "true native" of Colorado, as Crampton called him, proposed that the firm US-West from Denver take part in it.

For the last two years the TSL project has expanded to such an extent that now twelve partners are participating in it and this is not the limit. Apart from U. S.-West and the USSR Communications Ministry, Austrian OTC, Japanese KDD, South Korean KT, major telecommunications companies of Denmark, France, Great Britain, German Bundespost, Italian STET, Spanish Telefonica and Turkish PTT.

Three international lines will be extended from Moscow: one to the south, to the Black Sea and from there to Istanbul and the Mediterranean; the second—to the north, to Leningrad and the Baltics and then by underwater water cable to Scandinavia; the third to the west, to Central Europe. According to Crampton, the system will link Japan, Australia and other countries of that region with areas of economic interest to them: Great Britain, France, Germany, and via trans-Atlantic cable network, the North American market.

Yet one cannot help but ask: how real is this or any other great project to be carried out in the USSR? Crampton seems optimistic. "We believe that this is just a question of time," says he. "In any country the development of telecommunications infrastructure is one of the conditions for economic upswing. This is quite evident. "

The main thing is that Soviet bureaucrats seem to have acknowledged this truth. Crampton is sure that both his partners and the Soviet government have realized the importance of the development of telecommunications infrastructure.

A developed communications infrastructure is needed to attract Western business people. "The majority of them are used to making calls when and where they like; this is what they consider an innate right. Consequently the fact that it's not always possible to get a connection in this country is a heavy blow to them. If the Soviet Union is interested in attracting major Western firms and corporations, it must provide them with a good old telephone. "

Then why isn't the project getting off the ground? Unlike many other joint projects which remain grounded, U. S.-West did not meet any bureaucratic obstacles, and Crampton has no reason to complain about Soviet bureaucrats. "I think we're very lucky," he says, speaking warmly of federal and Russian ministers and deputy ministers of communications. "They are exceptionally competent people with a Western type of mentality. Their employees are no less enterprising in looking for solutions than their Western counterparts... It's great pleasure to work with them. "

The main enemies of U. S.-West are the US government and COCOM, which controls the export of Western technologies. Crampton claims that the fiber-optic cable which the firm is going to use does not fall under the category of advanced technology prohibited for import into the USSR. "The Soviet Union possesses the necessary technology for producing fiber-optic cables, though not always in the amount required. However there's a "gentlemen's agreement" between COCOM members not to export the cable. Why so? Because unlike satellite or microwave communications systems fiber optical cables are not subject to easy tapping. And this is what concerns both the US government and COCOM. In the middle of May COCOM inflicted another blow on the plans to lay the trans-Siberian line by confirming its ban on the import of fiber-optic cable into the USSR.

Crampton says that he foresaw such a development of events. However U. S.-West will continue its struggle against these restrictions, considering such delays temporary. So far the company is set to fill the gap in Soviet communications systems by developing alternative technologies:—digital microwave and wireless telephone communications—mostly to serve Western business people. COCOM allows the cable to be laid almost to the very border of the USSR, just ten kilometers away from it. And from there communications will be maintained by way of alternative technologies. In the long run, hopes Crampton, either COCOM will lift the restrictions or the USSR will produce more cables, and then it will become possible to lay them across the territory of the Soviet Union.

It's ludicrous, almost absurd that American intelligence services openly declare that they will be unable to eavesdrop on telephone conversations conducted via fiber-optic cables from their spy satellites. Yet that is the reason why the US is so far against the construction of the Trans-Soviet Line.

The name of the project itself—the Trans-Soviet Line—may have to the changed. This project of the century designed to set up a communications ring, must cease to be a ring of prohibitions. Of course, we can carry out this project ourselves. So far the above-mentioned companies and their colleagues from 23 countries of the world (38 firms) are busy with laying an analogous fiber-optic cable between Japan and Singapore. A cable 7,500 kilometers long for 7,560 communications channels will be put into operation at the end of July 1993.

One has to admit however that the Americans have achieved something on the territory of the former USSR. In late October 1991 an official ceremony for opening an international automatic telephone exchange was held in Yerevan. The president of Armenia, Levon Ter-Petrosyan and president of the international group of AT&T Sam Willcoxon were present at it.

Speaking at the ceremony of the "first call" Mr. Willcoxon said that it was a big day for Armenia and a great day for his company. In honor of opening the international telephone exchange a stamp of the republic of Armenia has been issued for the first time since 1922 to commemorate this event.

The new exchange linked simultaneously 180 subscribers in Yerevan with the USA. There are also 90 telephone channels with France. A person can now directly call Armenia from abroad and vice versa—from Yerevan to any location on Earth, without using the Moscow phone exchange.

The exchange cost about six million dollars. It will be paid off in two years. The exchange's first subscribers were enterprises which earn hard currency for the republic, representative offices of foreign firms as well as foreign correspondents. Citizens of the republic can call abroad from two phone exchanges in Yerevan if they pay in dollars, francs or any other currency.

The opening of the first satellite communications office will enable Armenian business people living abroad to take more active part in developing entrepreneurship on the territory of the republic.

The 5ESS telephone digital system is considered to be the most sophisticated today. Both the system and a ground satellite communications station connected with it were installed by AT&T in the suburbs of the Armenian capital. The Americans assured the Armenians that the first 500 phone numbers were just the beginning, that a second unit of the Yerevan Central Telephone Exchange will connect dozens of thousands of phone subscribers with the rest of the world. The technical achievement of AT&T consists in the fact that this first peripheral (built in a place other than Moscow) international telephone exchange was put into operation in a record time—it took only eight months from the signing of the contract to the "first telephone call".

AT&T has done business with the USSR for forty years, providing telephone connections between our country and the USA. During the earthquake in Armenia AT&T Network Systems International delivered by air a compact telephone exchange to earthquake-stricken areas for international telephone communications.

The American firm U. S.-West mentioned above, evoked Soviet press interest in it in September 1991. In St. Petersburg the company installed a portable radio telephone for 750 phone subscribers (by the beginning of 1992 there will be 3,000 and in 1995 500,000 of them) for maintaining links with a city phone exchange as well as national and international telephone lines. St. Petersburg became the first Russian city with a commercial cellular phone system of radio communication. One has to pay 2,000 dollars to be connected to it. A monthly phone fee which gives one the right to 210 minutes of conversation costs 195 dollars. Each minute above this limit costs 65 cents. A monthly fee of 25 dollars is charged for connection to the inter-city and international phone lines. U. S.-West serves up to one third of its St. Petersburg subscribers for rubles: the mayor's office, police, fire-fighting teams and first-aid ambulance service.

In early spring of 1992 an analogous system of cellular telephone radio communications was opened in Moscow by U. S.-West as well. That is how the monopoly of white telephones with a gold USSR coat of arms on their dials (used by top Soviet officials) ended in the former Soviet Union. In an interview with *Megapolis-Express* U. S.-West president Richard McCormack said: "I'm quite sure that if Gorbachev had had a radio telephone he would have never been cut off from all communications at his dacha in the Crimea. A cellular phone system would have given him and his associates, isolated from the rest of the world during the coup, quick access to local, national and international phone lines and high-quality communications."

Now a private individual in this country will be able to call the USA from his own car. A cellular system outperforms all other communication systems both in specifics and quality.

Meanwhile Soviet newspapers published articles like that which appeared in the Moscow-based youth daily *Moskovsky Komsomolets* (of August 3, 1991) on the occasion of President Bush's visit to Moscow. The article, written by Elina Nikolaeva under the headline "*Communication with Moscow established! Afterward to the summit meeting*", went as follows:

> The Moscow International Trade Center housed the press-center of the White House. The Intercongress company did all the necessary work to provide the center with communications. This time the company had to do everything hastily since the news that the Soviet information Center would house the White House press service came only on July 18, just ten days before the visit. All technical services, including communications, power supply, repairs and construction, had to work round the clock and accomplished the near impossible: they created all requisite conditions for the work of the world's major television companies, like CNN, ABC and NHK, as well as for other news agencies.
>
> A team of journalists which accompanied President Bush arrived by Boeing-747 on July 29 at night right after the government plane. But instead of going directly to hotels for accommodation, like people generally do in order to have a rest after travelling, the American journalists requested that they be driven to the Congress Hall, where, leaving all their hand luggage in the hall, they ran to occupy places so as to get in touch with their editorial offices.
>
> Vladimir Vartanov, a leading consultant at Intercongress believes that it's high time to set up a big Congress Center in Moscow with all the necessary infrastructure, service premises, large and small halls and a good press-center with telephone, fax, telex and satellite communications. For the recent Moscow visit alone CNN had to bring in almost seven trucks' worth of equipment and actually built a large telecenter. This not in besieged Belgrade but in the relatively peaceful capital of a big country! There is no other way to provide high quality communications from Moscow.

But there is! The Moscow branch of the *Washington Post* pays five thousand dollars for an ordinary telephone in its bureau. The telephone has a code for the American capital's phone system and an American correspondent talks with colleagues in the US as easily as if they were in the next room. It's just as easy to reach numbers of their friends living in the suburbs of Washington. He can speak over the phone as long as he likes, since the Moscow branch of the *Washington Post* pays that sum of money for this pleasure each month.

Of course, not only American companies work technical wonders in the Soviet Union. Austrian companies with American assistance were the first to connect the Georgian government in March 1991 with a phone switchboard in Vienna and from there with the rest of the world, bypassing Moscow. In such a way the center's monopoly on all international phone connections was done away with. Georgians then said, had they had such access to the outer world two years earlier the tragedy of April 9, 1989 could have been averted.

Turkish companies opened sixty channels for direct telephone links with Azerbaijan in 1991, using a Turkish satellite for this purpose. They also organized joint production of digital telephone equipment in Baku. For the first time direct telephone and mail connection was established between Georgia and neighboring Turkey. Previously, during seventy years of Soviet rule, all mail, telephone and telex communication as well as trips abroad were carried out only via Moscow.

It was much faster to reach Tokyo by ship from the Far Eastern port of Nakhodka than by phone via Moscow. The Japanese were pretty fed up with this state of things and in late 1991 they brought phone equipment to Vladivostok designed for 120 channels. This equipment makes it possible to allocate an equal number of channels for connection with the USA, Japan, China and Singapore.

Under Stalin, Khrushchev and Brezhnev it was not recommended to call abroad. Under Gorbachev it was allowed to make calls abroad from major cities for hard currency. A few more years of efforts of such corporations on the Russian market as the Japanese NEC, German Siemens, Belgian Alcatel Bell, and French Alcatel, let alone American firms, and one will be able to reach the world from far-away Russian provinces for rubles and in no time, for less than the monthly salary of a Soviet engineer.

Checking of All Mail

Russia lags two epochs behind the West—postindustrial and postinformational ones. The Soviet Union rates between fiftieth and sixtieth places in terms of living standards and still continues to drop. Human rights are constantly abused in this country; the cult of secrecy and militarism still prevails. The Soviet mail service had for decades been subordinate not to the communications ministry but rather to various services of party propaganda and political investigation.

Our mail service is responsible for periodical distribution, delivery of parcels, telegrams, letters, money remittance, and pension payments. In better times it took a week for a letter to arrive from one city to another; it took much more time to get a letter in the countryside. In many Soviet major cities, to say nothing of villages, newspapers and letters were delivered by a carrier only once a week.

For the urgent needs of Soviet senior officials the KGB maintained its own mail service as well as couriers. The latter, dressed in military uniform, delivered allegedly secret mail in big bags between Moscow and hundreds of republican and regional centers within a single day. Imported fax machines (because of the lack of domestic ones) came into fashion only by the beginning of the 1990s. Party functionaries however preferred coded messages or red envelopes of thick light-proof paper, plastered with heavy wax seals, like two centuries ago.

During the last months of its existence the CPSU made an attempt to clamp down on glasnost by raising tariffs for distribution of periodicals to subscribers and newspaper kiosks. In 1990 the party apparatus onslaught manifested itself in a ten-fold price increase on paper. In 1991 the USSR Communications Ministry declared it would charge publishers 52 per cent of the cost of each copy of a periodical in 1992, no matter where it was to be sold—in a kiosk in Moscow or in Magadan.

Journalists counted their losses and were horrified. As in the previous year they had to increase once again prices for their publications, which would inevitably lead to loss of potential subscribers. The Communications Ministry, as is understood, did not refer to the CPSU Central Committee or the KGB. G. Kudryavtsev, USSR minister of communications, had somehow to find a way out of the situation, and explained price hikes by saying that "...the country's defense calls for priority development of communications" (*Moskovsky Komsomolets*, July 11, 1991), a ludicrous argument of vile politics. It's not a secret that the Soviet Union has communications troops which must do their job. However, as we all know, there have never been civil ministers in our country, since all of them served the interests of the military. The result of such politics is frustrating.

This country lacks telephones and one has to subsidize the military-industrial complex as well as the CPSU, greedy for money and power, once again, if one wants to read a newspaper. As for the CPSU, it never left its "friends" in trouble and made rich contributions to them in 1990 and subsequent year. These friends included *People's Daily World* (USA), *L'Unita* (Italy), *Morning Star* (Great Britain), *Rizospastis* (Greece), *Globus* (Austria), *Land og Folk* (Denmark), *OPF* (France), *Pergamon Press* (Britain), *Editori Riuniti*

(Italy), *Avante!* (Portugal) and dozens (!) of other such pro-communist publications and publishers in the West (see Argumenty i Fakty, No. 42, 1991).

We all remember that for decades in each newspaper kiosk of our boundless empire one could always see the French communist newspaper *L'Humanite* and magazines of the French communist party *Les Cahiers du Communisme* and *Economie et Politique*. And for no particular reason one could also find an Algerian French-language newspaper. New editions of newspapers and magazines were regularly delivered to kiosks, and the old ones with yellowed pages, which remained unsold, were written off. But instead of pulp paper, dollars and francs were sent to France and Algiers. The circulation of Soviet periodicals, from Stalin to Gorbachev, was limited until 1990. However in previous years one could freely subscribe to or buy *Pravda*, republican party newspapers and a few theoretical party magazines, plus publications of the French and British communist parties.

Publications of other communist parties, even those of socialist countries of Eastern Europe, were not distributed by Soyuzpechat to its kiosks. The reason was simple: one could get a lot of interesting information even from the Polish communist paper *Trybunu Ludu*. Moreover, the Polish leadership itself sent parcels with millions of dollars to the Kremlin, and from there they went to the West, to support the "progressive public". On instructions from the CPSU Central Committee the USSR Communications Ministry and its satellite, Soyuzpechat, strangled any Soviet periodical which people wanted to read, and instead of it forced on them *Pravda* and *L'Humanite* at moderate prices while maintaining artificial shortages of toilet and wrapping paper.

In autumn 1991 the headquarters of the CPSU and KGB ceased to exist. The ominous abbreviation of the security service and Bolsheviks were changed yet another time since the beginning of the century. As usual, a wave of shattering revelations swept the country, a phenomenon so familiar to every Soviet citizen.

In the pre-Gorbachev epoch the mutinous (according to classifications by the propaganda department of the Communist Party Central Committee) Soviet newspaper *Literaturnaya Gazeta* published letters compiled by journalist A. Rubinov, which said that some mail, sent or received from abroad, arrived with a delay of one or two months. In the perestroika years the same Rubinov in an interview with the USSR communications minister, G. Kudryavtsev, which covered an entire page in *Literaturnaya Gazeta*, now complains that all mail sent abroad travels several months. The newspaper *Kuranty* (July 27, 1991) screwed up its courage and published a critical remark addressed to 'the respectful KGB chief' Kryuchkov, pointing out that it was not good to violate the secrecy of correspondence.

Argumenty i Fakty (No. 38, 1991), calling a spade a spade, placed a reproduction of a registration form with detailed information which a censor fills in for each(?!) mail dispatch abroad. The weekly also placed a photo with a huge heap of letters on the pavement. The text of the article is interesting as well:

> In No. 11 for the previous year *Argumenty i Fakty* published documentary evidence by a weekly's reader of the fact that international mail in the Soviet Union is checked by special security services. Officials from the USSR Communications Ministry continue to deny that such things happen at their agency (though they didn't send written refutation to us), while the weekly's office is inundated with letters containing new evidence. The following document labelled "for secret use only" was sent to *Argumenty i Fakty*. This registration form contains data on its author, his addressee abroad, summary of the letter itself and the signature of an employee who examined it. Though the form is dated 1967, it confirms the fact that such a service did exist in those times. If it has now ceased to exist then a question arises: when and on the basis of which document was it liquidated? Who took such a decision?"
>
> And then why should one bother issuing new registration forms? It's much easier to throw letters away. Letters from various countries written to various addresses (including ones to President Gorbachev) were found in a garbage container near a telephone exchange, at building 1, 38 Mozhaisk highway.
>
> Maybe postmen lost them accidentally at the garbage site? A whole box of these letters awaits them in our editorial board.

Megapolis-Express (October 31, 1991) placed a letter by A. Merkulov, Cand. Sc. whose post office F-284, located near his house, sent in October 1991 a COD parcel valued at nine rubles 96 kopeks.

> What did I discover when I opened the parcel? It contained 105 letters from Soviet citizens sent in December 1989 to the USA (including my own two letters), and also a letter from the GDR to the USA and a letter mailed to New York (to Soviet ambassador Dubinin) from Florida. None of the letters reached the States— there were no corresponding stamps on them. The fact that letters dispatched abroad either disappear or are lost does not surprise anyone now. However the employees of the Moscow International Post Office seemed to have found a unique way of combating letters undesirable to them. A hundred plus letters are at my house and I don't know what to do with them.

Usually women in the rank of sergeant peruse letters at the KGB. Correspondence within the Soviet Union is examined selectively, while international mail is looked at in the majority of cases. There are lists of people who are constantly checked by the KGB. Their correspondence is examined more thoroughly. An *Izvestia* correspondent, S. Mostovshchikov, who studied this question, believes that the so-called operative-technical department of the KGB is responsible for this work. According to him special equipment, like that used for screening by doctors or customs offices, makes it possible to read a letter without opening it.

The Moscow International Post Office located on Varshavskoye highway, as our Soviet journalists wrote, even in 1991 had a department for censorship of foreign periodicals and other printed and audio visual products coming into the USSR. There at the Post Office in the rooms of the former Glavlit more than a hundred people with higher education, polyglots, worked a lot before and after the coup, selecting what is called "dangerous literature" and is consequently sent to special storage rooms in organizations and libraries.

There are cases when one has to send something quickly abroad, or receive a letter from there. Some people use the courier service or give letters to pilots of Soviet and foreign airlines. Beginning in 1991 American post came to our help. The firm Emery International delivers from Moscow to any location in Europe (two days) and the USA (four days) a package weighing up to one kg. for 42-79 dollars. The French firm Sofipost does the same but for rubles and at a much lower price.

The national post, in conditions of transition to a market economy in the disintegrated Soviet Union, is simply dying out. Having failed to raise their salaries in conditions of galloping inflation and price hikes local post employees sell their premises and equipment to new business people. Thus the Russian Commodity and Raw Materials Exchange has found a place in a luxurious central hall of the old building of the Moscow Post Office.

CHAPTER XIII

WHAT LIES IN STORE: SOME FORECASTS

1. The press of free Russia will take long to develop into the Fourth Estate, but the radio and television will be the hot-house in which influential politicians will mature.

In the spring of 1992 Yeltsin had two Vice-Premiers, Yegor Gaidar and Mikhail Poltoranin, who used to work for *Pravda*. Ex-*Pravda* staffers Yevgeny Primakov and Tatiana Samoilis were the head and the press secretary of the Central Intelligence Service (former First Chief Directorate of the KGB), respectively. Valery Boldin, Gorbachev's assistant and an ideologist of the August 1991 coup, also spent his best years in *Pravda*.

Alexander Bovin, Russia's Ambassador to Israel, and Ivan Laptev, a one-time head of the ex-USSR Parliament, matured in *Izvestia*. On the day of the 75th anniversary of *Izvestia* (March 13, 1992), its journalists wrote that Boris Orlov, doctor of history, was sent to Prague on August 21, 1968 to sing praises to the aggressors, but when he refused to comply he was shooed from the newspaper with a stigma of an outcast.

Pavel Voshchanov, Yeltsin's PR man, and Boris Pankin, the Russian Foreign Minister until March 1992, both worked in *Komsomolskaya Pravda*.

Perestroika luminaries Georgy Shakhnazarov, Fyodor Burlatsky and Yevgeny Ambartsumov are professional journalists. In the spring of 1992 the most influential people in Moscow were Yegor Yakovlev (ex-chief of *Moscow News*), Vladimir Yakovlev (*Kommersant*), Vladislav Starkov (*Argumenty i Fakty*), Vitaly Tretyakov (*Nezavisimaya Gazeta*), Pavel Gusev (*Kuranty*), Andrei Malgin (*Stolitsa*), Igor Golembiovsky (*Izvestia*), and Len Karpinsky (*Moscow News*), as well as Vitaly Korotich, the ex-chief of *Ogonyok* currently lecturing in the USA.

The most popular TV mediators are Tatiana Mitkova, Yuri Rostov and Svetlana Sorokina, whom the people believe never to lie outrageously in any conditions. Alexander Nevzorov, a TV star of the first magnitude, has become the mouthpiece of pronationalist forces of free Russia.

In post-communist Russia the most talented journalists developed into prominent politicians. The bulk of them are consistently advocating a democratic development for Russia and the restoration of private property of land and the means of production.

Yet Russia's journalists of unmatched popularity live beyond its borders, working for Radio Liberty, The Voice of America, Deutsche Welle and BBC. It is not by chance that the Paris-based Russian-language weekly *Russkaya Mysl* has no rivals as regards the depth of analysis and the truthfulness of depicting developments in Russia. There are no newspapers of this magnitude in Moscow, and *Russkaya Mysl* is not sold here either.

2. There will be no free press in post-communist Russia because the ruling circles do not want it. What they need is a tame press.

Who likes to be scolded? The Russian Parliament and government and the thousands of clerks serving them have more than once demonstrated their displeasure with Moscow-based newspapers. *Izvestia* broke free from its founder, the USSR Supreme Soviet, in August 1991, but already in April 1992 Ruslan Khasbulatov, chairman of the Russian Supreme Soviet, demanded that the paper be returned to the protective wing of the Parliament. This paper's leaders answered curtly that they would bow only to a court decision.

In the spring of 1992 the Russian government allocated five billion rubles in subsidies to certain newspapers and magazines (meaning not only the dailies of the Parliament and the government). The Russian taxpayers are made to pay for the distribution of *Komsomolskaya Pravda* and *Rabochaya Tribuna* and the broadcasting of the first channel of Moscow TV throughout the new Commonwealth. Seems absurd, doesn't it? Mind you, the government asked not five but sixty billion rubles. I would rather spend this money on books for children and students, or give them to our poor old people and invalids.

What freedom of the press is there to speak of when our "main" newspaper, *Rossiiskaya Gazeta* (of the Russian Supreme Soviet), is filled to overflowing within minutes of parliamentary debates and full texts of reports to Moscow from local administrations? As Boris Mironov, first chief editor of the paper who was fired after he published the first issue, said, "They were absolutely right to fire me. Otherwise the newspaper would not have kept silent when on the eve of price rises in January 1992 our deputies hurried to buy cars meant for the farmers who sold their output to the state."

Now that democrats have come to power, we have a weekly newspaper of the Russian government, *Rossiiskiye Vesti*, into which the personnel of the former weekly *Pravitelstvenny Vestnik* was incorporated in February 1992 by resolution of President Yeltsin.

3. I would advocate the banning of both the Communist Party and communist ideas in Russia.

Otherwise a day will come when we would read only one newspaper, *Den*, or *Pravda*, or *Sovetskaya Rossia*. The former nomenclature will always find enough money to popularize their crazy national-socialist ideas. The Communist Party's billions of dollars have long been syphoned into proxy economic structures in Russia and beyond it. It is not surprising that "The Secrets of the Soviet Bank in Paris" by Jean Montaldo, which became a best seller in France in 1979 because it exposed the facts of mass transfer of party money to proxy structures in Western Europe, has not been translated into Russian yet.

The newspaper *Pravda* might cease to exist, following the ingenious design of our "fathers." Who knows? *Izvestia* has always had cleaver chief editors, but *Pravda's* bosses were all daft. Of the fifty-six *Pravda* bureaus outside the USSR, it owned only one, in Finland. In other words, it rented premises for dozens of years, when it could buy property instead.

The demonstrative idiocy of some communist structures was in fact a proof of their deeply echeloned defenses. For example, the Communist Party and its press was given up, but up to 80% of local nomenclature and the KGB was kept intact, to say nothing of the Russian Orthodox Church, which was a branch of political police in this country.

I would not be surprised if some expert said that the bastions of the powers that be also include the daily *Nezavisimaya Gazeta*, Interfax, and the weekly *Rossia*. Indeed, why should I be surprised when I know that cadre KGB officers head the brilliant Interfax agency and that very interesting newspaper, *Rossia*, and that one of the three chief persons in *Nezavisimaya Gazeta* faithfully served the KGB during his many-year-long Novosti-appointed job abroad? I also know that the current head of Russian Radio and Television, ex-board member of APN, the author of exulted books and films about Lenin and a friend of Gorbachev, has never been a dissident or an anti-Communist.

4. The KGB might be pushed back from its position of control over the distribution of periodicals and books within and beyond the new Commonwealth.

The USSR Copyright Agency was world-famous as the rapist of writers and journalists, musicians and scientists. From its inception it used dozens of high-ranking KGB officers "to protect authors' rights." In February 1992 President Yeltsin issued a resolution which replaced the Copyright Agency with the Russian Agency of Intellectual Property, headed by famous lawyer Mikhail Fedotov, ex-deputy of Poltoranian, Minister of the Press. But the leadership of the Copyright Agency did not intend to fold up and die. It announced that it would act parallel with the new agency, which promised to take 5–10% from its clients (the USSR Copyright Agency used to claim 70–90%).

On January 22, 1992 Boris Yeltsin issued a decree which eliminated the Novosti Press Agency (APN, later renamed IAN) and TASS, and created a new monster instead, ITAR-TASS (The Information Telegraph Agency of Russia). In 1991 the state allocated 680 million rubles and 57 million dollars to the ex-APN< spent mostly on the maintenance of KGB structures abroad. There was hardly a country in the world which did not have a KGB or GRU man with the passport of a TASS or APN correspondent. In the spring of 1992 it turned out that a large part of these fired pseudo-correspondents decided not to return to Moscow. I wonder, did the idea just dawn on them or were they ordered to defect by the KGB?

5. The spirit of the KGB will not die in Russia, not yet.

The bulk of Moscow correspondents abroad are closely linked with the disinformation department and other branches of the Soviet (now Russian) intelligence service of the KGB and GRU. Before Gorbachev and after him, throughout the 1980s and 1990s, APN/IAN and TASS, *Pravda, Izvestia, Komsomolskaya Pravda, New Times, Trud* and Central TV were represented abroad by a more or less stable corps of journalists, whose links with the Soviet secret services were the main condition for working aboard.

Maybe—just maybe!—there will come a time when the number of KGB-financed periodicals abroad, like the US-based *Guardian* or the Paris-based *l'Humanite*, will dwindle. I sincerely hope so.

When I say "KGB," I also mean the whole of the party and economic nomenclature, which merged with the KGB under Gorbachev. In early 1992 mysterious dark forces linked with the underground communist leadership continued to control the largest newspapers and magazines, in particular *Trud, Pravda, Rabochaya Tribuna, Sovetskaya Rossia* and the rest of the communist press. What does it matter that the magazine *Partiinaya Zhizn* (Party Life) changed its name to *Delovaya Zhizn* (Business Life)? All executives are dying to regain their privileges and power. The ex-Central TV is playing up to the old nomenclature, while the Russian channel is clearly enamored with Khasbulatov and other leaders of the Russian Supreme Soviet.

The military-industrial complex, which is represented in the government by Alexander Rutskoi, is eager to disrupt the work of the government. In 1992 Vice-President Rutskoi, who posed as the fighter of profiteers, became a political pillar of the shadow economy and the corrupt faction of the Russian administration.

The underground party structures will continue their covert civil war with the use of the legally existing branch trade unions. A general strike can be staged any minute now, largely thanks to Yeltsin's benevolent attitude to the communist apparatchiks. The latter would shower the President and the government with false information, just like they did to Gorbachev.

This is the price we are paying for not having a free press, which could give us objective information. Will we continue to hear the truth only on from Western radio stations? Who will provide information to us tomorrow? It is clear that the national mass media cannot yet do anything other than popularizing the views of their sponsors.

6. Some local newspapers and major press concerns have a chance to survive in Russia.

It is logical that in the autumn of 1991 the subscription list for 1992 was headed by local dailies, *Moskovsky Komsomolets* (726,000) and *Vechernyaya Moskva* (390,000). Next followed *Trud* (340,000), *Komsomolskaya Pravda* (260,000), *Moskovskaya Pravda* (201,000), *Izvestia* (183,000), *Kuranty* (143,000), *Pravda* (61,000), *Nezavisimaya Gazeta* (22,000), *Rabacohaya Tribuna* (14,000), and *Krasnaya Zvezda* (9,000).

The mastodons of propaganda, the chronic pathological liars TASS and APN will die or be replaced by more presentable and vigorous agencies, such as Interfax. Local regional newspapers of Russia, from St. Petersburg to the Far East, have broken free from the Moscow diktat and gained access to normal sources of information. The rich market of printed matter (a total of 140 newspapers were published in St. Petersburg alone in the spring of 1992) will no longer be dominated by central Moscow newspapers. Only a few of the dozens of Moscow dailies will survive.

Izvestia will most probably be one of the lucky ones. In the autumn of 1991, the death hour of Soviet power in this country, it created a major concern of the same name, printing newspapers, magazines and books. It has a large printing shop and lots of editorial premises in Moscow's central thoroughfare. Tverskaya Street.

7. The readers will prefer objective information to pointless "deliberations."

Here are the results of the 1992 subscription campaign, as of December 1991.

Name	1992 (thou.)	1991 (thou.)	% of 1991
Business:			
Ekonomika i Zhizn	585	515	115
Kommersant	220	113	194
Biznes i Banki	24	22	112
Deloviye Lyudi	20	21	97
Delovoi Mir	18	15	124
Socio-Political:			
Argumenty Fakty	22,599	23,840	95
Trud	12,320	18,292	67
Izvestia	2,781	3,873	72
Megapolis-Express	1,600	93	1,700
Table Continued on Next Page			

Name	1992 (thous.)	1991 (thous.)	% of 1991
Socio-Political:			
Moskovsky Komsomolets	1,338	1,538	87
Pravda	874	2,221	39
Sovetskaya Rossia	780	1,321	59
Rossiiskaya Gazeta	577	252	229
Moscow News	337	1,297	26
Nedelya	70	76	93
Nezavisimaya Gazeta	64	—	—
Ogonyok	1,492	1,723	87

The only surprise of last year's subscription campaign was the fantastic results achieved by *Megapolis-Express*, which increased its subscription by 1,700%. But this surprise has a very simple explanation, because Megapolis cleverly exploited the shortage of books on the market and offered lots of popular literature, from "The Three Musketeers" by Dumas, to "Neznaika on the Moon" by Nosov, in return for a yearly subscription to *Megapolis-Express*

Ogonyok did the same, but with less spectacular results: the future sale of Sir Arthur Conan Doyle and Fitzgerald hardly made up for the losses from dwindling subscription.

The results of the subscription campaign of the two political rivals, *Nezavisimaya Gazeta* and *Moscow News*, were quite unexpected: *Moscow News* lost 74% (960,000) of its 1991 subscribers, while *Nezavisimaya Gazeta* attracted only 64,000 subscribers, or much fewer than it had hoped for.

The results of subscription campaigns of other newspapers were quite predictable. *Izvestia* remained afloat, although it lost about a million subscribers, and *Argumenty i Fakty* remained the indisputable leader owing to its ability to satisfy the demands of the readers with lightning speed.

The structure of the business press hardly changed. *Ekonomika i Zhizn*, which used the "mass-reader-low-price" principle (29 rubles for 12-month subscription), increased the army of its subscribers to 585,000, or up by 15% on the previous year. *Kommersant*, whose motto is "elite readers and high price" (96 rubles for 12-month subscription), won itself 94% more subscribers (220,000). *Deloviye Lyudi* and *Delovoi Mir* were somewhat worse off.

8. The amount of information is plummeting in the impoverished post-communist Russia, just like the independence and democratic orientation of political press.

When they opposed the communist Politburo and the bulk of the USSR Parliament, the democrats won the approval of a basically good Law on the Press in August 1990. It eliminated censorship and allowed private citizens to establish newspapers, magazines and radio and TV stations. In late December 1991 the Russian Supreme Soviet approved the Law "On the Mass Media," which gave the procurator's offices a right to inspect editorial offices and persecute journalists for withholding their sources of information from law-enforcement bodies.

Publications are becoming ever more costly and their circulation is dropping. Books are no longer published, with the exception of dictionaries and erotic literature.

No government likes its critics. Communists, when they were in power, learned to tame and control their critics. Under Yeltsin, the printed word is simply vanishing out of sight. Three or four years ago newspapers, magazines and books were ideological goods of exceptional significance, and as such were published and delivered to the reader irrespective of costs. The year 1992 threatens to become a year of defeat for the Russian mass media, a year of death for the bulk of newspapers.

9. The bulk of traditional Moscow "central" newspapers have no future.

Dozens of central Moscow newspapers, most of them four-and eight-page ones, will succumb to the growth of prices for newsprint and printing services. The readers, impoverished by the galloping inflation, can now buy only one of the many newspapers they used to buy. Newspapers are quickly becoming a luxury item.

The rich will pay good money only for truthful, serous information that will satisfy their demands. Such newspapers as *Kommersant* and *Delovoi Mir*, and probably *Moskovsky Komsomolets*, might preserve their readers. The latter is ten time more popular in Moscow than its rival *Komsomolskaya Pravda*.

The bulk of journalists, who for decades fed half-truths or bare-faced lies to us, will not be able to work for much longer. The credit of public confidence will be given only to the new generation of journalists. Of course, Yelena Bonner and Yuri Mityunov, Felix Svetov and Sergei Grigoryants have nothing to fear: the people will always read their articles eagerly.

The West has the yellow press (for the mass reader), the quality press (for the elite), and specialized publications (professional). We seem to be following in its footsteps.

On the other hand, both *Pravda* and *Komsomolskaya Pravda* should know that the era of the yellow press has ended. TV and radio will show or tell their audiences nearly everything, any pornography, drama or tragedy, and much better than the above newspapers might do this for their not very well educated readers.

Well-fed and clever people don't read *Komsomolskaya Pravda* or watch TV non-stop. They need elite, that is, top quality, information. They are not interested in political parties; they want freedom and favorable conditions for their business, service, leisure time, etc.

When we have privatization, we shall have newspapers for the elite and for the middle class. When we have private printing shops, we shall have what the USSR did not have—hundreds of illustrated magazines for different categories of readers. It is a fact that our three main magazines—*Rabotnitsa*, *Krestyanka* and *Zdorovye*— were the only ones in 1992 not to lose in tens of millions of their subscribers. Regrettably, these monthly magazines are hardly presentable from the viewpoint of printing quality.

10. Market relations are benefiting the Russian press.

Articles 43 of the new, Russian Law on the Mass Media freed editorial boards from the trying task of answering readers' letters or forwarding them to concerned organizations. The Russian newspapers were only too happy to sack the staff from their letter departments.

Complaints are heard in courts now. But previously hundreds of people in big and small newspapers of Moscow read well-nigh a million letters a year. They were obliged to answer every letter and to forward complaints to concerned ministries and departments, for the latter to act on them. It was a madhouse, with the whole of the country engaged in bureaucratic correspondence with each other, designed to create a semblance of concern for the people.

Next on the agenda for 1992 is the opening of the House of the Russian Press in Pushkinskaya Street, in the building which was occupied only recently by the 1,800 staffers of the last USSR Cabinet of Ministers.

11. The press, radio and television in the new independent states of the ex-USSR will begin from scratch.

An *Izvestia* correspondent in Tajikistan is not unlike his *Washington Post* or *Le Figaro* counterparts. The only difference is that the former was expelled from Dushanbe in March 1992, while the latter visit the republic only rarely. But then, who would read their articles in Tajikistan?

Having got rid of the pressure of the Moscow-based and local Communist Party structures, local journalists in Tajikistan or Latvia remain in the eye-sights of the KGB, the former nomenclature, all kinds of law-enforcement bodies and the Mafia. After the ten-and twenty-time increase in prices in January 1992, the impoverished newspapers had to choose between death or communist, business, military and other sponsors. Lucrative offers of millions of rubles are to be repaid with the rights to newspapers. This means an end to independence and responsibility to the readers.

In this situation ex-Soviet journalists are dreaming of being bought by a rich American or West European "daddy." Indeed, this might be best for all concerned.

12. There will be no common information space in the ex-USSR.

The so-called central press and Central TV are doomed to death. The voice of Moscow as the ultimate truth is no longer listened to in the Baltics, Ukraine, the Caucasus or Central Asia. In the bulk of the above regions central Moscow newspapers are no longer printed from matrixes in the dead of night, as was the norm barely several months ago. Subscription costs for these papers will triple, and they will not be sold in kiosks.

Moscow TV is still broadcast all over the Commonwealth, but none of the Commonwealth states want to pay Russia for it, because the viewpoint and the interests of Moscow do not coincide with the views and expectations of the bulk of the people in other republics even now, when Moscow TV has stopped lying as outrageously as it did before August 1991.

An information vacuum is spreading throughout the bulk of the ex-Soviet territory. Young independent states, just like the Russian provinces, hurried to get rid of the information diktat of Moscow. Very soon you will not buy a Moscow newspaper or magazine a mere hundred kilometers from Moscow, because the people have long memories and they remember how the Kremlin press and TV spurred on the Cold War and provoked armed conflicts in the Third World. Under Gorbachev, they did the same on home ground, when the privileges of the military-industrial complex, the Communist Party and the KGB were threatened. Soviet power and communist ideas collapsed, but imperial thinking is still polluting the words and deeds of Russian democrats led by Yeltsin.

Social tensions are affecting reporters too. Reporting has become a dangerous profession in this country. We have as many killed and wounded journalists here as in Yugoslavia. Tales about the beatings and robberies of journalists are becoming professional lore.

Journalists are rightless persons in all ex-Soviet republics. Unlike medical workers or policemen, they have no law to protect them. Their Western colleagues have bullet-proof vests and thousands of dollars of insurance, and the warring sides in conflict areas offer information to Western journalists more readily. So, the Soviet journalists' credit of confidence remains negligible, owing to the lack of professionalism, poverty and dependence on everybody.

We have grown used to getting key information about developments in this country from the West. Our best journalists bring their best pieces of information to the Western media. TV reports, photographs, commentaries and news are paid a hundred times better in the West than here.

Our journalists find it much safer to publish sensational information in the West. The procurator's offices and militants in the Caucasus and Moldova are very angry with ex-Soviet journalists, but are much more friendly with their Western colleagues, who are not imprisoned, tortured or tried. However, stray bullets and beatings are the common trouble of both ex-Soviet and Western journalists.

In the near future the peoples of the ex-USSR will depend on the West as regards all kinds of information. The administrations and the population of all ex-Soviet republics have a very low opinion of local and Moscow journalists. The powers that don't like shrewd journalists, and the people don't like tame ones. Ukraine's most influential newspaper, *Nezavisimost* (circulation 1.3 million), nearly closed down in February this year, purportedly owing to the shortage of newsprint but in actual fact due to the actions of the authorities. The latter did not like it when the newspaper wrote that on the eve of the price rise all deputies of the Ukrainian Parliament were allowed—at the initiative of the Cabinet of Ministers—to buy a car each for 10,000 rubles instead of a million, as well as a package of consumer goods at "old," low prices.

Ex-secretaries and members of the Communist Party Central Committee, the KGB bonzas, and nationalism-preaching dissidents have climbed to the helm of many ex-Soviet republics. Can one say that they are convinced democrats? Gamsakhurdia persecuted the late Merab Mamardashvili, an outstanding philosopher, for his love of the truth and independent opinions, more actively than Brezhnev and Gorbachev taken together.

The middle class—intelligentsia—was victimized by the Soviet government back in 1917. The current generations of the so-called intelligentsia have learned to betray of their own free will. We have legions of lying writers and journalists. Musicians were taught to inform on their more talented colleagues. Moscow composer Mikeal Tariverdiyev wrote about that drama (or tragedy?) of our intelligentsia in his brilliant documentary book.

13. Our people have been corrupted well-nigh beyond any hope of improvement. The most graphic proof of this is the ethnic conflicts in the Caucasus. The people of the ex-USSR will get up from their knees and turn into civilized, free citizens only with foreign assistance.

The 16-page Russo-American newspaper *We/Mi*, which saw the light of day in February 1992, will soon be published weekly, thanks to the efforts of *Izvestia* and the Herst corporation. The first Russian-language issue of the magazine *Europe*, published by the mission of the Commission of the European Communities in Moscow, was printed in March 1992.

Back in June 1991 the USA, represented by Secretary of State James Baker, stated its desire to facilitate the strengthening of independence of the mass media in Eastern Europe, including Russia. By the spring of 1992 it became clear that few of their projects materialized in this country. For example, Americans promised to create, with the assistance of the Institute of US and Canadian Studies of the Russian Academy of Sciences, a center that would provide ex-Soviet journalists (and their foreign colleagues) with a wide range of information services, including direct access to all computerized data banks of the West. Another idea was to create a library of American and other foreign literature and periodicals in Moscow, to hold briefings of leading Sovietologists, etc.

The task now is to establish all these facilities in all Commonwealth capitals. Will the Americans agree to do this? If not, then Germans, Turks or Iranians will be ready to oblige. The French *Le Monde* might decide to establish branches of its brilliant computerized bank of data on Russia in all Commonwealth states, and that will be it. There is nothing of the kind in any of the Commonwealth capitals now, and not even in Moscow. After thinking it over, the French Foreign Ministry is on the verge of opening a French school for journalists in Moscow in 1993.

14. In the next few years the international community will do its best to save Russia's stock of valuable books and documents.

The French, for example, hope to get back the twenty carloads of their own archives (1.2 million entries), which this country confiscated from the Germans, who in their turn captured them in France in 1940. These archives include documents of the French intelligence service and defense ministry dating at least three centuries back.

And the German book, archive and museum collections? The Central State (Special) Archives of the USSR can be called the archives of Europe's documents. Only the KGB was allowed to use them for collecting compromising information about Soviet citizens.

In 1992 the Hoover Institute and the Library of the US Congress announced that they had reached an agreement with the Russian authorities on the joint use of the main Moscow archives and the State Library named after Lenin. Our military commissioned aircraft carriers. The KGB commissioned the construction of two very large buildings in the past five years and is restructuring a third one in downtown Moscow. And all the while the country's main libraries in Moscow and St. Petersburg have been turning into a symbol of ruination and degradation. The government just does not seem to be able to find a single dollar for the purchase of books and periodicals abroad. The delivery to Russia of nearly all of the 5,000 foreign scientific journals stopped several years ago.

The Hoover Institute will be allowed to microfilm documents kept in the Russian archives, most of which were closed to all and sundry in the past 70 years. Two copies will remain in the Russian Archives Committee and the Lenin Library, and two would go abroad. The Hoover Institute, which has the richest collection on the history of Russia of the 20th century, will give us a present of 20,000 rolls of microfilm of its archives, in exchange for our 20,000 rolls. We will also get three million dollars, with all technical problems tackled together with the Americans and with their assistance. I think the Americans would have gladly spent 300 million dollars if they had to, just to guarantee the preservation of our archives which tell about the most tragic social experiment in human history. The archives of the Communist Party Central Committee and the KGB are priceless and must be open to the people. Regrettably, they have already been "cleansed" by the criminals who wanted to remove the evidence of their crimes.

The Library of the US Congress and our Lenin Library seem to be merging, which will help the Lenin Library to overcome its primordial poverty. Although the Russian Parliament decided to finance its restructuring, it does not have the 150 million dollars which are needed to do this. A great number of resolutions were approved by the government and Gorbachev, but fires and floods in the two or three largest libraries of Moscow and St. Petersburg threaten to become a fact of life. Before 1991 major libraries, with secret funds that have since been declassified, were branches of the KGB, and so nobody thought twice about them. Meanwhile, these libraries, which are a part of the historical memory of the Earth, are rotting into decay.

The French have delivered several thousand modern books for the Muscovites who know French. Some of them are for sale in the Progress shop, but 10,000 copies were deposited for lease at the French Cultural Center, which the French Foreign Ministry opened in the Library of Foreign Literature in Moscow in 1992.

15. The Green press will become the most popular and widespread in this country, and very soon.

We don't yet have a law prohibiting the production and sale of polluted products. Our fresh water, air, land and foods have long been polluted. Air pollution, radioactive and beam exposure, polluted soil and deafening noise make life in the ex-USSR nearly intolerable. An average Muscovite suffers from the dangerous natural influences more than a scientist working in the Antarctic. Foreign diplomats accredited in Moscow get additional payment for health hazards. Only 14% of our 17 year olds are healthy. Since the 1970s the number of ecology-related (heart and cancer) diseases has increased by 50%. Babies die in Russia twice as frequently as in the USA. Our men live seven to ten years less than their peers in industrialized countries. In the north of Siberia men live 22 years less, and women 14 years less, than their counterparts in North European countries.

Human (children's, women's, old people's, invalids', prisoners', farmers', consumers', etc.) rights are a much spoken of and are a painful issue.

In 1992 there was hardly any life or property insurance in the Commonwealth, either for private citizens or legal bodies. As many as 130,000 energetic and imaginative economic managers are languishing behind bars, although the criminal code articles which sent them to prison for speculation and private enterprise have long been annulled. A total of 37,510 people died in traffic accidents in this country in 1991 (two times more than perished during the ten years of the Afghan war). About the same number dies in traffic accidents in the USA, but it has ten times more cars than the ex-USSR.

16. All newly-independent states will intensively exploit the right to information. The mechanism of competition was switched on at the market of telephone services in dozens of ex-Soviet cities in early 1992, sooner than in all other economic spheres.

The KGB has been (and remains?) the invisible master of all telephone lines in this country. That is why the Ukrainian government strengthened its independence from Russia by striking an agreement with AT&T in January 1992. The Americans promised Ukraine to increase the number of its telephone lines from the seven million that existed in early 1992 to three times the figure by the end of this century, for one billion dollars. The 150 long-distance lines going via Moscow will be immediately buttressed with 60 direct international long distance lines. In the summer of 1992 Ukrainian exchanges will launch a commercial communications satellite.

Russia has fewer apartment phones per 100 urban families than any other ex-Soviet republic. It needs at least 55,000 international communication lines, but in the spring of 1992 it had no more than 3,000.

The USA is resigned to reduce—but not annul—COCOM lists, in particular, as regards the export of optical fiber technologies to the new Commonwealth. This is not so much an attempt to protect the West from new rivals, as a sign of fear, for the high-speed optical fiber communication lines cannot be tapped. Not long ago the US Congress approved a decision on outfitting all homes in the USA with fiber cables by the year 2015. We cannot plan so big, although we produce nearly all components necessary for establishing digital fiber communication lines. But still, we cannot do without Western assistance in this field. And neither will we build a trans-Siberian communications trunk line, so the Americans should not fear that we would use it for military purposes.

By March 1992 the COCOM allowed the sale of low-velocity optical fiber cables to us. AT&T immediately created a joint venture with the Soviet defense star Dalnyaya Svyaz (Long-Distance Communications), with the noble aim of modernizing communications systems in Russia. It will be a costly enterprise, because the modernization of the Moscow city telephone exchange alone will cost six to eight billion dollars. AT&T has started laying the optical fiber cable from Copenhagen to Kingisepp, outside St. Petersburg, and in the future it will run on to Moscow. By the end of 1992 AT&T plans to finish the construction of an international telephone exchange in St. Petersburg.

17. Radio has been and will remain the most reliable source of information throughout the former USSR. Unlike periodicals and television, radio has a great deal of foreign rivals.

Back in 1990 the official Soviet propaganda called Western radio stations "enemy voices." Vladimir Kryuchkov, then the head of the KGB and an organizer of the August 1991 coup, was especially outspoken on this subject.

Today Russian newspapers and TV regard Western "Radio voices" as the only guarantor of their freedom to provide the people with information, and a model to emulate. In the spring of 1992 the Moscow press wrote much about the 50th anniversary of The Voice of America. Radio Russia has been relaying some Russian-language BBC programs since October 1991. Radio Liberty announced in March 1992 that its audiences in the former USSR increased. Its journalists advised their Russian colleagues to stop supplying the people only with negative information, because there should be a hope for the better, a kind of a practical "positive" element.

Journalists of Radio Liberty and The Voice of America have occupied the top seats in the journalists' hierarchy, which used to belong to a *Pravda* correspondent, in the bulk of newly-independent Commonwealth states. The broadcasts of the above stations in Russian and the languages of other Commonwealth states are an invaluable contribution to the development of democracy in this country. In February 1992 BBC announced that it would open a branch in Ukraine, with a staff of at least ten journalists fluent in English and Ukrainian. In addition to its many premises in Moscow, BBC has organized an exhibition branch in the Library of Foreign Literature, to operate for five years. Everybody is invited there to listen to BBC news.

We cannot find radio sets in shops now. The few that are produced are sold out quicker than any other kind of audio and video equipment. Latvia used to be the monopoly producer of radio sets. The sets of the Riga Radio Factory (RRR) were sold throughout the USSR. Now we don't get them. Four Russian factories are producing video recorders, but nobody seems to think that people still want to listen to radio. This is probably somebody's oversight. Hopefully, radio sets will return to our shops now that independent radio stations for businessmen, Delovaya Volna and Radio Maximum, are broadcasting their information.

18. Just like the power and the ideology of Communists, *Soviet* TV cannot be reformed. This last pillar of the evil empire is bound to be swept away by dozens of private and state companies of Russia and other ex-Soviet states, which will have equal access to our ears. Broadcasts from Tashkent, Yerevan or Kazan will be beamed from a satellite throughout Russia and other ex-Soviet states.

This is an optimistic forecast which will take quite a few billions of rubles to materialize. A more modest scenario advanced by the Ost company (Ostankino, which replaced the First Channel of ex-Central TV) suggests dividing the air time equally between all ex-Soviet republics, with Moscow acting as dispatcher and commentator.

Many republican leaders think that it would be impossible to divide the First Channel equally, and don't want Moscow to act as a commentator and arbiter. The kremlin and Ostankino are told that Polish or North Korean TV are represented on the First Channel better than national TV programs from, say, the capital of Kirghizia.

The greatest trouble is that our TV today is just a version of magazines and newspapers as we knew them in the era of "developed socialism." After the August 1991 coup, amateurs were again appointed to head our TV: former chief editor of the magazine *Selskaya Zhizn* Oleg Poptsov and former chief editor of *Moscow News* Yegor Yakovlev.

Poptsov is responsible for Russian Radio and TV, and Yakovlev, for Central TV and Radio, which soon shrank in size to become the modest Ostankino channel. The backbone of the Russian TV was made up of people who were fired from, or otherwise left Central TV. The latter hardly changed after Leonid Kravchenko, the faithful servant of the Communist Party Central Committee, and his closest associates left it. All those who provided the ideological backing to the KGB and Soviet Army pogroms in Alma Ata, Ferghana, Tbilisi, Baku, Sumgait and Stepanakert were still working in the Ost company in the spring of 1992.

Several hundred officials of the USSR State Committee for Radio and Television (Gosterleradio) are fit to be tried at a kind of Nuremberg Trials. Their clever professional lies stoked bloody conflicts in all outlying regions of the Kremlin empire. Central TV's cold-blooded disinformation campaigns brought blood and suffering to all "fraternal socialist countries," paved the way to the personality cults of Qaddafi, Hussein, Arafat and Najibullah, fanned the Iran-Iraq war, the Sikh revolts in India, wars in Africa and Latin America.

TV programs broadcast from Moscow in 1992 are crammed with debates in the Russian Supreme Soviet, are fostering fascism in the words of TV journalists Alexander Nevzorov and a bunch of such notorious politicians as Zhirinovsky, Makashev and Umalatova. *Pravda's* survival depends on the number of subscribers, but the Kremlin's TV continues to pollute the air of about a half of the globe, at the cost of billions of taxpayers' rubles.

Our Politburo "fathers" knew the worth of their TV, and so they watched CNN and allowed hundreds of their underlings to do the same. The Kremlin TV cannot be reformed, even if privatized through proxies and with the money of the military-industrial complex or the Communist Party and the KGB.

There is only one way out: to eliminate Kremlin's monopoly in the air by challenging it to a competition with other TV companies. Moscow mayor Gavriil Popov is resolved to establish "an independent broadcasting enterprise for Moscow Region." St. Petersburg TV, the most popular in this country, has become independent, and the number of private TV stations has been growing with every month in Russia.

In March 1992 the Ost TV company still did not allow independent states to broadcast their programs on its channel, although Soviet republics have been bombarded with broadcasts from Moscow around the clock for many decades. Fed up, Ukraine switched off the First Channel broadcast from Moscow. Later in March the Hungarian authorities stopped relaying TV broadcasts from Moscow too, and presidents Zhelev of Bulgaria and Havel of Czechoslovakia advanced the idea of an information network embracing Eastern Europe and called the Eastern Express.

In Central Asian republics TV broadcasts from Moscow will be soon ousted by the Turkish TV, because corresponding agreements have been signed at the highest level. An experiment of broadcasting TV programs from Ankara to Azerbaijan and Uzbekistan is underway, and seems to be a success. If these young Moslem states promise to forget the Cyrillic alphabet, Turkey will help them to modernize their printing facilities.

In March 1992 even Belarus officially refused to finance TV broadcasting from Moscow. It appears that Moscow TV will be sponsored by cable television owners from the USA, Canada, Israel, Germany and other states which agree to receive Ostankino round-the-clock programs for Russia, Ukrainian and Jewish communities abroad.

NAME AND SUBJECT INDEX

600 seconds 304
ABB USSR Business Development Inc. 26
Adzhubei, A. 84
Afanasyev, Viktor 81
Afghanistan 232, 269
Alexander Men 15
Alexeyev, Mikhail 118
Algimantas Cekuolis 53
All-Russia Conference of the Newspaper Editiors 175
All-Union Library of Foreign Literature 215
All-Union TV and Radio 205
Altaiskaya Pravda 65
Amerika (America) 6
Angliya (England) 6
Anninsky, Lev 146
APN 51
Argumenty i Fakty 6, 30, 114
Armenia 408
Atmoda 65
audio-visual equipment 370
Auditoria (Audience) 257
Avraamov, Dmitry 38
Babushkin 52
Baku 106
Baltic area 85, 105
Baturin, Yu. 11
Berezovsky, Igor 208
best educational program of all times 224
Birzheviye Vedomosti 207
black berets 26
Bloknot Agitatora (The Agitator's Notebook 29
Bobkov, Fillip Denisovich 113
book black market 236
Book-Publishing 211
bookstores 212
Broadcasting Company 111
Bugged 398
Bukovsky, Vladimir 131, 167
Burda 194
Burda Moden 199
Burkov, B. 55
Cable TV 376
Censorship in the USSR 10
censorship 15, 16, 39
Central Administration for the Protection of State Secrets in the Press and Other Mass Media 16
Central TV 296
Chase, James 225
Checking of All Mail 410
Chelovek i Zakon (Man and the Law) 30
Chernobyl nuclear accident 297
Chikin, V. 40, 79
children's books 224
Christian Information Agency 67
Churkin, Vitaly 44
Circulation by subscription 29
circulation of Soviet central newspapers 6
Classics in the Market Environment 225
CNN International 361

COCOM 404
Collective Newspaper 151
color television 368
Committee to Protect Glasnost 53
COMMUNICATION NETWORKS 393
communications satellite 354
Congress of Journalists 38
Contemporary) 6, 307
coup 142
criminal scene 312
Cultural Initiative 221
Culture and Charity 201
Czechoslovakia 44
Danilov, Vladimir 308
Delovoy Mir 192
Delovye Ludi 193
democracy 95, 115
Democratic Union 63
Demokraticheskaya Rossia 10, 167
Denikin, General 133
Deutsche Welle 271
developments in Lithuania 43
diamonds 81
dictionaries 220
Diena 26
Dlya Vsekh (For Everyone) 57
Dobrov, A. 224
Dossier of International Problems 49
Drozdov, Alexander 178
Druzhba Narodov (Friendship among Peoples) 117
Dukes, Karen 14
Dundurs, Kazimir 25
Dyen newspaper 83
Earthquake in Georgia 325
Echo of Moscow 257
Ecos 206
Education Publishing-House 237
Eho Planety (Echo of the Planet). 43
Ekonomika i Zhizn (Economics and Life) 6
Ekonomika Sovetskoy Ukrainy (The Economy of the Soviet Ukraine) 29
EkoTASS bulletin 50
Ekspress-Khronika 64
Emergency Committee's Decree No. 2 94
Entin, V. 11
erotica 209
Esvandjia, Vakhtang 145
Euroexpansion 188
Europe Plus 262
European Journalist Prize 110
Falin, Valentin 52, 55, 108
Federal Commission of Mass Communications 19
Fedotov, M. 10, 33, 38
Fedyashin, General 52
Felgenhauer, Pavel 146
Fesunenko, I. 37, 287
Fiber Optic Equipment 404
First All-Union Radio Program 253
Foreign Radio Stations 262
foreign policy issues 76
Foteyev, V. 14
freedom of speech 18, 36
freedom of the press 11
Friday program VID 336
Frolov, Ivan 78
Fronin, Vladislav 96, 177
Fund to Protect Glasnost 39, 53
Fyodor Burlatsky 136
Fyodorov, Nikolai 11
Gamsakhurdia 307
General Motors 397
Georgia 137, 145
Gerasimov, Gennady 53
Glasnost 13, 15, 18, 64, 91, 115, 162
Glasnost Committee 14
Glavlit 39
Golembiovsky, Igor 85, 177
Golos 33
Golovin, V. 49

Name and Subject Index

Gorbachev, Mikhail 82, 105, 123, 142
Gorbachev, Raisa 52
Gordievsky, Oleg 234
Gosteleradio 33, 59, 254
government communications 402
Green press 426
Grigoryants, Sergei 62, 91, 162
Grigoryev, Alexei 169, 170
Grossman, Vassily Semyonovich 228
Guinness Book of Records 219
Gusev, Pavel 94, 177, 180
Gushchin, Lev 127
Gutiontov, Pavel 36
History of Great Patriotic War 232
household appliances 369
Hussein, Saddam 83
Ignatenko, Vitaly 45, 141
Inostrannaya Literatura (Foreign Literature) 117
Institute of Books 216
Interconcepts 237
Interfax 57
Interfax Agency 59
international communications 394
Interquadro 57
Izvestia 6, 30, 86, 207
Izvestia TsK KPSS (CPSU Central Committee News) 6
Izvestia TsK KPSS 30
Izyumov, Yuri Petrovich 138
journalism 37
journalist profession 259
Journalistic Code of Professional Ethics 38
Journalists' Union 33
Journalists' Union Board 32
Kalinichev, Vladimir 205
Kalugin, Oleg 17, 76, 130
Karaulov, Andrei 146
Karpinsky, Len 112, 179
Karpov, Vladimir 153
KAS-KOR 57
KGB 329, 402, 413

KGB activities 76
KGB phone communications network 402
Kharlamov, A. 40
Khristianin (Christian) 67
Khristianskii Arkhiv (Christian Archive) 67
Khristianskiye Novosti (Christian News) 67
Klimontovich, Nikolai 117
Komissar, M. 58
Kommersant 185, 186, 207
Kommunist 6
Kommunist Gruzii (Communist of Georgia) 29
Komsomolka 96
Komsomolskaya Pravda 6, 30
Komsomolskaya Zhizn (Komsomol Life) 96
Korotich, Vitaly 122, 178, 179
Krasnaya Zvezda (Red Star) 6
Krasnoyarskii Rabochii 65
Kravchenko, L. 40
Krivitsky, Yevgeny Alexeyevich 138
Kryuchkov, V. 130, 398
Kuranty 152
Kurkova, Bella 179
Kuznetsov, Valery 53
Laptev, I. 84
Lavrova, Sasha 66
Law on the Mass Media 20
Law on the Press 6, 181
Lenin State Library 214
Leonid Kravchenko 33, 45, 334
Literary Magazines 116
literary criticism 117
literary journals 132
Literaturnaya Gazeta 6, 30, 121, 133
Literaturnaya Uchoba (Literary Education) 133
Litfond (Literary Fund) 135
Lithuanian OMON 101
Little Vera 382

Logunov, Valentin 23, 150
loss of trust 106
Lysenko, V. 40, 76
Lyubovtsev, Viktor 142
Lyudmila Batynskaya 20
Makler 207
Malgin, Andrei 154
Mamardashvili, Merab 132
Manannikov, Alexei 62
Martynov, Vladimir 14
mass media 39, 45
Maximov, Vladimir 168
Maxwell, R. 109
Mayak 253
Megapolis 195
Mezhdunarodniye Otnosheniya (International Relations) 92
Miloserdiye (Compassion) 205
Ministry for the Press and Information of the Russian Federation 7
Ministry of Culture 35
Ministry of Information 41
mob demands 312
Molchanov, Vladimir 178, 179, 285, 288
Molodaya Gvardiya (Young Guard) 6, 205
Molodoy Kommunist (Young Communist) 96
Molodyozh Gruzii 137
moral censorship 387
Moscow Commodity Exchange 51
Moscow Journalists' Union 94
Moscow Magazine 194
Moscow News 6, 92, 103
Moscow Radio 253
Moskovskaya Pravda 94, 155
Moskovsky Komsomolets 44, 93, 94
Moskva 117
multi-channel television 359
multi-standard TV sets 370
My (We) 206

Nabokov 118
Nadezhda (Hope) 253
Nash Golos (Our Voice) 14
Nashe Naslediye (Our Heritage) 202
Natalya Chaplina 180
National Center for Public Opinion 60
Nedelya (Week) 6
Nenashev, Mikhail 31
Neva 117, 132
Nevzorov, Alexander 304
Nezavisimaya Gazeta 80, 141
Novodvorskaya, Valeria 308
Novosti Information Agency 51
Novosti Press Agency 51
Novoye Russkoye Slovo 169, 209
Novoye Vremya (New Times) 92
Novy Mir 6, 117, 118
Oganesyan, Vardan 52
Ogni Sibiri 117
Ogonyok (Spark) 6
Ogonyok 122
Oktyabr (October) 117
OMON-men 173
On (He) 206
Ona (She) 206
Orbita broadcast 338
Orpheus 255
Ostretsov, V. 233
Our Motherland 222
Pamyat 336
Pankin, Boris 97
Pankov, Anatoly 161
Panorama Publishers 224
Paper 20
paper prices 28
Party newspapers 18
Paskaleva, Tsvetana 52
Pavlov, Valentin 192
perestroika 106
Perspektivy (Outlook) 96
Petrunya, V. 38, 44
Planet Service 49

Name and Subject Index

Podnieks and Slapins 53
Politicheskoye Samoobrazovanniye 77
Poltoranin, Mikhail 7, 36, 53, 54
Polzikov, Stanislav 55
Popov, Alexander 93
Popov, Gavriil 108
Popovsky, Mark 15
Poptsov, Oleg 316
pornography 383
Poroikov, Yuri Dmitriyevich 139
post-communist Russia 95
Postfactum Agency 62
power 115
power structures 95
Pozner, V. 288
Pravda 6, 30, 69, 77
Pravda Publishers 18
Pravotorov, O. 225
Press for business people 185
press 95, 115
private property 83
Problems of Peace and Socialism 29
Prokhanov, Alexander 83
Prostor (Expanses) 117
Protection of Writers and Artists 33
Puls (Pulse) 96
Pushkin, Alexander 224
Pyatoye Koleso 176
Rabochaya Gazeta 77
Rabochaya Tribuna (Workers' Tribune) 6
Raboche-krestyansky korrespondent (The Worker and Peasant Correspondant) 29
Radio 253
Radio Liberty 65, 275
Radio Moscow World Service 265
Radio Nostalgie 263
Radio Novosibirsk 64
Radio Russia 253
Reader's Digest 204
Referendum 64
RIA 62
Rights of Journalists 36
Rossia 152
Rossiiskaya Gazeta 150, 152
Rossiiskiye Vesti 95, 151, 152
Rost, Yuri 137, 333
royalties 216
Russia On the Air 346
Russian Information Agency (RIA) 52
Russian Information Agency 53, 62
Russky Kuryer 204
Sagalayev, Eduard 32, 62, 288
Sakharov Congress 146
Sakharov, Andrei 64, 297
Salnikova, Marina 66
SECAM color TV system 368
Seleznev, Gennady 40, 81
Selskaya Zhizn (Village Life) 6
Selskaya Zhizn 30, 77
Semenova, Galina 201
Semya (Family) 6
Sergei Grigoryant's "Glasnost 162
Sergei Korzun 258
Severny Telegraf 64, 66
Severo-Zapad 57
Sevruk, Vladimir 87
Shatunovsky, Ilya 76
Shchekochikhin, Yu. 139
Shevardnadze, Eduard 338
Shishkin, G. 40
Siberia 64
Siberian Information Agency 62
Sibirskaya Gazeta 64
Sibirskiye Ogni 64
Simonov, Vladimir 52
Slovo Lektora (The Word from the Lectern) 29
Small and Expensive Will Be Most Viable 186
Smena 93
Sobchak, Anatoly 105
Sobesednik (Interlocutor) 96

Social Science Scientific Information Institute 213
Soglasiye (Consent) 205
Solovyov, Anatoly 216
Solzhenitsyn, Alexander 220
Sotsialisticheskoye Sorevnovaniye (Socialist Emulation) 29
Sotsialistichesky Trud (Socialist Labor) 29
Sovetskaya Kultura (Soviet Culture) 6, 77
Sovetskaya Rossia 6, 79
Sovetsky Shkolnik (Soviet Pupil) 205
Spiridonov, Lev 48
Starkov, Vladislav 114, 178
Starovoitova, Galina 27
State Emergency Committee 52
Stolitsa 153
strikes in the Kuzbass coalfield 65
Svetov, Felix 239
Svobodnoye Obshchestvo 64
TASS 41, 43
TASS Reports 49
Tbilisi 106, 137
Telephone 393
TERRA Publishers 222
The 11 Club 191
The Gospels 133
The Massacre in Vilnius 175
The Publishing Business
The World and the USSR 49
Tolkunov, L. 55, 84
Tramvai (Tram) 206
Tretyakov, Vitaly 141
Tribune) 6
Trud (Labor) 6, 30, 77
Tsvetov, V. 287
Tsvetov, Vladimir 51
TV set 369, 371
Tyumenskii Komsomolets 66
Uchitelskaya Gazeta (Teachers' Gazette) 6

Uchitelskaya Gazeta 77
Udaltsov, Arkady 140
UN Secretariat 76
UNESCO 224
US Congress library 214
USSR Writers' Union 241
Vasiliyev, Andrei 106
Vechernaya Moskva 205
Vechernyaya Moskva 153
Verchenko 119
Verena 200
video clubs 382
Vilnius 106, 333, 389
Vilnius Press House 38
Vinogradov, Andrei 52
violence 385
Vlasov, Albert Ivanovich 52, 55
VNIKI 197
Voice of America 274
Volin, Vladimir 79
Volkogonov, Dmitry 232
Voronezh video equipment 372
Vremya 332
Vyacheslav Goncharov 75
Vyacheslav Leontyev 122
Vysotsky, Vladimir 245
Vzglyad 130, 340
Vzglyad program 302
Vzglyad" program 335
White TASS 49
Yakovlev, A. 122
Yakovlev, Yegor 104
Yanayev, Gennady 52, 94
Yefimov, N. 85
Yeltsin, Boris 84
Yezhednevnaya Glasnost 91
YMCA-Press 238
Yunost (Youth) 117, 132
Yurkov, A. 40
Za Rubezhom 92
Zamyatin, Leonid 45
Zarya Vostoka (Dawn of the East) 41
Zasursky, Ya.N. 20

Zavidiya, Andrei Fedorovich 83
Zhirinovsky, Vladimir 82
Znamya 6, 117, 133
Znaniye Society 115
Zubkov, Ivan 33
Zvezda (Star) 6